Accounting Theory

7TH EDITION

Accounting Theory

7TH EDITION

JAYNE GODFREY

ALLAN HODGSON

ANN TARCA

JANE HAMILTON

SCOTT HOLMES

WILEY

John Wiley & Sons Australia, Ltd

Seventh edition published 2010 by
John Wiley & Sons Australia, Ltd
42 McDougall Street, Milton Qld 4064

Typeset in 10/12.5 ITC Giovanni LT

Australian editions © John Wiley & Sons Australia, Ltd
1992, 1994, 1997, 2000, 2003, 2006, 2010

Authorised adaptation of the original edition,
Accounting Theory, published by John Wiley & Sons,
New York, United States of America. ©1986 in the
United States of America by John Wiley & Sons, Inc.
All rights reserved.

The moral rights of the authors have been asserted.

National Library of Australia
Cataloguing-in-Publication entry

Title:	Accounting theory/
	Jayne Godfrey . . . [et al.]
Edition:	7th ed.
ISBN:	978 0 470 81815 2 (pbk.)
Notes:	Includes index.
Subjects:	Accounting.
Other Authors/Contributors:	Godfrey, Jayne M. (Jayne Maree)
Dewey Number:	657

Cover and internal design images: © iStockphoto.com/© Lise Gagne;
© Photodisc

Typeset in India by Aptara

Printed in Singapore by
Craft Print International Ltd

10 9 8 7 6 5 4 3

Professor Jayne Godfrey

Professor Jayne Godfrey, BCom (Hons), DipEd, MEc, PhD, is President of Academic Board and Professor of Financial Accounting at Monash University. Her publications draw upon a range of accounting and auditing theories. For her service to Australian society through business leadership, Jayne was awarded Australia's Centenary Medal. A past member of the Australian Accounting Standards Board, and past president of the Accounting Association of Australia and New Zealand, she frequently addresses international and national audiences concerning accounting research issues. She is currently a member of Australia's Water Accounting Standards Board, applying principles consistent with accounting theories described in this book. Jayne's research focuses on the role of accounting and auditing in generating and distributing economic resources, including the contracting and capital market causes and consequences of earnings management, and auditor specialisation.

Professor Allan Hodgson

Professor Allan Hodgson, BEc (Hons), MEc, PhD, is Dean of the Amsterdam Business School and Director of Graduate Studies at the University of Amsterdam. Allan has lectured in accounting theory and financial statement analysis in Africa, Europe, Australia, the United Kingdom and the United States. His published research in international journals covers insider trading, derivative markets, banking, capital market research, corporate governance and intangibles. He is currently on the editorial boards of six international journals.

Professor Ann Tarca

Professor Ann Tarca, PhD, MAcc, BCom, is a professor in the Accounting and Finance group of the Business School at the University of Western Australia (UWA). She has over 20 years teaching experience, with the last 15 years being spent at UWA working with both undergraduate and post-graduate students. Following from her experience as a chartered accountant in public practice, her research has focused on financial reporting standards and practices. She has a particular interest in international issues including standard setting, regulation and enforcement.

Professor Jane Hamilton

Professor Jane Hamilton, BBus, MAcc, PhD, is Professor of Accounting at the Bendigo campus of the Regional School of Business, La Trobe University, and previously held academic positions at the University of Technology, Sydney. Jane has 20 years experience in teaching and has published the results of her auditing research in several Australian and international journals.

Professor Scott Holmes

Professor Scott Holmes, BCom, PhD, FCPA, is currently Pro Vice-Chancellor (Research), Dean of Graduate Studies and Professor of Accounting, The University of Newcastle and Honorary Professor, UQ Business School, The University of Queensland. Scott has held academic positions at a number of universities, including Australian National University, Queensland University of Technology, The University of Queensland, University of Arizona and University of Oregon. He has also acted as a consultant to several of the multinational accounting firms, and in 2007–08 was senior adviser to the New South Wales Treasurer. In 2004, Scott was made a life member of the Small Enterprise Association of Australia and New Zealand in recognition of his research in the area of small-firm financial management and reporting. Scott's current research focus is budget and reporting models in a health setting.

CONTENTS

About the authors   v
Preface   x
How to use this book   xii
Acknowledgements   xiv

Part 1

ACCOUNTING THEORY   1

1   Introduction   3
Overview of accounting theory   4
Content outline   14
Additional readings   16
Endnotes   17

2   Accounting theory construction   19
Pragmatic theories   20
Syntactic and semantic theories   21
Normative theories   24
Positive theories   28
Different perspectives   29
Scientific approach applied to accounting   37
Issues for auditing theory construction   39
Summary   42
Questions   43
Additional readings   45
Endnotes   51

3   Applying theory to accounting
regulation   53
The theories of regulation relevant to accounting
and auditing   54
How theories of regulation apply to accounting and
auditing practice   60
The regulatory framework for financial
reporting   69
The institutional structure for setting accounting and
auditing standards   74
Summary   80
Questions   82
Additional readings   84
Websites   84
Endnotes   88

Part 2

THEORY AND ACCOUNTING
PRACTICE   91

4   A conceptual framework   93
The role of a conceptual framework   94
Objectives of conceptual frameworks   97
Developing a conceptual framework   101
A critique of conceptual framework projects   111
Conceptual framework for auditing standards   119
Summary   122
Questions   123
Additional readings   125
Endnotes   130

5   Measurement theory   133
Importance of measurement   134
Scales   134
Permissible operations of scales   136
Types of measurement   138
Reliability and accuracy   140
Measurement in accounting   145
Measurement issues for auditors   150
Summary   152
Questions   153
Additional readings   154
Endnotes   159

6   Accounting measurement systems   161
Three main income and capital measurement
systems   162
Historical cost accounting   162
Current cost accounting   171
Financial capital versus physical capital   174
Exit price accounting   183
Value in use versus value in exchange   190
A global perspective and International Financial
Reporting Standards   191
Issues for auditors   201
Summary   203
Questions   206
Problems   207
Additional readings   210
Endnotes   215

7 Assets 227
  Assets defined 228
  Asset recognition 232
  Asset measurement 235
  Challenges for standard setters 241
  Issues for auditors 243
  Summary 247
  Questions 248
  Problems 249
  Additional readings 251
  Endnotes 255

8 Liabilities and owners' equity 257
  Proprietary and entity theory 258
  Liabilities defined 263
  Liability measurement 268
  Challenges for standard setters 275
  Summary 281
  Questions 283
  Problems 285
  Additional readings 286
  Endnotes 289

9 Revenue 291
  Revenue defined 292
  Revenue recognition 295
  Revenue measurement 301
  Challenges for standard setters 305
  Issues for auditors 311
  Summary 314
  Questions 315
  Problems 317
  Additional readings 321
  Endnotes 327

10 Expenses 329
  Expenses defined 330
  Expense recognition 332
  Expense measurement 333
  Challenges for accounting standard setters 342
  Summary 347
  Questions 348
  Problems 350
  Additional readings 352
  Endnotes 355

Part 3

ACCOUNTING AND RESEARCH 357

11 Positive theory of accounting policy and disclosure 359
  Background 360
  Contracting theory 361
  Agency theory 362
  Price protection and shareholder/manager agency problems 365
  Shareholder–debtholder agency problems 369
  Ex post opportunism versus *ex ante* efficient contracting 374
  Signalling theory 375
  Political processes 377
  Conservatism, accounting standards and agency costs 379
  Additional empirical tests of the theory 381
  Evaluating the theory 389
  Issues for auditors 392
  Summary 394
  Questions 396
  Additional readings 398
  Endnotes 400

12 Capital market research 403
  Philosophy of positive accounting theory 404
  Strengths of positive theory 405
  Scope of positive accounting theory 407
  Capital market research and the efficient markets hypothesis 408
  Impact of accounting profits announcements on share prices 412
  Trading strategies 426
  Issues for auditors 433
  Summary 435
  Questions 436
  Additional readings 437
  Endnotes 440

13 Behavioural research in accounting 445
  Behavioural accounting research: definition and scope 446
  Why is BAR important? 447

Representativeness: the evidence   462

Accounting and behaviour   464

Limitations of BAR   465

Issues for auditors   466

Summary   468

Questions   469

Additional readings   470

Endnotes   472

14 Emerging issues in accounting and auditing   477

Current factors influencing accounting and auditing research, regulation and practice   478

Issues surrounding the application of fair value accounting during the global financial crisis   481

Possible directions in future international accounting standard setting arrangements   483

Sustainability accounting, reporting and assurance   485

Other non-financial accounting and reporting issues   493

Summary   496

Questions   497

Endnotes   500

List of key terms   503

Index   513

During the period that the seventh edition of *Accounting Theory* was being prepared, the world financial system suffered its greatest crisis since the collapse of the US stock market in 1929. From mid-2007 financial markets experienced a number of economic shocks as borrowers in the United States began to default on home loans, and the 'sub-prime' crisis was born. An international liquidity crisis hit markets around October 2008 as banks in the United States, United Kingdom and elsewhere either failed or sought injections of capital from governments and other parties. As asset prices fell and market liquidity for investments disappeared, some commentators pointed to fair value accounting as the cause of the crisis. Political pressure on standard setters and regulators was intense as action to ameliorate the crisis was demanded and taken.

We must ask the question of where an accounting theory textbook fits in such an environment. Does the crisis mean that past material about accounting theory is no longer relevant? Our answer is no. We suggest that our existing knowledge can be used to understand current events and to equip us for future action. The primary strength of *Accounting Theory* is the balanced approach taken in explaining and discussing the alternative theories and perspectives of accounting and the rigour of the learning material presented. It will always be important for students to study accounting theory, and that relevant material is presented and discussed in an objective manner. In part one of the revised text, our objective is to help readers explore what is meant by theory and how theory relates to the practice of accounting. In this part, chapter 3 addresses the role of theory in regulation and provides material that helps us to evaluate an event such as the global financial crisis and the responses to it.

At the time the sixth edition was released in 2006, we noted a major change in the financial reporting environment, namely the adoption of International Financial Reporting Standards (IFRS). These standards are now used in more than 100 countries around the world, including Australia and New Zealand and the major European and Asian economies. The worldwide adoption of IFRS confirms our focus on these standards, their theoretical underpinnings and the process by which they are set. We include extensive material on IFRS, particularly in part 2, chapters 4 to 10. We do not aim to be a 'how-to' manual for IFRS but rather to explore the theory behind standards. We apply theories to practice and make extensive use of theory in action vignettes and case studies drawn from real-world examples.

One of the strengths of our book is that we provide a longer term perspective on issues; we relate theory to practice over time. Not only do we provide up-to-date materials about standards, regulation and practice to inform readers of the current situation, we also provide the background to critical developments. Our historical perspective is particularly important in understanding current events, such as fair value accounting. For example, the material about the development of current cost accounting from the 1960s onwards provides essential background for readers to understand today's fair value accounting. Thus, readers have a wealth of material to develop informed views about the issues faced in practice today. Differences in accounting practice are a function of differences in theoretical viewpoints on the part of those responsible for measuring and reporting accounting information. In order for students to argue for a particular approach and to apply a particular view, they must understand the principles and research that underlie their perspective.

An important new feature of this edition is our introduction of material about auditing in each chapter. The crucial role of external auditing has long been recognised in capital markets. Thus, in the face of considerable external scrutiny of corporate financial reporting, we considered it was timely to introduce material that specifically addresses issues relating to auditors and the audit function. This innovation is consistent with our approach in which we aim to build on the solid foundation of detailed, well-researched discussion and analysis in earlier editions of the book, but also to bring in new material that is relevant to understanding how theory applies in practice. By extending our text into the auditing area, we meet our goal of revealing as well as integrating material students will find useful in understanding the accounting domain. We also provide an objective analysis of issues to help students to understand and scientifically debate issues. Without such an approach we are in danger of producing students who are technically capable, but unable to exercise appropriate judgement to provide and present information that serves users' needs.

In part three, we include chapters on positive accounting theory, capital market and behavioural research. These chapters provide an overview of important theories and studies and are updated with new theory in action vignettes and case studies to provide current material illustrating topical issues. We conclude with a new chapter on emerging issues in accounting and auditing in which we refer again to IFRS and the global financial crisis as well as other topical issues.

We hope that all our readers find their exploration of the world of accounting theory through our book an informative and thought-provoking experience. We know that accounting theory often represents a major challenge to accounting students. We therefore thank instructors for their continued commitment to the text and to its approach to informed, rigorous debate. In this regard, we are always keen for feedback and encourage both academics and students to contact us with comments and suggestions for improvements or expansion of the issues covered.

Allan Hodgson thanks Brendan O'Dwyer at the University of Amsterdam for scholarly advice and support in mounting a course at Amsterdam Business School that draws heavily on this book. Ann Tarca thanks her students at the University of Western Australia, who provide lively discussions based on material in this book. She also acknowledges the contribution of her research colleagues, without whom developing an understanding of accounting theory and issues would not be possible. We also thank the professional editorial and management team at John Wiley & Sons for their hard work and persistence in updating and making the content relevant to students, and in their undoubted commitment to maintaining high academic standards in the accounting discipline. Finally, we thank our families for their continued support and understanding.

Jayne Godfrey

Allan Hodgson

Ann Tarca

Jane Hamilton

Scott Holmes

November 2009

Accounting Theory, 7th edition, has been designed with you — the student — in mind. The design is our attempt to provide you with a book that both communicates the subject matter and facilitates learning. We have accomplished these goals through the following elements.

LEARNING OBJECTIVES assist you to identify the essential elements of the chapter. They are clearly stated and linked to subsequent discussion in the chapter.

The **INTRODUCTION** outlines the key issues, topics, processes and procedures to be discussed in the chapter.

THEORY IN ACTION vignettes feature throughout the text, and profile industry experiences and professional events that reinforce the role of accounting theory in the profession. Questions are supplied with each, and the information that is included has been obtained from Australian and international newspapers and professional articles.

APPLICATIONS TO AUDITING — each chapter contains information on how accounting theory relates to auditing. Presenting an audit perspective, this information encourages students to appreciate how accounting theory underpins all aspects of what auditors and accountants do.

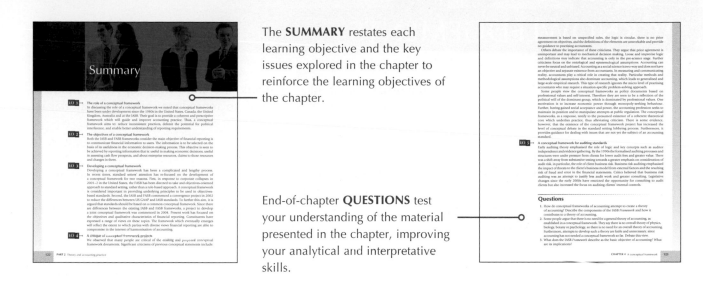

The **SUMMARY** restates each learning objective and the key issues explored in the chapter to reinforce the learning objectives of the chapter.

End-of-chapter **QUESTIONS** test your understanding of the material presented in the chapter, improving your analytical and interpretative skills.

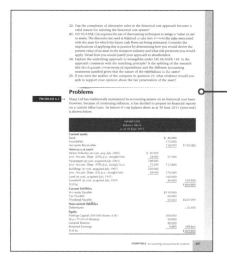

PROBLEMS included in selected chapters present more challenging activities to test your knowledge of the issues developed in the chapter.

CASE STUDIES encourage detailed evaluation of the issues explored in the chapter. The case studies are drawn from Australian and international sources that are ideal for individual and group-based activities.

KEY TERMS are presented at the end of the book, and provide an invaluable resource for your learning.

ACKNOWLEDGEMENTS

The authors and publisher would like to thank the following copyright holders, organisations and individuals for their permission to reproduce copyright material in this book.

Figures

• **p. 95:** Reproduced with joint permission of CPA Australia and the Institute of Chartered Accountants in Australia • **pp. 98, 181, 182:** Portions of various FASB documents, copyright by the Financial Accounting Standards Board, 401 Merritt 7, PO Box 5116, Norwalk, CT 06856-5116, USA, are reprinted with permission. Complete copies of these documents are available from the FASB • **p. 235:** © 2009 International Accounting Standards Committee Foundation. All rights reserved. No permission granted to reproduce or distribute • **p. 296:** CPA Australia, figure from Australian Accounting Research Foundation, ED 51B reproduced with the permission of CPA Australia Ltd and the Institute of Chartered Accountants in Australia • **p. 301:** © 2009 International Accounting Standards Committee Foundation. All rights reserved. No permission granted to reproduce or distribute • **pp. 413, 416:** From 'An empirical evaluation of accounting income numbers' by R. Ball and P. Brown, *Journal of Accounting Research*, vol. 6, no. 2, Autumn 1968. Wiley Blackwell Publishers • **p. 424:** Graphs from R. M. Bowen, D. Burgstahler and L. A. Daley, 'The incremental information content of accrual versus cash flows', *Accounting Review*, vol. 42, no. 4, 1987, p. 727 © American Accounting Association • **p. 425:** From 'Have financial statements lost their relevance?' by J. Francis and K. Schipper, *Journal of Accounting Research*, vol. 37, no. 2, 1999. Wiley Blackwell Publishing • **p. 450:** Robert Libby, *Accounting and Human Information Processing: Theory and Application*, 1st Edition, © 1981, p. 6. Adapted by permission of Pearson Education, Inc., Upper Saddle River, NJ • **p. 453:** Reprinted with permission of the Australian Graduate School of Management, publisher of the *Australian Journal of Management* • **p. 459:** From 'Human judgement accuracy: multidimensional graphics and humans versus models' by D. Stock, C. Watson, *Journal of Accounting Research*, Spring 1984, p. 202, Wiley Blackwell Publishers

Text

• IASB © 2009 International Accounting Standards Committee Foundation. All rights reserved. No permission granted to reproduce or distribute. © Commonwealth of Australia 2009. All legislation herein is reproduced by permission but does not purport to be the official or authorised version. It is subject to Commonwealth of Australia copyright. The *Copyright Act 1968* permits certain reproduction and publication of Commonwealth legislation. In particular, s. 182A of the Act enables a complete copy to be made by or on behalf of a particular person. For reproduction or publication beyond that permitted by the Act, permission should be sought in writing from the Commonwealth available from the Australian Accounting Standards Board. Requests in the first instance should be addressed to the Administration Director, Australian Accounting Standards Board, PO Box 204, Collins Street West, Melbourne, Victoria, 8007 • **pp. 8–9:** original article 'The man who saved the world' by Robert Samuelson, *The Washington Post*, 26/8/09 Issue © Reuters. All rights reserved. Republication or redistribution of Thomson Reuters content, including by framing or similar means, is expressly prohibited without the prior written consent of Thomson Reuters. Thomson

Reuters and its logo are registered trademarks or trademarks of the Thomson Reuters group of companies around the world. © Thomson Reuters 2009. Thomson Reuters journalists are subject to an Editorial Handbook which requires fair presentation and disclosure of relevant interests • **pp. 10–11:** 'Fresh blow to banking as rogue trader costs Societe Generale US$7.1 billion' by Sudip Kar-Gupta, 24/1/08, © Reuters. All rights reserved. Republication or redistribution of Thomson Reuters content, including by framing or similar means, is expressly prohibited without the prior written consent of Thomson Reuters. Thomson Reuters and its logo are registered trademarks or trademarks of the Thomson Reuters group of companies around the world. © Thomson Reuters 2009. Thomson Reuters journalists are subject to an Editorial Handbook, which requires fair presentation and disclosure of relevant interests • **p. 22:** From 'Bonuses soften wage freeze' by Sue Mitchell, 31/7/09, p. 45 • **pp. 26–7:** Blog post 'IFRS for local authorities: stop this madness now' by Richard Murphy, dated 18/1/08, accessed via http://www.taxresearch.org.uk/Blog/ • **p. 28:** From 'Shares set for a pullback, not new lows' by Glenn Mumford, *The Australian Financial Review*, 6/8/09, p. 23 • **pp. 32–7:** Extracts from 'Financial accounting: an epistemological research note' by Eduardo Schiehll, José Alonso Borba and Fernando Dal-Ri Murcia, *R.Cont. Fin.* USP. São Paulo, vol. 18, no. 45, pp. 83–90, December 2007 • **pp. 38–9:** Narelle Hooper and Fiona Buffini, *The Australian Financial Review*, 5/9/05 • **p. 39:** 'Telstra retains forecast for 2009 earnings to rise' by Andrea Tan, 6 November 2008 © 2008 Bloomberg L.P. All rights reserved. Used with permission • **pp. 45–6:** Originally published as 'UK's top groups in U-turn on accounts', *Financial Times* (London), 26/9/05 • **pp. 47–8:** 'The thrill is gone' by Philip Rennie, *BRW*, 1–7 September 2005, p. 79 • **pp. 49–50:** 'Tabcorp costs trouble market by Fleur Leyden, *Herald Sun*, 7/8/09, pp. 41–42 © *The Herald and Weekly Times* • **pp. 64–6:** 'Companies should come clean on the value of leases on their books' by Paul Kerin, *The Australian*, 2/10/07 • **pp. 68–9:** 'Accountants draw the line at regulating' by Patrick Durkin, *The Australian Financial Review*, 5/3/09, p. 5 • **pp. 72–3:** 'Executive in U.S. convicted for backdating share options', from *The New York Times*, © 8 August, 2007 *The New York Times*. All rights reserved. Used by permission and protected by the Copyright Laws of the United States. The printing, copyright, redistribution, or retransmission of this material without express written permission is prohibited • **p. 79:** 'Many small-cap reports to flash orange' by Damon Kitney and Patrick Durkin, *The Australian Financial Review*, 23/2/09, p. 9 • **pp. 84–5:** 'US's Snow urges balance in Sarbanes-Oxley rules', 2/6/05 © Reuters. All rights reserved. Republication or redistribution of Thomson Reuters content, including by framing or similar means, is expressly prohibited without the prior written consent of Thomson Reuters. Thomson Reuters and its logo are registered trademarks or trademarks of the Thomson Reuters group of companies around the world. © Thomson Reuters 2009. Thomson Reuters journalists are subject to an Editorial Handbook which requires fair presentation and disclosure of relevant interests • **pp. 85–7:** From *The New York Times*, © 1 July, 2008 *The New York Times*. All rights reserved. Used by permission and protected by the Copyright Laws of the United States. The printing, copyright, redistribution, or retransmission of this material without express written permission is prohibited • **pp. 100–1:** From 'Accounting for carbons' by Georgina Dellaportas, *Charter*, June 2008 © The Institute of Chartered Accountants in Australia • **pp. 102–3:** 'The accounting cycle. Arbitrary and capricious rules: Lease Accounting — FAS 13 v. IAS 17' by J. Edward Ketz, March 2008, first published at www.SmartPros.com • **pp. 106–7:** 'Mind the gap: AICD, Finsia set guidelines' by Marsha Jacobs, *The Australian Financial Review*, 10/3/09, p. 11 • **p. 108:** From 'Conceptual Framework — Joint Project of the IASB and FASB'. Reproduced with the FASB's permission. Copyright © 2009 International Accounting

Standards Committee Foundation. All rights reserved. No permission granted to reproduce or distribute • **pp. 127–9:** Extract from 'Enhancing not-for-profit annual and financial reporting: Best practice reporting: The essential tool for transparent reporting', 2nd edition by Stewart Leslie, The Institute of Chartered Accountants in Australia, March 2009, pp. 7–8 • **pp. 129–30:** Measurement: an international issue: from 'Revisiting the Concepts — A New Conceptual Framework Project', an FASB/IASB Special Report, May 2005. Reproduced with the FASB's permission. © 2009 International Accounting Standards Committee Foundation. All rights reserved. No permission granted to reproduce or distribute • **pp. 142–5:** 'The Impact of the accounting profession's movement toward fair value reporting in financial statements', and interview by Patrick A. Casabona, *The Review of Business*, vol. 27, no. 4, Special Accounting Issue, St John's University, pp. 6–9 • **pp. 147–8:** from 'True and fair' and 'fair value' — Accounting and legal will-o'-the-wisps' by Graeme Dean and Frank Clarke, *Abacus*, vol. 41, no. 2, 2005, pp. i–vi. Reproduced with the permission of the publisher, Wiley-Blackwell • **pp. 149–50:** 'Capital or income?' by Nadine Fry and David Bence, Accountancy Magazine (online version), April 2007, p. 81 • **pp. 154–5:** Ed Charles, *Australian CPA*, May 2002 • **pp. 155–6:** *Corporate Finance Magazine*, April 2005 © Euromoney Institutional Investor PLC • **pp. 156–7:** From 'The trend toward fair value accounting' by J. Russell Madray, *Journal of Financial Service Professionals*, May 2008, pp. 16–18. Reproduced by permission • **p. 158:** 'IFRS put damper on share option schemes' by Barney Jopson, *Financial Times*, 10/8/05 • **pp. 163–4:** From 'Bendigo boss makes small provision for big MIS exposure' by Adele Ferguson, *The Australian*, 5/8/09 • **p. 165:** From 'Client push drives Infosys jobs offshore' by Brian Corrigan, *The Australian Financial Review*, 3/8/09, p. 47 • **p. 167:** From 'Loss-making News pins hope on pay sites' by Dominic White, *The Australian Financial Review*, 7/8/09, p. 43 • **pp. 176–8:** From 'Reflections of an Australian Contemporary: The Complementarity of Entry and Exit Price Current Value Accounting Systems' © Allan Barton, *Abacus*, vol. 36, no. 3, 2000, pp. 305–307. Reproduced with the permission of the publisher, Wiley-Blackwell • **pp. 200–1:** From 'Revisiting the Concepts — A New Conceptual Framework Project', an FASB/IASB Special Report, May 2005. Reproduced with the FASB's permission. © 2009 International Accounting Standards Committee Foundation. All rights reserved. No permission granted to reproduce or distribute • **pp. 210–12:** 'Fair value or false accounting?' by Anthony Rayman, *Accountancy Magazine*, October 2004, p. 82 • **p. 213:** 'Rising dough: Domino's sales climb and costs fall' by Carrie LaFrenz, *The Australian Financial Review*, 1/8/09, p. 14 • **pp. 213–14:** 'Red ink flows, but Talent2 is looking up' by Paul Smith, *The Australian Financial Review*, 31/7/09, p. 47 • **pp. 214–15:** AAP content is owned by or licensed to Australian Associated Press Pty Limited and is copyright protected. AAP content is published on an 'as is' basis for personal use only and must not be copied, republished, rewritten, resold or redistributed, whether by caching, framing or similar means, without AAP's prior written permission. AAP and its licensors are not liable for any loss, through negligence or otherwise, resulting from errors or omissions in or reliance on AAP content. The globe symbol and 'AAP' are registered trade marks • **pp. 240–1:** From *The New York Times*, © 22 February, 2008 *The New York Times*. All rights reserved. Used by permission and protected by the Copyright Laws of the United States. The printing, copyright, redistribution, or retransmission of this material without express written permission is prohibited • **pp. 244–5:** 'Barclay's reveals £1.7bn loans write-off' by Patrick Hosking, *The Times Online*, November 16, 2007 • **p. 246:** 'Class action targets ABC and auditors' by Nabila Ahmed, *The Australian Financial Review*, 16/12/08, p. 6 • **pp. 253–5:** Reprinted with permission from CFO, April 2008. Visit our website at www.cfo.com © CFO

Publishing Corporation. All Rights Reserved. Foster Printing Service: 866-879-9144, www.marketingreprints.com • **pp. 262–3:** 'Worst may be over but thorny problems remain' by Peter Thal Larsen, *Financial Times*, 9/4/09 • **p. 267:** 'New public-private flexibility' by Annabel Hepworth, *The Australian Financial Review*, 1/4/09, p. 10 • **p. 269:** From 'The use of fair value in IFRS' by David Cairns, *Accounting in Europe*, vol. 3, iss. 1, pp. 5–22, reprinted by permission of the publisher, Taylor & Francis Group, www.informaworld.com • **p. 277:** Text box from 'Rainbow Connection' by Giles Parkinson, *Real Business*, Spring 2007, p. 31 • **pp. 287–8:** From article 'Zurich: Disclosure of Environmental Liability' by Lindene Patton, first published in 'CEO, Chief Executive Officer', 2006 by SPG Media Ltd, and found at http://www.the-chiefexecutive.com/projects/CEO008_insurance/ • **pp. 293–4:** 'No income gained from revaluations' by Robert Harley, *The Australian Financial Review*, 14/3/07, Accounting Debate, p. S13 • **pp. 306–7:** 'Revenue recognition is Isoft's curse' by Philip Stafford, *Financial Times*, 9/8/06 • **p. 308:** 'Banking group attacks IFRS with double set of accounts' by David Jetuah, Accountancy Age (online), 8/3/07 • **pp. 312–13:** 'EPG's auditor queried on sales' by Ashley Midalia, *The Australian Financial Review*, 9/5/08 • **pp. 321–3:** This article was reprinted with permission from the June 2004 issue of *Internal Auditor*, published by The Institute of Internal Auditors, Inc., www.theiia.org • **pp. 326–7:** Article by Professor Patricia Dechow, 5/7/07, Haas Research Intelligence, University of California, Berkeley's Haas School of Business, based on working paper 'Predicting material accounting misstatements' by Dechow, Larson, Ge, and Sloan • **p. 337:** 'Options deal dwarfs salary of ANZ chief' by Stuart Washington, *The Sydney Morning Herald*, 15/11/06, p. 21 • **pp. 338–9:** 'Share option plans worthless' by Patrick Durkin, *The Australian Financial Review*, 16/1/09, p. 4 • **pp. 342–3:** From 'Loophole lets banks rewrite the calendar', *The New York Times*, © 7 March, 2008 *The New York Times*. All rights reserved. Used by permission and protected by the Copyright Laws of the United States. The printing, copyright, redistribution, or retransmission of this material without express written permission is prohibited • **pp. 353–4:** 'Current developments in enviromental issues' by Charlotte Wright, *Petroleum Accounting and Financial Management Journal*, Spring 2007, vol. 26, no. 1, *Accounting for Emission Allowances*, pp. 64–65 • **p. 369:** 'Objections to crackdowns' by Steven Scott with Marsha Jacobs, *The Australian Financial Review*, 29/5/09, p. 13. • **p. 373:** 'CVC deal with UBS helps Stella performance', Market Wrap, edited by Jemima Whyte, *The Australian Financial Review*, 3/8/09, p. 18 • **pp. 376–7:** 'Education provider's earnings soar 32pc' by Sara Rich, *The Australian*, 5/8/09 • **pp. 378–9:** 'Drugs code set to get tougher' by Emma Connors, *The Australian Financial Review*, 4/8/09, p. 5 • **pp. 398–9:** 'Further concessions sought on share plans' by John Kehoe, *The Australian Financial Review*, 20/7/09, p. 5 • **pp. 399–400:** 'Results blamed on accounting' by Duncan Hughes, *The Australian Financial Review*, 4/8/09, p. 47 • **p. 409:** 'Deregulation aids earnings at GrainCorp' by Carrie LaFrenz, *The Australian Financial Review*, 4/8/09, Companies and Markets, p. 19. • **pp. 422–3:** 'New Wattyl boss to target costs' by Jeffrey Hutton, *The Australian Financial Review*, 4/8/09, p. 46 • **pp. 432–3:** 'AIFRS — A work in progress' from The Boardroom Report, vol. 4, iss. 11, 6/6/06. Reproduced with permission • **pp. 437–8:** 'DJ sales pick up but shares dive' by Rachel Hewitt, *Herald Sun*, 6/8/09 © The Herald and Weekly Times • **pp. 439–40:** 'Market cheers Axa's Asian plan' by Martin Collins: John Durie, *The Australian*, 6/8/09; • 'Nufarm buys US companies' by Geoff Easdown, *Herald Sun*, 6/8/09 © The Herald and Weekly Times • **pp. 457–8:** Media release, 'ASA seeks to remove NAB director', 8/10/08 © Australian Shareholders' Association • **p. 471:** 'Telstra opts for David Thodey as replacement for Sol Trujillo' by John Durie and Jennifer Hewett, *The Australian*, 8/5/09. • **p. 472:** 'Reporting season's moment of truth' by Barbara Drury,

The Age, 25/2/09. • **pp. 488–90:** From 'Trouble-entry accounting — revisited' by PricewaterhouseCoopers and the International Emissions Trading Association, pp. 27–28 © 2007 PricewaterhouseCoopers • **pp. 498–9:** 'Accounting related outcomes of the G20 meeting' © The Institute of Chartered Accountants in Australia, 14 April 2009 • **pp. 499–500:** 'Authority "fabricated" water data' by Carmel Egan, *The Age*, 29/3/09.

Every effort has been made to trace the ownership of copyright material. Information that will enable the publisher to rectify any error or omission in subsequent editions will be welcome. In such cases, please contact the Permissions Section of John Wiley & Sons Australia, Ltd.

Part 1

Accounting theory

1 Introduction   3
2 Accounting theory construction   19
3 Applying theory to accounting regulation   53

1

Introduction

LEARNING
OBJECTIVES

After reading this chapter, you should have an appreciation of the following:

1 what is meant by 'accounting theory' and the purpose it has served over time

2 the structure of this book and how it logically sequences its discussion of accounting theory.

This chapter traces the historical development of accounting theory and illustrates how the view of accounting has changed over time. It finishes by providing an overview of the chapters in this book.

LO 1 ⊢ OVERVIEW OF ACCOUNTING THEORY

Why do rockets need so much power to lift off? Why do humans walk on two legs? To answer these questions, we are likely to call upon the theories of gravity and evolution. These theories are generally held in high regard for their powers of explanation and prediction, but what is it that gives them their authority? In fact, what is a theory? Furthermore, what is the relevance of accounting theory to accounting?

In a perfect financial world there is no demand for published accounting reports and hence any accounting theory. We would simply look up freely available prices for the value of assets, revenues, or the costs of all inputs (including managerial costs). In such an Arrow-Debreu economy[1] all this information is available now and for all future time periods. But we do not live in such an economic world. Instead there is a demand for financial information to fill gaps in our knowledge and to reduce uncertainties about current and future values. This demand comes from a wide range of stakeholders — both internal and external.

In accounting theory a major issue is related to questions around measurement. In general, how should assets and liabilities be measured? By their historic cost, their selling price, updated by current costs to buy, or by the present value of future cash flows? Should we recognise all internally generated intangibles or only recognise them when they are evidenced by an external transaction, such as in a takeover price? Then again, what is the impact of implementing different measurement systems on the economy or market or on each individual stakeholder?

The term 'theory' can be used in different ways. As such, it can take on several meanings. One definition is that a theory is a deductive system of statements of decreasing generality that arise from an agreed or hypothesised premise. Another is that a theory is a set of ideas used to explain real-world observations. In his classic text on accounting theory, Hendriksen offered definitions of 'theory' and 'accounting theory' which are appropriate to this text. These are defined in points 1 and 2 below, respectively:

1. . . . the coherent set of hypothetical, conceptual and pragmatic principles forming the general framework of reference for a field of inquiry.
2. . . . logical reasoning in the form of a set of broad principles that (1) provide a general framework of reference by which accounting practice can be evaluated and (2) guide the development of new practices and procedures.[2]

Theory can be described simply as the logical reasoning underlying the statement of a belief. Whether the theory is accepted depends on:
- how well it explains and predicts reality
- how well it is constructed both theoretically and empirically
- how acceptable are the implications of the theory to a body of scientists, professionals and society as a whole.

It is important to understand that accounting theory is not simply an abstract process. It is not divorced from reality. In fact, its main objectives are to explain why and how current accounting practice evolved, to suggest improvements, and to provide the basis for developments in such practice.

Accounting theory is a modern concept when compared with, say, theories emanating from mathematics or physics. Accounting first developed as a set of tools to record activities or transactions. Even Pacioli's treatise (see next page) on double-entry accounting was focused on documenting the processes involved and not about explaining the underlying basis for this method of recording. Chambers summarised a view that accounting has mainly developed in an improvised fashion rather than systematically from a structured theory:

> Accounting has frequently been described as a body of practices which have been developed in response to practical needs rather than by deliberate and systematic thinking.[3]

That is, many accounting prescriptions on how to account were developed to resolve problems as they arose. Hence, the theory underlying those prescriptions also developed in a largely unstructured manner. This has led to inconsistencies in practice. Examples of such inconsistencies include different methods of depreciation and inventory expensing even within the same industry; and measuring some assets at fair value whereas others are measured at cost. In other cases, some transactions are kept off the financial statements completely. For example, the move to regulate disclosures concerned with the capitalisation of certain lease commitments was a direct response to practices being adopted that failed to recognise the lease liability in company accounts. More recently, in response to increasing demand, an accounting standard was introduced requiring firms to report the cost of providing executive remuneration in the form of share options. These examples are consistent with and illustrate the historical development of accounting methods (the inconsistency problem). It is worth pointing out at this juncture that some theoretical accountants argue that, because business situations vary across industry (and countries), we need a variety of accounting methods that can be adapted to fit the changing needs of business.

Accounting practices also have multiple demands from insiders, such as managers and employees, and outsiders such as investors, creditors, taxation, legislative authorities and society in general. This means that accounting theory is complex and one of the issues under intense debate is who should financial accounting reports serve? That is, who are the primary users of accounting information? We call this the 'objective problem' — the problem of determining the objective of financial information.

For many years, accounting standard setters have been trying to solve the objective and inconsistency problems by developing a conceptual (theoretical) framework that would lead to more consistent treatment of like items. However, conceptual framework projects have not resolved the inconsistencies in practice, and have often been used to justify or support such inconsistencies rather than resolve them. Because such frameworks seek to provide universal guidance, they have proved too general to provide a clear set of decision rules which lead to an obvious practical answer for the full range of choices required in preparing accounting reports.

Pre-theory

Before the double-entry system was formalised in the 1400s, very little was written about the theory underlying accounting practices. During the developmental period of the double-entry system, the main emphasis was on practice. It was not until 1494 that a Franciscan monk, Fra Pacioli, wrote the first book to document the double-entry accounting system as we know it. The title of his work was *Summa de Arithmetica Geometria Proportioni et Proportionalità* (Review of Arithmetic, Geometry and Proportions). For 300 years following Pacioli's 1494 treatise, developments in accounting concentrated on refining practice. This is referred to as the 'pre-theory period'.[4] Goldberg asserts:

> No theory of accounting was devised from the time of Pacioli down to the opening of the nineteenth century. Suggestions of theory appear here and there, but not to the extent necessary to place accounting on a systematic basis.[5]

Until the 1930s, developments in accounting theory were rather random and ill-defined, evolving as they were needed to justify particular practices. However, developments in the 1800s led to the formalisation of existing practices in textbooks and teaching methods. The rapid expansion in technology, accompanied by the large-scale separation of ownership from control of the means of production, increased the demand for both management and financial accounting information. In particular, growth of the business sector and the construction of railroad networks in the United States and the United Kingdom increased the demand for detailed accounting information, for improved techniques, and for accounting practices such as depreciation which addressed the long-term nature of assets. The introduction of taxation legislation and the 'teething' problems associated with the birth of the corporation led to increased government legislation regarding reporting requirements. Further, some government and corporate economic policy decisions were beginning to be based on accounting numbers. Also during this period, economic theory was progressing rapidly and was beginning to be linked to the demands for accounting information. These developments occurred mainly in the United Kingdom. They provided an impetus for the growth of theories explaining accounting practice to enable accountants to deal with new issues as they arose and to explain to students why certain procedures were adopted. After this, developments in accounting theory shifted from the United Kingdom to the United States.

Pragmatic accounting

The period 1800–1955 is often referred to as the 'general scientific period'. The emphasis was on providing an overall framework to explain why accountants account as they do; that is, based upon observation of practice.[6] Empirical analysis relies on real-world observations rather than basing practice on deductive logic that is critical of current practices. The major focus of accounting was on the use of historical cost transactions and the application of the conservatism principle. The scientific method was interpreted as being based on empirics.

However, while it has been labelled an empirical period in accounting development, there was a degree of logical debate about the merits of measurement procedures. This was especially the case after the Great Wall Street Crash in 1929. This led to the creation of the Securities and Exchange Commission (SEC) in the United States in the early 1930s. The SEC had a brief and legislative power to improve financial regulation and reporting, with many seeing the crash being caused by questionable accounting methods. Stephen Zeff reports that Healy and Kripke, two leading practitioners, were highly critical of the accounting write up practices in the United States in the 1920s. Such comments as '... write ups were used to create income or to relieve the income accounts of important charges' and '... you can capitalize in some States practically everything except the furnace ashes in the basement' and '... illustrated what they saw as the flagrant write up of assets in the 1920s'.[7]

The 1930s period also gave rise to several notable accounting publications and initiatives and saw the birth of professionally based conceptual theory. In 1936 the American Accounting Association (AAA) released *A Tentative Statement of Accounting Principles Affecting Corporate Reports*; in 1938 the American Institute of Certified Practising Accountants (AICPA) made an independent review of accounting principles and released

A *Statement of Accounting Principles* (authored by Sanders, Hatfield and Moore). In the same year, the AICPA established the Accounting Procedures Committee, which published a series of accounting research bulletins. The nature of these bulletins (and other accounting theory publications at the time) was summarised in the preface of Bulletin No. 43:

> Forty-two bulletins were issued during the period 1939 to 1953. Eight of these were reports on terminology. The other 34 were the result of research by the committee on accounting procedures directed to those segments of accounting practice where problems were most demanding and with which business and the accounting profession were most concerned at the time.

As a result of this sporadic approach to the development of accounting principles, the AICPA established the Accounting Principles Board and appointed a director of accounting research in 1959. Overall, this period focused on the existing practical 'viewpoint' of accounting and, as research gained momentum over the period, the theories promulgated to explain practice became more detailed and complex.

Normative accounting

The period 1956–70 is labelled the 'normative period', because it was a period when accounting theorists attempted to establish 'norms' for 'best accounting practice'. During this period researchers, such as Edwards and Bell in 1961 and Chambers in 1966, were less concerned about what *actually* happened in practice and more concerned about developing theories that prescribed what *should* happen. In the years before 1956, several authors produced preliminary normative works which related mainly to issues surrounding the appropriate basis for the valuation of assets and owners' claims. These theories made adjustments for the impact of inflation and specific increases in asset prices.[8]

The normative period was one of significant debate. It degenerated into a battle between competing viewpoints on the ideal approach to measuring and reporting accounting information. During this period, the debate was predominantly about measurement rather than the actual practice of recording and reporting information. However, the end result was no clear choice for changing practice to one ideal system of (inflation or price adjusted) accounting, leading to the continued use of the historical cost method. The accounting profession in Australia has been reluctant to reignite the debate about recommending on a specific and ideal measurement system and has failed to issue comprehensive measurement guidelines. Instead, in 2005 the profession adopted the measurement guidelines contained in the International Accounting Standards Board's (IASB) conceptual framework. The IASB has rather an unstructured approach, with the accounting standards allowing adoption of current value measurement concepts to be mixed with historical cost.

Normative theories are distinguished because they adopt an objective (ideal) stance and then specify the means of achieving the stated objective. They provide prescriptions for what *should* occur to achieve their stated objective. As mentioned, the major focus of the normative accounting theories during the period 1956–70 was the impact of changing prices on the value of assets and the calculation of profit (such theories were often seen as a consequence of the record levels of inflation experienced during this period).[9]

Two groups dominated the normative period — the critics of historical cost accounting and the conceptual framework proponents. There was some overlap between these two groups, especially when historical cost critics tried to develop theories of accounting where asset measurement and profit determination depended on inflation and/or specific price movements.

During the normative period, the idea of a 'conceptual framework' gained increased popularity. A 'conceptual framework' is a structured theory of accounting. Such frameworks are meant to encompass all components of financial reporting and are intended to guide practice.[10] For example, in 1965 Goldberg was commissioned by the AAA to investigate the nature of accounting. The result was the publication of *An Inquiry into the Nature of Accounting*, which aimed at developing a framework of accounting theory by providing a discussion of the nature and meaning of accounting.[11] One year later, the AAA released *A Statement of Basic Accounting Theory*, with the stated purpose of providing 'an integrated statement of basic accounting theory which will serve as a guide to educators, practitioners and others interested in accounting'. These frameworks had a common logical approach. They first stated the objective (purpose) of accounting and then worked downwards to derive accounting principles and rules that fulfilled that objective.

The normative period began drawing to an end in the early 1970s, and was replaced by the 'specific scientific theory' period, or the 'positive era' (1970–). The two main factors that prompted the demise of the normative period were:

- the unlikelihood of acceptance of any one particular normative theory
- the application of financial economic principles, increased supply of data and testing methods.

Because normative accounting theories prescribe how accounting *should* be practised, they are based on opinions of what the accounts should report, and the best way to do that. Opinions as to the appropriate goals and methods of accounting vary between individuals, and most of the dissatisfaction with the normative approach was that it provided no means of resolving these differences of opinion. Henderson, Peirson and Brown[12] outline the two major criticisms of normative theories in the early 1970s:

- Normative theories do not necessarily involve empirical hypothesis testing.
- Normative theories are based on value judgements.

Further, the underlying assumptions of some normative theories were untested, and it was unclear whether the theories had strong foundations or assumptions about the purpose of accounting. Pragmatically, it was also difficult to obtain general acceptance of any particular normative accounting theory.

**1.1
THEORY
IN ACTION**

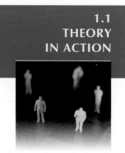

Theory implementation and politics

A depression scholar knows what it takes

by Robert Samuelson

It would have been insane for US president Barack Obama not to nominate Ben Bernanke to a second term as chairman of the Federal Reserve. The economics dictated it, as did the politics.

We will never know whether the world might have suffered a depression if Bernanke's Fed had not responded so aggressively.

Early this year, the Nobel Prize-winning economist and *New York Times* columnist Paul Krugman issued depression warnings.

Bernanke admitted similar fears in interviews with David Wessel, economics editor of *The Wall Street Journal* and author of *In Fed We Trust*. The fact that the global economy is no longer uncontrollably spiraling downward (for 2010, the Economist Intelligence Unit predicts growth of 2.7 per cent for the world and 1.8 per cent for the United States) was no foregone conclusion. Nor was it ordained that the panic gripping financial markets just six months ago would subside. From recent lows in March, the US stockmarket is now up roughly 50 per cent.

It is not that Bernanke's performance was flawless. Far from it. He made two blunders. First, he didn't see the crisis coming. Even after the collapse of the investment bank Bear Stearns in March 2008, he didn't foresee a widespread financial panic or a savage recession.

In the summer of 2008, the economy was weakening but seemed — to Bernanke and most economists — to be suffering from inflationary overheating. Consumer prices were rising at a 5 per cent annual rate, oil was peaking at $147 a barrel.

Second, along with the then-treasury secretary Henry Paulson, Bernanke allowed Lehman Brothers to go bankrupt in September. Both have said they lacked the legal power to rescue Lehman and that no one wanted to buy it.

If Bernanke and Paulson had fully anticipated the consequences of Lehman's failure, they almost certainly would have found a way to save it. Once Lehman collapsed, the crisis got much worse. Banks retreated from lending to each other, investors wouldn't buy new bonds, banks, consumers and businesses hoarded cash. The economy contracted at an annual rate of 5 per cent to 6 per cent.

Here is where Bernanke distinguished himself. A student of the Great Depression, and especially of the disastrous effects of bank failures, he went well beyond the standard response of lowering interest rates (the overnight Fed funds rate dropped effectively to zero by December). The Fed created a dizzying array of liquidity facilities to substitute more than $US1 trillion of Fed credit for retreating private credit. It supported markets for mortgages, money market funds, commercial paper, auto loans and student loans. The strategy was, as Wessel says, to do whatever it took to avoid a complete loss of credit and confidence — a loss causing continuous drops in spending and asset prices (for stocks, bonds, homes) and ending in depression.

Although there were other actors, the Fed's interventions were decisive in halting the panic. It is an open question whether any other Fed chairman — someone without Bernanke's detailed knowledge of the Depression — would have been so bold in supporting credit markets. Moreover, Bernanke's approach inspired similar moves abroad. But this is also Bernanke's burden. If the Fed doesn't withdraw all that extra credit quickly enough, it may spawn inflation. If it withdraws it too quickly, it may subvert recovery.

Source: Excerpts from *The Australian Financial Review*, 27 August 2009, p. 63, www.afr.com

Questions
1. The article describes how a particular theoretical approach has been replaced by another. Explain why one theory replaces another, and who, or what, determines whether an existing theory survives.
2. Does the reintroduction of a theory mean that it should not have been replaced in the first place?
3. Should a theory be discarded if it does not specify the means of achieving a stated objective? Explain your answer.

Positive accounting

The dissatisfaction with normative theories, combined with increased access to empirical data sets and an increasing recognition of economic arguments within the accounting literature, led to the shift to a 'new' form of empiricism which operates under the broad label of 'positive theory'.[13] In effect, positive theory was hardly 'new', as it was based on the empirical approach, which formed the basis of the general scientific period. Positive theory sought to provide a framework for explaining the practices which were being observed; that is, whether what practising accountants produced had a decision-usefulness objective, whether it filled other roles, and whether it was inferior or superior to proposed alternatives.

The objective of positive accounting theory is to explain and predict accounting practice. An example of a positive accounting theory is the theory that leads to what is known as the 'bonus plan hypothesis'. This theory relies on managers being wealth-maximisers who would rather have more wealth than less, even at the expense of shareholders. If managers are remunerated partly with bonuses based on reported accounting profits, the managers have incentives to use accounting policies that maximise reported profits in periods when they are likely to receive bonuses. This theory leads to the prediction (hypothesis) that managers who are remunerated via bonus plans use profit-increasing accounting methods more than managers who are not remunerated via bonus plans. Such theories are important since they explain the economic, or wealth, effects of accounting and why accounting is important to various parties such as shareholders, lenders and managers — all of whose personal wealth is affected by accounting decisions.[14] It is also important in assisting in the design of contracts based on accounting numbers that control such behaviour.

By explaining and predicting accounting practice, Watts and Zimmerman consider that positive theory has given order to the apparent confusion associated with the choice of accounting techniques. They argue that positive accounting theory helps predict the reactions of investors in the market (such as current shareholders) to the actions of management and to reported accounting information.[15] One benefit of such research is that it enables regulators to assess the economic consequences of the various accounting practices they consider. The problem with this approach is that wealth maximisation became the answer to every question. Basically, whatever the observed practice, it could be construed as a means of maximising wealth (normally for the firm, but sometimes for management). To give the argument symmetry, the reverse argument could also be applied — namely, that the observed practice was to minimise the impact of costs or some external event on the value of the firm. The positive literature involves developing hypotheses about reality which are subsequently tested by observation of impact, usually based upon the assumption of wealth maximisation. The approach has attracted criticisms which are largely based on the seemingly narrow approach that concentrated on agency theory and assumptions about the efficiency of markets.

The potential role of positive accounting theories in explaining and predicting behaviour is illustrated in theory in action 1.2.

1.2
**THEORY
IN ACTION**

Out of control

Fresh blow to banking as rogue trader costs Societe Generale US$7.1 billion

by Sudip Kar-Gupta

A "massive fraud" by a junior rogue trader has punched a US$7 billion hole in the finances of French bank Societe Generale, leaving its credibility in tatters and forcing it to get emergency cash.

France's central bank and government scrambled to shore up confidence in the banking system after Societe Generale, France's second-biggest bank, said it had been the victim of massive and "exceptional" fraud resulting in losses of 4.9 billion euros.

SocGen, one of France's oldest banks and a world leader in free-wheeling modern financial derivatives, blamed a young backroom trader whom it said had tried to cover up bad bets on the stock market. "It was an extremely sophisticated fraud in the way it was concealed", said Societe Generale chairman Daniel Bouton, who offered to resign but has been asked to stay on.

Shares in the bank fell more than 6% to 74 euros.

The Bank of France announced an enquiry by the Banking Commission. Governor Christian Noyer said SocGen had been able to overcome the crisis because it was "very solid".

If fraud is proved, the loss will be the biggest caused by a single trader, dwarfing the US$1.4 billion loss by trader Nick Leeson that brought down British bank Barings in the 1990s.

SocGen declined to name the trader, but said he had been suspended pending dismissal after confessing to his actions. It described him as a man in his thirties who had worked for SocGen since 2002 and earned less than 100 000 (US$146 500) euros a year. He now faces legal action from Societe Generale, which is in turn already being sued by a group of 100 angry shareholders.

The bank accused the trader of taking "massive fraudulent" positions in 2007 and 2008 on European equity market indexes, meaning he was gambling on broad movements in share prices. When the bank discovered the concealed trades, it decided to close the positions in the market as quickly as possible, but this coincided with a sharp market sell-off, and the bank's losses on the deals spiraled to 4.9 billion euros.

Like Leeson before him, the trader apparently benefited from knowledge of the bank's control systems after working in the back office of its trading rooms, according to SocGen.

It said he had used a "scheme of elaborate fictitious transactions" to try to cover up his mistakes, but did not accuse him of profiting personally from his actions.

The announcement sent a shiver through the world banking industry, which is suffering a credit crunch as high-risk U.S. mortgage borrowers default on their loans. Lehman Brothers chief executive and chairman Richard Fuld called it "everyone's worst nightmare" in a comment from the World Economic Forum in Davos, Switzerland.

"We get the feeling that the financial markets have become a big casino which has lost control. It seems incredible that the Societe Generale can lose 5 billion through one operator", said Alain Crouzat, a portfolio manager at Montsegur Finance.

Other said the crisis at SocGen, one of the top 10 banks in the eurozone by market value, could spell trouble elsewhere. "The most serious thing is that this puts into doubt the risk-management systems at some banks," said Fortis analyst Carlos Garcia. "You can't suddenly announce this from one day to the next a hit of $7 billion. In the light of this, what we've done is to downgrade banks that are very linked to trading income or whose capital base is weak."

Analysts said the episode would have a major impact on the reputation of SocGen, which was founded in 1864 and is one of France's most prestigious blue-chip companies. Several said the bank, which has for years been coveted by larger French rival BNP Paribas, could face a battle to remain independent. Shares in BNP rose 7%.

SocGen said it expected a 2007 net profit of between 600 and 800 million euros, well below its 2006 profit figure.

Source: Excerpts from Reuters, 24 January 2008; published online, *Financial Post*, www.financialpost.com.

Questions

1. 'Rogue' is defined in the Oxford dictionary as 'that which lacks appropriate control; something which is irresponsible or undisciplined'. Given this definition, who is ultimately responsible for the rogue trading outlined in the Societe Generale scandal — the trader directly involved; management, who are responsible for the high-risk framework in which the trader operated; or a combination of both?

2. Discuss the role played in the SocGen case by each of the following three elements: personality, institutional framework, and opportunity.

3. How could Societe Generale have been unaware of the activity of its trader and of the environment that it had created for the trader to operate within?

4. Do you think that the actions of 'rogue' traders are predictable under particular theories (such as agency theory)? Explain your answer.

This seemingly narrow approach of the positive theorists resulted in a resurgence, especially in the 1980s, in behavioural research. Behavioural research is concerned with the broader sociological implications of accounting numbers and the associated actions of key participants such as managers, shareholders, creditors and the government as they react to accounting information. An example is a theory that predicts that loan managers cannot process all the financial information they receive, so they assess firms' credit risk using the information that is most relevant to the background of the loan manager. If the loan manager had been involved with loans to firms that defaulted on their debt agreements because of poor cash flows, despite profitable activities, it is predicted that the manager will place more reliance on cash flow information than other information. On the other hand, if the loan manager had been involved with loans to firms that defaulted because of unprofitable operations, it is predicted that the manager will place more reliance on the reported profit or loss and earnings prospects of prospective borrowers. Behavioural accounting theory tends to focus on psychological and sociological influences on individuals in their use and/or preparation of accounting. Note that, although it had a resurgence in the 1980s and continues to be important, behavioural research in accounting emerged in the early 1950s and first appeared in the accounting literature in 1967.[16]

More recently, there has been a spate of very significant and dramatic corporate collapses or confessions of corporate wrongdoing. Many stakeholders (shareholders, government, and creditors) are concerned about the failure of accounting information to signal such financial catastrophes and the apparent manipulation of accounting information and of those meant to independently report on financial information (auditors). In fact, in some of these cases (such as Enron in 2001 and the collapses in the financial sector in 2008) it appears that the auditors colluded with management to mislead the external stakeholders. In one sense, this supports the positive view that at least one party was acting to maximise its wealth to the obvious detriment of others. This leads to an alternative view — if theory focused on the impact of accounting on behaviour rather than on explanations after the event of observed behaviour, the current corporate and reporting failures could well have been predicted. Instead, as occurred in the aftermath of the 1930s following the 'Great Crash' of the Wall Street exchange, the legislative reporting requirements have been increased significantly (e.g. the Sarbanes–Oxley Act (2002) in the United States), following the collapse of WorldCom and Enron.

One view is that it is impossible to develop a single theory of accounting, as human greed, opportunism, future uncertainty, and a degree of naivety on the part of some stakeholders can never be captured in a theory of accounting *per se*. Accounting standards and legislated reporting measures are the outcome of competing sets of interests and this may well be the place to begin developing a new theory of accounting behaviour. Either way, the current environment is one of increased disclosures and reporting requirements with legislated sanctions. But the key question is will this advance the development of theories relating to accounting measurements and disclosures?

Recent developments

Both academic and professional interests in theory development have tended to be aligned in the past. In recent times, however, academic and professional developments in accounting theory have taken somewhat different approaches. Whereas the academic research emphasis remains in the area of capital market, agency theory, and behavioural impacts, the profession has pursued a more normative approach. In particular, the profession has sought normative theories to unify accounting practice and make it more homogeneous, whereas academic researchers have sought to better understand the role and impact of different forms of accounting information. These positive and normative approaches are not incompatible, since an understanding of the impact of accounting is a factor that accounting standard setters consider in developing prescriptions for practice.

In the mid to late 1980s, the Australian accounting profession was heavily involved in the conceptual framework debate in an attempt to provide a definitive statement of the nature and purpose of financial reporting and to provide appropriate criteria for deciding between alternative accounting practices. In December 1987, the Australian Accounting Research Foundation (AARF) released ED 42A–D 'Proposed Statements of Accounting Concepts', which outlined the objective, qualitative characteristics and rules for the definition and measurement of assets and liabilities. It also included a detailed outline of the 'tentative building blocks of a conceptual framework for regulation of financial reporting'. This was closely followed by ED 46A–B in March 1988, which outlined the concept of a reporting entity and provided definitions of the measurement and recognition of expenses. In 1990, the AARF formally applied the basis of the conceptual framework in Statement of Accounting Concepts (SAC) 1, 2 and 3, followed in 1992 by SAC 4. SAC 5, the controversial measurement statement, had not been released prior to the adoption of international financial reporting standards (IFRS) in 2005.

The transition to IFRS saw the replacement of SAC 3 and SAC 4 with the IASB's conceptual framework, which together with SAC 1 and SAC 2 make up the conceptual framework in Australia. The IASB framework also forms the basis for the frameworks of other standard-setting nations such as the United Kingdom, Canada and New Zealand. The conceptual frameworks of the various countries are used in developing accounting standards and in attempting to reduce the inconsistencies arising from earlier fragmented theory and practice developments. The need for a single, consistent framework has gained widespread acceptance in recent years. The IASB, in a joint project with the US Financial Accounting Standards Board, embarked on a new conceptual framework project in 2005 to update and improve the conceptual framework for standard setters and preparers of financial statements to use.

The need for a single set of international accounting standards was acknowledged by the accounting profession in Australia with the adoption of IFRS in January 2005. International standards seek to harmonise practices across international reporting boundaries and to reduce the differences in reported information which are a direct consequence of different accounting choices. This approach aims to eliminate accounting disclosures and techniques specific to one or a small group of countries which subsequently affects the comparability or integration of information, particularly for multinational and listed corporations. The assumption is that the same theoretical issues apply whether the standards are specific to one country or designed for global application.

Figure 1.1, overleaf, summarises the main periods of theory development to the present.

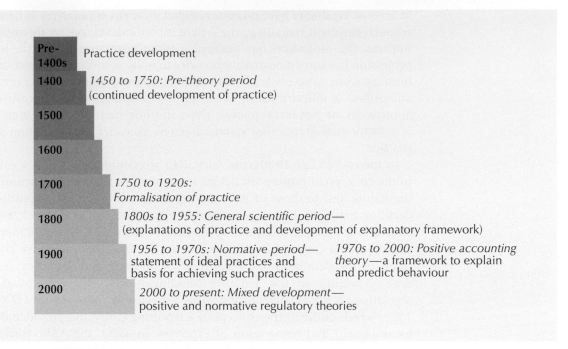

FIGURE 1.1 Accounting theory timeline

LO 2 ┤ CONTENT OUTLINE

This book provides a link between issues in accounting theory, research and practice. To reflect this, the book is divided into three parts:

Part 1: Accounting theory (chapters 1–3)

Part 2: Theory contributing to practice through accounting standards (chapters 4–10)

Part 3: Accounting and research (chapters 11–14)

Chapters 2 and 3 detail many different theory construction frameworks and then apply them to analyse examples from the accounting literature. The 'parts' of a theory are detailed, the means of testing theories are considered and the chronological development of accounting theory is traced. Understanding the components of theory development is important for accountants, not just those who will become academics, but also those who need to understand the choice of alternative accounting methods and explain this to clients and stakeholders. It is also important to distinguish between theory development as it relates to the natural versus human sciences. Accounting processes and information are the result of a complex set of human interactions and decisions which may not fit the traditional empirical (or scientific) process. When it comes to interpreting human behaviour, completely rational and systematic approaches may not apply. To be a complete professional accountant one needs to understand the mainstream approaches to theory development, in order to specifically consider theories of accounting, the behaviours accounting information demands, and the advice needed by clients. Thus, these chapters set down the fundamentals of taking a scientific perspective.

Chapter 4 describes how, over time, the different perspectives of the different users of financial statements have influenced the focus of accounting. It covers issues such as whether the focus of accounting is on reporting the ownership interest in the firm or the financial affairs of the firm as a separate operating entity. In addition, this chapter highlights a common view that accountants actually create their own 'reality'; that is, accounting measures and reports are an outcome of the boundaries drawn by accountants to construct the reporting entity. Basically, a significant number of choices and decisions are made to ensure the accounting methods fit the reporting entity. It is important to appreciate that human decisions, preferences and objectives will affect the accounting viewpoint adopted, which in turn drives the accounting choices made in recording, measuring and reporting accounting information. This is an important chapter in the context that the IFRS has adopted a shareholder perspective rather than an entity perspective when determining the focus of accounting.

Since measurement is fundamental to accounting, chapter 5 provides an introduction to some important technical issues in relation to measurement and to how it applies to accounting theory and practice. We learn that in fundamental measurement numbers can be assigned by reference to natural laws, but in accounting there is considerable debate over the nature of fundamental value. We also learn that accounting is derived measurement that depends on the previous measurement of two or more other quantities. For example, we calculate income and expenses before profit is determined. Fiat measurements are those that relate numbers to properties of objects or events on the basis of arbitrary definitions.

Chapter 6 provides an overview of the accounting measurement systems from which the principles of fair value accounting can be said to be derived. The first section describes conventional historical cost accounting and the theoretical bases, criticisms and defence of the system. During the normative period, the historical cost system came under attack, and theories were developed to deal with the effects of changing prices on asset valuation and profit determination. These theories focused on either buying prices (current costs) or selling prices (exit prices). This part of the chapter outlines the development of current cost and exit price accounting theories and techniques, reviews the application of such techniques, and analyses the perceived impact of reporting current cost and exit price information. Thus, this chapter enables the student to place into perspective arguments about accounting measurement and the current debates about measurement in IFRS.

The definition and measurement of assets and liabilities are fundamental in determining the net value of the firm and, in many cases, the income and equity. Chapter 7 provides the definition of an asset and addresses measurement issues related to tangible, intangible and financial assets. The mixed measurement attribute model applied by IFRS is outlined as well as the concepts and methods behind different measurement methods. Chapter 8 is concerned with the credit side of the balance sheet — liabilities and equity. Liabilities are first defined and applications associated with applying the recognition and mixed measurement criteria to employee benefits, pension liabilities, provisions and contingencies are discussed. Issues are currently under intense debate as the IASB and FASB attempt to improve accounting standards in these areas. The chapter finishes with the definition of equity as the residual interest in assets, discusses the concept of capital, and outlines the difference between debt and equity.

The calculation of profit has been a key component in accounting measurement over many years and forms a fundamental component in many valuation models, capital market research, agency contracts, taxation issues, social issues and the behaviour of individuals. Chapters 9 and 10 provide overviews of the issues faced in the two main components used to derive income — revenue and expenses. Discussion is provided about recognition criterion — from cash transactions through to more recent concepts such as the acquisition of a customer valued at exit price. We show that there is now less emphasis on the traditional notions of realisation and earned. We also discuss the concept of the comprehensive income. Expenses are defined and concepts such as economic benefits, expired costs and matching expenses and revenue are discussed in chapter 10. One outcome of these two chapters is the ultimate consideration of the nature of profit and the alternative measurement rules that can give rise to quite different levels of reported profit.

Positive empirical accounting theory has been at the forefront of the academic accounting research agenda for several decades. Chapters 11 and 12 focus on the philosophy, scope and impact of positive theory on accounting theory development. Chapter 11 details the development of theories of accounting policy choice and revenue management. It focuses on contracting, agency and signalling theories, as a result of the divergence between managers and shareholders (and debtors), that provide managers with incentives to manage accounting numbers to maximise the wealth of themselves or the firm. Chapter 12 describes and explains the development of theories about the role of accounting information in the share market. It focuses on evidence of how share prices respond to accounting information, and why the information should influence either the price or amount of shares that are traded. The role and development of behavioural accounting theory are described in chapter 13. This chapter explains how relaxing some of the assumptions underlying positive accounting theory and focusing on individual behaviour rather than on aggregate market behaviour influences an understanding of the role of accounting reports and their significance, in various contexts, to various parties. The final chapter, chapter 14, discusses some recent controversial issues in accounting theory and regulation. Issues covered are the use of XBRL — a system that enables users to extract accounting data at a micro (less aggregated) level, the impact of Sarbanes–Oxley on the accounting and auditing professions, the role of fair values in the global financial crisis of 2008–2009, the IASB and FASB convergence program, and the impact of IFRS on auditors. Finally, the chapter ends by summarising a number of issues in sustainability accounting. This research area is a growing extension to the traditional focus of accounting theory on financial issues. It examines social and environmental issues in an accounting context. Topics covered include the Global Reporting Initiatives, climate change issues and accounting for carbon emissions rights, assurance problems, and water accounting.

Overall, this book aims to assist students to develop the necessary skills to interpret, discuss, evaluate and criticise competing theories and concepts, and to apply the elements of these theories and concepts to current accounting issues. More specifically, it aims to help students evaluate the current issues surrounding the introduction of IFRS on a scientific basis, using logic and empirical perspectives.

Additional readings

Anthony, R, Hawkins, D, & Merchant, K 1999, *Accounting: text and cases*, 10th edn, New York: McGraw-Hill.

Barry, P 2002, *Rich kids: how the Murdochs and Packers lost $950 million in One.Tel*, Sydney: Random House.

Marshall, D, McManus, W, & Viele, D 2002, *Accounting: what the numbers mean*, 5th edn, New York: McGraw-Hill.

Scott, W 2006, *Financial accounting theory*, Toronto: Pearson.

Zeff, SA 2007, *The SEC rules historical cost accounting: 1934 to the 1970s*, Working paper, January, Rice University.

Endnotes

1. An Arrow–Debreu economy is when there are complete and perfect markets with all possible information available about current and future events.
2. E Hendriksen, *Accounting theory*, p. 1, Illinois: Richard D Irwin, 1970.
3. RJ Chambers, 'Why bother with postulates?', *Journal of Accounting Research*, vol. 1, no. 1, Spring, p. 3, 1963.
4. S Henderson, G Peirson and R Brown, *Financial accounting theory — its nature and development*, 2nd edn, Melbourne: Longman Cheshire, 1992.
5. For a detailed discussion of the historical development of the double-entry system, see L Goldberg, 'The development of accounting', *Australian Accountancy Student*, March, pp. 3–8; May, pp. 51–9; July, pp. 99–107; September, pp. 146–54, 1949.
6. Henderson, Peirson and Brown op. cit., p. 58.
7. SA Zeff, *The SEC rules historical cost accounting: 1934 to the 1970s*, Working paper, Rice University, January, 2007. See also David Alexander and Eva Jermakowicz, *Abacus*, vol. 42, no.2, 2006, p. 143, where they comment on conceptual frameworks that reinforced historic cost and conservatism 'This was a reaction (against deviations from transaction accounting) to the widespread practices of the 1920s to overstate assets and net income'.
8. Two examples of such books are: K MacNeal, *Truth in accounting*, Philadelphia: University of Pennsylvania, 1939; and H Sweeney, *Stabilized accounting*, New York: Harper, 1936.
9. See, for example, O Edwards and P Bell, *The theory and measurement of business income*, Berkeley: University of California, 1961; R Chambers, *Accounting, evaluation and economic behavior*, Englewood Cliffs, NJ: Prentice Hall,1966; A Barton, *The anatomy of accounting*, St Lucia: University of Queensland Press, 1975; S Gilman, *Accounting concepts of profit*, New York: Ronald Press, 1939.
10. A detailed analysis of the conceptual framework literature is provided in chapter 2 of this book.
11. L Goldberg, *An inquiry into the nature of accounting*, Iowa City: AAA, 1965.
12. Henderson, Peirson and Brown op. cit., p. 39.
13. Chapters 11 and 12 provide a detailed analysis of the positive accounting literature.
14. For further detail, see chapter 11.
15. R Watts and J Zimmerman, *Positive accounting theory*, Englewood Cliffs, NJ: Prentice Hall, 1986.
16. J Birnberg and J Shields, 'Three decades of behavioral accounting research: A search for order', *Behavioral Research in Accounting*, vol. 1, 1989, pp. 23–74.

2 Accounting theory construction

After reading this chapter, you should have an appreciation of the following:

1 how pragmatic approaches to theory development apply to accounting

2 criticisms that have been levelled at historical cost accounting as a theoretical model

3 normative true income theories and the decision-usefulness approach to accounting theory

4 how positive theories are constructed

5 alternative naturalistic approaches and the importance of ontology

6 misconceptions associated with scientific approaches to accounting research, and why they are misconceptions

7 issues for auditing theory construction.

A useful way to study and assess accounting theories is to classify them according to the assumptions they rely on, how they were formulated, and their approaches to explaining and predicting actual events. Some of the classifications that have proven most useful are pragmatic, syntactic, semantic, normative, positive and naturalistic approaches. Pragmatic approaches are based on observing the behaviour of accountants or those who use the information generated by accountants. Syntactic approaches rely on logical argument, based on a set of premises, and semantic approaches concern how theories correspond to real-world events. Normative theories rely on both semantic and syntactic approaches. Positive approaches test hypotheses against actual events, and naturalistic approaches consider individual cases and do not try to generalise.

This chapter provides some insight into how accounting theories in each of these classifications were formulated. We also note some of the weaknesses and criticisms of various theories. Later chapters consider the different types of theory in detail in relation to particular accounting issues.

LO 1 ⊢ PRAGMATIC THEORIES

Descriptive pragmatic approach

The descriptive pragmatic approach to accounting theory construction is an inductive approach — it is based on continual observation of the behaviour of accountants in order to copy their accounting procedures and principles. Hence, a theory can be developed from observations of how accountants act in certain situations. The theory can be tested by observing whether accountants do, in fact, act in the way the theory suggests. Sterling called this method the 'anthropological approach':

> ... if the accounting anthropologist has observed that accounting man normally records a 'conservative' figure and generalises this as the 'principle of conservatism', then we can test this principle by observing whether or not accounting man does in fact record a conservative figure. If the accounting anthropologist sets forth the 'principle of diversity', then we can test this principle by observing whether or not accounting man does in fact record similar occurrences in different ways. And so forth.[1]

The descriptive pragmatic approach is probably the oldest and most universally used method of accounting theory construction. Until quite recently, it was a popular way of learning accounting skills — future accountants were trained by being apprenticed or articled to a practising accountant.

However, there have been several criticisms of this approach to accounting theory construction:

- The descriptive pragmatic approach does not include an analytical judgement of the quality of an accountant's actions; there is no assessment of whether the accountant reports in the way he or she should.
- This approach does not provide for accounting techniques to be challenged, hence it does not allow for change. For example, we observe practising accountants' methods and techniques and teach those methods and techniques to students. Those students will become practising accountants whom we will observe in the future to learn what to teach, and so on.
- The descriptive pragmatic approach focuses attention on accountants' behaviour, not on measuring the attributes of the firm, such as assets, liabilities and profit. In taking a descriptive pragmatic approach, we are not concerning ourselves with the semantics of accounting phenomena.

Sterling comments:

> ... it is my value judgement that the theory of accounting ought to be concerned with accounting phenomena, not practising accountants, in the same way that theories of physics are concerned with physical phenomena, not practising physicists.[2]

Sterling concludes that such a pragmatic approach is inappropriate for accounting theory construction. His conclusion is, of course, in relation to normative theories of how accounting should be conducted rather than pragmatic theories that describe real-world practices.

Psychological pragmatic approach

In contrast to descriptive pragmatic approaches where theorists observe accountants' behaviours, psychological pragmatic approaches require theorists to observe users' responses to the accountants' outputs (such as financial reports). A reaction by the user is taken as evidence that the financial statements are useful and contain relevant information. A problem with the psychological pragmatic approach is that some users may react in an illogical manner, some might have a preconditioned response, and others may not react when they should. This shortcoming is overcome by concentrating on decision theories and testing them on large samples of people, rather than concentrating on the responses of individuals.

LO 2 — SYNTACTIC AND SEMANTIC THEORIES

One theoretical interpretation of traditional historical cost accounting is that it is largely a syntactic theory. This interpretation may be described as follows: the semantic inputs of the system are the transactions and exchanges recorded in the vouchers, journals and ledgers of the business. These are then manipulated (partitioned and summed) on the basis of the premises and assumptions of historical cost accounting. For example, we assume that inflation is not to be recorded and market values of assets and liabilities are ignored. We then use double-entry accounting and the principles of historical cost accounting to calculate profit and loss and the financial position. The individual propositions are verified every time the statements are audited by checking the calculations and manipulations. However, the accounts are rarely audited specifically in terms of whether and how people will use them (a pragmatic test) or in terms of what they mean (a semantic test). In this way, historical cost theory has been confirmed many times. If we assume a Lakatosian research program, the principles of historical cost accounting form the negative heuristic and, in a Kuhnian viewpoint, the dominant paradigm.

Some accounting theorists are critical of this approach. They argue that the theory has semantic content only on the basis of its inputs. There is no independent empirical operation to verify the calculated outputs, for example, 'profit' or 'total assets'. These figures are not observed; they are simple summations of account balances, and the auditing process is, in essence, simply a recalculation. The auditing process verifies the inputs by examining underlying documents and checks mathematical calculations. However, it does not verify the final outputs. This means that even if accounting reports are prepared using perfect syntax, they may have little, if any, value in practice.

Sterling comments:

> The inadequacy of this procedure to confirm a theory is immediately apparent. If one were to attempt to confirm a theory of astronomy, as exemplified by a particular planetarium, then one might begin by checking on the accuracy of the observational inputs and one might also check for errors in computation. However, at some point the

outputs of the system would be verified. One would look at the sky to see if the stars were in fact in the position indicated by the planetarium. In the absence of this last step, several absurdities could result. First, the set of equations could describe any situation whatsoever, e.g. a rectangular orbit. If one restricted the 'verification' procedure to a check on the accuracy of the inputs and a recalculation, then one would certify that this planetarium presents fairly the position of the stars. The only way to discover that the orbit ought or ought not to be rectangular is to perform a separate operation and compare the results of that operation with the outputs of the system. If enough of these outputs were subjected to independent verification, the theory of rectangular orbits would be either confirmed or disconfirmed. Second, if there were two planetariums concerned with the same phenomena but with different sets of equations resulting in contradictory outputs, then the auditing procedure would require that both of them be certified as correct when at least one of them is necessarily wrong. Finally, the number of different sets of equations with different outputs is limitless.[3]

The following article demonstrates the importance of ensuring that the syntax and semantics are not only correct, but also complete.

<table>
<tr><td>

2.1
THEORY
IN ACTION

</td><td>

Do share prices rise when profit improves?

</td></tr>
</table>

Bonuses soften wage freeze

by Sue Mitchell

Metcash has frozen employee salaries and non-executive directors' fees but has softened the blow for senior executives by offering $1 million long-term retention payments.

The ... retention offers are conditional on Metcash achieving a compound 8 per cent increase in earnings per share over the next five years while the previous offers, entered into in 2006 and 2007, were conditional on Metcash achieving compound earnings per share growth of 12.5 per cent and 10 per cent respectively.

The declining hurdle rate for retention bonuses reflects the slowing growth outlook for Metcash after its $900 million acquisition of Foodland's Australian operations in 2005 ... "Post that acquisition there was quite a lot of access to potential synergies ... to an extent most of that has flowed through," said Deutsche Bank analyst Kristan Walker.

Metcash increased earnings per share by 13.3 per cent in 2009 and is forecasting more growth this year, driving sales and earnings through a combination of organic growth and acquisitions.

Metcash shares rose 7c to close at $4.29 yesterday.

Source: The Australian Financial Review, 31 July 2009, p.45, www.afr.com.

Questions

1. The article describes a market reaction to accounting news. This description provides an example of which approach to theory?
  (a) pragmatic
  (b) syntactic
  (c) semantic
  Explain your answer.

2. Consider the following syllogism:
  When a company reports better prospects than previously, investors force that company's share price to increase.
  • Metcash is a company that has reported better earnings per share than previously.
  • Investors forced Metcash share prices to increase.
      (a) Is there a flaw in the syntax or semantics within the syllogism that means its conclusion is not true? If so what is the flaw? (*Hint:* Consider whether the general premise at the start of the syllogism must always be true.)
      (b) What is the practical significance of this theory being invalid and its conclusion false?

Historical cost accounting has also been criticised on the basis of its syntactic element, for example with respect to the practice of summing several different money amounts assigned to specific assets:

The sum of two weights means nothing unless they are measured by the same rules ... What, then, about the procedure of adding the amount of cash held by a company today to the amount of cash paid 20 years ago for a piece of freehold land which the company still holds today?[4]

Chambers adds further criticism:

The impression one gains from the internal inconsistency of many of the arguments upon which the justification of conventional accounting is made to rest is strongly reminiscent of the underlying philosophy of the rulers of Oceania in George Orwell's *Nineteen Eighty-Four*. The distinctive feature of this philosophy is doublethink. Doublethink means the power of holding two contradictory beliefs in one's mind simultaneously, and accepting both of them.[5]

Chambers goes on to give some examples of accounting doublethink:

Valuations are incorporated in balance sheets ... but the balance sheet is not a valuation statement.
    Fixed assets should be carried at cost ... in historical accounts, unless such cost is no longer meaningful.[6]

Questions have been raised also about the imprecision of definitions in accounting. In terms of a Popperian approach to science, many of the propositions of conventional accounting are not falsifiable. Take, for example, the following criticism of a definition of depreciation:

Definitions are unacceptable which imply that depreciation for the year is a measurement, expressed in monetary terms, of the physical deterioration within the year, or the decline in monetary value within the year, or, indeed of anything that actually occurs within the year.[7]

Sterling takes this point further by stating that the problem lies in the way accountants have defined the determination of costs and profit as a choice among conventions, which are in turn defined so that a present magnitude depends on a future magnitude. For example, depreciation depends on allocation, which in turn depends on a future sale (disposal value) and the expected useful life of the asset. The same is true for profit. Under this logic, true profit cannot be determined until the firm has been liquidated.

Theories based on historical cost conventions lead to cautious hypotheses. The hypotheses therefore are unable to be tested and, as per the falsificationist approach (in which a hypothesis is not informative and does not add to scientific progress if it is not worded or proposed so that it is falsifiable), they are not useful for financial decision making except to verify accounting entries. Hence, they are uninformative and do not add to knowledge or progress in accounting. The above criticisms of historical cost are essentially criticisms about measuring current values and were the forerunner of the current move of International Financial Reporting Standards (IFRS) towards 'fair value' accounting.

In defence of the historical cost system, accountants argue that there is no requirement that accounting outputs should have any semantic content (correspondence with current real-world events, transactions, or values) or be subject to falsification rules. They counter by using the argument that the role of accounting is to allocate the historical cost of resource usage against revenue — the matching concept — to determine the surplus secured from economic activity. In this case, assets, liabilities and equity are residuals from this process; they are not meant to measure or say anything about entity value or about the entity's financial state of affairs. If we adopt this allocation approach, the definition of depreciation is then in accordance with the matching concept. Although it may be syntactic, this cost allocation assumption can conflict with normative theories about how we should account to provide information that is useful for decision making. The assumption that accounting should be a measurement system, providing information useful for decision making, is a normative premise assumed by a large group of accounting theorists and regulators.

The criticism that there are many different and acceptable historical cost allocation systems can be explained within a 'positive accounting' framework which makes the assumption that accounting information is an economic good, subject to demand and supply forces.

Under positive approaches to accounting theory development, diversity of accounting techniques exists because diversity is required. This is because different accounting techniques are needed to account for different business situations. For example, where firms are regulated by agencies that allow them to charge prices only on a cost-recovery basis, historical cost could be useful for management accounting price setting and for informing outside users of financial statements about the firm's likely future profits, and also as a means of influencing price-regulation agencies regarding the appropriateness of their price-setting formula. The allocation of costs used for price setting might involve accelerated cost recognition, such as diminishing-balance depreciation over a short period of time because this gives high costs and leads to high prices being set for the firm's products. However, a slower cost allocation might better reflect to outside users the likely life and value of the assets. Agency theory suggests that the accounting technique required to minimise the costs of contracting will often differ from situation to situation. Moreover, different political and regulatory costs affect each firm. Since firms seek to minimise all costs, they will choose different accounting techniques and because historical cost allocation allows a substantial number of allocation techniques, then firms can simply choose the most efficient technique.

LO 3 — NORMATIVE THEORIES

The 1950s and 1960s saw what has been described as the 'golden age' of normative accounting research. During this period, accounting researchers became more concerned with policy recommendations and with what *should* be done, rather than with analysing and explaining the currently accepted practice. Normative theories in this period concentrated either on deriving the 'true income' (profit) for an accounting period or on discussing the type of accounting information which would be useful in making economic decisions.

True income: True income theorists concentrated on deriving a single measure for assets and a unique (and correct) profit figure. However, there was no agreement on what constituted a correct or true measure of value and profit. Much of the literature during this period consisted of academic debate about the merits and demerits of alternative measurement systems.

Decision-usefulness: The decision-usefulness approach assumes that the basic objective of accounting is to aid the decision-making process of certain 'users' of accounting reports by providing useful, or relevant, accounting data; for example, to help investors (current and potential) decide whether to buy, hold or sell shares. One test of usefulness already discussed is the psychological pragmatic reaction to data. Others do not identify a particular group but argue that all users have the same requirement for accounting data.

In most cases decision-usefulness theories of accounting are based on classical economics concepts of profit and wealth or rational decision making. They usually make adjustments to historical cost measures to account for inflation or the market values of assets. They are, in essence, measurement theories of accounting. They are normative in nature because they make the following assumptions:

- accounting should be a measurement system
- profit and value can be measured precisely
- financial accounting is useful for making economic decisions
- markets are inefficient or can be fooled by 'creative accountants'
- conventional accounting is inefficient (in an information sense)
- there is one unique profit measure.

These assumptions were rarely subjected to any empirical testing. Their proponents usually described their derived accounting system as the 'ideal'. They recommended it to replace historical cost and prescribed its use by all and sundry.

Normative researchers labelled their approach to theory formulation scientific and, in general, based their theory on both analytic (syntactic) and empirical (inductive) propositions. Conceptually, the normative theories of the 1950s and 1960s began with a statement of the domain (scope) and objectives of accounting, the assumptions underlying the system and definitions of all the key concepts. The domain of accounting was general. It was in relation to the entire income statement and balance sheet, not just specific accounting items such as accounting for doubtful debts only. Also, it was in relation to all users of financial statements and not confined to a specific user or user group.

The normative theorists also made assumptions about the nature of a firm's operations based on their observations. Detailed and precise accounting principles and rules and a logical explanation of the accounting outputs were outlined. The deductive framework was to be rigorous and consistent in its analytic concepts. Financial statements should mean what they say; they should have semantic connections with the real world. Although financial statements are abstractions and reductions of firms' economic affairs, since they summarise the stock and the movement of economic resources, they should be pragmatic only to the extent that they were surrogates for direct experience. The pragmatic tests were that, when observing financial statements, users should act as though they actually observed the events the financial statements represented.[8] Although this methodology has both syntactic and semantic features, it relies mainly on syntactic relations and therefore has been labelled 'hypothetico-deductive'.

An important question in this accounting research concerns the usefulness of accounting data. Are the quantitative data we derive from given sets of operations based on an overall theory of accounting useful to users of financial statements? To find the answer, what was usually done was to take the output data of specific accounting systems and determine whether this data helped decision makers make the right financial decisions. This is a direct approach to testing accounting theory. Figure 2.1 indicates the procedure. The arrows signify the output of each model. Decision makers use accounting data to make predictions about the company. Based on these predictions, they decide what to do, such as sell shares in the company or buy more.

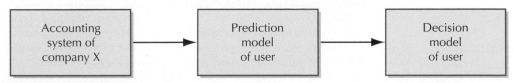

FIGURE 2.1 The decision process

In science, this decision-usefulness approach is referred to as either financial *instrumentalism* or *realism*. The suggestion that alternative accounting systems should be assessed according to their predictive ability is an extension of logical positivism and is termed 'instrumentalism' — that is, a theory has no utility except as an instrument for prediction. According to Friedman, theories cannot be tested by the realism of their assumptions; they can be judged only by their predictive power.[9] There are, however, some problems involved in applying this test. First, if the prediction is verified, it verifies the prediction model of the user, not the accounting system. There are, of course, other variables besides accounting data that affect a financial prediction. We do not know precisely how the accounting data were used. Second, if the decision turns out to be the right one, it verifies the decision model, not the accounting system. Therefore, it is difficult to interpret the validity of the accounting model based simply on decision making.

On the other hand, realism stresses the explanatory role of science; in essence, prediction in reverse. This methodological point of view stresses the feedback role of accounting. The 'realism' approach to accounting means that for an accounting theory to be valid it must be more than an instrument for forecasting; it must also hold as a description of the reality that underlies the accounting phenomena. Accounting, under this approach, gains predictive ability only because it gives relevant feedback or descriptive explanation of what has occurred. We can also question the logical validity of using prediction (forecasting) as a scientific test for an accounting theory in a dynamic environment where intervening variables cannot be controlled. Prediction in science is more valid when we can control variables such as air pressure, heat, weight and so on. When we cannot control variables in the economic environment, such as inflation and interest rates or consumer confidence, we have to assess predictions statistically, according to how probable it is that the evidence supporting the prediction is representative.

The following article is a comment on the way accounting theory has evolved, become accepted and then implemented.

2.1
INTERNATIONAL
VIEW

IFRS is a Big Four gravy train

by Richard Murphy

It's been announced that International Financial Reporting Standards are to be used by UK local authorities from 1 April 2010 for the preparation of their accounts.

Now, I'm not usually one of those who goes around suggesting the public sector is wasting money, largely because when all is said and done it seems to me no more prone to the frailty of human fallibility than the private sector, where I have witnessed waste on the most colossal scale. But on this occasion I'm going to, and I'm going to point a finger at those imposing the waste.

IFRS are completely and utterly inappropriate for use by local authorities. The reason is simply stated: IFRS are designed to produce what the IASB call 'decision useful information'. I question that, but for logical reason in this case.

The IASB defines decision useful information as that needed by an investor to decide whether to buy or sell shares in an entity. They do not consider there to be any other reason for financial reporting. That is why the entire focus of IFRS shifted from that in the previous UK GAAP, which was on reporting profit, to one of reporting changes in balance sheet value.

This is no minor issue: UK GAAP was accruals accounting and sought to match transactions in a period to provide a measure of what had happened in that time scale. Balance sheets are a residual measure in that process. So this GAAP was about stewardship, financial performance, delivery of value for money, and action over time.

IFRS on the other hand is about measuring value at a point of time and comparing that with value at another point of time. The difference is the result for the period.

So the balance sheet is predominant and the profit and loss account secondary because it is assumed that the investor in the entity will have a short time scale for involvement (usually less than a year — the UK stock exchange changes hands entirely well over once a year now, on average) and is therefore wholly uninterested in stewardship, performance over time or even delivery of results.

The IFRS belief is that the only issue of concern to the investors, who they believe to be the sole user of accounts, is in making a quick buck from dealing.

Now, let's get down to some basic facts here. No one invests in a local authority. They're not for sale. They do not provide an investment return. With rare exceptions (and I regret this) they do not even issue bonds to finance their capital projects.

So the user of the financial statements that IFRS assume to exist are not present in the case of local authorities. There are no investors. And the use for which the financial statements that IFRS assumes to exist, being the decision to buy and sell shares, does not exist in the case of local authorities. There is nothing to buy and sell.

This alone, at this most obvious and basic level, makes it abundantly obvious that IFRS is the wrong accounting system for local authorities (as it is for any unquoted company, incidentally, for much the same reason — an absence of any marketable security).

It's worse than that though: IFRS will not require accounting for stewardship of public funds entrusted, or for the supply of services, both of which are core to the management of local authorities. And we know that a failure to measure almost always means a failure to deliver in management terms. This means we have a potential disaster on our hands.

And whose fault is this? Well firstly, the IASB's. They do not act in the public interest, after all. They are a private cartel designed by and promoted for, in no small part, the benefit of their biggest sponsors — who are the Big 4 firms of accountants. Second, those firms have much to answer for.

They have just made a fortune from the IFRS transition for first tier listed companies, now they're selling similar services to the secondary markets and after that there was a void. So they've persuaded the professional bodies (which they dominate) to move IASB into local authorities which will give their teams work for several more years. You can call that cynical if you like — but actually, it's just a statement of fact.

What I really hate is when people say the public sector is inefficient when the entire reason is that the public sector was sold a completely dud product by the private sector. That's true of most of the IT debacles, for example. It will be true here.

Someone needs to wake up, smell the coffee and realise that UK local authorities are being sold a dud reporting system designed from the outset to be unfit for their needs. This project must be cancelled now before it is too late! This is not just a waste of money. This is a straightforward con.

I am angry. And so should all local authority tax payers in the UK. We're going to be taken for a ride unless we protest now.

Source: Tax Research UK, Richard Murphy on tax and corporate accountability, www.taxresearch.org.uk.

Questions
1. Murphy comments on the different theories of accounting under IFRS and UK GAAP. What are the differences and why is IFRS deemed inappropriate for local authorities?
2. Based upon the arguments by Murphy should we have different accounting systems? For local authorities? For different countries?
3. What approach is Murphy using when he addresses the question of accounting for local authorities?
4. Why do you think IFRS has been adopted for local authorities? Is it scientific or unscientific?

Normative theories of investment

Shares set for a pullback, not new lows

by Glenn Mumford

It's been a great run, but I'm starting to get very nervous. Australian equities are now about 40 per cent off bear-market lows. Ditto the Australian dollar. Commodity indices are at nine-month highs, while domestic interest rates are at 49-year lows.

I remain a bull — a true believer. My 2010 target on the S&P/ASX 200 Index is 5500. I'm still a supporter of the commodity super-cycle. And the little Aussie battler should test parity against an ailing greenback at some stage over the next 18 months.

So why in the world am I worried? I get the feeling we may be trading at interim highs on equities, the Australian dollar and commodities . . . I can't shake the feeling that investors have already factored in most of the market's medium-term positives. This inevitably leaves them prone to short-term negative surprises.

Commodities are a particular concern. I think Xstrata's Mick Davis caught the mood on Tuesday when he pointed to the "froth" that had accompanied the run-up in metal prices. "Sentiment has been driving prices, rather than fundamentals," he warned. I'm also expecting a more pragmatic reading of the domestic interest rate outlook to soften the local currency.

Equity investors appear to be searching for an excuse to take some profits. Many are still pinching themselves, as they come to terms with their recent good fortune. Selling pressure in the US would be the likeliest catalyst for this "judicious liquidation", though with reporting season about to get underway, some less-than-stellar 2008/9 profit outcomes could provide an added trigger.

So how should investors play this? As volatility returns, the market will inevitably wrong-foot many as it moves to find a new floor. Do you look to take advantage of gains that have accrued since the March lows and lock a little away? Or do you grit your teeth and ride out any short-term volatility, before the expected fourth-quarter resumption of the dominant market trend? Whatever path you take, view any correction as an added opportunity. Just remember what we said back in March. Forget selling rallies — it's time to buy dips.

Source: The Australian Financial Review, 6 August 2009, pp. 23, 25, www.afr.com.

Questions

1. What is a bull market? What is a bear market?
2. Why would high commodity prices and low interest rates help to maintain share prices?
3. What is the theory underlying the advice to buy the 'dips'? Is this a normative theory? Explain your answer.

LO 4 POSITIVE THEORIES

During the 1970s, accounting theory saw a move back to empirical methodology, which is often referred to as positive methodology. Positivism or empiricism means testing or relating accounting hypotheses or theories back to experiences or facts of the real world. Positive accounting research first focused on empirically testing some of the assumptions made by the normative accounting theorists. For example, by using questionnaires and other survey techniques, attitudes to the usefulness of different accounting techniques were determined. A typical approach was to survey the opinions of financial analysts, bank officers and accountants on the usefulness of different inflation accounting methods in their decision-making tasks (such as predicting bankruptcy or deciding whether to buy or sell shares). Another approach was to test the assumed importance of accounting outputs in the marketplace. Tests attempted to determine whether inflation accounting increased the information efficiency of share markets; whether profit is an important determinant in share valuation; whether the cost of gathering 'finer' accounting data outweighed the benefits; or whether the use of different accounting techniques affected value.

Today, the greater bulk of positive theory is concerned mainly with 'explaining' the reasons for current practice and 'predicting' the role of accounting and associated information in the economic decisions of individuals, firms and other parties that contribute to the operation of the marketplace and the economy. This research tests theories that assume that accounting information is an economic and political commodity, and that people act in their own self-interest. Positive accounting theory in particular covers questions such as: Do firms substitute alternative ways of financing assets when the rules governing the accounting for leases change? Which firms are more likely to use straight-line depreciation rather than diminishing-balance depreciation, and why? The theory used to answer these questions generally revolves around managers' incentives to maximise bonuses based on their companies' profits, their incentives to avoid breaching accounting-based debt covenants and thereby reducing the cost of debt, or their incentives to use accounting techniques to divert attention from their high profits if those profits would attract public or government scrutiny, and perhaps lead to higher taxes. In this book, chapters 11, 12 and 13 focus on different types of positive accounting theories.

The main difference between normative and positive theories is that normative theories are prescriptive, whereas positive theories are descriptive, explanatory or predictive. Normative theories prescribe how people such as accountants should behave to achieve an outcome that is judged to be right, moral, just, or otherwise a 'good' outcome. Positive theories do not prescribe how people (e.g. accountants) should behave to achieve an outcome that is judged to be 'good'. Rather, they avoid making value-laden prescriptions. Instead, they describe how people do behave (regardless of whether it is 'right'); they explain why people behave in a certain manner, for example to achieve some objective such as maximising share values or their personal wealth (regardless of whether that is 'right'); or they predict what people have done or will do (again, regardless of whether that is 'right' or 'best behaviour').

Many positive theory researchers are largely dismissive of normative viewpoints. Similarly, many normative theorists do not accept the value of positive accounting research. In fact, the theories can coexist, and can complement each other. Positive accounting theory can help provide an understanding of the role of accounting which, in turn, can form the basis for developing normative theories to improve the practice of accounting.

LO 5 ▸ DIFFERENT PERSPECTIVES

To this point, we have focused on what may be considered to be a highly structured approach to theory formulation — the scientific approach. We start with a theory based on prior knowledge or accepted 'scientific' theory constructions. When we observe real-world behaviour that does not concur with the theory, we treat that anomaly as a research issue and express it as a research problem to be explained. We develop a theory to explain the observed behaviour and use that theory to generate testable hypotheses that will be corroborated only if the theory holds. We then follow precise and highly structured or predetermined procedures for data collection and, after subjecting the data (usually) to mathematical or statistical techniques, we validate or refute the hypotheses tested. This approach has an inherent assumption that the world to be researched is an objective reality capable of examination in terms of large-scale or average statistics. This type of research is carried out by incremental hypotheses which are then combined to provide greater understanding, or better predictions, of accounting. The implied assumption is that a good theory holds under circumstances that are constant across firms, industries and time.

This approach to research is generally described as the 'scientific' approach and is the approach currently used by most researchers in accounting, and the approach that is published in most major academic accounting journals. It is important to note that it is based on certain ontological assumptions (the way we view the world), which imply different epistemologies (the way we gather knowledge, or learn) and different research methods. This, in turn, influences the types of research problems posed and the hypotheses that are tested. It is important for accounting researchers to clearly recognise the assumptions underlying their research and to consider whether alternative research approaches are more appropriate. There is a body of literature, loosely labelled naturalistic research, which is critical of the highly structured approach adopted by 'scientific' researchers. We briefly review some of their criticisms in this section. Most researchers now accept that the most appropriate approach depends on the nature of the research question being considered.

The first criticism of the scientific method is that large-scale statistical research tends to lump everything together. Hypotheses based on the use of stock market prices or surveys render much of accounting research remote from the world of practitioners. Also, they are not commensurate with the concerns of many individual accountants in their roles as accountants. Some researchers advocate the naturalist research focus as being more appropriate for gaining a knowledge of accounting behaviour in its natural setting. The idea is that we undertake research as naturally as possible. This approach has two implications. First, we do not have any preconceived assumptions or theories. Second, we focus on firm-specific problems. This is done by taking a flexible research approach using close observations and placing less emphasis on mathematical analysis, modelling, statistical tests, surveys and laboratory tests. The usual way to undertake naturalistic research is to use individual case studies and more detailed fieldwork. This type of research is much more micro in its perspective because it is aimed at solving individual problems which may be firm-specific. Therefore, results may be more difficult to generalise.

The naturalistic approach can be compared with 'scientific' accounting research, which is more prone to aggregating the results from testing a number of hypotheses in order to form 'general theories of accounting'. Naturalistic research starts from specific real-world situations; the main intention is to answer the question 'What is going on here?', not to provide generalisable conditions for wide segments of society.

The case-study approach is seen by some researchers as best fulfilling the role of exploring or crystallising the research problem for naturalistic research. For example:

> ... where it is not feasible to develop theoretical models prior to empirical observation, the next best alternative (an exploratory approach) may be followed.[10]

Tomkins and Groves disagree with this viewpoint. They see the naturalistic research approach as being more appropriate to different ontological assumptions.[11] Differences in ontological assumptions imply different research styles and influence the research questions asked and investigated. For example, we may view accounting as a social construction. We may wish to understand what self-images people hold, what underlying assumptions sustain that view, or what part this perception plays in controlling the way they perform their everyday role. These are the types of questions that might be researched using a subjective ontology.

To further explain ontology and the different research styles which may be used, we consider the article by Tomkins and Groves[12] and the Morgan and Smircich classification they used. First, they list a six-way classification of the nature of the social world (see table 2.1).

Categories 1–6 are alternative ways of looking at the world. Category 1 is a strict objectivist viewpoint of the world, where behaviour will always conform to a set of behavioural rules, and outcomes of decisions and actions are highly predictable. In relation to category 1, for example, researchers assume that all managers aim to maximise their personal wealth and that they are aware of how they can use accounting techniques to do so (e.g. by increasing reported earnings, thereby increasing their bonuses that are tied to reported earnings). This enables researchers to predict what accounting methods managers will use if accounting choice is unregulated. Researchers will predict that all managers behave in the same manner because they have a shared view of the world and of the outcomes of their actions, and because they share preferences for particular outcomes. When researchers view the world as a concrete structure (category 1), this enables them to use the scientific approach and statistical methods to test their predictions. The scientific approach is appropriate where the behaviour investigated is predicted to occur systematically, according to a model of behaviour and events.

Category	Assumption
1.	Reality as a concrete structure
2.	Reality as a concrete process
3.	Reality as a contextual field of information
4.	Reality as symbolic discourse
5.	Reality as social construction
6.	Reality as projection of human imagination

TABLE 2.1 Six basic ontological assumption sets

Source: C. Tomkins and R. Groves, 'The everyday accountant and researching his reality', *Accounting, Organizations and Society*, vol. 8, no. 4, 1983, pp. 361–74.

As we move down through the categories we are gradually relaxing our assumptions about the 'concreteness' of the world: category 1 assumes that the world is concrete and stable, category 6 views the world as unstable and human-specific. In category 6, humans are not expected to behave according to a set of behavioural rules that apply to everyone equally. Complex interrelationships and individualistic decision models are assumed. Individuals are not expected to think alike. Because individualism is expected in category 6, the scientific method and statistical tests are inappropriate because their assumptions are violated. Although individuals may behave rationally according to their personal understanding of the world and of the outcomes of particular actions, they do not share a common understanding of how the world works, and they have different preferred outcomes from their decisions. For example, some managers might prefer to maximise their personal wealth; others might prefer to maximise their subordinates' job satisfaction; and others might prefer to minimise their personal work effort. Understanding decision making involves understanding individuals' perceptions and preferences.

For categories 1–3, it is more appropriate to use the scientific approach. By appropriate observation and measurement, it is assumed that one has readily available, stable and usually very simple functions relating to isolated and small subsets of the social world that can be used for accurate predictions.[13]

For categories 4–6, Tomkins and Groves suggest that naturalistic or exploratory research is more appropriate. These three categories are generally labelled as 'symbolic interactionist'. Symbolic interactionists see their world as one in which people form their own separate impressions through a process of human interaction and negotiation. They believe that social action and interaction is possible only through exchange of shared interpretations of 'labels' attached to people, things and situations. Reality is not embodied in the rules of interpretation themselves, but only in the meanings that result from people's interpretation of the situations and events they experience. A 'scientific' approach to researching the interpretations people make might elucidate such rules through large-scale, statistical research in those areas where meanings held by individuals might be assumed to be stable. In contrast, the 'naturalist' would research the problem by placing emphasis on 'feeling one's way inside the experience of the actor' in order to gain an understanding of the problem. This process might identify many significant forms of social behaviour which cannot be related to a few well-specified variables with stable meanings, but which result from the nature of the interactions among a group of people.

As we have previously noted, the ontological assumption we make implies different epistemological approaches and certain research methods. This in turn influences the types of research problems asked and the hypotheses that are tested. To help you understand this, we present a comparison of the scientific and naturalistic approaches in table 2.2.

TABLE 2.2 A comparison of scientific and naturalistic research		
	Scientific research	**Naturalistic research**
Ontological assumptions	• Reality is objective and concrete. • Accounting is objective reality.	• Reality is socially constructed and a product of human imagination. • Accounting is constructed reality.
Epistemological approaches	• Piecemeal advancement of knowledge • Reductionism • Testing of individual hypotheses • Laws capable of generalisation	• Holistic • Complexity of the world cannot be solved by reductionism • Irreducible laws
Methodology	• Structured • Prior theoretical base • Empirical validation or extension	• Unstructured • No prior theory
Methods	• Syntactic model formulation • Empirical induction to form hypotheses • Appropriate statistical methods	• Case studies • Exploration by flexibility • Experience of events

In the following article as a further illustration of different perspectives on accounting theory formation, extracts from 'Financial accounting: an epistemological research note' (Schiehll, Borba, Dal-Ri Murcia 2007) provide an overview of accounting theory development and the authors' view on the development of accounting theories.

2.2
INTERNATIONAL VIEW

Financial accounting: an epistemological research note

by Eduardo Schiehll, José Alonso Borba, and Fernando Dal-Ri Murcia

What is accounting? It is amazing how this simple, basic question has never been answered precisely (Kam, 1986). A simple and widely-held concept of accounting is the process of identifying, measuring, recording, and communicating economic information about an organization so that it may be used for sound decision-making. This concept was derived from Wells (1976), and like other concepts of accounting, it emphasizes the application aspect of accounting knowledge. Viewing this definition from an epistemological perspective, one might argue that the object of study is not well defined, the methodology (truth criteria) is not identified, and the purpose of accounting research is poorly delimited. The aim of this document is not to criticize this specific definition, but to argue that one of the difficulties in understanding accounting as a scientific discipline resides in its definition as stated in the literature. Among others, the importance of viewing accounting as a scientific field is that fundamental or applied research is the only way to generate and improve knowledge in a scientific field. In other words, the relevance of, and incentives for, conducting research in a specific discipline like accounting depend on the extent to which specific methods may be applied to improve the discipline's body of knowledge.

Following this line of reasoning, we believe that in order to perceive and appreciate accounting as a scientific field, a first, essential step would be to understand the distinctions and associations between accounting theory and accounting practice. According to the framework proposed by Kuhn (1972), for example, we may conjecture that accounting theory is a body of statements or propositions connected by rules of inferential reasoning (i.e. testable hypotheses or premises and conclusions) that form the general frame of reference for the development or explanation of accounting practices. The study by Hendriksen (1982) corroborates this argument, adding that accounting theory may be defined as logical reasoning in the form of a set of broad principles that:

(1) provide a general frame of reference by which accounting practice can be evaluated, and
(2) guide the development of new practices and procedures.

According to these principles, we argue that the next step in perceiving accounting as a scientific field would be to identify the accounting theories that are being developed and how they are verified. In this respect, Popper (1982) suggests that accounting knowledge is a body of normative and positive empirical theories built around inductive inferences.

"Normative" means that accounting theories contain imperative value judgments stemming from factual statements about the object of study, e.g., the market value of firm equity. Another justification is that normative conclusions are very often the origin of policy recommendations, which may or may not be adopted by practitioners in the field. According to Watts & Zimmermann (1986), normative theories are almost entirely devoted to the examination of questions of "what ought to be done." Thus, this theory attempts to prescribe what information ought to be communicated and how it ought to be presented. In other words, the normative theories attempt to explain what accounting "should be" rather than what accounting "is."

On the other hand, positive theories attempt to explain why accounting is what it is. They describe not only what accounting information should and how it should be communicated to its users, but also why accountants do what they do and the effects of all this on people and resource utilization (Christenson, 1983). However, as suggested by Schroeder and Clark (1995), ideally there should be no such distinction (normative versus positive) because a well-developed and complete theory encompasses both what should be and what it is.

The empirical and inductive attributes of accounting theory are easier to justify. In fact, according to Sterling (1970), only mathematics and logic can be classified as non-empirical sciences. Accounting theories in particular are fundamentally based on experience and observation. For example, the qualitative and quantitative variations of firm equity studied in Financial Accounting, or the dysfunctional behaviors of budgetary control investigated in Management Accounting.

However, accounting premises and conclusions are connected by inductive inference. Double-entry bookkeeping system can serve to illustrate this point. The double-entry system is based on noting changes in the wealth of a firm and an attempt to translate the qualitative and quantitative variations in the firm's equity. The double-entry system, perhaps the first and most important paradigm* of accounting science, was invented in the commercial city-states of medieval Italy in response to the emergence of trade and commerce. According to de Roover (1938) the double-entry was born when people came to see that you could not take something out of one pigeonhole without putting it into another. It has emerged as a natural outcome of the evolutionary process to the need of times (Kam, 1986). The first published accounting work was written in 1494 by the Venetian monk Luca Pacioli (1450–1520). It summarizes principles that have remained essentially unchanged to this day.

Subsequent works written in the 16th century introduced the first formulations of the concepts of assets, liabilities, and income. In keeping with this theme, Lakatos (1978) suggests that a theory is constructed by a body of concepts. From this perspective, assets, liabilities, income, and other notions derived from these such as long and short term, revenue, costs, expenses, operational, no operational, etc., have a specific (or rather particular) meaning in the accounting field, and are fundamental elements for the building and understanding of accounting knowledge. In the same line of thinking, the study by Glautier and Underdow (1994) suggests that the concepts of financial accounting are particularly significant to the development of accounting theory in two ways:

(1) they are themselves part of an empirical process for developing rules of financial accounting, and

(2) they reflect the influence of institutional forces which shape the philosophy of accounting in a given and social environment.

Much later, the Industrial Revolution drove the need for accounting practices that could handle mechanization, factory-manufacturing operations, and the mass production of goods and services. With the rise of large, publicly held business corporations owned by absentee stockholders and administrated by professional managers, the accounting role was further redefined. According to Schoroeder, Clark and Cathey (2005) the Industrial Revolution brought the need for more formal accounting procedures and standards. In terms of epistemology, these two events may be interpreted as a crisis (Kunh, 1972) in accounting science. Organizations were immersed in a new social and economic reality. New paradigms were imposed onto management activities, calling for new accounting theories to support the new accounting practices. From that point on, research in the accounting field split off into two directions: financial accounting and management accounting.

While the first focuses on the outside user of accounting information, the second focuses on the internal user and the decision making process. However, independently of this split, theorists continue their quest: explain accounting practice. In the next section we discuss the purposes, evolution and methods of financial accounting research.

The sociological and discursive perspectives of accounting

The studies by Latour (1989) and Whitley (1984) suggest that the sociological and discursive perspectives of a science are basically determined by the extent and intensity of its interaction with society. Like every other social science, accounting conducts its research based upon assumptions about the nature of social science and the nature of society (Belkaoui, 1997). As it happens, financial accounting may be analyzed from both the sociological and discursive perspectives. Thus, accounting may be viewed as a "socio-systemic" structure, with input, process, and output. The idea is that financial accounting knowledge does not affect only the accountants and accounting practices, but also (directly or indirectly) impacts the management context in all its ramifications. As Beaver (1998) suggests, the current financial report environment consists of various groups (investors, information intermediaries, regulators, managers, auditors, etc.) who are affected by and have a stake in financial reporting requirements. Hereafter, the sociological and discursive perspectives of accounting will be analyzed assisted by the strong interdependence between science and society (the science "players"). Our argument is that, as an applied science, the accounting discipline is no exception to the rule. In this sense, the process of constructing accounting theories has been analyzed, culminating in the conclusion that market pressure, tax laws (institutional influence), management decision needs, and macroeconomic factors such as inflation are the main inputs to a sociological accounting system. These inputs are the starting points for an accounting translation process. Thus, the discursive result is the creation or improvement of accounting practices, while the sociological contribution is the correct incorporation of these aspects into the accounting framework to address user needs and serve as interpretation models. Therefore, the accounting "socio-output" is represented by better assessments of a firm's financial health by investors and stakeholders and improved decision-making by managers. Thus, selection of a financial reporting system might be viewed as a social choice, where bargain power will determine whoever gets their desires fulfilled. In a number of countries, such as the United States, where financial reporting information is directed primarily toward the needs of investors and creditors, decision usefulness is the overriding criterion for judging its quality (Mueller, Gernon and Meek, 1994). However, in some other countries, such [as] some Latin American countries, financial accounting is designed primarily to ensure that the right amount of tax is collected. In this sense, accounting is shaped by the environmental forces in which it operates. At the same time, scientific research in accounting has also been influenced by social and environmental forces, which resulted in two different streams of research: the North-American and the European. According to Lopes and Martins (2005) research in accounting cannot be considered independently of the social environment in which it is inserted. The research itself is a product of the social environment. The North American stream of accounting research, which is known as the mainstream, has been based on the economic concepts and in a framework based on the positive method, which basically relies on:

 (i) hypotheses development

 (ii) economic theories to support the hypotheses

(iii) empirical tests using econometrics techniques

(iv) conclusions that wish to construct a theory in order to explain and predict particle

This line of research has been largely disseminated by the Elite Schools (Chicago, MIT, Rochester, Stanford, etc.) and their PhDs programs. This research has also been stimulated by premier scientific journals like *The Accounting Review (TAR)*, *Journal of Accounting Research (JAR)*, *Journal of Accounting and Economics (JAE)*, *Contemporary Research (CAR)* and *Review of Accounting Studies (RAS)*. However, an alternative stream of research has emerged with the foundation of the journal *Accounting, Organization and Society*, in England. Here, we call it the European or British stream, as most of the researchers were originally British like Antony Hopwood, Michael Power and Peter Miler. However, we might note the existence of British authors that are adopters of the "North-American approach" and vice-versa.

The theoretical approach used by the British stream of research has been based on disciplines like sociology, psychology, history and political economy. In this line of research, the accounting phenomenon cannot be viewed within the best possible option (normative) or a set of hypotheses to be tested (positive); instead the proposition is that forces that shape accounting should be elaborated within a set of social interactions that act in a debate arena (Lopes and Martins, 2005).

Final remarks

This brief epistemological overview of the history of financial accounting research demonstrates how it gained importance as a hands-on activity before the accounting theorists arrived on the scene. Consequently, accounting practices were shaped by accounting practitioners and the government authorities, which took a keen interest in the protection of capital markets and creditors. The capital market still wields a strong influence over the sociological and discursive branches of financial accounting science. Research programs have been supported by regulatory bodies such as AICPA (USA) and CICA (Canada) and professional accounting associations such as AAA (USA) and CAAA (Canada)**. Financial accounting research has also been impacted by the corporative influence. This influence has taken the form of standards designed to control financial accounting practices instead of fostering discussion on the anomalies between the reality and evaluation of firm equity. As a consequence, few paradigms or accounting theories have been put forward to guide research avenues in financial accounting. When Positive Accounting Theory brought to accounting a theory-testing approach, researchers embarked on an efficient capital market approach, which led to improved utilization of rigorous research methods and statistical analysis. These factors may have shielded financial accounting from criticism, and therefore creativity, compared to other management disciplines, where there was more incentive for qualitative and interpretative investigation. At the same time recent accounting scandals involving highly known corporations have raised questions about financial reports' reliability, which seem to [have] somehow shifted the focus back to regulation that could result in less information usefulness, in order to recover the integrity of accounting information. As such, researchers in financial accounting need to be aware of the many dimensions and realities that they are attempting to "account for" and represent. Numerical Accounting highlights aspects of organizational reality that are quantifiable and built into the accounting framework, but oftentimes ignore aspects of organizational reality that are not quantifiable in this way. That said such challenges are part and parcel of all scientific fields.

* Both inductive and deductive inferences may generate positive or normative theories. Positive theories attempt to explain what and how accounting information is presented and how it should be communicated to users. Normative theories attempt to prescribe what data ought to be communicated and how they ought to be presented, that is, they attempt to explain what should be rather than what is. Watts & Zimmermann (1986).

** AICPA is the acronym for American Institute of Certified Public Accountants; CICA is the acronym for Chartered Accountants of Canada; AAA is the acronym for American Accounting Association; and CAAA is the acronym for Canadian Academic Accounting Association.

References

Beaver, W. *Financial Reporting: an accounting revolution.* 3rd ed. Prentice Hall, 1998.

Belkaoui, A. *Accounting Theory.* 3rd ed. Dryden Press, 1993.

Christenson, C. (1983), The Methodology of Positive Accounting. *The Accounting Review*, v. 58, n. 1, p. 1–22.

de Roover, R. Characteristics of Bookkeeping before Paciolo. *Accounting Review*, p. 146, 1938.

Glautier, M.; Underdown, B. *Accounting Theory and Practice.* 5th ed. Pitman Publishing, 1994.

Hendriksen, E. S. *Accounting Theory.* 4th ed. Illinois: Richard D. Irwin, Inc, p. 589, chap. 1–4, 1982.

Kam, V. *Accounting Theory.* 2nd ed. Wiley Inc, 1986.

Kuhn, T. S., The Structure of Scientific Revolutions, 1st. ed. Chicago: University of Chicago Press, 1972.

Lakatos, I. The Methodology of Scientific Research Programmes. In: *The Methodology of Scientific Research Programmes, Philosophical Papers*, v. 1. Cambridge: Cambridge University Press, p. 8–101, 1978.

Latour, B. La science en action. Paris: *Les Éditions de la Découverte*, p. 7–96, 1989.

Lopes, A; MARTINS, E. *Teoria da Contabilidade: uma nova abordagem.* Editora Atlas, 2005.

Mueller, G.; Gernon, H; Meek, G. *Accounting: an International Perspective.* Irvin Editors, 1994.

Popper, K. R. *Examen de certains problèmes fondamentaux: La logique de la découverte scienfitique.* Paris: Payot, p. 23–45, 1982.

Schroeder, R.; Clark, M. *Accounting Theory: texts and readings.* 5th ed. Willey Inc, 1995.

Schroeder, R.; Clark, M.; Cathey, J. *Financial Accounting Theory and Analysis: texts and readings.* 8th ed. Willey Inc, 2005.

Sterling, R. R. On Theory Construction and Verification. *The Accounting Review*, p. 444–457, July 1970.

Watts, R. L.; Zimmerman, J. L. *Positive Accounting Theor.* 1st. ed. Englewood Cliffs, New Jersey: Prentice-Hall, Inc, p. 388, chap. 1–3; 12–14, 1986.

Wells, M. C. Revolution in Accounting Thought? *The Accounting Review*, v. 51, p. 471–482, July 1976.

Whitley, R. *The Organizational Structures of Scientific Fields. The Intellectual and Social Organization of the Science*, Oxford, Clarendon Press, p. 153–218, 1984.

Source: *Revista Contabilidade & Finanças* [online] 2007, vol.18, no.45, pp. 83–90.

Questions

1. Outline at least two theories mentioned above and describe the ontological and epistemological assumptions made in each theory.

2. What do the authors mean when they say accounting theories contain 'imperative value judgements'?

3. Why are accounting theories about social choices? How does accounting affect society? How would you go about researching societal impact?

LO 6 # SCIENTIFIC APPROACH APPLIED TO ACCOUNTING

Misconceptions of purpose

A great deal of misunderstanding exists about the attempt to apply a scientific approach to accounting. Some believe that the attempt is to make scientists out of accounting practitioners. This view is not the aim of the approach. A scientist is one who uses the scientific method and, therefore, is mainly a researcher. The medical profession provides a good analogy of the difference between researcher and practitioner and the use and effect of the scientific method.

The medical researcher is a scientist, but the medical practitioner (the doctor) is not. The latter applies the tools of medicine. He or she is a professional person who is expected to use judgement to diagnose diseases and recommend treatments. The 'tools' the doctor applies consist mainly of knowledge gained through scientific research by medical investigators. But, as in many other fields, scientific research has not found all the answers to medical questions and some of the conclusions are not as persuasive as others. The conclusions of research are generalisations, but the practitioner is faced with specific cases that may not conform exactly with general conclusions.

For these reasons, the practitioner's judgement is always necessary in applying the 'tools' of his or her trade. What is significant is that the practitioner takes a scientific attitude in practice — that is, he or she takes seriously the view that evidence to support a diagnosis or treatment is important. Accountants who believe in a scientific approach want empirical evidence and logical explanation to support accounting practices so that practitioners can recommend the most appropriate methods for given situations based on this evidence. People find statements more convincing when substantiated by objective, empirical evidence than statements based only on debatable rationalisations.

Another common misunderstanding about the application of the scientific view in accounting is that 'absolute truth' is desired, which of course is not possible. Therefore, those who argue against the scientific approach to theory formulation contend that it is fruitless to seek that which is impossible. Such an argument is based on the misconception that science discovers absolute truth. The scientific method is not perfect. It is a human invention to help us ascertain whether a statement should be considered realistic or not. The structure of the process in which this determination is made is such that no one can claim absolute truth in science. Thus, scientific truth is provisional. A statement or theory gains the status of 'confirmation' only after scientists in the area from which the theory evolves decide that the evidence is sufficiently persuasive, for example, when statistical tests show that the results obtained have less than a 5 per cent probability of occurring by chance. The history of science discloses that substitutions, adjustments and modifications of theories are made in the light of new evidence.

Alternative approaches to accounting theory construction

Predicting profits is crystal-ball gazing

by Narelle Hooper and Fiona Buffini

Coles Myer chief executive John Fletcher previously set five-year annual profit growth targets in the company's initial revival plan, against the advice of his board.

'The downside risk of sharing that externally was that you get half way through it and people can check you along the way and if you're not delivering, the pressure gets built up. And he's missing targets and all of a sudden he's out of a job,' Mr Fletcher said.

'The five years is getting close so as a team we'll be going through that ... we definitely won't be sharing any targets again ... I've done that once,' he said, 'I don't need that now. And the risk of doing that twice with the market I don't want to take.'

While Mr Fletcher's experience has been more bruising than most, rival chief executives are following his lead by pulling back on making specific projections about earnings.

Perpetual Trustees announced a 27 per cent rise in 2004–05 earnings but chief executive David Deverall deferred first-half guidance until the annual meeting in October.

By contrast at the same time last year, he said the company expected improvement in operating profit after tax in excess of 10 per cent, subject to market conditions.

'This time last year, we thought we would exceed a 10 per cent increase in operating profit after tax and we ended up delivering 27 per cent so in our view that wasn't very helpful guidance,' said Perpetual Trustees chief financial officer John Nesbitt.

'So this year our view was to wait a little while until things settle and give more appropriate guidance at the AGM. I think that's consistent with the perceived trend in the market not to give guidance because of the general uncertainty.'

Sankar Narayan, the CFO of John Fairfax Holdings — publisher of *The Australian Financial Review* — said the company's practice was to give general directional guidance followed by much more precise guidance later in the year when advertising demand was more visible.

Mr Narayan agreed that other companies had been 'fairly general' in their guidance this reporting period and speculated that 'it may be because of the economic environment'.

Pacific Brands' investor relations executive Katherine Cooper said the company had decided against providing specific guidance. 'The problem with guidance is the market is so susceptible to expectations that even if you exceed your own forecasts but the market thinks something different you can be marked down,' she said.

Other companies such as BHP Billiton, IAG and Rio Tinto continue to provide broad outlook statements but not specific profit forecasts.

'If you can tell us what the Australian dollar is going to be at the end of the year and a few other variables we'll tell you what we're going to make, I think it's as simple as that,' Rio spokesman Ian Head said.

IAG investor relations chief Anne O'Driscoll said the insurer never provided a profit forecast, in part as a large equity portfolio made the figure unpredictable.

'People aren't very good at predicting what the market will do', she added.

Source: The Australian Financial Review, 5 September 2005, p. 19.

Questions

1. What market backlash do businesspeople fear if they do not meet their forecast earnings or growth targets? Why?
2. Mr Fletcher describes how he has learned not to publicly disclose 5-year annual profit growth targets. Explain what is likely to have caused him to learn that lesson. In coming to the conclusion, what approach to theory construction has Mr Fletcher applied? Explain your answer.

3. Can the scientific approach to theory construction and testing be useful in relation to predicting when and how investors will react to earnings announcements? Why or why not?
4. What is the importance to society of developing a theory to explain the relationship between earnings forecasts, earnings announcements, and share price movements?

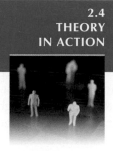

**2.4
THEORY
IN ACTION**

Alternative approaches to accounting theory construction

Telstra retains forecast for 2009 earnings to rise

by Andrea Tan

Telstra Corp., Australia's largest phone company, reaffirmed its forecast for earnings and sales to climb this year on growth from its mobile and internet units amid the global financial turmoil.

Earnings before interest, tax, depreciation and amortization will probably rise as much as 7 percent in the 12 months ending June 30, Telstra said today in a statement to the Australian stock exchange. Sales this year may climb between 3 percent and 4 percent, the company said.

Telstra, based in Melbourne, stuck to its forecasts even as the credit crisis forces some companies to cut earnings estimates. The phone operator is three years into a five-year plan to raise profit by slashing its workforce by as much as 12,000 and has said it will invest more than A$10 billion ($6.8 billion) to upgrade the speed and geographic coverage of its networks to counter failing revenue from fixed-line operations.

"Unlike most companies at this time, Telstra is in an enviable position," Chief Executive Officer Sol Trujillo told investors in Sydney today. "You can take it to the bank that we're going to grow earnings."

Mobile-phone unit sales rose by a "double-digit" percentage in the fiscal first quarter ended Sept. 30, he said.

Telstra, which has cut 9,584 jobs since it announced its five-year plan, expects to save between A$200 million and A$300 million in labor costs by June 2010, Chief Financial Officer John Stanhope said. The phone operator had 46,649 workers at the end of June 30, according to its annual report.

Questions
1. What market backlash do businesspeople fear if they do not meet their forecast earnings or growth targets? Why?
2. Can the scientific approach to theory construction and testing be useful in relation to predicting when and how investors will react to earnings announcements? Why or why not?
3. What is the importance to society of developing a theory to explain the relationship between earnings forecasts, earnings announcements, and share price movements?

LO 7 ISSUES FOR AUDITING THEORY CONSTRUCTION

As discussed earlier, auditing is a verification process that is applied to the accounting inputs and processes. Auditors are not verifying outputs for conformance to one unique economic measure of profit, but provide an opinion on whether the financial statements are in accordance with the applicable reporting framework. In addition, depending on the jurisdiction, auditors provide an opinion on whether the statements present fairly, in all material respects, or give a true and fair view.[14]

In general, the construction of a theory of auditing has followed, with a lag, the development of accounting theory. The early literature on auditing focused on issues arising in the conduct of an audit, such as the emphasis on fraud detection, discovery of errors of principle and the nature of account verification.[15] The pragmatic approach to auditing theory development is evident in early texts explaining the process and principles of auditing. For example, the concept of professional scepticism has its roots in principles laid down in nineteenth-century legal cases, such as Kingston Cotton Mill[16] (in 1896) and London and General Bank[17] (in 1895). The judgement of Lopes LJ in the Kingston Cotton Mill case defined the auditor's responsibilities with respect to the detection of fraud as the right to believe company representatives, provided reasonable care is taken. Further cases in various jurisdictions refined and developed the concept of professional scepticism,[18] and the auditing standards have adapted and developed over time to incorporate this concept. Today's standards still refer to the auditor's right to accept records and documents as genuine, provided the auditor investigates further if any condition creates doubt about that presumption.[19]

Mautz and Sharaf, in 1961, attempted to generalise the existing literature and provide a comprehensive theory of auditing.[20] Their motivation to write the monograph was to counter the prevailing view that auditing was a practical exercise, not only without any theoretical underpinnings, but not requiring theoretical development.[21] Mautz and Sharaf argued that practical issues could be resolved only by development and use of theory. They provided eight postulates as a foundation for the theory of auditing and developed the basic concepts of such a theory. These concepts were identified as evidence, due audit care, fair presentation, independence and ethical conduct. However, although these concepts are now embedded in the auditing standards and regulations, the development of an auditing theory progressed slowly in the years following Mautz and Sharaf's publication.[22]

The normative era of accounting theory and research also coincided with a normative approach to auditing theory. In the early 1970s the American Accounting Association (AAA) established the Committee on Basic Auditing Concepts to investigate the role and function of auditing, to make recommendations for research projects, examine the problems of evidence, and issue a position paper on the scope of auditing by accountants.[23] The report provides a normative statement on auditing with an emphasis on concepts that should be studied by students, and suggestions for research which may 'lead to better fulfilment of the role of auditing in society'.[24] The resulting Statement of Basic Auditing Concepts (ASOBAC)[25] emphasised the essence of auditing as the collecting and evaluating of evidence without fully developing the theory of how evidentiary material is used in the reasoning process to support the auditor's opinion.[26]

The growth of positive theories of accounting in the 1970s was accompanied by a change in direction of auditing research. Two major streams of research developed, both of which relied on empirical data and were designed in a positive or scientific framework. Experimentalists focused on a micro-level understanding of the audit testing/judgement process (known as JDM, or judgement/decision making research).[27] This research sought to explain how auditors make judgements and decisions so that they could predict how auditors would behave when placed in certain situations. The early research in this field provided somewhat disturbing evidence of differing judgements by auditors when presented with the same information,[28] although these effects appeared at least partly due to the problem of creating realistic audit tasks in an experimental setting.[29]

The other major stream of empirical auditing research that developed in this era examined questions of auditor choice by companies and the factors affecting the level of fees paid by companies to their auditors. This research was particularly interested in whether the quality of audits performed by different auditors in different circumstances differed. DeAngelo[30] argued that audit quality is positively related to audit firm size because larger auditors have 'more to lose' by failing to report a discovered breach in a particular client's records. That is, large audit firms have more clients to lose than small audit firms from compromising their independence on an audit in order to please the client. This theory helps explain why large audit firms dominate the audit services market. Simunic[31] developed a theory to explain that audit fees are based on client characteristics and reflected the forces of demand and supply. This literature is based on economic concepts of efficient markets and the role of the auditor in resolving agency conflicts between shareholders, managers and lenders. These theories are discussed further in later chapters.

Summary

A review of accounting theory construction reveals that there are many different approaches to theory formulation in accounting. This chapter classifies and explains some of these approaches. Whereas the previous chapter focuses on theory in general, this chapter extends that discussion to focus on theory construction in relation to accounting.

LO 1 — **How pragmatic approaches to theory development apply to accounting**

Accounting was dominated by descriptive pragmatic approaches to theory development or syntactic explanations of pragmatic relationships before the late 1950s. Pragmatic approaches are inductive approaches designed to learn from what accountants do (descriptive pragmatic approach) or how users respond to accounting information (psychological pragmatic approach), in order to replicate accounting procedures and principles.

LO 2 — **Criticisms that have been levelled at historical cost accounting as a theoretical model**

Historical cost accounting has been criticised for a number of reasons, some of which are explored in later chapters. In this chapter we explored why traditional historical cost has been criticised for poor syntax, whereby different types of monetary measures are added, and for semantic deficiencies since there is no independent empirically observable correspondent to concepts such as 'profit' or 'asset'. In later chapters we explore whether alternative accounting theories compensate for these deficiencies.

LO 3 — **Normative true income theories and the decision-usefulness approach to accounting theory**

The 1950s and 1960s saw accounting theory formulated using a normative approach to prescribe how accountants should report either to derive the 'true income' for an organisation or to generate information that is useful for decision making. 'True income' theorists concentrated on deriving a single, correct measure of income. However, 'true income' is a concept that was never defined to the satisfaction of all parties. Decision-usefulness approaches focused on developing theories to ensure that accounting reports would provide the information most useful for making the decisions that the theorists believed to be most important. This period saw accounting theory develop mostly in relation to measurement theories of value and adjustments to take into account how inflation affected values. Normative theorists relied mostly on syntactic logic in deriving theories, and concentrated on measurement.

LO 4─┤ **How positive theories are constructed**
From the early 1970s, accounting theory became more involved in empirical or positive theory development and testing. Positive accounting theorists concentrate on understanding the assumptions that normative theorists take for granted. Unlike normative theories, which prescribe particular courses of action, positive theories describe, explain, or predict observable phenomena, such as why accountants do what they do and what is the impact of historical cost accounting on capital markets. Positive theories start when anomalies to existing theory are observed, and researchers develop theories to explain those anomalies and then test them, generally using the scientific inductive approach to theory construction and evaluation.

LO 5─┤ **Alternative naturalistic approaches and the importance of ontology**
In contrast to the normative and inductive approaches to theory formulation and testing, the naturalistic approach is more an exploratory approach that does not attempt to draw large-scale inferences, but rather tries to explain complex and potentially unique situations using an unstructured approach. The naturalistic approach regards accounting as constructed reality rather than objective reality, and naturalistic research is more likely to use case studies and individual experiences of events than the scientific approach of syntactic model formulation and empirical induction to develop hypotheses, followed by statistical testing of the hypotheses.

LO 6─┤ **Misconceptions associated with scientific approaches to accounting research, and why they are misconceptions**
Some have contended that the scientific approach to theory construction in accounting is inappropriate because it tries to make scientists out of accounting practitioners or because the scientific method assumes that there is an 'absolute truth' that accounting should achieve. Both of these views are incorrect. Although an accounting researcher may apply the scientific method to theory construction, practitioners do not act as scientists; rather, they use the empirical evidence and logical explanations from the approach to support their practices. The scientific method does not claim to provide 'truth'. Instead, it attempts to provide persuasive evidence which, on the balance of probability, may provide as good a description, explanation, or prediction as theory can provide.

LO 7─┤ **Issues for auditing theory construction**
The development of a theory of auditing has followed, with a lag, approaches in accounting theory. Early writers attempted to document the process of auditing and the duties expected of auditors. Attempts to develop a general theory of auditing began in the 1960s and described and prescribed best auditing practice. More recently, experimental research has studied how auditors make decisions in an attempt to predict auditor behaviour, and positive theories explain demand for auditing and audit fees using economic models.

Questions

1. 'A theory that is purely syntactic is sterile.' Is this true? How can this statement relate to accounting?
2. One type of theory construction involves observing the practices and techniques of working accountants and then teaching those practices and techniques to successive accountants.
   (a) What type of theory construction is this?
   (b) What are the advantages of this approach compared with a decision-usefulness approach to theory construction?

(c) What are the disadvantages of this approach?

(d) Do you believe that this is a good approach to developing a theory of accounting? Why or why not?

3. Describe the semantic approach to theory construction.

(a) Should the outputs of accounting systems be verified?

(b) If so, how can this be achieved? If not, why not?

4. In the 1970s there was much debate about how to account for inflation.

(a) Did this debate involve positive theory or normative theory?

(b) Is it important to account for the effects of inflation? Why or why not?

5. Researchers who develop positive theories and researchers who develop normative theories often do not share the same views about the roles of their respective approaches to theory construction.

(a) How do positive and normative theories differ?

(b) Can positive theories assist normative theories, or vice versa? If yes, give an example. If not, why not?

6. Can accounting theory be constructed as a purely syntactical exercise? Why or why not?

7. Classify the following hypotheses according to whether they are the conclusions of positive or normative theories. Explain your answers.

(a) Historical cost accounting should be replaced by a market value system.

(b) Historical cost accounting provides information used by creditors.

(c) Historical cost accounting is used by many managers to allocate costs in determining divisional performance.

8. Give an example of the types of issues that might be resolved by accounting theories developed using the following methods of theory construction.

(a) psychological pragmatic approach

(b) scientific approach

(c) naturalistic approach

(d) normative approach

(e) positive approach

9. Explain the naturalistic and syntactic approaches to theory construction. Are these approaches mutually exclusive? Why or why not?

10. The decision-usefulness approach to theory development can be used to develop theories of accounting.

(a) Explain what is meant by the decision-usefulness approach to theory development.

(b) How can the decision-usefulness approach relate to accounting theory formulation?

(c) Give two examples of decisions that require data obtained from accounting reports.

11. What type of a theory is historical cost? How has it been derived? Do you have any criticisms of historical cost accounting?

12. Explain the psychological pragmatic approach to accounting theory. Give an example of how it can be applied.

13. Give an example of an accounting convention usually adopted in historical cost accounting. Conventions govern the way accounting is practised, and conventions are, by definition, known from practice.

(a) What theoretical approach is used to derive conventions?

(b) What does your answer to (a) imply about the potential for accounting theories based on conventions to be innovative in providing useful information?

14. How do you think the massive amounts of data now available from information technologies will affect
    (a) the development of accounting theories?
    (b) the testing of accounting theories?
15. What are some common criticisms of a scientific approach to professions such as accounting and law? Are they valid? Why or why not?
16. Early auditing theories were constructed by observing the practices of auditors. What type of theory construction is this? What are the advantages and disadvantages of this approach?
17. How would you design an experiment to provide evidence on how auditors make judgements? What competing issues would arise?

Additional readings

Burchell, S, Clubb, C, Hopwood, A, & Hughes, J 1980, 'The roles of accounting in organizations and society'. *Accounting, Organizations and Society*, vol. 5, no. 1, pp. 5–27.

Gaffikin, JMR 1987, 'The methodology of early accounting theorists', *Abacus*, vol. 23, no. 1, pp. 17–30.

Glautier, M & Underdown, B 2000, *Accounting — theory and practice*, 7th edn, London: Pearson Education.

Henderson, MS, Peirson, G, & Harris, K 2004, *Financial accounting theory*. Sydney: Pearson Prentice Hall.

Jones, S, Romano, C, & Ratnatunga, J 1995, *Accounting theory — a contemporary review*, Sydney: Harcourt Brace.

Ryan, RJ 1980, 'Scientific method.' In *Topics in management accounting*, edited by J Arnold, B Carlsberg and R Scapens, Oxford: Phillip Allan Publishers.

Scott, WR 2003, *Financial accounting theory*, 3rd edn, Toronto: Pearson Education.

Stamp, E 1981, 'Why can accounting not become a science like physics?' *Abacus*, vol. 17, no. 1.

Verrecchia, R 1990, 'Information quality and discretionary disclosure', *Journal of Accounting and Economics*, vol. 12, pp. 365–80.

Wells, MC 1976, 'A revolution in accounting thought', *Accounting Review*, July.

Whittred, G, Zimmer, I, Taylor, S, & Wells, P 2004, *Financial accounting incentive effects and economic consequences*, 6th edn, Southbank: Thomson Learning.

Woodward, D, Edwards, P, & Birkin, F 1996, 'Organisational legitimacy and stakeholder information provision', *British Journal of Management*, vol. 7, pp. 329–47.

| 2.1 CASE STUDY | The following article provides an example of alternative approaches to the construction and evaluation of accounting theory and policy. |

New accounting rules 'don't add up'

by Barney Jopson

Britain's biggest companies, once enthusiastic advocates of international accounting standards, have turned sour on the new rules, complaining that they are making accounts more opaque and less useful.

Jon Symonds, chairman of the influential Hundred Group of finance directors, said companies were being forced to present numbers to investors that almost defied explanation. 'I don't want a technical and theoretical approach (to accounting) to undermine communication between business and owners,' he told *The Financial Times*.

International Financial Reporting Standards have changed the face of accounts since their introduction in the European Union this year, requiring listed companies to dig out previously unreported figures and disclose much other information in a different way. The unhappiness of British companies is an ominous development for rule-makers at the International Accounting Standards Board (IASB) in London, which has generally found its British constituents more supportive than those in Europe.

Mr Symonds, chief financial officer of AstraZeneca, said he supported the goal of a single set of global reporting standards to make accounts clearer and more comparable.

But IFRS were developing in the wrong direction and he expressed reservations about the standards' conceptual foundations, the use of 'fair value' accounting, and growing US influence over their form.

The new standards are more complex than existing British accounting rules and require greater technical disclosure of a range of items from derivatives and employee stock options to pension fund deficits and off-balance-sheet finance. The introduction of 'fair value' accounting, requiring asset and liability revaluations to be passed through the income statement, has already sparked ire elsewhere in the EU.

Some companies say it introduces volatility into reported profits, distracting attention from underlying performance.

Tom Jones, vice-chairman of the IASB, rejected the criticism of fair value accounting but admitted that standard-setters were having little success in placating disgruntled companies.

'It's not our objective to get away from economic reality ... There is nothing more real than the value of an asset today,' he said.

Mr Symonds also voiced worries about an agreement between the IASB and the US Financial Accounting Standards Board to close differences between their accounting rules and thus reduce corporate compliance costs. 'There is some concern that the strength of the relationship between the IASB and FASB means we are heading down a US path without adequate debate.'

The Hundred Group is working on a more detailed list of desired changes to present to the IASB. Under pressure from the EU, standard-setters have tried in recent months to respond to the concerns of at least some constituents.

Source: The Weekend Australian, 27–28 August 2005, p. 35.

Questions

1. What are international financial reporting standards (IFRS)?
2. Many arguments are expressed in this article. List three factors that you think are causing British businesspeople to be upset about the prospect of adopting the IFRS.
3. Consider each of the three factors you mentioned in response to question 2.
   (a) Is there empirical evidence to support the factor?
   (b) Is the analysis leading from the factor to the complaints about adopting the IFRS scientific or naturalistic in its approach? Explain your answer.
4. How could researchers evaluate the decision usefulness of adopting the IFRS?
5. What role can positive theory play in resolving the issue(s) described in the article?
6. What role can normative theory play in resolving the issue(s) described in the article?

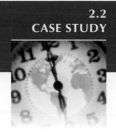

Numerous approaches can be taken to construct a theory of how and why investors use accounting numbers in making their investment decisions. The following case is an example of how more than one approach might be possible, or even appropriate.

The thrill is gone

by Philip Rennie

Although Lend Lease's 13.5% rise in underlying profit for 2004–05 and guidance of double-digit growth for 2006 were reasonable enough, the market was not impressed.

Against the 52-week high of $14.24, the price is now $12.91. The problem is lack of excitement, compared with its history as a glamour stock. Lend Lease has done well to produce a growth business after its disastrous plunge into United States property funds management, but what remains is largely a retail and residential development and construction group, with a property investment portfolio thrown in.

It is an international business, with substantial activities in the United States and Britain as well as Australia. It has undertaken prominent projects, including cleaning up the World Trade Center site after the September 11, 2001 terrorist attacks. But no one is getting excited about largely cyclical industries. Lend Lease has not entered the glamour infrastructure areas such as toll roads and tunnels, and has no plans to do so.

In private, competitors snigger at those behind Lend Lease naively selling its MLC funds management business just as the Australian superannuation boom was about to get going, to dive into the unknown world of US property.

Of course, that all happened before present chief executive Greg Clarke was hired. His job was to knock what remained into shape and he is generally seen as having done a good job. But there are questions about why Lend Lease's bid for General Property Trust failed and whether Clarke should have moved faster and more aggressively and put his foot on a sizeable unit-holding.

GPT was effectively Lend Lease's captive institution. The relationship had been mutually beneficial. Lend Lease made substantial fees as GPT's manager and this annuity income provided a balance to Lend Lease's more cyclical businesses.

There is still a substantial amount of investment income flowing from top-class investment properties such as the Bluewater shopping centre in Britain and the King of Prussia mall in the US. Investment income amounted to 22% of 2004–05 earnings and the long-term aim is to lift this to 30–35%. One benefit of this would be a strengthening of Lend Lease's credit rating, but Clarke concedes that this annuity income goal will take some years to achieve.

At $12.91, Lend Lease shares yield 4.4%, based on the 2004–05 dividend of 57¢. The payment is partly franked and the outlook is for more of the same. Chief financial officer Roger Burrows says that with about a third of earnings coming from Australia, the franking credits should be enough to provided 40–50% dividend franking on a 60–80% profit payout.

This means investors need a higher yield than would be required from a comparable company paying fully franked dividends. The present price reflects this. As a result, the return looks reasonable, certainly if double-digit earnings and dividend growth can be sustained.

Source: BRW, 1–7 September 2005, p. 79.

Questions

1. Lend Lease reported a 13.5 per cent increase in profit for 2004–05. Why was the share market unimpressed?

2. In trying to explain shareholders' subdued reaction to Lend Lease reported earnings, explain whether and/or how you could use the following approaches to accounting theory construction.
   (a) pragmatic
   (b) decision usefulness
   (c) positive accounting theory
   (d) normative theory
   (e) scientific approach
   (f) naturalistic approach
3. Which of the approaches described in answer to question (2) do you believe is most useful? Why?
4. Are the approaches you described in answer to question (2) mutually exclusive, or can they be used to complement each other? Explain.

2.3
CASE STUDY

The following article provides an example of alternative approaches to the construction and evaluation of accounting theory and policy.

Intergovernmental working group of experts on international standards of accounting and reporting

As this Group of Experts has underscored on many occasions, principles-based, high quality financial reporting standards are critical for the coherence and efficient functioning of the international financial architecture. A rapidly globalizing world economy needs global accounting, reporting and auditing standards. In a world economy that has been growing increasingly interdependent, resource mobilization and allocation has been taking place across borders. In the second half of this decade, we have witnessed the transformation of the financial reporting landscape. An unprecedented number of enterprises adopted International Financial Reporting Standards as the basis for the preparation of their financial statements.

The centrality of reliable and comparable information for financial stability and investors' ability to assess risk and allocate resources to different investment opportunities has been painfully demonstrated by recent events. The global financial crisis has shown how — in a world of unprecedented financial interdependence — intransparent financial market products and financial accounts can wreak havoc not only with investors' profits, but — more importantly — with the development prospects of innocent bystanders, including some of the most vulnerable populations.

At the heart of this crisis are problems with opacity and complexity, while financial institutions may have been reporting a lot of information, the question was whether or not those reports provided any meaningful insight or useful understanding of the companies' inherent risks. With hindsight, the answer is clearly no. It is now evident that even the boards of leading banks and their own accountants and internal auditors did not fully understand the risks of their own products.

Ultimately, regaining investor confidence will once again require full transparency, better accounting, reporting and auditing standards and practices. The current crisis has prompted a re-examination of several accounting, reporting and auditing requirements — including consolidation of off-balance sheet entities, fair value or mark-to-market valuation of financial instruments and related uncertainties. I understand that in light of the current crisis, standard setters have taken action to amend relevant standards . . .

Source: Excerpts from Statements by Supachai Panitchpakdi, Secretary-General of UNCTAD (2008–2009), Geneva, 5 November 2008, www.unctad.org.

2.4
CASE STUDY

Numerous approaches can be taken to construct a theory of how and why investors use accounting numbers in making their investment decisions. The following case is an example of how more than one approach might be possible or even appropriate.

Tabcorp costs trouble market

by Fleur Leyden

Tabcorp's full year profit may be back in the black but the gaming giant's shares were pounded almost 5 per cent yesterday, with investors worried about mounting licence fees and taxes and an extra $100 million to be spent upgrading Star City casino.

The fresh outlay of funds will take the cost of the Sydney casino refurbishment to $575 million in an environment Tabcorp chief executive Elmer Funke Kupper said remained challenging.

"I think we'll still have a soft patch in the economy over the next 12 months and, while we're all very encouraged by the housing market recovery and equity markets . . . I think that uncertainty is still there," he said.

Tabcorp unveiled a $521.7 million net profit for the year to June 30, a sharp turnaround from the previous year's $164.6 million loss, which had been weighed down by writedowns associated with the Victoria Government's decision to end the gambling duopoly between Tabcorp and Tatts in 2012.

Normalised profit for the past year, including the effect of one-off items and fluctuations in Tabcorp's theoretical win rate against high-rolling gamblers, rose 1.2 per cent to $496.2 million. Revenue rose 5 per cent to $4.2 billion.

However, investors dismissed the profit result — which was slightly ahead of expectations — with the scrip closing 35c weaker at $7.03 in a stronger overall share market. Analysts said investors were spooked by the company's grim outlook and the admission that licence fees to racing clubs could rise to $65 million — more than double the $30 million it had previously flagged. The company also will have to absorb higher taxes in Queensland.

"The outlook commentary was a bit underwhelming," said Austock analyst Rohan Sundram.

"Wagering will probably achieve low growth due to the full-year impact of race field charges, but casinos is where the biggest downside is — there will be a $30 million tax hit on the Queensland casino pokies and then a $20 million EBIT impact from refurb disruptions at Star City. It's going to be tough."

Mr Funke Kupper said the board gave the green light to the extra spend on Star City earlier this month. He said about a third of the extra $100 million would go towards beefing up gaming, a third towards food and beverage outlets and "nightlife", and the rest to electrical upgrades.

Tabcorp's casinos division booked a 2.6 per cent rise in revenue for the year, although EBIT fell 11 per cent to $328.1 million as labour and marketing expenses grew. Revenue from the wagering division kicked up 7.8 per cent, while EBIT fell 1.6 per cent to $251.7 million, crimped by a 5.1 per cent jump in expenses from setting up Luxbet.com.

The company declared a final dividend of 30c a share, to be paid on September 18 for shareholders on the books by August 17, taking the full-year payment to 65c, compared with the previous year's 94c, which included a special dividend.

Source: Herald Sun, 7 August 2009, pp.41–42, www.heraldsun.com.au.

Questions

1. Tabcorp reported an increase in profit for 2008–2009. Why was the share market unimpressed?
2. In trying to explain shareholders' subdued reaction to Tabcorp's reported earnings, explain whether and/or how you could use the following approaches to accounting theory construction.
   (a) pragmatic
   (b) positive accounting theory
   (c) naturalistic approach
3. Are the approaches you described in your answer to question (2) mutually exclusive, or can they be used to complement each other? Explain.
4. What is meant by 'normalised earnings'? Why would a firm disclose 'normalised' earnings?

**2.5
CASE STUDY**

The following case demonstrates how investors supplement their decisions using logical explanations in addition to accounting information.

Alumina jumps on bad news

Alumina has posted an 86.3 per cent fall in first-half profit after a tough year for the aluminium sector, but the company's shares rose after it said the worst of the downturn might be over.

Alumina, a minority partner in Alcoa World Alumina & Chemicals (AWAC) group, made a net profit of $6 million in the first half of the year, down from $43.8 million in the previous interim period. It also made an underlying loss of $14.6 million compared with a profit of $151.7 million previously, as the company curtailed production by 17 per cent. However, the result beat market expectations for an underlying loss of about $19 million.

Chief executive John Bevan said the latest June half was "extraordinarily difficult" for the aluminium industry. While he remained cautious, he said the situation was improving. "We firmly believe that the worst is behind us in terms of the impact of the global financial crisis and we are quietly confident that the market will begin to improve from here," he said.

Mr Bevan said the result reflected aluminium prices between last November and April, when they averaged below $US1400 a tonne. Prices had since rebounded to trade above $US2000 a tonne.

Shares in Alumina yesterday ended up 16c, or 9.79 per cent, at $1.795 — the stock's highest close since last November 10, when it ended at $1.945. "The market is liking the result, which is combined with the fact that aluminium was up 4 per cent overnight," said IG Markets research analyst Ben Potter.

The company did not declare a dividend, after previously paying a 12c a share interim dividend. It said it would continue to review the dividend issue every six months.

Source: Herald Sun, 7 August 2009, p. 56, www.heraldsun.com.au.

Questions

1. Alumina reported an 86.3 per cent fall in first half-year profit, and suspended its final dividend. Why did its share price rise by 9.79 per cent on the announcement date?
2. In trying to explain the positive response to Alumina's reported earnings, explain whether and/or how you could use the following approaches to accounting theory construction.
   (a) decision usefulness
   (b) normative
   (c) scientific
3. Which of the approaches described in answer to question (2) do you believe is most useful? Why?
4. Explain the importance to investors of developing a theory to explain the relationship between earnings announcements and share price movements.

Endnotes

1. R Sterling, 'On theory construction and verification', *Accounting Review*, July 1970.
2. ibid.
3. ibid.
4. R Chambers, 'Why bother with postulates?', *Journal of Accounting Research*, vol. 1, no. 1, Spring, 1965, pp. 587–8.
5. R Chambers, 'Implications of asset revaluations and bonus issues' in *Accounting, Finance and Management*, Sydney: Butterworths, 1969, p. 122.
6. ibid.
7. R Sterling, 'Towards a science of accounting', *Financial Analysts Journal*, Sept.–Oct. 1975, p. 32.
8. For a more detailed description see R Chambers, *Accounting, evaluation and economic behavior*, Englewood Cliffs, NJ: Prentice Hall, 1966.
9. M Friedman, 'The methodology of positive economics' in *Essays in positive economics*, Chicago: University of Chicago Press, 1953, pp. 3–43.
10. AR Abdel-Khalik and BB Ajinkya, *Empirical research in accounting: a methodological viewpoint*, Florida: AAA, 1979.
11. C Tomkins and R Groves, 'The everyday accountant and researching his reality', *Accounting, Organizations and Society*, vol. 8, no. 4, 1983, pp. 361–74.
12. ibid.
13. ibid., p. 367.
14. ISA 700, Forming an opinion and reporting on financial statements, September 2008. The meaning of the phrase 'present fairly' has been debated extensively, specifically whether it has any implications for the quality of the financial statements beyond their compliance with the relevant accounting standards; see for example, Y Toba, 'A semantic meaning analysis of the ultimate proposition to be verified by independent auditors', *The Accounting Review*, vol. 55 no. 4, October 1980, pp. 604–619.
15. For example, WA Staub, 'Mode of conducting an audit', *The Accounting Review*, vol. 18, no. 2 April 1943, pp. 91–98.
16. *Kingston Cotton Mill Co.* (No. 2) (1896) 2 Ch. 279, Lopes LJ: It is the duty of an auditor to bring to bear on the work he has to perform that skill, care and caution which a reasonably competent, careful and cautious auditor would use. What is reasonable skill, care and caution must depend on the particular circumstances of each case. An auditor is not bound to be a detective, or, as was said, to approach his work with suspicion or with a foregone conclusion that there is something wrong. He is a watchdog, but not a bloodhound. He is justified in believing tried servants of the company in whom confidence is placed by the company. He is entitled to assume that they are honest, and to rely upon their representations, provided he takes reasonable care. If there is anything calculated to excite suspicion, he should probe it to the bottom but, in the absence of anything of that kind, he is only bound to be reasonably cautious and careful.
17. *London and General Bank* (No. 2) (1895) 2 Ch. 673.
18. For example, *Pacific Acceptance Corporation Ltd v. Forsyth* (1970) 92 WN (NSW) 29; *Thomas Gerrard & Son Ltd* (1967) 2 All ER 525.
19. ISA 240, *The auditor's responsibilities relating to fraud in an audit of financial statements*, February 2009, paragraphs 12–14.
20. R Mautz and HA Sharaf, *The philosophy of auditing*, American Accounting Association, 1961.
21. HE Miller, 'Review', *The Accounting Review*, vol. 37, no. 3, July 1962, pp. 599–600.
22. HM Anderson, JW Giese and J Booker, 'Some propositions about auditing', *The Accounting Review*, vol. 45, no. 3, July 1970, pp. 524–531.
23. JA Silvoso, 'Report of the committee on basic auditing concepts', *The Accounting Review*, supplement to volume XLVII (1972), pp. 15–74.
24. Silvoso, op. cit., p. 16.
25. American Accounting Association Committee on Basic Auditing Concepts, 'A statement of basic auditing concepts', Sarasota, 1973.
26. Y Toba, 'A general theory of evidence as the conceptual foundation in auditing theory', *The Accounting Review*, vol. 50, no. 1, January 1975, pp. 7–24.

27. J Francis, in editorial, 'Roundtable on auditing research', *European Accounting Association Newsletter*, issue 1, 2009, pp. 12–16.

28. SF Biggs and TJ Mock, 'An investigation of auditor decision processes in the evaluation of internal controls and audit scope decisions', *Journal of Accounting Research*, vol. 21, no. 1, Spring 1983, pp. 234–255; TJ Mock and JL Turner, 'Internal Accounting Control Evaluation and Auditor Judgment', Auditing Research Monograph No. 3, New York: AICPA 1981.

29. KT Trotman, 'The review process and the accuracy of auditor judgments', *Journal of Accounting Research*, vol. 23, no. 2, Autumn 1985, pp. 740–752.

30. LE DeAngelo, 'Auditor size and audit quality', *Journal of Accounting and Economics*, vol. 3, no. 3, December 1981, pp. 183–199.

31. D Simunic, 'The pricing of audit services: theory and evidence', *Journal of Accounting Research*, vol. 18, Spring 1980, pp. 27–35.

3

Applying theory to accounting regulation

LEARNING OBJECTIVES

After reading this chapter, you should have an appreciation of the following:

1 the theories of regulation that are relevant to accounting and auditing

2 how theories of regulation apply to accounting and auditing practice

3 the regulatory framework for financial reporting

4 the institutional structure for setting accounting and auditing standards.

At the end of each quarter, half-year and financial year firms are busy preparing their accounts and (at least at year-end) having them audited by an independent auditor. Firms lodge their accounts with government agencies and listed firms provide reports and other information for their stock exchange. Firms issue press releases for investors and advisers. To what extent can theory help us to understand why these activities occur? Can theory explain why private sector bodies and governments and their agencies take an active role in the financial reporting process? This chapter addresses these questions.

First, we consider a number of theories that are relevant to the practice of accounting and auditing. We discuss the theory of efficient markets and agency theory to understand the setting in which financial reporting occurs. We consider three specific theories of regulation, which have been proposed to explain regulation in capital markets. The theories are public interest, regulatory capture and private interest theory. In the next section, we consider how the three theories apply in practice. Consider the case where a government changes financial reporting requirements or introduces more oversight of auditors following a major corporate collapse (e.g. as occurred in the United States with the Sarbanes-Oxley Act in 2002). Can public interest theory explain this intervention in the market place, or is private interest theory more applicable? If a major industry group is able to ensure production of an accounting standard which aligns with its preferences for accounting measurement and disclosure, has the group captured the standard setter? We consider the extent to which each of the three theories is helpful in understanding these and similar events.

In this chapter we identify many different parties that are involved in the preparation and regulation of financial reporting. In the third section we present a description of the regulatory framework and discuss the elements which are likely to comprise a 'proforma' (or example) framework. The elements considered are: statutory requirements; corporate governance; auditors and oversight; and independent enforcement bodies. We explore how these elements influence the output of the financial reporting process, that is, the financial statements.

Finally, we describe the international standard setting process. Accounting standards can be viewed as a key part of the regulatory framework as they influence the behaviour of preparers and auditors and thus the information provided for users of financial reports. Since accounting standards involve wealth transfers, many parties are concerned about their content and have become involved in their formulation. In recent years, standard setting has moved to the international arena, with the standards developed by the London-based International Accounting Standards Board (IASB) used in more than 100 countries. The goal of harmonisation of financial reporting has led the IASB to work closely with the United States's Financial Accounting Standards Board (FASB) on a number of joint projects. We also describe the development of auditing standards, which has become increasingly international.

LO 1 ▸ THE THEORIES OF REGULATION RELEVANT TO ACCOUNTING AND AUDITING

Capital market theorists suggest that managers have many incentives to voluntarily provide accounting information to parties external to the firm, and to have that information verified by independent auditors. So why do we observe regulation of financial reporting through company law and accounting standards? Why do most countries have legal requirements to produce audited financial statements? There are several theories which are relevant to understanding the regulation of financial reporting (i.e. the preparing, auditing and supply of accounting information about an entity). They include:

- theory of efficient markets
- agency theory
- theories of regulation — public interest, regulatory capture and private interest.

Theory of efficient markets

Free market economists would argue that markets function best without government intervention, and that maximum efficiency is achieved by allowing forces of supply and demand to dictate market behaviour. In the world's increasingly international capital markets, forces of demand and supply have a large influence on the flows of information and capital. However, governments also actively intervene in these markets, regulating not only how markets are conducted but also the provision of information which has been described as the 'lifeblood' of capital markets. At best, government intervention aims to assist market development and promote economic growth. Equitable and transparent markets, where there is a balance of wealth-enhancing opportunities and investor protection, are considered vital to attract participants. Nevertheless, optimal market regulation is an art rather than a science.

Accounting can be seen as an information industry; that is, the business of accounting is to produce information. Advocates of the free-market approach argue that, as with any other product, demand and supply forces should operate. There is a demand for accounting information by users and a supply of such information from companies in the form of financial statements. An equilibrium price therefore can theoretically be found for accounting information.

Suppose a new type of financial information is demanded by users and a supplier is willing to provide it for a price. The price will finally adjust to one where the supplier still finds it advantageous to furnish the information and users believe the cost is equal to or less than the benefits of the information. If not, then the information will not be provided. In other words, free-market forces can determine what type of accounting data to provide and the necessary standards that underlie them.

It is highly unlikely that authoritative, regulatory bodies will relinquish their present power in accounting. Because of that, critics of the free-market approach say the theory is unrealistic. Furthermore, they argue that the theory is unworkable because the market mechanisms will not be able to achieve a socially ideal equilibrium price for accounting information for the following reasons.

Accounting information cannot be considered in the same way as other products, because it is a 'public' good. Once the information is released by a company, it is available to everyone. Although the information may be sold to certain people only, others who did not pay for it cannot be easily excluded from using the information. This phenomenon is referred to as the 'free-rider' problem, outlined overleaf. In the accounting setting, examples of free riders include financial analysts and potential investors. Because not all users can be charged for the cost of producing the accounting information, suppliers will have minimal incentive to produce it. Only regulatory intervention can persuade companies to produce the information necessary to meet real demand and to ensure an efficient capital market.

A company has a monopoly on the supply of information about itself and, therefore, the tendency will be for the company to underproduce and sell at a high price. From society's point of view, mandatory reporting will result in more information at a lower cost.

Even if a free market existed for accounting information, a regulatory board would still be needed because users are unable to agree on what they want and accountants will not agree on the procedures to derive the desired information. Further, the value of information provided by companies to users is greatly enhanced if it can be compared with information from other companies.

Agency theory

The demand for financial information can be categorised as being either for stewardship or for decision-making purposes. Atkinson and Feltham state that agency theory considers mainly the stewardship demand for information.[1] The theory concentrates on the relationships in which the welfare of one person (e.g. the owner) is entrusted to another, the agent (e.g. a manager). Atkinson and Feltham explain that the demand for stewardship information relates to the desire to:

- motivate the agent
- distribute risk efficiently.

The demand for information for decision-making purposes relates to the role of information in statistical decision theory. Information is valuable if it improves the allocation of resources and risks in the economy. It does this by reducing uncertainty.

Uncertainty in agency theory can be classified as ex ante or ex post. Ex ante (before the event) uncertainty exists at the time a decision is to be made, such as uncertainty about controllable events that will affect production or uncertainty about the skill of the manager. Ex post (after the event) uncertainty exists after the decision has been made and the results realised. This uncertainty is the same as ex ante uncertainty except that it can be reduced by ex post reports on what actually happened. Agency theory focuses on the impact of alternative ex post reports that affect ex post uncertainty.

Atkinson and Feltham see the role of standard setting as one of identifying situations where welfare improvements will be obtained from a given policy on financial reporting. Welfare improvements relate to Pareto comparisons. Policy A would be preferred to policy B if under the former every person is at least as well off as under the latter and at least one person is better off. Policy A would also be preferred to policy B if it resulted in a more efficient allocation of resources and risk. Thus, under this view, it appears that perceived economic consequences of accounting standards play an important role.

Agency theory gives us a framework in which to study contracts between principals and agents and to predict the economic consequences of standards. For example, it is often logical that managers' compensation be tied to reported profits or they may have less incentive to achieve profits. In this situation, one type of contractual relationship is between users of accounting data and the company. Contracts for financial data can be alternatives to public reporting. If accounting were 'deregulated', the market mechanism could generate sufficient information and reach a socially ideal equilibrium point where the cost of providing the information equals the benefits. Supporters of this view argue that mandatory disclosures are therefore unnecessary and undesirable because market forces can be depended on to generate any desired information. Further, companies have incentives to disclose information voluntarily, as evidenced by the significant level of voluntary disclosures by listed companies. The possibility of over-legislating reporting requirements also relates to the 'free-rider' effect. Basically, where the marginal cost of information is perceived to be less than the possible (marginal) benefits, users will demand increased levels of disclosure. However, interested parties who bear little or none of the costs of disclosure have greater incentives to demand increased levels of disclosure, hence the term 'free rider'.

Moreover, advocates argue, required reporting tends to create overproduction of information. Since the cost of producing information is not borne by users, they will demand more and more information. An authoritative body, such as the IASB, may be misled by this exaggerated demand and, consequently, prescribe more disclosure of information than necessary. This may create a 'standards overload', about which many companies and accountants have complained.

Theories of regulation

Public interest theory

The central economic reason for the origins of government intervention in the operations of various markets in the 'public interest' is that of market failure.[2] Within this theoretical framework, regulation is intended by legislatures to 'protect consumer interests by securing improved economic performance . . . compared with an unregulated situation'.[3]

A potential market failure occurs when there is a failure of one of the conditions necessary for the best operation of a competitive market. Examples of potential failures include:

- lack of competition (monopoly, oligopoly)
- barriers to entry
- imperfect information gaps (information asymmetry) between buyers and sellers or certain market signals (e.g. seller reputation)
- the 'public-good' nature of some products (e.g. financial information), where the provision of the product to a single individual makes it equally and costlessly available to other individuals. Market failure occurs here because — since other individuals can receive the product free of charge — the normal pricing system in the market cannot function.[4]

Public interest theory is based on the assumption that economic markets are subject to a series of market imperfections or transaction failures, which, if left uncorrected, will result in both inefficient and inequitable outcomes. It is also based on three further assumptions that:

- the interest of consumers is translated into legislative action through the operation of the internal marketplace. Within this market, votes are seen as a form of currency. The policies, or at least the images, presented by the competing candidates for the office are the commodities being bought.[5]
- there are agents (entrepreneurial politicians and public interest groups) who will seek regulation on behalf of the 'public interest'. 'These agents may satisfy their self-interest instrumentally through pursuit of public interest objectives . . . but the theory requires that at least some preferences for the public interest be genuine and terminal.'[6]
- the government has no independent role to play in the development of regulations. Rather, government officials are simply neutral arbiters who intervene costlessly in markets at the request of 'public interest' agents.

Regulatory capture theory

A second theory proposed to understand regulation of financial reporting is capture theory. This theory maintains that although the 'purpose in fact' or origin of regulation is to protect the public interest as discussed above, this purpose is not achieved because, in the process of regulation, the regulatee comes to control or dominate the regulator. That is, the capture view singles out regulated entities as 'prevailing in the struggle to influence legislation . . . [It] predicts a regular sequence, in which the original purposes of a regulatory program are later thwarted through the efforts of the interest group'.[7]

Capture theory assumes, firstly, that all members of society are economically rational; therefore, each person will pursue his or her self-interest to the point where the private marginal benefit from lobbying regulators just equals the private marginal cost. Regulation has the potential to redistribute wealth.[8] Therefore, people lobby for regulations that increase their wealth, or they lobby to ensure that regulations are ineffective in decreasing their wealth.[9] Second, the capture view assumes, as with public interest theory, that the government has no independent role to play in the regulatory process, and that interest groups battle for control of the government's coercive powers to achieve their desired wealth distribution.

Capture is said to occur in any one of four situations, namely, if the regulated entities:

- control the regulation and the regulatory agency
- succeed in coordinating the regulatory body's activities with their activities, so that their private interest is satisfied
- neutralise or ensure non-performance (or mediocre performance) by the regulating body
- in a subtle process of interaction with the regulators, succeed in co-opting the regulators into a mutually shared perspective, thus giving them the regulation they seek.[10]

Regulatory agency capture involves capture of the administration, implementation and, to a large degree, evaluation of the effects of the policy process within any regulated area. It has been found to be especially pronounced where the following preconditions apply.

- There is a small number of client entities.
- Individuals within the regulatory agency have regular contact with a common set of individuals within the regulated entities and have either a regulated industry background or a potential for future employment opportunities in the regulated industry.
- The regulated industry controls the information needed for regulation.
- There is complexity of information and product.
- The regulatory agency has minimal resources in comparison to the industry it is regulating.

The main reason for the capture view centres on the fact that regulatory decisions usually have major effects on the interests of regulated industries. For example, the permission to operate a business or to provide a particular product or service may be granted or denied by regulatory agencies, and the level and structure of prices charged for an industry's output may be determined by statute. In turn, regulated industries perceive that their overall financial position can be significantly affected by regulatory decisions. Therefore, they generate intense activity aimed at influencing the regulatory agency.[11]

In contrast, non-industry groups such as the general public and consumers find themselves in a different situation with 'each person's individual stake in a regulatory decision [being] very small, perhaps imperceptible ... Moreover, even when they do become concerned about a regulatory issue, general interests lack pre-existing organisations through which their concerns can easily be channelled'.[12]

The regulatory capture theory would suggest that professional accounting bodies or the corporate sector will seek as much control as possible over the setting of accounting standards governing the reporting by their members. This involves either formal control over standard setting, representation on the relevant standard setting bodies, or significant influence/control over the decisions made by the relevant standard setting bodies.

Private interest theory

A third theory has emerged in response to dissatisfaction with explanations provided by both the public interest and the capture theories. The assumptions of these theories, that regulation comes into existence as a result of government response to public demands to rectify inefficient or inequitable practices by individuals and organisations, was strongly challenged in 1971 by George Stigler.[13] The basic theme of Stigler's challenge is that governments have one basic resource which 'is not shared even with the mightiest of its citizens: the power to coerce'.[14] This 'power to coerce' is a potential resource or threat to every business firm in that with its power to prohibit or compel and/or to provide or withdraw taxes and subsidies, the government can and does selectively help or hurt many businesses.

Stigler argues that regulatory activity reflects the relative political power of interest groups. Their interaction is with politicians who are not neutral arbiters (as in the public interest and capture theories) but, rather, are like business executives or consumers, and are thus rationally self-interested. The politicians seek to maximise their chances of future electoral success. Government officials will 'sell' aspects of their right to coerce others in the form of supplying regulatory programs and legislation, which will act to enhance their ability to win votes and raise money to finance election campaigns.

The essential commodity transacted in this political market is a transfer of wealth, with constituents on the demand side and their political representatives on the supply side. 'Viewed in this way, the market here, as elsewhere, will distribute more of the good to those whose effective demand is the highest. For Stigler, the question of which group will have the highest effective demand translated very quickly into a question of numbers.'[15]

Private interest theorists believe that there is a market for regulation with similar supply and demand forces operating as in the capital market. Within this political market there are many bidders. However, only one group will be successful, and that is the group that makes the highest bid. In this view, producer groups are most often the highest bidders and are thus able to use the power of the government to their own advantage for two reasons. First, the firms in any given industry are fewer in number than the persons outside the industry that may bear the costs of the regulation sought, such as restrictions on entry. Therefore, the firms seeking political protection find it easier to become an organised interest group capable of wielding political influence. Since the per capita gains to them are likely to be high, they have an incentive to combine their efforts to achieve mutually beneficial ends.

In contrast, much larger but more diffuse groups, such as consumer and public interest groups, are limited in their ability to make an effective bid, due to two major cost factors:

- the costs of organisation (e.g. the costs involved with mobilising their votes and contributing resources to the support of the appropriate political party)
- information costs (e.g. costs associated with obtaining information about government actions).

The basic assertion of private interest theory is that there is a law of diminishing returns in the relationship between group size and the costs of using the political process. Given this assertion, theorists believe that regulation does not arise as a result of a government's response to public demands. Instead, regulation is sought by the 'producer' private interest group and is designed and operated mainly for its benefit.

But even if a group has a strong incentive to organise, there must still be a mechanism by which the group acquires and uses its influence. Stigler's second assumption is that government officials, like business executives or consumers, are rationally self-interested.

They seek to maximise their votes (if they are elected officials) or their wealth (if they are appointed officials), or both. 'Producer' private interest groups can supply these resources by providing campaign contributions and political advertising to elected officials and lucrative opportunities for post-government employment.

Thus, regulation can simply be seen as a device for transferring profits to well-organised groups in the form of subsidies, price-fixing, control of entry of political competitors, and suppression of the production of substitutes if the groups will return the favour with votes and contributions to politicians. 'The theory [therefore] predicts that regulators will use their power to transfer income from those with less political power to those with more.'[16]

We will now apply these theories to practice.

LO 2 → HOW THEORIES OF REGULATION APPLY TO ACCOUNTING AND AUDITING PRACTICE

In the previous section, we explored a number of theories of regulation, which have been proposed to explain the regulation of accounting and auditing. We now consider the application of the public interest, capture and private interest theories in practice. We ask to what extent these theories explain and predict the regulation of accounting and auditing as observed in capital markets.

Application of public interest theory

Under public interest theory, governments intervene in the regulation of financial reporting in response to market failure and 'in the public interest'. The basic argument is that market mechanisms have failed and government action is necessary for the greater good. The introduction of the Sarbanes-Oxley Act in the United States in 2002 following the collapse of the Enron Corporation and the audit firm Arthur Andersen can be viewed through the lens of 'the public interest'. New financial reporting and corporate governance requirements were introduced and new standards and oversight structures for auditors were created.[17] Canada, Kuhn and Sutton argue that the Sarbanes-Oxley Act created, in the public interest, one of the greatest protections in financial markets and related corporate behaviour in history.[18] Case study 3.1 at the end of this chapter provides an opportunity to consider the costs and benefits of the Sarbanes-Oxley Act.

An earlier example is the Australian government establishing the Accounting Standards Review Board (ASRB) in 1984. The government's intervention in the accounting standard setting process is seen as justified by failures in the market for accounting information, evidenced by the significant number of corporate collapses even after auditors had certified accounts as 'true and fair'. Similarly, calls for stricter accounting standards or for changes in standard setting processes following major corporate collapses in the late 1990s and early 2000s (Enron and Worldcom in the United States; HIH and One.Tel in Australia) are seen as justified under the public interest theory.

Corporate collapses are deemed to indicate that there were serious violations of competitive conditions. The violations stemmed from information asymmetries between the suppliers (corporate management and accounting professionals) and external financial statement users (investors) who do not know what accounting information they need and/or are unable to determine the value of the accounting information they receive. Furthermore, financial information can be seen as a 'public good' which has led to a divergence between the marginal costs and benefits to (a) the users of financial information and (b) information producers (corporate management). Before government intervention (e.g. the establishment of the ASRB), standards were not legislatively backed and public interest theorists argue that it was not surprising to find that the amount of the information produced by corporate entities fell short of 'the quality necessary for informed investment decisions and optimal resource allocation in the economy'.[19]

Thus, the public interest theory framework suggests the government intervention in the accounting standard setting process is to rectify failures in the market for accounting information. In turn, public interest was served by a return of confidence in the capital markets by investors.

By concentrating on the necessity of government intervention in the marketplace to protect consumers, public interest theory generally ignores the findings of many research studies which indicate that the managers of business entities have strong incentives to 'correct' market failure perceptions about their business activities. This correction is achieved through the release of extensive voluntary disclosures of information which protects the users of financial information.[20] For example, market forces will exert pressure on firms to reduce uncertainty about the quality of the firm's product, the future viability of the firm, and the ability of current management to ensure appropriate returns to investors. It is claimed that failure to reduce this uncertainty leads to the firm being viewed as a 'lemon'.[21] This, in turn, can result in additional costs to the firm in the form of, for example, higher interest charges, increased security requirements for loans and an increased threat of takeover from competitors. Thus, we find examples where we can apply public interest theory, but it is not clear that the theory is the only explanation for the observed behaviours.

Application of capture theory

Walker argues that although the Australian government originally introduced the ASRB to ensure the protection of the 'public interest', he believes capture theory is more applicable in explaining the events. He argues that the board was successfully captured by the accounting profession, the regulated industry.[22] The ultimate signals of capture, according to Walker, centred on events such as the fact that the 'due process' provisions were abandoned in favour of 'fast-track' approval of standards submitted by the Australian Accounting Research Foundation (AARF).[23] Furthermore, a number of disputes between the ASRB and the AARF were settled in the latter's favour and the AARF (funded by the profession) merged with the ASRB (funded by the government). The ASRB formally had power to consider standards submitted to it from any source. This was an attempt to broaden political acceptability of approved standards; however, only one out of 23 approved standards came from a source outside the profession. Thus, as with ordinary standards, it could be argued that the 'due process' mechanism within the ASRB failed to achieve its purpose.

Basically, Walker's argument is that the accounting profession needed to legitimise accounting standards (that is, ensure compliance with the standards) which could be achieved only by standards that had the 'force of law' by ensuring that accounting standards were backed by legislation. However, the accounting profession had an economic interest in retaining the standard setting process, which it did not want to relinquish to the government. In turn, therefore, the only way the profession could both legitimise accounting standards and maintain its economic interests was to 'capture' the ASRB, the body that had the power to make accounting standards mandatory for corporate entities. Under the capture view, regulatory intervention in the accounting standard setting process was designed, as with the public interest theory framework, to protect the public interest. However, Walker's study portrays the accounting profession as an elite group that, in effect, was not accountable to the public interest, which sought and achieved control of the standard setting process for its own gain, and which was constrained only by the fear of state intervention.[24]

The international harmonisation of accounting has raised new questions in relation to the applicability of capture theory. While there was widespread support in Australia for the harmonisation of accounting standards, the adoption of international standards strongly reflect the interests and preferences of large companies, the Australian Securities Exchange (ASX) and sections of the accounting profession.[25] CLERP 1 directed standard setters to have a commercial focus and to be responsive to business needs, reflecting a response by government to lobbying against Australian Accounting Standards Board (AASB) standards by the corporate sector. The ASX was a strong supporter of early adoption of international standards, presumably because it saw benefits for the ASX and listed companies flowing from the use of international standards. In one sense, the interests of all these parties have been overtaken by international events. Having exercised their influence and achieved their preference for adoption of international standards, they are now in the position of having given up influence over the process of the development of those standards. It is unlikely that these parties (large companies, the accounting profession and the ASX) can influence future Australian accounting standards in the same way as they have in the past. None of them is in the position to control or 'capture' the standard setting process post-2005.

With Australia's and Europe's decisions to adopt international standards, and the IASB's mission to have its standards adopted in all countries throughout the world, the focus of regulatory capture has shifted to the IASB. Zeff notes that the IASB is under a 'steady flow of insistent views' from trade associations, major companies and banks in European countries.[26] He explains that there are many groups vitally concerned with the IASB output, so we can conclude that capture by any one group would be unlikely. However, the idea that the IASB has been 'captured' by the FASB has been flagged. The issue of IASB standards which are close to US Generally Accepted Accounting Principles (GAAP) does raise the question of the influence of US GAAP on IASB standards. Zeff reports that the dissent in Europe over IFRS 8, which closely follows a FASB standard, has raised afresh the question of whether convergence between the IASB and FASB is good for Europe.[27]

Application of private interest theory

Private interest theory provides another approach to understanding behaviour of parties with an incentive to influence the regulation of financial reporting. Rahman[28] sought to apply the private interest theory of Stigler, Posner and Peltzman to the establishment of the ASRB. Rahman's conclusion was that there were several limitations in Walker's study. He asserted that a systematic review of the Board's organisation and functions indicated that the Board was dependent on and susceptible to influence from several interest groups. Thus, while Rahman confirmed the influence of the accounting profession on the preparation and review of standards, he also found that other parties secured important roles that enabled them to constantly scrutinise and influence the Board's activities. These parties included the Ministerial Council which provided the Board with its basic authority. The Board had to operate with the notion that all its approved accounting standards were subject to political approval. This implied that the political consequences of its standards had to be minimal.

Rahman found that the Board also depended on the National Companies and Securities Commission (NCSC) for the enforcement of standards. The presence or absence of any standard which impeded the efficient administration of company law was thus liable to receive the attention of the NCSC (now the Australian Securities and Investments Commission or ASIC). Furthermore, Rahman argued that Walker failed to mention the presence of a number of company executives on the ASRB Board. This is particularly important, given that it was mainly the corporate managers and directors that were required to comply with mandatory accounting standards on the introduction of the ASRB. Thus, it was this sector which was, in reality, the 'regulated industry'. Auditors or the accounting profession as a whole were ultimately affected only because they were actively involved in the preparation and authentication of company financial statements. The considerable representation of company executives on the board was devised, presumably, to help secure the interests of that group of regulated parties.[29]

From this perspective, the accounting profession did not 'capture' the standard setting process in Australia. Rather, it could be argued that the producer group, which is well organised and capable of wielding significant political influence compared with either the accounting profession or the much larger but more diffuse 'user' group, became extensively involved in, and ultimately controlled, the debate on the regulation of the standard setting process in the 1980s. Arguably, it did so in order to achieve a particular form of regulatory intervention which 'secures them from over-deregulation'.[30] Other evidence of the lobbying power of the corporate preparers group (the managers/directors of the G100 public companies) can be seen in the pressure this group brought to bear on the accounting profession to effectively withdraw Statement of Accounting Concepts (SAC) 4 *Definition and Recognition of the Elements of Financial Statements* during the early 1990s.[31] Further examples of influence by parties from the corporate sector are seen in the government's CLERP 1 proposals to restructure standard setting processes and the subsequent 2005 adoption of international accounting standards.

A limitation of these theories of regulation is that they are not mutually exclusive, that is, events explained by one theory may be explained equally well by another theory. It is not clear that a single explanation can be defended. For example, in relation to the Sarbanes-Oxley Act it can be argued that the US government was obliged to take action following the collapse of Enron, to show that it was responding to serious levels of concern about the adequacy of corporate governance, financial reporting supervision and auditing. Thus, the private interest theory may apply equally well to explaining observed events. Private interest theory has many supporters as it recognises the fundamental self-interest of parties involved in regulation. It also fits well with the view that standard setting is a political process. We consider the influence of politics on standard setting in the next section.

Standard setting as a political process

Standard setting is viewed as a political process because of its potential to significantly affect the wellbeing of a wide variety of interest groups. Therefore these groups attempt to influence the introduction of regulation. This model of political behaviour is a summary of the 'public choice' theory of regulation. It was used by Watts and Zimmerman to argue that the political process is simply a means of pursuing individual or group self-interest.[32] Different groups are affected differently by accounting regulations. For example, a standard banning recognition of doubtful debts expense might be welcomed by firms that borrow heavily and are close to their borrowing agreement leverage constraints. On the other hand, large banks with high public profiles may be averse to the standard because it causes their profits to increase, understates their risk, and increases their apparent exploitation of their customers. In the presence of diverse and often conflicting interests, a decision-making body — a regulatory group — must strike a balance between them by making political choices.[33] For those decisions to be accepted by the people affected, the regulatory agency needs a mandate to make social choices; that is, it needs political legitimacy. Gerboth reinforces this view:

> … a politicisation of accounting rule-making [is] not only inevitable, but just. In a society committed to democratic legitimisation of authority, only politically responsible institutions have the right to command others to obey rules.[34]

In response to dissatisfaction with standard setting by professional accounting bodies, governments in many countries have set up independent standard setters in an attempt to produce high quality standards which meet decision making needs of financial statement users. The standard setting 'due process' should allow stakeholders to contribute to standard setting, but also prevent any one party, such as the accounting profession, from dominating the process. Conceptual frameworks, previously developed in the United States, United Kingdom, Canada and Australia, sought to provide standard setting bodies with a framework within which to develop accounting standards. Independent national standard setters have had mixed success in producing conceptually sound accounting standards that achieved the decision-usefulness objective. New standards that have extended the traditional boundaries of financial reporting include those incorporating fair value measurement methods. However, there are notable examples where progress toward a conceptually preferred position has been slow or where political lobbying has 'derailed' an accounting standard. An example of the former is leasing. A G4+1 study in 1996 recommended capitalising property rights inherent in all leases.[35] Standard setters have expressed a preference for recognising leases on the balance sheet, but have thus far been unable to secure a standard which satisfactorily achieves this objective. The IASB/FASB have a current joint project on lease accounting, which involves comprehensive reconsideration of all aspects of lease accounting and is expected to lead to fundamental changes in accounting for leases. The aim of the project is to develop a new common approach to lease accounting that would ensure that all assets and liabilities arising under lease contracts are recognised in the balance sheet. A discussion paper on the topic was issued in 2009.[36] Issues relevant to understanding standards for lease accounting are explored in theory in action 3.1.

3.1 THEORY IN ACTION

Companies should come clean on the value of leases on their books

by Paul Kerin

Investors should be very wary of the results reported by companies that rely heavily on leases.

Silly accounting rules can mean that the majority of many companies' assets and liabilities don't show up on their balance sheets. As a result, even terrific companies like Woolworths report grossly inflated returns on investment and provide financial risk measures that bear no relation to reality.

Following a spate of corporate crises such as Enron's collapse, the US Securities and Exchange Commission investigated off-balance-sheet arrangements. Its mid–2005 report made sobering reading. It estimated that US-listed companies had committed themselves to lease payments totalling $US1.25 trillion ($1.4 trillion) that did not appear on balance sheets. About 90 per cent of Australian leases are off balance sheet and most companies have some.

This smoke and mirrors trick is particularly rife in the retailing and airline sectors. David Tweedle, chairman of the International Accounting Standards Board, recently told a US congressional hearing of his ambition to "actually fly in an aircraft that's on an airline's balance sheet before I die".

He should fly Qantas — to its credit, some (though not all) of its aircraft leases are on balance sheet. Last year, *Business Week* valued the off-balance-sheet lease liabilities of two large US retailers, CVS and Walgreen, at $US11.1 billion and $US15.2 billion respectively.

If these were on the balance sheet, the companies' respective total liabilities would be 260 per cent and 366 per cent of their reported levels.

In reality, companies committing themselves to leases effectively buy assets (right to use things) funded by debt. Obligations to make regular lease payments are just like obligations to make regular interest repayments. Good analysts, bankers and equity investors adjust reported financial statements to reflect this fact.

Accountants distinguish between "capital" and "operating" leases. Capital leases must go on balance sheet but operating leases don't. While the Australian standard says that lease classification should be based on a lease's "substance", its guidance criteria on capital leases (such as the lease term covering the "major part" of an asset's economic life) leave much wriggle room.

The US standard provides hard criteria, such as the present value of minimum lease payments exceeding 90 per cent of asset value. But such criteria have created a huge financial engineering industry and provided a "how to" guide for structuring lease deals to keep them off balance sheet.

Retailers can commit themselves to multi-decade leases involving huge lease payments, yet keep them off balance sheet. Fund manager JF Capital Partners estimates the capitalised values of Woolworths' and Coles' off-balance-sheet leases to be $11.8 billion and $10.8 billion respectively. Adjusting for this off balance sheeting makes a huge difference to their recently reported 2006–07 results.

Woolies reported that net debt fell $1.3 billion, to $2.4 billion, in 2006–07. But adjusted for off-balance-sheet leases (which rose $1.3 billion in value), it really remained unchanged at $14.1 billion. Coles' adjusted net debt is really $11.8 billion, versus the $900 million reported. That is, 83 per cent and 92 per cent of these companies' real net debt, respectively, is off balance sheet. Likewise, reported invested capital (debt plus equity) numbers grossly understate reality. Woolies' 71.9 per cent adjusted debt/capital ratio is more than double the 30.7 per cent reported, while Coles' is almost quadruple (75.1 per cent versus 19.4 per cent). While off balance sheeting doesn't distort returns on equity, its impact on debt ratios falsely downplays risk — which may cause shareholders to make poor risk/return trade-offs.

In fairness, off balance sheeting also reduces reported earnings before interest and tax (EBIT), because it causes the entire lease charge to be expensed. If lease assets and liabilities were on balance sheet, the expense would be split between depreciation and interest; the former affects EBIT, the latter doesn't. Nevertheless, off balance sheeting inflates reported returns on invested capital (ROI), as it reduces the invested capital denominator by much more than the EBIT numerator. Using JFCP's lease value and depreciation/interest splits, Woolies' lease-adjusted ROI is 15.2 per cent — while very healthy, it is little more than half the 27.1 per cent reported. Coles' 13 per cent adjusted ROI is less than half the 27.3 per cent reported.

Off balance sheeting can also make ROI trends misleading. For example, Coles often claims that its ROI has more than doubled since 2001–02. It has — from 12.7 per cent to 27.3 per cent — because reported EBIT has doubled while reported invested capital has grown only 21 per cent, kept in check mainly through sorely needed working capital reductions. But as working capital is small relative to off-balance-sheet lease value, which grew 24 per cent, the adjusted ROI has only risen from 9.7 per cent to 13 per cent.

Given the market's views on Woolies (great) and Coles (poor), you may wonder why Woolies' reported ROI looks slightly worse than Coles'. The main driver is Woolies' $5 billion of intangible assets (such as goodwill from acquisitions) versus Coles' $1.7 billion. If intangibles are excluded to provide a better measure of real operating performance, Woolies' ROI before lease adjustments becomes 95 per cent — more than double Coles' 43.1 per cent. After lease adjustments, it is 21 per cent, much higher than Coles' 14.5 per cent.

The Woolies/Coles comparison shows that off balance sheeting can make inter-company comparisons of reported returns very misleading.

As companies differ in the mix of assets under direct ownership, capital leases and operating leases, the only way to make like-for-like comparisons is to put all leases on balance sheet.

Off balance sheeting can also distort comparisons across business units. Reported ROIs of Target (65 per cent) and Food & Liquor (24 per cent) do partly reflect genuine performance differences. But they also reflect the fact that off balance sheeting boosts ROI relatively less for units with higher earnings per square metre (as meterage drives lease charges, hence off-balance sheet lease values). Despite its current underperformance, Food & Liquor's $413 million EBIT is 24 per cent above Target's. On balance sheeting would narrow its apparent ROI gap.

Following the SEC's call, the International Accounting Standards Board plans to review lease accounting (with Australian participation). Unfortunately, a new standard won't emerge until at least 2009 — and it won't necessarily require full on balance sheeting. As current standards have fostered a huge industry and allowed companies to financially engineer rosy financial reports, big changes will meet heavy resistance.

Rather than wait for new standards to force on balance sheeting, companies that really care about shareholders should take the initiative to do it now.

Paul Kerin teaches strategy at Melbourne Business School and is a member of JF Capital Partners' Trinity Best Practice Committee.

Source: The Australian, 2 October 2007.

Questions

1. Describe current accounting practices for leases as outlined in this article.
2. Why does the author call leasing standards 'silly accounting rules'?
3. Standard setters propose revising leasing standards to require capitalisation of all leases. Explain the financial impact for Coles and Woolworths in 2007–08 of having 'off-balance sheet' leases.
4. What are the advantages of capitalising leases? Given that most companies usually reporting operating leases, will they oppose new leasing rules?

There are many examples where political lobbying has interfered with the standard setting process and with the standards eventually issued by boards. Zeff tracks the rising importance of financial accounting standards in different sectors of the United States economy and describes the special-interest lobbying which has occurred to obtain standards compatible with parties' desired outcomes.[37] Notable examples include the treatment of foreign currency translation gains and losses; unrealised holding gains and losses on current marketable equity securities; 'successful efforts' and 'full cost' policy choice for the oil and gas industry; as well as leasing, stock options, pensions, consolidated accounting and financial instruments. The US situation is not unique — Zeff describes lobbying of national standard setters in Canada, Sweden and the United Kingdom on a range of similar issues. He also notes significant lobbying of the IASB, in relation to the elimination of last in, first out (LIFO), share-based payment and financial instruments.[38] We describe below the case in relation to financial instruments and then conclude this section with a description of the political processes surrounding the adoption of IAS 38 *Intangible Assets* in Australia.

Financial instruments

Few accounting standards have been as controversial as those for financial instruments. Consequently, the adoption of IAS 39 *Financial Instruments — Recognition and Measurement* in the European Union (EU) has been a highly politicised process. Forming standards to account for financial instruments has challenged standard setters for several years. Early developments occurred in the United States, where there has been considerable demand for the use of fair value measurement (i.e. mark-to-market or use of an estimation model to record fair value at balance date) to more accurately reflect the risks and rewards of holding financial instruments.[39] Standard setters have viewed fair value measurement as useful for providing relevant information for decision making by users of financial information. The International Organization of Securities

Commissions (IOSCO) considered guidance for accounting for financial instruments essential and requested the International Accounting Standards Commission (IASC) to include a financial instruments standard among the core standards being prepared in expectation of endorsement by IOSCO for use by companies in cross-border listings. The IASB created IAS 39 based on the FASB standards relating to financial instruments (FAS 114, 115, 133 and 140) as an interim standard, noting that further development of IAS 39 would be required.[40]

Following the announcement in 2002 that international accounting standards (IAS) would be adopted in Europe, much greater attention was focused on the content of international standards. EU-listed companies, which had previously followed national GAAP, would now be required to follow IAS at least for consolidated accounts. In the area of financial instruments, the accounting change was potentially dramatic. Generally, companies used historical cost accounting for financial instruments, showing them at cost or amortised cost, and including gains in the income statement only when they were realised. In relation to financial assets and liabilities, companies had considerable discretion about when gains and losses were recorded in income. IAS 39 would require companies to include unrealised gains and losses on certain financial instruments in income when they occurred (not when they were realised), thus restricting companies' choices about the timing of recognition of gains and losses on some instruments.

The reaction to IAS 39 among some European companies was extremely negative. The idea of including unrealised gains and losses in income was not popular in some countries, such as France and Germany, where accounting practice was essentially conservative, use of the historical cost principle the norm and upward revaluation of assets or liabilities not widely practised.[41] Companies objected to possible subjectivity introduced into accounting measurement and expected volatility in reported earnings, as well as the costs incurred in meeting the requirements. Further, bank representatives argued that they would be forced to follow accounting rules (such as those proposed for hedge accounting) which did not reflect the underlying reality of their business, making accounting information less, rather than more, useful for decision making.[42]

The IASB gave careful consideration to the issues raised by stakeholders. In December 2003 it amended the 2002 exposure draft after an extensive due process which included numerous board meetings, discussion of the exposure draft with constituent groups in nine roundtable meetings, receiving and evaluating more than 270 comment letters and discussing the topic with advisory committees and national standard setters from around the world.[43] At the same time, financial statement preparers, notably the large French and German banks, were lobbying hard through all possible means to avoid the adoption of IAS 39. Lobbying efforts directed at the IASB were made by companies, individuals and their representative bodies such as professional associations, industry representative groups, national standard setters and European representative bodies including FEE and EFRAG.[44] The ultimate lobbying activity was observed: a letter from the French president, Jacques Chirac, to the European Commission (EC) president which objected to measurement of derivatives at fair value and claimed that the IASB standard would have 'nefarious consequences for financial stability'.[45]

The IASB responded as best it could to these concerns, but was committed to a standard based on the principle of recognition and measurement of financial instruments at fair value. Thus, IAS 39 was included in the standards submitted to the Accounting Regulatory Committee (ARC) for endorsement prior to adoption by the EC. The ARC endorsed all the IASB standards, but excluded certain provisions contained in IAS 39.[46] These related to the use of fair value measurement and to hedging. Companies were not required to comply with these sections of IAS 39 when preparing accounts in accordance with IAS/IFRS from 2005. Thus, the lobbying activities of economically powerful and politically well-connected groups succeeded in dictating the content of an accounting standard. One of the issues of the 'carve out' has been resolved, while the other remains.[47]

The ARC's decision was criticised by parties who saw the creation of 'European IAS' as a backward step, away from the goal of harmonised financial reporting. The UK standard setters did not agree with the ARC decision, and encouraged UK companies to comply with the full hedging requirements of IAS 39.[48] The political controversy in relation to IAS 39 has not decreased with the passage of time. The financial crisis, which began in 2007–08 resulted in the IASB amending IAS 39 (and IFRS 7 *Financial Instruments: Disclosures*) to allow companies the choice of reclassifying some financial instruments from categories where fair value measurement applies to categories where items are measured based on amortised cost. The board defended the changes, which were made without due process consultation, in the light of requests from EU leaders and finance ministers and that the fact that the accounting choice was available under US GAAP.[49] Both theory in action 3.2 and case study 3.2 address issues relating to regulation and accounting standards. They allow further exploration of the role of fair value accounting in the global financial crisis.

3.2
THEORY
IN ACTION

Accountants draw the line at regulating

by Patrick Durkin

The global accounting standards setter has defended its role in the financial crisis and blamed prudential regulators for lax rules that enabled banks to make risky bets, dole out excessive bonuses and pay too much in dividends.

Members of the International Accounting Standards Board, visiting Sydney yesterday, also defended fair-value accounting, which banks have criticised for exacerbating the crisis by forcing them to record massive write-downs in asset values.

"We are not set up to be focused on financial stability," board member Stephen Cooper said. "There are other [prudential regulators] who are already set up to do that, but they don't want to do it.

"It seems crazy to me that people are asking us to do something we are patently not equipped to do."

The IASB will present its views to the G-20 meeting of world leaders in London next month and will urge leaders to put the onus for oversight of banks on prudential regulators.

"The regulator should be focused on not allowing banks to pay dividends and do share buybacks if that is going to put the bank in danger, rather than trying to change the profit that is reported," Mr Cooper said.

The IASB said the problems with fair-value accounting — the method of valuing assets at market value rather than historical cost — arose because it was not adopted widely enough and should be applied to all financial instruments.

The major investment banks apply the method to only 60 per cent to 80 per cent of financial instruments on their balance sheets, and the major retail banks apply it to as little as 10 per cent to 20 per cent.

"People are asking us to take a haircut to fair value or other measurements when times are good and increase the fair value when times are bad," Mr Cooper said.

"But to decide by how much you haircut and by how much you increase, you have to be close to the banks and the markets. The banking regulator has that closeness."

IASB member Warren MacGregor said the banking industry should keep an additional capital buffer to protect against catastrophes, as insurers did.

He also said Australian companies should report quarterly, as in the US, rather than twice a year, to ensure the timely disclosure of asset prices "if the need for timely information is clearly there."

The IASB will lobby the G-20 to ensure the US continues towards adopting international accounting standards. If the US fails to adopt the standards, there will be an increased risk of regulatory arbitrage: companies looking for gaps to determine the best jurisdiction for them to report in.

Source: The Australian Financial Review, 5 March 2009, www.afr.com.

Questions

1. The article refers to a view circulating at the time, that fair value accounting contributed to the 'global financial crisis' (from October 2008, the near collapse of many banks caused capital flows to dry up and share prices to fall dramatically). How could fair value accounting exacerbate the financial crisis?
2. Why does the IASB member refuse to accept responsibility for the financial crisis?
3. The IASB considers adoption of IASB standards in the USA to be essential. Explain why it holds this view. To what extent does the IASB's position reflect self-interest?

Intangible assets

The adoption of IAS 38 *Intangible Assets* in Australia also illustrates the role of politics in the standards setting process. The AASB had not issued a specific standard on accounting for intangibles, having withdrawn its exposure draft in 1992 due to lack of consensus on the subject.[50] Many methods for valuing intangibles assets had developed and Australian companies used a variety of methods.[51] IAS 38 (issued by the IASB in 1998 and revised in March 2004) required methods of accounting that were significantly different from those adopted by some Australian companies. For example, internally generated intangibles cannot be recognised and intangible assets without an active market cannot be revalued. Australian companies with substantial intangible assets in either of these categories lobbied the IASB, the AASB and the federal government for relief from the IAS 38 requirements based on the impact that they would have on companies' financial statements.[52] The AASB requested that Australian companies be permitted to carry forward existing intangible asset values from 1 January 2005. However, the IASB declined their request. The AASB was unable to negotiate with the IASB to achieve an outcome that was considered important by some Australian companies. The result shows the relative power of the AASB and IASB and highlights the limited ability of the AASB to influence the IASB. It also illustrates the IASB's need to be seen to be a strong independent standard setter. The Australian government chose not to intervene in the process of adopting IAS 38, despite company requests for it to do so. Transferring a fundamental aspect of standard setting offshore (to the IASB in London) allows the government to refer to global market forces demanding international comparability and gives it a justification to stay out of the standard setting process. It also highlights the loss of influence of the corporate sector over the standard setting process.

LO 3 · THE REGULATORY FRAMEWORK FOR FINANCIAL REPORTING

In the preceding discussion, we have referred to many parties with an active role within the financial reporting environment. They include the preparers of the financial reports (company directors and their executives and managers) and a company's external auditors as well as the rule-makers, such as private sector groups, stock exchanges and governments and their agencies. The activities of these parties will be influenced by the environment in which financial reporting takes place; that is, its legal, economic political and social setting. The specific environmental features of the financial reporting environment make up what can be called the regulatory framework of financial reporting. While regulatory frameworks vary between countries, they often have common elements. We outline these elements below to provide an overview of the regulatory framework for financial reporting (that is, a proforma regulatory framework) and to demonstrate how the elements of the regulatory framework influence the output of the financial reporting process — the financial statements. The elements of the regulatory framework which we discuss are:

- statutory requirements
- corporate governance
- auditors and oversight
- independent enforcement bodies.

Statutory requirements

The key participants in the production of financial reports are corporate directors (and their executives and managers) and independent auditors. Elsewhere in this book, we have explained that there are many motivations for managers to voluntarily provide financial information and to have that information independently verified through the audit process. Now we turn to the role of statutory requirements as an incentive to produce financial statements and have them audited. In many countries company law mandates that directors provide audited accounts.[53] Thus a primary influence on directors and auditors is the need to fulfil statutory reporting requirements, as contained in company law. On the one hand, company law will likely mandate basic requirements relating to which reports are to be prepared and their frequency of preparation. But it may also include particular requirements relating to the information to be included; for example, in Australia companies must disclose information about their environmental performance. In some jurisdictions, notably the United States, reporting requirements are derived predominantly from securities market law rather than company law.[54]

Additional financial reporting requirements are derived from specific accounting standards and in many jurisdictions these standards have the force of law. For example, listed companies in the European Union that prepare consolidated financial statements are required by law to use IASB standards adopted by the EU. In Australia, company law requires all reporting entities to follow legally endorsed IASB-based accounting standards. Taxation law is another statutory influence on financial accounting in many countries, notably those following a French or German accounting tradition. In these countries, for single entity reporting, the financial accounting rules are the same as tax rules.[55] Company law, in turn, forms part of a wider legal system, which is likely to include ways of monitoring compliance with statutory requirements. For example, the FEE reports that many European countries have a body responsible for checking lodgement of accounts. In addition, the judicial system provides sanctions and penalties that promote compliance with company law.[56]

Corporate governance

Another important element within a country's regulatory framework is the system of corporate governance. Davis takes a broad view of corporate governance and states that it refers to 'the structures, processes and institutions within and around organizations that allocate power and resource control among participants'.[57] Some corporate governance practices are derived from laws which require directors to carry out specific actions in relation to the management for their companies. For example, requirements to hold meetings with shareholders and to disclose matters of interest such as directors' remuneration and related party transactions are basic corporate governance matters which may be covered by company law.[58]

However, a regulatory framework may contain additional corporate governance guidance and rules, arising from both private sector voluntary recommendations and stock exchange listing rules. Corporate governance guidance may take the form of voluntary best practice recommendations, which encourage directors to adopt appropriate governance mechanisms, to best suit the situation of their individual company. Both supranational and national bodies have produced corporate governance recommendations. The International Federation of Accountants (IFAC) guidelines are an example of the former and corporate governance codes issued in the United Kingdom and Australia are examples of the latter.[59] Governance requirements relating to financial reporting can be enforced by the stock exchanges or the government body responsible for enforcement of financial reporting requirements. For example, in the United Kingdom and Australia, the respective stock exchanges recommend compliance with the corporate governance codes and require companies not in compliance to provide explanations of the reasons for non-compliance, the so-called 'if not, why not' rule. EU directives on corporate governance can be enforced through member states' legal systems.

Auditors and oversight

In many countries auditors perform a vitally important function in providing assurance about the quality of information provided by companies in their financial statements.[60] It is common for the auditing profession to be regulated in some way. The most basic form of regulation of the profession is limiting of membership to persons with particular qualifications and experience and requiring registration to practise. Other forms of regulation involve requiring membership of a professional body and commitment to an ethical code of conduct. Professional bodies may also sanction members in breach of their rules.[61]

Many of these forms of regulation are self-imposed because a profession may agree to follow a body of rules to maintain its privileged position and to protect its right to practise as a profession. For example, private sector self-regulation of the accounting profession is an early form of auditor oversight. In the past, professional bodies have taken their role of oversight of the profession seriously, devoting considerable resources to developing standards for professional conduct at a national and international level. Many national bodies representing auditors have voluntarily adopted international standards of auditing (ISA) as an indication of their commitment to providing a high-quality service and demonstrating behaviour appropriate to members of a profession.

Self-regulation of the auditing profession has been widely observed, but there are some notable examples where regulation was from early times the responsibility of state authorities. For example, in France and Italy regulation of auditors was the responsibility of their respective independent enforcement bodies (the securities market regulators, Autorité des Marchés Financiers or AMF in France and Commissione Nazionale per le Società e la Borsa or Consob in Italy). In the case of the AMF and its predecessor organisation Commission des Opérations de Bourse (COB), the regulator works closely with the Compagnie Nationale des Commissaires aux Comptes or CNCC, the body representing the auditing profession in the process of carrying out oversight of auditors' activities.

The location of responsibility for auditor oversight with a statutory body, rather than allowing self-regulation, provides (at least in theory) for more independent regulation. The choice of a statutory regulator rather than self-regulation may reflect economic or political differences in approaches to management of capital markets. For example, until 2005 the United Kingdom had a longstanding tradition of self-regulation of auditors, consistent with a cultural position of minimising intervention in the operation of the capital market. Statutory regulation of auditors is consistent with a more centralised, interventionist approach to regulation of business observed in France and Italy.[62] In recent years, many countries have introduced statutory bodies responsible for auditor oversight, as discussed in the final section of this chapter.

Independent enforcement bodies

A study by the FEE includes an independent enforcement body as part of the overall system for enforcement of financial reporting requirements.[63] The role of such a body in the regulation of financial reporting is to promote compliance with the regulations governing the production of financial statements, which are contained in law, and accounting standards. An independent enforcement body is an extension of lodgement supervision, a basic part of the regulatory framework. While many countries have a body responsible for lodgement supervision, setting up an independent enforcement body is a more recent event, linked to the adoption of IFRS in 2005. Because of the importance of comprehensive and consistent application of IFRS in achieving the goals of IFRS adoption, each EU member state was required to set up an independent enforcement body. The Committee of European Securities Regulators (CESR) reported that by 2006, 20 of the 27 EU member states had set up an enforcement mechanism that met, at least in part, the requirements laid down by CESR standards for enforcement.[64]

A securities market regulator is the most commonly observed form for an independent enforcement body. Examples include the AMF in France, the Consob in Italy, the Autoriteit Financiële Markten (or AFM, Financial Market Authority) in the Netherlands, the Securities Exchange Commission in the United States and ASIC in Australia. Independent enforcement bodies may have extensive duties and powers in relation to the regulation of securities markets, which extend far beyond the monitoring of financial reporting. Nevertheless, such bodies can be very active in enforcing financial reporting requirements contained in law and accounting standards.[65] The SEC is a notable example of an active market regulator, which is involved in setting accounting requirements (either directly or through a delegated committee, FASB), providing interpretation advice and taking legal action against firms for non-compliance.[66] Theory in action 3.3 explores the role of both the FASB and the SEC in relation to the issue of backdating of stock options in the United States. We consider the extent to which FASB and/or the SEC can be considered responsible when there is non-compliance with an accounting standard.

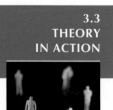

3.3 THEORY IN ACTION

Enforcing requirements of accounting standards

Executive in U.S. convicted for backdating share options

by Eric Dash and Matt Richtel

New York: U.S. prosecutors scored a guilty verdict in the first options backdating case to go to trial, securing a conviction that is expected to embolden them to pursue similar cases.

Jurors in U.S. District Court in San Francisco on Tuesday convicted a former chief executive of Brocade Communications Systems, Gregory Reyes, 44, on 10 counts of conspiracy and fraud.

The verdict ended a five-week trial in which Reyes was accused of intentionally changing the grant dates for hundreds of stock option awards without disclosing the move to investors.

Sentencing is scheduled for Nov. 21. Under U.S. sentencing guidelines, Reyes could face up to 20 years in prison for the most serious charges as well as pay millions of dollars in fines.

The verdict sent shock waves through Silicon Valley and law offices around the country that are representing dozens of companies and executives entangled in the widespread scandal.

In the wake of intense media attention, regulators cracked down on more than 100 companies over the unlikely coincidence of stock options being granted again and again to executives and employees on dates when the share price was low — a tactic that guaranteed the maximum profit when the options were later turned into cash.

Backdating is illegal if the company does not properly account for the discounted grants as an expense.

The U.S. Securities and Exchange Commission eventually investigated about 140 companies in connection with the practice, and prosecutors filed charges against at least five executives.

Yet lawyers have long argued that these cases were more winnable as civil rather than criminal courts where the burden of proof is much greater.

Most of the backdating cases, including the one against Reyes, hinged on proving that the defendants knowingly manipulated an option grant date to defraud investors.

But that claim can be obscured by the complexity of accounting issues. While lawyers on both sides acknowledge that these cases are difficult to win, the Brocade decision indicates that a guilty verdict is possible.

"It emboldens them in bringing other cases, but I don't think it means they will bring bushels of these cases," Sean O'Shea, a criminal defense lawyer in New York, said of prosecutors. "They will bring the strongest of those where they can show evil intent in trying to conceal information from shareholders."

Mark Zauderer, a trial lawyer in New York, said: "Defense lawyers are going to be keenly aware that where there is evidence of misleading documents, it will be difficult to rely on the defense that nobody knew it was illegal.

"Better to report something truthfully that is perhaps questionable than to risk misrepresenting the facts," he said.

In the Brocade case, prosecutors presented evidence that Reyes intentionally misled shareholders with a "systemic practice of cherry-picking stock prices" to build in gains for employees.

During the trial, a former human resources employee testified that Reyes told her that the practice was "not illegal if you don't get caught."

Prosecutors also said that Reyes denied backdating stock options when he was questioned by investigators about the pattern of favorable grant dates.

The lawyer for Reyes, Richard Marmaro, portrayed his client as a hard-working technology company executive who did not traffic in the accounting arcana of stock option grants.

Brocade, the defense argued, offered the low-priced grants as a way of attracting employees as the dot-com boom created an intense battle to hire talent.

Source: International Herald Tribune, the New York Times Company, Wednesday, 8 August 2007.

Questions

Accounting standards require that, in certain circumstances, companies record an expense for stock options granted to employees.

1. Do you consider that the company Brocade Communications complied with the requirement to record an expense for stock options?
2. Who benefits from the 'backdating' of stock options? Who is harmed?
3. If options can be backdated, has the standard setting board (in the United States, the FASB) been effective in the role of promulgating accounting regulations?
4. What is the role of the SEC in relation to the regulation of accounting practice?

In some countries, the stock exchange takes the role of market regulator. For example, stock exchanges are (or have been) involved in monitoring financial reporting in Switzerland, Sweden and Norway. Another form of independent enforcement body is a review panel, such as the United Kingdom's Financial Reporting Review Panel (FRRP). The FRRP was formed in 1991 with power to investigate matters relating to financial reporting brought to its attention. The FRRP was set up as a private sector trust and comprises members of the business community. Thus, it is a structure that involves the private sector in regulation, which is viewed by many as an effective alternative approach to regulation.[67] Another approach was taken by Germany following adoption of IFRS. They set up a two-tier enforcement system, comprising a review panel (Deutche Prüfstelle für Rechnungslegung, i.e. the Financial Reporting Enforcement Panel or FREP), which reports to a government department (Bundesanstalt für Finanzdienstleistungsaufsicht or BaFin, i.e. the Federal Institute for the Oversight of Financial Services).

Another part of the regulatory framework which arises because of widespread adoption of IFRS is a system to coordinate enforcement. A supranational organisation, the International Organization of Securities Commissions (IOSCO) established a system for participating IOSCO members and other independent enforcement organisations to share information and consult in order to improve coordination and convergence. Each national regulator retains the ability to deal with an issue in its own right but the system aims to facilitate consistency and provide a reference point for future regulatory decisions.[68] At a regional level, CESR has set up a coordination mechanism (European enforcers' coordination sessions or EECS) to maintain a database of enforcement decisions. The EECS focuses on decisions taken or to be taken by local enforcers and gives input and feedback on specific cases in order to achieve consistency among European enforcers.[69]

LO 4 — THE INSTITUTIONAL STRUCTURE FOR SETTING ACCOUNTING AND AUDITING STANDARDS

In our discussion of the regulatory framework for financial reporting, we saw that financial reporting requirements are commonly derived from statute law and accounting standards. In this section, we consider the development of an international standard setting body and the process of setting international accounting and auditing standards.

Background

The development of international accounting standards began formally with the formation of the International Accounting Standards Committee (IASC) in London in 1973. The committee comprised representatives of professional accounting bodies from nine countries (Australia, Canada, France, Japan, Mexico, the Netherlands, the United Kingdom and Ireland, the United States and West Germany).[70] Its aim was to develop accounting standards for the private sector suitable for use in countries throughout the world. Prior to 2005, International Accounting Standards (IAS) were influential in the following ways. They were adopted for use in countries without a national standard setting structure; for example in Papua New Guinea and Indonesia. In other cases, they were used in the development of national standards, such as in Singapore and Hong Kong. IAS were also used voluntarily from the early 1990s in the consolidated accounts of companies from countries such as Switzerland and Germany.[71] In these countries, national accounting reflected a stakeholder orientation arising from their code law legal framework and tax-based accounting systems. Companies used IAS to provide additional information for capital market participants in a more transparent and comparable format.

The members of the IASC hailed from countries with a range of accounting practices and different approaches to setting accounting standards. Early IASC standards often allowed a choice of accounting policy to include the preferences of various member nations. During the late 1980s the IASC began work on the Improvements Project, to improve the quality of IAS and remove many optional treatments. The IOSCO, a body representing securities regulators throughout the world, sought a set of standards which its members could use in cross-border listings. The revised standards were endorsed by IOSCO in 2000, albeit with the proviso that member countries could add further requirements.[72] The latter provision reflected the position of the market regulator in the United States, the SEC. It did not intend to remove the US GAAP reconciliation requirements (the so-called Form 20-F) for companies using IASC standards and listing on the more-regulated United States exchanges (such as the NYSE, NASDAQ and AMEX).[73]

Although use of IAS throughout the world was increasing, further acceptance was limited by the fact the IASC was not an independent standard setting board. Consequently, it was restructured in 2001 to create the International Accounting Standards Board (IASB), an independent board based on the structure of the Financial Accounting Standards Board (FASB) in the United States. The board comprised fourteen full-time members, chosen for their expertise and experience in professional accounting and standard setting. It was supported by dedicated technical staff, located in London. The IASC Foundation became the oversight body of the IASB and an interpretations committee was formed.[74] The formation of the IASB saw the disbanding of the G4+1 (a body comprising independent standard setters from Australia, Canada, New Zealand, the United Kingdom, the United States and the IASC), which was becoming influential in developing international standards. The IASB has responsibility for updating existing IAS (which still carry the IAS label) and producing International Financial Reporting Standards (IFRS).

The importance of the activities of the IASB increased dramatically with the decision in 2002 by the European Commission (EC) to adopt IASB standards in 2005. The EC announced that all listed companies in European Union (EU) member countries would prepare consolidated accounts based on IASB standards. This fundamental change was an important step promoting the production of more transparent and comparable financial information by listed European companies. It was prompted by the goal of developing a single, unified capital market in Europe. The decision prompted a flurry of activity at the IASB and in EU member countries. First, the IASB was required to produce a 'stable platform' of standards by 1 March 2004, to be reviewed by the EC's Accounting Regulatory Committee (ARC). The committee would recommend to the EC whether the standards should be endorsed for use in EU countries. Thus, the IASB had a heavy workload and tight timetable as it sought to finalise standards, including demanding and controversial projects such as accounting for financial instruments. Second, each EU member country had to prepare for adoption of international standards by considering how IFRS reporting would integrate with national reporting. For example, would parent company and private company accounts also use international standards or continue to use national GAAP? The setting up of independent national enforcement bodies, to promote compliance with international standards, was also required.[75] Third, the accounting profession (including external auditors and public accountants) had to prepare for IFRS adoption. This involved technical training to acquaint themselves with standards, which in some cases were markedly different to existing national GAAP. Companies also faced many challenges. Personnel had to become technically proficient in the standards and companies had to revise accounting systems to record information required by the new regime. In addition, they had to communicate with stakeholders such as investors and financiers about how IFRS adoption would impact on their financial statements.

The IASB and FASB convergence program

The work program of the IASB was further complicated by the announcement of the IASB/FASB convergence program, called the Norwalk Agreement, in 2002.[76] The FASB was formed in 1973 and is highly regarded throughout the world as a leading standard setter. The FASB has power delegated by the SEC to develop standards for financial reporting for listed companies. It has produced several accounting concept statements[77] and a series of financial reporting standards focusing on providing high quality financial information which is useful for decision making. The use of international standards in the United States has been discussed at length.[78] While some groups, such as the stock exchanges, mounted arguments in favour of acceptance of IAS based financial statements, the SEC until 2007 maintained that reconciliation to US GAAP was necessary to ensure a 'level playing field'. The SEC issued a concept release in 2000 which outlined its views about desirable attributes of the financial reporting framework.[79] They include high-quality standards developed by an independent standard setting board, and compliance promoted by independent enforcement bodies. With the adoption of IAS in 2005 by many companies, pressure to allow the use of IAS without reconciliation (e.g. from EU companies cross-listed in the United States) increased. In 2007, the SEC agreed to permit foreign registrants to file IFRS accounts with the SEC without the Form 20-F reconciliation.[80] The SEC then began the process of considering whether domestic registrants be permitted to use IFRS instead of US GAAP.[81] While there are some supporters for use of IFRS in the United States, de Lange and Howieson argue that political realities mean the US is unlikely to give up sovereignty over the setting of accounting standards.[82]

In the meantime, the IASB/FASB convergence program has generated considerable work for both Boards. It complicated the process of producing the 'stable platform' of standard for 2005 as the IASB was working to this aim while at the same time considering the extent to which standards could be revised to converge with US GAAP. The convergence program requires the FASB and IASB to identify differences between their respective standards, to review available solutions and to adopt the better treatment. In practice, convergence is a complicated process. Some of the differences arise because of underlying differences between the two sets of standards. US GAAP have been described as rule-based standards while IAS aim to be principles-based.[83]

The greater involvement of the United States means that international standard setting (and, in turn, national standard setting) is now dominated by the FASB and IASB. The convergence process can only be a two-way dialogue between the FASB and IASB because of its inherent difficulties, which would increase if more parties were involved. However, the IASB has a policy of working with national standard setters on projects where they are able to contribute to the standard setting process.[84] The current liaison standard setters are national standard setting bodies from Australia, France, Germany, Japan, New Zealand, the United Kingdom and the United States. They participate in the IASB's work through research projects, project teams and joint projects. The IASB is dependent on the contribution of national standard setters, yet it is unclear the extent to which these bodies will influence the final decisions of the IASB. Since 2005 bodies from the EU (such as national standard setting boards and EFRAG) have become more vocal in the process of developing accounting standards. The IASB may see itself as the global standard setter, but for the EU it is their 'local neighbourhood standard setter'.[85] Given that standards have economic consequences, there is vigorous debate in Europe about the content of IASB standards and the direction of standard setting, as discussed previously in this chapter in relation to financial instruments. Case study 3.3 provides an opportunity to consider a number of important developments relating to the adoption of international standards, which bring out key issues arising from use of common standards.

Accounting standards for the public sector

As noted above, the IASB sets standards for the private sector. Different standards could apply to the public sector, given that public sector entities may have different goals and objectives and different stakeholders compared with private sector entities. Individual countries must decide the extent to which IASB standards will be followed by public sector entities. In Australia and New Zealand, the approach to date has been to pursue one set of accounting standards, suitable for both public and private sector entities. Such standards are described as 'sector neutral standards'.[86]

In Australia the AASB has a number of functions, as described below by the then chairman, Professor David Boymal:
- produce accounting standards to be followed by reporting entities
- produce accounting standards for the public and not-for-profit sectors
- actively participate in development of international standards
- provide interpretation of accounting standards to ensure comparability of financial reporting by Australian reporting entities
- provide technical support to Australian representatives on international committees such as the IPSASB and SAC[87]
- produce standards for private sector and not-for-profit entities are a key board function. In addition, the Board notes that it supports the work of the International Public Sector Accounting Standards Board (IPSASB), a committee of the International Federation of Accountants (IFAC). In 2009, IPSASB was involved in developing a conceptual framework for public sector accounting.

International auditing standards

Finally in this chapter, we consider the regulation of auditing practice and the development of international auditing standards. Historically, auditing was self-regulated. Several professional accounting societies were founded in the nineteenth century to promote the profession and to provide training for members.[88] The formation of these societies occurred during a time when Companies Acts were being passed in the United Kingdom requiring audits and thus generating a significant source of revenue for accountants.[89] As Watts and Zimmerman have documented, there is evidence of audits in the early history of corporations and the development of professional auditing reflected the development of capital markets.[90] The authors conclude that audits were demanded to meet the needs of financial statement users and contracting parties and that legislation requiring audits merely codified the best existing practice.

As discussed in chapter 2, early auditing theory development documented the process of auditing and the duties expected of auditors. More general theoretical development followed which described and prescribed best auditing practice. These practices became enshrined in auditing standards issued by the profession. In the United States, the American Institute of Accountants was responsible for the first auditing standards in 1939.[91] In Australia, auditing standards were issued by the professional accounting bodies through the AARF. The profession was responsible for maintaining ethical standards, including disciplining members who did not follow accounting and auditing standards. However, this form of regulation was weakened if there was no legal requirement for accountants to be members of professional bodies. The American Institute of CPAs (AICPA) began a system of peer reviews in the 1960s, although it was voluntary until 1989.[92]

As noted previously, the accounting scandals at Enron and other companies in the early 2000s can be regarded as market failures and appear to have been used as justification for government intervention in auditing standard setting in the United States and Australia. Since the passage of the Sarbanes-Oxley Act (2002), reviews of audit firms in the US have been conducted by a government body, the Public Company Accounting and Oversight Board (PCAOB). The PCAOB is also responsible for setting auditing standards for the audit of public companies. In Australia, auditing standards have had legal backing through the *Corporations Act 2001* since 1 July 2006 following passage of CLERP 9.

Even though auditing standards are now set by government bodies, the early focus has been more on rewriting standards to enable them to be incorporated into legislation than on changing their content. International Standards on Auditing (ISA) are developed by the International Auditing and Assurance Standards Board (IAASB). In Australia, the Auditing and Assurance Standards Board (AUASB) rewrote the previous set of professional standards and is directed to use ISA as a base from which to develop new Australian standards, with any necessary amendment.[93]

The IAASB operates under the auspices of the IFAC. The IFAC's members are accounting organisations and most members of the IAASB have been practising auditors. This situation has led some commentators to suggest that the IAASB is 'captured' by the auditing profession in the same way that professional accounting bodies had 'captured' the national auditing standard setting process before the Sarbanes-Oxley Act in the US and CLERP 9 in Australia. Even though governments appear to have taken control of auditing standards, their reliance on the IAASB potentially undermines government authority.[94]

The IAASB appears to be aware of the threat to its credibility and power by its reliance on professional accountants for funding and expertise. The IFAC established the Public Interest Oversight Board (PIOB) in 2005 with the objective of increasing confidence in the standards issued by the IAASB and other IFAC bodies.[95] Its aim is to ensure that standards are set in a transparent manner that reflects the public interest, with input by the public and regulators, and to facilitate audit regulation. As discussed further in chapter 14, the future success of the IAASB relies on successful enforcement of the auditing standards and retaining the trust of the various stakeholders.

Governments appear to believe that accounting and auditing standards matter, and they have some support from research for their view. There is evidence that the strength of accounting and auditing standards and the effectiveness of their enforcement are factors in the successful development of financial markets around the world. Francis, Khurana and Pereira gathered evidence on the quality of auditing, the strength of auditing enforcement, and the quality of accounting standards and found that high-quality accounting and auditing are more likely to exist in corporate governance in countries with strong investor protection.[96] However, although higher quality accounting and auditing are also positively associated with financial market development in these countries, the evidence does not support the contention that they are sufficient to encourage the development of financial markets without strong investor protection. One example of how the actions of auditors can impact on individual companies and on the broader market is addressed in theory in action 3.4. The article presented considers the market impact of auditors giving an 'emphasis of matter' opinion, which may be necessary for some companies following the 2007–08 financial crisis.

Many small caps to flash orange

by Damon Kitney and Patrick Durkin

Hundreds of small Australian Securities Exchange-listed companies will have their half-yearly accounts flagged by auditors over the next fortnight because of concerns they may fail to stay in business over the next 12 months.

The ongoing impact of the credit crisis means directors of many small companies will be unable to guarantee that their company will continue as a going concern, especially where they face rolling over their debt.

The warning by directors and accountants follows a crackdown by the Australian Securities and Investments Commission on insolvent trading and comes as the half-year reporting season draws to an end over the next two weeks — when many cash strapped companies tend to report.

In December, ASIC said directors should focus on whether companies will remain solvent given their ability to refinance debt, raise funds and comply with lending covenants.

"Managing banking covenants in an environment where asset values are dropping can be a very difficult thing, said Jeff Lucy, chairman of the Financial Reporting Council — the oversight body for accounting and auditing standards in Australia.

"For a small mining company, for instance, a drop in commodity prices leads you to look at the carrying value of mines. This reduces asset values, which then affects banking covenants."

When signing off on accounts, auditors are also required to provide an assurance that companies will remain solvent over the next 12 months. Where there is uncertainty about whether a company can continue as a going concern, auditors are required to flag the accounts with "an emphasis of matter".

The technical accounting warning is one step below a "qualification", which is the most serious warning about potential irregularities in company accounts.

KPMG's national managing partner, risk and regulation, Michael Coleman, said he expected to see more accounts flagged with an "emphasis of matter" in the current environment because of uncertainty about their debt profile. But the high number of flagged accounts has created alarm among accountants and regulators amid concerns that investors may misinterpret the findings.

"In this environment, a simple event has a chain reaction," Mr Lucy said. "In putting the truth on the table, it can have a snowball effect. There needs to be a mature judgement applied. Does it mean that wheels are about to fall off? No. But rather than a qualification, which is a red flashing light, an emphasis of matter is really an orange glow."

The matter was discussed at a meeting of the Financial Reporting Council in Melbourne last week attended by Mr Lucy, Corporate Law Minister Nick Sherry and the new chairman of the Australian Accounting Standards Board, Bruce Porter.

"It is emphasising to the readers this particular point, it is saying go and have a look at this, go and have a read so you fully understand the accounts because of this uncertainty," Mr Porter said. "It is saying there is a lack of evidence to say 100 per cent [that this company will survive]," he said.

Source: The Australian Financial Review, 23 February 2009, p. 9.

Questions

1. What does the headline of the article mean by 'small cap' and 'flash orange'?
2. Explain the argument that merely by placing an 'emphasis of matter' section in an audit report you could start a chain reaction.
3. The article discusses bank covenants — explain the impact of asset values on bank covenants and the potential repercussions for a company.

Summary

LO 1 → **The theories of regulation which are relevant to accounting and auditing**

The aim of theory is to explain and predict real world phenomena. In this chapter we reviewed theories proposed to explain the practice of financial reporting and auditing. Theories from economics including the theory of efficient markets and agency theory are relevant to understanding the environment in which financial reporting occurs. Both these theories help us to understand the role of financial information and the incentives for its production. Specific theories of regulation also provide insights about how and why we observe the regulation of financial reporting.

Public interest theory proposes that governments or their agents introduce regulation to compensate for market failure. Regulation is intended to protect the interest of individuals and society as a whole; with regulation society is better off than otherwise. In relation to financial reporting, the assumption is that regulation will improve information flows thus improving capital market efficiency. In this theory the government is an independent party. Its agents respond to requests from 'entrepreneurial politicians' and public interest groups to intervene in the market. While it could be argued that these parties are acting in part with self-interest, the regulatory intervention is claimed to have some overall genuine public interest.

Regulation is not costless. It involves wealth transfers and therefore has economic consequences for the parties being regulated. Capture theory proposed that parties subject to regulation seek to control the government or its agents who are responsible for issuing the regulation. The theory assumes that individuals are economic rationalists and they will pursue their own self-interest. Thus, they act to increase and protect their wealth by seeking control of the regulating body. For example, they secure control by dictating the body's activities and agenda or by neutralising it (i.e. ensuring that its performance is ineffective).

A third theory takes a somewhat different perspective. Private interest theory proposes that, in contrast to the two prior theories, the government is not independent. It has the 'power to coerce' and will exercise this power in the way which best suits government objectives. Thus politicians are not neutral arbiters, but exercise their power to maximise their future electoral success. The government does not regulate in the public interest but rather in response to the private interest group with the most voting power. In capital markets the group with the most incentive and resources to lobby for their preferred regulation is often from the listed company or corporate sector.

LO 2 ━ **How theories of regulation apply to accounting and auditing practice**

In this section, we explored the extent to which public interest, capture and private interest theories can be applied in practice. We observed that governments in many countries have intervened in the process of setting accounting and auditing standards. Although standards were initially under the control of the private sector, a succession of events led to government control in many countries. For example, in Australia accounting standards were developed by the accounting profession. The government intervened in the accounting standard setting process from the 1980s by setting up bodies with the responsibility for promulgating accounting standards. We discussed the extent to which such bodies were 'captured' by the parties for whom they were creating regulations. We also considered the role of private interest groups in obtaining regulation favourable to their own interests.

The final part of this section expanded on the theme of the political nature of standard setting and regulation. Noted US academic Stephen Zeff has described standard setting as an inescapably political process. This view applies not just to the United States, but equally in other countries as well. We observed that the adoption of IASB standards in the European Union has taken the politicisation of accounting standard setting to a new level. Zeff explains that there are a range of parties involved, with different objectives and cultural preferences, which has resulted in a lengthy endorsement process subsequent to the IASB's standard setting process (already a highly political process). We reviewed the adoption of IAS 39 in Europe to illustrate some of the issues involved.

LO 3 ━ **The regulatory framework for financial reporting**

Financial reporting does not occur in a vacuum. There are many factors which influence the process of producing financial information. In this section we described a number of key elements which may be observed in a number of countries' financial reporting framework. Our aim was to provide a 'proforma' of the regulatory framework and to show how the elements affect the production of financial reports. First, we discussed statutory requirements, that is, the laws which require preparation and auditing of financial reports. Such laws may be contained in company, securities market and taxation law. Common requirements which affect preparation of financial reports are the duty to prepare accounts (in accordance with accounting standards and other legal requirements), to have them audited by an external auditor and to lodge them with a government body. Next we referred to corporate governance. Some corporate governance practices follow requirements of law, while others reflect 'best practice' recommendations developed by the private sector. Examples of the former include the EU directives on corporate governance and examples of the latter are the governance codes which have been adopted in the United Kingdom and Australia.

Compliance with financial reporting requirements is promoted by external auditors and independent enforcement bodies. We observed that in many countries auditors have traditionally been the most important parties for promoting compliance with accounting standards. As a result of adoption of IASB standards in 2005 many countries have set up independent enforcement bodies. While some people consider such bodies a waste of resources (they have been described as 'checking the checkers'), many commentators point to the necessity of consistent enforcement across countries to ensure comparable application of IFRS. It is argued that without coordinated enforcement the benefits of adoption of international standards will not be achieved. We described the types of body which have been set up and the enforcement coordination mechanisms which have been put in place. An evaluation of the role and effectiveness of these bodies will occur in the future.

The institutional structure for setting accounting and auditing standards

In the final section of this chapter we provided an overview of the development of international bodies that provide accounting and auditing standards. We discussed the background to the current processes for developing international accounting standards, beginning with the formation of the IASC in 1973 and then the IASB in 2001. Key issues discussed were: IOSCO's support for a set of core standards; the EU's decision to adopt IASB standards from 2005; and the greater involvement of the United States in international standard setting, resulting from the IASB/FASB convergence project, which commenced in 2002.

We also discussed the setting of auditing standards. The professional accounting bodies have a long history of involvement with standard setting, which parallels the history of legal requirements for audits. Regulation of auditing occurred despite evidence that audits are demanded in the absence of regulation. Professional accounting bodies wrote the first auditing standards but governments have used market failures to justify regulating auditing standards in the United States and Australia. However, the Australian auditing standards are based on the international standards which are written by a body controlled largely by practising auditors. An oversight body has been established to ensure the standards reflect the public interest and have due regard to the views of regulators. Empirical research supports the role of accounting and auditing standards and their effective enforcement in the development of financial markets around the world.

Questions

1. General acceptance of accounting standards is important to the accounting profession. By whom does the profession require general acceptance of the standards, and why is it important to the profession?
2. The standard setting process is highly political. Describe an accounting regulation that would be politically controversial, and the types of political pressures that could be brought to bear in the standard setting process.
3. The text describes a theory of regulatory capture.
    (a) What is regulatory capture?
    (b) How can standard setting bodies such as the AASB avoid regulatory capture?
    (c) If a standard setting body is 'captured' by the profession, are there any steps that the government can take to make the body independent? If so, should the government take those steps? Justify your answer.
    (d) Do you believe that the current international accounting standard setting arrangements, based around the IASB, are at risk of regulatory capture? Why or why not?
4. In under 500 words, provide an argument for the regulatory approach to standard setting. Then, in under 500 words, provide an argument for the free-market approach to standard setting. Finally, analyse the arguments and conclude in favour of one approach rather than the other (which approach you favour is up to you, but you must decide which approach is better, at least under a set of assumed circumstances).
5. If the IASB concludes that the economic consequences of a standard it is about to approve will disadvantage a powerful lobby group, what should the IASB do about the situation?

6. How do you think accounting standards should be set? Is that the approach currently taken by the IASB?

7. 'We should disband national standard setters. They are of no use following the adoption of international accounting standards'. Explain whether you agree or disagree with this statement.

8. What are 'free-riders'? How can a system ensure that those who benefit most from an accounting standard requiring certain disclosures also bear the greatest costs of it?

9. The setting of accounting standards requires some assessment of economic and other benefits and costs. What are the ethical issues involved? Is it possible to avoid ethical issues in developing accounting standards?

10. You have been appointed as chief accountant of a firm that will be adversely affected by the method of accounting that is proposed in an exposure draft for an accounting standard on leasing. Write a report of 500 words or less explaining to your Board of Directors how you could lobby the AASB and the IASB to adopt an accounting practice other than the one proposed in the exposure draft. Also comment on the costs and benefits of lobbying for the company.

11. In 2001 and 2002 there were several high-profile corporate collapses in the United States associated with misleading financial statements and accounting practices. Following these collapses, new laws were introduced to improve the quality of financial reporting.
    (a) In your opinion, will further regulation prevent deliberately misleading reporting? Explain.
    (b) Are additional laws likely to prevent corporate collapses? Why or why not?
    (c) How important is the enforcement of financial reporting requirements in promoting high quality reporting?

12. Each of the three theories of regulation discussed in this chapter has its strengths and limitations in describing accounting standard setting, either past or present. What do you believe are those strengths and weaknesses? Provide an example where you believe each of the theories has applied, or is likely to apply.

13. From 1 January 2005 Australia adopted IASB standards.
    (a) Do you agree with this change? Why or why not?
    (b) Who stands to gain from Australia's adoption of IASB standards? Explain.
    (c) Who stands to lose from Australia's adoption of IASB standards? Explain.

14. What is the role of the Financial Reporting Council? Do you think that all members of the Financial Reporting Council should be qualified accountants? Why or why not?

15. The IASB and FASB began a convergence project in 2002.
    (a) What are the expected benefits of the convergence project?
    (b) What factors make convergence difficult?
    (c) How is the future of the IASB tied to convergence?

16. Should the SEC allow the use of IASB standards for US domestic listed companies? Discuss reasons for and against the use of IFRS by US companies.

17. Why has IFAC established a Public Interest Oversight Board?

18. Why would the quality of accounting and auditing standards affect the development of financial markets? Why is the strength of enforcement of the standards and investor protection important in this relationship?

Additional readings

Alfredson, K, Leo, K, Picker, R, Pacter, P, & Radford, J 2009, *Applying international accounting standards*, John Wiley & Sons, Brisbane: Australia.

Alfredson, K 2003, 'Pathway to 2005 IASB standards', *The Australian Accounting Review*, vol. 13, no. 1, pp. 3–7.

Brown, P, & Tarca, A 2005, 'It's here, ready or not: a review of the Australian financial reporting framework', *Australian Accounting Review*, vol. 15, no. 2, pp. 68–78.

Collett, P, Godfrey, JM, & Hrasky, S 2001, 'International harmonisation: Cautions from the Australian experience.' *Accounting Horizons*, vol. 15, no. 2, pp. 171–82.

Georgiou, G 2004, 'Corporate lobbying on accounting standards: methods, timing and perceived effectiveness', *Abacus*, vol. 40, no. 2, pp. 219–237.

Laux, C, & Leuz, C 2009, 'The crisis of fair-value accounting: Making sense of the recent debate', *Accounting Organizations and Society*, vol. 6–7, pp. 826–34.

Miller, M 1995, 'The credibility of Australian financial reporting: Are the co-regulation arrangements working?' *Australian Accounting Review*, vol. 5, no. 2, pp. 3–16.

Watts, RL, & Zimmerman, JL 1986, *Positive accounting theory*. Englewood Cliffs, NJ: Prentice-Hall.

Zeff, S 2002, '"Political" lobbying on proposed standards: a challenge to the IASB', *Accounting Horizons*, vol. 16, no. 1, pp. 43–54.

Websites

Australian Accounting Standards Board (AASB) www.aasb.com.au

Australian Securities and Investments Commission (ASIC) www.asic.gov.au

CPA Australia www.cpaaustralia.com.au

Deloitte IASPlus www.iasplus.com

Ernst & Young www.ey.com.au

European Financial Reporting Action Group (EFRAG) www.efrag.com

Fédération des Experts Comptables Européens (FEE) www.fee.be

Financial Accounting Standards Board (FASB) www.fasb.org

Financial Reporting Council (FRC) www.asb.org.uk

Financial Reporting Council (FRC) www.frc.gov.au

Google scholar www.scholar.google.com

Institute of Chartered Accountants in Australia (ICAA) www.icaa.org.au

International Accounting Standards Board (IASB) www.iasb.org

KPMG www.kpmg.com.au

PricewaterhouseCoopers www.pwc.com.au

Securities and Exchange Commission (SEC) www.sec.gov

3.1 CASE STUDY

Balancing the costs and benefits of regulatory intervention

US's Snow urges balance in Sarbanes-Oxley rules

US Treasury Secretary John Snow on Wednesday warned against using Sarbanes-Oxley financial reporting rules in ways that might dampen economic growth, and he sympathized with the plight of corporate executives who are under regulatory scrutiny. 'We need to maintain balance in our enforcement,' Snow said in prepared remarks to the New York University Center for Law and Business. 'We need to make sure the emphasis is on substance and not form. We need to make sure that innocent mistakes are not criminal,' he said. Congress passed Sarbanes-Oxley in 2002 in response to a series of high-profile corporate scandals that felled Enron, WorldCom and the accounting firm Arthur Andersen. The law, named for Ohio Republican Rep. Michael Oxley and Maryland Democratic Sen. Paul Sarbanes, calls for strict financial reporting standards and accountability. Snow's comments come amid widespread complaints by businesses that Section 404 of the law, which requires managers to explain publicly how they look after corporate finances, is too costly and time-consuming. In a question and answer session with the audience, he said that he was sympathetic with the 'world' in which corporate executives and lawyers are living where they are 'under siege' from regulators. 'We've overdone this. We have got to find a way to rationalize this whole corporate governance regulatory process,' Snow said.

The treasury secretary warned that while Sarbanes-Oxley was essential in restoring public confidence in businesses after the scandals, it runs the risk of being a drag on US corporate effectiveness and willingness to invest in growing capital. 'This whole climate we find ourselves in, which Sarbanes-Oxley is only a part, may have altered the appetite for risk taking and may have engendered a risk-averse attitude,' Snow said in response to a question from the audience. He added that the ratio of capital spending to cash flows and corporate profit is lower than one would expect due perhaps to a reluctance among US companies to take risks. However, Snow maintained that passing Sarbanes-Oxley was necessary due to the acts of a few corporate miscreants and that modifying the law at this point would be ill-advised. 'Even though we all know there are ways that you could tweak (Sarbanes-Oxley) this way or that, the consequences of trying to amend it to deal with those issues this early in the process would have a political backlash that would be unfortunate and counterproductive,' he said.

Source: Reuters News, 2 June 2005.

Questions

1. Give reasons for the introduction of the Sarbanes-Oxley Act in the United States in 2002.
2. Why are some parties now opposed to the Act? Why has their view changed from when the law was first introduced?
3. According to John Snow, what criteria should be considered in determining financial reporting rules?
4. Would you recommend a repeal of the Act? Why or why not?

Are bean counters to blame?

by Andrew Ross Sorkin

Some blame the rapacious lenders. Others point to the deadbeat borrowers. But Stephen A. Schwarzman sees another set of culprits behind all the pain in the financial industry: the accountants.

That's right, the bean counters.

A new accounting rule — "an accounting rule!" — partly explains why the American financial system looks so wobbly these days, he says.

Mr. Schwarzman, the co-founder of the private equity giant Blackstone Group, has been espousing this view for weeks over lunches and at cocktail parties around the globe. It's a controversial hypothesis, which others have put forward before, and it has sparked plenty of debate within the industry. But Mr. Schwarzman is convinced that the rule — known as FAS 157 — is forcing bookkeepers to overstate the problems at the nation's largest banks.

"From the C.E.O.'s I talk with," Mr. Schwarzman said during an interview on Monday morning, "the rule is accentuating and amplifying potential losses. It's a significant contributing factor."

Some of his bigwig pals in finance believe that Wall Street is in much better shape than the balance sheets suggest, Mr. Schwarzman said. The president of Blackstone, Hamilton E. James, goes even further. FAS 157, he said, is not just misleading: "It's dangerous."

Huh? So the Citigroups and Merrill Lynches of the world are writing off billions of dollars — but they haven't actually lost the money?

Sort of. If Mr. Schwarzman is to be believed — and there's some evidence he might be right, at least partly — it all goes back to FAS 157, which went into effect Nov. 15, just as the credit hurricane tore through Wall Street. Remember, that was about the time Citigroup ousted Charles O. Prince III after the bank shocked investors by writing down $5.9 billion and Merrill Lynch showed E. Stanley O'Neal the door after it was forced to write down $8.4 billion. (The pain didn't end there, for either of those companies or the rest of the financial industry.)

FAS 157 represents the so-called fair value rule put into effect by the Financial Accounting Standards Board, the bookkeeping rule makers. It requires that certain assets held by financial companies, including tricky investments linked to mortgages and other kinds of debt, be marked to market. In other words, you have to value the assets at the price you could get for them if you sold them right now on the open market.

The idea seems noble enough. The rule forces banks to mark to market, rather to some theoretical price calculated by a computer — a system often derided as "mark to make-believe." (Occasionally, for certain types of assets, the rule allows for using a model — and yes, the potential for manipulation too.)

But here's the problem: Sometimes, there is no market — not for toxic investments like collateralized debt obligations, or C.D.O.'s, filled with subprime mortgages. No one will touch this stuff. And if there is no market, FAS 157 says, a bank must mark the investment's value down, possibly all the way to zero.

That partly explains why big banks had to write down countless billions in C.D.O. exposure. The losses are, at least in part, theoretical. Nonetheless, the banks, in response, are bringing down their leverage levels and running to the desert to raise additional capital, often at shareholders' expense.

Mr. Schwarzman and others say FAS 157 is forcing underserved write-offs and wreaking havoc on the financial system. There is even a campaign afoot in Washington to change the rule.

Some analysts, even insiders, say banks like Citigroup and Lehman Brothers marked down some of their C.D.O. exposure by more than 50 percent when the underlying mortgages wrapped inside the C.D.O.'s may have only fallen 15 percent.

Bob Traficanti, head of accounting policy and deputy comptroller at Citigroup, said at a conference last month that the bank had "securities with little or no credit deterioration, and we're being forced to mark these down to values that we think are unrealistically low."

As a result, Citigroup went hat in hand to Abu Dhabi, selling a significant stake and diluting existing shareholders in the process. According to the Securities and Exchange Commission, FAS 157 requires an institution "to consider actual market prices, or observable inputs, even when the market is less liquid than historical market volumes, unless those prices are the result of a forced liquidation or distress sale."

As a result, Christopher Hayward, finance director and head of holding company supervision initiatives at Merrill Lynch said: "There is a bit of this pressure, a bit of this atmosphere that says, 'Let's just mark it down, no one is going to question it if we mark it down.'"

Of course, Mr. Schwarzman's theory only holds up if the underlying assets are really worth much more than anyone currently expects. And if they are so mispriced, why isn't some vulture investor — or Mr. Schwarzman — buying up C.D.O.'s en masse?

For Mr. Schwartzman's part, he says that the banks haven't been willing to unload the investments at the distressed prices. Besides, the diligence required for most buyers is almost too complicated.

It is not clear that Mr. Schwarzman's view is correct. The folks at the University of Chicago — those the-market-is-always-right guys — take umbrage at the mere suggestion that marking-to-market is not always appropriate.

FAS 157 proponents say that if Mr. Schwarzman and his crowd get their way, financial companies might end up valuing investments based on market prices when it suits them, and just look the other way when it doesn't.

"He's entitled to his view, but I don't agree" said Daniel Alpert, managing director at the investment bank Westwood Capital. "I don't believe that people are taking write-downs that forces them to dilute their shareholders." If anything, Mr. Alpert says, "There is still a lot of sludge out there."

Mr. Schwarzman is suggesting that the market is somehow wrong, or wildly inefficient. (Of course, Mr. Schwarzman is a private equity guy, so the day-to-day swings in the market in his mind are always wrong.)

But some say Goldman Sachs proved why FAS 157 works: Goldman has been marking its books to market for years, and as a result, its risk officers were able to hold back its go-go traders from making bad bets when everyone else was throwing down their chips last year into the subprime game.

Of course, the purpose of FAS 157 was to make the market more transparent and efficient, which Mr. Schwarzman doesn't take issue with.

"The concept of fair value accounting is correct and useful, but the application during periods of crisis is problematic," he said. "It's another one of those unintended consequences of making a rule that's supposed to be good that turns out the other way."

Let's hope he's right.

This article has been revised to reflect the following correction: The DealBook column on Tuesday, about an accounting rule that a private equity executive says is causing bank write-downs to be exaggerated, misstated the name of the organization that establishes accounting standards. It is the Financial Accounting Standards Board, not the Federal Accounting Standards Board.

Source: New York Times, 1 July 2008 (correction appended 7 July 2008).

Questions

1. List possible factors contributing to the banking crisis (the problem of bad debts relating to collateralised debt obligations, i.e. the so-called sub-prime crisis, which began in mid-2007 and became a more general global financial crisis in October 2008).
2. Has the market benefited from the regulation requiring the use of fair value accounting for financial instruments?
3. According to people quoted in the article, did the US capital market efficiently price the collateralised debt obligations (CDOs)?

3.3
CASE STUDY

The following five events represent significant developments in relation to the adoption and use of international accounting standards.

1. **June 2002** — The European Commission announces plans to adopt international accounting standards (IAS) for consolidated financial statements of all listed companies in European Union (EU) member states from 1 January 2005.
2. **October 2004** — The European Commission endorses IAS for use in the EU, with the exception of certain provisions of IAS 39 relating to hedge accounting and fair value measurement of financial instruments. When complying with IASB standards from 2005, companies will not be required to follow the excluded provision of IAS 39.

3. **April 2005** — The European Commission seeks rule changes to make it easier for EU companies cross-listed in the United States to de-list from US stock exchanges. The Commission is seeking agreement from the United States securities market regulator, the SEC, to change the current requirement that companies show they have fewer than 300 shareholders before they are permitted to cease registration in the United States.

4. **November 2007** — The SEC announces that from 2007, companies cross-listed on US stock exchanges which prepare accounts based on IAS are permitted to file financial reports with the SEC without reconciling the reports in accordance with US GAAP.

5. **October 2008** — The IASB announces amendments to IAS 39 which permit companies to choose to reclassify items out of categories requiring fair value measurement into categories where amortised cost is used. The amendments were announced in response to the 2007–2008 financial crisis and were made without following the IASB's due process.

Question

After considering the material presented in this chapter, what would be possible explanations for each of these five events?

Endnotes

1. AA Atkinson and GA Feltham, 'Agency theory research and financial accounting standards', in S Basu and JA Milburn (eds), *Research to support standard setting in financial accounting: a Canadian perspective*, Hamilton, Ontario: Clarkson Gordon Foundation, McMaster University, 1982, p. 260.

2. Detailed discussions on this market failure concept can be found in F Bator, 'The anatomy of market failure', *Quarterly Journal of Economics*, vol. 72, 1958, pp. 351–79; R Posner, 'Theories of economic regulation', *Bell Journal of Economics and Management Science*, Autumn 1974, pp. 335–58; B Mitnick, *The political economy of regulation*, New York: Colombia University Press, 1980; and I Ramsay, 'Framework for the regulation of the consumer marketplace', *Journal of Consumer Policy*, vol. 8, December 1985, pp. 353–72.

3. A Fels, 'The political economy of regulation', *USSW Law Journal*, vol. 5, 1982, pp. 32–33.

4. K Cooper and G Keim, 'The economic rationale for the nature and extent of corporate financial disclosure regulation: A critical assessment', *Journal of Accounting and Public Policy*, vol. 2, 1983, p. 190.

5. G Rowe, 'Economic theories of the nature of regulatory activity', in R Tomasic (ed.), *Business regulation in Australia*, Sydney: CCH Australia Ltd, 1984, p. 154.

6. Mitnick, op. cit., p. 91.

7. Posner, op. cit., p. 342.

8. For example, governments can provide subsidies to corporate entities; create and enforce barriers to entry within industries; and allow corporate directors to avoid detailed disclosures on bonuses and benefits received. In turn, these 'regulated' benefits have the potential to transfer monies from other parties such as, respectively, taxpayers, consumers within the 'closed' industry, and shareholders and other investors to the management of the 'favoured entities'.

9. AJ Richardson and BJ McConomy, 'Three styles of rule', *CA Magazine*, May, 1992, p. 42.

10. Mitnick, op. cit., p. 95.

11. P Quirk, *Industry influence in federal regulatory agencies*, Princeton, NJ: Princeton University Press, 1981, p. 13.

12. ibid.

13. G Stigler, 'The theory of economic regulation', *Bell Journal of Economics and Management Science*, Spring 1971, pp. 2–21.

14. ibid., p. 4.

15. S Peltzman, 'Towards a more general theory of regulation', *Journal of Law and Economics*, August 1976, p. 212.

16. JQ Wilson, *The politics of regulation*, New York: Basic Books, 1980, p. 373.

17. J Riotto, 'Understanding the Sarbanes–Oxley Act — a value added approach for the public interest', *Critical Perspectives on Accounting*, vol. 19, 2008, pp. 952–62.

18. J Canada, J Kuhn and S Sutton, 'Accidentally in the public interest: the perfect storm that yielded the Sarbanes-Oxley Act', *Critical Perspectives on Accounting*, vol. 19, 2008, pp. 987–1003.

19. Cooper and Keim, op. cit., p. 191.

20. For detailed discussions of voluntary disclosures refer to such studies as G Benston, 'The value of the SEC's accounting disclosure requirements', *Accounting Review*, July 1969, pp. 515–32; R Morris, 'Corporate disclosure in a substantially unregulated environment', *Abacus*, June 1984, pp. 52–86; G Foster, *Financial statement analysis*, London: Prentice-Hall, 1986; G Whittred, 'The derived demand for consolidated financial reporting', *Journal of Accounting and Economics*, December 1987; D Skinner, 'Why firms voluntarily disclose bad news',

Journal of Accounting Research, Spring 1994; and L Yi, G Richardson, and D Thornton, 'Corporate disclosure of environmental liability information: Theory and evidence', *Contemporary Accounting Research*, Fall 1997.

21. G Ackerlof, 'The market for lemons: Quality uncertainty and the market mechanism', *Quarterly Journal of Economics*, August 1990, pp. 488–500.

22. Walker, op. cit.

23. The Australian Accounting Research Foundation was funded by the professional accounting bodies (ICAA and CPAA) to carry out research and participate in setting accounting and auditing standards for the public and private sector during the period 1966–2000.

24. This finding by Walker is consistent with that of Willmott op. cit., p. 63, who investigated the setting of accounting standards in the United Kingdom and the role of the accounting bodies in that process.

25. P Brown and A Tarca, 'Politics, processes and the future of Australian accounting standards', *Abacus*, vol. 37, no 3, 2001, pp. 267–96.

26. S Zeff, 'IFRS developments in the USA and EU, and some implications for Australia', *Australian Accounting Review*, vol. 47 no. 4, 2008, pp. 275–82.

27. S Zeff, 'Some obstacles to global financial reporting comparability and convergence at a high level of quality', *British Accounting Review*, vol. 39, 2007, pp. 290–302.

28. A Rahman, 'The Accounting Standards Review Board — the establishment of its participative review process', PhD thesis, University of Sydney, November 1988.

29. ibid., p. 2.

30. Rahman, op. cit., p. xvii.

31. For example, refer to M Dobbie, 'SAC 4: the great debate', *Financial Forum*, vol. 2, no. 4, May 1993, pp. 1, 3, 5; and D Soh, 'G100 pulls the rug on SAC 4', *New Accountant*, vol. 6, no. 7, 15 April 1993, pp. 1, 9.

32. R Watts and J Zimmerman, 'The demand for and supply of accounting theories: The market for excuses', *Accounting Review*, vol. 54, no. 2, 1979, pp. 273–305.

33. R Kaplan, 'Book review on Beaver: financial reporting, an accounting revolution', *Journal of Accounting and Economics*, vol. 3, no. 12, December 1981, pp. 243–52.

34. DL Gerboth, 'Research, intuition and politics in accounting inquiry', *Accounting Review*, vol. 68, no. 3, July 1973, pp. 475–82.

35. G4+1 Study title: Accounting for leases: a new approach, July 1996, www.iasplus.com.

36. IASB 2009, Discussion Paper DP/2009/1, Leases, preliminary views, www.iasb.org.

37. S Zeff, 'The evolution of US GAAP: The political forces behind professional standards', *The CPA Journal*, February, vol. 75, no. 2, 2005, p. 18.

38. S Zeff, Political lobbying on accounting standards — national and international experience, in C Nobes and R Parker, *Comparative international accounting*, ninth edition, London: Pearson Education, 2006, chapter 9.

39. L Johnson and R Swieringa, 'Anatomy of an agenda decision: Statement No. 115', *Accounting Horizons*, vol. 10, no. 2, 1996, pp. 149–79.

40. R Jones and E Venuti, 'Accounting and reporting for financial instruments: International developments', *CPA Journal*, vol. 75, no. 2, 2005, pp. 30–4.

41. C Nobes and R Parker, Accounting rules and practices of individual companies in Europe, *Comparative international accounting*, ninth edition, London: Pearson Education, 2006, chapter 14.

42. D Flint, 'A passion for clarity: IAS 39 is in the front line of the conflict pitting principles against rules', *Financial Times*, 6 February 2003, p. 2.

43. Jones and Venuti, op. cit.

44. Fédération des Experts Comptables Européens (European Financial Reporting Action Group).

45. A Parker, 'IASB to stand firm following French attack', *Financial Times*, 11 July 2003.

46. A Parker, 'EU states vote on se of IAS 39', *Financial Times*, 2 October 2004, p. 8.

47. Zeff, op. cit. *Australian Accounting Review*, 2008.

48. J Healy, 'Financial instruments: IAS 39: a moveable feast for accountants?', *Accountancy Ireland*, vol. 36, no. 6, 2004, pp. 16–8.

49. IASB 2008, press release, IASB amendments permit reclassification of financial instruments, October, www.iasb.org.

50. K Alfredson, 'Accounting for identifiable intangibles — an unfinished standard setting task', *The Australian Accounting Review*, vol. 11, no. 2, 2001, pp. 12–21.

51. K Chalmers and J Godfrey, 'Companies in the danger zone', *Australian CPA*, vol. 73, no. 10, 2003, p. 69.

52. T Ravlic, 'CCA's $1.9-billion teaser', *CFO*, 1 September 2004, p. 82; K Walters, 'Standards fightback', *Business Review Weekly*, 12 February 2004, p. 36.

53. L Orsini, JP McAllister and R Parikh, *World accounting*, New York: Matthew Bender, 2008.

54. Zeff, op. cit., *British Accounting Review*, 2007.

55. C Nobes and R Parker, *Comparative international accounting*, eighth edition, London: Pearson Education, 2004, p. 33.

56. Fédération des Experts Comptables Européens, *Enforcement mechanisms in Europe: A preliminary investigation of oversight systems*, April 2001, www.fee.be/publications/main.htm.

57. GF Davis, 'New directions in corporate governance', *Annual Review of Sociology*, vol 31, pp. 143–62, August 2005, http://ssrn.com.

58. Orsini, op. cit.

59. The Combined Code on Corporate Governance, United Kingdom, www.frc.org.uk; Principles of good corporate governance and best practice recommendations, Australia, www.nfcgindia.org.

60. Orsini, op. cit.

61. While cases have been taken against members, self-regulation is always limited by the disciplinary bodies' willingness to pursue cases against their peers.

62. S McLeay (ed.), *Accounting regulation in Europe*, Macmillan, 1999.

63. Fédération des Experts Comptables Européens 2001, op. cit.

64. The Committee of European Securities Regulators (CESR) CESR's review of the implementation of

enforcement of the IFRS in the EU. Ref 07-352. CESR, Paris, November 2007.

65. P Brown and A Tarca, 'A commentary on issues relating to the enforcement of International Financial Reporting Standards in the EU', *European Accounting Review*, vol. 14, no. 1, 2005, pp. 181–212.

66. Nobes and Parker 2006, op. cit. p. 178.

67. S Fearnley, T Hines, K McBride and R Brandt, 'A peculiarly British institution: an analysis of the contribution made by the Financial Reporting Review Panel to Accounting Compliance in the UK', Centre for Business Performance, Institute of Chartered Accountants in England and Wales, 2000.

68. International Organization of Securities Commissions (IOSCO) 2005, Annual Report, www.iosco.org.

69. Fédération des Experts Comptables Européens, Position paper financial reporting: convergence, equivalence and mutual recognition, March 2006, www.fee.be.

70. Nobes and Parker 2006, op. cit.

71. Nobes and Parker 2004, op. cit.

72. International Organization of Securities Commissions (IOSCO) 2000, 'IASC standards', May, www.iosco.org.

73. New York Stock Exchange; National Association of Securities Dealers Automated Quotations; American Stock Exchange.

74. IASB 'About us', www.iasb.org/about/index.asp.

75. Brown and Tarca 2005, op. cit.

76. Financial Accounting Standards Board & International Accounting Standards Board 2002, Memorandum of understanding: The Norwalk Agreement, Norwalk, Connecticut.

77. See chapter 4.

78. For an overview of the arguments, see RA Dye and S Sunder, 'Why not allow FASB and IASB standards to compete in the US?', *Accounting Horizons*, vol. 15, no. 3, 2001, pp. 43–54.

79. Securities and Exchange Commission 2000, 'The concept release on international accounting standards', www.sec.gov.

80. Zeff 2008, op. cit.

81. DL Street, 'The impact in the United States of the global adoption of IFRS', *Australian Accounting Review*, September 2008, pp. 199–208.

82. P De Lange and B Howieson, 'On a slow boat to convergence: the relationship between the USA and International Accounting Standards', working paper, University of South Australia, 2004.

83. See chapter 4.

84. IASB, 'How do national standard setters fit into the IASB's activities?', www.iasb.org.

85. A term used by Zeff; see Zeff 2008, *AAR*, p. 279.

86. See further discussion see ME Bradbury and RF Baskerville, 'The "NZ" in "NZ IFRS": Public Benefit Entity Amendments', *Australian Accounting Review*, vol. 18, no, 3, 2008, pp. 185–90.

87. Accounting Standards Interest Group, AFAANZ Conference presentation, Melbourne, July 2005.

88. CPA Australia was formed as the Australian Society of Accountants in 1952 from a merger of several professional accounting societies, the oldest of which, the Incorporated Institute of Accountants, was formed in 1886, www.cpaaustralia.com.au. Both the Institute of Accountants in Edinburgh and the Institute of Accountants in Glasgow were formed in 1853, www.icaew.com.

89. A Companies Act termed the 'accountants friend' is passed in 1862. The Act establishes the role of Official Liquidator, a person responsible for proceedings in the liquidation of public companies, the act creates a large source of revenue for accountants. Another Companies Act is passed in 1867, www.icaew.com.

90. RL Watts and J Zimmerman, 'Agency problems, auditing, and the theory of the firm: some evidence', *Journal of Law and Economics*, vol. 26, no. 3, October 1983, pp. 613–33.

91. AICPA 2002, *A brief history of selfregulation: the Enron Crisis: the AICPA, the profession and the public interest*, 20 February, http://thecaq.aicpa.org.

92. ibid.

93. Report from the Chairman of the Auditing and Assurance Standards Board, Bulletin of the FRC 2005/2, 8 April, www.frc.gov.au.

94. R Simnett, 'A critique of the International Auditing and Assurance Standards Board', *Australian Accounting Review*, vol. 17, no. 2, July 2007, pp. 28, 29–36.

95. Public Interest Oversight Board 2009, www.ipiob.org.

96. J Francis, I Khurana, and R Pereira, 'The role of accounting and auditing in corporate governance and the development of financial markets around the world', *Asia-Pacific Journal of Accounting and Economics*, vol. 10, no. 1, 2003, pp. 1–30.

Part 2

Theory and accounting practice

4 A conceptual framework   93
5 Measurement theory   133
6 Accounting measurement systems   161
7 Assets   227
8 Liabilities and owners' equity   257
9 Revenue   291
10 Expenses   329

4

A conceptual framework

After reading this chapter, you should have an appreciation of the following:

1 the role of a conceptual framework

2 the objectives of a conceptual framework

3 developing a conceptual framework

4 a critique of conceptual framework projects

5 a conceptual framework for auditing standards.

Worldwide, accounting academics and standard setters alike have attempted to develop a conceptual framework that provides a definitive statement of the nature and purpose of financial accounting and reporting and which provides guidance for all accounting practice. Individual academics drove most of the early attempts. Their main aim was to provide a solid theoretical base to explain accounting and to make it logical for their students. Since the early 1980s, standard setters and professional accounting bodies have shown strong interest in the development of a conceptual framework to guide the preparation and presentation of general purpose financial reports in the public and private sectors.

Conceptual framework projects were carried out in the 1980s and early 1990s in the United States, Canada, the United Kingdom and Australia. The International Accounting Standards Board (IASB) issued its *Framework* in 1989. Progress on conceptual frameworks in all jurisdictions has been slow, with disagreement about their content and applicability. In particular, standard setters encountered difficulties when attempting to address fundamental issues relating to measurement. Political intervention also hampered development of conceptual frameworks. In the latter years of the 1990s, greater progress was made in promulgating individual standards than through development of the conceptual framework. This chapter describes the role and objectives of a conceptual framework. It provides an overview of development of conceptual frameworks by the IASB and in the United States by the Financial Accounting Standards Board (FASB).

The establishment of the IASB/FASB convergence project in 2002 rekindled interest in the conceptual framework. The process of harmonising accounting standards highlights the need for a robust framework to guide standard setters in the task of converging and developing new standards. Thus, in 2004 the IASB and FASB began a joint project to develop a single, complete and internally consistent conceptual framework. The structure of the project is outlined in this chapter. It is likely that the project will face many of the difficulties encountered in previous attempts to develop conceptual frameworks, which we also discuss in this chapter. In addition, many criticisms of conceptual frameworks have been presented. A discussion of these critiques concludes the chapter.

LO 1 THE ROLE OF A CONCEPTUAL FRAMEWORK

A conceptual framework of accounting aims to provide a structured theory of accounting. At its highest theoretical levels, it states the scope and objective of financial reporting. At the next fundamental conceptual level, it identifies and defines the qualitative characteristics of financial information (such as relevance, reliability, comparability, timeliness and understandability) and the basic elements of accounting (such as assets, liabilities, equity, revenue, expenses and profit). At the lower operational levels, the conceptual framework deals with principles and rules of recognition and measurement of the basic elements and the type of information to be displayed in financial reports. Figure 4.1 provides a diagrammatic representation of the possible components of a conceptual framework. The diagram, created by standard setters from Australia, shows the matters which are considered in the various levels of a conceptual framework.

It is often argued that there should be a 'scientific' methodology behind the framework for it to be legitimate. The scientific methodology applied to determine principles and rules of accounting measurement is assumed to be deduced from previously defined objectives and concepts. For example, the FASB has defined the conceptual framework as:

> . . . a coherent system of interrelated objectives and fundamentals that is expected to lead to consistent standards and that prescribes the nature, function and limits of financial accounting and reporting.[1]

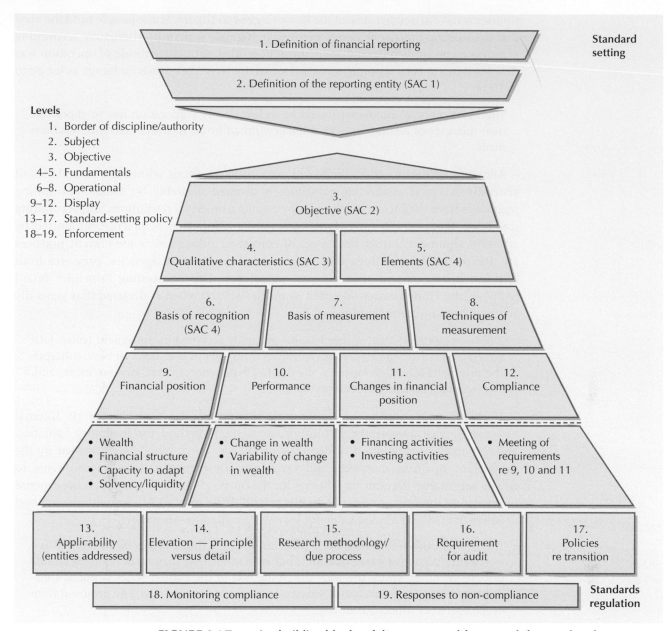

Levels
1. Border of discipline/authority
2. Subject
3. Objective
4–5. Fundamentals
6–8. Operational
9–12. Display
13–17. Standard-setting policy
18–19. Enforcement

Standard setting

1. Definition of financial reporting
2. Definition of the reporting entity (SAC 1)
3. Objective (SAC 2)
4. Qualitative characteristics (SAC 3)
5. Elements (SAC 4)
6. Basis of recognition (SAC 4)
7. Basis of measurement
8. Techniques of measurement
9. Financial position
10. Performance
11. Changes in financial position
12. Compliance

- Wealth
- Financial structure
- Capacity to adapt
- Solvency/liquidity

- Change in wealth
- Variability of change in wealth

- Financing activities
- Investing activities

- Meeting of requirements re 9, 10 and 11

13. Applicability (entities addressed)
14. Elevation — principle versus detail
15. Research methodology/ due process
16. Requirement for audit
17. Policies re transition

18. Monitoring compliance
19. Responses to non-compliance

Standards regulation

FIGURE 4.1 Tentative building blocks of the conceptual framework for regulated financial reporting

Source: Australian Accounting Research Foundation and Australian Accounting Standards Board, Statement of Accounting Concepts (SAC) 4 'Definition and Recognition of the Elements of Financial Statements', 1995.

Such words as 'coherent system' and 'consistent' indicate that the FASB advocates a theoretical and non-arbitrary framework, and the word 'prescribes' supports a normative approach.

Some accountants ask whether a conceptual framework is necessary. They argue that formulating a general theory of accounting through a conceptual framework is not necessary. We have not had a general theory of accounting in the past, so one is not necessary now. Although it is true that the profession has survived so far without a formally constructed theory, and could probably continue to do so, numerous problems have arisen because of the lack of a general theory. Some people hold the view that accounting practice is overly permissive because it permits alternative accounting practices to be applied to similar circumstances. This permissive mode of operation was described in a special report to a committee of the New York Stock Exchange as long ago as 1934:

> The more practical alternative would be to leave every corporation free to choose its own methods of accounting within the very broad limits to which reference has been made . . .[2]

Allowing entities to select their own accounting methods within the boundaries of generally accepted accounting principles is deemed desirable by some.[3] Accounting regulators have tried to establish order by issuing numerous resolutions and accounting standards. Some of the early regulations were a distillation of practice, supported by arbitrary arguments rather than a set of consistent principles. Some current practices are due to the direct influence of laws, rules of government agencies, pressures from business managers and even political expediency. The Accounting Principles Board (APB) in the United States admitted as much in 1970 when it declared that generally accepted accounting principles are:

> . . . conventional — that is, they become generally accepted by agreement (often tacit agreement) rather than by formal derivation from a set of postulates or basic concepts. The principles have developed on the basis of experience, reason, custom, usage, and, to a significant extent, practical necessity.[4]

There are many sources of authority in accounting. For example, the US Internal Revenue Service accepts the last-in-first-out (LIFO) method for inventory valuation and the accelerated method of depreciation; hence, the methods are accepted by the profession. Business managers and executives sometimes persuade accountants to devise 'acceptable' accounting schemes for the purpose of minimising their tax expense or increasing their reported profit. In this regard, Paton once took issue with the method of lower of cost and market value for inventory valuation. He said:

> The . . . enthusiasm for the device . . . was not a tribute to the merits of the scheme as a worthwhile accounting mechanism . . . but as an immediate method of reducing taxable income. In other words, the wide use of the rule in the United States is not as time-honoured as many think, and it waxed on account of considerations far removed from development of sound accounting.[5]

Inconsistency of practices has been seen as a problem. Gellein, a former member of both the APB and FASB, commented that because of the lack of a conceptual framework, 'Gresham's law sometimes takes over: bad practices at times triumph over good practices.'[6]

Before the conceptual framework debate, accounting standard setters followed the route of previous professional bodies in trying to provide answers to specific accounting questions. However, providing answers to particular problems presupposes a 'theory' which provides the basis for deriving these answers. Since no generally accepted theory of accounting exists, the recommendations of authoritative bodies can be viewed only as somewhat random solutions to pressing problems of the moment. On reviewing the history of formulating accounting principles, Storey concluded:

> The . . . solutions resulting from the play-it-by-ear approach have rarely turned out to be lasting solutions (even taking into consideration the dynamic nature of accounting) . . .[7]

Solomons argues that someone has to make a judgement about the type of accounting which is desirable. He argues against standards being set by inductive observation because the result of this process is that:

> A principle or practice would be declared to be 'right' because it was generally accepted; it would not be generally accepted because it was 'right'.[8]

Solomons also sees the conceptual framework as a defence against political interference in the neutrality of accounting reports. He notes that accounting policies can be implemented only by making a value judgement, but there is no way of proving that the value judgements of any individual or group are better for society than those of others. Thus, the provision of a 'coherent theoretical base' from which standards are derived provides a conceptual defence:

> If a standard setting body cannot show that its standards will lead to the production of information having the qualities and characteristics necessary to attain a defined accounting objective, it will have no defence against sectional interest that sees a standard as injurious to its welfare, for if a standard is not derived from a conceptual framework, how can it be shown that one standard is better than any other?[9]

The benefits of a conceptual framework have been summarised by Australian standard setters as follows:

(a) Reporting requirements will be more consistent and logical because they will stem from an orderly set of concepts.
(b) Avoidance of reporting requirements will be much more difficult because of the existence of all-embracing provisions.
(c) The boards that establish the requirements will be more accountable for their actions in that the thinking behind specific requirements will be more explicit, as will any compromises that may be included in particular accounting standards.
(d) The need for specific accounting standards will be reduced to those circumstances in which the appropriate application of concepts is not clear-cut, thus minimising the risks of over-regulation.
(e) Preparers and auditors will be able to better understand the financial reporting requirements they face.
(f) The setting of requirements will be more economical because issues should not need to be re-debated from differing viewpoints.[10]

LO 2 → OBJECTIVES OF CONCEPTUAL FRAMEWORKS

In 1978, the FASB Statement of Financial Accounting Concepts (SFAC) No. 1 (paragraph 34) stated the following basic objective of external financial reporting for business entities:

> Financial reporting should provide information that is useful to present and potential investors and creditors and other users in making rational investment, credit, and similar decisions.

Both the IASB and FASB frameworks consider the main objective of financial reporting is to communicate financial information to users. The information is to be selected on the basis of its usefulness in the economic decision-making process. This objective is seen to be achieved by reporting information that is:

- useful in making economic decisions
- useful in assessing cash flow prospects
- about enterprise resources, claims to those resources and changes in them.

In order to provide useful financial information, the accountant must choose which information to transmit. It therefore becomes necessary to develop a hierarchy of qualities which make information useful. Principal qualitative characteristics include: understandability to decision-makers, relevance, reliability and comparability (and aspects of those qualities such as materiality, faithful representation, substance over form, neutrality, prudence and completeness). The hierarchical arrangement of the qualitative characteristics presented in SFAC No. 2 is shown in figure 4.2.

SFAC No. 2 and the IASB *Framework* explain the qualitative characteristics. Understandability refers to the ability of information to be understood by users. Users are assumed to have a reasonable knowledge of business and economic activities and accounting, and a willingness to study the information with reasonable diligence. Information has the quality of relevance when it influences the economic decisions of users by helping them evaluate past, present or future events or confirming or correcting their past evaluations. To be reliable, financial information should faithfully represent transactions and events without material bias or error (IASB *Framework*, paragraphs 24–42).

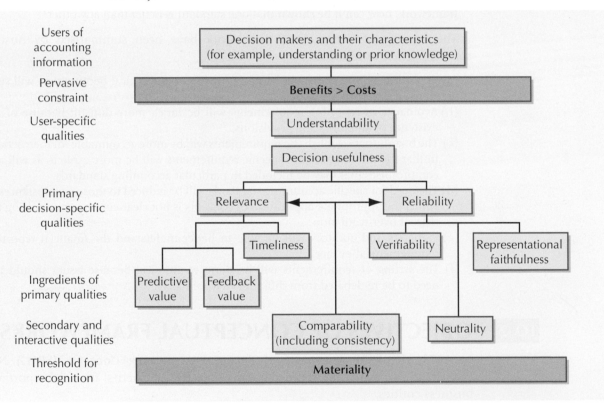

FIGURE 4.2 SFAC No. 2 Qualitative characteristics of accounting information

Source: FASB/IASB, 'Revisiting the concepts: A new conceptual framework project', diagram p. 4.

The IASB's *Framework* was developed following the lead of the United States standard setter, the FASB. In the period 1987–2000 the FASB issued seven concept statements covering the following topics:
- objectives of financial reporting by business enterprises and non-profit organisations
- qualitative characteristics of useful accounting information
- elements of financial statements
- criteria for recognising and measuring the elements
- use of cash flow and present value information in accounting measurements.

The IASB has just one concept statement, the *Framework for the Preparation and Presentation of Financial Statements*. It was issued by the International Accounting Standards Committee (IASC), the predecessor organisation to the IASB, in 1989 and subsequently adopted by the IASB in 2001. The *Framework* describes the basic concepts by which financial statements are prepared. It serves as a guide to the IASB in developing accounting standards and as a guide to resolving accounting issues that are not addressed directly in an International Accounting Standard (IAS) or International Financial Reporting Standard (IFRS) or Interpretation. The IASB states that the *Framework*:

- defines the objectives of financial statements
- identifies qualitative characteristics that make information in financial statements useful
- defines the basic elements of financial statements and the concepts for recognising and measuring them in financial statements. The framework acknowledges that a variety of measurement bases are used in financial reports (e.g. historical cost, current cost, net realisable value and present value) but it does not include principles for selecting measurement bases (paragraphs 1, 100, 101).

IAS 1 *Presentation of Financial Statements* and IAS 8 *Accounting Policies, Changes in Accounting Estimates and Errors* deal with the presentation of financial statements and make reference to the *Framework*. IAS 8 (paragraph 10) requires that in the absence of an IASB standard or interpretation that specifically applies to a transaction, other event or condition, management must use its judgement in developing and applying an accounting policy that results in information that is:

- relevant to the economic decision making needs of users
- reliable, in that the financial statements:
  - (i) represent faithfully the financial position, financial performance and cash flows of the entity;
  - (ii) reflect the economic substance of transactions, other events and conditions, and not merely the legal form;
  - (iii) are neutral, i.e. free from bias;
  - (iv) are prudent; and
  - (v) are complete in all material respects.

IAS 8 (paragraph 11) provides a 'hierarchy' of accounting pronouncements. It requires that in making the judgement required in paragraph 10

management shall refer to, and consider the applicability of, the following sources, in descending order:
- the requirements and guidance in Standards and Interpretations dealing with similar and related issues; and
- the definitions, recognition criteria and measurement concepts for assets, liabilities, income and expenses in the *Framework*.

This statement articulates the relationship of the *Framework*, the standards and interpretations of the standards. It also makes material in the *Framework* binding on preparers. Consequently, the development of the revised framework is being closely scrutinised by constituents. Deliberations about its content are being and will be subject to the political process which accompanies standard setting.

Since the *Framework* was issued in 1989 many new standards have been issued, including standards that conflict with the *Framework*. For example, Bradbury outlines many inconsistencies between IAS 39 *Financial Instruments: Recognition and Measurement* and the *Framework*.[11] They arose because of the demand for a standard to be part of the set of core standards presented to the International Organization of Securities

Commissions (IOSCO) in 2000, the complexity of accounting for financial instruments, the incompleteness of the *Framework*, and the lack of acceptance of a *Framework* based solution by preparers. Areas where the *Framework* provides inadequate guidance include accounting for derecognition of financial assets and hybrid financial instruments. Further, Bradbury suggests that the *Framework* ignores risk, one of the main attributes of financial instruments. Not only should *Framework* guide the standard setting process, it should also assist practitioners to interpret standards. Theory in action 4.1 explores whether the *Framework* appears to have assisted in deriving an interpretation, in this case IFRIC 3 (released by the International Financial Reporting Interpretations Committee), which relates to emissions trading.

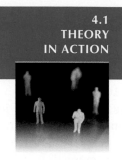

**4.1
THEORY
IN ACTION**

IFRIC 3 and Emissions Trading

Accounting for carbons

by Georgina Dellaportas, ICAA

Development of IFRIC 3
Cap-and-trade schemes have been in operation in Europe for a number of years. In December 2004, the International Accounting Standards Board (IASB) issued IFRIC 3 Emission Rights to address accounting for emission rights arising from such schemes. However, the interpretation met with significant resistance on the basis that it resulted in accounting mismatches between the valuation of assets and liabilities leading to potential volatility in the profit and loss. Consequently, the IASB decided to withdraw the Interpretation in June 2005 despite the fact that it continued to consider it to be an appropriate interpretation of existing IFRS.

Possible approaches
Until definitive guidance on accounting for cap-and-trade emission rights schemes is issued, an entity has the option of either:
* applying the principles of IFRIC 3 (UIG 3 in Australia); or
* developing its own accounting policy for cap-and-trade schemes based on the hierarchy of authoritative guidance in IAS 8/AASB 108 *Accounting Policies, Changes in Accounting Estimates and Errors*.

IFRIC 3 approach
IFRIC 3 takes the view that a cap-and-trade scheme gives rise to various items that are to be accounted for separately:
(1) *An asset for allowances held:* allowances, whether allocated by government or purchased, are to be accounted for as intangible assets under IAS 38/AASB 138 *Intangible Assets*. Allowances issued for less than fair value are to be measured initially at their fair value. On a go-forward basis, entities have the choice to carry the intangibles at cost or at fair value (to the extent that there exists an active market for the allowances).
(2) *A government grant:* this arises when allowances are granted for less than fair value and represents the differential between the fair value and the nominal amount paid. The grant is accounted for under AASB 120 *Accounting for Government Grants* and is recognised as deferred income in the balance sheet and subsequently recognised as income on a systematic basis over the compliance period for which the allowances are issued regardless of whether the allowances are held or sold.
(3) *A liability for the obligation to deliver allowances equal to emissions that have been made:* as emissions are made, a liability is recognised as a provision under IAS 37/AASB 137 Provisions, Contingent Liabilities and Contingent Assets. The liability is the best estimate of the expenditure required to settle the obligation at the balance sheet date. This would usually be the present market price of the number of allowances required to cover the emissions made up to the balance sheet date.

The application of IFRIC 3 met with significant resistance on the basis that it results in the following accounting mismatches:

- a measurement mismatch between the assets and liabilities recognised
- a mismatch in the location in which the gains and losses on those assets are reported; for example, to the extent that the intangibles are carried at fair value any upward revaluation would be recognised in equity while changes in the liability would be charged to the income statement
- a possible timing mismatch as allowances would be recognised when they are obtained, typically at the start of the year, whereas the emission liability would be recognised during the year as it is incurred.

Given these mismatches, very few overseas companies in countries where such schemes exist have applied IFRIC 3 on a voluntary basis.

Source: An excerpt from an article by Georgina Dellaportas, CA, *Charter* magazine, June 2008. The Institute of Chartered Accountants in Australia.

Questions
1. What would be the likely impact of the 'mismatch' arising under IFRIC 3?
2. To what extent is 'matching' a principle proposed by the IASB *Framework*?
3. In what ways can you see the influence of the IASB *Framework* on IFRIC 3?
4. In relation to IFRIC 3, do you consider that the IASB *Framework* provides a 'theory of accounting' That is, does the *Framework* explain and predict accounting practice?

LO 3 DEVELOPING A CONCEPTUAL FRAMEWORK

The development of conceptual frameworks is influenced by the following key issues, which we will discuss in detail:

- principles versus rules-based approaches to standard setting
- information for decision making and the decision-theory approach.

Principles-based and rule-based standard setting

Conceptual frameworks have an important role in the standard setting process as they provide a framework for the development of a body of coherent standards based on consistent principles. The IASB aims to produce principles-based standards and thus it looks to the conceptual framework for guidance. It represents the basic ideas which underpin the development of the standards and assist users in their interpretation of the standards. While the IASB aims to be a principles-based standard setter, standards such as IAS 39 have been criticised as being overly rule-based. Nobes suggests that the reasons standards become rules-based is that they are inconsistent with the conceptual frameworks of standard setters. He argues that the use of appropriate principles could lead to clearer communication and more precision without the need for detailed rules currently included in standards.[12]

Nobes identifies six examples where IASB standards have detailed technical rules, namely lease accounting, employee benefits, financial assets, government grants, subsidiaries and equity accounting. He argues that the need for rules results from lack of principles or use of an inappropriate principle (i.e. one that is inconsistent with higher level principles applicable in the standard). However, rule-based standards have some advantages which explain their popularity. These include increased comparability and increased verifiability for auditors and regulators. Rule-based standards may reduce the opportunities for earnings management; however they allow for the specific structuring of transactions to work around the rules.[13] Determining principles-based standards is not a simple matter. The issues are illustrated in relation to lease accounting in theory in action 4.2.

Arbitrary and Capricious Rules: Lease Accounting — FAS 13 v. IAS 17 Op/Ed

by J Edward Ketz

One of the main arguments against a rules-based accounting standards-setting system is that resulting rules are sometimes arbitrary; correspondingly, proponents of principles-based accounting claim that resulting standards will not be arbitrary, but rather logical, consistent, transparent, and informative to financial statement users. Lease accounting is often presented as an exemplar of this point. Since the IASB standards are purportedly principles-based, let's compare the FASB rule against the international accounting rule — er, principle — and look at the differences. FAS 13 versus IAS 17.

IAS 17 classifies leases as finance leases or operating leases, but this is mere words. Finance leases correspond to the Financial Accounting Standards Board's capital leases. There are five criteria for determining whether a lease is a finance lease; they are:

- The lease transfers ownership to the lessee;
- The lease contains a bargain purchase option to purchase that is expected to be exercised;
- The lease is for the major part of the economic life of the asset;
- The present value of the minimum lease payments amounts to substantially all of the fair value of the leased asset;
- Only the lessee can use the leased asset.

The first four criteria correspond strongly with those of FASB; the last one is also contained in FAS 13 even though it is not specifically included as one of the criterion to determine whether a lease is a capital lease.

Critics are correct inasmuch as FASB included bright lines in criteria 3 and 4 (the 75 percent and the 90 percent thresholds), whereas IASB did not. One wonders, however, whether that change eliminates or enhances arbitrariness in financial reporting. True, FASB chose thresholds that cannot be defended while IASB does not contain them. The upshot might be to move the threshold from the standard-setter to the preparer and the auditor, without the investor's being privy to the debate. For example, the preparer might have a lease in which the present value of the minimum lease payments amounts to (say) 95 percent of the fair value of the asset and argues for operating lease treatment. What power and authority does an auditor have to challenge that assertion?

Yes, FAS 13 contains bright lines that are inherently arbitrary, as no economic theory supports the 75 percent or the 90 percent thresholds. But, the lack of bright lines does not solve the issue at all — it merely shifts the decision about the threshold from the standard-setter to the preparer and to the auditor. This adds subjectivity to the determination of an appropriate cutoff point between what is a capital or an operating lease. Unfortunately, this reality places the decision in the hands of the one being evaluated by the investment community, and the last decade has shown us what happens when we entrust accounting policy making to managers.

To my way of thinking, the arbitrariness in FAS 13 is significantly less than the arbitrariness inherent in IAS 17. To say it another way, the transparency of FASB's arbitrariness to the investment community trumps the opaqueness of IASB's rule.

The present value of the lease is calculated with the interest rate implicit in the lease, if practicable; otherwise, the present value is determined with the business enterprise's incremental borrowing rate. Notice that IASB thereby allows financial engineering by the managers of the entity. Managers can argue that they do not know and cannot find out the implicit rate, obtain a lower present value of the leased item, and then be in a better position to argue that the lease is an operating lease. IASB's position conceptually is no better than FASB's on this point.

IASB defines assets and liabilities as follow:

An asset is a resource controlled by the entity as a result of past events and from which future economic benefits are expected to flow to the entity.

A liability is a present obligation of the entity arising from past events, the settlement of which is expected to result in an outflow from the entity of resources embodying economic benefits.

These definitions are not substantially different from FASB's definitions. Most importantly, notice that if one is truly principled, he or she must conclude that leased items are assets and lease obligations are liabilities. There is no room for operating leases if managers or auditors are adhering to the principles imbedded in the definitions that IASB gives assets and liabilities.

Both FASB and IASB have ignored their own conceptual frameworks in FAS 13 and IAS 17. Under both sets of definitions, leased items are assets and lease obligations are liabilities. The only logical conclusion for FASB and IASB is to require capitalization of all leases.

When American corporations are allowed to employ international rules, as seems highly probably, then U.S. managers will have a field day in hiding their lease obligations, assuming IASB doesn't have the courage to amend IAS 17. Justice will come when class action suits will be filed against the managers and directors of such companies and perhaps their auditors as well. When the plaintiffs' attorneys read these IASB definitions and note that the managers did not follow the principles in these definitions, they will go a long way in proving the defendants' intent to deceive. Europeans may quash legal redresses on their continent, but American courts are not so easy to intimidate.

FAS 13 is one of the most deficient standards ever issued by FASB. Yet, IAS 17 contains most of the same errors and shortcomings. Its only improvement — removal of the bright lines — is actually a detriment because it assists managers in their efforts to obfuscate meaningful communications with investors and creditors. If that's the best example of principles-based accounting, give me rules any day.

Source: SmartPros © 2008 SmartPros Ltd. All Rights Reserved, http://accounting.smartpros.com.

Questions

1. What are the criteria in IASB and FASB standards for classifying a lease as a finance lease?
2. What is meant by 'bright lines' in accounting standards? Give examples of the 'bright lines' in US leasing standards.
3. Mr Ketz does not believe the IASB approach of principles-based standards will be effective for leases. Provide details of the arguments he presents in favour of his case and consider the alternative view.
4. Do accounting practices under current IASB leasing standards comply with the definition and recognition criteria of the IASB *Framework*?

The accounting standards of the United States have often been described as rule-based standards because they contain many detailed requirements in relation to treatments which must be followed to comply with the accounting standards. Schipper points out that in fact United States' standards are initially formed in relation to principles, which represent a starting point on which the rules are based.[14] In 2002 the Sarbanes-Oxley Act required the United States regulator (the Securities and Exchange Commission or SEC) to conduct a study of the use of principles in the standard setting process. The study recommended that accounting standards be developed using a principles-based approach and that standards should have the following characteristics.

- Be based on an improved and consistently applied conceptual framework.
- Clearly state the objective of the standard.
- Provide sufficient detail and structure that the standard can be operationalised and applied on a consistent basis.
- Minimise the use of exceptions from the standards.
- Avoid use of percentage tests (bright lines) that allow financial engineers to achieve technical compliance with the standards while evading the intent of the standard.[15]

The greater emphasis on the conceptual framework, principles and objectives arises from events in 2001–2002 in the United States. It follows the corporate collapses at Enron and WorldCom, which have been blamed in part on the rule-based approach taken in preparation of financial statements. The Sarbanes-Oxley Act 2002 introduced many changes to improve the quality of financial reporting and auditing. This overhaul of financial reporting regulation also changed the approach to standard setting. Establishing a principles-based approach as a FASB objective is timely in terms of the IASB/FASB convergence program. The production of converged standards by the IASB and FASB demands that the approach to developing the standards is the same. A lack of the same underlying approach would make converging standards and producing standards for use in both jurisdictions more difficult. Thus, the SEC decision to refer to objectives in the production of standards is necessary and timely in terms of international convergence of accounting standards.

One of the reasons for the preponderance of rules in standards in the United States was that SEC staff requested rules from FASB to use in interpreting accounting standards. One role of SEC staff is to determine whether companies have complied with the financial reporting requirements contained in accounting standards. However, the interpretation of accounting standards may require skill and judgement, particularly where the standards refer more to principles and rely less on rules. In some cases, two different experts (such as auditors from the 'Big 4' audit firms) could interpret the requirements of an accounting standard differently. The SEC has in the past requested rules from the FASB to clarify how accounting standards should be interpreted to ensure compliance with standards. Auditors have sought guidance in the form of rules to protect them from litigation.[16] Rules assist reporting entities to apply the requirements of accounting standards in the same way, thus increasing the comparability of financial reporting. While both the FASB and SEC have supported the emphasis on producing standard based on principles and objectives, they operate in an environment where many rules exist and listed companies, auditors and the SEC staff are used to having rules to follow. Consequently, Zeff raises the question whether US standards will become any shorter or less detailed and whether SEC staff will become less insistent on company compliance with detailed norms. He points out that highly specific and prescriptive standards are part of the United States accounting culture and cultural change is not easily achieved.[17] The depth and complexity of GAAP has led the IASB to produce a standard for small and medium enterprises (IFRS for SMEs) that can be used by entities for which compliance with the full set of IFRS is not cost effective. Case study 4.1 allows students to explore the benefits of IFRS for SMEs.

Information for decision making and the decision-theory approach

It is widely accepted that accounting data are for decision making or evaluative purposes in relation to a specific entity. Accounting information for decision making begins with the stewardship function. In earlier times, the steward in charge of the estate had to account to the master. In Pacioli's era, an accounting had to be made to the 'silent' partners after a venture was completed. Today, managers are accountable to the equityholders of the company. Those who supply the capital to a business want to know what the stewards, or managers, have done with the economic resources entrusted to them. The information on how managers have discharged their stewardship responsibility is used by the equityholders to evaluate the performances of the managers and the firm.

Since the early 1960s, emphasis has been placed on the decision-making aspects of accounting information. For example, Moonitz stated:

> Quantitative data are helpful in making rational economic decisions, i.e. . . . in making choices among alternatives so that actions are correctly related to consequences.[18]

One reason for this emphasis was, perhaps, the development of decision theory. Information for decision making, however, is not seen to replace information relating to stewardship or accountability. Information for decision making implies more than information on stewardship. First, the users of financial information are greatly expanded to include all resource providers (such as potential investors and creditors), recipients of goods and services and parties performing a review or oversight function (*Framework*, paragraph 9). Second, accounting information is seen as input data for the prediction models of users. We must, therefore, ask the question: What kind of accounting information is relevant to users' predictions of future performance and position? Third, whereas stewardship is concerned mainly with the past in order to assess what has been accomplished, prediction looks towards the future. Accounting information for external users is, of course, based on past events, but the future cannot be ignored when decision making is emphatically stated as the objective of accounting.

For many, the emphasis on decision making strongly implies the use of current values. If it were possible, users would prefer to have actual information about the future events affecting the company. However, we can only predict these events. As they have not yet occurred, future events and values are not objective and cannot serve as a reliable basis for decision making. For many accountants, current value is the most relevant value for decision making because the present is closest to the future and still grounded in reality. However, advocates of conventional accounting believe that historical cost is still relevant for decision making.

The decision-theory approach to accounting is helpful to test whether accounting achieves its purposes. The theory should serve as a standard by which accounting practices are judged. In other words, it should be the 'blueprint' for the construction of the many individual systems in practice. If the individual systems provide useful information, then the theory on which the systems are based can be considered effective or valid. The process is presented in figure 4.3. The arrows indicate the output of the theory, system or model.

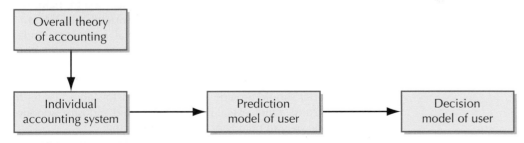

FIGURE 4.3 The decision-theory process

The model maps the process by which the outputs of the accounting system provide inputs to the decision model of the user. Financial information may have a wider range of users. For example, the IASB *Framework* includes investors, employees, lenders, suppliers and trade creditors, customers, governments and their agencies, and the public as potential users (paragraph 9). The *Framework* further states that users have different information needs, some of which will not be met by accounting information (paragraphs 6–11). Thus as we evaluate the output of accounting systems, we must consider the extent to which information is useful for a range of decision makers. Theory in action 4.3 explores a situation where preparers were dissatisfied with performance measures based on accounting standards. They provided other measures (of 'underlying earnings') which they considered better to meet users' information needs.

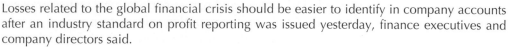

Guidelines for reporting 'proforma' earnings

Mind the gap: AICD, Finsia set guidelines

by Marsha Jacobs

Losses related to the global financial crisis should be easier to identify in company accounts after an industry standard on profit reporting was issued yesterday, finance executives and company directors said.

The Financial Services Institute of Australasia (Finsia) and the Australian Institute of Company Directors (AICD) issued voluntary guidelines outlining seven key principles for reporting underlying profit, which they said would lead to more consistent reporting and give investors a better understanding of company performance.

The issue of underlying profit was elevated last year after a long list of major companies, including Lend Lease, Axa Asia Pacific, Foster's Group, Newcrest Mining and St George Bank, reported huge differences between their statutory and underlying profit figures.

Underlying profit normally excludes one-off items or unusual adjustments and is considered by media and analysts as a better indicator of a company's performance.

However, the calculation of underlying profit is not done using the same strict accounting rules as the statutory profit figure, allowing greater opportunity for malleability in the underlying profit figure.

John Colvin, chief executive of AICD, said directors were encouraged to follow the principles 'so that any references to underlying profit are easily understood, consistent and any potential controversies over one-off adjustments are limited, particularly given the scrutiny of results announcements in the current economic environment.

"These principles are designed to both promote good reporting practices, and also to discourage any poor practices, such as inappropriate adjustments to statutory profits or window dressing," Mr Colvin said.

KPMG director Michael Coleman, who is the chairman of the AICD reporting committee, said directors were concerned that statutory results did not focus on the same issues that directors were focused on in a company.

He said directors were more and more concerned to make sure shareholders had a good level of understanding about what is actually driving a business.

"With greater use of international financial reporting standards, greater use of market value accounting, greater focus on impairment of assets and write-downs of goodwill, many directors believed a statutory result was not a proper reflection of what the underlying nature of the business was," Mr Colvin said.

"The paper should provide guidance to directors about issues they should consider."

Martin Fahy, chief executive of Finsia, said industry adoption of the principles would improve the overall quality of company reporting.

"Too often, analysts contend with contradictory and opportune adjustments to statutory profit figures from one reporting period to the next," Dr Fahy said. "These principles establish a new benchmark for companies to clearly articulate the adjustments made in calculating an underlying profit figure."

Source: The Australian Financial Review, 10 March 2009, p. 11.

Questions

1. According to the article, what is meant by 'underlying profit'? How does underlying profit differ from statutory profit?
2. Why did the AICD and Finsia release guidelines about reporting underlying profit?

3. According to the article, why do some directors consider that statutory profit is not a 'proper reflection' of the underlying business? Explain whether you agree with the directors' view.
4. Discuss whether the actions of (a) directors in releasing an underlying profit figure and (b) the AICD/Finsia guidelines are supportive of the IASB/FASB's conceptual framework project.

Dean and Clarke describe many issues that are relevant to understanding why the development of conceptual frameworks at a national level has been problematic.[19] The authors argue that development of conceptual frameworks has been more a search for a rationale for current practice than a re-affirmation of the legal, social and economic framework within which accounting is to function. They suggest that current conceptual framework projects have sought to develop a constitution-based framework for accounting, instead of focusing on concepts underpinning ordinary, everyday commerce. This analysis is highly relevant to international standard setting. It will be difficult to obtain support for a framework that departs from existing practice, and difficult to determine a framework to represent practice, when this differs between countries.

International convergence of accounting standards and adoption of IASB standards in the European Union, Australia and many other countries has increased the importance of the IASB. Ironically, it has also made standard setting more difficult for the IASB as many parties are now actively concerned about the content of accounting standards. In this environment, the conceptual framework that underpins the accounting standards becomes more important. Jones and Wolnizer suggest that the conceptual framework has a crucial role in stating the agreed scope, objectives, qualitative and measurement characteristics of accounting which influence standard setting.[20] Such a framework would assist the IASB to withstand the political pressures in the standard setting process. However, Jones and Wolnizer argue that convergence to the IASB *Framework* will mean that initiative and innovation in development of conceptual frameworks will decline as national setters no longer work independently on conceptual framework projects. As part of its convergence project with the FASB, the IASB has undertaken a project to revise its *Framework* which is discussed in the next section.

International developments: the IASB and FASB Conceptual Framework

In October 2004, the FASB and IASB added a joint project to their agendas to develop an improved, common conceptual framework. The revised framework will build on the existing IASB's and FASB's frameworks and consider developments subsequent to the issuance of those frameworks. The Boards state that such a framework is essential to fulfilling the Boards' goal of developing standards that are principles-based, internally consistent, and internationally converged. They maintain that such standards will lead to financial reporting that provides the information capital providers need to make decisions in their capacity as capital providers. The FASB states that the project will do the following:

1. Focus on changes in the environment since the original frameworks were issued, as well as omissions in the original frameworks, in order to efficiently and effectively improve, complete, and converge the existing frameworks.
2. Give priority to addressing and deliberating those issues within each phase that are likely to yield benefits to the Boards in the short term; that is, cross-cutting issues that affect a number of their projects for new or revised standards. Thus, work on several

phases of the project will be conducted simultaneously and the Boards expect to benefit from work being conducted on other projects.

3. Initially consider concepts applicable to private sector business entities. Later, the Boards will jointly consider the applicability of those concepts to private sector not-for-profit organisations. Representatives of public sector (governmental) standard-setting Boards are monitoring the project and, in some cases, considering the potential consequences of private sector deliberations for public sector entities.[21]

The boards are conducting the joint project in eight phases. Each of the first seven phases will address and involve planning, research, initial Board deliberations, public comment, and redeliberations on major aspects of the Boards' frameworks. The phases are shown in figure 4.4.

Phase	Topic
A	Objective and Qualitative Characteristics
B	Elements and Recognition
C	Measurement
D	Reporting Entity
E	Presentation and Disclosure, including Financial Reporting Boundaries (Inactive)
F	Framework Purpose and Status in GAAP Hierarchy (Inactive)
G	Applicability to the Not-for-Profit Sector (Inactive)
H	Remaining Issues (Inactive)

FIGURE 4.4 IASB/FASB Conceptual Framework Project

Source: Conceptual Framework — Joint Project of the IASB and FASB, project information page, www.fasb.org.

For each phase, the Boards plan to issue documents that will seek comments from the public on the Boards' tentative decisions. The Boards will consider these comments and redeliberate their tentative decisions. While the Boards plan to seek comments on each phase separately, they have not precluded seeking comments on several phases concurrently.[22] By 30 June 2009 the Boards had issued and received comments on an exposure draft (ED) relating to Phase A Objectives and Qualitative Characteristics. A discussion paper relating to Phase D Reporting Entity had been issued and work was continuing on Phase B Elements and Recognition and Phase C Measurement.

The decision to defer consideration of not-for-profit sector issues has been contentious. In countries such as Australia and New Zealand, which follow a 'sector-neutral' approach to standard-setting issues relating to the not-for-profit sector need to be addressed at the same time the concepts are developed for the for-profit sector. (A sector-neutral approach means that the same standards are applied in the public, not-for-profit and private sectors). Feedback from national standard setters (from Australia, New Zealand, Canada and the UK) has suggested three areas where current Board deliberations raise issues for the not-for-profit sector.

They are:
- an insufficient emphasis on accountability and stewardship
- a need to broaden identified users and establish an alternative primary user group
- the inappropriateness of the pervasive cash flow focus.[23]

McGregor and Street[24] state that the IASB has some sympathy for the arguments advanced by constituents. However, extending the scope of the conceptual framework project at this time to include not-for-profit entities will increase the work load of the Boards and expose the project to the risks of further time delays and greater difficulty in reaching decisions. In an interesting development, which challenges the IASB's focus on the for-profit sector, the IFAC's International Public Sector Accounting Standards Board (IPSASB) has began a project to develop a conceptual framework for the public sector entities. The objective of the project is to develop a Public Sector Conceptual Framework which is applicable to the preparation and presentation of general purpose financial reports of public sector entities. A discussion paper was released in September 2008.[25] Case study 4.2 at the end of this chapter focuses on financial reporting in the not-for-profit sector. Specifically, it allows students to consider the quality of financial reporting in this sector using reporting guidelines proposed by a professional accounting body (the Institute of Chartered Accountants in Australia, or ICAA).

Comments on the Phase A exposure draft (ED) identify several key issues for stakeholders. Whittington[26] states that these issues were considered to be uncontroversial, but this has not proved to be the case. The ED discussion adds to material in the existing IASB *Framework* (i.e. its form and argument) and brings it under the scrutiny of stakeholders who were not involved in the development of the 1989 *Framework*. Controversial matters include the perspective underlying financial reporting (entity vs proprietorship), the primary user group and the objective of financial reporting, and the qualitative characteristics of financial reporting. Each of these issues is discussed below.[27]

Entity vs proprietorship perspective

As discussed later in this book, the entity and proprietorship perspectives represent different approaches to financial reporting. The Boards recommended that financial reports should be prepared from the perspective of the entity rather than the perspective of the owners or a particular class of owners. Many respondents agreed that the entity is distinct from its owners and thus concurred with reporting from the perspective of the entity. Others noted that the notion of reports being produced from an entity perspective was being introduced for the first time (i.e. it was not part of previous frameworks) and that the boards did not provide enough information to justify the choice of the entity perspective over other perspectives (such as the proprietorship and parent company perspectives). The perspective adopted is important as it affects work in Phase D, Reporting entity, where alternative perspectives are under discussion.[28]

Primary user group

The Boards proposed that the primary user group for general purpose financial reporting is present and potential capital providers. Most respondents agreed with the Boards' approach that present and potential capital providers (equity investors, lenders and other creditors) of the entity are the primary user group. However, it was noted that having a diverse primary group could oversimplify the relationship between the entity and individual users. Other respondents were concerned about the focus on a primary user group and the effect this could have on recognition of needs of other parties, such as charities and corporate governance monitoring groups.

Decision usefulness and stewardship

According to the Boards, the objective of financial reporting should be 'broad enough to encompass all the decisions that equity investors, lenders, and other creditors make in their capacity as capital providers, including resource allocation decisions as well as decisions made to protect and enhance their investments'.[29] Many respondents agreed with the Boards' view. However, many other respondents were concerned that the objective of stewardship is not sufficiently emphasised, while the role of financial statements in providing information to enable users to forecast future cash flows is overemphasised. For example, a group representing European national standard setters produced a report specifically addressing stewardship/accountabilty as an objective and concluded that there is broad consensus in support of stewardship/accountability as a separate objective of financial reporting.[30]

Whittington considers that the objective of stewardship has been 'sidelined' in the ED and notes that this is not acceptable to many constituents, particularly in Europe, where stewardship is a key part of corporate governance and company regulation.[31] He states that stewardship has been subsumed into the decision usefulness objective in the ED. However, it can be argued (and was argued by some IASB Board members during discussions of the issue) that accountability entails more than the prediction of cash flows and that stewardship is about monitoring the past as well as predicting the future cash flows. It may be as much concerned with integrity of management as with economic performance.

Qualitative characteristics

The IASB *Framework* includes four principal qualitative characteristics, namely understandability, relevance, reliability and comparability (paragraphs 24-42). The exposure draft proposes that the qualitative characteristics that make information useful are relevance, faithful representation, comparability, verifiability, timeliness and understandability; and that the pervasive constraints on financial reporting are materiality and cost. The qualitative characteristics are distinguished as either fundamental (relevance, faithful representation) or enhancing (comparability, verifiability, timeliness and understandability), depending on how they affect the usefulness of information.

Nearly every respondent commenting on the ED agreed that relevance is a fundamental characteristic. A majority agree in relation to faithful representation, but suggested the Boards have not adequately justified replacing reliability with faithful representation and that the terms have different meanings. Whittington notes that the 1989 *Framework* allowed for a trade off between relevance and reliability but the ED fails to acknowledge that relevance and faithful representation are relative not absolute properties of accounting information.[32] He considers that this approach has implications for practice: relevance will be considered first, followed by representational faithfulness, rather than allowing for a trade-off which recognises the relative importance, in the particular situation, of the each characteristic. Penno argues that an accounting conceptual framework must acknowledge the necessity of what he describes as 'vagueness' in its terms.[33] The difficulty in capturing concepts in the terms used in the *Framework* and the implications which follow from the use of particular terms is well-illustrated in the following IASB discussion about reliability and faithful representation:

> Although some Board members were cautious about losing the term 'reliable' from the general IFRS lexicon, other Board members and IASB senior staff noted that 'reliable' was one of the most problematic terms in that lexicon. Some used it to imply precision; others used it as an excuse to avoid recognising liabilities; others to imply verifiability. The Board concluded that the only way to avoid this misuse and the consequent miscommunication was to focus on what the *Framework* was trying to communicate was to use a different term. 'Faithful representation' was perhaps not the ideal term, but it was the best they had.[34]

Not surprisingly, many people suggested changes to the qualitative characteristics listed in the ED. Respondents suggested that understandability and verifiability be elevated, as well as the addition of prudence or concepts such as substance over form, true and fair view, and transparency. The ED rejects the concept of prudence as inconsistent with neutrality (which is freedom from bias). Some constituents, for whom stewardship is an important objective, may be uncomfortable with removing prudence. Whittington queries the removal of prudence as a qualitative characteristic because of its importance in restraining managerial opportunism.[35] In addition, he claims the concept is still actively used by the IASB, for example in a recent standard IAS 36 *Impairment* (i.e. recognise impairment losses but not increases in asset values).

The boards are continuing their work on Phase B and Phase C Measurement. In relation to Phase B, the existing definition of the elements of financial reporting (assets, liabilities, equity, revenue and expense) are being modified and new recognition criteria are being proposed.[36]

As noted earlier, prior conceptual frameworks have struggled to deal effectively with the issue of measurement. For the same reasons, Phase D will be controversial. Whittington notes that given the current reality of financial reporting, the pursuit of one universal measurement method may be fruitless.[37] He suggests that a more appropriate approach could be to define a clear measurement objective and to select the measurement method that best meets that objective in the particular circumstances that exist in relation to each item in the accounts.

The IASB and FASB need to make progress on the conceptual framework as it is fundamental to developing standards and it underpins convergence efforts. Case study 4.3 at the end of this chapter provides an opportunity to consider further the issues raised in this chapter in relation to the IASB/FASB conceptual framework project. The boards need some measure of consensus and support about objectives of financial reporting and qualitative characteristics of financial information to be able to issue framework chapters that are acceptable to constituents. Feedback comments represent many individual perspectives and views about key attributes of information, which relate back to individual views about the purpose of accounting information. We have seen that stakeholders are making their views known through the consultation process. The project has many challenges ahead and it is a test of whether parties can set aside individual differences to achieve the goal of harmonisation of financial reporting.

LO 4 → A CRITIQUE OF CONCEPTUAL FRAMEWORK PROJECTS

The development of conceptual frameworks met with criticisms in the United States, Australia and elsewhere. An analysis of the criticisms will help explain reasons for the previous slow development of the frameworks and highlight issues relevant to achieving progress in the current IASB/FASB project.

There are two approaches we can use in our analysis. The first is to assume that the conceptual framework should be a 'scientific' approach based on the methods used in other areas of scientific inquiry. Accounting prescriptions or observations arising from such an approach must justify their validity by recourse to logic and empiricism, or both. The second is a professional approach which concentrates on prescribing the 'best' course of action by recourse to 'professional values'. This is similar to a constitutional approach to rule setting.

We will discuss two broad areas in our analysis:
• scientific criticisms
• descriptive and non-operational.

In all questions of accounting standard setting or debate on accounting principles we find ourselves asking the same basic questions: What is value? How do we value the basic elements of accounting such as assets and liabilities? One purpose of a conceptual framework is to answer such questions, thereby avoiding repetitious arguments over the meaning of such terms. Prior agreement on these fundamentals should minimise inconsistencies and inequities arising from differences in judgement. Given the order and efficiency of this approach — where terms are previously defined and agreed upon and concepts fit together like building blocks — it is clear that the conceptual framework is intended as a fundamentally prescriptive project. The aim is to provide guidance and prescriptions to practising accountants on how to account for information which is relevant for economic decision making.

Within the FASB's conceptual framework project, it is on these crucial issues of recognition and measurement that dissension arose. The SFAC No. 5 on measurement and recognition problems, released in 1984, was basically a description of the elements of accounting reports based on the observation of current practice. By the time SFAC No. 5 was issued the Board's approach had become almost totally descriptive. Indeed Statement No. 5 shows that the aims and philosophy of the conceptual framework had been lost by the time it was issued. SFAC No. 5 states in several places (paragraphs 35, 51, 108), that concepts are to be developed as the standard setting process evolves. Such an evolution philosophy, which sees concepts as being the residual of the standard setting process, is in direct contradiction to the purpose of the conceptual framework.[38]

Further, Dopuch and Sunder consider that the definitions of the main elements of financial statements — assets, liabilities, owners' equity, revenues, expenses, gains and losses — depend on unspecified rules and conventions:

How can a conceptual framework guide choices from among alternative principles and rules if the elements of the framework are defined in these very same terms?[39]

Dopuch and Sunder argue that nothing in the FASB's conceptual framework seems to be of much help in resolving contemporary measurement and disclosure issues. They support this assertion by selecting three issues: deferred tax credits, treatment of costs of exploration in the oil and gas industry, and current value accounting. They conclude:

1. The definition of liabilities is so general that we are unable to predict the Board's position on deferred taxes;
2. The framework supports two opposing principles of accounting (full cost and successful efforts) and is preliminary evidence that the framework is unlikely to be a useful guide in resolving the measurement issue; and
3. It does not address the problem of estimation, on which past efforts to encourage publication of current costs have foundered.[40]

We can make similar criticisms of the IASB *Framework*. In this document, assets and liabilities are defined in very similar terms to those in the United States project. Not only is the definition of assets rather vague, but the recognition criteria are couched in terms of probability — a subjective concept. In addition, the recognition criterion fails to offer any guidance on the measurement problem, which is fundamental to accounting. Again the definition is open-ended and it appears that any measure would be acceptable as long as the cost or value can be 'reliably' measured. Recent work by the IASB/FASB in the conceptual framework project is addressing these criticisms.

Is it important, as it is in science, that prior agreement is reached on the precise definitions of the elements of accounting? Gerboth contends that real knowledge comes from investigation of the subject matter, not from prior agreement on definitions. He claims that to base an accounting framework solely on the limited understanding conveyed by such definitions would be irrational.[41]

In order to reinforce what Gerboth perceives to be the negligible role that definitions play in both human affairs and science, he quotes from Popper:

> In science, we should take care that the statements we make should never depend on the meaning of our terms. Even where the terms are defined, we never try to derive any information from the definition, or to base any argument upon it. That is why our terms make so little trouble. We do not overburden them. We try to attach to them as little weight as possible.[42]

This is not the approach of the conceptual framework projects. When they attempt to define 'assets', 'liabilities' and other elements, accounting regulators intend that the valuation decisions should depend on the definitions. Contrary to Popper, the FASB sought to make the definition bear as much weight as possible.[43]

Some argue that the attempt to base accounting practice on preconceived definitions risks a kind of mechanical decision making. Although a conceptual framework may provide a consistency in that it is efficient and orderly, it is a consistency of a trivial sort; consistency with an abstraction, not consistency with real ends. This trivial consistency is a direct consequence of dogmatism whereby pronouncements issued by the FASB, or other authoritative bodies, are accepted by the profession. This approach carries the danger that the framework may become an end in itself, consuming time and effort which may be better focused on filling the gaps in accountants' substantive knowledge. Definitions and prior agreement on the meaning of terms are important to the development of a consistent, interrelated and meaningful system. However, it is the over-reliance on definitions that Popper criticises. A contrary argument is that the conceptual framework is necessary and a common understanding of definitions is crucial to consistent preparation and interpretation of financial statements.

Ontological and epistemological assumptions

Throughout the conceptual framework projects, the focus has been to provide information to users of financial reports in an unbiased and objective manner. Freedom from bias, or neutrality, has been defined as 'an information quality that avoids leading users to conclusions that secure the particular needs, desires or preconceptions of the preparers'.[44] Solomons explains freedom from bias as 'financial mapmaking'. Accounting is financial mapmaking: the better the map, the more completely it represents the complex phenomena that are being mapped. We do not judge a map by the behavioural effects it produces. The distribution of natural wealth or rainfall shown on a map may lead to population shifts or changes in industrial location which the government may like or dislike. That should be no concern of the cartographer. We judge their map by how well it represents the facts. People can then react to it as they will.[45]

This philosophy of realism comes about in accounting from the assumption that we can observe, measure and communicate an objective economic reality. Some philosophers of science, for example Feyerabend, argue that scientific truth is not absolute — it refers only to a statement about a constructed reality. A given statement or belief warrants acceptance only after the evidence conforms with prescribed and agreed-upon rules about what is scientific methodology. Hines points out that the problem with the economic realism/measurement approach adopted by the conceptual framework project in the United States (and this applies to the IASB framework as well) is that within many scientific communities, reality is now viewed as being constructed and sustained by social practices, thereby polluting accountants' perceptions of economic reality.[46] In the social sciences, the undermining of the realism philosophy is even more complete. Within the social sciences, actors act in accordance with prevailing definitions and concepts of reality. By doing this, they maintain and perpetuate that reality.

> ... but we have not so much grasped reality, as created it, by thinking of it in a certain way, and treating it that way ... But when people have a preconceived notion of what reality is, well we can't afford to go against it! Why not?

> We are supposed to communicate reality in accounting. If people have a certain conception of reality, then naturally, we must reflect that. Otherwise people will lose faith in us.[47]

This makes it questionable whether theories forming the basis of a framework can ever be neutral, independent and free from bias. The extension of this argument is that a conceptual framework cannot provide a completely objective means of measuring economic reality since such a reality does not exist independent of accounting practices. Hines considers that it is a two-way interactive relationship in which financial accountants, by the process of measuring and communicating a picture of reality, play a critical role in deciding what is reality. Therefore, they create that reality.

Hines further claims that mainstream accounting research is based on 'taken-for-granted' commonsense conceptions and assumptions, which run counter to questions on how social reality arises and is maintained and legitimised. For example, conceptual frameworks avoid relying on deductive and empirical evidence for asserting their correctness. If they did take such an approach, generally accepted accounting principles would be deduced from the higher level beliefs, objectives and assumptions of the framework. Instead, the reverse seems to occur. These elements are held to be truths through an inductive process of deriving accounting principles which have never been formally tested against logic and empirical evidence. The 'authority' equivalent of science for the conceptual framework is traceable to the opinions of authoritative bodies and individuals. This is where science and accounting, as manifested in the conceptual framework, seem to diverge.

Further, the structure of conceptual framework projects bears some resemblance to a hypothetico-deductive approach. The hypothetico-deductive approach to scientific explanation has two main consequences. The first leads to universal laws or principles from which lower level hypotheses may be deduced. Secondly, there is a tight connection between explanation, prediction and the techniques applied. For example, the IASB and FASB conceptual frameworks have generalised assumptions and objectives from which principles (standards) and procedures (methods and rules) should be able to be deduced. The essential purpose of this approach to science is to arrive at an understanding of our environment in order to be able to operate more effectively in that environment. However, some authors disagree with this approach to science:

> ... accounting researchers believe in a (confused) notion of empirical testability. Despite this lack of clarity as to whether theories are 'verified' or 'falsified', there is widespread acceptance of Hempel's [1965] hypothetico-deductive account of what constitutes a 'scientific explanation'.[48]

This hypothetico-deductive approach influences the epistemological and methodological assumptions about 'tests of truth' and the manner in which most accounting research is undertaken. For example, emphasis is placed on large-scale sample surveys and empirical analyses using 'statistically sound techniques' and on deriving general theories. Assumptions are also made about behavioural characteristics (e.g. rational wealth maximisation and information needs of users, relating to future cash flows and current values) and about the way people relate to one another and to society. These approaches preclude, to some extent, research techniques which are individualistic and/or focus on case studies. As Horngren comments:

> Each person has characteristics that limit the usefulness of a conceptual framework ... Almost everyone says he or she wants a conceptual framework, but his or her conceptual framework may not be yours.[49]

Circularity of reasoning

As we have seen, one of the stated objectives of a conceptual framework is to guide the everyday practice of accountants. A superficial view of the conceptual frameworks indicates that accountants at least follow one scientific path — that of deducing principles and practice from generalised theory. However, various countries' existing conceptual frameworks are typified by an internal circularity. For example, within FASB Statement No. 2, information qualities such as reliability are stated to depend on the achievement of other qualities, such as representational faithfulness, neutrality and verifiability. However, these qualities, in turn, depend on other non-operationalised information qualities. For example, the discussion of neutrality relies on relevance, reliability and representational faithfulness, but the necessary and sufficient conditions for obtaining any of these qualities are not stated. The FASB framework attempts to break out of, or justify, this circularity of reasoning by referring to the notion of an informed accounting person who will have sufficient and appropriate knowledge to determine and interpret financial reports. However, it provides no specific guidance as to how this should be achieved.

An unscientific discipline

Is accounting a science? Conceptual frameworks may have attempted to adopt the deductive (scientific) approach, but this approach is questionable if accounting does not qualify as a science to begin with. Accounting has been variously described as an art or a craft in addition to its scientific description. In 1981, Stamp said:

> Until we are sure in our minds about the nature of accounting, it is fruitless for the profession to invest large resources in developing a conceptual framework to support accounting standards.[50]

Indeed, Stamp considers that accounting is more closely aligned to law than to the physical sciences, since both the accounting and legal professions deal with conflicts between different user groups with varying interests and objectives. He describes law as a normative discipline which is prescriptive in nature and full of value-laden concepts. Accounting faces imperfect markets and involves subjectively based, human decision-making processes. In contrast, the physical sciences are considered to be positive disciplines, descriptive in nature and characterised by value-free concepts.

Theoretical and empirical elements are somewhat loosely defined and applied in accounting, and it lacks a definitive scientific paradigm. Early (normative) accounting theory had many weaknesses. Positive accounting theory is still in its embryonic, possibly pre-scientific, stage. This does not necessarily indicate the lack of a scientific approach, however. Provided the theoretician is rigorous in applying the ontological, epistemological and methodological rules relating to the field of study, the scientific methodology may be said to be applied.

Positive research

It has been argued that the basic focus of the conceptual framework projects — providing financial information to help users make economic decisions — ignores the empirical findings of positive accounting research. Early market research has cast doubt on the ability of published accounting data to influence share prices and on the importance of accounting data for making economic decisions relating to the share market. Some argue that the share market does not appear to be fooled by creative accounting techniques, the valuation of assets and liabilities is not a real issue and that the market is relatively efficient in the semi-strong form. Furthermore, agency theory offers an explanation for the observation of many different accounting techniques. These accounting techniques are demanded by agents who seek to minimise monitoring costs in the most cost-efficient manner. The accounting technique of least cost will naturally vary between firms and industries and variation in accounting practice is therefore desirable. Nonetheless, for decisions with multiple choices, accounting information may be useful. This is an area that behavioural research has not yet fully considered.

Furthermore, those who argue that positive accounting research and a conceptual framework are in conflict sometimes ignore the mounting evidence that capital markets are not completely efficient. Even if they are efficient, the fact that the market responds immediately to information in financial reports does not mean that individuals process the information efficiently or that individuals or groups cannot make incorrect investment, lending, supply, or purchase decisions. If a conceptual framework could ensure that these people received useful information, it would serve a useful purpose.

The conceptual framework as a policy document

As a generalised body of knowledge, the conceptual frameworks fail a number of 'scientific' tests. Even if we argue that reality is merely a social construct anyway, there is no deductive process inherent in the frameworks to apply them to empirical phenomena in order to change the reality to a more preferred state in terms of assumed goals. Whether the frameworks can be considered completely normative models for accounting practice is also a problem, because accepted practice has been determined largely by adopting existing procedures which the frameworks attempt to legitimise.

An alternative to viewing the conceptual frameworks as either scientific or deductively derived normative models is to consider them as policy models. Ijiri differentiates between normative and policy models.[51] He says that a normative model is based on certain assumptions concerning the goals to be served; the researcher does not necessarily subscribe to the assumed goals. Thus, although a normative model has policy implications, it is different from a policy judgement, which involves a commitment to goals. Whether descriptive or normative, a model is a theory which can be scientifically verified. This is different from policy statements based on value judgements and opinions. Ijiri points out that theories and policies are intermingled in accounting, whereas in other empirical sciences the distinction is well established. For example, economic policies are treated quite differently from economic theories. In contrast, accounting theories always seem to be tied to policies.

Controversies among accounting theorists centre mainly on how accounting practices should be carried out — an issue that clearly belongs to accounting policy according to Ijiri.[52] Further, if one accepts Tinker's view, then even the positivist, descriptive approach of researchers is simply an attempt to legitimise an ideological position at the theoretical level.[53] Perhaps a more realistic approach is to reject the conceptual frameworks as bodies of 'scientifically' derived theory and accept them as policy statements based on value judgements and opinions. This approach also has implications in relation to the question of whether conceptual frameworks are largely a reflection of professional values.

The distinction between theories and policies is important. Policy issues are generally resolved by political means. This can be crucial when looking at conceptual frameworks in terms of their interpretation of reality and political processes. Political power can be defined 'as the ability of an individual or group to impose their definition of reality on another individual or group'.[54] Since accounting does not operate in a social, economic or political vacuum, it may be that the resulting conceptual frameworks are to some extent a reflection of either the will of the dominant group or, alternatively, a consensus between competing and conflicting political influences. This view tends to conform with Buckley's 'constitutional' approach to policy models, whereby principles are derived from axioms.[55] Such truths as continuity, objectivity, consistency, materiality and conservatism are considered self-evident. The conceptual frameworks appear to reinforce this constitutional approach, largely re-endorsing pre-existing principles. The FASB, in fact, defines a conceptual framework as a 'constitution', as well as a 'coherent system of interrelated objectives and fundamentals'.[56]

The constitutional approach conforms with Bunge's assertion that people claim they can have instinctive knowledge independent of controlled experience:

> They left science the boring task of finding the details of this knowledge but its essence they held, without proof, to be attainable either by special intuition or by reason alone (rationalism), in any case without extrospection and experiment.[57]

The constitutional approach also conforms with the assertion that accounting largely relies on self-evident or dogmatic bases for establishing criteria for truth. Extending this to the conceptual framework, truth may simply be the ideas embodied in the conventions and doctrines of accounting. That is, in line with the historical-constitutional approach, the conceptual framework is little more than the perpetuation of unquestioned accounting conventions. This approach is expressed in Chambers' claim:

> ... all we have as fundamental or basic is a set of propositions that are more or less arbitrarily established, or which are plain dogmas. There is no body of ideas or knowledge by reference to which we can judge whether or not these propositions are preferable to others, we must simply accept them.[58]

In defending the FASB approach to building a conceptual framework, its chairman at the time, Kirk, claimed that the view that standards can be set by consensus is part of a belief that standards are conventions and conventions are formed by agreement. He promotes the idea that a conceptual framework best serves the public interest, because it is a conceptual approach. Standard setting by consensus, compromise or consequences does not serve the public interest, because it is a political approach.[59] However, this is problematic since the public interest is represented by users who have conflicting needs. Kirk's remarks are compromised by a research survey which he quotes. The survey showed that a majority of respondents from universities, government, the financial media and the large accounting firms wanted a framework that would result in significant changes in financial reporting. In contrast, a majority of company managers and security industry officials favoured a framework that affirmed the status quo.

The fact that the FASB conceptual framework in many instances describes existing practice tends to indicate that the political process prevailed in the development of the framework. Miller has claimed that the FASB and its conceptual framework will survive only by maintaining a position that reflects the interests of the beneficiaries of the capital market. He rejects Kirk's claim that the FASB managed to avoid having to develop a conceptual framework based on consensus, claiming that standards emerge from 'a vested set of political processes that create inconsistencies as the search for a consensus continues'.[60]

The political nature of accounting and its reflection in conceptual framework projects has been stressed in the accounting literature. For example, Burchell and his colleagues state:

> ... the roles which [financial accounting] serves are starting to be recognised as being shaped by the pressures which give rise to accounting innovation and change rather than any essence of the accounting mission.[61]

If we accept that the conceptual framework will develop to be a description of present accounting practice, then it will also be merely an outgrowth of institutional and social processes. This is the very reason Hines believes that the FASB's conceptual framework and, by implication, the IASB/FASB's current joint project, will fail. Its stated objective embraces truthfulness and realism. The success of the accounting profession is judged against this objective. Solutions to accounting controversies will always be determined by social interaction and will be situation-specific.[62]

Professional values and self-preservation

An explanation of conceptual frameworks in terms of self-preservation and professional values may at first appear to be a contradiction in terms. 'Self-preservation' implies the pursuit of self-interest, whereas 'professional values' suggests idealism and altruism. However, 'professional values' can mean several things. Greenwood points out that professional organisations emerge as an expression of the growing consciousness-of-kind on the part of the profession's numbers. They promote group interests and aims.[63] The outcome of this social interaction is a professional culture with social values. The social values of a professional group form the basic fundamentals: the unquestioned premises on which its very existence rests. Foremost among these values is the perceived worth of the service which the professional group provides to the community, together with a strong sense of responsibility to the community.

Gerboth considers that this sense of personal responsibility — the essence of professionalism — is what makes accountants' decisions objective. The key to objectivity lies in the values of those who practise accounting. Accounting must take its direction not from its concepts or from its intellectual structure, but from its professional conduct. Gerboth argues:

> Of necessity, accountants make many judgements. And when they do, their decisions may differ from those that other accountants would make. But that does not make the decisions arbitrary. Accountants' freedom to decide is not freedom to decide as they please. Their personal responsibility for the decisions forces a diligent search for the best obtainable approximation of accounting truth, and that responsibility leaves no room for arbitrariness.[64]

It was stated earlier in this chapter that conceptual frameworks do not operate in a social vacuum. Where complex human affairs are involved, it is probably impossible to develop a comprehensive, prescriptive framework and decision model. For example, Agrawal, in reference to the United States' framework, cites a series of issues ranging from comparability to cost-effectiveness which cannot be resolved by recourse to the framework.[65] These can only be decided by judgements which will inevitably be subjective. Judgement is also largely based on professional values. Greenwood refers to this as the value of rationality where there is a commitment to objectivity in the realm of theory and technique.[66] More controversially, he claims that, because of this orientation, nothing of a theoretical or technical nature is regarded as sacred and unchallengeable simply because it has a history of acceptance and use.

The impossibility of agreeing on normative accounting standards, and therefore a prescriptive framework, is supported by Demski.[67] Demski offers mathematical evidence that, in general, no set of standards exists that will identify the most preferred accounting alternative, without specifically incorporating an individual's beliefs and preferences. Such beliefs and preferences may be a mix of personal and professional values. Therefore, Bromwich believes that the best approach to accounting standard setting is to issue a stream of 'partial' standards which consider accounting problems in isolation (similar to current practice before the conceptual framework projects).[68] With a narrowly defined partial standards approach, consensus may be more easily obtained among accounting users and limited resources can be targeted and decentralised. A steady stream of standards provides more explicit evidence of activity to alleviate pressures on the accounting profession for immediate reform.

The less idealistic aspects of professional values are the concepts of professional authority and monopoly.

> Thus, the proposition that in all service-related matters the professional group is infinitely wiser than the laity is regarded as beyond argument![69]

This concept conforms with the constitutional approach argued by Buckley. It is extended by the proposition that standard setting is connected with monopoly-seeking behaviour by the profession.[70] This is achieved by issuing increasingly complex standards and concepts. The result is that the general public does not understand the paraphernalia of complex accounting principles and rules. The public therefore has to rely increasingly on accountants and auditors to prepare and interpret financial reports. This caters to the economic enhancement of the profession by establishing and perpetuating a monopoly on professional knowledge. It could actually be inconsistent with the stated objective of conceptual frameworks to give a service to users by producing objectively derived, relevant and reliable information.

Hines argues that the ability of the accounting profession to retain legitimacy as a profession will be judged by society in terms of the apparent theoretical defensibility of the profession's body of knowledge. This leads to the need for a conceptual framework:

> Viewing conceptual framework projects as constituting a strategic manoeuvre to assist in socially constructing the appearance of a coherent differentiated knowledge base for accounting standards, thus legitimising standards and the power, authority and self-regulation of the accounting profession, may help in explaining why conceptual framework projects are continually undertaken by the profession . . .[71]

Hines further argues that if accounting practice is seen by society as nothing more than an arbitrary collection of unrelated methods, then the social legitimacy of the profession would suffer. The fact that attempts to construct a conceptual framework may result in failure is not important. The existence of standard setting bodies comprising members skilled in accounting theory and practice, together with a conceptual framework, testifies to the presumed existence of a coherent theoretical core which underlies practice. This provides the accounting profession with a continued legitimacy.

LO 5 — CONCEPTUAL FRAMEWORK FOR AUDITING STANDARDS

As discussed earlier, the first major attempt to state a general comprehensive theory of auditing was by Mautz and Sharaf in 1961.[72] In a contemporary review of the text, Miller emphasised that Mautz and Sharaf attempted to provide theoretical underpinnings for a discipline which at that time was primarily regarded as a practical exercise.[73] Fundamentally, Mautz and Sharaf saw auditing not as a subdivision of accounting, but as a discipline based in logic. This led them to the conclusion that auditors are not naturally limited to a verification of accounting information.[74] Modern developments in some of these extensions of auditing services are surveyed in chapter 14. However, Mautz and Sharaf also questioned the compatibility of auditing and consulting services and recommended separation of these two types of services in order to protect auditor independence, one of their auditing theory's key concepts.[75]

Mautz and Sharaf's work was developed further in the early 1970s by the Statement of Basic Auditing Concepts (ASOBAC), issued by the American Accounting Association.[76] ASOBAC had a strong focus on the process of collecting and evaluating evidence, another of the fundamental concepts identified by Mautz and Sharaf. The focus of theoretical debate in auditing during the 1980s was the role of structure and quantification in the evidence gathering and evaluation process.[77] Knechel describes this as a period of rapid growth in audit practices, the expansion of the professional personnel pool, improvements in technology, and the perceived need to reduce costs in the audit process. All these contributed to the movement towards highly structured and formalistic processes in accounting firms.[78]

However, Knechel argues that by the 1990s the traditions of auditing and the profession's efforts to formalise audit processes began to face opposition from other forces. These forces included pressure from clients on auditors to reduce audit fees and deliver more value. Knechel proposes that one interpretation of the interplay between these factors was that it led to change in traditional auditing methods. There began to be less emphasis on direct testing of transactions and balances and more reliance on testing clients' control systems as a means to gather evidence on the financial statements that are produced by those systems. This involved a reduction in time devoted to an audit, and a reduction in substantive testing and sample sizes. This process became known as business risk auditing.

Business risk auditing is a form of auditing that considers client risk as part of the audit evidence process.[79] The formalisation of audit risk occurred in the 1970s.[80] The audit risk model requires an auditor to consider the risk of an inappropriate audit opinion as a function of the inherent risk of errors occurring, the risk that the client's control system will not prevent or detect those errors, and the risk that the auditor's procedures will not detect the error.[81] The focus on audit risk was not new; even in the 1940s, auditors were instructed to begin their audit with a thorough investigation of the client's system and consider its safeguards against fraud and error.[82] However, Knechel argues that the profession's perceptions of risk began to change dramatically with the release of the 1992 report 'Internal Control — Integrated Framework' by the Committee of Sponsoring Organizations (COSO). Auditors became more aware of the relation between internal controls and the conduct of an audit. Clients with more effective internal controls were seen to be at lower risk of fraud and error, and this provided the opportunity to justify a reduction in resources, costs and audit fees for these clients. In addition, gaps in clients' internal controls provided an opportunity to sell non-audit services.[83]

Business risk auditing emphasises the threats to a client's business model from the complexities in its business environment, and business risk is seen to drive audit risk.[84] The key conceptual change that business risk auditing brought to auditors was the requirement to think through the causal relation from the client's business model and operations to the financial accounts, rather than to think in terms of accounting errors first.[85] For example, the decline in 2007–08 global financial markets would cause auditors to consider the risk to a bank's loan loss provisions and going concern assessment, in addition to focusing on specific asset and liability valuations. Business risk auditing meant the audit had to expand its horizon beyond the strict confines of the client to include key process owners outside the organisation.[86]

Development of the business risk model was primarily undertaken at the large accounting firms. For example, KPMG's audit methodology during the period 1997–2006 has been formalised as 'Strategic Systems Audit'.[87] However, although the new approach was supposed to emphasise planning and business understanding processes, there is some evidence that auditors were reluctant to do so, and the claimed efficiency benefits were slow to materialise.[88] Other commentators suggest that business risk auditing was not really very revolutionary. The large auditors already had a focus on business risk, although it was not necessarily clearly articulated until the 1990s.[89]

Critics argue that not only was business risk auditing used to justify a push to sell consulting services; it ultimately led to the accounting scandals at Enron and elsewhere.[90] This criticism implies auditors misused business risk auditing methodology to justify opportunistic behaviour. Regulators have acted through with the Sarbanes–Oxley Act (2002) in the US and the CLERP 9 revisions to the Australian Corporations Act to restrict the opportunities for auditors to provide consulting services to their clients, and there is evidence of increased emphasis on fraud detection in the 2000s.[91] Knechel suggests that the future of business risk auditing could be constrained, but the focus on auditing clients' internal controls in the US legislation still provides a clear focus for auditors to consider risks in the client's processes and environments as part of the financial statement audit.

Summary

LO 1 The role of a conceptual framework

In discussing the role of a conceptual framework we noted that conceptual frameworks have been under development since the 1980s in the United States, Canada, the United Kingdom, Australia and at the IASB. Their goal is to provide a coherent and prescriptive framework which will guide and improve accounting practice. Thus, a conceptual framework aims to: reduce inconsistent practices, delimit the potential for political interference, and enable better understanding of reporting requirements.

LO 2 The objectives of a conceptual framework

Both the IASB and FASB frameworks consider the main objective of financial reporting is to communicate financial information to users. The information is to be selected on the basis of its usefulness in the economic decision-making process. This objective is seen to be achieved by reporting information that is useful in making economic decisions, useful in assessing cash flow prospects, and about enterprise resources, claims to those resources and changes in them.

LO 3 Developing a conceptual framework

Developing a conceptual framework has been a complicated and lengthy process. In recent times, standard setters' attention has re-focused on the development of a conceptual framework for two reasons. First, in response to corporate collapses in 2001–02 in the United States, the FASB has been directed to take an objectives-oriented approach to standard setting, rather than a rule-based approach. A conceptual framework is considered important in providing underlying principles to be used in objectives-based standards. Second, the IASB and FASB commenced a convergence project in 2002 to reduce the differences between US GAAP and IASB standards. To further this aim, it is argued that standards should be based on a common conceptual framework. Since there are differences between the existing IASB and FASB frameworks, a project to develop a joint conceptual framework was commenced in 2004. Present work has focused on the objectives and qualitative characteristics of financial reporting. Constituents have expressed a range of views on these topics. The framework which eventually emerges will reflect the extent to which parties with diverse views about financial reporting are able to compromise in the interest of harmonisation of accounting.

LO 4 A critique of conceptual framework projects

We observed that many people are critical of the existing and proposed conceptual framework documents. Significant criticisms of previous conceptual statements include: measurement is based on unspecified rules, the logic is circular, there is no prior agreement on objectives, and the definitions of the elements are unworkable and provide no guidance to practising accountants.

Others debate the importance of these criticisms. They argue that prior agreement is unimportant and may lead to mechanical decision making. Loose and imprecise logic and definitions may indicate that accounting is only in the pre-science stage. Further criticisms focus on the ontological and epistemological assumptions. Accounting can never be neutral and unbiased. Accounting as a social science is two-way and does not have an objective and separate existence from accountants. In measuring and communicating reality, accountants play a critical role in creating that reality. Particular methods and methodological assumptions also dominate accounting, which leads to generalised and large-scale empirical research. This type of research ignores the micro level of practising accountants who may require a situation-specific problem-solving approach.

Some people view the conceptual frameworks as policy documents based on professional values and self-interest. Therefore they are seen to be a reflection of the political will of the dominant group, which is dominated by professional values. One motivation is to increase economic power through monopoly-seeking behaviour. Further, having gained social acceptance and power, the accounting profession seeks to maintain its position and to manipulate attempts at public regulation. The conceptual frameworks, as a response, testify to the presumed existence of a coherent theoretical core which underlies practice, thus alleviating criticism. There is some evidence, however, that the existence of the conceptual framework project has increased the level of conceptual debate in the standard setting lobbying process. Furthermore, it provides guidance for dealing with issues that are not yet the subject of an accounting standard.

LO 5 | A conceptual framework for auditing standards

Early auditing theory emphasised the role of logic and key concepts such as auditor independence and evidence gathering. By the 1990s the formalised auditing processes and structures were under pressure from clients for lower audit fees and greater value. There was a shift away from substantive testing towards a greater emphasis on consideration of audit risk, in particular the role of client business risk. Business risk auditing emphasised the impact of threats to the client's business model from external factors and the resulting risk of fraud and error in the financial statements. Critics believed that business risk auditing was an attempt to justify less audit work and greater consulting. Legislative changes since the early 2000s have restricted the opportunity for consulting to audit clients but also increased the focus on auditing clients' internal controls.

Questions

1. How do conceptual frameworks of accounting attempt to create a theory of accounting? Describe the components of the IASB *Framework* and how it contributes to a theory of accounting.
2. Some people argue that there is no need for a general theory of accounting, as established in a conceptual framework. They say there is no overall theory of physics, biology, botany or psychology, so there is no need for an overall theory of accounting. Furthermore, attempts to develop such a theory are futile and unnecessary, since accounting has not needed a conceptual framework so far. Debate this view.
3. What does the IASB *Framework* describe as the basic objective of accounting? What are its implications?

4. What type of information do you think is useful for shareholders, lenders and creditors? Is this the type of information that is currently provided?

5. The expressions 'truth', 'justice' and 'fairness' have all been applied to describe desirable characteristics of accounting information. What role do you think they play in practice? Are they included in the IASB *Framework*? If so, how? If not, why not?

6. Explain the role of accounting in relation to:
   (a) individuals
   (b) firms
   (c) the Australian economy.

7. Can accounting ever provide an unbiased map of economic reality? Why or why not?

8. Some argue that the development of a conceptual framework is inappropriate because accountants constantly deal with specific issues that will not be envisaged by an overall, general conceptual framework. In particular, a conceptual framework makes no allowance for differences in the social contexts where accounting is applied. They also argue that it would be preferable to develop case-specific solutions to accounting issues, based on case study research, and bearing in mind the social contexts of all accounting decisions. Discuss this view, presenting arguments for and against it.

9. What is the difference between art and science? Is accounting an art or a science? Does it matter? Why or why not?

10. 'The development of a SME standard by the IASB will defeat the purpose of international harmonisation.' Explain why you agree or disagree with this statement.

11. In Australia, the conceptual framework did not proceed to SAC 5 concerning measurement.
    (a) Why do you think that was the case?
    (b) Do you think that accounting standards have been moving towards a particular measurement method? If so, what is that method?
    (c) How can standards lead the development of a formalised conceptual framework?

12. Give reasons for your answers to the following questions.
    (a) How important is it that standard setters agree on objectives, concepts and definitions before they develop a conceptual framework of accounting?
    (b) How important is it that the conceptual framework is generally accepted by the business community before it is applied to develop accounting standards?
    (c) Why do the FASB and IASB require a common conceptual framework?

13. Explain the advantages and disadvantages of principles-based and rule-based standards.

14. Why has the FASB been directed to produce more objective-based standards? Do you consider this to be a realistic standard setting objective?

15. Discuss whether the IASB *Framework* is merely a policy document based on professional values and self-interest, without scientific foundation. In your discussion, state your opinion on whether the conceptual framework should serve as a policy document in this manner.

16. Assume that you have been contracted by the Australian Accounting Standards Board to develop a proposal regarding whether to issue an accounting standard on accounting for the costs of environmental damage. Draft a proposal of 1500 words or less outlining why you think it is appropriate, or inappropriate, to develop an accounting standard on this issue. Also outline the key issues that would need to be covered by the standard and how the conceptual framework can contribute to resolution of those issues.

17. Write a report of 1500 words or less to the chairpersons of the Financial Reporting Council and the Australian Accounting Standards Board, commenting on the following argument:

'Attempts to bring about radical change through the introduction of a conceptual framework have failed. When it appeared as though SAC 4 would require firms to report their true liabilities, lobbying began in earnest and business ensured that any innovation was quashed. As such, the best that can be hoped for from a conceptual framework is that it legitimises current practice, maintains existing social and economic status, and staves off public sector attempts to control accounting standard setting.'

18. What is business risk auditing? How does it differ from traditional substantive auditing? Why do critics believe it is used to justify selling more consulting services to audit clients? How could business risk auditing be blamed for failures such as Enron?

Additional readings

Alfredson, K, Leo, K, Picker, R, Loftus, J, Clark, K, & Wise, V 2009, *Applying international financial accounting standards*, Brisbane: John Wiley & Sons Australia, Ltd.

Bradbury ME, & Baskerville, RF 2008, 'The "NZ" in "NZ IFRS": Public Benefit Entity Amendments'. *Australian Accounting Review*, vol. 18, no. 3, pp. 185–90.

Foster, J, & Johnson, L 2001, 'Understanding the issues: why does the FASB have a conceptual framework?', www.fasb.org.

Loftus, J 2003, The 'CF and accounting standards', *Abacus*, vol. 39, no. 3, pp. 298–324.

Nobes, C 2008, 'Accounting Classification in the IFRS Era', *Australian Accounting Review*, vol. 18, no. 3, pp. 191–98.

Page, M & Spira, L 1999, 'The conceptual underwear of financial reporting', *Accounting Auditing and Accountability Journal*, vol. 12, no. 4, pp. 489–501.

Psaros J & Trotman, K 2004, 'The impact of the type of accounting standards and preparers judgements', *Abacus*, vol. 40, no. 1, pp. 76–93.

Walker, RG & Jones, S 2003, 'Measurement: a way forward', *Abacus*, vol. 39, pp. 356–74.

4.1
CASE STUDY

Big GAAP, small GAAP: accounting for SMEs

Note: in this article IFRS for SMEs is referred to by a prior title, IFRS for Private Entities.

IFRS for Private Entities: a practical guide

by Irene O'Keeffe

Comparability of companies' financial information

The application of IFRS for Private Entities will significantly improve the comparability of entities within an industry and across different industries, regardless of where the reporting entity is domiciled. Under the IFRS for Private Entities, similar transactions and economic circumstances are accounted for and presented more consistently than under varying national requirements.

Internationally, financial indicators are not comparable because different recognition and valuation principles are applied in each country. This makes it difficult for users of financial statements to make informed decisions on a private entity's performance and cash flows. Private companies that move to widespread use of IFRS for Private Entities should find that it improves both the comparability of information and the quality of communications to stakeholders.

Acquisitions, partnerships and cooperation agreements

The adoption of IFRS for Private Entities will often make it easier to implement planned cross-border acquisitions and to initiate proposed partnerships or cooperation agreements with foreign entities. Furthermore, maintenance of financial information under this IFRS-based standard may simplify the sale of the reporting entity itself, either as a whole or on a piecemeal basis. This is because financial statements are key documents for evaluating an acquisition and negotiating a purchase price, as well as for assessing potential partnership or cooperation agreements. Interpreting the performance of the other party's business becomes significantly easier, and agreement is more likely, when both sides already have financial statements prepared using a similar accounting framework. If financial information is based only on national requirements, additional time and expense must be invested in order to understand the different basis of accounting and reach a clear assessment of the other party's performance. Post acquisition, the costs of integrating the financial reporting systems are lower where both the acquirer and the acquiree use the same accounting framework.

Building relationships with overseas customers

The use of IFRS-based information should help private entities involved in buying/selling goods or services across national borders to initiate new relationships with customers and suppliers. As the spread and acceptance of IFRS-based standards grows internationally, so should the importance of IFRS-based financial statements as a tool to cultivate a positive image. It is not only large foreign groups that now demand financial statements from companies as part of the process of supplier selection and evaluation. Suppliers that only prepare financial statements under their national GAAP may well find themselves at a disadvantage compared to competitors with IFRS-based financial statements. To eliminate disadvantages in the global competition for new contracts and allow businesses to compete on their merits, an entity must be able to provide high-quality information that, at the very least, is as convincing and as relevant for decision-making as the information its competitors provide. This is particularly important when entering into long-term trading relationships: in these circumstances, potential customers or suppliers usually want reassurance about the entity's solvency before committing to a relationship. This information can be better conveyed using an internationally-accepted accounting framework, such as the proposed IFRS for Private Entities, rather than a national framework that needs to be explained.

Dealing with finance providers

Demonstrating compliance with an IFRS-based accounting framework should strengthen a company's position in negotiations with credit institutions and reduce the costs of borrowing because of the positive effect it can have on credit ratings. IFRS can also result in more accurate risk evaluations by lenders and, in many cases, a lower risk premium. This is because financial information prepared using an IFRS-based standard emphasises the economic substance of transactions and tends to provide higher-quality information, with better disclosures and transparency than many national accounting frameworks.

Compliance with an IFRS-based accounting framework may also help private companies to take advantage of alternative forms of finance. Equity financiers, just like credit institutions, want top-quality information to help them assess the risks and rewards of the entity or project to be financed. IFRS-compliant information should facilitate clearer comparison of investment opportunities in various countries to be made, and help investors to identify the specific advantages of each. The better the information for investors, the easier it should be to attract them and the lower the risk premium for the company.

Source: *Accountancy Ireland*, vol. 40, no. 6, December 2008, pp. 30–31.

Question

The international harmonisation of accounting standards raises questions about which entities should use international standards and whether one set of standards is suitable for all entities. For example, should use of international standards be limited to large international companies for which international comparability is important? Can one set of standards be used for all entities, regardless of size and structure, independent of whether the entity is from the private, public or not-for-profit sector?

UK GAAP has for many years incorporated differential reporting. That is, it has different reporting rules for companies based on size. UK GAAP includes a standard for small and medium enterprises (SMEs) called the Financial Reporting Standard for Smaller Entities (FRSSE) which exempts certain companies from compliance with the full set of UK accounting standards. In recognition of concerns about the applicability of the full set of IASB standards for some entities, the IASB included the IASC's SME project on its agenda. An exposure draft was issued in 2007 and the International Financial Reporting Standard for Small and Medium-sized Entities (IFRS for SMEs) followed in July 2009.[92]

The SME standard is the result of extensive consultation over a five-year period. The aim of the standard is to provide a set of financial reporting principles, based on IFRS, which meet the needs of entities that are not publicly accountable. These entities are estimated to be over 95 per cent of all companies worldwide. It is a self-contained document which has modified IFRS requirements based on the needs of users of SME financial statements and cost-benefit considerations. Simplifications include the omission of irrelevant topics, reduction in accounting policy options, simplification of IFRS recognition and measurement principles and a reduction in disclosures.[93]

Based on this information and the article by Irene O'Keeffe, answer the following question:

Under the four headings in the article, discuss the possible benefits of an SME standard identified by the author. In your discussion, name the parties most likely to benefit from the SME standard and explain the extent to which you agree or disagree with the views presented by the author. You should also consider what factors may inhibit the success of the SME standard.

**4.2
CASE STUDY**

Usefulness of accounting information

Public sector and not-for-profit entities

In the existing IASB and FASB conceptual framework documents, standard setters have identified 'decision usefulness' as an objective for financial reporting. To meet this objective financial information should have the following qualitative characteristics: understandabilty, relevance, reliability and comparability (*Framework*, paragraphs 24–42).

Reproduced below are guidelines which may assist in enhancing the quality of information provided by not-for-profit entities (NFPs).

3. Overall recommendations

3.1 Recommendations to enhance NFP annual reporting
The following recommendations are designed to enhance the quality of annual reporting by NFPs. The recommendations are based on research carried out by the Institute and information gathered in the review of submissions to the 2007 PricewaterhouseCoopers Transparency Awards.

Objectives	Provide more information about what NFPs are trying to do (their mission), their objectives, explanations of activities to achieve those objectives, and how those activities are funded.
Strategy	Provide a summary of the strategy to assist readers reviewing an NFP's performance for the year. NFPs striving for best practice should consider the inclusion of measurable, quantified strategic targets and progress reporting against those targets. Make the strategic plan or, at a minimum, the strategic goals for the period available on the website. A link or cross reference to the website could be included in the annual report.
Future plans	Provide more information regarding future plans.
Governance structure and processes	Greater transparency around governance structures and processes through inclusion of a comprehensive governance statement will: > Initially, lead to improved governance reporting as the NFP strives to demonstrate best practice > Assist Board members in protecting their reputation > Potentially provide a competitive advantage. Examples of governance statements can be found in section 4.2 in this publication. Additionally, specific guidance exists for sporting body NFPs.[1]
Risk management	Ideally readers of the annual report should be provided with sufficient information to understand the risks faced by the NFP and the ongoing management of those risks. This could be achieved by providing a summary of policies on risk oversight and management of material risks in the governance statement.
Stakeholder reporting	Identify major stakeholders — people, groups or organisations who impact or could be impacted by the NFP's actions — and provide an overview of the relationship with each stakeholder. Specific attention should be paid to employees and volunteers. Consider disclosing employment policies, policies for engaging volunteers, an overview of the training provided to both employees and volunteers, and recognition of employee and volunteer achievements.
Funding	Provide more detail about sources of funds as well as fundraising activities. Although the quantum of funds raised and used by NFPs can be determined from their financial statements, additional information on the sources of funds would enhance transparency. Consideration should be given to providing information regarding: > The processes to secure government funding > Policies for public fundraising > Which costs are included in fundraising costs > The revenue models and the NFP's approach to funding > The use of websites to generate donations.

1. Sporting body NFPs can achieve best practice in governance reporting by comparing their structure to the Australian Sporting Commission's *National Sporting Organisation Governance Principles of Best Practice*. If necessary, they can take remedial action to align their governance structure with this best practice.

Source: Extract from 'Enhancing not-for-profit annual and financial reporting', ICAA reports, March 2009, Extract p. 7, www.charteredaccountants.com.au.

4.3
CASE STUDY

In 2004, the IASB and FASB announced a joint project to revisit their conceptual frameworks. The following material provides some background about the project and raises questions for discussion.

Revisiting the conceptual framework

The FASB and IASB began a joint agenda project to revisit their conceptual frameworks for financial accounting and reporting in 2002. Each board bases its accounting standards decisions in large part on the foundation of objectives, characteristics, definitions, and criteria set forth in their existing conceptual frameworks. The goals of the new project are to build on the two boards' existing frameworks by refining, updating, completing, and converging them into a common framework that both Boards can use in developing new and revised accounting standards. A common goal of the FASB and IASB, shared by their constituents, is for their standards to be 'principles-based'. To be principles-based, standards cannot be a collection of conventions but rather must be rooted in fundamental concepts. For standards on various issues to result in coherent financial accounting and reporting, the fundamental concepts need to constitute a framework that is sound, comprehensive, and internally consistent.

Without the guidance provided by an agreed-upon framework, standard setting ends up being based on the individual concepts developed by each member of the standard-setting body. Standard setting that is based on the personal conceptual frameworks of individual standard setters can produce agreement on specific standard-setting issues only when enough of those personal frameworks happen to intersect on that issue. However, even those agreements may prove transitory because, as the membership of the standard-setting body changes over time, the mix of personal conceptual frameworks changes as well. As a result, that standard-setting body may reach significantly different conclusions about similar (or even identical) issues than it did previously, with standards not being consistent with one another and past decisions not being indicative of future ones. That concern is not merely hypothetical: substantial difficulties in reaching agreement in its first standards projects was a major reason that the original FASB members decided to devote substantial effort to develop a conceptual framework.

The IASB *Framework* is intended to assist not only standard setters but also preparers of financial statements (in applying international financial reporting standards and in dealing with topics on which standards have not yet been developed), auditors (in forming opinions about financial statements), and users (in interpreting information contained in financial statements). Those purposes also are better served by concepts that are sound, comprehensive, and internally consistent. (In contrast, the FASB Concepts Statements state that they do not justify changing generally accepted accounting and reporting practices or interpreting existing standards based on personal interpretations of the concepts, one of a number of differences between the two frameworks.)

Another common goal of the FASB and IASB is to converge their standards. The Boards have been pursuing a number of projects that are aimed at achieving short-term convergence on specific issues, as well as several major projects that are being conducted jointly or in tandem. Moreover, the Boards have aligned their agendas more closely to achieve convergence in future standards. The Boards will encounter difficulties converging their standards if they base their decisions on different frameworks.

The FASB's current Concepts Statements and the IASB's *Framework*, developed mainly during the 1970s and 1980s, articulate concepts that go a long way toward being an adequate foundation for principles-based standards. Some constituents accept those concepts, but others do not. Although the current concepts have been helpful, the IASB and FASB will not be able to realise fully their goal of issuing a common set of principles-based standards if those standards are based on the current FASB Concepts Statements and IASB *Framework*. That is because those documents are in need of refinement, updating, completion, and convergence.

The planned approach in the joint project will identify troublesome issues that seem to reappear time and time again in a variety of standard-setting projects and often in a variety of guises. That is, the focus will be on issues that cut across a number of different projects. Because it is not possible to address those cross-cutting issues comprehensively in the context of any one standards-level project, the conceptual framework project provides a better way to consider their broader implications, thereby assisting the boards in developing standards-level guidance.

As noted in the chapter, the boards have issued and received comments on an exposure draft relating to Phase A Objectives and Qualitative Characteristics. A discussion paper relating to Phase D Reporting Entity had been issued and work is continuing on Phase B Elements and Recognition and Phase C Measurement.

Source: Excerpts from Halsey G. Bullen and Kimberley Crook, 'Revisiting the concepts: A new conceptual framework project', May 2005, FASB and IASB, www.fasb.org or www.iasb.org.

Questions

1. Explain why principles-based standards require a conceptual framework.
2. Why is it important that the IASB and FASB share a common conceptual framework?
3. It is suggested that several parties can benefit from a conceptual framework. Do you consider that a conceptual framework is more important for some parties than others? Explain your reasoning.
4. What is meant by a 'cross-cutting' issue? Suggest some possible examples of cross-cutting issues.

Endnotes

1. Financial Accounting Standards Board (FASB), Statement of Financial Accounting Concepts No. 1, 'Objectives of Financial Reporting by Business Enterprises', November 1978, p. 1.
2. The American Institute of Certified Public Accountants (AICPA), 'Audits of corporate accounts', New York, 1934, p. 9.
3. See R Watts and J Zimmerman, *Positive accounting theory*, Englewood Cliffs, NJ: Prentice-Hall, 1986.
4. Accounting Principles Board (APB), Statement No. 4, 'Basic Concepts and Accounting Principles Underlying Financial Statements of Business Enterprises', para. 139, 1970.
5. W Paton, 'Comment on "A statement of accounting principles"', *Journal of Accountancy*, March 1938, pp. 201–2.
6. O Gellein, 'The conceptual framework: Needs and uses', FASB Viewpoints, 19 August 1980.
7. R Storey, *The search for accounting principles*, New York: AICPA, 1964, p. 52.
8. D Solomons, 'The political implications of accounting and accounting standard setting', *Accounting and business research*, Spring 1983, p. 109.
9. ibid., p. 115
10. Australian Accounting Research Foundation (AARF), Series No. 1, 'Guide to Proposed Statement of Accounting Concepts', December 1987.
11. M Bradbury, 'Implications for the conceptual framework arising from accounting for financial instruments', *Abacus*, vol. 39, no. 3, 2003, pp. 388–97.
12. C Nobes, 'Rules based standards and the lack of principles in accounting',

Accounting Horizons, vol. 19, no. 1, 2005, pp. 25–34.

13. MW Nelson, 'Behavioural evidence on the effects of principles and rules based standards', *Accounting Horizons*, vol. 17, no. 1, 2003, pp. 91–104.

14. K Schipper, 'Principles-based accounting standards', *Accounting Horizons*, vol. 17, no. 1, 2003, pp. 61–72.

15. Securities and Exchange Commission (SEC), 'Study pursuant to Section 108(d) of the Sarbanes-Oxley Act of 2002 on the adoption by the United States Financial Reporting System of a principles-based accounting system', 2003, www.sec.gov.

16. SA Zeff, 'A perspective on the US public/private sector approach to the regulation of financial reporting', *Accounting Horizons*, vol. 9, no. 1, 1995, pp. 52–70.

17. SA Zeff, 'The evolution of US GAAP: The political forces behind professional standards', *The CPA Journal*, vol. 75, no. 2, 2005, pp. 18–29.

18. M Moonitz, *The basic postulates of accounting*, New York: AICPA, 1961, p. 21.

19. G Dean and F Clarke, 'An evolving conceptual framework?' *Abacus*, vol. 39, no. 3, 2003, pp. 279–97.

20. S Jones and P Wolnizer, 'Harmonization and the conceptual framework: An international perspective', *Abacus*, vol. 39, no. 3, 2003, pp. 375–87.

21. Conceptual Framework Joint Project of the IASB and FASB, Project Information Page, Latest revisions as of 3 August 2009.

22. ibid.

23. Accounting Standards Board, UK, Conceptual Framework project.

24. W McGregor and D Street, 'IASB and FASB face challenges in pursuit of joint conceptual framework', *The Journal of International Financial Management and Accounting*, vol. 18, no. 1, 2007, pp. 39–51.

25. International Public Sector Accounting Standards Board, 'Conceptual Framework for General Purpose Financial Reporting by Public Sector Entities: The Objectives of Financial Reporting, The Scope of Financial Reporting, The Qualitative Characteristics of Information Included in General Purpose Financial Reports, The Reporting Entity', September 2008, International Federation of Accountants, www.ifac.org.

26. G Whittington, 'Fair value and the IASB/FASB conceptual framework project: An alternative view', *Abacus*, vol. 44, no. 2, 2008, pp. 139–68.

27. IASB, Comment letter summary: Objectives and Qualitative Characteristics (Agenda paper 2A), IASCF: London, December 2008.

28. IASB, Comment letter summary: Discussion paper Reporting Entity Phase D (Agenda paper 4), IASCF: London, November 2008.

29. IASB, Agenda paper 2A comment letter summary, op. cit., p. 7.

30. Pro-active Accounting Activities in Europe (PAAinE), 'Stewardship/accountability as an objective of financial reporting: A comment on the IASB/FASB Conceptual Framework project', June 2007, European Financial Reporting Advisory Group, www.efrag.org.

31. Whittington, op. cit.

32. ibid.

33. M Penno, Rules and Accounting: Vagueness in Conceptual Frameworks, *Accounting Horizons*, September, 2008, vol. 22, no. 3, pp. 339–51.

34. IASB Board Meeting, January 2009, www.iasplus.com.

35. Whittington, op. cit.

36. FASB/IASB Project update, Conceptual Framework Phase B: Elements and Recognition, www.fasb.org.

37. Whittington, op. cit.

38. R Hines, 'Why won't the FASB conceptual framework work?', AAANZ Conference paper, August 1987.

39. N Dopuch and S Sunder, 'FASB's statements on objectives and elements of financial accounting', *Accounting Review*, January 1980, p. 4.

40. ibid., pp. 6, 7, 8.

41. D Gerboth, 'The conceptual framework: Not definitions, but professional values', *Accounting Horizons*, September 1987, p. 5.

42. K Popper, *The open society and its enemies*, Princeton, NJ: Princeton University Press, 1966, p. 19.

43. Gerboth, op. cit., p. 5.

44. FASB, Statement of Financial Accounting Concepts No. 2, 'Qualitative Characteristics of Accounting Information', 1980, p. xvi.

45. E Solomons, 'The politicization of accounting', *Journal of Accountancy*, November 1978, p. 71.

46. R Hines, 'Financial accounting: In communicating reality, we construct reality', *Accounting, Organizations and Society*, vol. 13, no. 3, 1988, pp. 251–61.

47. ibid., pp. 254–55.

48. WF Chua, 'Radical developments in accounting thought', *Accounting Review*, October 1986, p. 607.

49. CT Horngren, 'Uses and limitations of a conceptual framework', *Journal of Accountancy*, April 1981, p. 92.

50. E Stamp, 'Why can accounting not become a science like physics?', *Abacus*, vol. 17, no. 1, 1981, p. 14.

51. Y Ijiri, 'Theory of accounting management', Studies in Accounting Research No. 10, Florida: AAA, 1975, pp. 9–10.

52. ibid., p. 10.

53. T Tinker, 'Panglossian accounting theories: The science of apologising in style', *Accounting, Organizations and Society*, vol. 13, 1988, no. 2, pp. 165–89.

54. Hines 1987, op. cit.

55. J Buckley, 'Policy models in accounting: A critical commentary', *Accounting, Organizations and Society*, vol. 5, no. 1, 1980, p. 52.

56. FASB, An Analysis of Issues Related to the Conceptual Framework for Financial Accounting and Reporting: Elements of Financial Statements and Their Measurement, 1976, p. 2.

57. M Bunge, *Scientific Research II: The search for truth*, New York: Springer Verlag, 1967, quoted in Buckley, op. cit., p. 53.

58. R Chambers, 'Conventions, doctrines and common sense', *Accountants' Journal*, February 1964, p. 183.

59. D Kirk, 'Concepts, consensus, compromise and consequence: Their roles in standard setting', *Journal of Accountancy*, April 1981, p. 84.

60. P Miller, 'The conceptual framework: Myths and realities', *Journal of Accountancy*, March 1985, p. 62.

61. Burchell et al., 'The roles of accounting in organizations and society', *Accounting, Organizations and Society*, vol. 5, no. 1, 1980, p. 12.

62. Hines 1987, op. cit., p. 15.

63. E Greenwood, 'Attributes of a profession', in SE Loeb, *Ethics in the accounting profession*, John Wiley and Sons Inc.: New York, 1978, p. 60.
64. Gerboth, op. cit., p. 7.
65. S Agrawal, 'A conceptual framework for accounting: The American model', *Chartered Accountant in Australia*, June 1987, p. 27.
66. Greenwood, op. cit., p. 60.
67. J Demski, 'The general impossibility of normative accounting standards', *Accounting Review*, vol. 50, October 1973, pp. 718–23.
68. M Bromwich, 'The possibility of partial accounting standards', *Accounting Review*, April 1980, pp. 288–300.
69. Greenwood, op. cit., p. 60.
70. Buckley, op. cit., p. 58.
71. R Hines, 'Financial accounting knowledge, conceptual framework projects and the social construction of the accounting profession', *Accounting, Auditing and Accountability Journal*, vol. 2, no. 2, 1989, p. 85.
72. R Mautz and HA Sharaf, *The philosophy of auditing*, American Accounting Association, 1961.
73. HE Miller, Untitled review of *The philosophy of auditing* by RK Mautz and HA Sharaf, in *The Accounting Review*, vol. 37, no. 3, July 1962, pp. 599–600.
74. Mautz and Sharaf 1961, cited in Miller 1962, p. 600.
75. ibid.
76. American Accounting Association Committee on Basic Auditing Concepts, A Statement of Basic Auditing Concepts, Sarasota, 1973.
78. WR Knechel, 'The business risk audit: Origins, obstacles and opportunities', *Accounting, Organizations and Society*, vol. 32, no. 4/5, 2007, pp. 383–408.
78. ibid., p. 386.
79. ME Peecher, R Schwartz and I Solomon, 'It's all about audit quality: Perspectives on strategic-systems auditing', *Accounting, Organizations and Society*, vol. 32, no. 4/5, 2007, pp. 463–85.
80. Knechel (op. cit.) notes that the first audit risk statement in the US was issued in 1983; Statement on Auditing Standards 47, Audit Risk and Materiality in Conducting the Audit, AICPA, 1983; cited in Knechel, 2007.
81. ISA 330 The Auditor's Responses to Assessed Risks/ASA 330 The Auditor's Procedures in Response to Assessed Risks.
82. WA Staub, 'Mode of conducting an audit', *The Accounting Review*, vol. 18, no. 2, April 1943, pp. 91–8.
83. Knechel, op. cit., p. 388.
84. A Eilifsen, WR Knechel and P Wallage, 'Use of strategic risk analysis in audit planning: A field study', *Accounting Horizons*, September 2001, pp. 193–207; WR Knechel, *Auditing: risk and assurance*, 2nd ed, Southwestern Publishing Co. 2001; cited in Knechel op. cit., 2007.
85. Knechel 2007, op. cit., p. 393.
86. M Power, 'Business risk auditing — Debating the history of its present', *Accounting, Organizations, and Society*, Vol. 32, No. 4/5, 2007, pp. 379–82.
87. Peecher, Schwartz, and Solomon op. cit.; T Bell, F Marrs, I Solomon and H Thomas, 'Auditing organizations through a strategic-systems lens: The KPMH business measurement process', 1997. KPMG LLP, cited in Power, M 2007.
88. E Curtis and S Turley, 'The business risk audit — a longitudinal case study of an audit engagement', *Accounting, Organizations and Society*, vol. 32, no. 4/5, 2007, pp. 439–61.
89. C Flint, IAM Fraser and DJ Hatherly, 'Business risk auditing — A regressive evolution? A research note', *Accounting Forum*, vol. 32, 2008, pp. 143–47.
90. See Knechel op. cit. 2007, for an extensive discussion of the criticisms of business risk auditing.
91. ibid.
92. IASB, Fact Sheet: IFRS for SMEs Fact Sheet, 9 July 2009, London: International Accounting Standards Committee Foundation.
93. Institute of Chartered Accountants in Australia (ICAA), News and Issues, 'IASB releases SME standard', 23 July 2009, www.charteredaccountants.com.au.

5

Measurement theory

LEARNING OBJECTIVES	*After reading this chapter, you should have an appreciation of the following:*

1 the importance of measurement

2 the nominal, ordinal, interval and ratio scales of measurement

3 the permissible operations of scales

4 the difference between fundamental, derived and fiat measurements

5 what is meant by reliability and accuracy in measurement

6 measurement in accounting

7 measurement issues for auditors.

Measurement is a significant part of scientific inquiry. Measurements are made, as demonstrated in accounting, because quantitative data can impart greater information than qualitative data in many instances. Because measurement of attributes reported in accounting reports (e.g. assets, income and liabilities) is an important function in accounting, it is worthwhile for us to examine measurement theory and to outline a number of basic measurement assumptions in accounting.

LO 1 — IMPORTANCE OF MEASUREMENT

Campbell, one of the first to deal with the issue of measurement, defined measurement as 'the assignment of numerals to represent properties of material systems other than numbers, in virtue of the laws governing these properties'.[1] Stevens, a noted theorist in the area of measurement in the social sciences, referred to measurement as the 'assignment of numerals to objects or events according to rules'.[2] Campbell makes a distinction between systems and the properties of those systems. The 'systems' in Campbell's definition are what Stevens calls 'objects or events'. These could include houses, tables, people, assets or distance travelled. Properties are the specific aspects or characteristics of the systems, such as weight, length, width or colour. We always measure properties and not the systems themselves. In this respect, Campbell's definition is more precise than Stevens's.

Campbell's definition requires numerals to be assigned to properties according to the laws governing the properties, whereas Stevens's definition requires only that the assignment be done 'according to rules'. Sterling objects to the broadness of Stevens's definition, arguing, 'One needs restrictions upon the kind of rule that can be used'.[3] Otherwise, any assignment of numbers can be called measurement. In the usual understanding of measurement, semantic rules (operational definitions) are devised and used to link the formal number system with the property (of objects or events) to be measured. When the semantic rules assign numbers to objects or events in such a way that the relationships among the objects or events (in respect of a given property) correspond to mathematical relationships, a scale has been established and the property is said to be measured. Stevens states:

> When this correspondence between the formal model and its empirical counterpart is close and tight, we find ourselves able to discover truths about matters of fact by examining the model itself.[4]

Under this view, the measurement process is similar to the approach to theory formulation and testing mentioned earlier. A statement, expressed mathematically, is advanced. Semantic rules (operations) are devised to connect the symbols of the statement to particular objects or events. When it is demonstrated that the relationships in the mathematical statement correlate with the relationships of the objects or events, then measurement of the given aspect of the objects or events has been made.

In accounting we measure profit by first assigning a value to capital and then calculating profit as the change in capital over the period after accounting for all economic events that affect the wealth of the firm.

LO 2 — SCALES

Every measurement is made on a scale. A scale is created when a semantic rule is used to relate the mathematical statement to objects or events.

The scale shows what information the numbers represent, thus giving meaning to the numbers. The type of scale created depends on the semantic rules used. According to Stevens, scales can be described in general terms as nominal, ordinal, interval or ratio.[5] These classifications were arrived at by examining the mathematical group structure of scales. The mathematical structure is determined by considering the kind of transformation that leaves the structure of the scale invariant, i.e. unchanged.

Nominal scale

In the nominal scale, numbers are used only as labels. The numbering of football players is an example given by Stevens.

Many theorists object to the nominal scale as representing measurement. Torgerson states:

> In measurement, as we use the term, the number assigned refers to the relative amount or degree of a property possessed by the object, and not to the object itself, whereas, in the different nominal scales, the numbers refer to the objects or classes of objects: it is the object that is named or classified.[6]

The nominal scale simply represents classification, which is not what measurement is considered to be in the ordinary usage of the term. As Torgerson points out, measurement refers to properties of objects, whereas in the nominal scale the numbers often denote the objects themselves, such as numbering or naming players in sporting teams. The major property the numbers have is to identify players or objects. In the accounting system, the closest we have to the nominal scale is the classification of assets and liabilities into different classes.

Ordinal scale

An ordinal scale is created when an operation ranks the objects in question with respect to a given property. For example, suppose a certain investor has three feasible investment opportunities for a given amount of money to invest. They are ranked 1, 2, 3 according to their net present values, with the highest ranked as 1 and the lowest as 3. The operation (calculation of net present value) gives rise to an ordinal scale, which is the set of numbers referring to the investment alternatives. The numbers indicate the order of the size of the net present value of the options and, therefore, their profitability.

A weakness of the ordinal scale is that the intervals between the numbers (1 to 2, 2 to 3 and 1 to 3) do not tell us anything about the differences in the quantity of the property they represent. In our example, in terms of the aspect measured (net present value), option 2 may be very close to option 1, and option 3 may be considerably less than option 2. Another weakness is that the numbers do not signify 'how much' of the attribute the objects possess.

Torgerson argues that some ordinal scales have a 'natural origin', that is, a natural zero point.[7] Applied to our example of ranking investment alternatives, the natural zero point could be a neutral point where in one direction are all the expected profitable alternatives and in the other direction are the expected unprofitable ones. The numbers assigned to the options on one side of the zero point would have positive signs and, on the other, negative signs.

Interval scale

The interval scale imparts more information than the ordinal scale. Not only is the ranking of the objects known with respect to the given property, but the distance between the intervals on the scale is equal and known. A selected zero point also exists on the scale. An example is the Celsius scale of temperature. Equal intervals of temperature are noted by equal volumes of expansion with an arbitrary zero point agreed on for the scale. The temperature differential is divided between freezing and boiling into 100 degrees, with the freezing point arbitrarily set at zero degrees. If the temperature of two different rooms is measured with a Celsius thermometer and gives readings of 22 degrees and 30 degrees, we can say not only that the second room is hotter, but also that it is 8 degrees higher in temperature. The differences between the numbers can be translated directly to represent the differences in the characteristic of the objects.

The weakness of the interval scale is that the zero point is arbitrarily established. For example, suppose we were to measure the height of a group of men on an interval scale and assign a number to each according to his height with respect to the average of the group. The average represents the zero point on the scale. If A is 3 centimetres above the average, then we would assign him the number +3; and if B is 5 centimetres below the average, then we would assign him the number –5. On this scale, we do not know how tall A or B is in an absolute (actual) sense. B may be the shortest man in the group, but the group may consist of tall basketball players.

Mattessich mentions standard cost accounting as one example where the interval scale is used in accounting.[8] The standard may be based on theoretical, average, practical or normal performance. Because the choice is more or less arbitrary, the calculation of standards and variances generates an interval scale. If the variance is zero, this signifies neutrality, but this point is arbitrarily selected.

Ratio scale

A ratio scale is one where:
- the rank order of the objects or events with respect to a given property is known
- the intervals between the objects are equal and are known
- a unique origin, a natural zero point, exists where the distance from it for at least one object is known.

The ratio scale conveys the most information.

The measurement of length is a good example of a ratio scale. When A is 10 metres long and B is 20 metres, we can say not only that B is 10 metres longer but also that it is twice as long as A. The ratios of the numbers are also directly interpretable as ratios of the quantities of the property measured. Thus, it makes sense to say that A is half as long as B or B is twice as long as A, whereas we cannot say that 40 degrees Celsius is twice as hot as 20 degrees Celsius.

An example of the ratio scale in accounting is the use of dollars to represent cost and value. If asset A cost \$10 000 and asset B cost \$20 000, we can state that B cost twice as much as A. A natural zero point exists, because 0 denotes absence of cost or value, just as 0 for length means no length at all.

LO 3 ⊢ PERMISSIBLE OPERATIONS OF SCALES

One reason for discussing scales is that certain mathematical applications are permissible only for different types of scales. The ratio scale allows for all the fundamental arithmetical operations of addition, subtraction, multiplication and division, and also algebra, analytic geometry, calculus and statistical methods. A ratio scale remains invariant (fixed) over all transformations when multiplied by a constant.[9] For example, consider the following:

$$X' = cX$$

If X represents all the points on a given scale, and each point is multiplied by a constant c, the resulting scale X' will also be a ratio scale. The reason is that the structure of the scale is left invariant, that is:

- the rank order of the points is unchanged
- the ratios of the points are unchanged
- the zero point is unchanged.

This means that if we measured the length of a room and found it to be 400 centimetres and then converted the 400 centimetres to 4 metres by multiplying by the constant 1/100, we can be assured that the length of the room is unchanged, even though the number representing length has changed. This is the same point we make in chapter 6 regarding the conversion of historical cost of, say, $100 000 of equipment under the nominal dollar scale to the purchasing power of the dollar scale by applying a constant, say, 120/100, to derive $120 000. The $120 000 is still historical cost.

The invariance of a scale permits us to know the extent to which a theory or rule remains basically the same, even though the scale is expressed in different units, such as from centimetres to metres or from nominal dollars to constant dollars. An invariant transformation of a ratio scale will leave intact the same general form of the relationship of the variables.

Without invariance, it is possible to find that X is twice as long as Y when measured in centimetres, but three times as long when measured in metres. In accounting, the scale for current cost is variant from that of historical cost, because the attributes to be measured are different. When machine A is measured under historical cost it may be $90 000, but when measured under current cost it may be $110 000. The unit of measure, the dollar, is used in both cases but the scales are different: they are variant. But changing from the nominal dollar scale to the purchasing power of the dollar scale for the same attribute (historical cost or current cost) leaves the structure invariant.

With an interval scale, not all arithmetical operations are permissible. Addition and subtraction can be used with respect to the particular numbers on the scale as well as the intervals. However, multiplication and division cannot be used with reference to the particular numbers, only to the intervals.[10] The reasons are due to the conditions of invariance. An interval scale is invariant under any linear transformation of the form:

$$X' = cX + b$$

The transformation of one interval scale for measuring a specific property to another interval scale for measuring the same property is made by multiplying each point of the first scale X by a constant c and adding to it a constant b. The reason for b is that there is no absolute zero point on an interval scale. For example, to transform from Celsius temperature to Fahrenheit temperature, we multiply each degree by 9/5 and add 32. The 9/5 is used because the Celsius scale has 100 degrees as opposed to 180 degrees for Fahrenheit, and 32 is added because that is the freezing point for the latter scale.

The conditions of invariance show that we can multiply and divide with respect to the intervals, but these arithmetical operations cannot be used for the particular numbers on the scale. To illustrate, consider the following transformation:

$$X' = X + 10$$

Consider the objects on points 3 and 6 on scale X. Transforming to scale X', we now have 13 and 16. The ratio of 13 to 16 is not the same as the ratio of 3 to 6 because of the addition of the constant. Multiplication and division (i.e. ratios) are therefore not permissible for the particular numbers. Thus, if Robyn receives 90 points on her accounting exam and Maria receives 45 points, we cannot say that Robyn knows twice as much as Maria regarding the subject matter of the exam. The reason is that there is no natural zero point for the exam for 'no knowledge'. Even if a student receives '0' on the exam, we cannot say that he or she has no knowledge of the subject matter. In this example, what we can say is that Robyn passed the exam and Maria failed the exam, but we cannot infer comparatively the amount of knowledge to the numbers. Likewise, if the quantity variance is $5000 favourable, as opposed to the previous month's variance of $10 000 favourable, we cannot say that the use of materials this month is only half as efficient as in the preceding month.

With ordinal scales, none of the arithmetical operations can be used. We cannot add, subtract, multiply or divide the numbers or the intervals on the scale. Ordinal scales, therefore, convey limited information.

LO 4 ― TYPES OF MEASUREMENT

As we said earlier, the measurement process is similar to the scientific approach of theory construction and testing. Our discussion of scales relates to the question of the construction and implementation of theory. There must be a rule to assign numbers before there can be measurement. This rule is usually a set of operations which must be devised for the given task. The formulation of the rule gives rise to a scale. Measurement can be made only on a scale.

The question of testing of a theory relates to the question of the different kinds of measurement. Campbell mentioned two kinds: fundamental and derived.[11] Recall that in Campbell's definition of measurement he stated that the numbers are assigned according to the 'laws' governing the property. For Campbell, measurements can take place only when there are confirmed empirical theories (laws) to support the measurements. A further type of measurement, fiat measurement, was mentioned by Torgerson as being additional to the fundamental and derived measurements discussed by Campbell. All three measurements are discussed on the following pages.

Fundamental measurements

A fundamental measurement is one where the numbers can be assigned to the property by reference to natural laws and which does not depend on the measurement of any other variable. Properties such as length, electrical resistance, number and volume are fundamentally measurable. A ratio scale can be formulated for each of these properties on the basis of laws relating the different measures (quantities) of the given property. The interpretation of the numbers depends on the confirmed empirical theory that governs the measurement operation.

As it turns out, the fundamental properties are additive. Because of this, it is simple to find physical parallels to the operations of arithmetic.[12] For example, adding the length of object X to the length of object Y is paralleled by the actual operation of placing two straight rods end to end, with one rod having the same length as X and the other the same length as Y. We can physically determine the total length of X and Y. Because of these physical parallels, the scientist can simply perform the mechanical operations of mathematics without having to conduct an experiment for length.

Derived measurements

According to Campbell, a derived measurement is one that depends on the measurement of two or more other quantities. The measurement of density is an example. It depends on the measurement of both mass and volume. Derived measurement operations depend on known relationships to fundamental properties. They are based on a confirmed empirical theory relating the given property to other properties. Mathematical operations can be performed on the numbers from derived measurements because of the parallel mathematical and physical operations on the fundamental properties.

It has been pointed out that there are measurements, such as temperature, that depend only on one rather than two or more other measurements.[13] To measure temperature, we need only to measure pressure, volume or electrical resistance. However, even in these cases the measurement is based on natural laws.

Today, because natural scientists are aware of so many known relationships among physical properties, they can simply derive measurements based on a few fundamental properties. But this cannot be said of social scientists, because there is no agreement as to what the fundamental properties are in the social sciences. In accounting, an example of a derived measurement is profit. It is derived from the addition and subtraction of income and expenses.

Fiat measurements

It is typical in the social sciences, and in accounting, to use an arbitrarily established definition to relate certain observable properties (variables) to a given concept, without having a confirmed theory to support this relationship.

For example, in accounting we do not know how to measure the concept of profit directly. Rather, we assume that the variables of revenues, gains, expenses and losses are related to the concept of profit and can therefore be used to give us an indirect measure of profit. We use an arbitrary definition to relate the variables to the concept. In this instance, we consider the algebraic sum of the measurement of the variables to be a measure of profit.

However, under Campbell's stringent classification, measurements can be made only if confirmed empirical theories exist to support them. Under Campbell's requirement, then, many of the measurements in the social sciences, including our measurement of profit, cannot be considered measurements.

In order to justify most of the measurements in the social sciences, Torgerson argues that one other category of measurement should be added to Campbell's list: measurement by fiat.[14] (*Fiat* means decree, edict.) Such measurements would encompass those based on arbitrary definitions (e.g. the measurement of profit in accounting). However, Torgerson points out that the major problem with measurement by fiat, because it is not based on confirmed theory, is the numerous ways in which the scales can be constructed. In accounting, for example, the various accounting standards boards determine accounting scale by fiat, not by reference to confirmed measurement theories. Therefore, there are many measurement alternatives so confidence in any particular scale may be low. Coming back to our earlier example, do we know, for example, that the specific way we measure profit is valid? It may be one of a hundred ways to measure profit and as long as the particular way we measure it is not based on confirmed theory, there is no good reason for confidence in its results.

One of the reasons for a measurement approach to accounting theory formulation is the hope that if accounting theory can be empirically tested, then instead of fiat measurements we can have fundamental measurements. One can be justifiably more confident in fundamental measurements than in fiat measurements as a measurement tool.

To test for the validity of their measures, social scientists have attempted to relate the property under study to other variables to see if they are meaningful. For example, if we wanted to measure people's arithmetical ability, we might choose to make them sit an arithmetic test. However, there is no confirmed empirical theory to justify our test and we therefore make assumptions when we establish the measurement scale (i.e. when we set the number and type of items in the test and the form of the test). We can predict that, given a large number of people, those who score high on our test will also perform well in a university maths course. The correlation between scores on the test and the grades received in the university course would be one way to validate the particular measurement operation (i.e. our test). In this way, assuming a significantly high positive correlation, we can have some confidence in the validity of the given measurement operation.

LO 5 → RELIABILITY AND ACCURACY

What is meant by the reliability of a measurement or the accuracy of a measurement? To answer this question, we should state first that no measurement is free of error except counting. We can count the number of chairs in a certain room and be exactly correct. But except for counting, all measurements involve errors.

Sources of error

The sources of error in measurement include the following, which are not mutually exclusive.

- *Measurement operations stated imprecisely.* The rule to assign numbers for a given property usually consists of a set of operations. A set of operations may not be stated precisely and therefore may be interpreted incorrectly by the measurer. For example, the calculation of profit involves numerous operations, such as cost classifications and allocations between assets and expenses which are often interpreted differently by different accountants. Another reason is that frequently the 'fit' of the mathematical operation does not match well the actual relations of the properties to be measured.
- *Measurer.* The measurer may misinterpret the rule, be biased, or apply or read the instrument incorrectly. For example, if ten people measured the length of a certain room, there would probably be ten different results, which may all be close, but still at variance with one another. One concern in accounting is that managers have certain biases to increase the recorded profit or asset base and then place pressure on the accountant to bias the accounts.
- *Instrument.* Many operations call for the use of a physical instrument, such as a ruler or thermometer or barometer, which may be flawed. There is potential for error even when the instrument is not a physical tool but is, for example, a chart, graph, table of numbers or a price index. For instance, some consider the CPI for general price level adjustments to be defective.
- *Environment.* The setting in which the measurement operation is performed can affect the result. For example, weather conditions may affect the instrument or the measurer. More generally, noise may distract the measurer or, in accounting, pressure from management may affect the accountant's decisions. If the pressure causes bias by the accountant, the 'error' is deliberate and non-random. If the pressure (e.g. from heavy workload) causes concentration lapses and distraction, the source of error can be labelled 'environmental'. Random errors are often caused by environmental factors. Another factor is the environment in which the firm's management is operating in. For example, the manager may be paid his or her bonus according to the amount of profit earned or the cost of debt funds may be determined by the amount of gearing (assets/equity).
- *Attribute unclear.* What is to be measured may not be clear, especially if the measurement involves a concept which cannot be measured directly. For example, suppose we want to measure the mechanical ability of people, which is not a directly observable property. What do we look at to measure? Or suppose we wish

to measure the 'masculinity' of each boy in a given group. First of all, the attribute is difficult to define. Measurement of it can only be indirectly inferred from a variety of responses. The problem of vagueness of the attribute is not uncommon in accounting. What is the value of a non-current asset? Is it the present value, acquisition cost, current cost or selling price? Given that a major purpose of accounting is to reflect 'values', it is important to clearly define the attribute 'value'. Is it value in use, value in exchange, or some other attribute that the accountant should measure? The problem lies in defining the attribute to be measured, not the measurement method *per se*.

• *Risk and uncertainty*. This relates to the distribution of returns on a tangible asset. For example, future returns on tangible assets such as plant and equipment are risky but they are (more or less) homogeneous and prices observable. That is, when pricing the asset one may under- or overestimate the amount of returns but the distribution of returns is more or less known (i.e. the estimate of value is risky but the risk is comparably narrow). However, intangible assets face the problem of risk as well as uncertainty. Risk exists because the amount of returns is unknown, and uncertainty means that we face a relatively unknown distribution of returns. This is usually caused by highly uncertain returns from intangible investments (e.g. human capital, research and development and marketing), and returns from these investments that vary greatly across firms and industries.

If all measurements except counting inherently involve errors, then how can any statement that includes a measurement be regarded as true? The problem is that many expect perfection when there cannot be any. What we need is to establish limits of acceptable error. If any measurement falls within these limits then it can be considered true and fair in accounting terms.

Reliable measurement

It is often required that before elements such as assets, liabilities, income and expenses are recognised in financial statements, the elements should be capable of reliable measurement (e.g. IAS 8/AASB 108 *Accounting Policies, Changes in Accounting Estimates and Errors*, paragraph 10(b)). What is meant by a reliable measurement? Reliability refers to the proven consistency of either an operation to produce satisfactory results or the results (the numbers) themselves for a particular use. In statistics, reliability demands that measurements be repeatable or reproducible, thereby demonstrating their consistency.

The notion of reliability incorporates two aspects: the accuracy and certainty of measurement, and the representative faithfulness of disclosures in relation to the underlying economic transactions and events. The measurement aspect concerns the precision of measurement.

The term 'precision' is often used in two contexts. First, it may refer to a number, in which case it is opposite to the notion of approximation. For example, the number 90.4 is more precise than 90 if the real score is 90.44. Second, it can refer to a measurement operation, in which case it relates to:

• the degree of refinement of the operation or its performance

• the agreement of the results among repeated use of the measurement operation as applied to a given property.

This last meaning is essentially the same as that of reliability. Putting together the two terms, we can say that the reliability of a measurement pertains to the precision with which a specific property is measured by use of a given set of operations.

Accurate measurement

Although a measurement procedure may be highly reliable, giving very precise results, it may not produce accurate results. A certain rifle in the hands of an expert sports shooter may be highly reliable in enabling successive shots to be placed close together, but if the sight is not properly aligned, those shots will not be around the bullseye. Consistency of results, precision and reliability do not necessarily lead to accuracy. The reason is that accuracy has to do with how close the measurement is to the 'true value' of the attribute measure, the 'bullseye', so to speak.[15]

Fundamental properties, such as the length of an object, can be determined to be accurate by comparing the object with a standard that represents true value. We can, for example, use a ruler as a representation of the standard. For many years, a platinum-iridium bar kept in Paris represented the standard metre. In 1983, the standard metre was defined as the length of the path travelled by light in a vacuum during a time interval of $1/(299\ 792\ 458)$ of a second.

The problem is that for many measurements the true value is not known. In order to determine accuracy in accounting, we need to know what attribute we should measure to achieve the purpose of the measurement. The objective of accounting mentions the 'usefulness' of the information. Accuracy of measurements therefore relates to the pragmatic notion of usefulness, but accountants are not in agreement as to what the specific, quantitative standards are that are implied. We should note, however, that repetition of operations does not ensure accuracy. We can calculate the cost of the inventory by FIFO and repeat the calculation a hundred times and get the same answer, but that does not mean the answer is accurate, except in the sense of checking for arithmetical error. We can also be very precise in our calculation to derive a figure of $1 018 412.18 and still not necessarily be accurate. Instead of using the term 'accuracy', which is so often understood to mean arithmetical precision, it may be prudent to use the term of the social scientists, 'validity'.

The following interview provides a perspective regarding the meaning of reliability and relevant measurement. Importantly, note the comments on the hierarchy of reliability in measurements, increased complexity, the new role of auditors and university courses.

5.1 INTERNATIONAL VIEW

The impact of the accounting profession's movement toward fair value reporting in financial statements: an interview with Theresa Ahlstrom, Long Island Office Managing Partner, KPMG LLP.

Interviewed by Patrick A. Casabona, The Peter J. Tobin College of Business, St. John's University

KPMG LLP, the audit, tax and advisory firm, turns knowledge into value for the benefit of its clients, people, communities and the capital markets. Its professionals work together to provide clients access to global support, industry insights, and a multidisciplinary range of services. KPMG LLP (www.us.kpmg.com) is the U.S. member firm of KPMG International. In 1993, KPMG International was the first multidisciplinary professional services organization to establish itself along industry-specific lines of business. This enabled KPMG to tailor services and strategies to the needs of clients across a range of global industry markets. KPMG International's member firms have 103,000 professionals, including 6,700 partners, in 144 countries.

Theresa P. Ahlstrom is KPMG's Long Island Office Managing Partner and the Northeast Audit Quality Support Partner, supporting the Northeast Audit Area Risk I Management Partner, and playing a key role in the development and execution of the area's quality enhancement initiatives. She started her career at KPMG, LLP, in 1982 as a pre-professional in the firm's

National Department of Professional Practice (DPP), and joined the audit professional staff of the Long Island office in 1983. In 1993, after a two-year rotation in DPP and the Office of General Counsel, she was admitted into the partnership.

Ms. Ahlstrom has served as lead engagement partner for numerous clients in the healthcare, biotech, consumer and industrial market, and non-profit industries. Because of her technical experience and client service record, she was designated an SEC Reviewing Partner, Professional Practice Partner, Employee Benefit Resource Partner, Primary Campus Recruiter, and National Training Instructor.

Graduating summa cum laude with a B.S. degree in accounting from St. John's University in 1983, she was inducted into the YWCA Academy of Women Achievers in 1998 and the Long Island's Top 50 Women Hall of Fame in 2000, 2001 and 2003. Ms. Ahlstrom is also very active in numerous community activities and professional associations, and received the 2003 Long Island Fund for Women and Girls Achievers Award. She resides in South Huntington, New York, with her husband Bob and their two young sons.

Q: **How do you think fair value affects the reliability and relevancy of the financial statements?**

A: There have been grumbles within Corporate America for well over a decade that financial statements are irrelevant to financial analysts, in light of the current techniques analysts use to value the health and projected financial performance of an entity. The objective of fair value accounting, on the other hand, provides users of financial statements with a clearer picture of the current economic state of a company, making a company's financial statements more useful or "relevant" in the marketplace. Clearly, historical cost accounting, while perhaps easier to follow and "bookkeep," has seen its day and more than outlived its usefulness. So I think most preparers and users of financial statements are sold on the enhanced relevancy point. However, I am not convinced on the topic of reliability of financial reporting using more fair value accounting methods. The increased subjectivity and estimation process that underpins all aspects of fair value accounting calls the "reliability" of such information into question for me. Having said that, I do believe that fair value has a far better chance of providing more reliable information in most cases than the old historical cost model.

Look at the last four Statements on Financial Accounting Standards (SFAS) issued by the Financial Accounting Standards Board (FASB), which all require some form of fair value reporting (i.e., SFAS 155, Accounting for Certain Hybrid Financial Instruments, SFAS 156, Accounting for Servicing of Financial Assets, SFAS 157, Fair Value Measurements, and SFAS 158, Employers' Accounting for Defined Benefit Pension and Other Postretirement Plans, an amendment of FASB Statements No. 87, 88, 106, and 132(R), and SFAS 159, The Fair Value Option for Financial Assets and Financial Liabilities, Including an amendment of FASB Statement No. 115). It is very clear from these standards that the "fair value train" has left the station, has accelerated quickly, and in my view will not to return anytime soon.

Q: **Similarly, what is your view on whether employing fair value accounting measures increases or decreases the complexity and "quality" of financial reporting?**

A: While I, and probably most other practitioners, think that today's accounting couldn't possibly get more complex, I believe the trend to recording more assets, liabilities, and the associated transactions at fair value will prove us wrong. Fair value accounting does not ensure, in my eyes, enhanced "quality" in financial reporting. As has always been the case, the quality of the financial statements still hinges on the soundness of internal controls over financial reporting and the thoroughness and technical competency of the preparers. I have heard many proponents of fair value accounting thought that it is the end of earnings management (and, therefore, improved quality of earnings) because there would be more of a focus on the assets and liabilities on the balance sheet than on the income statement. I would suggest that the inherent subjectivity and complexity of fair value valuation techniques makes it ripe for manipulation, if that is the objective. Of course, the astute reader of the financial statements could detect some cases of manipulation if there is robust disclosure of the assumptions underlying the valuations.

Q: During September 2006, the FASB issued SFAS 157, "Fair Value Measurements." Please comment on what impact this will have on the current accounting standards that require fair value measurements. Does this standard add to the complexity? Does it enhance the consistency of fair value reporting?

A: In my view SFAS 157 was long overdue. With numerous existing accounting standards requiring varying degrees of fair value estimates, SFAS 157 clearly provides some consistent "how to" requirements for calculating fair value. However, it is likely to add some complexity in financial reporting, as well as audit risk, associated with such reporting and disclosures. Moreover, based upon the assumptions within the "inputs" used to make the fair value calculations, the Financial Accounting Standards Board established a hierarchy of fair value measurements for financial disclosure, referred to as Levels 1, 2 and 3. This hierarchy, which is explained thoroughly in some of the articles presented in this journal issue, is intended to convey information about the nature of the inputs, with Level 1 being the "most reliable," which includes inputs that are only quoted prices in active markets, versus Level 3, which consists of unobservable inputs [that may reflect the Company's own assumptions].

Of course, this new standard will require that entities expend more effort than in the past, as they are forced to use more complex valuation models and calculations that are claimed to produce more reliable valuation estimates. Who is to make the final decision as to what valuation technique is most appropriate in each situation, especially when economists have been arguing about these issues for years? I also foresee many instances where there will be a lively debate about what the most appropriate "hierarchical level" a particular valuation estimate should be classified as, as Level 3 valuation requires more detailed and costly reconciliations and roll-forward disclosures for all activities that occurred during the period. Nonetheless, this debate is healthy as it should improve the transparency of fair value estimates to the astute reader and analyzer of the financial statements. The benefit of having one set of guidelines for calculating fair value measures codified within one accounting standard will hopefully improve consistency and transparency which may outweigh the costs associated with the complexity of the calculations. The disclosures within the financial statements should be a good step in allowing investors to understand the inputs and assumptions used by a Company to determine fair value and in turn, make their own judgments on the reliability and relevance of the information within the financial statements.

Q: How does the greater use of fair value accounting measurements affect the audit procedures of the independent auditor?

A: The impact on the independent audit has been relatively extensive, particularly in auditing the more complex fair value calculations using valuation models, for example as required by SFAS 123(R), Share-Based Payment, or in situations (which are becoming more and more common) where a company uses third-party specialists to determine a fair value measurement. In short, in these situations the subjectivity and complexity has had a direct impact on audit risk and the cost of the audit.

At KPMG, timely, extensive and on-going training programs for its professionals worldwide are developed and delivered on each new accounting and audit standard. Additionally, our engagement teams are typically armed with a list of procedures and steps they use to effectively and efficiently audit complex accounting areas, such as fair value measures, referred to as audit program guides. Our firm also specifically trains experienced audit and advisory professionals to assist engagement teams in working through more difficult accounting standards, such as SFAS 157.

More often than not, our core audit engagement teams are assisted by valuation specialists, actuaries, financial derivative resources or share-based payment specialists. These professionals, most of whom are specially-trained audit partners and senior managers, principally assist the auditors in assessing the qualifications of third-party specialists engaged by a client to calculate fair value measurements and disclosures and determining the reasonableness of the assumptions and methodologies used in such measurements. Of course, where valuations and estimates are used to determine fair values, there are numerous other audit procedures that are employed. These include documentation and testing of management's process over calculating fair value measures, including assumption development, as well as testing completeness, accuracy, and relevancy of the underlying data used in the valuations and other calculations.

Q: How could accounting programs appropriately prepare students for the fair value accounting measurements they will inevitably deal with when they enter the business world?

A: There is no doubt that the movement toward the increased use of fair value accounting and estimation methods requires additional skill sets in accountants, auditors, analysts and financial reporting specialists, than were previously required. I would argue that the enhanced fair value requirements may significantly increase the workloads of these individuals, given the complexity and the need for more continuous updating of fair values estimates than before. Unfortunately, this comes at a time of already stretched resources of both corporate accounting and financial reporting staffs and external auditors. Accounting programs are going to have to ensure that there is a focus on teaching the next generation of CPAs valuation techniques and in-depth financial statement analysis tools. Additionally, higher education institutions may need to consider providing more opportunities for students to specialize in areas of economics, finance, and statistics [in addition to accounting degrees], to ensure that today's students are adequately prepared to tackle tomorrow's challenges.

Source: Review of Business, pp. 6–9. College of Business Administration at St. John's University, New York. Copyright of *Review of Business* is the property of St John's University College.

LO 6 → MEASUREMENT IN ACCOUNTING

Measurement in accounting falls into the category of derived measurement for both capital and profit. Accounting profit is now derived, under international accounting standards, from the change in capital over the period from all activities including increases and decreases in the fair value of net assets excluding transactions with owners. Capital is derived from the net of 'fair value' measure of assets and liabilities. That means we have to measure the value of opening capital, the amount of income received, the amount of capital usage, and the change in the fair value of net assets. The increase in capital over the period will then measure the amount of profit from various sources including operations and remeasurements (after adjusting for the infusion of new capital or payment of dividends). The restated fair value of net assets will then constitute opening capital in the next period.

Contrast this measurement approach with the approach taken before the introduction of international accounting standards. Revenue received was matched against net assets used up in a period and if income was greater than net capital usage (or expenses), then we had an increase in capital. Profit was not earned until initial opening historical cost capital was maintained and profit realised. That is, capital was always stated at historical costs and changes in net assets were not considered as profit. Hence, we can see that derived profit depends very much on how we measure opening capital and how we measure expense and capital allocation. We can also see that the concept of capital valuation in accounting has evolved over time with the result that we have several capital maintenance measurements and profit concepts. A brief historical overview will illustrate this point.

In the first thousand years AD, the economic structure was represented by decentralised, self-contained fiefdoms. The purpose of accounting was to count and safeguard the assets of the steward using single-entry accounting. Under this system, capital was measured as the stock of land, animals and agricultural produce with the purpose of producing output (income) for sustenance. Capital was not usually measured in financial terms but simply counted and itemised.

After the crusades to the Holy Land in the eleventh century, the opening up of the Middle Eastern and Asian trade routes created a demand for tradeable goods (silk, spices, carpets). The Italian trading cities played a major role transporting crusaders to the Holy Land and returning with goods. This activity created a requirement for venture capital. Profit was based on the returns from (usually) single return voyages, which were financed by venture partners and calculated after returning original capital. Thus, ending capital was measured as the accumulation of wealth from individual ventures plus original capital. From a venture shareholder's point of view, profit represented an increase in wealth. Moreover, the use of the Arabic numbering system together with the concept of returnable capital led to the evolution of double-entry accounting. This system was used widely by Italian merchants from the twelfth to the sixteenth centuries and was first documented by Luca Pacioli as the 'System of Venice' in 1494.

The eighteenth century in England saw the development of joint stock companies with limited liability, a separate management class, and transferability of shares. A number of these companies were declared bankrupt, resulting in large losses to creditors, which in turn, led to the introduction of the 1844 Joint Stock Companies Regulation and Registration Act. This Act emphasised creditor protection and conservative accounting valuations. Thus, the definition of derived capital moved towards 'creditor capital' and resulted in an acceptance of the lower of cost and market value rule as a measurement principle. In the nineteenth century another concept of capital emerged following the railway expansion in the United States. This concept of capital revolved around maintaining intact the stock of going concern assets (railroad assets such as engines, coaches and track) so as to continue the ability of railroads to provide the same level of transport services. This resulted in the concept of depreciation as a method to retain funds (capital) in order to replace assets, and the going concern concept of capital maintenance.

To this point in history there was little developed theory of capital maintenance and profit, only a collection of vague concepts. However, in 1940 Paton and Littleton[16] produced the first definitive statement on the concepts of capital and profit. They defined profit as being derived from the matching or allocation of historical costs against revenue earned. Profit measurement was seen as the major focus of accounting with the derived balance sheet simply the repository of all yet-to-be-allocated historical costs. Hence, the balance sheet was not seen as a measurement of the net market value (or fair value) of a business. The concepts and principles of the Paton and Littleton system formed the basis of the conventional historical cost accounting system which was the dominant system before the introduction of international accounting standards in 2005.

The normative period of the 1960s saw a number of challenges to the historical cost principle of valuation and hence capital maintenance. Critics deductively argued that the valuation of firms based on outdated historical costs was not all that useful for economic decision making, and the derived profit did not measure contemporary resource usage. They developed several capital maintenance and profit systems based on maintaining intact opening capital adjusted for general and specific inflation. Thus, profit was derived after maintaining intact some concept of 'market priced' capital, and viewed as a real increase in purchasing power or an ability to maintain the supply of goods and services. There was robust debate about which was the 'dominant' profit measurement system, but the debate was never settled and lapsed somewhat in the literature. These debates can be considered the forerunner of the 'fair value' approach to derived accounting measurement.

Consequently, we were left with a number of accounting measurement systems. These different perspectives reflect various boundaries of accounting and a lack of agreement on measurement principles, but with the historical cost allocation system as the conventional and dominant model. Added to this were a number of academic accounting papers that suggested the value relevance of conventional profit had significantly declined over time, but balance sheet items and intangible assets had become more important.[17] More recently, the International Accounting Standards Board (IASB) has taken the view that globalisation of business supports the need for one set of accounting standards to be used throughout the world in order to produce comparable financial information.

This has resulted in two notable developments in international accounting standards[18] as signalled through accounting standards such as IAS 39/AASB 139 *Financial Instruments: Recognition and Measurement* and the IASB/FASB joint project on reporting financial performance[19] — (1) that profit measurement and revenue recognition should be linked to timely recognition, and (2) that the 'fair value' approach should be adopted as a working measurement principle. Thus, from 2005 we see the use (in part) of a measurement principle that focuses on the change in the value of assets and liabilities rather than the completion of an earnings process. In short, this means that changes in the fair value of assets and liabilities are recognised immediately they occur and reported as a component of income. Furthermore, the focus has shifted towards a valuation concept, with the balance sheet the major repository of value-relevant information, and the main users of accounting information stated to be shareholders and investors. At no stage has the principle of capital maintenance been explicitly discussed. These measurement concepts are not without controversy. Theory in action 5.1 comments on fair value measurement within IASB and FASB standards and raises a number of concerns surrounding fair value accounting and whether it has an underlying measurement principle.

<table>
<tr><td>5.1
THEORY
IN ACTION</td><td>**Fair value measurement**</td></tr>
</table>

'True and fair' and 'fair value' — accounting and legal will-o'-the-wisps

by Graeme Dean and Frank Clarke

This issue of *Abacus* goes to press as the convergence to an international financial reporting standards (IFRS) regime begins. More than thirty years since the lengthy gestation of the International Accounting Standards (IAS) Committee, application and enforcement of international standards under the guidance of the International Accounting Standards Board (IASB) is nigh . . .

Within this setting the suggestion by many commentators (including the IASB in its public documents) that the IFRS regime is principles- rather than rules-based is contestable. This matter has been discussed in several recent *Abacus* editorials and is further examined here. Whereas those promoting the principles rather than rules mantra have failed to specify what those principles are, the general tenor of their comments gives reason to imagine that such a distinction is underpinned by the qualitative criterion, 'true and fair view' (or its equivalent) legal or professional override. Frequent recourse to 'fair value' in many IFRS adds further support to a principled approach to things commercial. It will be shown that both settings, however, illustrate the contestable nature of what is meant by those preferring principles. Those settings represent potential difficulties in achieving convergence of an effective IFRS regime . . .

Richard Macve in his submission adopts a different, albeit equally critical, perspective. An extract from his conclusion is followed by an earlier summary paragraph outlining specifics:

> Even though it [FASB] argues that 'conceptually, fair value is a market-based measurement that is not affected by factors specific to a particular entity' (para C2), this ED necessarily acknowledges that there may be different market prices available to different enterprises, and correspondingly different measures of fair value. It proposes to resolve this divergence by requiring that entities choose as their reference market the most advantageous market to which they have immediate access (para C45). This issue is discussed further below. However, the more fundamental issue of 'entry' versus 'exit' prices is left undiscussed and unresolved (and the definition of fair value is therefore itself necessarily left ambiguous) primarily because there is no discussion of the underlying conceptual framework of valuation which has been fully explored elsewhere in the academic and professional literature using the concept of 'deprival value' for assets (and the related concept of 'relief value' for liabilities) (e.g., Baxter, 1975, Chapter 12; AARF, 1998; ASB, 1999). It is not clear whether the Board has come to a view on these conceptual issues or whether they are still to be addressed in the conceptual phase of the project. At present the ED gives the impression that the Board is merely avoiding these issues — but until they are addressed and explained the implications of the definition of fair value and related requirements of this proposed standard are necessarily left incomplete and essentially unclear. (For further discussion see Horton and Macve, 2000.) [R. Macve, FASB Submission #6, p. 2]

Brief discussion of those two events reveals the difficult path ahead for the IASB countering such will-o'-the wisp issues to achieve a convergence regime that produces financial reporting comparability across countries.

Source: Excerpts from *Abacus*, vol. 41, no. 2, 2005.

Questions

1. What do you think the authors mean by a principles- versus a rules-based system of accounting?
2. What are the measurement problems they allude to?
3. What does Macve mean by the underlying conceptual framework? What problems does he see with a 'fair value' approach?
4. Do you think there is any difference between 'measures' and 'values'?

For some firms it is argued that fair value accounting fundamentally changes the focus of risk management. That is, firms will decrease their hedging activity because they are worried about the accounting impact of profits under IAS 39/AASB 139. One other consequence is that a company's pension fund now shows up as a liability on the balance sheet (IAS 19/AASB 119 *Employee Benefits*) and this may need to be hedged. The derivatives a firm uses to hedge this liability might depend on whether the pension scheme is in surplus or deficit. Thus, international accounting standards may reduce hedging activity if it results in an increased volatility in income while increasing hedging and risk management for pension liabilities.

The IASB also makes a trade-off between reliable measures and relevant measures. Sometimes that judgement is made by the IASB. For example, in IAS 39/AASB 139, for available-for-sale securities the IASB determines that fair value (selling price) must be used instead of historical cost. However, for IAS 41/AASB 141 *Agriculture*, although fair value is required where possible, the Board states that it may be difficult to obtain reliable measures of fair value. In this case the reliability exception allows preparers to make a trade-off between fair value and reliability when measuring value.

Capital or income?

Dr Nadine Fry and Dr David Bence are senior lecturers at the Bristol Business School

Despite the established link between asset and liability measurement and capital maintenance, the latter represents a second order issue for the IASB, say Nadine Fry and David Bence.

In May 2005, the International Accounting Standards Board (IASB) and the US Financial Accounting Standards Board (FASB) launched a joint project to develop a common conceptual framework that could be used to develop new and revised International Accounting Standards (IASs), As part of the project, much time will be spent considering the measurement of business income.

The 'debit' side of the problem has received a substantial amount of attention in recent years with the IASB's drive towards fair value as a solution to accounting measurement problems. Yet despite the established link between asset and liability measurement and capital maintenance, the latter represents a second order issue for the IASB. So if a futures contract has a fair value of £10m but an historical cost of zero, should one credit income or capital?

Interestingly, although the IASB's Framework claims that financial statements should enable users to determine distributable profits and dividends, the IASB argues that such issues constitute part of the legal framework of individual countries for which there is little international convergence.

Regrettable

However, even if one accepts that there will always be different distributable profit rules around the world, the IASB's failure to decide on a capital maintenance concept is regrettable as users have no idea as to whether total gains represent income or capital and are therefore unable to identify a meaningful 'bottom line'.

The IASB does not appear willing to tackle capital maintenance issues. IAS 1, *Presentation of Financial Statements*, permits companies to produce either a 'statement of recognised gains and losses' or a 'statement of changes in equity', but both ignore capital maintenance. Although it may be argued that sophisticated users can make up their own minds as to the nature of total gains, this decision is not in line with the FASB/IASB conceptual framework project, which aims to deal explicitly with the issue of capital maintenance.

The approach currently adopted by IASs generally provides a measurement of income based on the nominal unit of currency, a mixed system for measuring assets and liabilities and money capital maintenance (see for example, IAS 19, *Employee Benefits*; IAS 21, *The Effects of Changes in Foreign Exchange Rates*, IAS 39, *Financial Instruments: Recognition and Measurement*, and IAS 40, *Investment Property*).

Inconsistent

Surely a mixed measurement system and money capital maintenance do not go together well? However, the concept of money capital maintenance is not consistently applied across international standards. For example, IAS 29, *Financial Reporting in Hyperinflationary Economies*, has the effect of real financial capital maintenance, whereas IAS 16, *Property, Plant and Equipment*, and IAS 38, *Intangible Assets*, apply physical capital maintenance.

It seems fair to conclude that even if the IASB continues to apply capital maintenance on a line-by-line (or element-by-element) basis, an additional financial accounting element, a 'capital maintenance adjustment', should be included below 'total gains' in the 'statement of recognised income and expense'.

The IASB could provide guidance on the items that would make up the capital maintenance adjustment, presumably including changes in the unit of currency, unrealised gains, realised gains where replacement is required, and so on. Such a financial accounting element would enable users to determine the proportion of total gains represented by capital and income and would help to alert users to the fact that some gains may reverse because they are unrealised.

Source: Accountancy, April 2007, p. 81, www.accountancymagazine.com.

Questions
1. Why is the measurement distinction between capital and income important?
2. What do you think is real financial capital maintenance and what is physical capital maintenance?
3. Is the increase in the value of a house you live in income or capital? Provide explanations.
4. Does your answer to question 3 change if your house is an investment property? Give reasons for your answer.

The FASB/IASB joint project on Financial Statement Presentation (previously Reporting Comprehensive Income or Performance Reporting) highlights the IASB's thinking on income and asset measurement, particularly the application of fair value measurement. Some agreed concepts include the following.[20]

1. Accounting information should be aimed at decision makers making economic decisions about the entity.
2. Entities should present a single statement of all recognised income and expense items as a component of a complete set of financial statements.
3. The statement should be all-inclusive:
   (a) It should include the effects of all changes in net assets and liabilities during the period, other than transactions with owners.
   (b) Assets and liabilities should be valued at fair value which presumes market prices but substitutes such as discounted future cash flows, depreciated market prices or asset-pricing models can be used in the absence of a liquid market.
   (c) Income determination should be split between profit before remeasurement and remeasurement effects.
4. All income and expenses should be categorised and displayed in a way that
   (a) enhances users' understanding of achieved performance
   (b) assists in forming expectations of future performance.
5. Profits should not be based on a notion of realisation.
6. The focus should be on
   (a) greater transparency
   (b) useful information to investors and relevance of data for decision making
   (c) the concept of reliability has been replaced by representational faithfulness.

Under this approach the income statement would become the residual between opening net assets and closing net assets, rather than the balance sheet becoming the residual of unallocated costs after the matching process, which is the case under historical cost measurement. The concepts stated above give an indication of the Boards' thinking about financial statement presentation and measurement issues.

LO 7 ⊢ MEASUREMENT ISSUES FOR AUDITORS

Several issues are created for auditors by the shift in focus for profit measurement from matching revenues and expenses to assessing the change in the fair values of net assets. When profit is determined by matching revenue and expense transactions for the period the auditor can concentrate on gathering evidence that those transactions have been handled appropriately by the client's accounting system. However, when profit is derived from changes in fair values more difficult questions arise for the auditor around gathering evidence on management's estimates.

For example, one aspect of measuring profit by assessing changes in fair value of net assets is addressed by the accounting standard IAS 36/AASB 136. This standard requires a decline in an asset value to be recognised as an impairment loss. Management of the entity is required to assess at reporting date whether there is any indication that an asset may be impaired. If any such indication exists, management shall estimate the recoverable amount of the asset. If the recoverable amount of an asset is less than its carrying amount, the carrying amount of the asset shall be reduced to its recoverable amount. That reduction is an impairment loss. The impairment loss shall be recognised immediately in profit in most cases.

The international auditing standards guidance for auditing impairment losses and other fair value estimates is contained in ISA 540.[21] Auditors are required to gather evidence to judge if management has followed the accounting standard appropriately and if the amount recognised as an impairment loss is reasonable. To do this, the auditor must determine whether management has chosen appropriate and reasonable valuation methods and assumptions. If the accounting standards do not prescribe the valuation method for the particular assets and liabilities being considered, the auditor could accept any reasonable valuation method. As explained in detail in case study 5.1, there are at least twelve methods of valuing intangibles and brands from which management could choose. This means that it is difficult for an auditor to disagree with management's choice of a particular valuation method that is being used by other entities. The auditor must gather evidence that the method is applied consistently, so that managers do not pick and choose methods from year to year depending on their desired profit result. Auditors must also assess whether the asset or liability values are properly determined from management's significant assumptions, the valuation model and the relevant underlying data. Such data would include the interest rates used for discounting cash flows, market values used by comparison companies, royalty data, and so on.

Overall, given the existence of different reasonable valuation methods and possible assumptions, it is possible for several different but reasonable amounts to be recognised by management for impairment losses. These different amounts would therefore be acceptable to the auditors if the audit evidence suggests that management has applied the valuation models correctly and used appropriate data. In these circumstances, it is possible that auditors face pressure from managers to agree with their valuation choices or else lose the audit to another auditor who is more agreeable.

In addition to the issues related to the use of fair values and associated issues, auditors also face problems caused by variability in the level of reliability and accuracy of measurement of historical costs. For example, standard costing manufacturing systems are based on historical costs of various inputs, assumptions about processing volumes and methods, and issues surrounding the assignment of overhead costs between products, processes, and departments. All these factors affect the costs of inventory on hand at the end of the period and goods sold during the period. In this context, the auditor needs to test the reasonableness of the procedures adopted in developing the standards from the engineering specifications. This includes gathering evidence about the reasonableness of the underlying assumptions and consistent use of the data. The inventory cost per unit will appear to be very precise, but changes in operating conditions could produce significant variances and render the underlying assumptions for cost allocation to be invalid.

Summary

LO 1 **The importance of measurement**
Measurement involves the formal linking of numbers to some property or event by means of semantic rules. The semantic rules in accounting are represented by transactions in markets, and the allocation of the use of capital resources against incoming revenue over the period.

LO 2 **The nominal, ordinal, interval and ratio scales of measurement**
The rules used to assign numbers are determined according to four scales: nominal, ordinal, interval and ratio. In accounting, we use the ratio scale to measure the financial attributes of profit, assets and liabilities. However, we may also apply the ordinal scale to rank investment projects or the profitability of firms, or the interval scale in standard cost accounting.

LO 3 **The permissible operations of scales**
Invariance of a scale means that, regardless of the measure used, the measurement system will provide the same general form of the variables and the decision maker will make the same decisions. This is not the case in accounting, as different systems are variant to each other. Income measured under one system will lead to different decisions from income measured under another system. The systems won't provide the same information.

LO 4 **The difference between fundamental, derived and fiat measurements**
There are three different types of measurement. Fundamental measurement is when numbers, which do not depend on other properties, can be assigned by reference to natural laws. In accounting there is considerable debate over the nature of fundamental value. Derived measurement depends on the previous measurement of two or more other quantities, for example, the determination of income and expenses before profit is determined. Fiat measurements are those that relate numbers to properties of objects or events on the basis of arbitrary definitions. All measurement involves errors and for many measurements the true value is not known.

LO 5 **What is meant by reliability and accuracy in measurement**
Reliability refers to the proven consistency of the measure, that is, the same (or similar) measure would be reproduced by different observers. Accurate measure refers to the representation of the fundamental value of the property being measured. Measurement theory also teaches us that many of our measurements in accounting are on a ratio scale, which is the most informative scale, but they have the weakest theoretical foundation because they are fiat measurements. Greater confidence in such measurements can be attained if there is theoretical or empirical evidence to support the relationships of the properties or the need for such theories. However, all accounting measures contain

measurement risk and there is considerable debate in accounting as to what constitutes fair value and what are the acceptable distribution ranges. An understanding of the concepts of risk and uncertainty help us to understand the valuation problem.

LO 6 Measurement in accounting

The two fundamental measures in accounting are capital and profit and they are both derived measures. Capital is derived from transactions and revaluations that occur in financial markets, and profit can be derived from the matching of expenses with revenue or the change in capital over the period. Capital can be defined and derived in various ways, including historical cost, operating, financial, or 'fair value'. History shows us that the concepts of capital and profit have changed and evolved over time so that there are a number of concepts of fundamental measurement. More recently, international financial reporting standards have made greater use of the concept of 'fair value'. A number of commentators argue that this concept diverges from allocation principles to a valuation approach, which will differ according to the circumstances and subjective interpretations. These changes focus more on balance sheet valuation, moving accounting away from a simple profit allocation measurement system and placing more emphasis on relevance for commercial reality and investor decision making rather than reliability.

LO 7 Measurement issues for auditors

The existence of alternative valuation methods for some assets creates issues for auditors. There could be many different asset values that are acceptable to the auditor if the valuation method is applied appropriately and consistently, reasonable assumptions are used, and the data used to generate the valuations are valid. The auditor could face pressure from managers to accept their valuation or the entity will seek another auditor. There are also issues in auditing historical costs, such as standard inventory costs, where the costs are precisely stated, but based on assumptions about engineering processes that are influenced by changing conditions.

Questions

1. Technically, what do we mean when we say 'X was measured'?
2. How is a scale related to the process of measurement?
3. Describe the following scales: nominal, ordinal, interval, and ratio. Give an example of each. Which scales are applied in accounting and where?
4. Determine whether the following statements are correct and state why:
    (a) The historical cost of inventory is $60 000 at year-end. When it is converted to constant end-of-year dollars by multiplying by 110/100 to get $66 000, the $66 000 is still the historical cost of the inventory.
    (b) Last month the quantity variance was determined to be $12 000 favourable, and this month it is $24 000 favourable: therefore, the efficient use of materials has been doubled.
    (c) On the basis of saving income tax, Company X ascertained that the diminishing-balance depreciation method is better than the straight-line method. By using the diminishing-balance method for depreciation rather than the straight-line method, Company X saved $10 000 in income tax this year; therefore, the former method is 10 000 times better than the latter.
    (d) On the basis of the amount of assets, we can say that Company X is twice as large as Company Y, because its total assets amount to $1 000 000 compared with $500 000 for Y.
5. Describe the following types of measurement: fundamental, derived, fiat. In what sense are fiat measurements 'weak'? What type of measurement is inventory costing?

6. What are the sources of error in measurement?
7. Explain whether the following statements are facts:
    (a) Canberra is 320 kilometres from Sydney.
    (b) Depreciation expense for Kambah Pty Ltd for 2008 was $1 294 000. (This is the amount reported on the income statement.)
    (c) Smoking leads to lung cancer.
    (d) Sales revenue for Telex Ltd for 2009 was $2 800 000. (This is the amount reported on the income statement.)
    (e) Equipment (net of accumulated depreciation of $400 000) for McNair Ltd for 2008 was worth $1 800 000. (This is the amount reported on the statement of financial positon.)
8. What is the difference between accuracy and reliability in measurement? How are these notions related to the testing of a theory?
9. Discuss whether accounting measurement is fiat or fundamental. Can accounting numbers ever be related to fundamental values? If so, what are some possible measurements that can be used?
10. Discuss how recent accounting standards using 'fair value' accounting such as IAS 39 and IAS 41 have moved away from fundamental measurement.
11. Why will international financial reporting standards induce an increased demand for risk management techniques?
12. How will the use of fair values affect the role of auditors and the audit function? Do you think it will affect the training of accounting students? How so?
13. What would be included in overhead costs assigned to inventory? How many ways can you think of assigning these costs when there are multiple products and departments? What are the audit implications?

Additional readings

Alfredson, K, Leo, K, Picker, R, Loftus, J, Clark, K, & Wise, V 2009, *Applying international financial reporting standards*, 2nd edn, Brisbane: John Wiley & Sons.

Charles, E 2002, 'Mixed bag', *Australian CPA*, May, pp. 26–30.

Churchman, CW, & Ratoosh, P (eds) 1959, *Measurements: definitions and theories*. New York: John Wiley.

Institute of Chartered Accountants in England and Wales (ICAEW) 2006, *Information for better markets: measurement in financial reporting*, ICAEW, www.icaew.co.uk/bettermarkets.

Kam, V 1973, 'Judgements and the scientific trend in accounting', *Journal of Accountancy*, February.

5.1
CASE STUDY

The following article discusses 12 different ways to value intangibles and brands using 'fair values'. The article highlights the difficulty involved in requiring reliability and accuracy and in providing relevant information.

12 ways to value intangibles and brands

1. **Net present value** The mainstream discounted cash method, used by the Big Five and Interbrand. This method looks at the proportion of business profits driven by brand and the relative security of branded profit streams.
2. **Capital asset pricing model** The main method used by Brand Finance, which assigns a brand to the intangible. This is interchangeable with the CAPM's discount rate.

3. **Cost of creation** This attempts to calculate the cost of building from scratch. Some say this technique is unworkable and unrealistic.
4. **Market-based comparisons** This is literally what it says. A comparison is made to a similar brand in the market. In practice difficult to achieve. One only need compare two similar tasting drinks, Coke and Pepsi, and their respective brand values of US$68.95bn and US$6.21bn respectively.
5. **Royalty relief method** If a brand is licensed from a third party, a royalty is paid. Here future sales are estimated and applied to a royalty rate to arrive at future brand value. The cashflow is discounted back to a net present value or brand value.
6. **Relative value** This looks at valuing the progress a company has made towards meeting target. For example: have 80 per cent of employees been with the customer in some meaningful way?
7. **Balanced scorecard** Supplements traditional financial measures with three additional perspectives such as customers, internal business processes, and learning/growth.
8. **Competency models** This would typically calculate the market value of the behaviours of a company's most successful employees.
9. **Benchmarking** Involves identifying companies that are recognised leaders in leveraging their intellectual assets, determining how well they score on relevant criteria, and then comparing your own company's performance against them.
10. **Business worth** This approach centres on three questions. What would happen if the information we now use disappeared altogether? What would happen if we doubled the amount of key information available? How does the value of this information change after a day, a week, a year?
11. **Business process auditing** This measures how information increases value for a specific business process, such as accounting, production or marketing.
12. **Knowledge bank** This turns around traditional accounting by saying that capital spending is an expense rather than an asset. In contrast, salaries are treated as an asset rather than an expense as they create future cashflows.

Source: Australian CPA, May 2002, p. 29 (using the sources of Montague Institute Review, Interbrand, Brand Finance).

Questions

1. Evaluate the advantages and disadvantages of each suggested measurement technique.
2. Make a recommendation as to which measurement technique should be used.
3. Would you consider using more than one measurement technique? Why or why not?

5.2
CASE STUDY

The following article raises concerns about the impact of international accounting standards on risk management strategies. In particular, it highlights the impact of IAS 39/AASB 139.

Risk management survey 2005: Take a risk. No chance

by Edward Thornton

How is IAS affecting corporates
'For some clients it's decreasing their hedging activity because they are worried about the accounting impact,' says Rashid Hoosenally, head of client strategies and product innovation at Deutsche Bank. 'But I think other clients have turned the corner.' Having

been initially fearful of IAS 39, Hoosenally believes many corporates are determined to implement strategies that are in the long-term economic interests of their company, even if it means bearing the pain of volatility in the short term . . .

This observation is certainly borne out in [*Corporate Finance's*] survey. While nearly half of respondents say that accounting considerations were 'very important', the vast majority (89.36%) of corporates surveyed say the ratio of their hedging done via options and structured forwards had not changed since IAS 39 became an issue. Corporates seem to be in a quietly defiant mood: acknowledging the importance of accounting issues, but refusing to be cowed.

On the other hand, says Russell Schofield Bezer, managing director of the corporate financial engineering group at JPMorgan, the issue of stricter accounting regulations has fundamentally changed the focus of risk management. Before, much of a corporate's time was spent worrying about the steepness of the dollar curve or the Federal Reserve's next interest rates announcement. 'We don't have many conversations around those micro topics anymore,' he says. 'All the conversations we have with our corporates are fundamental in terms of "what's the impact on the business now of risk management?" '

One consequence of the stringent accounting regulations is that a company's pension fund now shows up as a liability on the balance sheet. And, like any other liability, it needs to be hedged. The derivatives a corporate uses to hedge this liability might depend on whether the pension scheme is in surplus or deficit.

'The companies that have large deficits are thinking, if they start to hedge their liabilities now they effectively lock themselves into this large liability that has real losses,' says Deutsche Bank's [Rich] Herman.

Source: Excerpts from *Corporate Finance*, Issue 241, April 2005.

Questions

1. Why would firms be concerned with increasing or reducing hedging activities under different accounting systems?
2. What impact will international financial reporting standards have on the income statement?
3. Why is the measurement and reporting of pension liabilities and assets a concern for risk management?

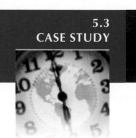

The trend toward fair value accounting

by J Russell Madray, CPA

The Debate

Critics contend that GAAP is seriously flawed. Some in the accounting profession go so far as to pronounce financial statements almost completely irrelevant to the financial analyst community. The fact that the market value of publicly traded firms on the New York Stock Exchange is an average of five times their asset values serves to highlight this deficiency. Many reformers, including FASB chairman Robert Herz, believe that fair value accounting must be part of the answer to making financial statements more relevant and useful.* Advocates of fair value accounting say it would give users of financial statements a far clearer picture of the economic state of a company.

But switching from historical cost to fair value requires enormous effort. Valuing assets in the absence of active markets can be very subjective, making financial statements less reliable. In fact, disputes can arise over the very definition of certain assets and liabilities.

The crux of the fair value debate is this: Each side agrees that relevance and reliability are important, but fair value advocates emphasize relevance, while historical cost advocates place greater weight on reliability.

Relevance versus Reliability

The pertinent conceptual guidance for making trade-offs between relevance and reliability is provided by FASB Concepts Statement No. 2, *Qualitative Characteristics of Accounting Information*. It provides guidance for making standard-setting decisions aimed at producing information useful to investors and creditors. Concepts Statement No. 2 states:

> The qualities that distinguish "better" (more useful) information from "inferior" (less useful) information are primarily the qualities of relevance and reliability ... The objective of accounting policy decisions is to produce accounting information that is relevant to the purposes to be served and is reliable.

Critics of fair value generally believe that reliability should be the dominant characteristic of financial statement measures. But the FASB has required greater use of fair value measurements in financial statements because it perceives that information as more relevant to investors and creditors than historical cost information. In that regard, the FASB has not accepted the view that reliability should outweigh relevance for financial statement measures.

Some critics also interpret reliability as having a meaning that differs in at least certain respects from how that term is defined in the FASB's Conceptual Framework. Some critics equate reliability with precision, and others view it principally in terms of verifiability. However, Concepts Statement No. 2 defines reliability as "the quality of information that assures that information is reasonably free from error or bias and faithfully represents what it purports to represent." With respect to measures, it states that "[t]he reliability of a measure rests on the faithfulness with which it represents what it purports to represent, coupled with an assurance for the user, which comes through verification, that it has that representational quality." Thus, the principal components of reliability are representational faithfulness and verifiability.

Although there are reliability concerns associated with fair value measures, particularly when such measures may not be able to be observed in active markets and greater reliance must be placed on estimates of those measures, present-day financial statements are replete with estimates that are viewed as being sufficiently reliable. Indeed, present-day measures of many assets and liabilities (and changes in them) are based on estimates, for example, the collectibility of receivables, salability of inventories, useful lives of equipment, amounts and timing of future cash flows from investments, or likelihood of loss in tort or environmental litigation.

Even though the precision of calculated measures such as those in depreciation accounting is not open to question since they can be calculated down to the penny, the reliability of those measures is open to question. Precision, therefore, is not a component of reliability under Concepts Statement No. 2. In fact, Concepts Statement No. 2 expressly states that reliability does not imply certainty or precision, and adds that any pretension to those qualities if they do not exist is a negation of reliability.

* Robert H. Herz's remarks to the Financial Executives International Current Financial Reporting Issues Conference, New York Hilton Hotel, November 4, 2002.

Source: Excerpts from 'The trend toward fair value accounting', *Journal of Financial Service Professionals*, May 2008, pp. 16–18.

Questions

1. What you think is the fundamental problem with financial statements based upon the historic cost measurement principle used under US GAAP ?
2. What do you think of the principle '. . . accounts must reflect economic reality' as a core principle of measurement in accounting?
3. How would you measure economic reality?
4. What is reliability in accounting?

The following article discusses share option schemes in the light of the international financial reporting standards.

IFRS put damper on share options schemes

by Barney Jopson

International financial reporting standards have triggered a sharp drop in the popularity of share option schemes, realising the fears of critics who said the rules would kill off a vital recruitment tool.

Under IFRS, companies are required to deduct the cost of issuing options from earnings for the first time. This has led to sudden reductions in reported profit at some companies.

As a result, stock options are falling out of favour in the remuneration of FTSE 100 chief executives. The proportion of incentive awards made up by options has dropped to 21 per cent this year from 36 per cent, according to PwC.

Graham Ward-Thompson, partner at PwC, said: 'IFRS is creating a fundamental shift in the design of stock-based incentive plans.'

Options have enabled many companies — notably small technology groups — to recruit elite and rank-and-file staff who are attracted by the chance of earning far more than cash salaries when share prices rise.

Opponents of option expensing have warned that its effect on profits could make the instruments unusable, leaving companies unable to attract good staff and inhibiting innovation.

PwC's research showed that granting actual shares had become a viable option. 'Performance share plans' now account for 68 per cent of FTSE 100 chief executive incentives, up from 57 per cent.

Performance share plans must also be expensed under IFRS, but Mr Ward-Thompson said they enabled companies to get the same 'incentive and retentive effects' for a lower accounting charge. 'Employees don't see as much value in options as they do in free shares.'

Companies that have introduced performance share plans for senior management or employees include BAA, British Land, Carphone Warehouse, Emap and Legal & General.

Stock option expensing is expected to exert a drag of about 13 per cent on the pre-tax profit of LogicaCMG, an IT services group. Seamus Keating, chief financial officer, said the company was considering changes to remuneration but would have done so irrespective of IFRS.

'Stock options have probably been a less effective tool to incentivise employees recently because the stock market has been flat and the tech sector has gone through some difficult years,' he said.

James Wheaton, finance director of Business Systems Group, which is listed on Aim, said: 'I don't think you should run the company on a change in accounting policy.

'If options were the right way to find and retain people we would use them and explain it to shareholders.'

Source: Financial Times, 11 August 2005.

Questions

1. How do share options schemes affect the measure of income under international financial reporting standards?
2. Why has this led to the reduction in stock-based packages for staff?
3. How is the form of structuring and reporting financial statements important to
   (a) management?
   (b) shareholders?

Endnotes

1. N Campbell, 'Symposium: measurement and its importance for philosophy', Proceedings of the Aristotelian Society, 1938, p. 126.
2. SS Stevens, 'Mathematics, measurement and psychophysics', in SS Stevens (ed.), *Handbook of experimental psychology*, New York: John Wiley, 1951, p. 1.
3. R Sterling, *Theory of the measurement of enterprise income*, Kansas: Kansas University, 1970, p. 70.
4. Stevens, op. cit., p. 2.
5. Stevens, op. cit., p. 23.
6. W Torgerson, *Theory and methods of scaling*, New York: John Wiley, 1958, p. 17.
7. ibid., pp. 21, 30–1.
8. R Mattessich, *Accounting and analytical methods*, Homewood, Ill.: Irwin, 1964, p. 71.
9. Stevens, op. cit., p. 25; Jum Nunnally, *Psychometric theory*, New York: McGraw-Hill, 1967, p. 15.
10. Nunnally, op. cit., pp. 16–17.
11. N Campbell, *Physics, the elements*, Cambridge: Cambridge University Press, 1920; N Campbell, *An account of the principles of measurement and calculations*, London: Longmans, Green, 1928.
12. W Hays, *Quantification in psychology*, New York: Brooks/Cole, 1967, p. 17.
13. B Ellis, *Concepts of measurement*, Cambridge: Cambridge University Press, 1966, p. 53.
14. Torgerson, op. cit., p. 24.
15. SS Wilks, 'Some aspects of quantification in science', in Harry Woolf (ed.), *Quantification*, New York: Bobbs-Merrill, 1961, p. 7.
16. W Paton and AC Littleton, *An introduction to corporate accounting standards*, Florida: AAA, 1940.
17. See J Francis and K Schipper, 'Have financial statements lost their relevance?', *Journal of Accounting Research*, Autumn 1999, pp. 319–52.
18. International accounting standards were adopted from 2005 in Australia and the EU countries (for consolidated accounts of listed companies) and from 2007 in New Zealand.
19. Deloitte Touche Tohmatsu *IASPlus* website, IASB Agenda Project: Reporting Comprehensive Income (Performance Reporting), www.iasplus.com.
20. Financial Statement Presentation, www.iasb.org; see also Project Updates: Financial Statement Presentation — Joint Project of the IASB and FASB, www.fasb.org.
21. International Standard on Auditing 540: *Auditing accounting estimates, including fair value accounting estimates, and related disclosures*. The equivalent Australian Auditing Standards are ASA 540 *Audit of Accounting Estimates*, and ASA 545 *Auditing Fair Value Measurements and Disclosures*.

6 Accounting measurement systems

LEARNING OBJECTIVES

After reading this chapter, you should have an appreciation of the following:

1 an overview of the three main income and capital measurement systems in accounting — historical cost, current cost (entry value), and current selling price (exit value)

2 the historical cost model (arguments for and against)

3 current cost accounting: business profit, holding gains and operating capital (arguments for and against)

4 financial capital versus physical capital

5 exit price accounting (arguments for and against)

6 the difference between value in use and value in exchange

7 global initiatives and relationships with 'fair value' accounting under International Financial Reporting Standards (IFRS)

8 issues for auditors.

THREE MAIN INCOME AND CAPITAL MEASUREMENT SYSTEMS

The study of accounting practice normally starts with a consideration of the range of technical issues relating to recording and reporting financial or economic activity. However, the basic technical processes have changed very little since the double-entry accounting system was described by Pacioli in the fifteenth century. Over the years that followed and with increased momentum during the industrial revolution, especially after the Wall Street collapse in 1929, the traditional historical cost system emerged. However, the historical cost system was not systematically codified as the fundamental basis for measuring capital, and for recording and reporting the economic and related activities of an entity, until the late 1930s. In the 1960s, several alternative systems were then developed that challenged historical cost as the fundamental accounting system. The first was an updated cost system that proposed to measure the current costs of resource usage and to value capital at current buying prices. The second applied current selling prices.

There were two basic current buying price systems. In 1961, Edwards and Bell proposed a system of current cost accounting in *The Theory and Measurement of Business Income*.[1] Because the system was based on current market costs, it can be regarded as the first methodical presentation of a fair value accounting system. The Edwards and Bell system was based on the concept of financial capital maintenance but, as illustrated in the second version of current cost that uses physical capital maintenance, the choice of the capital concept significantly affects the derived measure of profit. The second major system used selling prices or exit values to derive measures of income and capital. Support for different versions has varied, and the chapter goes on to outline and describe the advantages and disadvantages of each accounting system. We also note that the systems have attained varying support in a global context and recent international accounting standards partially incorporate each system within the notion of 'fair value'.

LO 2 **HISTORICAL COST ACCOUNTING**

The rationale for historical cost came from several sources with the most influential a book by Paton and Littleton, *An Introduction to Corporate Accounting Standards*.[2] We rely on their book for many of the arguments for the theoretical support of historical accounting today.

Objective of accounting

With the growth of the corporation over the last century and a half, accounting information took on greater significance as a source of information about firms. One reason for this is that the corporate form for a large business caused a separation of business ownership and control. Absentee owners do not possess first-hand knowledge of the operations and conditions of the firm and, therefore, must depend to some extent on accounting reports for information. The large company also has made evident that the firm has an identity of its own, separate and distinct from owners, creditors and all other interested parties. Although owners and creditors supply the funds to the business entity, they are in most cases considered 'outsiders' and have no special access to the records and accounts of the entity. Accountability, therefore, is seen to be the most critical objective of the reporting function. In particular, the stewardship function of managers was seen as the focus of attention of accountants in reporting to external parties. Owners and creditors are concerned mainly about what management has done with the funds entrusted to them. Paton and Littleton highlighted this stewardship function:

> Corporation reports should rest upon the assumption that a fiduciary management is reporting to absentee investors who have no independent means of learning how their representatives are discharging their stewardship.[3]

The historical cost stewardship objective emphasises a conservative 'contractual' relationship between a firm and those who provide resources to it by making management accountable for the input of assets to operations and the subsequent outputs on the net value of equity from operations. Thus, the income statement is the key communication mechanism.

Critics of historical cost argue that reporting only income (that matches inputs on an historical cost basis) with no recognition of the changing value of assets and liabilities is misleading and results in incorrect dividend policies. This is because there may be losses or gains simply from holding assets (or liabilities), and this should be recognised when evaluating performance on a regular basis. Instead, under the historical cost view, changes in asset values are basically ignored until the asset is sold or disposed of by sale or 'write-off/write-down'. That is, a transaction must occur in order for the accounting event to be recognised. These valuation issues are a repeated theme in the literature. In summary, under historical cost theory, determining the residual 'net value' of the firm is not of any high importance.

6.1
THEORY
IN ACTION

The effect of asset provisioning on earnings

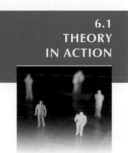

Bendigo boss makes small provision for big MIS exposure

by Adele Ferguson

Bendigo and Adelaide Bank's decision to book a paltry $20 million provision against a messy and litigious exposure to the collapsed management investment scheme Great Southern will undoubtedly come back to haunt it.

In a market update before its annual profit results next week, the bank's new boss Mike Hirst reserved 3 per cent of the $556 m in loan exposures against bad debts, while the total arrears are 22 per cent. Using as much spin as possible, Hirst did his best to play down the risk in this exposure on the basis that the credit quality of these loans was "very strong". By "very strong" he meant about 80 per cent of Great Southern investors earned more than $100,000 a year, 60 per cent were professionals and 75 per cent had a loan size of less than $250,000.

The problem with this is, by its own admission in slide 8 of the presentation titled strategic arrears, it is Bendigo's wealthiest investors who are causing it the most grief by not paying back their loans. The presentation shows that investors with net assets to loan value at drawdown of greater than five times are in arrears with the bank to the tune of $52 m, compared with $4.6 m for the least wealthy investors, or those with net assets to loan value at drawdown of less than two times.

What this means is, the richest are playing hardball and basically telling the bank to get nicked. Given Great Southern collapsed in May, and more and more law firms are preparing class actions on behalf of investors, it's a nightmare scenario. If these investors, plus others, are able to challenge the validity of the loans in the hands of Great Southern, then the bank has a $550 m problem on its hands.

The writeoffs (announced) yesterday will reduce the group's net profit by almost 16 per cent. It said cash earnings per share would be 63 c for 2009, which means the second half EPS is 19 c compared to 44 c in the first half.

Source: Excerpts from *The Australian*, 5 August 2009, p.32, www.theaustralian.com.au.

Questions

1. How does a provision for underperforming loans affect the earnings of a firm? Should a reduction in equity be recognised?
2. What are the implications of a change in accounting policy affecting provisions for (1) shareholders, and (2) analysts such as credit rating agencies?
3. Should the $20 million provision or a larger provision be used in analysing the performance of the company? If so, how would you determine the size of the adjusted provision?

Capital and profit

In order for historical cost profit to be determined, the accounting entity must first retain the same amount of capital (assets minus liabilities) that it had at the beginning of the period — where all assets and liabilities are valued at their historical purchase cost. Thus, income is the increment in historical cost capital at the end of the accounting period.

Paton and Littleton described profit determination as follows:

> Accounting exists primarily as a means of computing a residuum, a balance, the difference between costs (as efforts) and revenues (as accomplishments) for individual enterprises. This difference reflects managerial effectiveness and is of particular significance to those who furnish the capital and take the ultimate responsibility.[4]

Income indicates the accomplishments of the firm for the given period, expenses represent the efforts expended (in matched historical costs terms) and profit correlates with the effectiveness of the firm as an operating unit. The income statement is therefore the most important financial statement, since it reveals the results of the operations of the business. The balance sheet is not of great significance; it serves merely as a 'connecting link joining successive [income statements] into a composite picture of the income stream'.[5] The permanence of the operating income stream reflects the fundamental value of the firm, which, in the final analysis, is the basis of value for any enterprise.

At one time in the United States, the Financial Accounting Standards Board (FASB) used the term 'revenue–expense view' for the theory that emphasises the definition and measurement of profit by direct reference to revenues and expenses. It used the term 'asset–liability view' for the theory that emphasises the changes in value of assets and liabilities in the definition and measurement of profit. There are two fundamental concepts to the historical cost revenue–expense viewpoint: matching of costs and conservatism.

Matching of costs theory

The historical cost accountant keeps track of the flow of costs. Because costs attach, this is just another way of saying that the accountant keeps account of the transactions of the business. As the firm purchases goods and services, the accountant's task is to trace the movement of costs and attach (match) them to the revenues received as they flow through the business. In other words, the accountant must decide which costs have 'expired' and therefore are to be matched against income in the income statement, and which costs remain 'unexpired' and are to be placed on the balance sheet as the residual (unmatched assets). In describing this process, Paton and Littleton, somewhat poetically, declare that 'inventories and plant are ... cost accumulations in suspense, as it were, awaiting their destiny'.[6] Their destiny, of course, is to expire on the income statement. Thus, we can see that the matching concept is of critical importance in historical cost accounting. It is this concept which guides the accountant in deciding which costs are to be considered expenses. Terms such as 'expired costs' for expenses and 'amortised costs' for non-monetary assets stem from the costs attach theory as applied to the allocation of historical costs.

6.2
THEORY
IN ACTION

Outsourcing and costs

Client push drives Infosys jobs offshore

by Brian Corrigan

Indian outsourcer Infosys Technologies is sending more of its local work offshore as profit margins come under increasing pressure from cost-conscious customers.

Financial reports lodged with the Australian Securities and Investments Commission show that Infosys Australia posted revenue of $152.5 million for the year ended March 31, 2009, down by $6.5 million from the previous 12 months.

Net profit slumped from $28.9 million to just under $13 million for the same period. However, because some of the work booked with local clients is conducted overseas as part of the company's global delivery model, this revenue is recorded through parent company Infosys Technologies.

According to internal Infosys figures, revenue for work done on behalf of clients in Australia and New Zealand was up 22.3 per cent for the financial year, indicating that the company is providing more services from offshore.

Despite the drop in local net income Ms Korhonen (Infosys chief executive) said Infosys was quite comfortable with profit levels across the entire business.

"It is fair to say there is pressure on our margins because the market-place is very competitive," she said.

Source: Excerpts from *The Australian Financial Review*, 3 August 2009, p. 47, www.afr.com.

Questions

1. Identify the potential problems associated with allocating costs that 'attach' to services provided by firms such as Infosys Technologies.
2. What criteria would management use when deciding to expense or capitalise expenditures associated with its services?
3. Why is the decision to expense or capitalise expenditures so important to the costs attach principle which underlies the historical cost system?

Conservatism

Another important component is the application of conservative matching procedures. Expenses should be allocated as soon as possible, while revenues should not be recognised until there is a high probability that they will be received. That is, there is a biased skewness towards expense recognition vis-à-vis revenue recognition. Another cornerstone of the conservatism concept is that increases in the value of assets should not be recognised, but decreases in value should be — the lower of cost or market rule. The application of such procedures means that profit is calculated in a conservative manner and means that any potential revenue streams flow into the income statement slowly over time. For example, if the value of an asset increases because of its increased potential future economic cash flows; then it is only recognised slowly in income as those potential increased revenue flows are realised. Thus, the conservatism concept reinforces the transaction approach to accounting (a transaction must be evidenced by either credit or cash) and the non-recognition of events that do not result in such a transaction (such as price increases).

Arguments for historical cost accounting

Historical cost accounting has been attacked by many, mainly on the basis that it does not report commercial reality or provide an up-to-date valuation of net worth. Defenders have presented the following arguments:

1. *Historical cost is relevant in making economic decisions.* As managers make decisions concerning future commitments, they need data on past transactions. They must be able to review their past efforts and the measure of these efforts is historical cost. Littleton argued:

   > Cost to management is an investment, a calculated risk; management dare not lose sight of that investment as a risk-cost; to do so will deprive them of the basis for judging, in retrospect, the wisdom of having entered upon that risk.[7]

2. *Historical cost is based on actual, not merely possible, transactions.* Under historical cost accounting, a record of the actual transactions is made. A supporting record of the figures on the financial statements is therefore provided and is observable. This is not the case as in other 'current value' systems which recognise current prices as value or even income — these events may or may not occur.

3. *Throughout history, financial statements based on historical cost have been found to be useful.* Littleton argued that modern industrial and managerial accounting practices are the direct descendants of the many years of trial and error spent by owner-operators developing data that would be useful to them in running their businesses.[8]

4. *The best understood concept of profit is the excess of selling price over historical cost.* This notion of profit is accepted as a measure of successful performance. Decisions on whether to continue a product line or division or factory depend to a large extent on whether there is a favourable spread between revenue and cost. People understand this basic notion of business success.

5. *Accountants must guard the integrity of their data against internal modifications.* Most would argue that historical cost is less subject to manipulation than current cost or selling price. In reference to current prices, Littleton said, 'these are still wholly outside the prior decisions and the recorded experience of the enterprise'.[9] Mautz asks, 'Whom would you trust to value the assets of any major company?'[10] How are current values to be determined? How would an accountant ascertain that the values are a fair presentation? Can an accountant withstand the pressure by managers to accept optimistically valued assets? This gets back to the conservative notion of value and income determination. Records of past transactions are necessary for accountability and as long as accountability is important — this being the main objective under the stewardship function — historical cost must be used.

6. *How useful is profit information based on current cost or exit price?* Is it useful to show as profit an increase in the value of an asset that the firm has no intention of selling? Suppose a company has a long-term investment in securities of another company in order to ensure a supply of raw materials. It has no intention of selling the securities regardless of fluctuations in their market price. How useful is it to users to show variations in the market price as profit? Current value proponents argue that managers must be held accountable for changes in value, because the securities could have been sold. Mautz asks:

   > How far should we indulge in such 'might have been' accounting? Is this accounting? Or only wishful thinking?[11]

   Ijiri further asks:

   > Why should it care that the disposal value of the plant has decreased from $5 million to $4 million if management expects to earn $10 million from the

plant during the economic life of it? Why should management performance be penalised or rewarded because of environmental changes (the changes in price) when such changes are so remote for current decision making?[12]

Consider the example of reduction in asset values presented in theory in action 6.3.

6.3
THEORY
IN ACTION

Review of deteriorating assets leads to write-downs

Loss-making News pins hope on pay sites

by Dominic White

Rupert Murdoch has declared that News Corp is planning to charge for all of its news websites after the newspaper-to-cable TV conglomerate plunged to a US$3.4 billion ($4.03 billion) annual loss, stung by heavy write-downs, structural upheaval and the worst advertising slump since World War II.

The News Corp chairman predicted a return to revenue growth and a high single-digit rebound in underlying operating profits this financial year, saying "the worst may be behind us" as he reported some "good signs of life in the advertising market".

News of the strategic volte-face, which Mr Murdoch first hinted at in May, came after News Corp plunged deep into the red after booking US$8.9 billion in impairment charges, some of which related to its US$5.6 billion acquisition of Dow Jones, owner of *The Wall Street Journal*. News Corp was dragged to a fourth-quarter net loss of US$203 million after taking US$680 million in impairment and restructuring charges at Fox Interactive Media, owner of social networking site MySpace, which has cut more than 700 jobs as it seeks to cope with the rapid rise of rival website Facebook.

Stripping out one-off charges, the company reported adjusted operating income down almost a third to US$3.6 billion as gains at the cable television networks and magazines and inserts business failed to offset declines in newspapers, movies, books, satellite TV and at Fox Interactive Media.

The profit figure was in line with analysts' guidance, and shares in News Corp closed up 44 c at $14.86.

Source: Excerpts from *The Australian Financial Review*, 7 August 2009, p. 43, www.afr.com.

Questions

1. What criteria would management use to decide when to write down impaired assets on the statement of financial position? Discuss the reasons underlying the write-down of Fox Interactive Media.
2. Comment on the timing of the decision by News Corp management to write down the MySpace networking site, given the 'rapid rise of rival Facebook'.
3. What effect would amortisation of News Corp's media assets have on reported earnings under the historical cost system?

---

7. *Changes in market prices can be disclosed as supplementary data.* Supplementary data on current prices are a practical and efficient way of dealing with such information without having to shift from historical cost to a current cost basis. Based on studies of the relationship between accounting data and the market reaction to the data, the efficient markets hypothesis states that securities prices reflect publicly available information. In other words, any information made public by a firm is immediately taken into account by the market as revealed by the firm's securities price.

8. *There is insufficient evidence to justify rejection of historical cost accounting.* Traditional accountants argue that there is no persuasive empirical evidence that indicates that current cost or exit price accounting information is more useful than historical cost information. Most of the research studies indicate that current cost data do

not provide any more information than historical cost data. Beaver and Landsman came to this conclusion after analysing the impact of changing prices on more than 700 companies.[13] However, Duncan and Moores presented a contrary view.[14]

Criticisms of historical cost accounting

Objective of accounting

In historical cost accounting, the objective of providing useful information for economic decision making is taken to mean providing information on the stewardship function of management. Although important, this is a relatively narrow interpretation of the objective. The history of accounting reveals that another role of accounting is to meet the decision-making needs of users. In turn, a decision-usefulness approach calls for a 'forward-looking' position rather than a preoccupation with the past. Furthermore, information on the stewardship function does not necessarily restrict accountability to the original amounts invested directly or indirectly by equity holders. Investors are also interested in knowing about the increases or decreases in the value of their investments as represented by the net assets of the company.

Further, the critics of historical cost accounting have repeatedly argued that the system fails in its underlying function of providing objective information. There are so many decisions associated with the recording, measurement and reporting of information that the historical cost system is far from objective and is open to manipulation. In 1998 the AARF released Accounting Theory Monograph 10, *Measurement in Financial Accounting*. Monograph 10 (p. 22) questions the validity of historical cost information and attacks a basic tenet of the system, which is that historical information ensures the maintenance of an entity's capital base:

> An entity's capital is equal to its equity (or net assets). Therefore, the policies adopted for the recognition and measurement of an entity's assets and liabilities will determine the measurement of its capital. However, this does not identify the *concept* of what it is that should be measured, because the measure of equity is a mere residual. For example, adopting the conventional accounting model yields a measure of equity under the modified historic cost convention, but it is extremely difficult to explain just what the concept of capital is under this model. The best one can suggest is 'money valuations attributed to capital contributed, augmented by retained profits plus ad hoc revaluations of assets which are viewed as additions to capital'. However, this is more a description of a measurement process than a concept of what is intended to be measured.

Information for decision making

Proponents of historical cost argue that managers need historical data in order to evaluate their past decisions as they contemplate future commitments.

Whether a past decision was right or wrong must ultimately be ascertained by what happens in the marketplace. Edwards and Bell argue that a proper evaluation of past decisions must entail a division of the total profit in a given period between profit from operating activities and profit from gains (or losses) due to holding assets or liabilities while their prices changed. Further, the operating profit and holding gains must be separated into the element that was expected and the element that was a surprise.[15]

Historical cost is insufficient for the evaluation of business decisions. When assets are acquired, their historical cost is pertinent because it refers to current events. However, once the period of acquisition passes it is no longer current and therefore no longer consequential. Profit in a given year is supposed to represent the net increase in the value of the entity's capital for that year — that is, activities that transpired in a given year that increased the capital of the entity. Capital can be defined in several ways. For example, to be useful for decision making, 'capital' may mean the operating capability of the firm (its ability to sustain production), or the purchasing power of the firm (its ability to transact in the market). In terms of historical cost, capital is the original monetary investment in the firm.

If capital is defined to be the operating capability of the firm, profit is the change in the firm's operating capability during a reporting period. That is, profit is the amount earned after maintenance of the firm's physical capital. This information is useful to decisions that focus on the ability of the entity to maintain production and to compete with others in the industry in the future. If profit is the change in purchasing power, the concept of capital being maintained is financial capital measured in terms of current prices. Again, the information is useful because it provides information regarding changes in the entity's future capacity to transact in the market.

Critics argue the profit reported under historical cost has no such 'prospective' interpretation. Rather, it is entirely 'retrospective'. Historical cost accounting adopts a financial capital concept — capital is regarded as the nominal dollar investment in the firm — rather than the purchasing power of the investment. After the year of acquisition, historical costs do not correlate with the events of that year. It is a fiction created by accounting procedures to believe that historical costs are entirely related to current operations. To match historical costs against current revenues does not allow for the division of the total profit into its operating and holding components.

Further, historical cost overstates profit in a time of rising prices because it offsets historical costs against current (inflated) revenues. As such, it could lead to the unwitting reduction of capital where capital is defined in terms of the entity's ability to produce, transact, or otherwise operate into the future. The profit figure under historical cost may deceive management to the extent that dividends paid could exceed annual 'real' profit and erode the capital base.

Historical cost may be more objective than current prices but critics state that its relevance for decision making is highly questionable. The fact that numerous exceptions (e.g. the lower of cost and net realisable value rule for inventories) reveals that its rationale is flawed. Sterling remarks, 'Cost is not a fundamental tenet of accounting; instead it is a derivative of the conservatism principle of valuation.'[16]

Basis of historical cost

One of the justifications for the use of historical cost is the going concern assumption. The supposition is that the life of the firm is indefinite, so that normal expectations concerning the non-monetary items will be fulfilled. Inventory can be expected to be sold, and non-current assets to be fully used in the business. Therefore, the historical cost of the assets, or an allocated portion of it, is the appropriate amount to match with revenues. It is the *use* of the non-current assets, according to the argument, not their possible sale or repurchase, that is relevant. Sterling, however, questions the validity of the assumption:

> The high rate of business failures would make it difficult to build an evidential case for a projection of continuity. No business has ever continued 'indefinitely' into the future. All businesses, except those presently in existence, have ceased operations. Thus, it would seem more reasonable to assume cessation instead of continuity.[17]

Sterling wonders why the assumption leads to the historical cost model. The actual justification, he argues, is that the firm is 'locked in'; that is, it has no alternative but to use its non-current assets. Obviously, such a premise is unrealistic.

Matching

On a closer examination of conventional theory, we find that the going concern assumption does not underlie the use of historical cost. Rather, the costs attach concept drives historical cost reporting. The matching concept requires that when revenues are earned, the expenses incurred in earning those revenues are matched (offset) against the revenues to calculate profit. Conventional accounting puts emphasis on deciding whether a cost should be deducted from revenues in the current period or be deferred to future periods. Sprouse argues that 'matching does not require a concept of income to serve as a basis for making those judgements'. In fact, he says, 'in most cases the matching of costs and revenues is a practical impossibility'.[18] What we know as matching is essentially a process calling for random decisions to be made, rather than consistent analysis. Sprouse describes the process as one similar to judging a beauty contest where the judges cast their votes according to their personal preferences to decide the winner, because no established concepts exist to ascertain beauty, just as there are none to determine proper matching.

Along the same lines, Thomas argues that statements about matching, and in particular allocation of costs, are 'incorrigible', that is, they are not capable of being verified or refuted.[19] There is no way to select one method over another except arbitrarily. If we believe in matching, then we should be able to support given methods of matching with empirical evidence.

One of the consequences of the matching concept is that it relegates the balance sheet to a secondary position. The balance sheet becomes merely a summary of balances that result after applying the rules to determine profit. It serves mainly as a repository of unamortised costs. But the balance sheet has an importance of its own; it is the main source of information on the financial position of the firm. Sprouse contends that the balance sheet embodies the most fundamental elements of accounting theory and that all transactions should be analysed in terms of their effect on assets, liabilities and equity. The conventional matching concept is responsible for deferred charges that are not assets and deferred credits that are not liabilities. Traditional accounting assumptions complicate the evaluation of the financial position of a company when the balance sheet is considered mainly as a 'dumping ground for balances that someone has decided should not be included in the income statement'.[20] However, with the release of the revised Statement of Accounting Concepts (SAC) 4 in March 1995, the matching concept came under attack. The Australian Accounting Standards Board (AASB) advocated that in some instances use of the matching concept may lead to volatility in reported results and profit smoothing over different reporting periods. The *Framework* issued in July 2004 supersedes SAC 4 and provides support for the matching concept in paragraph 95 as follows:

> Expenses are recognised in the income statement on the basis of a direct association between the costs incurred and the earning of specific items of income. This process, commonly referred to as the matching of costs with revenues, involves the simultaneous or combined recognition of revenues and expenses that result directly and jointly from the same transactions or other events.

The concerns outlined by the AASB previously in SAC 4 are not reflected in the new *Framework* apart from the following qualification to paragraph 95:

> the application of the matching concept under this *Framework* does not allow the recognition of items in the balance sheet which do not meet the definition of assets or liabilities.

Notions of investor needs

It has been argued that historical cost accounting, with its focus on determining net profit, causes either a distortion or concealment of important company disclosures.

Whitman and Shubik argue that the problem arises because the goals of conventional historical cost accounting are ill-conceived; that:

- accountants have a naive, simplistic view of investors and their needs
- accountants accept the old-fashioned, fundamentalist view of how companies and their shares should be analysed.[21]

Note that there is a difference between share market analysis and corporate analysis. For the former, analysis consists mainly of trying to ascertain what other investors are thinking. Followers of this perspective are not really concerned about corporate facts, but about the psychology of the market. They are interested in what Keynes called 'the average opinion of the average opinion'. According to Whitman and Shubik, the reasons for this emphasis on investor psychology rather than corporate reality are that:

- investors usually have little knowledge about a company, its management, its policies and objectives, its opportunities and problems
- investors as shareholders take a passive role because they are in no position to change the way the company's resources are used
- investors deal with highly marketable securities and therefore move in and out of situations readily
- investors develop a short-term view because the economics of share market investing is directed towards that end. Psychology has a greater effect on market prices in the short term.[22]

For the above reasons, many investors have no interest or confidence in analysing a company for underlying values. Instead, they have embraced market analysis with its concentration on the psychology of the market and its effect in the short term on share prices. Conventional accounting assumptions are formulated to meet the needs of this type of investor who is not truly concerned about what is happening in the business.

Whitman and Shubik argue that accounting should provide information for the sophisticated, intelligent investor who is interested in what is really going on in the business.[23] These investors are interested in underlying long-term values. However, historical cost accounting practice emphasises current rates of return rather than long-term profitability, and investors are assumed to be naive. This encourages creative financial reporting. There is an incentive to produce financial statements that contain misleading data, such as overstated revenues and assets or understated expenses and liabilities, or vice versa. This leads us into the systems proposed in the 1960s as alternatives to the historical cost system. We start with another cost system which is updated to reflect current costs to buy.

LO 3 ⊢ CURRENT COST ACCOUNTING

There are two systems. We start with the Edwards and Bell system, which is based on the concept of financial capital maintenance, but then move onto the current cost system which uses physical capital maintenance and the entity concept.

Objective of current cost accounting

Current cost accounting (CCA) is an accounting system in which assets are valued at current market buying prices and profit is determined by allocation based on current costs (i.e. current cost to buy). What is the objective of current cost accounting? To answer the question, we need to consider the kinds of decisions managers are faced with in running a business. One assumption we can make is that managers of a firm want to know how they should allocate the firm's resources in order to maximise profits.

Edwards and Bell express this fundamental problem in terms of three questions:

- What amount of assets should be held at any particular time? This is the *expansion* problem.
- What should be the form of these assets? This is the *composition* problem.
- How should the assets be financed? This is the *financing* problem.

Managers make decisions regarding these three questions based on expectations about future events. To formulate relatively accurate expectations, managers need to evaluate past activities and decisions. A useful tool in this evaluation is a comparison of accounting data for a given period with expectations originally specified for that period. If this comparison reveals that expectations were inaccurate, current events or expectations should be altered. For example, if accounting data reveal that the total cost of raw materials was higher than budgeted for because the price of raw materials was higher than expected, the company needs to alter its expectations of future raw material prices and its decision on how much to budget for the total cost of raw materials in the future. For accounting information to be useful in decision making, it must measure the actual events of a period as accurately as possible. If the information includes events of earlier periods mixed with current events or if it omits some current events, the evaluation process becomes confused and the usefulness of the evaluation will be diminished. Edwards and Bell consider that price movements in a given period are events that are important to management.

Although Edwards and Bell emphasise the information needs of management, they argue that much of the data are also relevant to outsiders, such as shareholders and creditors. Shareholders and creditors are also interested in evaluating the performance of the managers and, thus, of the company. Under this theory, accounting information therefore serves two purposes:

- evaluation *by* managers of their past decisions in order to make the best possible decisions for the future
- evaluation *of* managers by shareholders, creditors and others.

Evaluation by both insiders and outsiders provides the means for the successful functioning of the economy because, theoretically, resources will then be allocated more efficiently.

Concept of business profit and financial capital

With regard to profit, management often faces two decisions:

- *holding decisions* about whether to 'hold' assets and liabilities or to dispose of them (e.g. through sale of assets or repayment of debt)
- *operating decisions* about how to use and finance the entity's operations.

In order to evaluate both the holding and operating decisions of managers, Edwards and Bell offer a profit concept that they call 'business profit' comprising (1) current operating profit and (2) realisable cost savings. *Current operating profit* is the excess of the current value of the output sold over the current cost of the related inputs. Realisable cost savings are the increase in the current cost of the assets held by the firm in the current period. They include both realised and unrealised cost changes. The business profit is therefore calculated on a real basis; that is, the 'fictional' element due to changes in the general price level is eliminated. The term we use for realisable cost savings is 'holding gains/losses', which can be realised or unrealised. Because the costs of resource usage are matched at current buying prices, all assets and liabilities are also measured at current buying prices and appear in a statement of financial position at contemporary values. Capital is a real financial proprietorship concept which means that profit is determined after restating opening buying values (capital) at the general price level; that is, profit is the increase in business profit and holding gains and losses after adjusting for any increases or decreases in the general price level.

Holding gains and losses

An assumption underlying business profit is that mixing holding gains/losses and operating gains/losses confuses the evaluation of management decisions and hinders the allocation of resources in the economy. The concept of business profit allows the separation of these components. Holding a certain composition of assets and liabilities is one way management tries to enhance the firm's market position. Managers and others want to know if these holding activities are successful. Under historical cost accounting, gains are recorded only when the assets are disposed of. Therefore, determining whether management's holding activities are successful or not is virtually impossible unless assets are bought and sold in the same period. Also, under historical cost accounting, when comparing firms we may be misled as to which firm is more efficient. Suppose all the firms in a given industry are equally efficient, but Company A started 10 years earlier than the others. The operating profit of A will be larger because of lower depreciation expenses, thus giving the impression that A is more efficient than the others. But this larger profit is not due to the efficiency of the managers in operating the firm in the current year. Rather, it reflects the efficiency of the managers of 10 years ago in starting the business and purchasing the assets at that time. Therefore, the separation of holding gains and operating profit gives credit to the appropriate managers.

Why holding gains are a component of profit

Edwards and Bell believe that holding gains represent 'a saving attributable to the fact that the input was acquired in advance of use. This saving is attributable to holding activities . . .'[24] But why should the increase in the current cost of an asset be considered as part of profit? They never directly provide an answer to this question, but Revsine suggests that the theory they advance reveals a possible response as follows:

> A firm benefits from the increase in the price of its assets because, otherwise, a greater cash outflow would be necessary if it were to purchase them now. The cash savings due to the fortuitous timing of the purchases are thus a real benefit, and should be included in income. This is essentially an opportunity cost notion. The cost saving is a component of income; it represents an 'opportunity gain', because the company purchased its asset at the time it did rather than at a later date when the price was higher.[25]

Revsine offers another explanation of a cost saving:

> A cost saving measures a firm's cash position advantage relative to other firms in the industry that were not fortunate to hold the given asset while its price rose. When these other firms do buy the asset, they will have to do so at higher prices. As a consequence, their cash outflow will exceed the cash outflow of the firm which experienced the cost saving.[26]

Thus, the opportunity gain argument implies a comparison of the firm with other firms.

Another possible justification for the inclusion of holding gains as profit is to say that the appreciation of value is an actual economic phenomenon that could be realised if the firm were to sell the asset. However, some accountants argue that a company purchases most assets to use in its operations, regardless of price changes. Therefore, the possible liquidation of the assets is unrealistic. Besides, this rationale is inappropriate for a current cost concept because its emphasis is on liquidation value or exit price, whereas current cost accounting measures assets at entry (cost) values. Revsine contends that a liquidation-oriented profit component is inconsistent with the information needs of investors. Investors are concerned about the future cash flows of the company, especially in terms of dividends to themselves and proceeds from the sale of their shares. In the long run, profits and dividends are directly related to using the operating assets, not liquidating them.

Revsine suggests that the inclusion of holding gains as profit may also be justified on the ground that changes in the current cost of the given asset reflect changes in the future cash flows expected to be generated from the use of the asset. Holding gains qualify as profit because the price increases on which they are based are a reflection of greater future earning power. If this assertion is true, then a profit figure that includes holding gains is highly relevant to users who are trying to predict the future cash flows of a company.

Revsine's argument implies that current cost profit is a lead indicator of future cash flows. The theoretical justification of this relationship is the connection between current cost profit and economic profit. Economic profit is defined as the difference between the present (discounted) value of the expected net cash flows of a firm at two points in time, excluding additional investments by and distributions to owners. Economic profit can be divided into two component parts: distributable cash flow or expected profit and unexpected profit. These components are defined as:

Expected profit = Market rate of return × Beginning value of net assets
Unexpected profit = Sporadic increases or decreases in present value of net assets due
to change in expectations regarding the level of future cash flows

Expected profit measures the cash flows the firm is capable of generating into the indefinite future, whereas unexpected profit measures the changes in cash flow due to environmental factors that were not predicted at the beginning of the period. In a perfectly competitive economy, current cost profit is virtually identical to economic profit. The current operating profit under current cost is equal to the distributable cash flow component or expected profit. Holding gains are directly related to unexpected profit.[27]

Including holding gains as a component of profit reflects a financial capital view. Any amount at the end of the period that exceeds the amount invested at the beginning of the period, excluding additional investments by and distributions to owners, is profit. Therefore, holding gains are part of profit. The return on investment is that sum of money in excess of the amount invested (adjusted by inflation). Appendix 6.1 provides a fully worked example.

LO 4 ┤ FINANCIAL CAPITAL VERSUS PHYSICAL CAPITAL

Under market value accounting systems, the calculation of profit depends on the measure of capital. That is, profit is more precisely defined as the change in capital over the reporting period and not as an allocation of historical costs determined by a multitude of accounting conventions. In current cost accounting there are two fundamental and competing views on what constitutes beginning and ending capital — the financial concept and the physical concept. There is no dispute over the valuation concept which is accepted by both paradigms as current market buying prices (current costs), but the dispute revolves around the definition of capital and how profit is measured from that definition.

From a practical point of view, the main difference between the financial capital concept and the physical capital concept is whether or not holding gains (or losses) are included in profit. In quantitative terms, the difference between the two viewpoints is that holding gains are included in profit under financial capital and excluded under physical capital. To illustrate the difference, consider a company that begins operations with $1000 cash on 1 January and immediately purchases 100 units for $10 each. On 31 January, it sells all the units for $18 each. On this date, the current cost has risen to $12 a unit. Assume that profit is paid out as dividends at the end. The calculation of profit is as follows:

	Financial capital view	Physical capital view
Sales revenue (100 × $18)	$1800	$1800
Cost of sales (100 × $12)	1200	1200
Current operating profit	600	600
Holding gain (100 × $2)	200	0
Profit	$ 800	$ 600
Paid as dividends	$ 800	$ 600

In support of physical capital

Advocates of physical capital argue that capital is the physical units denoting the firm's operating capability. In this case, the firm had 100 units at the beginning; if capital is to be maintained, then it must be in a position to purchase 100 units at the end of the period. Because the price has risen $2 per unit, the firm needs $200 more at the end of the period to maintain its beginning operating capability. Therefore, the $200 is not a holding gain, but a capital maintenance adjustment. The following analysis illustrates the point.

Profit after maintaining operating capability of 100 units:

Beginning capital	$1000
Purchase of 100 units (outflow of cash)	−1000
Sale of 100 units (inflow of cash)	+1800
Needed at end to maintain capital (100 units × $12)	1200
Profit for January	$ 600

If $800 were paid as dividends, the company would have $1000 at the end, which could purchase only 83 units in February. Capital, or the ability to maintain the same level of operations, would not have been maintained.

As previously noted, the inclusion of holding gains as profit is based mainly on two arguments:

- they are cost savings
- they represent increases in the future cash flow of the asset in question.

Samuelson attacks both premises. He argues that these changes in current cost should be a capital maintenance adjustment.[28] Concerning cost savings, he points out that the separation between holding activities and operating activities is not as clear-cut as Edwards and Bell assume. Samuelson further argues that cost savings are an opportunity gain resulting from taking one course of action as opposed to another. But the alternative was forgone when the actual course of action was taken. Once the asset is acquired, its cost is a 'sunk cost' that cannot be avoided by any future action. The only alternative is to sell the asset or continue using it. However, holding gains are not based on these options, but the one that was not taken and which no longer exists. Conceptually, profit relates to net cash flows, either realised or expected. Samuelson wonders why cost savings should be part of profit when they are neither realised cash flows nor expected cash flows, but forgone cash flows. If they are to be included in profit, then what about other types of cost savings, such as purchasing asset *X* rather than asset *Y*, or borrowing money at a time when interest rates are low rather than high?

Concerning the argument that a correspondence exists between changes in current cost and the present (discounted) value of an asset, the assumption is that changes in current cost are positively correlated with changes in the net realisable value of the asset. For non-current assets, however, individual cash flows cannot be identified. It is necessary, therefore, to view the correlation as between the current cost of the asset and the present value of the entire firm, because the cash flows attributed to non-current assets are represented by cash flows realised from the sale of the output of the firm. Samuelson contends that the change in current cost of non-current assets, which are also used by other industries, does not necessarily imply a corresponding change in the present value of the cash flows from product sales for a particular firm. For example, industry *A* may experience a greater demand for its product so that it acquires more of non-current asset *X*, thereby driving up the price of *X*. The increase in the cost of *X* does not necessarily mean greater future sales for a company which is in industry B and also uses *X*. Because of these difficulties, Samuelson believes that holding gains should not be included in profit. He supports the physical capital position.

Physical capital maintenance is based on the theory of optimum resource allocation and obtaining the required rate of return on resource inputs. Theory in action 6.4 sets out these arguments.

**6.4
THEORY
IN ACTION**

Optimum resource allocation and required rate of return

Resource allocation theory and CCA

by Allan Barton

In the modern terminology of market opportunity cost, the relevant resource prices to use for resource allocation decisions are their normal buying prices where it is profitable for the firm to purchase them. These are the prices at which producers are willing to supply the resource. They are the opportunity costs of the resources in the market, and unless the firm is willing to pay the market price it cannot acquire them and the resources will be purchased by other buyers. Where it is no longer profitable for the firm to acquire resources at their normal buying prices, but the firm has some stock of the resources on hand, the appropriate opportunity cost of those resources is their current market resale price (Marshall's market period).

CCA should be based on the economic theory of optimum resource allocation, though it is not always evident from the literature that it is so. The theory demonstrates why current market prices of resource inputs (based on the appropriate measure of market opportunity cost) are always relevant for resource allocation and control decisions; and, secondly, why a firm must keep on adapting its production methods, product mixes and levels of output as changes occur in the buying prices of its resource inputs and in the selling prices of its products if it is to be an efficient, profit-maximizing firm. The analysis covers investors as well. Investors must be rewarded at least the market opportunity cost of their funds for them to subscribe and retain their investment in the firm; otherwise they will withdraw them and invest them elsewhere. The market opportunity cost of capital funds is included in the cost functions of the firm.

The appropriate valuation bases to use for assets used as resource inputs to a productive process are their normal buying prices or, in the case of existing assets no longer worth acquiring, their lower market resale prices. Furthermore, the measures of income, financial position and rate of return on investment are conceptually valid and relevant ones for the measurement and evaluation of operating performance and financial position. The CCA income statement charges the expenses of all resources consumed over the period, measured at their current market prices, against the sales revenue of the period. According to whether a real purchasing power concept or a physical capital maintenance concept is adopted, profit is the surplus which can be distributed to investors while maintaining capital (as defined) intact. In realistic market conditions the two concepts are likely to give similar measures. A firm which distributes the whole of its income is able to maintain intact its physical capability to continue its operations into the future. The statement of financial position shows the current market prices of the firm's investment in its assets, the current market prices of its liabilities, and the owners' residual equity in the firm. The rate of profit on the investment in net assets, when compared with the market cost of equity funds, indicates whether the firm is a going concern or not. If it is so, the statement of financial position indicates that the firm should be able to meet its existing financial commitments from expected future cash operating inflows, existing financial assets and sale of surplus or obsolete assets ... Subject to the reliability of the asset valuations, the financial statements can faithfully represent the financial performance and position of a firm within the context of the accounting valuation model.

In addition to the above general uses of CCA information for resource management and the measurement and evaluation of income earned and financial position, CCA information is useful for a number of specific purposes. These include:

Physical asset management policies In addition to decisions to acquire or dispose of physical assets, CCA information is relevant to the determination of asset maintenance policies. Repair and maintenance policies affect the productivity and lifespans of depreciable assets and their resale prices. Optimizing these policies involves consideration of buying and selling prices over time. In the case of building maintenance, for example, current costs of building reconstruction are often used as the basis for determining long-term and annual maintenance budgets. Maintenance needs to maintain the physical quality of a building are calculated as a percentage of the current cost of the building, and this is upgraded annually through the use of detailed building cost price indices ...

Pricing and output determination As the economic theory demonstrates, the costs that are relevant in determining the optimum output in competitive markets where firms are price-takers are the current costs of supplying the product. Conversely, where the firm has market power and is a price-maker, the relevant costs are again the current costs of supplying the product. Pricing and output determination are fundamental areas of management decision making and profit generation.

Dividend policy CCA income forms a rational basis for the determination of dividend policy and its associated decision to retain funds for profitable reinvestment in expanding the firm's asset base or otherwise.

The going concern status of the firm The concept and measure of the going concern status of the firm are based on the ability of the firm to earn a normal rate of profit on owners' investment, where all measures are based on the current market opportunity costs of the resources. The normal rate of profit earned must at least cover the opportunity cost of investors' capital funds ...

Maintenance of a going concern status is particularly important for firms having a substantial investment in assets whose current resale values are less than their current market buying prices. The losses incurred from the forced liquidation of such assets can be substantial. Such firms must strive to maximize the ex ante value in use of their assets to remain as going concerns as they do not have the option of recovering their investment expenditures from resale of the assets.

Investors are also particularly interested in knowing whether the firm remains as a going concern because of its impact on share prices and future operations. In the case of a listed company, the earning of a normal rate of profit should, [other things being equal], maintain the share price at its current level; the earning of additional profit should boost its share price; and conversely for below normal profits. Investors' confidence in the ability of the firm to continue profitable operations into the future are boosted by its present going concern status.

Source: Excerpts from *Abacus*, vol. 36, no. 3, 2000, pp. 298–312.

Questions

1. How will CCA based on physical capital maintenance help managers to make better resource allocation decisions?
2. How will the use of CCA help investors make decisions about whether to buy or sell shares in a particular company?
3. Will income and dividend decisions change under CCA? Explain.
4. Explain in your own words what is meant by the going concern assumption.

Major features of the physical capacity system

Capital maintenance

The system of current cost is based on the entity concept of maintaining intact the ability of the firm to continue to deliver the same amount of goods and services — its operating capability.

If there is no technological change, capital maintenance requires that the initial physical stock of net assets is retained. This is achieved by matching resource usage by using current buying prices and ensuring the general purchasing value of monetary items is maintained. Using this concept, sufficient funds are maintained within the firm to finance all asset replacement from expense recovery. This information can also be used to calculate prices that must be paid to acquire inputs and to calculate the minimum price at which the firm is willing to sell its outputs under the assumption of continuity and non-liquidation.

The system is based on economic concepts of marginal analysis in factor markets. Market forces, such as changing demand and supply, are continually operating to affect prices in factor markets. The result is that wages and other variable inputs to production, as well as the buying prices of fixed assets, are continually changing. It is argued that firms must adjust operations to take advantage of these continual changes in factor markets in order to remain competitive and efficient. Economic logic suggests that optimum operating efficiency occurs where a given volume of output is produced at the minimum total market opportunity cost of its factor inputs. For example, if a variable cost (such as wages) increases, then more capital-intensive methods of production will be required to reduce labour input and minimise costs. Using fixed costs as a further example, if the market price of the firm's land and buildings increases, they should be used more intensely in the production process, rented out, or sold up and operations moved to a cheaper location. Current buying prices or entry prices are the relevant measure of opportunity cost in factor markets and should be used in this system.

Valuation principles

Non-monetary items

Monetary and non-monetary items are subject to different effects and risks during inflation. Monetary items are claims to a fixed number of dollars. In nominal terms they do not change during price inflation. In contrast, the value of non-monetary items (such as land and buildings) will be adjusted by market forces in nominal dollar terms.

For balance sheet purposes, non-monetary assets should be valued and shown at their current cost. Values are obtained by reference to:

- current market buying prices, or
- specific indexes where market prices are unavailable, or
- the service potential of an identical or like item for superseded or specialised assets.

For depreciating assets, the new value less the accumulated depreciation is used to derive the value of that asset.

When a non-monetary asset is restated (usually at the date of the balance sheet), the adjustment is made to the Current Cost Reserve account in the equity section of the balance sheet statement. However, when a decrease in value permanently decreases the operating capability of the entity, then the debit adjustment is made straight to the income statement.

Monetary items and loan capital

Monetary assets are shown at the amounts at which they were originally brought to account and represent losses in purchasing power. Monetary liabilities are valued at the amounts which are expected to be paid, and provide a gain to firms if held when money loses purchasing power.

Monetary items should be split into two different components. The first component is based on the entity concept and comprises all monetary items that are not loan capital. These mainly constitute trade creditors and debtors, cash, prepayments and short-term bank overdrafts. The monetary item gain or loss should be calculated by the appropriate index of change in the current cost of goods and services. For example, a building company would apply a construction cost index to monetary items that finance the operating inputs (such as trade creditors and debtors). For a financing entity such as a bank, the relevant index would be the general price index. When the application of specific input indexes is not practical or cost effective, the use of a general price index is recommended.

The current cost operating system is based on an entity concept. All long-term sources of finance, such as loans, debentures and bonds (both marketable and non-marketable) as well as shareholder contributions and reserves, are deemed to constitute the capital base of the firm. Gains and losses on loan capital are calculated mainly to assess the extent to which shareholders have benefited from the entity having used long-term loan capital to fund operations. Because this measure is related to shareholders — the proprietorship concept — a general price index should be used for calculations. Further, whenever trade creditors and other monetary liabilities exceed monetary assets and inventories, the excess would be used to fund non-monetary assets. In this case the excess should be treated as loan capital and any gain on this excess treated in the same manner as loan capital.

Non-monetary assets bought and sold on the same market

Shares and certain marketable commodities such as gold, silver and other assets that are held as speculative or financial assets are bought and sold in the same markets. These assets do not directly add to the operating capability of the entity. Nor are they consumed or used up during the process of rendering goods and services. They are usually held for profit-generating purposes or for resale at a capital gain. In these cases the operating capability of an entity is enhanced or reduced by the reinvestment ability of these assets. This ability remains unchanged in a period when the market price of the particular asset moves in line with general inflation. However, if the value of the asset increases at a greater rate than general inflation, then reinvestment ability or operating capability is enhanced. The asset is debited with the price increase, the general inflation adjustment is credited to the current cost reserve and any gain, over and above inflation, is credited to the income statement. If a loss occurs, then the entries are reversed. A fully worked example is presented in appendix 6.2.

Arguments for and against current cost

Recognition principle

Advocates of historical cost accounting argue that current cost accounting violates the conservatism principle that a profit should only be recognised at the time a non-monetary asset is disposed of. This is true for unrealised holding gains when a financial capital view is taken because the financial capital view recognises unrealised holding gains. Proponents of current cost point out that the unrealised holding gains represent actual free movement phenomena occurring in the current period and therefore should be recognised if there is sufficient objective evidence to support the price changes.

Physical capital theorists also argue that because the firm intends to use non-current assets rather than sell them, changes in the market price of those assets are irrelevant for profits. Whether holding gains on assets constitute income or revaluation adjustments is a major debating point in accounting theory and practice (and is one of the contentious issues under the International Accounting Standards Board (IASB) comprehensive income proposal). Historical cost and physical capital theorists argue that holding gains should not be recognised, whereas Edwards and Bell (current cost theorists) argue that they constitute income and should be recognised.

Objectivity of current cost

Those who favour a strict historical cost concept argue that current cost accounting lacks objectivity because in most instances the current cost to be used is not based on actual transactions in which the firm is a participant. Objectivity, however, is relative — even under conventional historical accounting with its myriad allocation techniques, some figures are more objectively determined than others. The question, therefore, is whether current costs, in general, meet a certain minimum level of objectivity that the accounting profession is willing to accept.

For items whose market prices are relatively easy to obtain, the objectivity of their current costs may be acceptable to accountants. Inventories of raw materials and finished goods purchased from others fall into this category. In fact, the current cost of these inventories is more objective, in the sense of less dispersion, than historical cost determined on the basis of an assumed flow, such as LIFO or FIFO. For most large companies, it is virtually impossible to calculate the actual historical cost flow of goods. Because of this difficulty, an assumed flow for accounting purposes is used that may have no correspondence with the actual physical flow. In contrast, current cost accounting demands that the ending inventories be priced at the prevailing cost on the reporting date, and that cost of sales be stated at the current cost at the time the goods were sold.

Ascertaining the current cost of non-current assets involves some complex issues. For standard assets, however, such as vehicles and office equipment, the current cost can be obtained from second-hand dealers with little difficulty. Revsine states:

> Used asset markets are surprisingly well developed for many types of industrial equipment and machinery. Numerous dealers and well-organised informal markets exist for a wide range of general purpose manufacturing components and for many more specialised items where the demand is sufficiently deep. Thus, market prices for the 'old' assets currently in use will frequently be available by reference to used equipment dealers' price lists and similar sources.[29]

For non-current assets where no market prices are available, appraisals, calculations of reproduction costs and use of index numbers will be necessary. These methods entail a great deal of subjective judgement. Many accountants find the latitude of current cost in this particular area unacceptable.

Technological change

According to Edwards and Bell, current operating profit is an indication that the firm is making a positive long-term contribution to the economy and that the production process in use by the firm is effective.[30] This is especially the case for current operating profit determined under physical capital maintenance. It is representative of the long-term profit capability of the firm under the existing production process, assuming that existing conditions remain relatively the same.

Current cost accounting has been criticised because it appears to ignore technological advances. Lemke notes that the main interest of current operating profit is the long term prospects of the firm, but wonders why 'these long-run prospects would be indicated by the prospects of the present mode of production when it is becoming obsolete'.[31] If future operations will be based on a different set of techniques, then the operating profit of today will not be a valid indicator of future operating profits.

Revsine also argues that when a new machine changes the cost of production, the price of the old machine must adjust. This is due to the cross-elasticity of demand between the old and new machines, assuming a market in which entry barriers are minimal. Once this adjustment takes place, the price of the old asset will reflect the technological change.[32] An example is when a bigger and more technically refined tractor is invented; the prices of all the outdated tractors fall to reflect their now lower relative efficiency.

More specific criticisms

Advocates of historical cost

Advocates of historical cost accounting reject current cost accounting, mainly because it violates the traditional realisation principle. A related problem is the subjectivity of determining the amount of the increase in cost. If there is no reliable second-hand market, then the basis for determining the current cost of a fixed asset used by the firm must be the new asset expected to replace the old. The notion of current cost calls for an adjustment to be made for any operating advantage or disadvantage between the actual asset owned and its replacement to arrive at the current cost of the former. It is no easy task to calculate the amount of any operating advantage or disadvantage. An editorial in *Business Week* summarised the problem as follows:

> ... to calculate earnings on a replacement cost basis, accountants must not only charge more depreciation, they must also adjust for differences in output and operating costs. When they have done so, they wind up in a curious dream world where companies subtract savings they did not realise from costs they did not incur to derive earnings they did not make.[33]

Comparison of the results with historical cost

The FASB compiled data on all the companies subject to Statement 33 in 1980 into a composite, which reflected the average results of these companies. The aggregate results taken from the annual reports of 846 industrial companies are shown in table 6.1.

TABLE 6.1 Comparison of earnings under historical cost and current cost			
	Historical cost (Nominal dollars)	Historical cost (Constant dollars)	Current cost (Nominal dollars)
	(US billions of dollars)		
Profit from continuing operations (before taxes)	$172	$120	$107
Taxes	73	73	73
Profit from continuing operations	$ 99	$ 47	$ 34

Source: FASB, *Highlights of Financial Reporting Issues*, 14 October 1981.

The difference between the historical cost and current cost profits from continuing operations (US$65 billion) is due to unrealised holding gains. If we follow the rationale of Edwards and Bell, we can conclude that of the US$99 billion of historical cost profit:

- US$34 billion is due to operating activities that are mainly under the control of management
- US$65 billion is due to holding activities, which are usually much less subject to management's control.

Under the physical capital concept, the US$34 billion represents the amount of distributable profit.

Industry variations become apparent when profit from continuing operations on constant dollar and current cost bases is stated as a percentage of that under historical cost. This is shown in table 6.2. Capital-intensive industries, such as primary and fabricated metals, transportation and communication, show a great disparity between current cost profit from continuing operations and profit under historical cost. The reason is probably due to the much greater amount of depreciation expense under current cost accounting.

TABLE 6.2 Profit by industry under historical cost and current cost			
	Historical cost (Nominal dollars)	Historical cost (Constant dollars)	Current cost (Nominal dollars)
	As a percentage of historical cost		
	%	%	%
Chemicals	100	58	63
Food, tobacco, textiles	100	66	69
Timber, paper, allied products	100	54	43
Machinery	100	66	73
Mining and construction	100	71	45
Other nonmanufacturing	100	56	35
Other manufacturing	100	73	68
Petroleum and rubber	100	52	32
Primary and fabricated metals	100	30	9
Transportation and communication	100	25	11
Transportation equipment	100	−221	−473
Utilities	100	−129	5
Wholesale and retail trade	100	77	69
Composite	100	47	34

Source: FASB, *Highlights of Financial Reporting Issues*, 14 October 1981.

Advocates of exit price

Exit price theorists contend that the term 'cost' implies the opportunity cost or sacrifice of the next best alternative. In almost all cases, the current sacrifice faced by a company is to sell the asset rather than use it, but not to buy it because the company already has it. Therefore, current cost, the price to purchase the item, is not the relevant amount. It is the exit price or realisable value that is the logical expression of opportunity cost.

The allocation problem brought to light by Thomas continues to be an issue. Instead of allocating historical cost, the allocation is of current cost. But it is still arbitrary and lacking in real-world counterparts. An additional point at issue is the need for backlog depreciation. Whether backlog depreciation is charged to income or to a capital account will make a difference in the amount of profit reported.

Exit price advocates insist that current cost accounting entails a mathematical problem of additivity because models recommended for practice involve a variety of measurement methods. Chambers explains the issue as follows:

> the amounts of assets must be of the same kind as the amounts of liabilities. They must be money amounts or the money equivalents of non-money assets at balance date. The money equivalents of non-money assets are the net cash values of those assets at balance date.[34]

Chambers contends that the following total is meaningless:

Cash	$1000
Some assets at present value	2000
Some assets at exit value	3000
Some assets at current cost	2000
Total	$8000

In order to be additive, figures must be of the same nature or of the same domain.

For similar reasons, Chambers argues against the use of specific price indexes. A price index is simply an average of prices. It is not likely, except by chance, that a particular company is affected by changes in prices in the same manner as every other company. And if an asset can no longer be purchased, it is senseless to calculate an indexed cost 'as if' the price 'would have' moved in the same direction and at the same rate as some index number series.

Chambers also maintains that the notion of value to the business overlooks a number of other reasons for value. Assets are valuable to a business for:
- the use that can be made of them
- the borrowing that can be based on them
- the cash they may bring in
- the potential hedge against inflation in the case of non-monetary assets.

Advocates of exit price accounting believe that current cost information, in general, is irrelevant to most investment decisions. It does not focus on the firm's ability to command financial resources in the firm's quest to adapt itself to the environment.

Finally, Sterling considers that the physical capital concept is fraught with weaknesses.[35] He argues that profit under the physical capital view is meaningful only if four conditions are met. These conditions are that the firm:
- continues to replace identical units
- faces continuously increasing costs
- buys and sells in different markets
- is fully invested in the physical unit.

If any one of these conditions is not met, serious measurement problems are encountered. This leads us to consider exit value.

LO 5 — EXIT PRICE ACCOUNTING

Income and capital

Exit price accounting is a system of accounting which uses market selling prices[36] to measure the firm's financial position and financial performance. It has two major departures from conventional historical cost accounting:
- The values of non-monetary assets are adjusted to measure changes in market selling prices specific to those assets and they are included in income as unrealised gains.
- Changes in the general purchasing power of money are taken into consideration when measuring financial capital and the results of operations.

The assets in the balance sheet are restated at exit values (selling prices) so that they represent the 'fair market value' to the firm in an orderly liquidation, that is, not in a 'fire-sale' situation. The income statement represents profit (and losses) from operations as well as the inflation-adjusted gains from holding assets. Hence, profit is measured under a 'comprehensive' concept which measures the total real change in the value of all recognised elements of equity,[37] and represents clean surplus accounting. (Clean surplus accounting is when the income statement links the opening balance sheet to the closing balance sheet, and no adjustments are made directly to reserves.)[38]

Exit price accounting is associated mainly with the works of Raymond Chambers and Robert Sterling, and an early advocate Kenneth MacNeal, whose proposal was not taken seriously by the accounting profession at the time it was presented. Chambers, in particular, made an important distinction between measurement and valuation. Measurement is obtaining prices objectively and independently from the measurer (the accountant), whereas valuation is concerned with expectations of future benefits that could be generated by the underlying asset. Therefore, the distinction is made between the past (historical costs), the future (valuation) and the present measurement (contemporaneous exit prices).

Objective of accounting

Adaptive decision making

Chambers presented a comprehensive proposal for exit price accounting, which he originally called 'continuously contemporary accounting' (CoCoA) and then upgraded to current cash equivalents (CCE). Chambers sees the business firm as an adaptive entity engaged in buying and selling goods and services. It is governed by the decisions of its managers who represent the owners' objectives. Owners consider the firm to be an instrument by which they hope to increase their real financial wealth; that is, their command over goods and services in general. The notion of adaptive behaviour implies a continual attempt to adjust to the competitive business environment for the sake of survival. Thus, the firm survives and continues operations by having the ability to go into the market place with cash to take advantage of opportunities as they arrive. The assumption is that the business world is dynamic (not static) and business must adapt to survive. Ultimately, Chambers also argues, investors are also interested in personal cash receipts from their association with the firm. Therefore, all major parties are interested in cash equivalents.

To continue in business, a firm must be able to engage in market transactions, and this is revealed by its financial position. In a market society, the monetary value of assets and liabilities can be determined objectively by reference to market prices; that is, the purchase price and the selling price. The purchase price, or current cost, does not reveal the firm's ability to go into the market with cash for the purpose of adapting itself to present conditions, but the selling price does. The selling price of a non-monetary asset is the asset's realisable price on the basis of an orderly liquidation. Chambers calls this price the asset's 'current cash equivalent'. Market selling prices of non-monetary assets are used, Chambers states, '... not because we expect a company to sell any of its assets (though it may do so when it finds its financial position), but because that is the only way to find the money (cash) equivalent of assets'.[39] In the last analysis, the survival of the firm depends on the amount of cash it can command.

When a firm purchases a non-current asset, it changes its ability to adapt. If the asset is purchased for cash, the reduction in the firm's cash balance diminishes its freedom to lay out cash for other investments. If the asset is bought on credit, this reduces the firm's ability to obtain further credit. But the concept of adaptive behaviour sees the firm as always being ready to dispose of the asset if this action is in its best interest. Hence, the firm will keep a non-current asset only if the present (discounted) value of the future net cash flow from the use of the asset is greater than the present value of the expected net cash flow from an alternative investment of the exit value of the asset. At all times, therefore, the firm must consider whether an alternative opportunity for greater returns exists for its non-current assets if they were sold and the proceeds invested. This is an opportunity cost concept, which uses the selling price and not the replacement price of the assets, as a measurement base.

Adaptive behaviour, therefore, calls for knowledge of the cash and current cash equivalents of the firm's net assets. Chambers states:

> the single financial property which is uniformly relevant at a point of time for all possible future actions in markets is the market selling price or realisable price of any or all goods held.[40]

He admits that every asset has, in principle, a value in exchange (exit price) and a value in use. Value in use (present value) is basically a calculated amount of a present expectation and Chambers argues that it represents beliefs about the future, not present facts.[41] It is subjective and not interpretable or understandable by people who are not familiar with the subjective expectations it is based on.

Arguments for exit price accounting

Providing useful information

After examining the history of accounting, MacNeal concluded that conventional accounting principles were based on 'primitive conditions' that have largely ceased to exist. He divided accounting history into three phases: the first era, from about the twelfth century to the seventeenth century; the second era, the eighteenth and nineteenth centuries; and the third era, the twentieth century onwards.[42] From the twelfth to the seventeenth century, the role of the accountant was to provide information to the business owner–manager about the total costs incurred in ventures and projects. This information could then be used to ascertain the (often extreme) profit or loss at the conclusion of the venture or project. Because the venture was not indefinite and usually concluded within a few years, costs were calculated using original or historical cost.

In the second era the situation changed, in that business firms were more established and transactions did not involve as great a risk as in the first era. The more stable business climate enabled creditors to lend money on the basis of the owner's net worth. The practice arose whereby creditors required owners to submit a statement of net worth and of profits before extending credit. To ensure that the statements were reliable, creditors insisted they were prepared by an independent accountant. Thus, public accounting as a profession was born.

Business firms were mainly owned outright by one person or a small group of partners. The accountant who prepared the financial statements had an obligation to only two interested parties: the owner, who managed the business and knew all of its details, and the creditor, who was interested mainly in the ability of the owner to pay the account or loan when due. Creditors were concerned about the possible overstatement of the financial reports and accountants learned that a conservative approach satisfied both parties. Valuation of assets at original cost was expedient and acceptable to both owners and creditors. Because the owner was fully conversant with the business, personal adjustments could be made to determine a more accurate measure of financial position.

Towards the end of the nineteenth century, however, firms grew larger and many became companies with a multitude of shareholders and hired managers. In the twentieth century, firms were generally owned by numerous shareholders who relied on financial statements and the media for their information about the company they owned. Unlike the situation in the first and second eras, accounting became an important information function for shareholders. MacNeal contended that conventional accounting principles based on historical cost provided potentially false and misleading financial statements that did not serve decision-oriented shareholders — they could not learn the current values of the assets of the companies they held shares in. Moreover, they were at a disadvantage compared with insiders who did have this information.

The ideal solution was seen to be for accountants to report all profits and losses and values as determined in competitive markets. However, not all assets have a ready market. MacNeal suggested therefore that a workable compromise should be to value:
- marketable assets at market price (exit price)
- non-marketable reproducible assets at replacement costs
- occasional non-marketable, non-reproducible assets at historical costs.

Profit should include all realised and unrealised profits and losses in accordance with the clean surplus principle.

Relevant and reliable information

Sterling believes that there is one method to determine profit that is superior to all others.[43] Using a simple model — a wheat trader in a perfect market with a stable price level — he defines profit as the difference between capital at two points in time exclusive of additional investments by and distributions to owners. Sterling assumes that the wheat trader wishes to maximise utility, the sources of which are consumption of goods and services and command over goods and services. The criterion to decide which valuation method is the best for the determination of profit is, therefore, a valuation method that yields more information and is superior to others that yield less information.

To be relevant, information must be useful in the decision models of accounting report users. The decision models, in turn, enable users to decide which course of action to take from several alternatives. If there were no constraints, information could be gathered that was relevant to each user for his or her given problem and decision model. However, constraints do exist because information production resources are scarce and costly. The problem is to select an appropriate decision model by assessing the ability of the model to predict the consequences of currently available alternative courses of action.

For the wheat trader, three decision problems are posed:
- the continuing decision to enter and stay in the market
- the continuing decision to hold either cash or wheat
- the evaluation of past decisions.

Sterling determined that the following items of information are relevant to the above decisions:
- the expected future price of wheat
- the expected future price of alternatives
- the present selling price of wheat
- the present buying price of alternatives
- the price at the last evaluation
- the quantity of wheat and money at the last evaluation
- the present quantities.

Sterling states that the present selling price of wheat is the only item of information that is relevant to all decisions. The others are relevant to one or more, but not all, decisions. Even when the assumption of perfect competition and stable prices is relaxed, the present market (exit) price is superior.

Additivity

Chambers considers the question of additivity to be a key factor in support of CCE accounting. The main products of an accounting system are the accounting statements — the balance sheet and income statement. If we assign different values to different characteristics of the particulars and use different measurement scales, then no practical or commercial meaning can be deduced from the aggregate — they cannot logically be added together. For example, we cannot value liabilities at historical cost (debentures), some assets at replacement cost (inventory), others at present value (leased assets) and still others at cash equivalents (debtors) and obtain a meaningful balance sheet. Nor can we use a jumble of historical costs on different dates and place any meaning on the calculation of net assets. Chambers comments:

> Such features of the financial characteristics of companies such as gross wealth, net wealth, current ratio, debt to equity ratio, rate of return are all aggregative. A balance sheet is not a series of isolated statements about particulars; it is a series of particular statements which yield aggregates of features of the whole company. Those particular statements must be such that they can quite properly be aggregated and that the aggregates can quite properly be related to one another.[44]

Hence, the valuation of all elements in the balance sheet and income statement at their money equivalents (exit values), provides one rule that can be applied consistently to any company. This system concentrates on measuring the financial capacity of the business at the end of the accounting period. It concerns itself exclusively with financial matters — money and money equivalents. 'It makes no use of physical or other characteristics of assets. It is self consistent.'[45]

Allocation

Thomas laments the fact that cost accounting systems (historical and current) rely heavily on cost allocation for asset valuation and profit determination. He argues that a positive feature of exit price accounting is that the financial statements are allocation-free.[46] The income statement is not a report of changes in allocated amounts, but of asset inflows and changes in the exit values of a firm's assets and liabilities in a given period. Profit displays the amount of change in real purchasing power of the net assets, excluding additional investments by and distributions to owners.

Reality

Exit price accounting involves references to real-world examples because, it is argued, every figure refers to a present, actual market price. Depreciation is not defined in the conventional way, but in the economic sense of a decline in the market price. Depreciation may not occur in some years if prices increase or remain constant. If no realisable value can be attributed to an item, then the item will have a zero balance. Moreover, exchangeability is part of the definition of an asset so that goodwill, which cannot be sold separately, is excluded from consideration. With these two constraints — exchangeability and existence of a selling price — all items on the financial statements can be corroborated by real-world evidence.

Objectivity

It is often argued that current market prices are not objective. Yet some research studies indicate that market prices are relatively more objective than most people believe. Parker carried out a research study on the relative comparability and objectivity of exit values and historical cost carrying amounts.[47] Objectivity was defined as a consensus among valuers. Comparability was defined as a consensus in measurements. Using 148 business firms, Parker showed that for measures of objectivity and comparability, exit values revealed less dispersion than carrying amounts. The major cause of the lack of objectivity of carrying amounts was the dispersion of accounting estimates on useful life and residual value. McKeown also applied the Chambers model to a medium-sized road construction company, and concluded by statistical analysis that the methods used to determine exit prices were more objective (verifiable) than the methods under GAAP.[48] In another study, McKeown compared four proposed models with methods under GAAP for their objectivity (verifiability) and concluded that the CCE model was the most objective.[49]

A measure of risk

Exit prices and changes in exit prices can also be an indication of the financial risk of purchasing an asset. For example, if a firm purchases an asset and its exit value differs significantly from its entry price, then the asset is a risky proposition. This financial information indicates that the purchase of such an asset should be a long-term proposition whereby economic value is recovered by value in use. Conversely, if exit prices rise dramatically, the opportunity cost of return increases and it must be operated more efficiently.

Jim Dixon, in an article in *Australian CPA*, commenting about the Joint Working Group of Standard Setters (JWG) draft accounting standard on 'Financial Instruments and Similar Items' effectively summarised risk assessment:

> To enable users of financial reports to evaluate risk positions and performance in managing significant financial risks the draft standard would require:
> - a description of each significant financial risk and of the enterprise's objectives and policies for managing those risks;
> - information about the impacts of these risks on the statement of financial position (balance sheet) and statement of financial performance; and
> - information about the methods and key assumptions used to estimate the fair value of financial instruments.[50]

Arguments against exit price accounting

Profit concept

Given that profit is a measure of the effectiveness of the actual performance of a firm in using the resources entrusted to it, Bell states:

> Certain assets were purchased with a plan of operations in mind. That plan, those operations, indeed those people who developed that plan must first be evaluated before alternatives about the future can be considered, and it is the accountant's task to provide the data for that evaluation.[51]

Once this evaluation is made, the firm can decide whether to continue to use the assets for the purpose they were acquired or to sell them and use their proceeds in some other alternative. A meaningful concept of profit, therefore 'is the measurement of performance in terms of what was originally intended'. Only after the expected plan is evaluated in terms of the profit made can we proceed to the next stage of deciding whether the plan should be changed and the assets sold. On the other hand, exit price measurement requires a concept of profit where the plan is always to maximise the cash equivalent of the net assets over successive short-term periods. Bell believes that for a company other than one which deals in the simplest trading operation, such as that examined by Sterling, 'such a view of the enterprise, its objectives, and its mode of thought, would just not seem to be applicable'.[52]

The argument against exit price accounting is that accounting must measure past events, those that actually happened, rather than those that might happen if a firm does something other than what was planned.

Weston[53] further argues that exit price accounting provides relevant information only if the company plans to liquidate its assets. If the company plans to continue in business, the information is not relevant. It may be that in a world of perfect markets, managers must decide to liquidate at year-end. However, in the real world, it is unrealistic to assume that such a decision is faced by management on a continual basis. Therefore, preparing financial statements on an exit price basis as the main published data is not realistic. Weston also argues that using exit price accounting does not provide a meaningful profit. Because inventories are restated at exit price, the effective profit from sale is zero. The emphasis is on changes in prices and not the actual selling transaction.

Additivity

Exit price proponents claim that accounting measurements, if they are to be objective, must be based only on past and present events. Anticipatory calculations cannot be added together with current figures. Critics point out, however, that Chambers's current cash equivalent of assets is determined on the assumption of a gradual and orderly liquidation. If that is the case, then future events must be assumed when the current cash equivalent is recorded on the balance date. The realisable value for an asset that has to be sold immediately in a forced liquidation may deviate greatly from that in a gradual, orderly liquidation. If, in fact, anticipations cannot be avoided in ascertaining current cash equivalent, then the exit price model itself violates the principle of exclusion of anticipatory calculations.

Larson and Schattke have indicated that the cash equivalents of individual assets sold separately and the same assets sold as a package may be quite different.[54] For example, the specialised assets of a factory may have little resale value, but when the factory is sold together with the assets, they may command a high price. The concept of current cash equivalent, with its emphasis on severability of assets, does not recognise the possibility of selling assets as one package. As assets are combined in different sets, the current cash equivalent of the different sets may be greater or less than the sum of the assets if sold individually. This is due to intangible factors, positive or negative, usually categorised as goodwill in accounting. Thus, Larson and Schattke conclude that current cash equivalents are themselves not additive, and exit theory does not recognise the ability of the firm to adapt in terms of combinations of assets.

The valuation of liabilities

Chambers argues that bonds payable is effectively a form of capital and should be stated at face value, rather than at market value. This has led some to charge Chambers with inconsistency of treatment, because bonds as an asset are to be stated at market value. In defence, Chambers maintains that at any given time, regardless of the price in the market, the firm owes the bondholders only the contractual amount of the bonds; therefore, it is the contractual amount that is relevant in assessing present financial position.[55] In most cases, this is equivalent to face value. But critics are not persuaded because, by Chambers's own definition, the financial position indicates the firm's ability to engage in transactions. This logically implies the ability of the firm to go into the market to purchase its own bonds at the market price. Horton and Macve state:

> The issues here relating to fixed-interest securities — whether assets or liabilities — were clearly understood more than a hundred years ago by an English judge in the case of *Verner v. The General and Commercial Investment Trust* (63 Ch. D. 456) in 1894, who,

mercifully untrammelled by any accounting standard-setters' conceptual framework, realised that a fall in value of fixed-interest investments did not reduce a company's ability to continue to meet its interest obligations on its issued debentures and to pay dividends to its shareholders out of the unchanged cashflows it was still receiving. The JWG and FASB would benefit from adopting accounting concepts that showed a similar understanding of economic and commercial reality.[56]

Current cost or exit price

One question is crucial in deciding whether to use current cost or exit price: At what stage of the operating cycle should exit price dominate asset valuation? Current cost theorists argue that an entry price is the 'normal' method of valuation for the following reasons.[57]

- Using exit prices leads to anomalous revaluations on acquisition because immediately after purchase value usually falls so that it is less than acquisition cost.
- Using exit prices implies a short-term approach to business operations since one is interested in disposition and liquidation values. A positive profit under exit price accounting simply indicates it is worth staying in business in the short term, not that it is worth replacing assets and inputs and staying in business over the longer term.
- Using exit prices for finished goods inventory leads to the anticipation of operating profit before the point of sale because the inventory is valued in excess of current cost.

LO 6 → VALUE IN USE VERSUS VALUE IN EXCHANGE

Adam Smith was the first to make a distinction between value in use and value in exchange. Solomons maintains that value to the owner/firm is the relevant perspective.[58] An asset that is held rather than sold must be worth more to its owner than its exit price, otherwise it would be sold and not selling does not directly cause its owner to suffer in economic terms after a price fall.[59] This is especially the case of non-marketable fixed assets. Such assets are usually highly specific to a particular business and may in fact be excellent investments for the firm. Because no alternative use exists for the assets outside the business their resale value may effectively be zero. Chambers would require the firm to record a loss because of the zero resale value and according to Solomons this leads to an 'absurdity and a flagrant failure to measure up to the criterion of correspondence with the economic events which are being recorded'.[60]

Because of his insistence that value is determined by exchange, Chambers defines an asset as the 'severable means in the possession of an entity'.[61] Critics find the stipulation of severability, or individual exchangeability, to be unduly restrictive. Chambers believes that something that cannot be sold separately, such as goodwill, does not help the firm increase its ability to adapt to a changing environment. Critics argue that exchangeability emphasises only one way to ascertain value.

Hence, in summary, a firm can consider an asset to have value because of its use in the business rather than its sale and the synergistic value added by combining with other assets. Moreover, the above discussion highlights the fact that an asset can have two important components — value in use, which emphasises a long-term approach, and value in exchange, which concentrates on a short-term approach to valuation. They reflect two different perspectives on the purpose of financial accounting.

A value-in-use approach uses an external investor or a production-oriented entity as the relevant benchmark. Such an investor (firm) rarely focuses on current liquidation values but is interested in the prospects for future cash flows, which are more accurately predicted by operating earnings rather than current cash flow. So what is required is a measure of income that matches the current costs of asset inputs against outputs. This approach concentrates on obtaining the most efficient results from asset in use and does not consider adaptability as an option.

On the other hand, exit prices as a value-in-exchange approach takes the viewpoint of an internal manager or creditor who has to make decisions related to the liquidity of the firm and current spending power; that is, the short-term performance of the firm is more important. This approach is particularly important for firms with liquidity problems (high-debt firms), or firms engaged in tradeable goods and which are able to quickly adapt their operations to market conditions (such as mutual funds that invest in tradeable bonds or shares).

Staubus[62] points out that a number of factors are common to each viewpoint:
- Up-to-date observations of market prices are more relevant for financial decision making.
- Reliability is required of the measurement system; that is, valuation does not depend on a subjective allocation.
- Additivity (measurement) of economic phenomena is made in the same unit, adjusted for inflation and price movements.

Barton[63] states that in liquid markets there is very little friction between entry (CCA) and exit prices (EXA) and the accounting outputs are similar. However, when prices vary significantly both systems are required to give important (but different) information on value in use and value in exchange. Because cost of maintaining financial accounting systems can be an issue, a choice has to be made on which system is more cost-effective to the firm — the short-term approach or the long-term approach. Regardless, Barton still views these accounting systems as complements and not substitutes. This can be illustrated by a few simple decision rules that use the accounting returns (CCE and CCA) in conjunction with the net present value requirement (NPV):
- If CCA > EXA; and CCA > NPV, then assets have value in current use — maintain current operations.
- If EXA > CCA; and CCA > NPV, then liquidate assets currently used — continually adapt assets to other alternative investments.
- If EXA > CCA; and CCA < NPV, then liquidate and discontinue all operations.

LO 7 → A GLOBAL PERSPECTIVE AND INTERNATIONAL FINANCIAL REPORTING STANDARDS

Variants of current cost and price level accounting have been trialled or adopted in several countries.

Current cost in the United States

In 1976, the US Securities Exchange Commission (SEC) amended Rule 3-17 of Regulation S-X to require that replacement cost data be disclosed in the filed 10-K reports by firms with inventories and productive assets totalling more than US$100 million and constituting more than 10 per cent of total assets. This requirement was published in Accounting Series Release (ASR) 190.

In 1979, the FASB repealed ASR 190 and issued Statement 33 requiring supplementary disclosures of general inflation adjusted accounts and current cost data. The requirement to provide current cost data met with tremendous resistance from companies. After much debate about the usefulness of the supplementary information, the FASB issued Statement 89 in 1986, rescinding the requirement but urging companies to continue disclosing the data.

In Statement 33, the FASB required companies to disclose information on:

- profit from continuing operations on a current cost basis for the current financial year
- the current cost of inventory and property, plant and equipment at the end of the current financial year
- changes in the current cost for the current financial year of inventory and property, plant and equipment, using a constant dollar basis.

Changes in cost were not to be included in profit from continuing operations and companies were required to disclose the following current cost information on a nominal dollars basis for each of the most recent 5 years:

- profit from continuing operations
- profit per ordinary share from continuing operations
- net assets at financial year-end.

The FASB was undecided whether to support the financial capital view or the physical capital view. Because of this, it decided in Statement 33 to call the changes in current cost 'increases or decreases in current cost', rather than holding gains (or losses) or capital maintenance adjustments. However, it claimed that profit from continuing operations based on current costs is a guide to assessing the maintenance of the operating capability of a firm.[64] Statement 33 was meant to be a 5-year experiment. After considering the evidence on and reactions to the supplementary data, the FASB, in Statement 82 issued in November 1984, eliminated the requirement to report.

Current cost in the United Kingdom

In 1975 the Sandilands Committee, established by the UK government, recommended a system of current cost accounting. The committee concluded that historical cost statements, including those directly adjusted for changes in the general price level (constant dollar), were of limited usefulness. In considering the information needs of a variety of users, it decided that the assessment of the future benefits obtainable from a firm's net assets is of particular relevance to users. Information for such an assessment was decided to be best communicated by asset values that are based on a concept of 'value to the business'. This placed an emphasis on the business firm as an entity separate from its owners and the generation of profit as a means to continue current operations. Hence, an operating capacity and physical capital view underpinned current cost accounting in the United Kingdom.

Further, Sandilands determined that holding gains reflect current economic conditions that are generally out of the control of management, and are not indicative of normal activities. They decided that holding gains should be disclosed, but not included in profit.

The proposal by the Sandilands Committee was endorsed by the government and accepted in substance by the accounting profession as represented by the Accounting Standards Steering Committee. It was agreed that implementation should be left to the accounting profession. The Inflation Accounting Steering Group (IASG) was then established in early 1976 and produced an exposure draft (ED 18) in late 1976 that specified guidelines to be used by companies. After much debate, revisions and experimentation, the Accounting Standards Committee (ASC) issued a statement (SSAP 16) on current cost accounting in March 1980. The requirements of SSAP 16 could be satisfied by supplementary current cost data prominently displayed, or current cost for the main statements and historical cost as supplementary data. The standard applied to listed and large companies but in 1985, after much debate, the ASC withdrew the mandatory status of SSAP 16.

Current cost in Australia

In Australia, the accounting profession issued DPS 1.1, Statement of Provisional Accounting Standards (PAS) *Current Cost Accounting* in October 1976. An amended version of that statement (PAS 1) and a working guide were issued in August 1978. The recommended system of current cost was based on maintaining the firm's operating capacity intact. At the time, it was envisaged that the new system would completely replace historical cost statements once users became familiar with it. However, due to criticisms, lobbying by firms and individuals, and the lack of any material effect by the provisional standard on reporting practices, a 'downgraded' Statement of Accounting Practice (SAP) 1 *Current Cost Accounting* was issued in November 1983.

Thus the release of SAP 1 signalled a significant change in direction. A statement of practice *recommends*, whereas a standard *requires*, compliance. SAP 1 'strongly' recommended that all entities present supplementary current cost accounting statements in addition to their conventional historical cost financial statements, but it was not a requirement. An alternative was that current cost statements could be presented as the main financial statements, completely replacing the historical cost reports. SAP 1 was not widely adopted in Australia.

International accounting standards and current costs

The above overview reveals that a number of countries in the past have attempted to implement some form of current cost accounting but the systems were not widely adopted. On 15 July 2004, the AASB voted to adopt international accounting standards for all reporting entities preparing general-purpose financial reports after 1 January 2005. In Europe they were also adopted for all firms listed on stock markets that applied consolidated accounting. IASB standards make greater use of fair value measurement than some national GAAP.

IAS 39/AASB 139 *Financial Instruments: Recognition and Measurement* (paragraph 9) and IFRS 3/AASB 3 *Business Combinations* (Appendix A) define fair value as 'the amount for which an asset could be exchanged, or a liability settled, between knowledgeable, willing parties in an arm's length transaction'. In active markets, fair value is normally the current transaction price and if there is no active market then a number of surrogates for fair value can be used, such as discounted cash flows, option pricing models, depreciated replacement cost, market indexes, and appraisal value.

Although fair value is normally accepted as the market transaction price, the definition of a transaction cost is not consistent and a single transaction price is not consistently applied in IFRS. Under IAS 16/AASB 116 *Property, Plant and Equipment* the fair value is the cost price at the date on which the acquirer obtains control of the asset, being the date of acquisition. After acquisition, each entity for each class of assets must decide the measurement model to be used. All assets within a class must be valued under the same principles, but not all classes must use the same valuation model. There is no specified period that the assets have to be revalued. Effectively IAS 16/AASB 116 allows entities a choice between a cost model and a current (revaluation) cost model. Under IAS 40/AASB 140 entities may choose between a cost–depreciation–impairment model or a fair value model with value changes recognised in the income statement, when measuring investment property.

Thus, under international accounting standards the definition of fair value can vary substantially from a cost model to buying and selling prices through to valuation models based on discounted cash flows or option pricing. There is no mention in the standards of capital maintenance concepts and, hence, no consistent application of income measurement rules based on changes in capital.

How is historical cost applied?

There is no question that the amount *actually* paid for an item is more concrete and objective than an amount that one *would* have paid. Acquisition costs represent a more ontologically hard view of reality to a particular firm than market prices. Underlying the acceptance of the objectivity of historical cost is the assumption that an arm's-length transaction is involved. This is why transactions between related parties must be looked at carefully. In an arm's-length transaction, the cost is considered to be equivalent to the fair value of the item at that time.

However, remember that the acquisition cost of an asset in accounting is not simply the invoice price. It is generally regarded as the outlay necessary to bring the asset to its existing condition and location. There are numerous items that may be included in the cost of the asset. For example, according to paragraph 10 of IAS 2/AASB 102 *Inventories* (issued in July 2004), 'cost of inventories' comprises 'all costs of purchase, costs of conversion and other costs incurred in bringing the inventories to their present locations and condition'.

Costs of purchase comprise the purchase price, import duties and other taxes, and transport, handling and other costs directly attributable to the acquisition of finished goods, materials and services. Trade discounts, rebates and other similar items are deducted in determining the costs of purchase.

Costs of conversion include costs directly related to the units of production, such as direct labour, as well as a systematic allocation of fixed and variable production overheads incurred in converting materials into finished goods.

Other costs include only those that are incurred in bringing the inventories to their present location and condition. Costs to be excluded from the cost of inventories and recognised as expenses in the period in which they are incurred include abnormal wastage costs; storage costs; administrative overheads that do not contribute to bringing inventories to their present location and condition; and selling costs.

Thus, in historical cost accounting the main basis for measuring inventories held at reporting date is cost. The United States Committee on Accounting Procedure considers such rules to be more easily stated than applied. As examples of the difficulties involved, the Committee reported:

> under some circumstances, items such as idle facility expense, excessive spoilage, double freight, and rehandling costs may be so abnormal as to require treatment as current period charges rather than as a portion of inventory cost ... general and administrative expenses should be included as period charges, except for the portion of such expenses that may be clearly related to production and thus constitute a part of inventory costs.[65]

Kieso and Weygandt present the procedure for calculating inventory cost more specifically as follows:

> Charges directly connected with the bringing of goods to the place of business of the buyer and converting such goods to a saleable condition are accepted as proper inventoriable costs. Such charges would include freight and hauling charges on goods purchased, other direct costs of acquisition, and labour and other production costs incurred in processing the goods up to the time of sale ... It would seem proper also to allocate to inventories a share of any buying costs or expenses of a purchasing department, storage costs, and other costs incurred in storing or handling the goods before they are sold.[66]

In practice, it is not surprising to find variations in the application of the procedure. Should cost be net of cash discounts, even if they are not taken? Should insurance of the items while in transit be included? The rule stated by Kieso and Weygandt specifies freight charges as an inventory cost, but in practice some companies exclude them. Most firms disregard storage charges in the cost of inventories. Clearly, judgement is necessary in ascertaining the acquisition cost of an asset. It is also evident that practice is inconsistent.

It is interesting to note the requirements of the provisions of the *Income Tax Assessment Act 1936*, as amended. For taxation purposes, the Australian Taxation Office requires the inclusion of specific indirect costs in calculating inventory for work-in-progress and manufactured trading stock. For example, Taxation Ruling IT 2350 'Value of Trading Stock on Hand at End of Year: Cost Price: Absorption Cost', outlines that the following costs should be taken into account when valuing inventory under the absorption costing method:

- factory light and power and administration expenses
- factory rent, insurance, maintenance and repairs
- factory rates and taxes
- indirect labour and production supervisory wages
- indirect materials and supplies
- royalties in respect of production process
- tools and equipment
- depreciation on factory plant and equipment.

Income tax law has no relevance to generally accepted accounting principles. However, in practice and for the sake of convenience, many firms will apply the same procedures for both tax law and external reporting.

The question of capitalising or expensing expenditures also affects the cost of an asset. For some items the answer is obvious, but for others it is not. If the interior of an office building is repainted, should the expenditure be capitalised or expensed? Should the cost of rearrangement of equipment be placed in an asset or expense account? IAS 38/AASB 138 *Intangible Assets* requires all research and development costs to be expensed as incurred, except for those development costs where all of the following can be demonstrated by the entity:

(a) the technical feasibility of completing the intangible asset so that it will be available for use or sale;
(b) its intention to complete the intangible asset and use or sell it;
(c) its ability to use or sell the intangible assets;
(d) how the intangible asset will generate probable future economic benefits. Among other things, the entity can demonstrate the existence of a market for the output of the intangible asset or the intangible asset itself or, if it is to be used internally, the usefulness of the intangible asset;
(e) the availability of adequate technical, financial and other resources to complete the development and to use or sell the intangible asset; and
(f) its ability to measure reliably the expenditure attributable to the intangible asset during its development.

Given the nature of research and development expenditure, it would be appropriate in most cases to expense them immediately if the above criteria are applied. On this basis, if research and development ultimately leads to a patent, the cost of the patent will be essentially the legal fees involved. Is this truly the cost of the patent?

In the past, many Australian firms capitalised development expenditure prior to the generation of profit-earning activities. But the *Framework*, which defines the elements of financial statements (namely assets, liabilities, equity, income and expenses) and specifies criteria for their recognition in financial statements, basically adopts a conservative historical cost perspective. For example, with respect to the criteria for measuring an asset, paragraph 89 states: 'An asset is recognised in the balance sheet when it is probable that the future economic benefits will flow to the entity and the asset has a cost or value that can be measured reliably.' In addition, there is some inconsistency — paragraph 100 identifies the different measurement bases used in financial reporting as historical cost, current cost, realisable (settlement) value and present value and in paragraph 101 states: 'The measurement basis most commonly adopted by entities in preparing their financial report is historical cost. This is usually combined with other measurement bases.' However, no guidance is provided on selecting the appropriate base, again creating inconsistencies in reporting practices.

One of the major accounting issues that arises with respect to non-current assets is not so much whether they qualify as assets or not, but what is to be included as part of their cost, as reported in the balance sheet. The majority of non-current assets in Australian balance sheets are carried at depreciated historical cost, or revalued and depreciated cost. However, the calculation of depreciation involves subjective assessments in determining both the useful life of the asset and its residual value. These cannot be considered fully objective as they are still in the future. Furthermore, it is common practice in Australia for businesses to reassess the value of some or all of their non-current assets. This assessment may lead to a revaluation or devaluation of selected non-current assets. The amount by which the carrying amount of an asset exceeds its recoverable amount is known as an impairment loss.

'Recoverable amount of an asset' is defined in paragraph 6 of IAS 36/AASB 136 *Impairment of Assets* as 'the higher of its fair value less costs to sell and its value in use', where 'fair value less costs to sell' is 'the amount obtainable from the sale of an asset or cash-generating unit in an arm's length transaction between knowledgeable, willing parties, less the costs of disposal' and 'value in use' is 'the present value of the future cash flows expected to be derived from an asset or cash-generating unit'.

Accordingly, the notion of 'recoverable amount' takes into account the value of the asset from its continued use and subsequent disposal. An estimate must be made as to the future cash flows of the asset, as well as its subsequent sale price.

From 2005, IAS 36/AASB 136 requires the discounting of future cash flows in assessing the recoverable amount of an asset. Further, paragraph 55 specifies that the discount rate to be used is the 'pre-tax rate that reflects current market assessments of (a) the time value of money and (b) the risks specific to the asset for which the future cash flow estimates have not been adjusted'. In estimating the discount rate, IAS 36/AASB 136 suggests an entity take into account the following rates:

- the entity's weighted average cost of capital determined using techniques such as the capital asset pricing model (CAPM)
- the entity's incremental borrowing rate
- other market borrowing rates.

Before 2005, the superseded standard permitted but did not require the use of present value techniques in determining recoverable amount and, where an entity elected to use present value techniques, provided no guidance on the discount rate to be used. The new standard therefore prescribes the use of a method which offers a high level of choice to account preparers in selecting an appropriate discount rate, thereby increasing the possibility of reporting inconsistencies and creating compliance costs associated with estimating discount rates.

The prescribing of present value discounting techniques in IAS 36/AASB 136 is generally viewed as a significant improvement over the previous standard. Alternative cost methods applied to the same set of facts can provide different results. For example, assuming prices are changing, if a company used FIFO, it would have a different measure for its inventories than if it had used LIFO or average cost. Although the results are different, each is historical cost. An example from the United States is provided by FASB Statements 19 and 25 which allow oil- and gas-producing companies to use either the successful efforts method or the full cost method. When an oil or gas reserve is discovered, the first method requires only that the cost related to that particular discovery be capitalised, whereas the second also includes costs of unsuccessful activities. Obviously, there can be a large difference between the two amounts.

In consolidating financial statements, if a parent company has less than 100 per cent interest in a subsidiary, the nature of the 'costs' on the consolidated balance sheet is difficult to describe. Assume a parent has an 80 per cent interest in a subsidiary and that the carrying amount of a particular non-monetary asset of the subsidiary is $100 000 and its market value is $180 000 on the acquisition date. Under the parent company theory, the parent will recognise only 80 per cent of the $80 000 increase in value. The asset will be shown on the balance sheet at $164 000, which is 100 per cent of the carrying amount plus 80 per cent of the $80 000. It may be argued that the $164 000 represents the cost of the asset to the parent, but the fact is that the parent did not acquire the asset directly. It did not pay $164 000 for the asset. By definition, if an entity has control of the future services of a resource then the resource qualifies as an asset, not just a portion of it. The $164 000 is a strange figure.

Subjectivity is involved in the determination of the acquisition cost of an asset. Yet, for the most part, accountants accept this and do not appear to be unduly disturbed about it. Familiarity with the subjective elements associated with historical cost may be the reason. In relating this issue to the contention that current values are subjective, Sterling states:

> for the accountant to reject present values because they are 'subjective' is the pot calling the kettle black. Like Paton, we 'marvel' at accountants who consider cost to be objective.[67]

An example of the mix of approaches being allowed is provided in IAS 16/AASB 116 *Property, Plant and Equipment*. This standard allows a reporting entity to choose either a cost or revaluation model as its accounting policy subsequent to initial recognition at cost and to apply that policy to an entire class of property, plant and equipment. The standard gives management the option of revaluing specified groups of property, plant and equipment on an ongoing basis and of recognising any changes in the value of these assets as a direct credit to equity. This means that businesses can nominate a group or groups of assets for ongoing revaluation, and leave others reported at cost, or subject to the intermittent write-down in accordance with IAS 36/AASB 136. However, the point is that the cost basis underlies the adoption of and support for the historical cost approach by the Australian accounting profession and the standard-setting body. The AASB allows entities to have a mixed approach, where current values are applied to some groups of assets and not to others. Further, the determination of 'fair value' is somewhat broadly defined and allows for different methods of valuation, both between classes of assets and over time.

Paragraph 6 of IAS 16/AASB 116 defines fair value as 'the amount for which an asset could be exchanged between knowledgeable, willing parties in an arm's length transaction' and according to paragraph 32 is usually the market value determined by appraisal. Where there is no market-based evidence of fair value, paragraph 33 states that an entity may need to use an income or a depreciated replacement cost approach to estimate fair value. Although an underlying principle expressed in the standard is to determine an appropriate fair value, the standard provides considerable discretion, even with respect to the frequency of valuation. Basically, where there are significant changes in fair value, the value should be revised annually. However, where there are insignificant changes in fair value, then no adjustment is required, but the standard suggests that a revaluation should occur every 3 to 5 years.

IAS 16/AASB 116 introduces the option of current value accounting, which is inconsistent with the provisions of many other accounting standards and the historical cost model with its underlying principle of objectivity.

Historical cost under attack

The above discussion shows that the use of historical costs has not been abandoned but it has come under continual criticism. For several years, we have witnessed a gradual move away from traditional historical cost reporting, possibly signalling the beginning of the end of historical cost reporting. According to Shanahan:

> The hints are coming thick and fast: historic cost accounting has had it. Balance sheets that contain outdated cost prices or valuations that don't represent current market value can hardly be said to be true and fair. Does knowing what an asset cost several years ago help investors assess whether a company is a worthwhile investment? It has long been accepted at law that a balance sheet is not a valuation statement — but do users of accounts know this?[68]

For example, standards requiring or permitting market value accounting for at least some assets include IAS 39/AASB 139 *Financial Instruments: Recognition and Measurement* and IAS 16/AASB 116.

The prescribing of present value techniques in determining the recoverable amount of an asset required by IAS 36/AASB 136 *Impairment of Assets* also represents a major shift from historical cost principles. Furthermore, standard-setters have also advocated that liabilities are to be measured using present value techniques. Standards such as IAS 19/AASB 119 *Employee Benefits* require that liabilities are to be measured at their present values, using discounting techniques.

The move away from traditional historical cost reporting is probably best reflected in paragraph 101 of the IASB *Framework*, which recognises the blending of alternative costing methods and the perceived benefits of current cost accounting as follows:

> The measurement basis most commonly adopted by entities in preparing their financial report is historic cost. This is usually combined with other measurement bases. For example, inventories are usually carried at the lower of cost and net realisable value, marketable securities may be carried at market value and pension liabilities are carried at their present value. Furthermore, some entities use the current cost basis as a response to the inability of the historic cost accounting model to deal with the effects of changing prices of non-monetary assets.

However, by their own admission, the IASB recognises that the issue of measurement is one of the most underdeveloped areas of the *Framework*. A joint project paper issued in May 2005 comparing the frameworks of the IASB (adopted by Australia) and the US Financial Accounting Standards Board (FASB) states:

> Measurement is one of the most underdeveloped areas of the two frameworks ... Both the IASB and the FASB frameworks contain lists of measurement attributes that are used in practice. Those lists are broadly consistent, and comprise historic cost, current cost, gross or net realizable (settlement) value and present value. Both frameworks indicate that the use of different measurement attributes is expected to continue. However, neither provides guidance on how to choose between different measurement attributes that exist. In other words, the frameworks lack fully developed measurement concepts.[69]

Despite the push from the standard setters away from traditional historical cost reporting, the Group of 100 categorically stated that they consider a move away from historical cost as 'unacceptable'. In the *New Accountant* on 25 June 1992, Michael Gillian, Chairman of the G100, was quoted as saying:

> The accounting framework is based on the historic cost concept. The piecemeal introduction of present value measurement into Australian standards is unacceptable without debate as to what the balance sheet represents.[70]

The business community also does not appear to share the standard setters' enthusiasm for mixed measurement models.

The previous two sections outlined conflicting areas. Various forms of historical cost (while strongly criticised) are applied, while a number of current and future valuation techniques are also applied under IFRS. The question then is what underlies IFRS? This question is addressed in the next section.

A mixed measurement system and international standards

The above discussion raises the question as to how current value techniques are applied into financial statements. In particular, the issue of accounting for financial assets provides an example of how exit prices may be used in financial statements. Financial assets may include trading securities and held-to-maturity assets. For trading securities, the existence of a ready market means that market prices are available and can be incorporated into financial statements. Trading securities are measured at market value under IAS 39/AASB 139 *Financial Instruments: Recognition and Measurement* and under US and Japanese GAAP.

Held-to-maturity financial assets are currently valued at amortised cost in most countries. However, the use of market values (current selling prices) for all financial instruments is an ideal for some standard setters.

Although market valuations are implied in the 'fair value' approach in some international financial reporting standards, the approach has been implemented in a crude fashion basically because accounting regulators do not have a theoretical concept of valuation, capital maintenance or income measure. Staubus[71] argues that they have not really adopted a decision-usefulness theory. Instead they have adopted their own term — attributes of an asset or liability — instead of distinct measurement methods. This has led to a mixed measurement system. Figure 6.1 shows the movement away from strict historical cost and the use of different measurement concepts under international standards.

FIGURE 6.1 Some examples of the use of different measurement concepts in IFRS

1. IAS 2/AASB 102: Permits measurement of inventory at net realisable value even if it is above cost for producers' inventories of agricultural and forest products, mineral ores, and broker–dealers' inventory of commodities or stock.
2. IAS 16/AASB 116: Property, plant and equipment may be valued at historical cost or revalued amount where revalued amount is fair value less subsequent accumulated depreciation and impairment losses.
3. IAS 17/AASB 117: Leasehold interest in land is accounted for as investment property under IAS 40/AASB 140 and measured at fair value with value changes recognised as a gain or loss in the income statement.

FIGURE 6.1 *(continued)*

4. IAS 19/AASB 119: Measurement of a curtailment gain or loss comprises (a) the change in the present value of the defined benefit obligation, (b) any resulting change in fair value of the plan assets, and (c) a pro rata share of any related actuarial gains and losses.

5. IAS 29/AASB 129: Adjustments to the financial statements of an entity that operates in a hyperinflationary economy can be done by using a general price level index.

6. IAS 36/AASB 136: Impairment of assets, where the asset is valued at the recoverable amount, which is the higher of the asset's value in use and the current cash equivalent.

7. IAS 36/AASB 136: Treats the residual value of an asset as the current cash equivalent.

8. IAS 37/AASB 137: Measurement of provisions is determined by the expected present value method.

9. IAS 40/AASB 140: Investment property can be measured by a choice between (a) cost–depreciation–impairment or (b) fair value with value changes passed through the income statement as a gain or loss.

Horton and Macve argue that the FASB's and IASB's interpretation of fair value is valuation by exit prices. However, until a system of accounting is decided and globally agreed on the IASB project must forever remain a mixed system of accounting. The international view below outlines this perspective.

Measurement: an international issue

Before the adoption of international financial reporting standards (IFRS) in 2005, the conceptual framework project in Australia had seen the release of four concept statements: SAC 1 *Definition of the Reporting Entity*, SAC 2 *Objective of General Purpose Financial Reporting*, SAC 3 *Qualitative Characteristics of Financial Information*, and SAC 4 *Definition and Recognition of the Elements of Financial Statements*. The next statement targeted for development by the AASB was to be SAC 5 *Measurement of the Elements of Financial Statements*. However, the contentious and complex nature of the measurement issue saw a delay in the development of this statement and at the time of adoption of the international standards, no real progress had been made towards filling this 'measurement' gap in the AASB's conceptual framework.

The IASB's *Framework for the Preparation and Presentation of Financial Statements* adopted by Australia from 2005 replaced SAC 3 and SAC 4. The *Framework*, like all IFRSs, is intended to provide consistency in reporting practices across international boundaries by providing preparers with fewer alternative accounting treatments, thereby enhancing comparability. However, the measurement concepts outlined in the *Framework* appear to fall short of this objective and are in need of further development.

The *Framework* contains three paragraphs (99–101) on measurement. The first defines measurement as 'the process of determining the monetary amounts at which the elements of the financial statements are to be recognised and carried in the balance sheet and income statement'. The second paragraph goes on to state that 'a number of different measurement bases are employed to different degrees and in varying combinations in financial reports', including historical cost, current cost, realisable (settlement) value and present value. And the final paragraph states:

The measurement basis most commonly adopted by enterprises in preparing their financial report is historic cost. This is usually combined with other measurement bases.

For example, inventories are usually carried at the lower of cost and net realisable value, marketable securities may be carried at market value and pension liabilities are carried at their present value. Furthermore, some enterprises use the current cost basis as a response to the inability of the historic cost accounting model to deal with the effects of changing prices of non-monetary assets.

The *Framework*, although recognising the existence of a range of acceptable measurement alternatives, provides no guidance on which to use. It also does not distinguish between initial and subsequent measurement, nor does it resolve issues such as the unit of account (i.e. level of aggregation) and measurement techniques such as present value.

Until these issues are tackled, a consistent international approach to the issue of measurement will remain unresolved.

Reference

IASB and FASB 2005, 'Revisiting the concepts: A new conceptual framework project', May, www.iasb.org and www.fasb.org.

LO 8 → ISSUES FOR AUDITORS

Auditors seek evidence to support their opinion on whether the financial statements are presented fairly and in accordance with the relevant standards and laws. This evidence must be sufficient and appropriate; that is, in sufficient quantity and of a reasonable standard of quality. The quality of evidence is determined by its relevance and reliability in providing support for, or detecting misstatements in, the transaction classes, account balances and disclosures of the entity (ISA/ASA 500). Where the auditor believes there is a greater risk of misstatement, the requirement to gather sufficient and appropriate audit evidence is more onerous.

As discussed in this chapter, auditors must contend with a mixed measurement model. For any one entity the measurement bases could include, at a minimum, fair values (e.g. exit prices for financial instruments), discounted cash flows (e.g. asset impairment assessments) and amortised costs (e.g. depreciated fixed assets). Even within each of these broad categories, there are a variety of application issues. For example, for assets stated at amortised cost there are decisions to be made about whether certain costs are capitalised or expensed; for example, costs associated with installation of fixed assets, self-constructed assets, and development expenditures.

Each measurement model creates certain types of misstatement risks. Exit prices could be difficult to determine when markets are thinly traded. Discounted cash flows require consideration of future cash flow projections and choice of discount rate. Deciding whether certain expenditures are in the nature of maintenance or capital improvement can be difficult, and assessing the future prospects of development expenditure relies on product sale forecasts. Auditors deal with some of these valuation issues by seeking expert opinions (ISA/ASA 620), and others by testing the basis for management assumptions and the data input to the valuation models rather than directly testing the values for correspondence to an external market value (ISA 540/ASA 540 and 545).

Although auditors can reduce their audit risk by obtaining an expert opinion about a valuation, evidence suggests that such valuations are not necessarily more reliable than those made by management. Cotter and Richardson (2002)[72] examined the properties of asset valuations made by boards of directors and independent external appraisers. They found that boards of directors were more likely to revalue investments, plant and equipment and identifiable intangibles. External appraisers were more likely to be used for revaluations of land and buildings and for other assets if the boards were less independent. This suggests that boards of directors are sensitive to perceptions that they are biasing their valuations because they are less independent. Also, Cotter and Richardson find that although external appraisers' valuations of plant and equipment were more reliable than those made by directors, there was no detectable difference between reliability of the valuations for other assets. It should be noted that the data used in this study came from audited financial statements. This suggests that any problems detected by the auditors in either type of valuations were resolved prior to publication of the financial statements. It is an empirical question whether the unaudited valuations made by directors are so reliable.

A specific asset that is valued at accumulated cost but tested against a value derived from estimates of future cash flows is the intangible asset arising from development activities. Development is the application of research findings or other knowledge to a plan or design for the production of a new or substantially improved material, device, product, process, system or service, prior to the start of commercial production or use (AASB 138/IAS 38). Research costs are not to be capitalised, but development costs are allowed to be recognised as assets under strict conditions laid down in the accounting standard. In addition to a consideration of the evidence of the costs of development, auditors need to obtain sufficient evidence about the specific capitalisation conditions to distinguish research from development. Auditors must also test the assumptions and data used by management to assess the future economic benefits from the development activities.

Another factor which increases the risk of misstatement in measurement is the involvement of related parties. Where transactions with related parties exist, the auditor requires specific evidence that the transactions have been property recorded and disclosed (ISA 550/ASA 550). In an arm's-length transaction the auditor is likely to be satisfied that the cost of the transaction is reasonable, and that any resulting assets, liabilities or profit elements are measured appropriately. However, the involvement of related parties adversely affects the quality of the evidence provided by the transaction record. The auditor must seek additional evidence from third parties, inspect all the documents and/or assets, and discuss the details of the transactions with management and members of the audit committee, as appropriate in the circumstances.

Summary

LO 1 An overview of the three main income and capital measurement systems in accounting — historical cost, current cost (entry value), and current selling price (exit value)

After the Wall Street collapse in 1929, the traditional historical cost system that applied conservative accounting principles emerged. This was systematically codified as the fundamental basis for measuring capital and calculating income using cost matching in the late 1930s. In the 1960s several alternative valuation systems were developed that challenged historical cost as the fundamental accounting system. The first was an updated cost system that matched the current costs of resource usage to valued capital at current buying prices. There were two versions of current cost: financial and operating capital. The other valuation system used exit values or selling price as the valuation base.

LO 2 The historical cost model (arguments for and against)

The objective of accounting is seen as monitoring the stewardship function of management by calculating income and valuing net assets in a conservative way. The income statement is maintained as more important than the balance sheet which records the unexpired costs of assets. Since the income statement is emphasised, the principles of revenue recognition and matching play a crucial role. Historical cost is considered to be objectively determinable and costs 'attach' to the assets and services acquired. By keeping track of the flow of costs, the accountant is also keeping account of the operations of the firm. Thus, the accountant's main task is to determine which costs have expired and are thus allocated to the income statement, and which have not yet expired and are thus placed in the balance sheet. Critics point out that stewardship is far too narrowly construed and effectively rules out the role of accounting in economic decision-making purposes; such as current valuations and making predictions about the company's future cash flows. The more current is information, the more relevant it is; therefore, using historical cost is outdated and not logical in a commercial sense. Finally, the task of deciding which costs have expired and which have not, is basically arbitrary and rules driven — because making such judgements are virtually impossible.

LO 3 Current cost accounting: business profit, holding gains and operating capital (arguments for and against)

Edwards and Bell argue that a comparison of past accounting data that reveals the amount, composition and financing of assets aids managers in making informed economic decisions. They determine that the fair value of assets for these decisions is valuation using current cost (entry) prices. The major departures from conventional historical cost are that holding gains and losses are measured and incorporated as part of income on the basis that they are cost savings to managers, and expenses are matched as the current cost of resource usage. Business profit rewards managers for profits actually made in the current accounting period and does not hide higher profits made from lower asset charges under the historical cost system. Operating capacity theorists diverge by arguing an entity concept, that increased costs of inputs are a capital maintenance item that must be maintained as capital in order to continue the same level of operations or services. Increases in costs are not income but a signal of increased costs of input that require higher funding from operations.

Critics point out that current cost accounting violates the traditional revenue recognition principle by recognising increases in the value of assets before they are sold. They also believe that too much subjectivity is injected into the accounting process by allowing revaluations of assets and liabilities, especially when markets are thin and prices unreliable. In defence, exponents of current cost believe that the main objective of accounting is to provide useful information for economic decision making. That means relevant current events of the period should be accounted for and reported, whether they give rise to realised transactions or not, because they represent opportunity cost. Current events include not only the acquisition and disposition of assets and liabilities, but also the change in their cost value throughout the current period. Operating theorists maintain the traditional going concern concept works better by using current rather than historical costs.

LO 4 Financial capital versus physical capital

While proponents of current cost accounting are convinced that it provides more useful information than historical accounting, they do not agree on all issues. In general, supporters can be divided into two camps: (1) those who believe in the financial capital concept, and (2) those who believe in the physical capital concept. Each measure of capital leads to different derived profits, with physical capital profit generally lower and less volatile. In quantitative terms, the difference between the two viewpoints is that holding gains are included in profit under financial capital and excluded under physical capital. Supporters of the physical capital view emphasise the need to know that the firm's operating capability has been maintained in order for it to continue in business. This is supported by the theory of optimal resource usage that uses current costs as a measure of input opportunity cost, as a signal that the cost of operations has increased, and as a base for calculating revised return on assets.

LO 5 Exit price accounting (arguments for and against)

MacNeal argued that profits included realised and unrealised components based on current market selling prices; Chambers concentrated on the adaptive behaviour of firms and its implications; and Sterling examined the types of decisions users are likely to make. Additional support for current exit prices is that they are additive because they pertain to the same property for assets and liabilities, which is cash and current cash equivalents. Exit price financial statements are also seen to be allocation-free and have references to real-world prices. Adaptive behaviour is the driving assumption and implies a continual attempt to adjust to the competitive business environment in order to survive. The purpose of the firm is to satisfy its main group, shareholders, whose major objective is to increase real financial wealth. In order to adapt, a firm must be able to engage in market transactions and this is revealed by its net financial position (monetary value of assets and liabilities). In the last analysis, the economic survival of the firm depends on the amount of cash it can command and the balance sheet is critical to these decisions. Critics argue that exit price accounting is too narrow in its interpretation of economic value — it ignores the concept of value in use. Entry price and historical cost theorists both emphasise revenue recognition and matching in the income statement, which in turn concentrates on operating performance as the critical activity undertaken by the firm. However, the critical event in exit price accounting does not relate to the performance of the firm but, instead, concerns price changes of assets and liabilities. Because the emphasis is on price changes rather than operations, it can be difficult to evaluate the firm with reference to its operating efficiency because it concentrates on financial liquidity and short-term decision making.

LO 6

The difference between value in use and value in exchange

When markets are very liquid and efficient, there is very little difference in the measurement of value. Further, Staubus points out that there are a number of factors common to both the liquidation (value in exchange) and value in use viewpoints. They include the belief that market prices are more relevant for financial decision making, additivity and reliability are prime requirements of both accounting measurement systems, and conventional historical cost accounting has many defects. Barton also states that when there is very little friction between entry and exit prices the outputs are similar, but when prices vary significantly both systems are required to give important (but different) information on value in use and value in exchange. Value in use assesses the firm's ability to survive in the long term (solvency) and value in exchange assesses the firm's ability to adapt in the short term (liquidity).

LO 7

Global initiatives and relationships with 'fair value' accounting under International Financial Reporting Standards (IFRS)

Current cost accounting has been used, or recommended to be used, at some stage during the 1970s and 1980s in the United States, the United Kingdom and Australia and then effectively abandoned. Most systems were based on physical capital and did not recognise holding gains as income. Today, no complete current cost system dominates but there are mixed measurement systems in use. An examination of IFRS shows that while historical cost accounting is still generally applied there are several current value type accounting standards. However, the measurement methods are not fundamentally driven by any distinct principles and recent IASB accounting standards have taken a piecemeal approach to valuation. Different measurements have been used to value assets and liabilities according to the generally argued specifics of the situation. Standard setters have compromised on the issue by supporting a vague definition of 'fair value' rather than recommending one all-encompassing accounting measurement method. This is reflected in the different measurement concepts used in the standards and some may argue that it reflects compromise rather than measurement from a theoretical concept of capital maintenance. According to Horton and Macve, the IASB is moving towards an exit value approach and, in 2004, proposed a system based on fair value accounting where all fair value increments or decrements would be deemed to be part of the income statement. However, at the current stage, the IASB approach can be described as a mixed valuation approach with fair value accounting sometimes defined as current market entry cost prices but also as historical cost, selling price and discounted future cash flows.

LO 8

Issues for auditors

Auditors need to obtain sufficient and appropriate evidence on the fair presentation and compliance of financial statements. A variety of audit risks arise with the mixed measurement model. Some of these risks are dealt with by the auditor by obtaining independent expert valuations and others by testing the basis for management assumptions and the data input to the valuation models. Risks of misstatement are higher under certain conditions, such as the involvement of related parties.

Questions

1. According to the historical cost system, what is the objective of accounting and the role of profit? What criticisms are made of profit calculated under the historical cost system?
2. Explain the concept of 'costs attach'. What do critics say about the concept? What is meant by the terms 'unexpired cost' and 'expired cost'.
3. Would market value-adjusted statements be more 'decision useful' than those prepared applying historical cost measures? Would using current market values reduce the number of decisions required to prepare financial statements?
4. What are the three types of decisions managers are faced with in running a business? How does accounting enter the decision-making process?
5. Explain the Edwards and Bell concept of 'business profit'.
6. What are the benefits of separating out the holding gains (or losses) in profit determination? What are some shortcomings of this separation?
7. There are several explanations to justify the inclusion of holding gains as profit. Discuss them.
8. Explain the difference between financial capital and physical capital.
9. Explain Samuelson's argument for changes in current cost as a capital maintenance adjustment.
10. According to MacNeal, why was the 'going value' theory, which assumes the firm is a going concern, formulated?
11. Explain the concept of 'adaptive behaviour' of the firm by Chambers, and how 'financial position' relates to it.
12. Why is Chambers critical of the notion of 'value in use'?
13. What is the basis of Sterling's conclusion that exit price should be used for the valuation of items?
14. What is Chambers's argument concerning the question of 'additivity'? Is it fundamentally important to be able to add together 'like' valuations in the balance sheet?
15. What are the criticisms of the profit concept under exit price accounting?
16. Assume that you favour exit price accounting. Give at least three reasons for your support.
17. How can exit value accounting can be used to assess the financial risk of a balance sheet?
18. Evaluate the argument that a mixed or piecemeal approach to standard setting is required in order to 'better' measure profit and financial position.
19. Explain how both exit price and current entry price accounting systems can be used to make decisions about retaining or selling assets.
20. Explain the concept of 'fair value' as defined in IAS 16/AASB 116 and outline the benefits to financial statement users of continually revaluing assets to their current value.
21. The following questions relate to the apparent divergence in view between the standard setters and the private sector, with respect to the need to shift from historical cost to current value accounting:
    (a) In your opinion, why do standard setters require measurement methods other than traditional historical cost accounting?
    (b) Why do you think that some in the business community and the public accounting firms are so strongly opposed to a move away from historical cost accounting?
    (c) Measurement principles are fundamental to any accounting system. Why does the *Framework* lack fully developed measurement concepts?

22. Has the complexity of alternative rules in the historical cost approach become a valid reason for rejecting the historical cost system?
23. IAS 36/AASB 136 requires the use of discounting techniques to assign a 'value in use' to assets. The discount rate used is required to take into account the risks associated with the asset for which the future cash flows are being estimated. Consider the implications of applying this in practice by determining how you would derive the present value of an asset in the transport industry and what risk premium you would apply. Detail how you would justify your approach to shareholders.
24. Explain the underlying approach to intangibles under IAS 38/AASB 138. Is the approach consistent with the matching principle? Is the splitting of the research and development components of expenditure and the different accounting treatments justified given that the nature of the expenditure is the same?
25. If you were the auditor of the company in question 23, what evidence would you seek to support your opinion about the fair presentation of the asset?

Problems

PROBLEM 6.1

Sharp Ltd has traditionally maintained its accounting system on an historical cost basis. However, because of continuing inflation, it has decided to prepare its financial reports on a current value basis. Its historical cost balance sheet as at 30 June 2011 (year-end) is shown below.

SHARP LTD			
Balance Sheet			
as at 30 June 2011			

Current assets			
Bank		$ 46 000	
Inventories		172 000	
Accounts Receivable		112 000	$330 000
Non-current assets			
Motor Vehicles (at cost, acq. July 2005)	$ 85 000		
Less: Accum. Depr. (20% p.a., straight-line)	34 000	51 000	
Equipment (at cost, acquired July 2003)	188 000		
Less: Accum. Depr. (10% p.a., straight-line)	75 200	112 800	
Buildings (at cost, acquired July 1997)	220 000		
Less: Accum. Depr. (2% p.a., straight-line)	44 000	176 000	
Land (at cost, acquired July 1997)		160 000	
Goodwill (at cost, acquired July 1997)		40 000	539 800
TOTAL			$ 869 800
Current liabilities			
Accounts Payable		$110 000	
Tax Payable		60 000	
Dividend Payable		50 000	$220 000
Non-current liabilities			
Debentures			250 000
Equity			
Paid-up Capital (300 000 shares of $1)		300 000	
Share Premium Reserve		50 000	
General Reserve		40 000	
Retained Earnings		9 800	399 800
TOTAL			$ 869 800

The company had its assets valued at their current buying prices on 30 June 2011, with the following results:

Inventories	$182 000
Motor vehicle (as new)	115 000
Equipment (as new)	260 000
Buildings (as new)	400 000
Land	380 000

Transactions for 2010–11 consisted of:

Sales (all credit)	$2 330 000
Purchases (all credit)	1 490 000
Wages paid	461 000
Other cash operating costs	227 000
Interest paid	25 000
Cash paid to creditors	1 444 000
Cash received from debtors	2 259 000
Tax paid	60 000
Dividend paid	50 000
Equipment purchased for cash (31 December 2010)	70 000
Motor vehicles purchased for cash (30 June 2011)	30 000
Share issue for cash: 100 000 shares at $1.20 (31 December 2010)	120 000

The following information should also be taken into account.

1. The new motor vehicles and equipment are subject to the same straight-line depreciation rates as the existing ones.
2. Income tax to be provided for is $75 850.
3. Dividends of 15 per cent on the shares (including the new issue) are to be provided for.
4. The historical cost of 30 June inventories is $236 000.
5. The 30 June buying prices of equivalent physical assets owned by the company are:

Inventories	$284 000
Motor vehicles, as new, including new vehicles	160 000
Equipment, as new: owned on 1 July	294 000
purchased in December	75 000
Building, as new	420 000
Land	400 000

6. The 31 December buying price of 1 July inventories was $204 000, while the 31 December buying price of 30 June inventories was $220 000.
7. Overall, the cost of original inventory increased by 35 per cent during 2007–08 and the CPI increased from 100 to 110.

Required
A. Present a set of financial statements in accordance with the requirements of SAP 1 and physical capital maintenance for the 2010–11 reporting period.
B. Show all calculations and appropriate general journal and ledger entries.
C. Explain why you calculated the adjustments for backlog depreciation and the gain/loss on monetary items in the manner you chose.

PROBLEM 6.2 Company Y had the following transactions in Year 2. The perpetual FIFO inventory system is used.

1. Purchased on credit, 4000 units of inventory at $5 each.
2. Sold 3000 units for $12 each on credit. Replacement cost at this time is $7 each. There were 1000 units in beginning inventory at $4 each, which represents both current and historical cost. The exit price of the 1000 units is $12 each.

3. At year-end, the building's current value is $150 000. The gross historical cost was $100 000. The building is 2 years old at year-end and is depreciated 10 per cent per year. The current value at the beginning of the current year was $125 000.
4. At year-end, the value of the land is $50 000. The historical cost was $30 000 and the current value was also $30 000 at the beginning of the year.
5. At year-end, the market price of the debentures, which were issued by the company at the beginning of the year, is $40 168. The debentures were sold at par for $44 000 at the rate of 8 per cent. The current rate of interest on 31 December is 10 per cent and the average for the year was 9 per cent. The remaining life of the debentures on 31 December is 6 years.
6. Accounts receivable of $20 000 has an exit price at year-end of $19 000. The other receivables were collected during the year.
7. At year-end, the selling price of the inventory is increased to $14 each.
8. On 31 December, operating expenses of $12 000 are paid, including interest of $3520.

Required

Record the transactions as journal entries under the following methods:
(a) conventional accounting (historical cost)
(b) exit price accounting. Assume debentures are capital.

PROBLEM 6.3

Consider the balance sheet of Circle Ltd on an exit price basis at the beginning of the year:

CIRCLE LTD Balance Sheet as at 1 January Year 10			
Cash	$ 20 000	Accounts Payable	$ 20 000
Inventory (1000 × $15)	15 000	Debentures Payable 10%	50 000
Investment in Y shares	20 000	Ordinary Capital	75 000
Building	90 000	Capital Maintenance Adjustment	8 333
Land	10 000	Retained Earnings	1 667
TOTAL	$155 000		$155 000

The building was purchased for $90 000 and the shares and debentures were issued when the general price index was 90 on 1 January Year 9. The beginning inventory has an historical cost of $5 each. A FIFO basis is used. The general price index is 100 at the beginning of the year. The following events are mentioned in chronological order for Year 10.
1. Purchased on account 5000 units of inventory at $6 each. The exit price is $15 each. The general price index is 105.
2. Sold on account 5000 units for $15 each. The general price index is 105.
3. At year-end, the building's current value is $200 000 and the value of the land is $20 000. The sales price of the inventory is increased to $19 each. The market price of the share investment is $25 000. The market price of the debentures is $45 032 on 31 December. The current rate of interest is 12 per cent. The average market rate of interest was 11 per cent for the year. The remaining life of the debentures is 8 years on 31 December.
4. On 31 December, half the land is sold for $10 000.
5. On 31 December, operating expenses of $15 000 are paid. Interest of $5000, which is not included in the $15 000, is also paid.
6. The general price index at the end of the year is 120. The average for the year is 108.

Required

Prepare journal entries to record the events, as well as the income statement for Year 10 and balance sheet as at 31 December Year 10, under the exit price method. Assume the debenture is not part of capital and is a financial investment.

Additional readings

Al-Hogail, AA, & Previts, GJ 2001, 'Raymond J. Chambers' contributions to the development of accounting thought', *Accounting Historians Journal*, vol. 28, no. 2, pp. 1–30.

Barton, A 2000, 'Reflections of an Australian contemporary: the complementarity of entry and exit price current value accounting systems.' *Abacus*, vol. 36, no. 3, pp. 298–312.

Chambers, R 1975, 'Accounting for inflation — the case for continuously contemporary accounting', *Australian Accountant*, December.

Carlon, S, Mladenovic, R, Loftus, J, Palm, C, Kimmel, PD, Kieso, DE, & Weygandt, JJ, 2009, *Accounting: building business skills*, 3rd edition, John Wiley & Sons Australia, Ltd.

Miller, M, & Loftus, J 2000, 'Measurement entering the 21st century: A clear or blocked road ahead?', *Australian Accounting Review*, vol. 10, no. 2, July, pp. 4–18.

Ryan, J 2000, 'Measurement — or market?', *Charter*, vol. 71, no. 11, December, pp. 56–7.

Staubus, GT 2004, 'Two views of accounting measurement', *Abacus*, vol. 40, no. 3, pp. 265–79.

6.1
CASE STUDY

The following article strongly criticises the notion of fair values and the measurement of financial assets under IAS 39/AASB 139.

Fair value or false accounting

by Anthony Rayman

Forget Enron; forget WorldCom; forget Parmalat. Dishonest accounting can do enormous damage — but nowhere near as much as the honest variety.

'Fair value accounting' is the most recent example. The title sounds wonderful, but its promotion by the International Accounting Standards Board (IASB) threatens to bring the profession into even greater disrepute by institutionalising false accounting on a global scale.

According to IAS 39, *Financial Instruments: Recognition and Measurement*, financial instruments are to be stated at their 'fair value' — defined as 'the amount for which an asset could be exchanged, or a liability settled, between knowledgeable, willing parties in an arm's length transaction'.

'If the market for a financial instrument is not active, an entity establishes a fair value by using a valuation technique . . . [including] discounted cashflow analysis and option pricing models,' says IAS 39. 'A gain or loss on a financial asset or financial liability classified as at fair value through profit or loss shall be recognised in profit or loss.'

As far as financial instruments are concerned, fair value accounting is notable for its closeness to the long-cherished academic ideal of 'income as present value growth'.

What possible objection can there be to fair value accounting? On the face of it, IAS 39 looks like a passport to the promised land of 'truth and fairness of view'.

Before leaping on to this particular bandwagon, however, it may be a good idea to try it out on a test-track — an economic utopia of perfectly competitive markets.

The beauty of an economic utopia is that it provides the most favourable conditions for fair value accounting: the change in recorded equity based on 'fair value' coincides with the academic ideal of 'present value growth' as a measure of economic performance.

A cautionary tale

With the (perfect) market rate of interest at 8% per annum, the Fair Value Company invests the whole of its investors' capital of £100m in 'financial instruments'. These are various equity shareholdings with expected cash dividends totalling £8m pa. The company has no other assets or liabilities.

Suppose an 'event' occurs — perhaps fear of a previously unexpected economic recession. Suppose this event causes (1) the market expectation of the annual dividends to be revised downwards to £5.5m, and (2) the monetary authority to lower the rate of interest to 5% pa. As a consequence, the market value of the company's financial instruments rises from [£8m/0.08 =] £100m to [£5.5m/0.05 =] £110m.

The £10m increase in the 'fair value' of the company's 'financial instruments' is based on observable market prices. According to IAS 39, it is to be reported as a 'gain'.

Since these financial instruments are the whole of the company's net assets, the market value of the company's share capital also rises from £100m to £110m. Investors in the Fair Value Company therefore have the opportunity of selling their shares and spending £10m more than before.

From every point of view, it looks like an open-and-shut case in favour of IAS 39 and reporting a gain of £10m — but appearances can be deceptive.

Only if investors actually take the opportunity of realising the market value and spending it immediately, are they able to spend £10m more than they could before the 'event'. If they save for one year before actually spending, the extra spending made possible by the 'event' is only £7.5m; and the equivalent present sum (at 5% pa) at the balance sheet date is £7.1m.

The effect of the 'event' on investors depends on how long they choose to save.

For investors intending to save for more than just over 3½ years, the effect of the fall in the rate of interest from 8% pa to 5% pa outweighs the initial increase in 'fair value'. If all the investors intend to save for eight years, the 'event' reduces the amount available for spending by £22.6m. To cover this shortfall, the compensation that would be required at the balance sheet date (in order to accumulate at 5% pa for eight years) amounts to no less than £15.3m.

If the consequence of the 'event' is £300,000 worse than being robbed of £15m, is it 'true and fair' to report a gain of £10m? Or is it fraudulent misrepresentation?

It is certainly misrepresentation, and it can be massive; but it is not intentional. The belief in the relevance of 'value change' as a measure of financial performance is the result of a fallacy deeply entrenched in the conventional academic wisdom.

The present-value fallacy

At any given moment, a higher market value is unquestionably preferable to a lower market value. Irrespective of subjective preferences, £110m will (through borrowing or lending) support a higher level of spending of any chosen pattern than will £100m. But, as the table demonstrates, this is not always true of sums available at different moments. That is why it does not necessarily follow that a £10m increase in market value over a period represents a gain. The fallacy underlying the IASB's standard on fair value accounting lies in following the conventional wisdom and assuming that it does.

The tale of the Fair Value Company is simply one particular example of the 'present-value fallacy'. But, because it takes place on the test-track of an economic utopia, it is sufficient to demonstrate that the academic ideal is false and that growth in present value (= 'fair' market value) is not reliable as a measure of economic performance.

(For readers with the patience to endure a spot of general economic equilibrium analysis complete with Fisher diagrams, a rigorous proof is available in the author's book on accounting reform: *Accounting Standards: True or False?* London: Routledge, 2006.)

The accounting implications

The moral of the story is that there is nothing wrong with fair values in the balance sheet; there is everything wrong with fair-value changes in the profit and loss account.

In a balance sheet intended to present a 'true and fair view' of a firm's financial position, the disclosure of fair values is a development to be welcomed — as an indication of the available market opportunities. On the balance sheet of the Fair Value Company after the 'event', no figure has a greater claim to relevance as a measure of the net assets than their fair value of £110 m.

But opportunities are not the same as actual transactions. The very fact that an item appears in a balance sheet, means that by definition it has not been exchanged. Its 'fair' market value represents a rejected opportunity.

The fundamental mistake is to report 'value change' as a 'gain or loss'. For 'value change' may simply be the difference between hypothetical opportunities that have actually been discarded. What is in question, therefore, is the relevance of fair value for reporting financial performance.

An accounting standard which generates a fair value 'gain' of £10 m in response to a fall in the expected annual returns from the Fair Value Company's net assets from £8 m to £5.5 m does not inspire confidence. The 'event' is responsible for an increase in fair value of the company's net assets from £100 m to £110 m. A gain of £10 m is a 'true and fair view' of the result on one assumption only: that the fair value is realised and actually consumed at the balance sheet date. The most common reason for investing, however, is to save for the future. Of all the assumptions that could have been chosen, immediate consumption is the least likely. It is ruled out almost by definition.

Many savers and pensioners in the UK have become materially worse off as a direct consequence of events that would be reported in 'fair value' accounts as substantial 'gains'. The propagation of the market-value fallacy has made a substantial contribution to the housing bubble and the pensions crisis.

Truth in accounting?

As a result of the 'event', the rate of return on investment in the Fair Value Company has fallen from 8% pa to 5½% pa. IAS 39 requires the accounts to report a gain of £10 m equal to 10% on capital. This is in clear breach of English criminal law: 'Where a person . . . in furnishing information for any purpose produces . . . any account . . . which to his knowledge is or may be misleading, false or deceptive in a material particular; he shall, on conviction on indictment, be liable to imprisonment for a term not exceeding seven years' (s17, Theft Act 1968).

IAS 39 is calculated to bring the profession into disrepute. But who is really responsible — those who do their best to operate, with honesty and integrity, in accordance with the standards — or the IASB which sets them?

Source: Excerpts from *Accountancy*, October 2004, pp. 82–3.

Questions

1. How are assets and liabilities measured under IAS 39?
2. What impact according to the author, will fair value accounting have on the balance sheet and income statement?
3. What measurement requirement of historical cost accounting is violated?
4. Is a change in asset value an increase in wealth or income? Are they the same?
5. What do you think fundamental value in accounting should be? Refer to the debate regarding value in use and value in exchange outlined in this chapter when answering this question.

The following article discusses the impact of exchange rates on earnings.

Rising dough: Domino's sales climb and costs fall

by Carrie LaFrenz

Domino's Pizza Enterprises has upgraded its full-year earnings by up to 30 per cent on the back of foreign exchange benefits, tax breaks and higher sales from its stores. The company is one of the few that has benefited from the downturn as customers flocked to cheaper takeaway options, helping boost its network sales. It is also a beneficiary of large declines in commodity costs that has helped bring down process for key inputs such as flour and cheese.

Chief executive Don Meij said following strong network sales performance, foreign exchange gains and better than expected tax outcomes, Domino's expected full-year earnings to be about $15.4 million, an improvement of between 28 per cent and 30 per cent on last year's earnings.

"The new menu in Australia has gone well and is suited to the economy," he said.

In February, Domino's said it expected to achieve market guidance for a lift in full-year profit of between 10 per cent and 15 per cent.

"The Australian dollar was quite weak for the majority of the 2009 financial year so we have benefited from that in our European business," Mr Meij said during a media briefing. But he admitted that the foreign exchange gains made last year won't be around this year given the recent strength of the Australian dollar. "The Australian dollar versus the euro is now going to be stronger so that will have an impact on [earnings] this year," he said.

Foresight Securities analyst Todd Guyot said Donino's positive momentum was previously flagged and while the upgrade was good news, it was mostly due to tax gains and foreign exchange benefits. When you dig through the underlying numbers, the tax rate last year was about 30 per cent and this year it's about 24 per cent," he said. "It's a good upgrade and proves Domino's resilience, but I would argue that it's more to do with tax and currency and that operationally it's pretty much what they said it would be."

Source: The Weekend Australian Financial Review, 1–2 August 2009, p. 14, www.afr.com.

Questions

1. Discuss the implications for Domino's shareholders of the upgrade in reported earnings due to the weaker Australian dollar for the 2009 year, given that the operational margins were in line with analysts' expectations.
2. How concerned should shareholders be with changes (increases or decreases) in earnings caused mainly by fluctuations in exchange rates?
3. How will Domino's forecast earnings be affected by the relatively significant increase in the strength of the Australian dollar since the end of the 2009 financial year?

This article discusses the impairment of assets.

Red ink flows, but Talent2 is looking up

by Paul Smith

The recruitment division returned to profitability in the June quarter as demand for placement services stabilised and cost cutting took effect, listed recruiter and software services firm Talent2 reports.

However, the economic downturn has taken its toll. The company said it would swing to a full-year loss of $2.5 million before interest, tax, depreciation and amortisation, from a profit of $10.8 million a year ago, and there were doubts it would pay a final dividend.

Talent2 chief executive John Rawlinson said he was disappointed the overall result was worse than the previous year's but it was not bad in the context of the global financial crisis crippling the jobs market.

"We returned to profitability in the recruitment part of the business during the fourth quarter and the managed services part of the business performed strongly, so there are some things to be very positive about," he said.

"Also we are very confident about what happens moving forward. From what we can see, we would expect a continued improvement in conditions in every geography we operate in. It will not necessarily be back to the heady days when recruitment was booming, but certainly a reasonable profit contribution."

His sentiment reflects that of Peoplebank chief operating officer Peter Acheson, who said earlier this month that his company had also recorded a marked upturn in hiring intentions across its 50 largest clients in July. Mr Acheson said the positive hiring intentions were largely limited to contract positions and the company forecast no change to the flat market for permanent recruitment this year.

Mr Rawlinson said Talent2 had begun to see some upturn in permanent recruitment in its Asian business, and Singapore in particular was firming up. However, he said growth in Australia was largely restricted to contract staff.

Recruitment revenue would fall 16 per cent year on year to $114.4 million and overall revenue was expected to total $228.7 million.

Revenue from Talent2's managed services business, which provides outsourced human resources, was up 21 per cent to $114.4 million.

"Our strategy once recruitment ground to a halt after last October was to make the necessary cost reductions and get the business better focused on areas of the economy that were still active," Mr Rawlinson said.

"We have since been able to align our business to win more of the available permanent recruitment market. If the current trends continue we would expect that the permanent market would pick up in the coming months."

Although the company traditionally declared an annual dividend, it looked likely that would not be possible this year, he said.

Because of impairment charges related to its operations in Hong Kong and the United Kingdom, Talent2 predicted a net loss before tax of $5.5 million, which would make a return to shareholders unviable.

Source: The Australian Financial Review, 31 July 2009, p. 47, www.afr.com.

Questions

1. What is the impact of the impairment charges on the income statement and on the statement of financial position of the company?
2. Should shareholders be concerned about the asset impairments on the Hong Kong and United Kingdom operations given that the expected improvement was largely restricted to 'contract positions'? Explain your answer.
3. What is meant by the statement that 'a net loss . . . would make a return to shareholders unviable'?

6.4
CASE STUDY

This article considers the costs attaching to business divisions.

Bradken forecasts a flat year ahead

by AAP

Bradken has posted a solid rise in annual earnings despite the slowdown but expects flat profits this financial year. The mining and engineered products provider reported net profit for the year ended June 30 of $64.3 million, up 11 per cent on $58 m for the

2007–08 financial year. Sales revenue for the 2008–09 financial year totalled $1.209 billion, up 59 per cent from $760.3 m.

"The year's result was a tale of two halves, with strong trading conditions in the first half and the global economic conditions impacting the second half through destocking and order cancellation by customers," managing director Brian Hodges said. "The ability to reduce variable costs in line with demand levels is an important feature of Bradken's business, allowing it to maximise gross margins in tough economic times." Bradken said it expected 2009–10 profit to be similar to the previous period, weighted towards the second half.

The rail division delivered sales growth of 19 per cent due to strong demand for freight wagons, including from BHP Billiton's iron ore division. Bradken's industrial division achieved a sales revenue increase of 3 per cent, although the underlying industrial business was down 13 per cent reflecting the slow-down across a range of industrial sectors, particularly large structural fabrication.

Sales revenue for Bradken's mining products division increased by 14 per cent, with growth in all product groups.

"After a strong start to the year, volumes in the second half were impacted by customer destocking due to ... economic conditions and the lack of expansion projects affecting the plate and block business," the company said. "Gross margins held up, influenced by reduced costs."

The company said strategies remained unchanged, with long-term aims of global expansion focused on design, manufacture and supply of products for mining and power stations.

Net debt at the end of June was $398.5 m, down by $28 m from December. Bradken declared a fully franked dividend of 13 c per share, bringing the full-year dividend to 23 c per share. Shares rose 76 c to $5.98.

Source: The Australian, 7 August 2009, p. 20, www.theaustralian.com.au. © 2009 AAP. See full copyright notice on the acknowledgements page.

Questions

1. Contrast 'displacement' cost and 'embodied' cost.
2. Identify the potential problems associated with allocating costs to various products and services.
3. Comment on the impact on Bradken's revenues in the second half of the year from customers 'destocking'.
4. Is the impact you identified in question (2) likely to have an influence on the amount of product and/or services cost that can be separated and categorised into new groups? Explain your answer.

Endnotes

1. E Edwards and P Bell, *The theory and measurement of business income*, Berkeley: University of California Press, 1961.
2. W Paton and AC Littleton, *An introduction to corporate accounting standards*, Florida: AAA, 1940.
3. ibid., p. 97.
4. ibid., p. 16.
5. ibid., p. 67.
6. ibid., p. 14.
7. AC Littleton, 'Significance of invested cost', *Accounting Review*, April 1952, p. 168.
8. ibid., p. 169.
9. ibid., p. 171.
10. R Mautz, 'A few words for historical cost', *Financial Executive*, January 1973, p. 26.
11. ibid., p. 25.
12. Y Ijiri, 'Theory of accounting management', *Studies in Accounting Research No. 10*, Florida: AAA, 1975, p. 97.
13. W Beaver and W Landsman, *Incremental Informational Content of Statement 33 Disclosures*, Stamford, Conn.: FASB, 1983.
14. K Duncan and K Moores, 'Usefulness of CCA information for investor decision making: A laboratory experiment', *Accounting and Business Research*, Spring 1988, pp. 121–32
15. Edwards and Bell, op. cit.
16. R Sterling, 'Conservatism: The fundamental principle of valuation', in S Zeff and T Keller (eds), *Financial Accounting Theory 1*, New York: McGraw-Hill, 1973, pp. 524–25.
17. ibid., p. 536.
18. R Sprouse, 'The balance sheet — embodiment of the most fundamental

elements of accounting theory', in S Zeff and T Keller (eds), op. cit., pp. 166–7.

19. A Thomas, 'The FASB and the allocation fallacy', *Journal of Accountancy*, November 1975.

20. Sprouse op. cit., p. 173.

21. M Whitman and M Shubik, 'Corporate reality and accounting for investors', in S Zeff and T Keller (eds) op. cit., pp. 62–72.

22. ibid.

23. ibid.

24. Edwards and Bell op. cit., p. 93.

25. L Revsine, *Replacement cost accounting*, Englewood Cliffs, NJ: Prentice Hall, 1973, p. 88.

26. ibid.

27. ibid.

28. R Samuelson, 'Should replacement cost changes be included in income?', *Accounting Review*, April 1980; see also Appendix 2, Statement of Accounting Practice (SAP) 1, *Current Cost in Australia*, November 1983.

29. L Revsine, 'Technological changes and replacement costs: a beginning', *Accounting Review*, January 1979.

30. Edwards and Bell, op. cit., pp. 98–9.

31. K Lemke, 'Asset valuation and income theory', *Accounting Review*, January 1966.

32. Revsine, op. cit.

33. 'Accounting in Erewhon', *Business Week*, 9 August 1976, p. 80.

34. R Chambers, 'Accounting for inflation — part or whole', *Accountant's Magazine*, March 1976; 'Value to the business', in GW Dean and MC Wells (eds), *Current cost accounting: identifying the issues*, Lancaster, UK: International Centre for Research in Accounting, 1977.

35. R Sterling and K Lemke (eds), *Maintenance of capital: financial vs. physical*, chapter 1, Kansas: Scholars Book Company, 1982.

36. Market selling prices and exit values are used interchangeably in this chapter.

37. Australian Accounting Research Foundation, *Measurement in financial accounting, Accounting Theory Monograph No. 10*, Melbourne: AARF, 1998, 15.1.

38. See JA Ohlson, 'Earnings, book values, and dividends in security valuation', *Contemporary Accounting Research*, no. 11, Spring 1995, pp. 661–87 for a full explanation.

39. R Chambers, *Accounting for inflation — methods and problems*, Sydney: University of Sydney, 1975, p. 16.

40. R Chambers, *Accounting, evaluation and economic behaviour*, Englewood Cliffs, NJ: Prentice Hall, 1966, p. 92.

41. Chambers, op cit., p. 21.

42. K MacNeal, *Truth in Accounting*, Kansas: Scholars Book Co., 1970, originally published in 1939.

43. R Sterling, *Theory of the measurement of enterprise income*, Kansas: University Press of Kansas, 1970.

44. Chambers op. cit., p. 19.

45. ibid., p. 47.

46. A Thomas, The allocation problem, *Studies in Accounting Research No. 9*, Florida: AAA, 1974, pp. 112–14.

47. Parker, 'Testing comparability and objectivity of exit value accounting', *Accounting Review*, July 1975.

48. J McKeown, 'An empirical test of a model proposed by Chambers', *Accounting Review*, January 1971.

49. J McKeown, 'Comparative application of market and cost based accounting models', *Journal of Accounting Research*, Spring 1973.

50. J Dixon, 'Setting the standards', *Australian CPA*, March 2001, pp. 62–3.

51. P Bell, 'On current replacement costs and business income', in R Sterling (ed.), *Asset valuation and income determination*, Houston: Scholars Book Co., 1971, pp. 27–8.

52. ibid.

53. F Weston, 'Response to evidence for a market selling price accounting system', in Sterling, op. cit.

54. K Larson and R Schattke, 'Current cash equivalent, additivity, and financial action', *Accounting Review*, October 1966.

55. R Chambers, 'Second thoughts on continuously contemporary accounting', *Abacus*, September 1970, p. 50.

56. J Horton and R Macve, '"Fair value" for financial instruments: How erasing theory is leading to unworkable global accounting standards for performance reporting', *Australian Accounting Review*, vol. 11, no. 2, 2000, pp. 26–39.

57. E Edwards, 'The state of current value accounting', *Accounting Review*, April 1975, p. 240.

58. D Solomons, review article, *Abacus*, December 1966, p. 208.

59. ibid.

60. ibid.

61. R Chambers, *Accounting, evaluation and economic behavior*, Englewood Cliffs, NJ: Prentice Hall, 1966, p. 92.

62. GJ Staubus, 'Two views of accounting measurement', *Abacus*, vol. 40, no. 3, 2004, pp. 265–79.

63. A Barton, 'Reflections of an Australian contemporary: The complementarity of entry and exit price current value accounting systems', *Abacus*, October 2000, pp. 298–312.

64. FASB, Statement 33 'Financial Reporting and Changing Prices', September 1979, para. 121.

65. Accounting Research Bulletin 43, chapter 4, 'Inventory pricing', Statement 3, para. 5.

66. D Kieso and J Weygandt, *Intermediate accounting*, 4th edn, New York: John Wiley, 1983, p. 344.

67. R Sterling, 'Conservatism: The fundamental principle of valuation', in S Zeff and T Keller (eds), *Financial Accounting Theory 1*, New York: McGraw-Hill, 1973, p. 540.

68. J Shanahan, 'Historic cost accounting is passé, but is market value the future?', *Financial Review*, March 1992.

69. FASB and IASB, 'Revisiting the concepts', May 2005.

70. J Shanahan, 'Group of 100 opposed to market value accounting', *New Accountant*, 25 June 1992, p. 9.

71. Staubus, 2004, op. cit.

72. J Cotter and S Richardson, 'Reliability of asset revaluations: the impact of appraiser independence', *Review of Accounting Studies*, vol. 7, no. 4, December 2002, pp. 435–57.

EXAMPLE USING CURRENT COST (BUYING PRICES) — PHYSICAL CAPITAL CONCEPT

The summary of transactions of Brumbles Ltd for the year ended 30 June 2010 is:

Sales (all credit)	$4 200 000
Purchases (all credit)	2 800 000
Cash operating costs	919 000
Tax paid	105 000
Dividend paid	85 000
Cash paid to creditors	2 760 000
Cash received from debtors	4 052 000

Incorporate the following additional information in the reports:

1. Straight-line depreciation to be charged on equipment at 12.5 per cent per year on current cost and on buildings at 2 per cent per year on current cost. The equipment was purchased on 1 July 2007 and the building on 1 July 2009.
2. Provide for income tax of $138 000.
3. Provide for a 20 per cent annual dividend on paid-up capital.
4. The historical cost of 30 June 2010 inventories was $482 000, and their current cost is $490 000.
5. The 31 December 2009 current cost of opening inventories is $515 000 and for closing inventories is $460 000.
6. The 30 June 2010 current costs of other assets are:

Equipment (as new)	$560 000
Building (as new)	690 000
Land	180 000
Share investments	125 000

7. The price of the firm's inventory increased by 14 per cent during 2009–10 and the CPI increased from 100 at the beginning to 115 at the end.

The balance sheet of Brumbles Ltd at 30 June 2010 in current cost dollars is shown below.

BRUMBLES LTD
Balance Sheet
as at 30 June 2010

Current assets			Current liabilities	
Accounts Receivable		$ 302 000	Bank Overdraft	$ 290 000
Inventories		480 000	Accounts Payable	310 000
Share Investments		100 000	Tax Payable	105 000
		882 000	Dividend Payable	85 000
				790 000
Non-current assets				
Equipment	$520 000		**Non-current liabilities**	
Less: Accumulated			Term Loan	500 000
Depreciation	130 000	390 000		
Building	660 000		**Equity**	
Less: Accumulated			Paid-up Capital	500 000
Depreciation	132 000	528 000	Current Cost Reserve	186 000
Land		200 000	Retained Earnings	24 000
		1 118 000		1 210 000
		$2 000 000		$2 000 000

Required

A. Present a set of financial statements in accordance with the requirements of SAP 1 for the 2009–10 reporting period.

B. Show all calculations and appropriate general journal and ledger entries.

SOLUTION

A. Financial statements

BRUMBLES LTD Income Statement for the year ended 30 June 2010		
Sales		$4 200 000
Less: Cost of Sales		
Opening Inventory	$ 515 000	
Purchases	2 800 000	
	3 315 000	
Closing Inventory	460 000	
Cost of Sales		2 855 000
Gross Profit		1 345 000
Less: Cash Operating Costs	919 000	
Depreciation of Equipment	67 500	
Depreciation of Building	13 500	1 000 000
Current Cost Operating Profit before Tax		345 000
Add: Gain on Holding Monetary Items		53 295
Current Cost Entity Profit		398 295
Less: Income Tax		138 000
Current Cost Entity Profit after Tax		260 295
Less: Dividend		100 000
Retained Entity Earnings for 2009–10		160 295
Add: Retained Earnings, 1 July 2008		24 000
RETAINED EARNINGS CARRIED FORWARD		$ 184 295

A proprietary result may also be calculated as follows:

Current cost operating (entity) profit after tax	$260 295
Add: Gain on loan capital	75 000
Current cost proprietary profit after tax	$335 295

BRUMBLES LTD Balance Sheet as at 30 June 2010					
Current assets			**Current liabilities**		
Accounts Receivable		$ 450 000	Bank Overdraft		$ 107 000
Inventories		490 000	Accounts Payable		350 000
Share Investments		125 000	Tax Payable		138 000
			Dividend Payable		100 000
		1 065 000			695 000
Non-current assets			**Non-current liabilities**		
Equipment	$560 000		Term Loan		500 000
Less: Accumulated					
Depreciation	210 000	350 000			
Building	690 000		**Equity**		
Less: Accumulated			Paid-up Capital		500 000
Depreciation	151 800	538 200	Current Cost Reserve		253 905
Land		180 000	Retained Earnings		184 295
		1 068 200			1 438 200
TOTAL		$2 133 200	TOTAL		$2 133 200

Notes

Balance sheet

1. *Inventories:* Inventories are valued at middle-of-the-period replacement costs for both opening and closing stock. As there are generally active markets for inventories, values should be obtained from transaction or price lists. They may be estimated from specific indexes if market prices are unavailable.

2. *Buildings and equipment:* The depreciation expense from these assets is based on average buying costs during the period. Current market prices can be obtained from similar sales in the area, by valuation or by applying the relevant index from the Australian Bureau of Statistics.

3. *Monetary items:* Monetary items are split into two different components. The first component is based on the entity concept and comprises all monetary items which are not loan capital. These mainly constitute trade creditors and debtors, cash, prepayments and short-term bank overdrafts. The monetary item gain or loss should be calculated by the appropriate index of change in the current cost of goods and services. The second component of monetary items is the entry for the gain on loan capital. The SAP 1 current cost operating system is based on an entity concept. All long-term sources of finance such as loans, debentures and bonds (both marketable and non-marketable) as well as shareholder contributions and reserves, are deemed to constitute the capital base of the firm. The main purpose of calculating gains and losses on loan capital is to assess the extent to which shareholders have benefited from the entity having used long-term loan capital to fund operations. Because this measure is related to shareholders — the proprietorship concept — it is suggested that a general price index should be used for calculations. Further, note that whenever trade creditors and other monetary liabilities exceed monetary assets and inventories, the excess would be used to fund non-monetary assets. In this case the excess is treated as loan capital. Any gain on this excess is treated in the same manner as loan capital.

Income statement

1. *Land, buildings, equipment, inventories:* All non-monetary assets are brought to account at their current buying prices as at the reporting date.

2. *Goodwill:* As there is no separate market value for goodwill, it is not recognised.

3. *Debenture assets:* As marketable assets, any price variations are recognised and gains or losses brought to account in the Profit and Loss Summary account. As liabilities they are deemed to be part of the pool of funds used to finance the continued operations of the firm. As a consequence, price variations are ignored and they are brought to account in the balance sheet at nominal values (see also treatment in the Profit and Loss Summary account).

Supporting calculations

Calculation of gain/loss on monetary items excluding loan capital

(a) Calculate loss on holding monetary assets using average holdings.

Accounts Receivable	$\dfrac{(302\,000 + 450\,000)}{2} \times 14\%$	$	$52\,640
Loss on monetary assets		$	$52\,640

(b) Calculate gain on monetary liabilities using average holdings (excluding loan capital).

Overdraft	$\dfrac{(290\,000 + 107\,000)}{2} \times \dfrac{115 - 100}{100}$	$ 29\,775
Accounts Payable	$\dfrac{(310\,000 + 350\,000)}{2} \times 14\%$	46\,200
Other Payables	$\dfrac{(190\,000 + 238\,000)}{2} \times 14\%$	29\,960
Gain on monetary liabilities		105\,935
Net gain on monetary items		$ 53\,295

Note: The inventory index is applied to payables and receivables on the assumption that they are used to finance the purchase and sale of inventory.

(c) Calculate gain on loan capital using average holdings.

Term loan:	$\dfrac{(500\,000 + 500\,000)}{2} \times \dfrac{115 - 100}{100}$	$ 75\,000
Total gain on holding monetary items (—52\,640 + 105\,935 + 75\,000)		$128\,295

B. General journal entries and ledger accounts

General journal

1. (a) 30 June 2010	Current Cost Reserve	$128\,295	
	Profit and Loss Summary		$128\,295
	(Total gain and holding monetary items)		
(b) 30 June 2010	Profit and Loss Summary	$75\,000	
	Gain on Loan Capital Reserve		$75\,000
	(Transfer gain on loan capital to reserve (leaving entity gain in profit))		
2. (a) 31 Dec. 2009	Opening Inventory (480–515)	$35\,000	
	Current Cost Reserve		$35\,000
	(Revaluation of opening inventory from middle-of-year values)		

(b) 30 June 2010	Closing Inventory (460–490)	$30 000	
	Current Cost Reserve		$30 000
	(Revaluation of closing inventory from middle-of-year to end-of-year values)		

(c) 30 June 2010	Equipment (520–560)	$40 000	
	Buildings (660–690)	30 000	
	Share Investments (100–125)	25 000	
	Accum. depr., Equipment (197.5–210)		$12 500
	Accum. depr., Building (145.5–151.8)		6 300
	Land (200–180)		20 000
	Current Cost Reserve		56 200
	(Revaluation of assets at end-of-year values)		

Ledger accounts

1. Backlog depreciation on Equipment

3 years at 12.5% on $560 000	$210 000
Less: Depreciation charged (130 000 + 67 500)	197 500
Backlog	$ 12 500

2. Backlog depreciation on Building

11 years at 2% on $690 000	$151 800
Less: Depreciation charged (132 000 + 13 500)	145 500
Backlog	$ 6 300

The Current Cost Reserve ledger account is shown below:

Current Cost Reserve ledger account

	Debit	*Credit*	
		186 000	Balance b/f
Inventory		35 000	
Inventory		30 000	
Plant		40 000	
Building		30 000	
Plant	12 500		
Building	6 300		
Land	20 000		
Shares		25 000	
Gain on Monetary Items	53 295		
		253 905	Balance

APPENDIX 6.2

Example using exit value (selling prices) — financial capital concept

EXAMPLE PROBLEMS

The balance sheet of Asia–Pacific Ltd prepared under the CCE exit price system for 31 December 2010 is as shown below.

ASIA–PACIFIC LTD Balance Sheet as at 31 December 2010			
Cash	$ 50 000	Creditors	$ 120 000
Debtors	140 000	Other Short-term Liabilities	40 000
Inventory	220 000	Marketable Debentures 15%	400 000
Equipment	540 000	Paid-up Capital	1 000 000
Land and Buildings	800 000	Capital Maintenance Reserve	220 000
Investments	200 000	Retained Earnings	170 000
TOTAL ASSETS	$1 950 000	TOTAL LIABILITIES AND EQUITY	$1 950 000

Asia–Pacific Ltd is in its second year of operations and has used exit value accounting for reporting since its incorporation. In addition, a periodic FIFO inventory system is used and the historical cost of opening inventory was $200 000. The general price index at the beginning of 2011 was 120.

1. During 2011 the following transactions and events occurred:

Sales on account	$2 400 000
Purchases on account	1 600 000
Cash paid to creditors	1 670 000
Cash collected from debtors	2 320 000
Cash operating costs (including interest)	480 000
Tax paid	40 000
Equipment purchased for cash on 30 June 2011	200 000
Dividends received	30 000

2. Resale values of physical assets on 31 December 2011 are:

Inventories (cost $210 000)	$280 000
Equipment	500 000
Land and Buildings	830 000

3. The market value of the debentures declined to $340 000 by 31 December 2011 and investments to $185 000.
4. Tax payable on 2011 profits is $45 000.
5. The general price level index rose from 120 to 130 over the year.

Required

Record the journal entries on an exit price basis and prepare the financial statements. Allow for changes in the general price level.

SOLUTION

Journal entries

The journal entries on the next page are made to adjust the historical cost accounts to CCE.

1. To adjust accounts to their exit market value at year-end

Land and Buildings	$ 30 000	
Inventory (closing)	70 000	
Price Variation	155 000	
Equipment		$240 000
Investments		15 000

Notes

(a) The adjustment for closing inventory is simply the price appreciation of holding closing inventory from $210 000 to $280 000.

(b) All accounts are adjusted to record the difference in exit values from the beginning to the end of the financial year.

(c) The entry for equipment takes into account the purchase mid-year as follows:

Opening exit value	$540 000
Add purchases	200 000
Total	740 000
Closing exit value	500 000
Adjustment	$240 000 Cr

(d) The Price Variation account is closed off to the income statement. This entry records the net price effect from holding assets over the year and is the combined net effect of all price variations. Note that the total of $155 000 is listed separately, according to individual price variations.

(e) Note that an alternative treatment of negative price variations (e.g. equipment) is to debit operating activities and to treat this fall in value as depreciation.

2. To restate opening inventory at historical cost

Price Variation	$20 000	
Inventory (opening)		$20 000

The adjustment for opening inventory is made to reverse the price change adjusting entry of 31 December 2010 in order to record cost of sales at cost, that is, the price appreciation from $200 000 to $220 000.

3. To restate shareholders' equity in dollars of current purchasing power

Price Level Adjustments	$115 833	
Price Level Reserve		$101 666
Retained Earnings		14 167

Calculation for purchasing power adjustment
The calculation for purchasing power adjustment is shown below.

	Dollars of 31 December 2010			Dollars of 31 December 2011	Adjust. 2011
Paid-up Capital	$1 000 000	× 130/120	=	$1 083 333	$ 83 333
Price Level Reserve	220 000	× 130/120	=	238 333	18 333
Retained Earnings	170 000	× 130/120	=	184 167	14 167
Shareholders' Equity	$1 390 000			$1 505 833	$115 833

The $83 333 and $18 333 will be added to the Price Level Reserve, the $14 167 to Retained Earnings as shown in journal entry 3.

Financial statements

ASIA–PACIFIC LTD
CCE Income Statement
for the year ended 31 December 2011

Operating activities

Sales Revenue			$2 400 000
Less: Operating Expenses			
Opening Inventory (at cost)		$ 200 000	
Add: Purchases		1 600 000	
		1 800 000	
Closing Inventory (at cost)		210 000	
Cost of Sales (at cost)			1 590 000
Cash Operating Costs			480 000
Operating Profit (at cost)			330 000
Opening Inventory Price Variation		(20 000)	
Closing Inventory Price Variation		70 000	50 000
Exit Value Operating Profit			380 000
Add: Dividends			30 000
Current Profit			410 000
Other price variation activities			
Land and Buildings			
Investments		30 000	
Equipment		(15 000)	
		(240 000)	
			(225 000)
			185 000
Less: Price level adjustment			
Paid-up Capital	(10/120 × 1 000 000)	83 333	
Price Level Adjustment	(10/120 × 220 000)	18 333	
Retained Earnings	(10/120 × 170 000)	14 167	115 833
PROFIT			$ 69 167

ASIA–PACIFIC LTD
Appropriation Statement
for the year ended 31 December 2011

Retained Earnings 2010	$170 000
Add: Price Level Adjustment	14 167
	184 167
Profit 2011	69 167
Total	253 334
Less: Tax	45 000
RETAINED EARNING (31 December 2011)	$208 334

ASIA–PACIFIC LTD
Balance Sheet
as at 31 December 2011

Current assets			Current liabilities		
Cash	$	10 000	Creditors	$	50 000
Debtors		220 000	Tax Payable		45 000
Inventories		280 000			95 000
		510 000			
Non-current assets			**Non-current liability**		
Equipment		500 000	Debentures 15%		400 000
Premises		830 000			
Investments		185 000	**Equity**		
		1 515 000	Paid-up Capital		1 000 000
			Price Level Adjustment		321 666
			Retained Earnings		208 334
					1 530 000
TOTAL		$ 2 025 000	TOTAL		$ 2 025 000

Notes

(a) The income statement is split between historical operating activities, current operating activities and price variation activities.

(b) All price level adjustments are closed to the income statement.

(c) Debentures as a liability or bonds payable are not adjusted in this system. As liabilities, they are deemed to be part of the pool of funds used to finance the continued operations of the firm. As a consequence, any price variation is ignored and they are brought to account in the balance sheet at nominal values. However, if debentures or bonds are held as an investment asset, any price variation is recognised and taken to the Price Variation account.

(d) All adjustments for inflation are made directly to equity accounts. Note the calculation of retained earnings. The Price Level Adjustment account is retained only for adjustments to nominal capital. This is to retain Paid-up Capital accounts in nominal values in order to fulfil statutory requirements.

(e) Cost of sales may also be derived from the Inventory ledger account as follows:

Inventory

	Debit	Credit	Balance	Dr
Opening Balance (exit price)			$ 220 000	
Price Variation Adjustment		$ 20 000	200 000	
Purchases (cost)	$1 600 000		1 800 000	
Cost of Sales		1 590 000	210 000	
Price Variation Adjustment	70 000		280 000	Dr

This procedure ensures that the Inventory account will enable calculation of historical cost profit from trading activities (the derived historical cost of sales figure) and profit from holding activities (price variation adjustment).

(f) Other price variation activities may be summarised as follows:

Plant (opening)	$540 000		Land and building (opening)	$800 000	
Add: Purchases	200 000		Land and building (closing)	830 000	
	740 000			$ 30 000	Cr
Plant (closing)	500 000				
	240 000	Dr	Investments (opening)	$200 000	
			Investments (closing)	185 000	
				$ 15 000	Cr

(g) A further note on inflation and the gains on holding debt: a contentious issue regarding long-term debt is how to account for the change in the market price of marketable bonds and debentures. For example, if interest rates fall, the value of marketable debt will increase and vice versa. Should these gains and losses be recognised as part of profit or ignored? One school of thought argues that long-term debt constitutes part of the capital investment funds of the firm. Therefore, if the market value of the debt falls and the debt is redeemed, no gain will be made because in order to maintain current operations the debt will have to be refloated. Secondly, this 'gain' is offset in subsequent years as the market price progressively returns to its nominal value at maturity date and 'losses' would be incurred in each of these years. Also, the recognition of the 'gain' will result in the understatement of the financial obligation to repay the nominal or face value of the debt.

Against these arguments it is pointed out that the fall in market prices is an observable economic event and should be recognised as it occurs, in any current value accounting system. The non-reporting of debt price movements presupposes that the present debt to equity ratio is optimal and that leverage levels should remain fixed. One alternative would be to redeem long-term debt and refinance with equity, thus realising any potential market gains. The point is that if market price variations are not reported, it is contended that relevant information is missing and economic decisions cannot be made.

7 Assets

After reading this chapter, you should have an appreciation of the following:

1 issues involved in defining assets and applying those definitions

2 why recognition and measurement criteria are both important and controversial

3 the relationship of asset recognition and measurement of income and equity

4 the implications of use of a mixed attribute measurement model and fair value measurement methods

5 issues arising for standard setters and auditors from current asset recognition and measurement methods.

Is a firm's land an asset? Most of us would argue that it is. But would you hold that view if the land was so badly radioactively contaminated that it would be unusable for the next 1000 years and if employees who worked on the site were suing the firm? Is the land then a liability rather than an asset? What if the firm carries out restoration work on the land and in the process develops a technology which deactivates previously contaminated land and has the potential for enormously profitable global sales? Has the firm incurred an expense or developed an asset?

These examples remind us that classification of items in the financial assets is fundamental to accounting. Classification will influence the way users interpret a firm's financial performance and position and consequently their decision-making process. Classification can influence perceptions of risk and solvency. In this chapter we explore how assets are defined and consider the various elements of the IASB's asset definition. We also investigate recognition and measurement criteria and consider the implications of various approaches to asset measurement. Given the importance of asset measurement, we conclude the chapter by exploring current asset measurement issues from the perspectives of standard setters and auditors.

LO 1 — ASSETS DEFINED

Although assets are the subject of several accounting standards and numerous references are made to them in company law, it was not until the development of conceptual frameworks in the 1980s that there was an authoritative definition of the term 'asset'. The IASB (AASB) *Framework for the Preparation and Presentation of Financial Statements* (para 49) defines an asset as follows:

> an asset is a resource controlled by the entity as a result of past events and from which future economic benefits are expected to flow to the entity.

> This chapter examines definitions of assets in relation to three essential characteristics:
> * future economic benefits
> * control by an entity
> * past events.

It also presents the debate about the inclusion of exchangeability as a fourth component and, finally, discusses the need for additional 'recognition rules' when identifying assets.

Future economic benefits

The IASB *Framework* definition pinpoints the essence of an asset as future economic benefits. The benefits for a for-profit business entity are associated with the activities that generate profit. However, the definition is broad enough to be applied to any entity, including not-for-profit organisations.

Paragraph 53 is important in its recognition that future economic benefits embodied in assets are the potential to contribute, either directly or indirectly, to the flow of cash and cash equivalents to the entity. This could be through the revenue-generating operating activities of an entity or from a capability to reduce cash outflows such as through reduced manufacturing costs of production.

Taking the definition of assets and applying it to both profit-seeking and not-for-profit entities makes it clear that, to qualify as an asset, the future economic benefit must help the entity pursue its objectives, whatever those objectives may be. The benefit may be reduced cash outflows (e.g. for a replacement monument or park).

It is in relation to assets that have no cash-generating capacity that most problems arise in applying the asset definition. Case study 7.1 probes this issue, by considering the application of the asset definition in relation to heritage assets.

The notion of future economic benefits (or service) is not new; it relates to economic resources. There are two main characteristics of an economic resource: scarcity and utility. If a resource was not scarce (there was enough of it for everyone who wanted it) then the resource would not be 'economic'. Utility relates to the future benefits or services mentioned above. Technically, in economic theory, the utility of a commodity is its ability to satisfy human wants. However, we can include in the notion of utility all future economic benefits on the basis that such benefits ultimately relate to the satisfaction of human wants. Thus, if there is an insufficient supply of a given commodity, and if the commodity has utility so that it is desired or demanded by people, then it has economic value. Therefore, all economic resources have value. Paton referred to assets as 'properties' that have value:

> a property is any consideration, material or otherwise, owned by a specific business enterprise and of value to that enterprise.[1]

The notion of future benefits, the main element of an economic resource, is emphasised by several writers. Sprague saw an asset as 'a storage of services to be received'.[2] Canning said 'it is the assured, separable service series . . . that constitutes the essence of enterprise assets'.[3] Some years later, Paton and Littleton stated:

> 'Service' is the significant element behind the account, that is, service-potentialities, which, when exchanged, bring still other service-potentialities into the enterprise.[4]

Vatter followed the same line of reasoning in defining assets as:

> embodiments of future want satisfaction in the form of service potentials that may be transformed, exchanged, or stored against future events.[5]

Peirson provided an example of this concept of future service:

> a motor vehicle owned by a reporting entity is an asset not because it is a physical object, but because it can provide the entity with future services in the form of transport. The services or benefits may arise from the use or from the sale of the object or right. For example, a machine is an asset because it provides future services from use. Inventory is an asset because it can generate future economic benefits from sale.[6]

Note that the idea expressed is that an asset is something that exists now, and has the capability of rendering service or benefit currently or in the future. The 'thing' that exists is referred to as a property, or right to property, or economic resource, or an 'embodiment' or 'storage' of future services. It is a bundle of future services, and that bundle exists in the form of something tangible, such as a building, or something intangible, such as a right. The *Framework* definition does not emphasise the present existence of something real when it equates an asset with future benefits. Something in the future is not reality; it has not happened yet.

The concept of an asset distinguishes between the object, such as a building or machine, and the services embodied in it. When a building is called an asset, basically the 'space services' is the asset rather than the bricks and mortar themselves. Future services are the essence of an asset, but the distinction between the object and the services is a nebulous one. If the bricks and mortar were not put together the way they are, the 'space services' could not be rendered. Future services can be rendered only through some vehicle or instrument. Without the existence of the latter, the former could not occur. The nature of an asset is that it is capable of providing future economic benefits. Although future economic benefits may be the essence of an asset, we must be careful to explain it in real-world terms if the definition is to have real-world application.

Control by an entity

The economic benefit must be controlled by the entity in question to qualify as an asset. As Ijiri states:

> Accounting is not concerned with economic resources in general, but only those which are under the control of a given entity.[7]

Must an asset be 'owned' (must an entity have 'title' to the asset?) before it can be considered to be an asset of that entity? Sprague commented, 'possession of a thing is merely the right to use it or control it'.[8] When using the term 'own' or 'ownership', we must be careful to appreciate that we simply mean owning the right to use or control. Furthermore, the control an owner has of property is not absolute. Paton points out that the scope of private interest is always subject to the general rights of the state, as well as the particular statutory limitations.[9] For example, the government may prohibit the possession or manufacture of certain products. Through its power, it can nullify a person's control over property. It can also confiscate property for taxes, dictate methods of operations and demand that products and assets conform to certain standards or that they be used for given purposes only. Ownership of your home, for example, does not entitle you to use it for commercial purposes such as a boutique or a cafe unless permitted by local government ordinances. Even in cases where no particular regulation or statute exists, public opinion may exert a powerful restraint so that, in effect, an entity's control over its assets is limited. Therefore, an entity's right to use or control an asset is never absolute. The right to use or control an asset as stated in the definition does not imply that an entity must be able to do absolutely whatever it pleases with the asset.

Ownership is often concurrent with control, but it is not an essential characteristic of an asset. For example, consider an agent who holds goods for sale on behalf of a principal. The goods are not assets of the agent but the agent has possession and therefore control. The alternative position is also possible, where there are benefits from possession without ownership, as in the case of a rental lease agreement.

The term 'title' can also confuse the issue. Most people think of title as a legal document which conveys ownership rights. The fact is that title is divisible. Several people can have different parts of the title of a particular asset. For example, suppose a transport company purchases a truck for $300 000, paying $150 000 now and agreeing to pay the balance in instalments over the next 3 years. Is the truck an asset of the company? Despite the fact that the company does not possess the legal document called the 'title' until it has fully paid for the truck, it owns the legal right to use the truck. Therefore, in accounting, we say the truck is an asset of the company. Technically, the real asset is the right to use the truck, not the truck itself. The company has the right to obtain the services of the truck and it has control over the truck.

Legal concepts are used in accounting as guidelines only. The objective of accounting is not achieved by focusing on the precision of legal concepts but, rather, by concentrating on the economic substance of the transactions and events that affect a firm's financial performance and condition. Thus viewed, certain economic objects called 'assets' arise. The overriding factor is control, which the IASB considers provides a definition which does not rely solely on 'legal enforceability', but allows weight to be given to economic and social sanctions.

Past events

Including the qualification that assets must be controlled by the reporting entity as a result of past events in the *Framework* definition of assets ensures that 'planned' assets are excluded. For example, a machine already acquired by a company is an asset, but a machine which is to be acquired according to the budget is not an asset until it has been acquired, since the event, a purchase transaction, has not yet taken place.

The qualification is somewhat ambiguous because the term 'event' can be interpreted in different ways. Is the signing of a contract an 'event'? If a company signs a contract with a construction firm to have a new office building erected in the future for a given price, does this qualify as an 'event' so that an asset is to be recorded? This type of contract is commonly called a 'wholly executory contract'. Wholly executory contracts arise where each party to the contract has yet to perform exactly the same percentage of its obligations under the contract.

Standard setters, such as the AASB, have in the past explored the implications of executory contracts. In the pre-2005 Australian conceptual framework (Statement of Accounting Concepts 4) the board considered that such contracts as leases, non-cancellable purchase contracts and forward exchange contracts gave rise to assets and liabilities that should be reported as assets and liabilities in the financial statements. Preparers were opposed to this approach. They argued that reporting executory contracts on the balance sheet increased leverage (both assets and liabilities would be recognised, but the value of liabilities would be greater) despite no real change in the underlying economic indebtedness of firms.

In the 1970s the FASB commissioned Ijiri to undertake a research project about executory contracts. Ijiri reasoned that wholly executory contracts 'seem to meet the first test for recognition as assets in financial statements'.[10] In the construction example above, both parties have 'rights to future performance' which exist presently and these are not future rights to be created in the future. Ijiri concluded that after a contractual right meets the definition of an asset (the first test), it should then meet certain 'recognition criteria' before it is recorded. One criterion is usefulness; another is the 'firmness' of the contract.[11]

At present some executory contracts are recognised as assets while others are not, depending on the requirements of accounting standards. For example, under IAS 17/AASB 117 a finance lease gives rise to an asset and liability, while an operating lease does not. The distinction between a finance and operating lease is not based on a theoretical principle but whether the lease transfers substantially all the risks and rewards incidental to ownership of a an asset (IAS 17, para. 4). Preparers (and auditors and regulators in turn) must decide what constitutes 'substantially all of the risks and rewards'.

The IASB framework provides definitions of assets and liabilities (see chapter 8) which, taken together, suggest that leases should be capitalised. The G4+1 standard setting group argued that lessees should recognise, at the beginning of a lease, the fair value of rights and obligations conveyed by the lease. This approach is consistent with both the IASB and FASB conceptual frameworks, while current practices under IAS 17/AASB 117 and US GAAP (FAS 13) are not. Issues relating to accounting for leases are explored further in the next section of this chapter and in chapters 3 and 4.

Exchangeability

Some researchers argue that the definition of an asset should include the condition that an asset be exchangeable. Exchangeability means that an item is separable from an entity, and that its disposal value is separate from the value of the entity. In 1939, MacNeal stated:

> A good that lacks exchangeability must lack economic value because its purchase or sale must forever remain impossible, and thus no market price for it can ever exist.[12]

The asset especially affected by this condition is goodwill, since it cannot be sold separately from the other assets. Chambers gives the following reasons for insisting on separability and for excluding goodwill as an asset:

> the definition arose from the necessity of considering the capacity of an entity to adapt itself to changes in its state and its environment. Adaptive behaviour implies that the goodwill subsisting in any collection of assets and liabilities is so susceptible to variation as to have no enduring quality . . .[13]

Chambers also argues that determining financial position involves the measurement of the values of assets and liabilities, but goodwill is subject to 'evaluation', not measurement. Its value can only be calculated 'anticipatively'. In making the calculation, the past performance of a firm can be used as a basis, but the whole calculation and the norms used for comparison are 'hypothetical', and are not subject to independent corroboration. The value ascertained for goodwill is not of the same kind as the value of the other assets and liabilities.[14] In Chambers's opinion, this is tantamount to adding apples and oranges.

Those who oppose the condition of exchangeability argue that exchange is only one way to obtain the benefits of assets. For example, inventories are one type of asset whose benefits are derived mainly through exchange. But the benefits of most assets such as manufacturing plant and machinery and office buildings are obtained through their use. The benefits of these assets are not affected by whether they are exchangeable. Critics also point out that economic value depends on scarcity and utility, but not on exchangeability. As Moonitz states, 'exchange does not make values, it merely reveals them'.[15] Finally, opponents argue that the inclusion of intangibles such as goodwill as assets is not an attempt to value the business as a whole, but simply an attempt to identify and value particular sources of future benefits to the firm.

Exchangeability is a characteristic that supports the existence of an asset. However, it is not an essential characteristic. Does it really matter whether exchangeability is a criterion? The evidence indicates that the answer to this question is 'yes'. Part of the reason is that, even if goodwill is excluded from the calculation of leverage for debt covenant purposes, and even if the current-period goodwill impairment is excluded from measures of return on equity, the equity number in leverage ratios and in some returns ratios is affected by prior-period impairment of goodwill, and this can affect whether a firm breaches a debt covenant. Also, there is some evidence that investors perceive value in the amount of goodwill reported on balance sheets, and that managers signal the value of their unidentifiable intangibles (goodwill) via their goodwill accounting policies.[16]

LO 2 → ASSET RECOGNITION

It is obvious that there is more to recording assets than simply defining them. Recognising assets on the balance sheet also involves conditions that can be called 'recognition rules'. These rules have been formulated because accountants require evidence to support their records in an environment of uncertainty. Accountants want to be sure that particular assets exist and that their inclusion in the balance sheet provides useful information that is both relevant and reliable.

Some recognition rules are informally expressed as conventions, and others are formally designated in authoritative pronouncements. Two examples of conventional recognition rules are:

- An account receivable is recorded as an asset when a credit sale is made.
- Equipment is recorded as an asset when it is purchased.

An example of a recognition guideline that is formally specified is the guideline adopted for the recognition of finance leases as assets. For a lessee, as stipulated in paragraph 10 of IAS 17/AASB 117, meeting one of the following criteria indicates that a non-cancellable lease is to be capitalised unless there are other reasons that would require the lease to be deemed an operating lease:

(a) the lease transfers ownership of the asset to the lessee by the end of the lease term;
(b) the lessee has the option to purchase the asset at a price that is expected to be sufficiently lower than the fair value at the date the option becomes exercisable for it to be reasonably certain, at the inception of the lease, that the option will be exercised;
(c) the lease term is for the major part of the economic life of the asset even if title is not transferred;
(d) at the inception of the lease, the present value of the minimum lease payments amounts to at least substantially all of the fair value of the leased asset; and
(e) the leased assets are of such a specialised nature that only the lessee can use them without major modifications.

In surveying existing accounting practices, it appears that the many recognition rules used to identify particular assets can be generalised into several criteria. Note that there is a distinction between a recognition rule, which is a specific rule to identify a particular asset, and a recognition criterion, which is a general guideline used to formulate recognition rules and a recognition guideline that provides assistance rather than prescription. The objective of accounting provides the basis for recognition criteria. In particular, the recognition criteria contained in the *Framework* are extensions of the subsidiary objectives (qualitative characteristics) of relevance and reliability of accounting information (*Framework*, paragraphs 26–28, 31–32).

Business and other economic activities occur in an environment characterised by uncertainty. Few outcomes are definite, including the receipt of future economic benefits that have arisen as the result of past transactions or events. Therefore, it is not surprising that the *Framework* recognition criteria incorporate consideration of the probability of economic benefits being forthcoming and that to qualify for recognition in the accounts, the asset must be capable of being measured reliably.

Numerous recognition criteria have been applied in the past to assist accountants to decide when to record assets. Not all of these criteria are now formalised in the *Framework*, and some have little or no theoretical foundation. The following list is not intended to be complete and the criteria are not mutually exclusive.

- *Reliance on the law*. Do we have a legal right to the future benefits? Recognition of many assets depends on the legal concept of an asset. The recording of accounts receivable due to the sale of inventory and the purchase of fixed assets giving the legal right to use them are examples. This criterion relates to both the relevance and the reliability of accounting information. Control, rather than legal ownership, is used to determine the existence of an asset. Nonetheless, the passing of legal title generally indicates the passing of control, and can be used in determining when to recognise an asset's existence. Although legal rights of ownership or control of benefits from use of property are often used as recognition criteria, the overriding recognition criterion is that of economic substance rather than legal form. According to the *Framework* paragraph 35, 'If information is to represent faithfully the transactions and other events that it purports to represent, it is necessary that they are accounted for and presented in accordance with their substance and economic reality and not merely their legal form.' The existence of legal rights is an indicator, but not a criterion for asset recognition.

- *Determination of the economic substance of the transaction or event.* Ascertaining the economic substance of a transaction relates to the objective of reporting relevant and reliable information. Materiality is also a factor: if the event is economically significant, it is important enough to record and to report. Indeed, materiality is defined in the *Framework* paragraph 30 as follows:

> Information is material if its omission or misstatement could influence the economic decisions of users taken on the basis of the financial report.

There are different facets to the economic substance and materiality criteria and therefore it is difficult to generalise. However, many rules are based on them. Sometimes the economic substance criterion is applied in contradiction to the law. One example is the wholly executory contracts previously discussed. The present rule is that there is no economic substance to the exchange of promises until there is performance by at least one of the parties. Finance leases are recognised mainly on the basis of whether there is a transfer of ownership benefits to the lessee. That is, a leased asset is recognised by the lessee when the lessee has acquired, in substance, the rights and obligations of ownership and has control over the property leased.

Although both finance and operating leases involve probable future benefits, the substance of the benefits, according to the rules, is different. Finance leases convey 'in-substance' ownership (style rights and obligations) whereas operating leases are in the nature of short-term hire, and do not have such rights and obligations attached. Therefore, the former brings forth an asset, but the latter does not. While the *Framework* does not treat operating and finance leases differently for purposes of asset definition, standards treat the leases differently for purposes of asset recognition. The reason for the difference reflects preferences of financial statement preparers which have influenced standard setters.

- *Use of the conservatism (prudence principle): anticipate losses, but not gains.* The *Framework* states in paragraph 37:

> Prudence is the inclusion of a degree of caution in the exercise of the judgement needed in making the estimates required under conditions of uncertainty, such that assets or income are not overstated and liabilities or expenses are not understated.

This approach seems inconsistent with the concept of neutrality, which is advocated in the *Framework*. Neutrality occurs when information is free from bias and is not selected or presented in a manner that would influence judgement to achieve a predetermined result or outcome (para. 36). Arguably, prudence biases decisions towards risk aversion rather than equally weighting risks and benefits. Conservatism implies that liabilities can be recorded early, but not assets. For example, if a company loses in a lawsuit, even if it appeals, conservatism implies that it would record a liability. However, if the company is the plaintiff in a lawsuit against another firm and it wins but the defendant appeals, no asset is recorded.

Another example of conservatism relates to accounting for long-term construction projects. In using the completed contract method, if in the process of constructing a long-term project a loss is anticipated, it is recorded even before the project is completed; but if a profit is expected, no gain is recorded until the completion of the project. Asymmetric treatment of recognition of gains and losses is widely practised.

Standards may also restrict asset recognition. For example, IAS 38/AASB 138 *Intangible Assets* paragraph 48 prohibits recognition of internally generated goodwill. The standard states that internally generated goodwill is not an identifiable resource (it is not separable or does not arise from contractual or other rights) which is controlled by the entity that can be measured at cost (para. 49). Recognition is not permitted because there are difficulties in identifying whether and when the intangible asset will generate future economic benefits. In addition, the costs of generating the asset (i.e. the outflows which give rise to the goodwill) cannot be determined reliably.

Similarly, IAS 38/AASB 138 restricts recognition of internally generated assets arising from research expenditure. All research expenditure is expensed as incurred because, in the view of the standard setters, an entity cannot demonstrate that future economic benefits will be generated. Recognition of internally generated assets arising from development expenditure are permitted, but only if strict criteria are met. The criteria are shown in figure 7.1. The inconsistent treatment of various types of intangible assets has been recognised by standard setters. For example, internally generated brands cannot be recognised but brands acquired as part of a business combination are recorded at fair value. A discussion paper focusing on the initial accounting for internally generated intangible assets was released by the AASB in 2008 and provides an opportunity for discussion of these issues.[17]

57. An intangible asset arising from development (or from the development phase of an internal project) shall be recognised if, and only if, an entity can demonstrate all of the following:
(a) the technical feasibility of completing the intangible asset so that it will be available for use or sale;
(b) its intention to complete the intangible asset and use or sell it;
(c) its ability to use or sell the intangible asset;
(d) how the intangible asset will generate probable future economic benefits. Among other things, the entity can demonstrate the existence of a market for the output of the intangible asset or the intangible asset itself or, if it is to be used internally, the usefulness of the intangible asset;
(e) the availability of adequate technical, financial and other resources to complete the development and to use or sell the intangible asset; and
(f) its ability to measure reliably the expenditure attributable to the intangible asset during its development.

FIGURE 7.1 IAS 38 paragraph 57, Recognition criteria for development expenses

LO 3 → ASSET MEASUREMENT

Once recognition criteria are met, the accountant must decide how to measure the asset. As discussed in chapters 5 and 6, several measurement approaches are possible. Which measurement basis should be adopted? Is there a theoretically justified 'best' approach? Standard setters have struggled to agree on conceptual guidance for measurement. Measurement at acquisition cost is argued to be objective and to provide reliable and verifiable information. On the other hand, fair value measurement provides relevant information. The IASB *Framework* outlines qualitative characteristics of financial information and thus gives guidance about the preferred attributes of financial information. However, what has not been resolved is which measurement approach (or approaches) should be used to achieve the desired qualitative characteristics.

Present measurement practice for assets varies and reflects both managers' incentives and past accounting practices. It is beyond the scope of this chapter to endorse one measurement approach over another. However, we can investigate some of the issues relating to choice of measurement method by considering measurement of tangible, intangible and financial assets. The choices relate to both measurement on acquisition and measurement in subsequent periods. Once measured, the information about asset values can be included in the financial statements (that is, asset values are recognised) or it can be included as a note disclosure. In the latter case, asset remeasurements may be disclosed in the notes to the accounts, but not recognised in the financial statements.

Tangible assets

As explained in chapter 5, the traditional approach has been to measure assets at historical cost. Historical cost has been firmly embedded in US Generally Accepted Accounting Principles (GAAP) through the SEC's position. Zeff describes the SEC's commitment to historical cost as following from the exposure of firms' questionable capitalisation and revaluation practices prior to the 1929 US stock market collapse. He comments that:

> From its founding, the SEC rejected any deviations from historical cost accounting in the body of the financial statements.[18]

The SEC held this position until 1978, when it proposed that oil and gas reserves be periodically revalued, with changes in value taken to the income statement. Like US GAAP, IASB standards are built on the assumption that the main measurement approach in accounting is the cost (or modified cost) model. For example, IAS 16 and IAS 40 require property, plant and equipment, and investment property (respectively) to be measured initially at cost, including transaction costs (IAS 16, para. 15; IAS 40, para. 20).

The cost model reflects a conservative approach to asset measurement. Some national GAAP favour the use of historical cost; for example, the national GAAP in France and Germany, and EU Directives prior to 2005. Subsequent measurement based on historical cost means that assets are measured at acquisition cost less any accumulated depreciation and impairment charges. Supporters of the cost model argue that cost of acquisition provides objective and verifiable evidence of the cost of the asset and that the application of depreciation and impairment ensures that its current value is reflected in the balance sheet. Consistent with a conservative approach to measurement, losses in value of the asset are recognised in the financial statements but gains are not.

However, IASB standards permit subsequent remeasurement of tangible assets. The options included in IAS 16 *Property, Plant and Equipment* and IAS 40 *Investment Property* reflect long-standing practice in UK GAAP which was adopted into IASC/IASB standards.[19] These standards permit, but do not require, the use of a current value measurement model. In relation to IAS 16, managers may choose to use the revaluation model for subsequent measurement (para. 31). Measurement can be based on market values provided by professionally qualified appraisers (para. 32) or may be estimated by the entity based on an 'income or depreciated replacement cost' approach (para. 33). Revaluations must be keep up to date at each balance date (para. 34). Similarly, in relation to IAS 40 managers can choose the cost model or the fair value model for measurement after recognition.[20]

Why would preparers choose one measurement model or another? It can be argued that revalued assets provide relevant information for financial statement users.

Revaluation can provide more current information about value than historical cost. However, this argument is less persuasive if assets are recently purchased or not subject to fluctuating market prices.

Managers may revalue land in times of rising prices, to ensure that assets are not understated on the balance sheet. A current value on the balance sheet may be relevant to decision making, it may be favourable for calculation of financial ratios or it may prevent the firm from becoming a takeover target.

In the United Kingdom and Australia firms have for many years used values other than historical cost for tangible assets. Aboody, Barth and Kasznik showed that in the United Kingdom 43 per cent of firms recorded an asset revaluation reserve (based on firm-years between 1983 and 1995).[21] Barth and Clinch reported that 45 per cent of Australian firms revalued property, plant and equipment (based on firm-years in the period 1991–1995).[22] The use of asset revaluations in Australia has been explained in terms of contracting theory and political costs.[23] Lin and Peasnell found that similar explanations were relevant in the United Kingdom, but that specific national factors, particularly equity depletion resulting primarily from the writing off of goodwill, influenced revaluation decisions.[24] Another suggested motivation for asset revaluations is to communicate managers' expectations for their firms. Aboody et al. concluded that revaluations of fixed assets by UK firms were related to subsequent changes in performance.[25]

Prior to the adoption of IAS/IFRS in 2005, firms in both the United Kingdom and Australia were observed to make less use of the revaluation model compared to prior periods. Possible reasons are the relatively low inflation environment, which reduces the demand for current value information, and the introduction of new accounting standards in the late 1990s, which required that the value of a revalued asset would not be materially different to its carrying amount at balance date. The cost of revaluation increased as firms would need to review asset values each balance date. These examples show than many factors can influence a firm's choice of measurement model. Diversity in practice would make it difficult for the IASB to promote one measurement model, even if the board could agree on a preferred model.

One of the arguments against use of a current measurement model is that measurement is unreliable and subjective. By unreliable, opponents refer to cases where fair value is estimated rather than observed, for example, when the fair value of stock options are determined using a model, rather than market prices. Measurement is subjective when it involves valuation inputs which are obtained by management. Managers may be self-interested in their choice of inputs to valuation models. Zeff notes that the SEC's long experience of observing corporate behaviour gives rise to the view that:

> Companies could not be trusted to use their discretion to make balanced and fair minded judgements on accounting treatments when given the flexibility to do so.[26]

Nevertheless, despite managers' discretion in asset measurement, Barth and Clinch report that asset revaluations are value relevant.[27] This result suggests investors make use of managers' information about asset value. In a similar vein, Horton reports that non-GAAP measures of values of assets and liabilities of UK life insurance companies are relevant to market participants.[28] These studies suggest that 'fair value' measures of assets potentially provide useful information for financial decision making. They provide support for standards setters who want to introduce fair value measurement into accounting standards.

Gain on remeasurement of assets, resulting from use of the revaluation model (IAS 16, para. 31) were traditionally included directly in equity. Assets were increased (debit asset) thus increasing assets on the balance sheet and the credit entry went directly to an asset revaluation reserve in equity (credit asset revaluation reserve). Thus, increases in asset values were shown without any impact on profit and loss. The clean surplus notion of income (that income should include all items of revenue, expense, gain and loss) was violated and the unrealised increase in assets, while communicated to financial statement users, did not affect income, so a conservative income figure was presented. The gain on the asset was realised when sold, but the accounting practice meant that revaluations could sit in equity long after the asset was sold. The treatment of unrealised gains and losses arising from a current value measurement model is one of the most controversial issues in accounting today, as discussed further later in this chapter.

Intangible assets

We have seen that current accounting practice makes use of both the cost and fair value (or revaluation) models for tangible assets. Should we take the same approach to measuring intangible assets? The asset, a bundle of future economic benefits to be realised by an entity, may relate to tangible or intangible items. Indeed, some of the most valuable assets held by corporations today are intangible. Consider the brands of Coca Cola, Louis Vuitton or Billabong or the self-developed intellectual property of Microsoft and Apple or the patents over pharmaceuticals innovations under development held by GlaxoSmithKline or Bayer.

Accounting practice in relation to measurement of intangible assets has, generally speaking, been conservative. As for tangible assets, accounting standards require that we measure intangible assets initially at cost of acquisition (IAS 38, para. 24). The use of a current value model for intangible assets is rare. IAS 38 (para. 75) permits the revaluation model but, unlike IAS 16, requires that fair value be determined with reference to an active market. Since most intangible assets by their very nature do not have an active market, cost (less accumulated amortisation and impairment) is the widely used measurement method (para. 81).

In addition, IAS 38 prohibits recognition of internally generated intangible assets (para. 48, 63). Although the expenditure may give rise to future benefits, it is written off on the basis that it does not produce a separately identifiable asset (para. 49, 64). One way internally generated intangible assets can appear in the balance sheet is via capitalisation of development costs, as explained previously. The valuation of intangible assets is contentious, involving as it does subjective estimations of the fair value of the asset. Case study 7.2 explores alternative approaches to the valuation of identifiable intangible assets.

Financial instruments

A third category of assets that we will now consider is financial assets. IAS 39 created a separate category of financial assets and liabilities and introduced associated measurement rules. How should these assets and liabilities be measured? Are the recognition and measurement rules applied to tangible and intangible assets appropriate? We know that the dominant measurement model is historical cost. However, it has been argued that historical cost principles are inappropriate to measure some financial instruments. For example, consider derivatives, which have no cost. Over time, their value can change dramatically, but under the cost model the changes in value would not be recorded in the financial statements. Should the changes in the value of the derivatives be included in the balance sheet, to reflect their value to the entity? Should the gain or loss on holding the derivatives be included in income of the period? How can investors adequately assess risk if derivatives and other financial contracts are not recognised?

The FASB and IASB have concluded that derivatives should be measured at fair value rather than cost. In IAS 39 (para. 9) fair value is defined as

> The amount for which an asset could be exchanged or a liability settled, between knowledgeable willing parties in an arm's length transaction.

Standard setters argue that by measuring financial assets at market value, information users are provided with relevant information about their value. Standards setters such as the FASB and IASB, considering the 'decision usefulness' objective, incorporated fair value measurement for financial instruments in several pronouncements. Since the 1980s the FASB has required fair value measurement (either directly in the financial statements or in note disclosure) in standards such as SFAS Nos. 107, 115, 119, 123, 125, 133, 140, 142, 143 and 144. SFAS 107, issued in 1991, defined fair value as 'the amount at which the instrument could be exchanged in a current transaction between willing parties, other than in a forced or liquidation sale' (para. 5). The standard further described how fair value could be determined. Quoted market price was preferred but management estimates (based on market price of a similar security or present value estimation of future cash flows discounted at a risk adjusted rate) could be used. These financial instrument standards have increased the relevance of information provided, however some argue that its reliability is reduced because of the inexact measurement methods used to determine fair value.[29]

The FASB's pronouncements have been influential in the development of financial instrument standards promulgated by the IASB. In fact, the IASB has followed FASB's lead in standard setting for financial instruments. In order to provide a set of core standards to the International Organization of Securities Commissions (IOSCO) in 2000, the original IAS 39 *Financial Instruments: Recognition and Measurement* was based on SFAS 133.[30] The IASB has been committed to the use of fair value measurement for financial instruments in order to provide relevant information for financial statement users. Standard setters have argued that gains and losses on financial instruments should be recognised as they arise in order to report on their associated risks, to make financial statements more transparent and to avoid the complexity of existing accounting treatments (such as hedge accounting).[31] On the other hand, some preparers have opposed aspects of IASB pronouncements, claiming that fair value measurement will not promote relevant, reliable, understandable and comparable reporting.[32]

Measurement of financial instruments reflects their complexity. A single measurement model has not been endorsed by the standard setters in IAS 39. In fact, a number of measurement methods are used. All financial instruments are categorised into four types, each with a required measurement method. These are shown in table 7.1. On initial recognition, all financial instruments are measured at acquisition cost (which, at this stage, is equivalent to a fair value). In subsequent recognition, an entity may elect to value all or any of its financial instruments at fair value, with changes in fair value recognised in income, by designating them as 'fair value through profit and loss'. Alternatively, an entity may classify assets into the other categories, subject to the requirement of IAS 39/AASB 139. A discussion of the measurement process in relation to financial instruments is provided in theory in action 7.1. In this vignette, Credit Suisse reported to the market that they had 'got it wrong' in relation to the valuation of investment securities, thus providing an illustration of the complexity of measurement of these assets.

TABLE 7.1 Classification and measurement of financial instruments

Type of financial asset	Measurement method
Originated loans and receivables	Amortised cost. The asset is not affected by the intention to sell or hold to maturity.
Held-to-maturity investments	Amortised cost, subject to review for impairment in value. An entity is prohibited from using the held-to-maturity classification if it sells or transfers more than a small portion of its held-to-maturity investments prior to maturity, during the current or preceding two financial years.
Available-for-sale securities	Fair value, with gains or losses from remeasurement recognised in equity.
Financial assets held for trading, or classified as fair value through profit and loss, and derivatives	Fair value, with gains and losses arising on remeasurement taken to profit and loss. All financial assets carried at amortised cost and available-for-sale securities are required to be assessed for impairment at each reporting date.

Source: AASB 139 *Financial Instruments: Recognition and Measurement.*

7.1
THEORY IN ACTION

Outdated prices blamed in Credit Suisse error

by Julia Werdigier

LONDON — The surprise $2.85 billion write-down at Credit Suisse this week underscored the difficulty banks face in valuing complex investments. But the cause of the blunder may be simple: traders at the bank used old prices.

Two managers in Credit Suisse's investment banking division said Thursday that several traders probably used out-of-date prices to value asset-backed securities. It is unclear whether the traders did so intentionally, according to the managers, who declined to be identified because the bank was still reviewing the episode.

A spokeswoman at Credit Suisse declined to comment. The bank said Tuesday that the traders had been temporarily suspended.

The mispricings were detected during a review of trading positions that the bank conducted as it prepared to sell bonds. Credit Suisse disclosed the write-down on Tuesday, a week after the bank reported fourth-quarter earnings.

The news sent shudders through the financial industry, six months into a global credit market crisis. The episode raised new questions about how banks manage risk and value complicated financial instruments, particularly those linked to mortgages.

Concerns about banks' risk controls are particularly urgent in Europe, where, even apart from the rogue trader case that has rocked Société Générale, banks have shocked investors over the last three months by repeatedly restating write-downs.

"Accounting practices in Europe differ from the mark-to-market approach in the U.S., and accountants often have to change the models as the market develops," said James Hyde, a bank analyst at European Credit Management, a fund management company in London. "We will continue to struggle with valuations as the goal posts continue to move."

In marking to market, traders value their positions based on actual market prices. The chief executive of Credit Suisse, Brady W. Dougan, said Tuesday that while most of the write-down was attributable to "pretty adverse market conditions," the mismarkings mostly involved "delinquencies of updating of pricing" and "some valuation issues where the pricing did not meet our standards."

Like most investment banks, Credit Suisse requires traders to value positions daily under management supervision. Those valuations are then checked weekly, monthly or when needed by independent controllers. The mismarkings were detected during such a cross-check, D. Wilson Ervin, chief risk officer at Credit Suisse, said Tuesday.

Credit Suisse is now under pressure to complete its internal review of the trades and reconsider the terms of $2 billion of subordinated bonds that it sold last week.

Standard & Poor's, the rating agency, put the debt rating of Credit Suisse under review for a possible downgrading on Tuesday, saying "the incident raises significant questions about the adequacy of control" and "it is not clear why the year-to-date losses are so much larger than those in 2007."

Credit Suisse said on Feb. 12 that it wrote down a net 2 billion Swiss francs ($1.8 billion) for 2007 on debt and loans. The bank's total write-downs are still far below the $19 billion reported by its larger Swiss rival, UBS.

Source: The New York Times, 22 February 2008, www.nytimes.com.

Questions
1. How do European bankers determine the valuations of asset-backed securities?
2. What is meant by these phrases used in the article?
   (a) 'pretty adverse market conditions'
   (b) 'delinquencies of updating of pricing'
   (c) 'some valuation issues where the pricing did not meet our standards'
3. What are the repercussions of the 'errors' at Credit Suisse? Are they reasonable or do they represent an over-reaction?

LO 4 — CHALLENGES FOR STANDARD SETTERS

Which measurement model?

The FASB and IASB intend to address the issue of measurement in Phase C of the conceptual framework project. Issues to be considered include potential measurement bases: past entry or exit prices, modified past amount, current entry, exit or equilibrium price, value in use or future entry or exit price. As part of the project, the boards will consider measurement concepts, principles and terms. They will evaluate and rank measurement methods according to the extent to which they meet required qualitative characteristics of financial information.

The conceptual framework project suggests that the standard setters are open to considering a range of measurement models. Commentators claim that IASB standards introduced widespread use of fair value measurement, although Cairns strongly denies this claim.[33] He states that IFRS has introduced fair value measurement for derivatives at each balance date and some other financial assets and liabilities (under IAS 39) as well as the requirement to measure share-based payments to employees at fair value (under IFRS 2). Further, Cairns argues that there is considerable misunderstanding about the extent of use of fair value under IFRS. Fair values are used to measure assets on initial recognition, for example in IAS 16 *Property, Plant and Equipment*, IAS 17 *Leases*, IAS 39 *Financial Instruments: Recognition and Measurement* and IAS 41 *Agriculture*. Subsequent measurement at fair value is more rare. It is mandatory for some financial assets under IAS 39 (for derivatives, held-for-trading financial assets and liabilities and those classified as fair value through profit and loss) and for pension assets and liabilities under IAS 19. In several other standards, fair value measurement is not mandatory but rather is an option, as discussed above in relation to IAS 16 and IAS 40.[34]

Cairns argues that widespread use of fair value measurement under IFRS is more a perception than a reality. Nevertheless, support by the IASB and FASB for greater use of fair value measurement, for example for all financial instruments, is the focus of considerable concern in some sections of the financial community. We explore the views of participants in the financial reporting process (preparers, analysts and standard setters) about fair value measurement of financial instruments in case study 7.3.

How to calculate fair value measurement

Given the use of fair value measurement, standard setters have provided guidance about how to measure fair value. The FASB's SFAS 157 *Fair Value Measurements* (effective 2007) provides examples of valuation techniques to be used to estimate fair value. They include:

- the market approach — use of observable prices and information from actual transactions for identical, similar or comparable assets or liabilities;
- income approach — conversion of future amounts (such as cash flows or earnings) to a single discounted present amount; and
- cost approach — the amount that currently would be required to replace its service capacity (current replacement cost).

The FASB has indicated that, irrespective of which approach is used, the valuation must emphasise market inputs, namely the assumptions and data that market participants would use in their estimates of fair value. An example of how market value inputs are used in practice is given in theory in action 7.2, in relation to the Swedish group Stora Enso, which holds agricultural assets.

The FASB statement also provides a 'fair value hierarchy'. That is, it nominates three categories or levels for the inputs to be used to estimate fair value (FASB, 2004, p. 5, para. 14). The levels are as follows:

- Level 1— use quoted prices for identical assets and liabilities in active reference markets whenever the information is available. Quoted prices shall not be adjusted.
- Level 2 — if quoted prices for identical assets and liabilities in active markets are not available, fair value shall be estimated based on quoted prices for similar assets or liabilities in active markets, adjusted as appropriate for differences.
- Level 3 — if quoted prices for identical or similar assets and liabilities in active markets are not available, or if differences between similar assets and liabilities are not objectively determinable, fair value shall be estimated using multiple valuation techniques consistent with the market, income and cost approaches.

As part of the international convergence of accounting standards, the IASB issued a discussion paper about fair value measurement in 2009. It issued an exposure draft which considers both the comments received and the recommendations of SFAS 157 in 2006. The IASB's deliberations in relation to fair value measurement will be influenced by events in the financial crisis of 2008–09. For example, considerable pressure was applied to the standard setters to modify existing fair value requirements, which were blamed by some as contributing to the financial crisis.

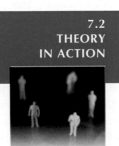
Agricultural assets: IAS 41 *Agriculture*

The following information is provided in the financial statements of the Swedish group Stora Enso in relation to Biological Assets:

At 1 January 2004, 95 per cent of the group's biological assets were in Sweden; however, these were divested in March when the group's recently created forest holding company Bergvik Skog AB was divested to institutional investors. Stora Enso's remaining biological assets had a fair value of EUR 64.6 million and were located by value in Portugal (83%), Canada (3%) and China (14%). In addition, the company now has three associated companies where IAS 41 is taken into account when computing results (Bergvik Skog AB, the new 43.3% owned Swedish associate has biological assets at a fair value of EUR 2 622.6 million;

Tornator Timberland Oy, a 41% owned associate, which acquired the group's Finnish forest interests in 2002, had biological assets at a fair value of EUR 614.9 million; Veracel, a 50% owned associate in Brazil, also has substantial forest plantations valued at EUR 70.0 though with a growing cycle of only seven years).

Biological assets (EUR million)	As at 31 December 2003	As at 31 December 2004
Assets reclassified from fixed assets	705.9	
Fair valuation surplus	855.8	
Initial IAS 41 valuation at 1 January 2003	1 561.7	
Carrying value at 1 January	1 561.7	1 587.8
Translation difference	8.3	6.4
Additions	7.2	4.5
Disposals	−1.0	−1 541.2
Change in fair value	116.2	37.5
Decrease due to harvest	−104.6	−30.4
Carrying value at 31 December	1 587.8	64.6

Question

Explain what is represented by the items shown in the above table.
(a) Assets reclassified from fixed assets, €705.9 m
(b) Fair valuation surplus, €855.8 m
(c) Carrying value at 31 December 2003, €1 587.8 m
(d) Additions €4.5 — and disposals, €−1 541.2 m
(e) Change in fair value, €37.5 m
(f) Decrease due to harvest, €−30.4

LO 5 ISSUES FOR AUDITORS

Auditing fair values creates difficulties for auditors because it requires the application of valuation models and, frequently, the use of valuation experts. Auditing fair values for assets has been identified by the chief executive officer of the global auditing firm Grant Thornton LLP as one of the top 10 topics for further research:[35]

> Historically and predominantly, auditors have attested to verifiable assertions. Although, as a profession, we have addressed issues related to impairment in value, to date, nothing as broad in scope as auditing fair value in the absence of a ready market has been asked of us. Assessing the reasonableness of fair values under such conditions requires an abundant supply of valuation experts.[36]

In a synthesis of research to date, Martin, Rich and Wilks argue that as more assets (and liabilities) are measured at fair value, auditors need to understand more about valuation models and the management processes that determine the inputs to those models, even when specialist valuers are used.[37] To develop an effective audit approach, auditors need to understand the client firm's processes and relevant controls for determining fair values, and make a judgement on whether the client firm's measurement methods and assumptions are appropriate and likely to provide a reasonable basis for the fair value measurement.[38]

Martin et al. also point out that auditors need to appreciate management's potential biases and likely errors in applying valuation models, identifying market inputs, and making the required assumptions. If managers have incentives to overstate assets, then auditors need to be aware of the critical components of valuation models that would make this easier for managers to achieve.

Using fair values for assets could appear more attractive to management (and less risky for auditors) during periods of rising asset values. During a share market boom investments in listed securities generally rise and the accounting rules (e.g. IAS 39/ AASB 139) require them under specified conditions to be measured at fair value with the increase in value recognised in profit and loss. The fall in share and bond markets during late 2008 and early 2009 prompted some investors and managers to blame fair value accounting rules for exaggerating losses for financial firms. Reilly reports claims by some managers that because the losses on investments in shares and bonds are 'unrealised', writing down such assets is 'exaggerating' the market turmoil.[39] However, others suggest that fair values give more disclosure and investors and managers 'will get through the problem that much quicker'.[40]

Theory in action 7.3 explores these issues in the context of write-downs of investment securities by Barclays Bank in 2007.

7.3
THEORY
IN ACTION

Impairment

Barclays reveals £1.7 bn loans write off

by Patrick Hosking

Barclays has written off £1.7 billion on sub-prime mortgages and buyout loans in the past four months, the bank disclosed yesterday as it sought to soothe market fears of a much larger black hole in its accounts.

Despite the write-offs, the bank's investment banking arm, Barclays Capital, made record profits of £1.9 billion in the first ten months of the year, it said.

The bank was rewarded with an initial 6 per cent rise in its shares, but the positive mood evaporated on closer reading of its trading statement and because of souring sentiment over banks generally. The shares ended down 2½p at 530½p.

There was also concern about the steepness of the slide in loan quality in recent weeks — £1 billion of the write-offs came in October alone, compared with a £700 million deterioration over the previous three months.

However, the writedowns were still a fraction of the £10 billion rumoured last Friday, when trading in the shares was briefly suspended and the bank was forced to issue a denial.

Bob Diamond, president of Barclays and chief executive of BarCap, told *The Times* that the bank had been far more open with the market than most of its peers. "We have been clinical, conservative, forward-looking and very transparent," he said.

In some cases, securities secured on US sub-prime mortgages had been written down to zero, he said. Second-lien mortgages — home loans where Barclays has only second claim on the collateral — had also been written off.

Barclays said that it had also adopted a more conservative accounting treatment, projecting cashflows through to the end of 2008, rather than just looking at historic cashflows.

Collateralised debt obligations — the investment vehicles in which many of the sub-prime mortgages are contained — have been hard to value because there has been little or no trading of them to set a market price. Even after the writedowns, Barclays still has total exposure to US sub-prime loans of about £10.8 billion.

Barclays also gave details of its exposure to warehoused leveraged buyout debt — loans given or promised to company buyers but no longer wanted by syndicated buyers because of the credit crunch.

Barclays said it now had £7.3 billion of such debt, down from £9 billion in September, and that it had written down the loans' value by £190 million. After taking account of £130 million of fees, the loss was likely to be only £60 million.

Jonathan Pierce, a Credit Suisse analyst, applauded the level of disclosure, but questioned whether the sub-prime writedowns were enough. At 12 per cent of the exposure, net of tax, they were in line with other European banks, but not as conservative as Merrill Lynch and Morgan Stanley, which have written down about 30 per cent, he said.

Alex Potter, of Collins Stewart, said: "We cannot categorically state that this is the end of the writedowns, but this gives us confidence that we should be materially through the problems."

The write-off blow was softened by a quirk of international accounting rules that let Barclays book a £400 million profit because of the deterioration in the market value of its own debt securities, reducing the net write-off for the four months to £1.3 billion. The rule let HSBC book a $1.3 billion offsetting profit when it revealed its $3.3 billion of sub-prime losses on Wednesday.

Analysts said the Barclays statement would add to pressure on Royal Bank of Scotland for a trading statement. RBS, which also has major exposure to US sub-prime loans on its own books and through acquisition of ABN Amro, is not due to report until December 6. Its shares fell 18½p to 448½p yesterday.

Fitch, the rating agency, downgraded Barclays' outlook score from "stable" to "negative". It said expansion of BarCap might expose the bank to greater risks.

Source: The Times, 16 November 2007.

Questions

1. What is a write-down?
2. At the time of the article, why were banks reporting write-downs?
3. What guidance is there about how to calculate the write-down?
4. Do all banks use the same model to calculate a write-down?

Whether the fair value rules ultimately are found to have helped investors by providing relevant information or caused problems by providing unreliable loss estimates, there is the potential that any corporate failures during this period will lead to legal action against auditors who failed to approach their audit of asset fair values appropriately.

Failures by audit teams to use adequate procedures to test and conclude on the value of various long-lived assets (both tangible and intangible) were reported by the Public Company Accounting Oversight Board (PCAOB) in its 2007 report summarising its findings from audit firm inspections.[41] Most problems found by the PCAOB related to the testing of asset values for recoverability within the historical cost model, but similar issues would arise when assessing fair value assertions. The PCAOB noted instances where auditors did not challenge management's assertions surrounding asset values, or test the reasonableness of management's significant assumptions and underlying data used to assess the recoverability of assets.[42] Theory in action 7.4 focuses on a situation where auditors are the target of a class action by disgruntled investors who claim the auditors signed off on inflated profits and asset values.

A specific situation that requires the use of fair values for a wide range of assets is in a business combination. The purchase price must be allocated appropriately to the individual assets acquired and liabilities assumed, with any balance being designated as goodwill. The cost allocated to goodwill is based on the fair values of the individual assets and liabilities at the date of the acquisition.[43] The PCAOB identified failures by auditors to perform adequate audit procedures to test the allocation of the purchase price and the reasonableness of the estimated fair values assigned to the assets acquired.[44] It is not clear from the PCAOB report whether the problems arose from auditors' failure to understand the fair value valuation models applied, or more generally a failure to challenge management's assertions surrounding the acquisition.

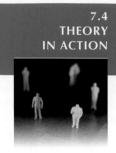

Class action targets ABC and auditors

by Nabila Ahmed

The long-term auditors of collapsed child-care giant ABC Learning Centres are set to come under fire as a Sydney law firm begins organising a new shareholder group action for damages worth "hundreds of millions of dollars".

Dennis & Company Solicitors is planning to run its case in competition to the shareholder class action being organised by litigation funder IMF and will target both ABC and its former auditors, Pitcher Partners.

Dennis & Company principal Bruce Dennis said ABC should be held to account for misrepresentation of profits and the value of the child-care centres and Pitcher Partners for "signing off on what we believe were inflated profits and inflated values".

"It seems that they (ABC) booked payments in as revenue and profit when it really wasn't. And they really pushed the boundaries I think way too far in terms of valuing the child-care centres," Mr Dennis said yesterday.

"They had people external to ABC building child-care centres, selling them to ABC at a certain price and there was an agreement that they (the sellers) would be guaranteeing the revenue for the first couple of years ... and then the auditors allowed them to book those guarantee payments as revenue."

Mr Dennis said he had already written to Pitcher partners asking the auditor to hold safe any information that may be relevant to the dispute.

ABC Learning employed Russell Brown of Pitcher Partners in Brisbane to audit its accounts between 2001 and 2005. Mr Brown handed over to colleague Simon Green, who signed off on the 2006 and 2007 accounts. Pitcher Partners' Brisbane arm ceased operation from December 1 and its partners have joined two other firms.

"It's a matter that I see very seriously in terms of the audit situation because they ought to have been a bit more careful about qualifying the audit report and saying some of this revenue constitutes profit guarantee and therefore the underlying model for the valuation of the child-care centres may be flawed," Mr Dennis aid.

The audit of ABC's accounts had been a major issue in the lead-up to the company's collapse early last month. ABC's new auditors, Ernst & Young, had been working for months to finalise the company's 2008 accounts and preparing to restate at least two prior years' earnings in a bid to clean up accounts previously audited by Pitcher Partners.

ABC's board, led by chairman David Ryan, had also brought in KPMG to provide an independent opinion when Ernst and Young decided to change the way certain items were treated by Pitcher Partners. KPMG thought both auditors' positions were defensible.

Mr Dennis, whose firm started the group action after being approached by an ABC shareholder, said Pitcher Partners had failed investors. Claims against ABC and Pitcher Partners could run into "hundreds of millions of dollars".

Mr Dennis is hoping to be able to put claims to ABC's administrators on behalf of shareholder clients by about March next year.

Source: The Australian Financial Review, 16 October 2008 p. 6, www.afr.com.

Questions

1. The article states that 'the auditors allowed them to book those guarantee payments as revenue'. What are the implications of this action for assets?
2. What is a class action? Why is it being brought against the auditors?
3. What do you think the auditor's legal defence will be?

Summary

LO 1 — **Issues involved in defining assets and applying those definitions**

Assets give rise to future economic benefits, a concept that is clear but not always easy to apply in practice. Some people have interpreted the definition of assets very narrowly to exclude things such as monuments and statues that help to satisfy the objectives of not-for-profit organisations; others have argued that an asset must be owned by an entity before it can be recorded. Both these views are incorrect under the IASB *Framework*. Similarly, determining the past event that gives rise to a future benefit is sometimes challenging. We have seen that the *Framework* and standards provide guidance, but many issues arise in practice when applying definitions.

LO 2 — **Why recognition and measurement criteria are both important and controversial**

The extent and timing of recognition of assets is important because it can have economic consequences for preparers and users of financial statements. The information presented affects how investors interpret the company's position and performance, thus influencing their investment decisions which can in turn affect the value of the firm. Also, the recognised measures of assets are often used in the calculation of ratios, which are important inputs for debt covenants or rate of return ratios applied in management compensation plans. As such, the application of definition and recognition criteria can affect whether a firm violates its debt covenants and have a bearing on management remuneration.

LO 3 — **The relationship of asset recognition and measurement of income and equity**

We understand that all the elements of accounting are linked and that measurement of income flows from measurement of the change in net assets. Thus, asset measurement is crucial in accounting. Determining asset values which are relevant and also a faithful representation is essential for determining changes in wealth in any given period. Standard setters argue that measurement of assets is the starting point for measuring income; indeed, that it is not possible to measure income in any other way than by considering the change in net assets. Consequently the rules and practices governing asset recognition and measurement will also affect measurement of income and, in turn, equity.

LO 4 — **The implications of use of a mixed attribute measurement model and fair value measurement methods**

Although historical cost (or modified historical cost) is the traditional and dominant measurement method in accounting, there are many instances where alternative measurement methods are used. Financial statement users (such as analysts and investors) have argued that effective decision making requires relevant information and that, in some cases, historical cost measures of assets are simply not adequate. For example, in relation to financial instruments, market values provide a measure of current value which is important when assessing firm value. For some categories of financial assets, historical costs do not capture essential aspects of value of the asset. Current IASB standards make use of a number of valuation approaches, including the common written down (or amortised) cost method which is used for many tangible and intangible assets. Methods which approximate current values include 'fair values'; these may be based on an exit value (an actual or estimated market value) or a value in use (such as a net present value estimation of future cash flows associated with the asset).

LO 5 **Issues arising for standard setters and auditors from current asset recognition and measurement methods**

The mixed attribute measurement model gives rise to many challenges for both standard setters and auditors. We have seen that the IASB's standard setting objective involves producing information which is useful for decision making, an objective which has led the board to incorporate more fair value measurements in accounting standards to improve the relevance of information provided. However, the board's approach is not without its critics, who claim that fair value measurement is too unreliable and subjective to be useful. In this setting, auditors have a crucial role to play. They must be satisfied that all measurements provided in a firm's accounts are appropriate and not unduly and inappropriately influenced by managers' incentives. The 2008–09 financial crisis has brought more attention to the measurement of assets (and liabilities) and to the role of auditors in ensuring that investors and others can rely on measures presented in the accounts.

Questions

1. What attributes must something possess in order to be defined as an asset? Why?
2. The *Framework* defines assets, liabilities and equity by reference to economic benefits.
   (a) What are the economic benefits that would be assets for AlexCorp, a government business enterprise that constructs the physical infrastructure (roads, bridges, etc.) for the city of Huntersville?
   (b) Must economic benefits be revenue-generating, or can parks, roads or statues provide economic benefits?
3. The *Framework* definition of assets requires future economic benefits to be controlled by an entity before they can be regarded as an asset. How does ownership differ from control? Which criterion (ownership or control) do you think should be applied in defining assets? Why?
4. According to the *Framework*, assets do not exist unless they result from past events. Determining whether a past event has occurred to give rise to an asset is not always straightforward. Explain the past event that triggers the existence of the following assets.
   (a) Accounts Receivable
   (b) Prepaid Insurance
   (c) Work-In-Process Inventory
   (d) Raw Materials Inventory
   (e) Finance Lease of Manufacturing Plant
   (f) Goodwill (internally generated or purchased)
5. What is an agreement equally proportionately unperformed (AEPU)? According to strict interpretations of the *Framework* definitions of assets, liabilities and equity, should AEPUs be reported on the balance sheet? Why or why not?

6. Under some market-based systems of accounting, asset definitions require that to be defined as an asset, an economic benefit must be both 'severable and saleable', sometimes described as 'exchangeability'. Is that a requirement in the *Framework* definition of assets? Why or why not? Do you think that severability is necessary to a definition of assets? Why or why not?
7. Are the following assets? If so, whose assets, and why?
    (a) members of the Australian hockey team
    (b) a nine-month lease agreement to rent a business office
    (c) expenditure on research and development
    (d) an unsigned, documented contractual agreement to build specialised equipment for a client
    (e) a building bequeathed to a firm
    (f) a five-year option to acquire property, where the option was purchased by the company a year ago

Problems

PROBLEM 7.1

Su Lamp Ltd, an electrical goods manufacturer, entered into the following transactions during the year 2009. Show how they should have been recorded by Su Lamp Ltd under Australian accounting regulations that year, and comment whether there are any differences in that reporting from what would be recorded if the company reported solely on the basis of *Framework* requirements.

1. Su Lamp Ltd experienced strong profit growth during the early 2000s. However, an industrial dispute in the transport industry affected the supply of electrical parts and the company sustained a $400 000 loss during 2009. The management of Su Lamp Ltd believed that it would be advantageous to carry the loss forward to 2010 for income tax purposes and was confident that there would be sufficient profit in 2010 to absorb the loss carry-forward. The 2009 income tax rate was 30 per cent.
2. At the start of 2009, Su Lamp Ltd entered into a contract with Pollett Ltd. Pollett Ltd was to build a new factory for Su Lamp Ltd, with building to start in January 2010. The contract price was $1 000 000 and the project was estimated to take two years to complete. Su Lamp Ltd was to pay Pollett Ltd $300 000 when the project was 10 per cent completed, $300 000 when it was 50 per cent completed and $400 000 when it was 100 per cent completed.
3. Kin Ltd filed a lawsuit against Su Lamp Ltd for $1 000 000 for patent infringement in April 2009. The companies expected that it would take approximately 18 months before the lawsuit was settled.
4. An employee suffered eye damage when a piece of glass exploded as she worked on the production line. She sued the company for damages and was awarded $400 000. Su Lamp Ltd planned to appeal.
5. Su Lamp Ltd contracted with the local city council to provide high-powered lighting for all function areas at the City Hall. The cost was estimated to be $1 000 000. The contract specifies a payment to Su Lamp Ltd of 15 per cent above cost.
6. At year-end, the executives decided to pay a bonus of $15 000 to their Danish sales manager, Rasmus Winters, for his performance during the year. However, due to cash constraints, the bonus was not to be paid until February 2010.

PROBLEM 7.2

Zanadriana Ltd is a start-up pharmaceuticals company with 50 per cent of its operations in research and development. The following transactions and events occurred in year 1. Record them in the company's accounts in accordance with IFRS. If needed, an appropriate rate of interest is 8 per cent p.a.

1. Zanadriana Ltd spent $250 000 on researching and developing a new product. The research shows high promise of becoming commercially viable.
2. In December, Zanadriana Ltd acquired all the common shares of Austin Power Ltd to ensure a supply of electricity to its remote research facilities. The acquisition was paid for with cash, $2 000 000. Austin Power Ltd will be absorbed into Zanadriana Ltd as a division rather than retaining a separate legal identity. The carrying amounts and market values of the assets on the acquisition date are:

	Carrying amount	Market value
Current assets	$ 140 000	$ 140 000
Land and buildings	1 500 000	1 700 000
Liabilities	150 000	150 000

3. In December, Zanadriana Ltd purchased all the ordinary shares of Bazza's Hickory Ltd in order to acquire the land and buildings of the organisation. The acquisition was paid for with cash, $1 900 000. Bazza's Hickory Ltd will be absorbed into Zanadriana Ltd as a division rather than retaining a separate legal identity. The carrying amounts and market values of the assets on the acquisition date are:

	Carrying amount	Market value
Current assets	$ 240 000	$ 240 000
Land and buildings	1 700 000	1 900 000
Liabilities	150 000	150 000

4. Three years ago, Zanadriana Ltd scientists developed a formula that has not yet been patented, but which is deemed to be worth at least $5 000 000.
5. On 30 November, Zanadriana Ltd entered into a non-cancellable lease of machinery for three years at $50 000 per month, payable at the start of the month, with an option to renew for five years at $3000 per month or to purchase the machines for $40 000 after the three-year lease term. Record whatever entry would be made on 30 November.
6. Zanadriana Ltd has good key staff with ten top-ranking executives who earn combined salaries of $4 000 000 p.a. Each of the executives has contracted to remain in the employ of Zanadriana Ltd for two years, following which a new contract will be negotiated. Confidentiality clauses, forbidding them to disclose information to competitors, have been signed by all of the top executives.

PROBLEM 7.3

Kalmers & Meehan, a taxation partnership, is preparing its 30 June 2011 financial statements, and seeks advice from PK & Slug, a firm of reputable accountants. What advice would PK & Slug offer in relation to accounting for each of the following situations? If a journal entry is required, what should it be?
1. Steph's Tennis World Ltd owes $70 000 for taxation advice throughout the year. The invoice was forwarded in May. Steph's Tennis World Ltd refuses to pay any part of the invoice, on the grounds that it is dissatisfied with the advice it received from Kalmers & Meehan, since the taxation partnership did not 'take a few risks' to reduce the company's tax bill.
2. When Kalmers & Meehan's client Ranch Vineyards Ltd suffered liquidity problems during the year, it agreed to pay Kalmers & Meehan in kind: 50 bottles of its best wines, normally retailing at $100 per bottle, but costing $5 per bottle to produce. Ranch Vineyards Ltd was invoiced on 15 May and has not yet delivered the wine.
3. Kalmers & Meehan spent $3000 on a paved walkway to their firm during May. The entrance was paved in May.

PROBLEM 7.4

Pip Lax Ltd manufactures high-quality sports equipment and sells it under a two-year warranty. The company guarantees to replace any defective parts and repair equipment at no cost to its customers. Record the following events of 2009. The company has a calendar reporting year.

1. During 2009, Pip Lax Ltd spent $800 000 repairing a certain brand of elite-level lacrosse equipment under warranty. Of this, $360 000 related to equipment sold during 2007; the rest related to equipment sold during 2008 and 2009.
2. At year-end, the company estimated repair costs for the outdoor sports equipment it had already sold to be approximately $900 000 in 2010. Of that, $500 000 related to repairs of equipment sold in 2008 and 2009.

PROBLEM 7.5

Sleech Ltd operates an information systems company. The firm is preparing its 30 June financial statements, and requires advice concerning the proper treatment of the following situations. Explain how to deal with each situation, and prepare any required journal entries.

1. Sleech Ltd owns a research laboratory which is uninsurable because of the high risk of competitor spying, and poor security systems. Based on previous experience, management firmly believes that a loss of information systems designs will occur during the year. The average loss per year over the last five years has been $500 000. The company self-insures via an appropriation of retained profits.
2. Ms Shazlick, a key manager of the organisation, is currently contracted to receive incentive payments on the basis of share price movements for the firm. During the year, Sleech Ltd has won some key tenders, and the share price has doubled, meaning that Ms Shazlick has earned shares with a market value of $500 000 for the year just ended.
3. The Freight Transport Union has threatened 14-day national strike action unless certain of its wages demands with another company are met. Negotiations have terminated, and it is expected that the union will strike during February the following year. It is estimated that a strike of 10 days would cause losses of earnings of approximately $1 000 000 because of loss of supply and delivery facilities.
4. During the year, Sleech Ltd completed a contract for Danlon Ltd and Dolland Ltd, organisations collaborating in the development of information systems to enable communications in remote cold locations. Sleech Ltd auditors have uncovered what appears to be overcharging on one invoice. Sleech Ltd is of the opinion that its clients will demand a refund of $75 000.
5. The finance minister of a foreign country in which one of its subsidiaries is located, T.G. Cee, has informed Sleech Ltd of her government's intention to expropriate funds from the subsidiary. T.G. Cee indicates that the best outcome Sleech Ltd could expect is to receive 60 per cent of the fair value of the subsidiary's property as settlement. The carrying amount of the (wholly owned) subsidiary is $12 900 000 and the estimated fair value is $15 000 000.

Additional readings

Deloitte, IAS PLUS, IAS 41 *Agriculture*, www.iasplus.com.

Feltham, GA, & Ohlson JA 1995, 'Valuation and clean surplus accounting for operating and financial activities', *Contemporary Accounting Research*, Spring, vol. 11, no. 2, pp. 689.

G4+1 Study 1996, 'Accounting for leases: a new approach', July, www.iasplus.com.

Landsman, W 2007, 'Is financial accounting information relevant and reliable? Evidence from capital market research', *Accounting and Business Research*, Special issue, pp. 19–30.

Langendijk, H, Swagerman, D, & Verhoog, W (eds) 2003, *Is fair value fair? Financial reporting from an international perspective*, Chichester: John Wiley & Sons, Inc.

Staubus, GJ 1985, 'An induced theory of accounting measurement', *The Accounting Review*, vol. 60, no. 1, pp. 53–75.

Watts, R 2003, 'Conservatism in accounting, Part I: Explanations and implications', *Accounting Horizons*, vol. 17, no. 4, pp. 207–21.

Watts, R 2003, 'Conservatism in Accounting Part II: Evidence and research opportunities', *Accounting Horizons*, vol. 17, no. 4, pp. 287–301.

Wyatt, A 2008, 'What financial and non-financial information on intangibles is value relevant? A review of the evidence', *Accounting and Business Research*, vol. 38, no. 3, pp. 217–256, http://ssrn.com.

Zeff, S 2007, 'The SEC rules historical cost accounting 1934 to 1970s', *Accounting and Business Research*, vol. 37, no. 1, p. 48.

7.1
CASE STUDY

Heritage assets

In 2006, the United Kingdom Accounting Standards Board proposed that heritage assets such as art collections and buildings be shown on the balance sheets of the institutions which hold them. Barker (2006) explains that heritage assets are defined as assets with historic, artistic, scientific, technological, geophysical or environmental qualities that are held and maintained principally for their contribution to knowledge and culture when this purpose is central to the objectives of the reporting entity. She adds that since most heritage assets do not move through the market place frequently, there is a problem in valuing heritage assets. The UK exposure draft proposed that heritage assets should be capitalized if it is practicable to obtain valuations and such valuations provide useful and relevant information.

Answer the following questions about the issue of recognising the value of heritage assets in the financial statements of the organisations which are responsible for the assets.

Reference
Barker, P 2006, 'Heritage assets can accounting do better?', *Accountancy Ireland*, vol. 38, iss. 4, p. 48.

Questions
1. In what ways are heritage assets similar to the assets of for-profit entities and in what ways are they different?
2. Is it appropriate to recognise a heritage asset in the financial statements of the entity which has custody of and responsibility for the asset?
3. Are there users for the information about the value of heritage assets?
4. Can a financial value be assigned to a heritage asset?

7.2
CASE STUDY

Intangible assets

The value of intangible assets is important in a knowledge-based economy. The market value of many listed companies exceeds their book value, reflecting intangible assets which are not recognised on companies' balance sheets. Such intangible assets include brands, innovation and customer relationships. Despite the importance of intangible assets, accounting standards permit only limited recognition of such assets, partially because of the difficulties associated with reliable measurement. We list below a number of intangible assets and also several approaches which can be used when valuing intangible assets.

Question

Consider the following four valuation methodologies.

1. *cost approach* (the after tax cost which would be incurred in reproducing the asset)
2. *market transaction* (actual transaction value for identical or similar asset based on an arm's length market transaction)
3. *income method* (excess earnings: the present value of future earnings generated by the intangible asset net of a reasonable return on other assets contributing to the stream of earnings)
4. *income method* (relief from royalty approach: the present value of the likely future royalty stream which would be earned from licensing out the intangible asset to a third party)

Reference

Anderson, N 2004, 'Financial reporting — Implementing IFRS 3 and IAS 38 value judgements', *Accountancy*, 12 October.

Which of the above approaches are appropriate for each intangible asset listed below? Explain your answers.

(a) brands and trade marks
(b) patents
(c) customer contract
(d) internally generated computer software

7.3
CASE STUDY

Bankers: Fair value is like throwing gasoline on a fire

Claiming a "mixed attribute" accounting model provides a better picture of a company's business and earnings engine, bank trade groups blast full fair value.

by Marie Leone

Trade groups representing the international banking community say that current accounting standards requiring fair-value measurement of financial instruments are, as American Bankers Association president and CEO Edward Yingling put it in a statement, "a step in the wrong direction."

The ABA and its international counterpart, the International Banking Federation, contend that full fair-value measurement, as proposed by U.S. and international accounting standard setters, is appropriate for financial instruments that are held for trading purposes. However, for assets and liabilities that are not based around short-term trading, or are held to maturity — such as loans, deposits, and receivables — fair-value measurement leads to income statement volatility (undertatements and overstatements), according to the groups.

The bankers are complaining about FASB and IASB's recent "Invitation to Comment" discussion paper, which calls for fair value for financial instruments, and rules such as the Financial Accounting Standards Board's FAS 159 *The Fair Value Option for Financial Assets and Financial Liabilities*, and the International Accounting Standards Board's IAS 39 *Financial Instruments: Recognition and Measurement*, as well as FAS 157, *Fair Value Measurement*. Indeed, FAS 159 give companies the irrevocable option to use the fair value option for most financial instruments, but bankers are not keen on rules that mandate the full fair value model. (Fair-value measurement is not required for non-financial assets, so far.)

Instead, bankers prefer a mixed-attribute financial reporting model to a strict fair-value regime for financial instruments. A mixed-attribute model is one that uses both fair value and historical cost calculations. To illustrate the bankers' point, the banking groups suggest looking at a loan.

Consider that loans are held to generate income via receiving interest over time until final maturity or until called. As a result, the expected cash flows of a loan and the matching receivables are known, because they are contractual, and the asset and liabilities are recorded as amortized costs. Further, the amortized costs are transparent to investors, as is the impact of the loan payments or receivables on future income statements, explains an IBFed report, "Accounting for Financial Instruments Conceptual Paper." However, in this case, a fair value calculation that requires a periodic mark-to-mark update of the loan could lead to a less predictive value because expected future cash flows are not always represented, argues IBFed.

"Fair-value accounting may have value where it is both relevant and can be reliably determined," acknowledges Yingling. But, absent relevance and reliability, IBFed is calling for a more "useful" way to measure the real financial conditions and value of assets and liabilities. "Under the stress of current market conditions, accounting policy should focus on measuring the heat of the flame instead of pouring gasoline on the fire," declares Yingling.

The discussion paper on fair-value measurement released by the International Accounting Standards Board, "offers a choice between full fair value today and full fair value tomorrow," noted Sally Scutt, CEO of IBFed, in a press statement. "This is at odds with the banking industry's view that a mixed measurement model is essential for the faithful representation of an entity's business model and how it generates earnings."

The bankers' reaction to full fair value underscores their fervor about an issue that is still up for debate. While FASB released FAS 157, *Fair Value Measurement* — the rule that tells companies how to fair-value assets and liabilities — in 2007, the board is still discussing fair value proposals — including how to fair value leases and pension obligations. What's more, the idea of full fair value remains a part of the gargantuan effort by FASB and IASB to shape a conceptual framework that defines fair value for accounting purposes. "Nothing is happening real quickly to change those things," says FASB chairman Robert Herz.

Nevertheless, Herz thinks bankers may be somewhat off-base about using a mixed-attribute model for financial instruments. He points out that currently, companies are required to take a write-down if asset value falls significantly, and carry whole loans at cost. "If the banking community is arguing that it doesn't want to take that kind of write down, it is being a little Pollyanna-ish," Herz tells CFO.com.

The ABA says that while impairment is a different issue, it agrees that items permanently impaired should be written down. However, the group does not believe other assets or liabilites should be written up or down for the purposes of fair value measurement.

Regarding the concept of measuring loans at fair value, Herz points out three counter arguments to the bankers' claims: loans are a financial instrument and should be covered by any rule that affects those instruments; loans are not always held to maturity; and loans are increasingly parceled out through securitizations, which gives them a short-term feel. "The old originate and hold model has been replaced by the originate and distribute model," contends Herz.

Meanwhile, investors are calling for more fair value. In a March survey that polled 2,000 investment professionals, the CFA Institute found that 79 percent of the respondents said that fair value requirements for financial institutions improve transparency and contribute to investor understanding of the risk profiles of the institutions. Meanwhile, 74 percent thought fair value requirements "improve" market integrity, in general.

In addition, in its 2007 report, "A Comprehensive Business Reporting Model: Financial Reporting for Investors," the CFA Institute, argued that fair value accounting was "useful" in calculating whether loans would be repaid, "because fair values are likely to reflect the most up-to-date market assessments of that probability."

On the flip side, the CFA Institute complained that the mixed-attribute model unduly burdens investors that rely on fair values to make decisions. That's because reworking historical cost calculations depends on the quality of the reporting company's disclosures. "Most, if not all, of this effort would be eliminated if the financial reporting standards were to require that companies record assets and liabilities at fair value at the inception with periodic revaluation."

Source: 'Today in Finance for April 14, 2008', CFO.com US, www.cfo.com , © CFO Publishing Corporation 2009. All rights reserved.

Question
Based on the material presented in this article and in the chapter, compare and contrast views about the fair value measurement model and the mixed attribute measurement model.

Endnotes

1. W Paton, *Accounting theory*, Kansas: Scholars Book Company, 1962, originally published 1922, p. 30.
2. C Sprague, *The philosophy of accounts*, New York: Scholars Book Co., 1907, p. 46.
3. J Canning, *The economics of accountancy*, New York: Ronald Press, 1929, p. 188.
4. W Paton and AC Littleton, *An Introduction to corporate accounting standards*, Florida: AAA, 1940, p. 13.
5. W Vatter, *The fund theory of accounting and its implications for financial reporting*, Chicago: University of Chicago, 1947, p. 17.
6. G Peirson, 'ED 42 Proposed Statement of Accounting Concepts (part 2)', *Accounting Communique*, no. 10, Melbourne: Australian Society of Certified Practising Accountants, 1988, p. 1.
7. Y Ijiri, *The foundations of accounting measurement*, Englewood Cliffs, NJ: Prentice-Hall, 1967, p. 69.
8. Sprague op. cit., p. 44.
9. W Paton op. cit., p. 56.
10. Y Ijiri, *Recognition of contractual rights and obligations*, Stamford, Conn.: FASB, 1980, p. 8.
11. ibid., pp. 65–7.
12. K MacNeal, *Truth in accounting*, Houston, Texas: University of Pennsylvania, 1939, p. 90.
13. R Chambers, *Accounting, evaluation and economic behaviour*, Englewood Cliffs, NJ: Prentice-Hall, 1966, pp. 209–10.
14. ibid., p. 210.
15. M Moonitz, The basic postulates of accounting, Accounting Research Study No. 1, New York: AICPA, 1961, p. 18.
16. For evidence of this see J Kirkness, 'The impact of AAS 18', *Chartered Accountant in Australia*, December 1987, pp. 49–51; ME Bradbury, JM Godfrey and PS Koh, 'Investment opportunity set influence on goodwill amortisation', *Asia Pacific Journal of Accounting and Economics*, vol. 10, iss. 1, 2003, pp. 57–79; T Abrahams and BK Sidhu, 'The role of R&D capitalizations in firm valuation and performance measurement', *Australian Journal of Management*, vol. 23, no. 2, 1998, pp. 169–84; JM Godfrey and PS Koh, 'The relevance to firm valuation of capitalising intangible assets in total and by category', *Australian Accounting Review*, vol. 11, iss. 2, 2001, pp. 39–48.
17. Australian Accounting Standards Board (AASB) Discussion Paper Initial Accounting for Internally Generated Intangible Assets, October 2008, www.aasb.gov.au.
18. S Zeff, 'Evolution of US Generally Accepted Accounting Principles (GAAP)', www.iasplus.com.
19. D Cairns, 'The use of fair value in IFRS', *Accounting in Europe*, vol. 3, iss. 1, 2007, pp. 5–22.
20. IAS 40 is a newer standard than IAS 16. Its terminology reflects the passage of time. The term 'fair value model' is used rather than 'revaluation model' as in IAS 16. In practice, there would seem to be no difference between a revaluation model of IAS 16 and a fair value model of IAS 40.
21. D Aboody, M Barth, and R Kasznik, 'Revaluations of fixed assets and future company performance: evidence from the UK', *Journal of Accounting and Economics*, vol. 26, 1999, pp. 149–78.
22. M Barth and G Clinch, Revalued financial tangible and intangible assets: Associations with share prices and non market based value estimates, *Journal of Accounting Research*, vol. 36, Supplement, 1998, pp. 199–233.
23. P Brown, H Izan, and A Loh, 'Fixed asset revaluations and managerial incentives', *Abacus*, vol. 28, 1992, pp. 36–57; J Cotter and I Zimmer, 'Asset revaluations and assessment of borrowing capacity', *Abacus*, vol. 31, 1995, pp. 136–151; G Whittred and Y Chan, 'Asset revaluations and mitigation of underinvestment', *Abacus*, vol. 28, 1992, pp. 58–74.
24. Y Lin and K Peasnell, 'Fixed asset revaluation and equity depletion in the UK', *Journal of Business, Finance and Accounting*, vol. 27 nos 3 & 4, 2000a, pp. 359–94; Y Lin and K Peasnell, 'Asset revaluation and current cost accounting: UK corporate disclosure decisions in 1983', *British Accounting Review*, vol. 32, 2000b, pp. 161–87.
25. Aboody et al. 1999, op cit.

26. Zeff op cit., p. 11.
27. Barth and Clinch 1998, op. cit.
28. J Horton, 'The value relevance of 'realistic reporting': evidence from UK life insurers', *Accounting and Business Research*, vol. 37, no. 3, 2007, pp. 175–97.
29. C Casey and M Sandretto, 'Internal uses of accounting for inflation', *Harvard Business Review*, November–December 1981.
30. P Frishkoff, *Financial reporting and changing prices: A review of empirical research*, Stamford, Conn.: FASB, 1982.
31. R Adkerson, 'Discussion of DAAM: The demand for alternative accounting measurements', *Journal of Accounting Research*, Supplement, 1978.
32. S Basu, *Inflation accounting, capital market efficiency and security prices*, Ontario: Society of Management Accountants of Canada, 1977.
33. Cairns, op. cit.
34. ibid.
35. E Nusbaum, 'Top 10 wish list for audit research', *Current Issues in Auditing*, vol. 1, 2007, C3–C9.
36. ibid., C7.
37. R Martin, J Rich and T Wilks, 'Auditing fair value measurements: a synthesis of relevant research, *Accounting Horizons*, vol. 20, no. 3, 2006, pp. 287–303.
38. Auditing Standard ASA 545 *Auditing Fair Value Measurements and Disclosures*, April 2006 paragraphs 15, 47.
39. D Reilly, 'Wave of write-offs rattles market; Accounting rules blasted as Dow falls; A $600 billion toll?' *Wall Street Journal (Eastern Edition)*, March 1, 2008, A1.
40. J Morrissey, 'Panel calls fair value scapegoat of credit mess', *Pensions & Investments*, April 28, 2008, vol. 36, no. 9, p. 37.
41. Public Company Accounting Oversight Board (PCAOB), 'Report on the PCAOB's 2004, 2005, and 2006 inspections of domestic triennially inspected firms', Release No. 2007-010 October 22, 2007, p. 10, www.pcaobus.org.
42. PCAOB, op. cit., p. 10.
43. Accounting Standard AASB 3 *Business Combinations*, October 2007, paragraph 36.
44. PCAOB, op. cit., p. 10.

8 Liabilities and owners' equity

LEARNING OBJECTIVES

After reading this chapter, you should have an appreciation of the following:

1 the proprietary and entity perspectives of the firm

2 issues involved in defining liabilities and equity, applying those definitions, and why the definition and recognition criteria are important

3 current measurement practices in relation to liabilities and equity

4 challenging issues for standard setters and auditors.

A firm holds assets because either owners or other parties have supplied funds to acquire the assets. Therefore, the total amount of assets is subject to claims by some party or parties, usually to pay money. There are two kinds of claims: by creditors (liabilities) and by owners (owners' equity). The rights of creditors and owners are different. Creditors have a prior claim on the assets in case of liquidation and their claims are almost always more specific than those of owners with respect to the amount and the timing of payment. The claims of creditors are obligations of the reporting entity, whereas the entity is not obliged, usually, to make any specific transfer of assets to the owners. Indeed, when an obligation arises, such as when a dividend is declared, the claim of owners becomes a liability (i.e. dividends payable). As such, liabilities are present obligations of an entity, whereas owners' equity is a residual interest or claim, but not an obligation to transfer assets.

In this chapter, we first consider two theories which underlie accounting, namely the proprietary and entity theories. Next, we explore the definition, recognition criteria and measurement of liabilities and owners' equity. As in other chapters, we refer to the IASB/AASB *Framework for the Preparation and Presentation of Financial Statements* to examine the guidance provided by standard setters. We also discuss issues arising in practice when applying the definition and recognition criteria for liabilities and equity. Finally, we consider current challenging issues for standard setters and auditors in relation to liabilities and equity.

LO 1 ⊢ PROPRIETARY AND ENTITY THEORY

In this section we outline two theories which have been proposed to help us understand accounting, namely proprietary theory and entity theory. Proprietary theory is based on the idea that the proprietor (or owner) is the centre of attention. Under this view, all accounting concepts, procedures and rules are formulated with the owner's interest in mind. In contrast, entity theory proposes that the business is a separate entity and accounting records the transactions of the entity.

Proprietary theory

Proprietorship represents the net worth of the business and can be represented in the accounting equation:

$$P = A - L$$

Where proprietorship (or owner's equity) is equal to assets less liabilities. P represents the net worth of the owner of the business. As Sprague states:

> The balance sheet of proprietorship is a summing-up at some particular time of all the elements which constitute the wealth of some person or collection of persons . . . The whole purpose of the business struggle is increase of wealth, that is, increase of proprietorship.[1]

Assets belong to the proprietor and liabilities are the obligations of the proprietor. In this light, we can see that the objective of accounting is to determine the net worth of the owner. The economic theory of the firm takes a proprietary view, with its emphasis on the role of the entrepreneur-owner. The concept of income, which increases net worth, is seen as a return for 'entrepreneurship'.

Income is earned, and expenses are incurred, because of the decisions and actions of the owner or the owner's representative. Income and expense accounts are subsidiary accounts of P, which are temporarily segregated for the purpose of determining the profit of the owner. Income is the increase in proprietorship; expense is the decrease in proprietorship. Vatter explains:

> The theory of double entry is based on the idea that expense and revenue accounts have the same algebraic characteristics as 'net worth', i.e. accounts tending to increase net worth are increased by credits, accounts tending to decrease net worth are handled in reverse order.[2]

Net income is, therefore, the increase in the wealth of the owner from business operations during a given period. If this is what income represents, then it should include all aspects that affect the change in the owner's wealth in that given period. Thus, change in net worth derives from income-generating activities as well as changes in value of assets. For example, the intrinsic value of a newspaper masthead may increase in value and could attract a significant premium to the owner if realised (sold). In such cases, the argument is that the increase in net wealth of the proprietor should be recognised, even though the change in wealth is notional until such time as the newspaper is actually sold to a third party. The problem for accounting is measuring the notional change in value.

To a large extent, present accounting practice is based on the proprietary theory. Dividends are considered a distribution of profits rather than expenses because they are payments to owners. On the other hand, interest on debt and income tax are considered expenses because they reduce the owner's wealth. For a sole proprietorship and partnership, salaries paid to owners who work in the business are not considered an expense, because the owner and the firm are the same entity and one cannot pay oneself and deduct that as an expense. The equity method for long-term investments recognises the ownership or proprietary interest of the investor company. It therefore authorises the investor company to record as profit its percentage share of the investee's profit. In consolidating financial statements, the parent company method is based on the proprietary theory. The parent company is seen as 'owning' the subsidiary. Minority interest, from the point of view of the 'owner' of the subsidiary, represents the claims of a group of outsiders. The extent of the minority interest is shown as a reduction in proprietorship.

A financial capital rather than a physical capital view is appropriate under proprietary theory. The former emphasises the financial investment of the owners, whereas the latter focuses on the firm's ability to maintain its physical operating level without any regard to ownership claims. The proprietary view sees no distinction between the assets of the proprietor and the assets of the entity. Therefore, all of the entity's profit is distributable to the owners of the firm. If the entity requires additional resources, these funds are available from the proprietor's own personal resources. Capital represents the cash invested by the owners plus profits reinvested by retention in the business. Most people adopt a financial view of capital and it is also the position taken in traditional conventional accounting practices.

The proprietary view of accounting was developed at a time when businesses were small and were mainly proprietorships and partnerships. However, with the advent of the company, the theory has proved inadequate as a basis for explaining company accounting. By law, the company is a separate entity from the owners and has its own rights. As such, the company, not the shareholders, takes possession of the assets and assumes the obligations of the business. Not only do companies assume the obligations of the business, but also the feature of limited liability makes it absurd to say that shareholders are responsible for the liabilities of the company. If shareholders of a large company wished to exercise their presumed rights of ownership by withdrawing assets from it, they would run foul of the law. Withdrawals of cash (dividends) are really distributions by formal legal procedures.

Accountability to owners is a significant function for a large company because of the gap between management and shareholders. For the small firm, owners are aware of the financial status of the business so that the notion of accountability or stewardship is not as meaningful. In contrast, the contact of shareholders with the affairs of the large company is at best minimal. Shareholders therefore depend on the information reported to them by management.

However, there are cases where large companies are linked to one or a few key individuals or a controlling organisation, in which the wealth of the key owner(s) and the organisation are practically inseparable. An example is Rupert Murdoch and News Corporation. In such cases, proprietary theory is still relevant.

Entity theory

The entity theory was formulated in response to the shortcomings of the proprietary view concerning the separate legal status of a company. The theory starts with the fact that the company is a separate entity with its own identity. The theory goes beyond the 'accounting entity assumption' regarding the separation of business and personal affairs. Martin outlined the two related assumptions embodied in the notion of an accounting entity:

- *Separation.* For accounting purposes, the enterprise is separated from its owners.
- *Viewpoint.* Accounting procedures are conducted from the viewpoint of the entity.[3]

Although the entity theory is especially suitable for corporate accounting, supporters believe that it can be applied to proprietorships, partnerships and even to not-for-profit organisations, providing:

- the accounts and transactions are classified and analysed from the point of view of the entity as an operating unit; and
- accounting principles and procedures are not formulated in terms of a single interest, such as proprietorship.

Paton states, for any business firm:

> It is the 'business' whose financial history the bookkeeper and accountant are trying to record and analyse; the books and accounts are the record of 'the business'; the periodic statements of operations and financial condition are the reports of 'the business'.[4]

It is true that the entity is not a person and cannot act of its own accord. It is an institution, but nonetheless it is a 'very real thing', argues Paton.[5] It has a real and measurable existence, even a personality of its own. For a company, once the share capital is issued, the life of the company does not depend on the lives of its shareholders. Broadly speaking, from an accounting perspective, an entity can be defined as any area of economic interest that has a separate existence from its owners.

When an entity perspective is taken, the objective of accounting may be stewardship or accountability. The traditional version of the entity theory is that the business firm operates for the benefit of the equityholders, those who provide funds for the entity. The entity must therefore report to equityholders the status and consequences of their investment. The newer interpretation sees the entity as in business for itself and interested in its own survival. Because it is concerned about its survival, the business entity reports to equityholders in order to meet legal requirements and to maintain a good relationship with them in case more funds are needed in the future.

Although both versions focus on the entity as an independent unit, the traditional view looks on the equityholders as 'associates' in business, whereas the more recent view sees them as outsiders. The information content of accounting statements for decision making, which has been emphasised in recent years, can be easily assimilated into both interpretations of the entity theory.

Under entity theory, the focus of the accounting equation is assets and equities. Net worth of the proprietor is not a meaningful concept, because the entity is the centre of attention. Owners and creditors are seen simply as equityholders, providers of funds. The accounting equation is thus:

$$\text{Assets} = \text{equities}$$

The balance sheet shows the assets of the entity, which Paton refers to as representing a 'direct' statement of value for the entity, and equities, which he calls an 'indirect' expression of the same total.[6] The assets belong to the firm and the liabilities are the obligations of the firm, not the owners. It has been argued that because the amount invested by the equityholders must be accounted for, this objective logically leads to the use of historical cost for non-monetary assets, because the total on the right side of the statement of financial position must equal the total on the left. After receiving the funds provided by the equityholders, the firm invests the funds in assets. For non-monetary assets, this is the original purchase price. But accountability does not necessarily imply keeping track of the original amount of investment. Equityholders are also interested in changes in the value of their investment. Current value advocates point out that the entity theory assumes that investors are not close enough to the business to make their own adjustments of values. Therefore, accountability should imply that these adjustments, namely changes in values, are reported. It can also be argued that the entity needs to know the current values of its assets in order to make correct decisions.

Under the entity view, income is defined as the inflow of assets due to the transactions undertaken by the firm and expense relates to the cost of the assets and other services used up by the firm to create the income for the period. Expenses reduce the worth of the entity's assets. The proprietary concept concentrates on the P of the accounting equation. The entity concept focuses on the other side of the equation, the assets. This is because assets are seen as the 'real' things the firm has to work with, whereas the equities are more abstract, having to do with claims on the assets — an 'indirect' way, as Paton put it, of viewing the value of the assets.

Assets and expenses are essentially the same in nature; they provide services. It is simply a question of whether the services are used up or remain for future use. The basic characteristic of income is that it creates more assets whereas expenses eventually diminish assets:

> Accounting theory, therefore, should explain the concepts of revenue [income] and expense in terms of enterprise asset changes rather than as increases or decreases in proprietors' or shareholders' equities.[7]

Net income accrues to the firm. If that is so, why then is it closed to retained earnings as though it belongs to the shareholders? Paton and Littleton argue that the shareholders have a contractual residual claim on the total assets, and it is for this reason that net income is placed in retained earnings.[8] The shareholders get the residual, the remainder, after the creditors have been paid in the event of liquidation of the firm. This explanation evolves from the conventional version of equity theory. The newer interpretation sees the retained earnings account as the firm's equity or investment in itself.[9] Payments for the use of money are expenses because both creditors and shareholders are considered external parties. Therefore, interest charges and dividends, as well as income tax, are expenses of the business. They reduce the amount of equity the entity has in itself.

In conclusion, we can say that both proprietary and entity theories are influential in practice. Conventional accounting theory is based on the entity concept, and financial reports reflect an entity view, with their focus on dividends and earnings per share. Companies trade in their own shares, which suggests the market accepts that they are separate entities. However, the proprietary view is also influential. For example, based on the proprietary concept, interest charges are considered an expense and dividends a distribution of profit. Theory in action 8.1 considers proprietary and entity theory in a practical setting by examining the ownership structure of the United Kingdom's Barclays Bank.

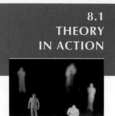

8.1 THEORY IN ACTION

Entity vs proprietorship perspective

Worst may be over but thorny problems remain

by Peter Thal Larsen

When John Varley and Marcus Agius take the stage at Barclays' annual meeting in a fortnight's time, the chief executive and chairman of the banking group will be braced for some strident words from shareholders. But they will also be hoping they are over the worst.

Just a few months ago, Barclays was fighting off speculation the bank would be forced to turn to the British government for financial help. Investors were still seething about the bank's decision to turn to Middle Eastern investors for £7bn in fresh capital last autumn, bypassing existing shareholders. Opposition politicians were raising questions about Barclays' aggressive tax structuring activities.

The episode was the culmination of a frenzied 18-month period in which Barclays executives tried in vain to persuade critics who questioned whether the bank had genuinely weathered the financial crisis in better shape than rivals such as Royal Bank of Scotland, which was forced into national ownership after suffering hefty losses.

In the past few weeks, however, there have been signs that the storm is easing. Most notably, the Financial Services Authority last month concluded the bank had enough capital to withstand even a severe global economic downturn. The bank is close to boosting its capital reserves further by selling iShares, its exchange-traded funds subsidiary, to CVC, the private equity group. Barclays shares have trebled in value since late January. They closed yesterday at 157.8p, up 0.1p.

Barclays Capital — the investment banking business that prompted much suspicion and speculation during the credit crisis — is also one reason for the bank's new bounce. Its opportunistic acquisition of the US assets of Lehman Brothers, combined with troubles at some rivals, have boosted revenue. The bank traded twice as much foreign exchange in the first quarter as in the same period two years ago. Fixed-income trading volumes were up 65 per cent in the same period.

Nevertheless, Mr Varley and Mr Agius continue to face several thorny problems. First, the bank's capital ratios continue to look weak. Though Barclays' tier one ratio — a key measure of balance sheet strength — is roughly the same as HSBC's, its capital base includes a higher proportion of hybrid debt. The sale of the exchange-traded funds business of iShares, which could be announced as early as today, will help boost its equity capital. The bank could boost its capital ratios further by buying back hybrid debt instruments at a discount to face value, though it would have to be careful not to upset the investors who are large buyers of debt that Barclays Capital issues on behalf of other borrowers.

Some investors remain concerned about aspects of Barclays' balance sheet, such as packages of corporate loans whose value is protected by ailing monoline insurers. But people close to the bank point out that the FSA's stress test, which took several weeks and assumed a severe five-year downturn in the bank's main markets, including the UK, US and Spain, would have examined these exposures.

Barclays also badly needs to patch up strained relations with the British government. That is why the bank is expected in the next few weeks to sign up to commitments to new lending in return for increasing its use of the government's credit guarantee scheme.

If the recent revival can be sustained, Mr Varley's determination to keep Barclays clear of government intervention will have been vindicated. Given the ongoing recession and the precarious state of parts of the financial system, however, it is probably too soon for the bank to declare victory.

Source: The Financial Times Limited, 9 April 2009.

Questions
1. Explain the ways in which Barclays Bank has increased its equity in the past year. Why was raising more equity important in the 2007–08 economic conditions?
2. Describe the process by which the sale of its funds subsidiary iShares could 'boost capital reserves further'?
3. Does the writer of the article take an entity view or proprietorship view of Barclays Bank?
4. Could the proprietorship perspective apply to Barclays Bank if the UK government took an ownership (equity) interest in the bank, as occurred at Royal Bank of Scotland?

LO 2 — LIABILITIES DEFINED

Liabilities are a key element in accounting. We now consider how to define liabilities, when they should be recognised in the accounts and how to measure them.

The IASB *Framework* paragraph 49(b) defines a liability as:

a present obligation of the entity arising from past events, the settlement of which is expected to result in an outflow from the entity of resources embodying economic benefits.

We examine this definition in terms of its two main components:
- the existence of a present obligation, requiring a future settlement
- the result of a past transaction or other past event.

Present obligation

The *Framework* definition states that liabilities are expected to give rise to an outflow of economic benefits. This definition, similar to that for assets, focuses on a 'future event'. As such, the actual sacrifices are yet to be made. The underlying consideration is that an obligation is already present in relation to the future sacrifice. For example, accounts payable are a current obligation, arising from the provision of services (the past event) by external parties. Planned maintenance can be a liability if there is a present obligation to an external party (i.e. a contract) to complete the maintenance. A plan to complete maintenance in the future without the commitment to an external party will not give rise to a present obligation under the *Framework*.

The *Framework*, paragraph 62, recognises that settlement of the obligation could occur in several ways such as cash payment, transfer of other assets, provision of services, replacement of the obligation with another obligation, conversion of the obligation to equity, or a creditor waiving the obligation. Of these methods of settling an obligation, only the first two necessarily involve the outflow of assets recognised by the entity. For example, accounts payable will be settled by cash (the outflow of an asset) while a liability for unearned revenue (revenue paid in advance) is settled by the provision of goods or services.

Past transaction

The requirement that an obligation must be the result of a past event ensures that only present liabilities are recorded and not future ones. As in the maintenance example on the previous page, the past event of signing the contract for maintenance gives rise to the present liability. However, the condition of past event may be difficult to interpret. What kind of past event is acceptable? This qualification is critical in determining whether there is an obligation in the first place. When a company places an order with a supplier to purchase inventory, present rules prescribe that there is no obligation until the goods are received or until title passes. Therefore, the past event in this case is the receipt of the goods, not the placement of the order.

Wholly executory contracts provide an interesting case for interpreting the term 'past event'. The question is whether the signing of a contract creates a liability? For example, is an unconditional purchase obligation a liability? Consider the situation where the purchaser agrees to pay a certain amount periodically in return for products or services, and these payments are to be made regardless of whether the purchaser takes delivery of the products or services. The purchaser is obligated to make the periodic payments, even if the service fails to ship the minimum quantity. At this stage, there is an agreement between two parties, which is unperformed by both. Assuming that the purchaser must make payments regardless of whether the products or services are received, an obligation to sacrifice future economic benefits (by paying cash) to another entity exists from the signing of the contract. Therefore, the unconditional purchase obligation constitutes a liability, which arises from the past event of signing the contract. The obligation exists even though it is unperformed.

Other examples can be used to illustrate the importance of correct interpretation of present obligation and past event. When an extractive industry company commences mining, does it have a present obligation to restore the mine site? The answer is yes, if under law the company has an obligation for restoration in the future as a result of the past event of beginning mining operations. Restoration will involve the outflow of future economic benefits (cash payments in relation to restoration activity). Another example relates to airline reward schemes. Do frequent flyer points give rise to a liability for the airline? One must consider whether the awarding of points creates a present obligation to sacrifice benefits in the future. We can argue that it does and that the past event is the act of buying a ticket and travelling on the flight. Following the flight, the airline awards points, which creates an obligation to be settled in the future by providing a service (giving a free seat to the holder of the points).

Liability recognition

Background

Once the definition of a liability is met, accountants need rules to determine if it should be recognised. The type of rules which have been applied in the past are similar to those applied to the recognition of assets. They include:
- reliance on the law
- determination of the economic substance of the event
- ability to measure the value of the liability
- use of the conservatism principle.

If there is a legally enforceable claim, there is little doubt that a liability exists. Although equitable or constructive obligations are embraced in the definition of a liability, most liabilities are determined on the basis of whether there is a legal claim against the entity that it is obliged to meet. The obligation for restoration of mining operations is a legal obligation if the law requires restoration but it could also be considered an equitable one (i.e. it is only fair that the land be restored to allow use by others in the future).

The second criterion requires that we consider the economic substance of a transaction. Has some 'real' obligation arisen? How important to users is the recording and eventual display of a liability in the balance sheet? The James Hardie Company found that some of its employees and their families were developing illnesses as a consequence of mining and living among asbestos in Wittenoom in Western Australia. The company recognised it had a 'real' obligation to provide compensation for sufferers of asbestos-related diseases. It also knew that shareholders, investors and employees (the users of financial information) would be vitally concerned with the amount shown in the balance sheet for the liability (i.e. the estimate of the company's obligation). Shareholders and investors were concerned about the magnitude of the outflow of economic benefits associated with settling compensation claims, while the employees and their families were concerned about how much the company had provided to meet their present and potential future claims. In recent years, many stakeholders (such as shareholders, creditors, employees and community groups) have become increasingly concerned about the liability of companies in relation to their impact on the environment. Questions about accounting for environmental liabilities are considered in case study 8.1.

Another example about economic substance relates to how we account for a converting note transaction (a hybrid security). Suppose a company borrows $10 000 from a bank and promises to repay the loan by giving 1000 of its own ordinary shares. In essence, this is a converting note but does it give rise to a liability? Converting notes are instruments that confer a stream of interest payments for a defined period of time, after which the notes must be converted into shares. Should we recognise a liability until such time as the note converts, when equity is created, even though there is no future outflow of economic benefits? It can be argued that we should, because a failure to record the obligation of the transaction until equity is issued may fail to record its economic substance.

The third criterion relates to determining the value of liabilities. For some liabilities, value is represented by a contract price, such as the amount of cash to be paid for the goods and services received. In the case of employee leave benefits, the nominal amount of the liability represents the amount to be paid to extinguish the liability. However, the value of the liability may be different to its nominal amount. For example, if the liability involves a period longer than 12 months (such as in the case of long service leave) we must consider the time value of money. Therefore the calculation of the value of the liability will be based on the present value of expected future cash flows, not its nominal amount.

Historically, accountants have taken a conservative approach to the recognition of assets and liabilities. Generally speaking, they are more likely to record liabilities earlier than assets. After all, it is 'safer' to understate assets than liabilities. For example, a company may adopt the higher of estimates of expected future damages in a legal case, to ensure that the liability is sufficiently covered and to avoid an additional outflow in the future. Such an approach is described as prudence in the IASB/AASB *Framework* paragraph 37. However, there is a major problem with a company's decision to adopt a conservative approach to measurement. At what point is the company too conservative, so that a bias is introduced into measurement? Decision makers seek neutral (i.e. unbiased) information in order to make decisions. If information is biased, because the company wants to portray a particular picture through its financial information, decision makers have 'noisy' information on which to base their decision. In fact, they could even make a different decision if unbiased information was presented. Thus, it can be argued that 'information free from bias' (*Framework*, para. 36) is essential for effective decision making.

IASB *Framework*

The IASB *Framework* provides guidance in relation to the recognition of balance sheet and income statement elements. Paragraph 82 states that an item that meets the definition of an element should be recognised if:

(a) it is probable that any future economic benefit associated with the items will flow to or from the entity; and
(b) the item has a cost or value that can be measured with reliability.

Paragraph 91 gives additional specific guidance. It states that a liability is recognised in the balance sheet when it is probable that an outflow of resources embodying economic benefits will result from the settlement of a present obligation and the amount at which the settlement will take place can be measured reliably. Therefore, the key issues to be considered in relation to recognising liabilities are (a) the probable outflow of economic benefits and (b) reliability of measurement. In practice, it may be difficult to apply these criteria. For example, what does *probable* mean? It can be argued that it means more likely rather than less likely. However, individual differences in estimates of the probability of an event may vary, leading to inconsistency in measurement.

What is meant by *reliable measurement*? The *Framework* states that reliable measurement is that which is 'free from material error and bias'; further, that an item is measured so that it 'faithfully represents' what it purports to represent (para. 31). The *Framework* states specifically that liabilities cannot be included if they cannot be measured reliably (para. 86). One example is a legal action. If the damages to be paid cannot be estimated reliably then the items cannot be recognised as a liability. The legal action example illustrates the trade off made between relevance and reliability. A probable future outflow of economic benefits associated with the lawsuit is relevant information, but to recognise an incorrect amount may be misleading to users of financial information.

Some people take the view that reliable measurement means verifiable measurement; that is, the measurement of the liability can be linked to objective evidence such as a contract amount or a market value. However, in many cases accountants must use judgement to make their best estimate of a liability. Consider for example the liability for warranty claims. The accountant uses relevant past data (such as the level of prior claims) and predicted information (such as the level of sales) to estimate the liability. If the estimate is sufficiently reliable (which will only be known in the future) then the information will also be relevant for users of financial information. Evidence that there are different views about how to define and when to recognise liabilities is emerging as part of the IASB/FASB's project on the conceptual framework. In October 2008 the boards tentatively adopted new working definitions for assets and liabilities. Discussion by the boards about when assets and liabilities should be recognised and derecognised is continuing.

A practical example of recognition of liabilities relates to accounting for public–private partnerships. These partnerships refer to the situation where the public sector (e.g. a government-controlled or -funded entity) contracts with the private sector (e.g. a company) for the construction of public-use assets such as roads, prisons and schools. The question is: Which entity should record the assets and liabilities associated with the transactions? To answer this question, accountants must apply the definition and recognition criteria outlined in accounting standards and the *Framework*. However, a number of outcomes are possible, depending how standards are applied. A key question to guide application of the relevant standards relates to where the risks and benefits of ownership lie. These issues are explored further in theory in action 8.2.

8.2 THEORY IN ACTION

New public-private flexibility

by Annabel Hepworth

Public-private partnership projects might be recorded on government balance sheets under new global accounting rules, a new Productivity Commission paper suggests.

There are concerns that having outlays off-balance sheet can cloud the liability and costs facing taxpayers and consumers to meet cost-recovery and other requirements under PPP contracts.

PPPs, where government and private sector work as joint partners, grew in popularity in the last decade and because they often were off-balance sheet, use of the model helped lower state government borrowing levels and support credit ratings.

Most economic PPPs have been treated by government as operating leases which, under accounting standards, typically meaning the risks and benefits of the project are treated as though they are with the private sector.

But following Australia's introduction of the International Financial Reporting Standards a few years ago, some PPP deals have already been re-classified as finance leases, which would tend to see them recorded on the balance sheet. Social PPPs, such as schools, are generally treated as finance leases.

"Most economic infrastructure PPP projects are not recorded on government balance sheets, bypassing expenditure controls and reducing parliamentary and public scrutiny of projects," says the staff working paper, *Public Infrastructure Financing: an International Perspective*.

"Off-balance sheet accounting can obscure the level of government liabilities or fiscal costs required to meet future PPP contractual service payments and guarantees. However, it is possible that more PPP projects could be reclassified and recorded on government balance sheets under new accounting rules."

Experts say that treatment can vary project-by-project depending on the risk transfer in contractual arrangements. The PC estimated about 5 per cent of public infrastructure was delivered using PPPs, compared with about 16 per cent in the UK. The commission also found PPPs could ensure efficiency by bundling design, construction and operation of projects, but the off-budget treatment of future obligations for some PPPs could "reduce the scrutiny applied to the investment".

"PPPs offer considerable potential to reduce project risk, but are costly to transact," it said.

"If such transactions are off-budget, this may inhibit the scrutiny needed to ensure efficient investment," NSW and Victoria had keenly embraced PPPs, but the credit crisis had led to new caution of the "innovative financial products utilised in some PPP financing arrangements".

Source: The Australian Financial Review, 1 April 2009, p. 10.

Questions

1. Describe what is represented by a public–private partnership project (PPP)?
2. What is meant by the phrase 'off-balance sheet' liabilities?
3. Why did the government favour PPPs which allowed debt to be off-balance sheet?
4. Explain the reasons in favour of recording economic infrastructure PPP projects on government balance sheets.

LO 3 → LIABILITY MEASUREMENT

The *Framework* provides little guidance about how to measure liabilities which meet the definition and recognition criteria. Paragraph 100 states that a number of different measurement bases may be employed. Under IFRS, the most commonly used measurement method for liabilities is historical cost (or modified historical cost). 'Fair value' measurement is used on initial measurement of transactions involving liabilities in relation to IAS 17 *Leases*, IAS 39 *Recognition and Measurement of Financial Instruments*, IFRS 2 *Share-based Payment* and IFRS 3 *Business Combinations*. What do we mean by fair value? The concept is defined in standards such as IAS 17 (para. 4) to be:

> The amount for which an asset could be exchanged or a liability settled between knowledgeable, willing parties in an arm's length transaction.

Thus, the liability arising under a finance lease is recognised at inception based on the fair value of the lease (which according to the above definition could be a market price for the leased property) or the present value of the minimum lease payments if lower (IAS 17, para. 20). In subsequent years, the liability is measured based on the method 'amortised cost'; that is, the 'cost' of the liability at inception (fair value or present value of minimum lease payments, if lower) adjusted on a yearly basis to reflect its estimated current value. The outstanding balance of the liability is based on the effective interest rate method of amortisation (para. 25). In the case of finance leases, the standard gives clear guidance for determining the value of the lease liability. However, in other cases, fair value measurement of liabilities presents some challenges. For example, how do we estimate the fair value of a liability for which there is no market value? Many liabilities are settled, not sold.

Table 8.1 shows the variety of measurement methods used under IFRS for subsequent measurement of liabilities.[10] We can see that historical cost (or rather modified historical cost, in this case amortised cost) is the most commonly used method for subsequent measurement of liabilities. Two examples where fair value measurement is required subsequent to acquisition are post-employment obligations such as pensions (superannuation) under IAS 19/AASB 119 *Employee Benefits* and long-term provisions under IAS 37/AASB 137 *Provisions, Contingent Liabilities and Contingent Assets*. Note that in both cases the liability is long term and likely to be affected by the time value of money. In present value terms, the longer the time period until settlement of the liability, the lower its value. This is because an entity benefits from the ability to earn interest on the funds which have not been used today to settle the liability. The next section explores the measurement of the liabilities associated with pensions (superannuation) and provisions and contingencies.

Employee benefits — pension (superannuation) plans

In many countries pension (or superannuation) plans are established by employers to provide retirement benefits for employees. Employers make payments to pension funds which hold assets, in trust, to fund payments when employees retire. The pension funds are legal entities, separate from the employer firm.

Pension plans may be contributory (both the employer and the employee contribute to the fund) or non-contributory (where only the employer makes contributions). For a defined benefit fund, the amounts to be paid to the employee are at least partially a function of the employee's final or average salary. In contrast, a defined contribution (or accumulated benefit) fund pays an amount that is a function of the contributions made to the fund.

TABLE 8.1 Subsequent measurement of liabilities in IFRS consolidated financial statements

	Usual measurement basis allowed by IFRS and adopted in practice	Fair value option*
Non-current liabilities		
Long-term borrowings	Amortised cost	No
Finance lease obligations	Amortised cost	No
Defined benefit post employment obligations	Present value of expected payments less fair value of plan assets	No
Deferred tax	Expected payments	No
Long-term provisions	Present value of expected payments	No
Current liabilities		
Trade payables	Amortised cost	No
Derivatives	Fair value	—
Short-term borrowings	Amortised cost	No
Current portion of long-term borrowings	Amortised cost	No
Other financial liabilities	Amortised cost	Yes
Current tax payable	Expected payments	No
Short-term provisions	Expected payments	No

Source: Cairns 2007.

* The fair value option may be used for financial liabilities only when there is an 'accounting mismatch' or when the liabilities are managed and evaluated on a fair value basis in accordance with a documented risk strategy (IAS 39, para. 11A).

Pension funds may be fully funded, partially funded or unfunded. Fully funded plans have sufficient cash or investments to meet the fund's obligation to members. In contrast, unfunded plans do not have cash or investments to cover the potential payouts under the plans. To the extent that amounts held in trust and being paid into the pension fund are insufficient to meet obligations under the plan as they fall due, the pension plan is underfunded.

Since pension funds are separate legal entities, it might be presumed that unfunded commitments of the plans are not liabilities of an employer firm that pays into a fund. However, it can be argued that the firm has an equitable obligation to meet unfunded commitments and, therefore, has a liability. In support of this argument, Whittred, Zimmer and Taylor offer the example of a firm that lets its sponsored superannuation fund default and suffers loss of reputation in labour and other markets as a consequence, thereby incurring a sacrifice of economic benefits.[11] Although some firms traditionally have not recognised unfunded commitments as liabilities, under the *Framework* and IAS 37/AASB 137 it is difficult to argue that they are not liabilities.

Another issue relates to when to recognise liabilities for pension (superannuation) payouts. Is it:

- as the employee renders services? The notion is that the payout is a form of compensation earned by the employee as services are rendered. However, it is paid in the future, after retirement.
- when the employee retires?
- when the fund is required to make payments under the pension plan?

Pension plans can be regarded as a promise by the entity to provide pensions to employees in return for past and current services. Pension benefits are a form of deferred compensation offered by the firm in exchange for services by employees who have chosen, either implicitly or explicitly, to accept lower current compensation in return for future pension payments. These pension benefits are earned by employees, and their cost accrues over the years the services are rendered. The critical past event is the rendering of services by employees and, therefore, an obligation arises for those pension benefits that have not yet been funded. Case study 8.2 considers issues relating to accounting for pensions (superannuation) in the United Kingdom and Australia by focusing on pension (superannuation) liabilities of a number of large listed companies.

Provisions and contingencies

Provisions and contingencies occur where there is a blurring of the line between present and future obligations. IAS 37/AASB 137 *Provisions, Contingent Liabilities and Contingent Assets* acknowledges the overlap of definitions in paragraph 12, when it states that all provisions are contingent because they are uncertain in timing or amount. Trying to distinguish between present, future and potential (or contingent) obligations is not as simple as it may appear. The distinction depends to a large degree on the nature of the 'past event'

IAS 37/AASB 137 paragraph 10 defines a contingent liability as:

(a) a possible obligation that arises from past events and whose existence will be confirmed only by the occurrence or non-occurrence of one or more uncertain future events not wholly within the control of the entity; or

(b) a present obligation that arises from past events but is not recognised because:
   (i) it is not probable that an outflow of resources embodying economic benefits will be required to settle the obligation; or
   (ii) the amount of the obligation cannot be measured with sufficient reliability.

The IAS 37/AASB 137 paragraph 14 recognition criteria for provisions are consistent with the *Framework* criteria for recognition of a liability. As such, liabilities and provisions are permitted to be recognised only when there is a present obligation, it is probable that an outflow of resources embodying economic benefits will be required to settle the obligation, and the amount of the obligation can be reliably measured. Contingent liabilities do not meet these criteria (just as contingent assets do not meet the criteria for recognition as assets). Hence, paragraph 27 of IAS 37/AASB 137 states categorically that contingent liabilities are not to be recognised in the financial statements. IAS 37 is presently under review by the IASB as part of the Liabilities project. One of the proposals is to eliminate the terms 'provision' and 'contingent liability', replacing them with 'non-financial liability'. The proposals aim to extend and clarify the application of IAS 37; however, as is usual, the proposals have received mixed responses from stakeholders.[12]

The effect of IAS 37 is to limit the use of provisions. For example, a company may consider it prudent to create a provision for uninsured losses (i.e. the process of self-insuring), however, a liability cannot be recognised under IAS 37 until the occurrence of an event necessitating the sacrifice of assets by the reporting entity. Another example relates to 'provision for possible losses' or a 'provision for restructuring' which may be created following poor performance. Since there is no existing obligation to an external party (i.e. a commitment to transfer resources from the entity to an external party which cannot be avoided) such a provision would not be permitted under the *Framework* or current standards.

Certainly, there are circumstances when the users of financial information want to know about potential losses or outgoings. IAS 37 (para. 86) states that in some circumstances a note to the accounts is required because the knowledge of the liabilities is relevant to the users of the financial report in making and evaluating decisions about the allocation of scarce resources. That is, future settlement may be required, but the estimated probability is not high enough to warrant formal recognition. This subjective probability test provides opportunities for firms to exclude liabilities from their financial statements. However, the liabilities should still be disclosed when knowledge of them is likely to affect users' decision making. Theory in action 8.3 provides an example of a contingent liability note from the Public Transport Authority of Western Australia (a public-sector entity). It is a worthwhile exercise to consider the extent of disclosure included in the note and the reasons it has been provided.

<table>
<tr><td>**8.3**
THEORY
IN ACTION</td><td>The following extracts are from the Public Transport Authority (PTA) Annual Report 2006/2007 Notes to the Financial Statements and detail the current legal actions in progress against the entity.</td></tr>
</table>

Contingent Liabilities

In addition to the liabilities included in the financial statements, there are the following contingent liabilities:

Litigation in progress

Quantifiable Contingencies

Leighton Contractors Pty Ltd, the contractor engaged by the PTA to design and construct the City portion of the Southern Suburbs Railway, has commenced Supreme Court actions against the PTA. Two of the actions relate to contractual disputes between the PTA and Leighton Contractors, on Leighton Contractors' alleged entitlements under the rise and fall and contaminated material provisions of the contract. The estimated value of these two claims is $64 million. The PTA has denied all liability and is vigorously defending the action.

The amount that has been claimed by John Holland Pty Ltd, the contractor engaged by the PTA to construct a package of three stations on the Southern Suburbs Railway, but rejected by PTA, which is now subject to dispute, is $6.89 million. PTA is defending the claims.

The amount that has been claimed by RailLink Joint Venture, the contractor engaged by the PTA to construct the civil, rail and structures portion of the Southern Suburbs Railway, but rejected by PTA, which is now subject to dispute, is $2.62 million. PTA is defending the claims.

Unquantifiable Contingencies

As at 30 June 2007, PTA has a number of claims lodged against it by several contractors engaged in construction of the Southern Suburbs Railway. One significant claim is from Leighton Contractors on allegations of misleading and deceptive conduct in relation to the contracts work insurance effected by the PTA pursuant to the contract. PTA has denied liability and is defending the claim. It is not possible to estimate the amount of any eventual payments in relation to these claims at balance sheet date.

Source: The Government of Western Australia, Public Transport Authority, Annual Report 2006/2007, Note 38, Notes to the Financial Statements, pp. 112–113.

Questions

1. Name the parties listed in the note that are taking legal action against the PTA. State the matters or matters under dispute and the amount of the claim if provided.
2. To what extent has the PTA incurred losses of economic benefits in relation to these matters?

3. 'Contingent liabilities are not liabilities of an entity; in fact, they may never eventuate so their disclosure is misleading.' Explain whether you agree or disagree with this statement and provide reasons for your view.
4. The PTA is a government business enterprise, with one shareholder, the Western Australian State Government. Discuss whether disclosure of contingent liabilities is less relevant for the PTA than for a publicly listed company with widely held shares.

Owners' equity

Owners' equity is the third of the fundamental accounting concepts captured in the accounting equation. It represents the net assets (assets minus liabilities) of the entity ($P = A - L$). Thus, owners' equity (or proprietorship) captures the owners' claims against the entity's net assets, which the entity has no current obligation to pay. It represents the owners' interest or capital in the firm. Owners' equity (the residual interest) is a claim or right to the net assets of the entity. The *Framework* defines equity in paragraph 49(c) as follows:

> 'Equity' is the residual interest in the assets of the entity after deducting all its liabilities.

Therefore, owners' equity is not an obligation to transfer assets, but a residual claim. Further, it cannot be defined independently of assets and liabilities. As such, the definitions of assets and liabilities must be agreed on before a definition of equity can be finalised and applied in a sound theoretical or practical sense. As a result of its residual nature, the amount shown in the balance sheet as representing equity is dependent on not only the assets and liabilities which are recognised but also how they are measured. For example, assume Firm A undertakes an upward revaluation of property under IAS 16/AASB 116 *Property, Plant and Equipment* but Firm B, which holds an identical asset, does not. Firm A will report higher assets and equity than Firm B.

A fundamental question to be addressed in arriving at the amount of equity is whether an item represents a liability or equity of the entity. There are two essential features which can help us to distinguish between liabilities and owners' equity. They are:
- the rights of the parties
- the economic substance of the arrangement.

Legal rights are a very important consideration. However, they should not be the only basis of distinction between creditor and owner. After all, the definition of a liability includes constructive and equitable obligations as well as legal obligations. Another reason is that the legal viewpoint is too narrow a focus to be useful in achieving the decision-usefulness objective of accounting. Therefore, economic substance must also be studied.

Rights of the parties

One feature of the rights given to the parties either by law or by company policy relates to the priority of rights to be (re)paid in the event that the entity is wound up. Legally, for a sole proprietorship or partnership, a creditor has a claim on the owner(s) and, for a corporation, a claim on the company. However, in accounting theory, no matter what the legal form of the organisation, the entity is recognised as a unit of accountability. Therefore, creditors have a claim on the entity and thus on its assets.

Creditors have the following rights:
- settlement of their claims by a given date through a transfer of assets (goods or services)
- priority over owners in the settlement of their claims in the event of liquidation.

Note that creditors' claims are limited to specified amounts (which may vary over time according to the terms of the agreement). In contrast, the owners have a residual interest only, although by contractual arrangement different classes of owners may have different priorities in the return of capital.

Another aspect of the rights of creditors and owners relates to the use of the assets or to the operations of the business. Creditors do not have the right to use the assets of the firm other than as specified in contracts. Except in an indirect way in some cases, they do not possess rights in the decision-making process in the operations of the business. In a limited way, by contract, they may intrude on operations by requiring that retained earnings be restricted, or that a given asset not be sold without their approval. On the other hand, owners have the right or authority to operate the business.

Economic substance

Both liabilities and owners' equity represent claims against the entity. All claimants against the entity bear a risk of loss but, because of the prior claims of creditors, their risk is less than that of owners. Owners must bear any losses stemming from the activities of the firm. They carry the brunt of the risk in the business. In each firm, the degree of risk for creditors and owners depends on their rights. As such, a key difference between the rights of creditors and owners is that creditors have a right to settlement, whereas owners have rights to participate in profits (the residual). The difference reflects the economic risk and return features of the two types of claims: creditors bear less risk and earn a relatively fixed return (interest and settlement of the principal), whereas owners bear greater risk and accordingly earn a variable (and often higher) rate of return through their participation in profits. Figure 8.1 provides a diagrammatic representation of the relationship between economic substance and rights.

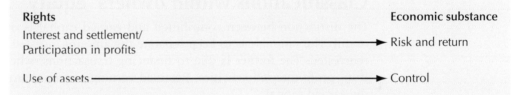

FIGURE 8.1 The relationship between economic substance and rights

Owners or their representatives have control of the acquisition, composition, use and disposition of the firm's assets. They have control of operations and the responsibility for running the business and for its survival and profitability. Generally speaking, company owners (shareholders) delegate most of these responsibilities and control to directors and managers.

These arguments correspond with the notions of the entrepreneur in economics. The concept of entrepreneur may be idealistic when applied to the average shareholder in a large, publicly owned company but this misfit is due to the insistence of accountants that a distinction is made between liabilities and owners' equity for all business enterprises. The recognition of owners' equity presumes a proprietary theory position, which, to begin with, is awkward when imposed on a large company.

Concept of capital

Accounting for shareholders' equity is influenced by legal prescriptions. For example, in the United Kingdom and Australia company law includes statutes relating to accounting for capital. Foremost is the requirement of 'capital maintenance', which demands that companies maintain intact their initial (and any subsequent) capital base. The *Framework* recognises that whether or not a firm maintains its capital intact is a function not only of the definition of equity as a residual interest in an entity, but also of the concept of capital. Capital can be conceptualised as the invested money or invested purchasing power (financial capital) or as the productive capacity of the entity (physical capital). Further, capital can be measured on either a nominal dollar or a purchasing power ('real') scale. Various combinations of the concept of capital and the measurement scale are used in different models that yield different measures of capital under identical circumstances. The *Framework* provides no guidance regarding which model is most appropriate, but does recognise in paragraphs 108 and 109 that firms would need to retain different amounts of resources to maintain different concepts and measures of capital.

Another objective of capital maintenance requirements is to protect creditors by providing a 'cushion' or 'buffer'. For example, suppose an entity holds no more than the legal capital of $10 000. If total assets are $100 000, this means that liabilities amount to $90 000. That is:

$$A = L + P$$
$$\$100\,000 = \$90\,000 + \$10\,000$$

If the entity were to be liquidated and the carrying amount of the assets realised only $80 000, there would be enough to pay the creditors. This is possible because of the existence of the capital of $10 000. Without it, the creditors would not be paid in full. Capital is not a guarantee for the protection of creditors, but it does offer some safety. The importance of capital reserves was highlighted in the banking and liquidity crises of 2007–08.

Classifications within owners' equity

The distinction between contributed and earned capital is one that accountants find useful. The rationale is to keep separate the amount invested from the amount that is reinvested. The former is due to financing transactions, whereas the latter is derived from profit-directed activities. Retained earnings, or unappropriated profits, make up the earned capital.

Retained earnings may be appropriated for specific purposes. Remember that retained earnings are not assets in themselves and therefore the appropriations of retained earnings to specific reserve accounts do not represent particular assets. In 1950, a special committee of the American Accounting Association explained that appropriations are of three types:
- those that are designed to explain managerial policy concerning the reinvestment of profits
- those that are intended to restrict dividends as required by law or contract
- those that provide for anticipated losses.[13]

The committee stated the following.
- The first type did not effectively achieve the objective and would be best explained in narrative form elsewhere.
- For the second type, the committee believed a note to the accounts would be preferable to an appropriation.
- For the third type, the committee felt an appropriation was unnecessary and often misleading; a note would be more suitable.

The committee emphasised that appropriations must not affect profit determination. There is little that can be accomplished by appropriations. Some accused companies of using appropriations as a ploy to decrease the amount available for dividends, hoping thereby to lessen complaints by shareholders about the level of dividends paid. Such arguments assume that managers believe shareholders are naive. The demarcation between contributed and earned capital cannot be strictly maintained because of transactions that do not fall neatly into these categories. For example, share dividends (i.e. dividends that are 'paid' in the form of an allocation of shares) represent a change in classification from earned to contributed capital.

LO 4 → CHALLENGES FOR STANDARD SETTERS

The IASB has several current projects which will affect the definition, recognition and measurement of liabilities, including those relating to the conceptual framework, financial instruments, provisions and employee entitlements. The Board is amending IAS 37 *Provisions, Contingent Liabilities and Contingent Assets* and IAS 19 *Employee Benefits* as part of the Liabilities project. The objective of the project is to (a) converge IASB standards with US GAAP and to (b) improve current standards in relation to the identification and recognition of liabilities.[14] The work on the Liabilities project illustrates how standards are interconnected and changes likely affect a number of standards; for example, the work on IAS 37 will be relevant to projects on leasing, insurance and the conceptual framework.

To illustrate challenges currently faced by standard setters, we now discuss three key topics which are relevant to issues discussed in this chapter. First, we consider the distinction between the classification of items as liabilities or equity, the so-called debt versus equity distinction. Second, we discuss when liabilities are extinguished; that is, when it is appropriate for companies to remove liabilities from their balance sheets. Third, we examine share-based payment transactions and consider the extent to which they give rise to liabilities or equity.

Debt vs equity distinction

Based on the definitions and recognition criteria discussed in this chapter, we can agree that shares issued to investors form part of equity and that loans from creditors are liabilities. However, questions are raised about hybrid instruments which have the characteristics of both debt and equity. For example, preference shares have traditionally been regarded as capital and, therefore, as part of owners' equity, but they have characteristics that also align them with liabilities, such as the following:
- they are fixed claims
- they might not participate in dividends other than at a pre-specified rate (akin to interest)
- they have priority over ordinary shares in the return of capital (as do liabilities)
- they generally carry no voting rights.

Although they are called shares, it is likely that they sometimes meet the definition of liabilities, and should be classed as liabilities. IAS 32/AASB 132 paragraph 18 comments:

> The substance of a financial instrument, rather than its legal form, governs the classification ... Substance and legal form are commonly consistent, but not always. Some financial instruments take the legal form of equity but are liabilities in substance and others may combine features associated with equity instruments and features associated with financial liabilities.

IAS 32/AASB 132 goes on to state that preference shares that provide for mandatory redemption by the issuer for a fixed or determinable amount at a fixed or determinable future date, for example, are financial liabilities. Similarly, a financial instrument that gives the holder the right to return the instrument to the issuer for cash or another financial asset (a 'puttable instrument') is a financial liability. Preference shares, convertible debt and 'perpetual' capital notes are examples of securities whose names may not accurately describe the dominant characteristics of the securities.

The classification of financial instruments as liabilities or equity has effects beyond the balance sheet since the classification determines whether interest, dividends, losses or gains relating to that instrument are recognised as income or expenses in calculating net income, or whether they are treated as a distribution of the calculated profits. Distributions of interest, dividends, losses and gains relating to financial instruments or components of financial instruments that are liabilities are recognised as income or expenses. In contrast, distributions to holders of an equity instrument are treated as a distribution of the profits once they have been calculated.

In summary, consistent with the theoretical bases of the definitions, IAS 32/AASB 132 requires classification of financial instruments to be based on their economic substance rather than their legal form. Consequently, preference shares redeemable at the option of the holder are classified as a liability. Compound financial instruments have both debt and equity characteristics and the component parts are to be accounted for separately. For example, the issuer of convertible notes providing their holders with the right to convert the interest-bearing note into ordinary shares of the issuer should allocate the proceeds from the convertible note issue into liability and equity components. The equity components reflect the holders' right to convert the security into ordinary shares. Thereafter, payments to the holders (other than any return of principal) are classified as interest or dividends on a pro rata basis according to the proportion of the security that is defined as debt or as equity.

The purpose of distinguishing between owners' equity and liabilities is to enhance the usefulness of information for decision making. Interesting questions are raised about how investors view so-called hybrid securities, which combine features of both debt and equity such as convertible notes, redeemable preference shares and subordinated debt (see theory in action 8.4). In their study of the usefulness of hybrid security classifications, Kimmel and Warfield found that the dichotomous classification of redeemable preference shares as straight debt or straight equity does not reflect the risk–return relationship that can be useful for decision making. Interestingly, though, Kimmel and Warfield concluded that the merit of classification within financial statements as a means of conveying information about hybrid securities is questionable when the nature of securities does not correspond to the elementary classification and the securities are non-divisible.[15]

The IASB has a current project on IAS 32/AASB 132, which aims to improve and simplify its requirements. Stakeholders have made criticisms of the standard, claiming that the principles are difficult to apply and that the application of those principles can result in inappropriate classification of some financial instruments. The IASB wants a better distinction between equity and non-equity instruments. It is currently considering how best to define what is, and what is not, an equity instrument. A starting point is the idea that all perpetual instruments (i.e. those that lack a settlement requirement) are equity. In addition, an instrument redeemable at the option of issuer would be equity. In contrast, a liability is mandatorily redeemable at a specific date or dates or is certain to occur.[16] The Board is exploring feedback on the discussion paper issued in February 2008. One of their challenges will be to provide the guidance sought by preparers without compromising the Board's principles-based approach.

A dynamite solution

by Giles Parkinson

When Australia's Orica bought the international assets of explosives group Dyno Nobel for $902 million in late 2005, it was faced with a delicate funding problem. It had already used a lot of debt to fund other acquisitions and investments, and it was important to protect its strong BBB plus credit rating.

Borrowing more might have placed that rating at risk. It raised $500 million in new equity through a rights issue, but issuing more equity would have been costly and reduced its earnings per share, an important calculation for investors.

Fortunately, Orica had done a lot of planning ahead of time. According to Frank Micallef, general manager of treasury operations, the company had been working for four years on developing a new form of hybrid security that combined the elements of debt and equity and best suited the needs of both the investor and the issuing company.

In early 2006, Orica introduced a new generation of hybrid securities, which it called Step-Up Preference (SPS) Securities. It offered to sell $400 million, but in the end demand was so great that it sold $516 million to institutional investors.

The key features of these securities were that they were treated as equity for accounting purposes, and so strengthened its balance sheet, and were viewed as a form of subordinated debt by investors, who received a higher interest payment than they would for corporate bonds.

The SPS offered a return of 135 points (or 1.35 per cent) over the prevailing bank bill rate — then 5.45 per cent. The payments are discretionary, but they can only be suspended if all dividend payments were suspended. The securities are also perpetual, but they can be redeemed by Orica at the conclusion of five years. If they are not redeemed by the company at this time, the interest rate payable on the securities, or the coupon, will "step up" by another 2.25 per cent.

"It was a good transaction," says Micallef. "It enabled us to minimise the ordinary equity that we could issue, and that helped in the earnings-per-share calculation. "Even though these instruments were more expensive than vanilla debt, we looked at it as a form of cheap equity rather than expensive debt."

Source: Extract from 'Rainbow Connection', *Real Business*, Spring 2007, pp. 30–1.

Questions

1. Outline the debt and equity situation of Orica at the time of the purchase of Dyno Nobel in 2005.
2. Describe the features of Step-Up Preference Securities (SPS) created by the company.
3. Explain how the securities could be considered as equity for accounting purposes but as debt by investors?

Extinguishing debt

A debt may be settled in ways other than by direct payment or rendering of services to the creditor. The obligation, for example, may be 'forgiven' by the creditor, thus releasing the debtor from making any future sacrifice. IAS 32/AASB 132 outlines offsetting a financial asset and liability in paragraph 42. The situation it deals with is referred to as the 'set-off and extinguishment of debt' or 'in-substance defeasance'. This allows a debtor to remove a debt from the balance sheet and to report a net financial asset or liability only if the entity has a current legally enforceable right to set off the recognised amounts, and intends either to (a) settle on a net basis or (b) realise the assets and settle the liability simultaneously.

The economic substance of the transaction involved in placing risk-free assets (i.e. government securities) or cash in an irrevocable trust for the purpose of payment of the debt is tantamount to extinguishing the debt. However, the company (debtor) is still legally liable for the debt so it is potentially misleading that the debt is not shown on balance sheet.

To illustrate why the in-substance defeasance arrangement became popular during the 1980s, consider the following example. Suppose Company A has bonds payable of $10 000 000, sold originally at par with a stated interest rate of 8 per cent and 10 years life remaining. Presently, because interest rates are higher, the market value of the bonds is lower than their maturity value. Company A will purchase government bonds with a face value of $10 000 000, stated interest rate of 8 per cent and 10 years life remaining, for $7 500 000. These will be placed in an irrevocable trust for the purpose of paying off the company's bonds payable. The following entries will be made:

| (1) | Investment in Government Bonds | $ 7 500 000 | |
| | Cash | | $7 500 000 |

(2)	Bonds Payable	$10 000 000	
	Investment in Government Bonds		$7 500 000
	Gain on Bonds Payable		2 500 000

The advantages to the company are:
- the debt is removed and, therefore, the company's debt to equity ratio improves
- profit for the current year increases by the amount of the gain
- for tax purposes, the gain is not recognised because the company is still legally obligated to pay the bonds
- for tax purposes, the interest from the government bonds will be offset by the interest expense of the company's bonds
- defeasance permits the company to manage the liability side of the balance sheet as it would its marketable securities on the asset side.

In-substance defeasance raises the question: When should a liability cease to be recognised? The *Framework* definition of a liability implies that it is settled when assets or services have been transferred to other entities. On the other hand, although an obligation may be removed from the accounts, the liability may in fact revert to the debtor. The question remains as to what would happen if the trustee proved to be unreliable and the assets were lost or misappropriated. In such a case, the debtor would have to reinstate the liability. As is clear from this example, there can sometimes be many variations of transactions and events that challenge the theoretical structure of accounting standards.

The importance of reliable recognition and measurement of assets and liabilities has been highlighted through the events of the 'sub-prime crisis' which emerged in the United States in mid-2007 and led to global financial market turmoil and a more general economic crisis (referred to at the time as the 'global financial crisis'). Given the central role of financial instruments in the crisis, the ways in which financial instruments are regulated came under close scrutiny by a broad range of parties. The relevant standards of the IASB and FASB were put under the spotlight and changes made to ease the effect of mark-to-market accounting for instruments without liquid markets.[17] The IASB published an exposure draft related to derecognition of financial instruments in March 2009. Amendments are proposed to IAS 39 *Financial Instruments: Recognition and Disclosure* and IFRS 7 *Financial Instruments: Disclosure*. As explained above, companies may respond to incentives to remove items from their balance sheets, or to ensure that items do not appear on their balance sheet. Such activities interfere with financial statement users' ability to assess company risk. In the derecognition project, the IASB proposes to a new approach for derecognition based on a single concept of control rather than multiple concepts (risks and rewards, control, continuing involvement). In addition, disclosures will be extended and improved so that users can better understand the relationship of transferred assets and associated liabilities so as to assess risk exposure.[18]

Employee shares (share-based payment)

Accountants debate whether share-based payment gives rise to an expense. Another aspect of the issue is whether the remuneration 'paid' to employees by way of company shares or stock options (options to buy shares) gives rise to liabilities or equity. Share-based payment plans normally cover a number of years. When shares or options have been offered under a plan, but prior to the issue of shares, does the company have a liability? If so, what is the economic benefit to be sacrificed in the future? When shares are issued under the plan, has equity increased, or merely been redistributed? Those who argue that the issue of shares creates an expense and a liability contend that the employee is obtaining something of value to the employee; therefore, there is a cost to the company. This cost is an expense, and a corresponding liability exists until it is settled with shares, when equity is increased accordingly. Those who argue that the issue of shares in a share-based payment plan does not constitute payment of an expense maintain that the entity perspective deems that an entity cannot sacrifice future economic benefits through the issue of its own equity since it is not giving up anything. They argue that the firm is no worse off for issuing additional shares. Rather, it is the shareholders whose individual holdings may have been diluted in value.

The IASB has decided to treat share based remuneration as an expense. IFRS 2/AASB 2 *Share-based Payment* distinguishes between share-based payments that are cash-settled and those that are equity-settled. When goods and services are received or acquired in a share-based payment transaction, the entity records the event when it obtains the goods or as the services are received. If the goods or services were received in an equity-settled share-based payment transaction, the credit side of the entry is to owners' equity. In contrast, if the goods or services were received in a transaction that will be settled in cash (e.g. an amount of cash equal to the value of the entity's shares at the time the payment is made), the corresponding credit entry is to a liability. The current approach in IFRS 2/AASB 2 leads to a differential treatment for the fair value changes associated with equity-settled compared with cash-settled plans. The fair value of transactions in equity-settled plans is determined on grant date and subsequent changes are ignored. However, the transactions classified as liabilities under cash-settled plans are adjusted to fair value at each balance date, with gains and losses included in income. The differential treatment raises the question whether items which are the same in substance (share-based payment) should be accounted for in different ways.[19]

Issues for auditors

The completeness of liabilities recognised on the balance sheet and the note disclosures about contingencies and other obligations are major issues for auditors. They are required to gather evidence that accounts payable, accruals, and other liabilities include all amounts owed by the entity to other parties. Auditors need to consider the possibility of timing irregularities, where a liability incurred prior to the end of the financial period is not recorded by the entity until the commencement of the new accounting period. Cut-off tests are designed to gather evidence that transactions are recorded in the proper period. In addition, auditors need to test whether the liabilities are recorded at the proper value.

Concealment by managers of the entity's obligations, such as contingent liabilities, loan guarantees, or commitments under various contractual agreements, understates liabilities and creates an impression of greater solvency for the company. In an extreme case, such concealment means that it is inappropriate for the financial statements to be prepared on a going concern basis, and the auditor will fail to qualify the audit opinion. Auditing standard ASA 570[20] requires an auditor to specifically consider whether management's use of the going concern basis is appropriate and, if there is any doubt, whether the relevant circumstances have been disclosed correctly. If the auditor concludes that the entity will not be able to continue as a going concern, the auditor is required to express an adverse opinion if the financial report had been prepared on a going concern basis (ASA 570 para. 63).

An example of a company which appeared to have problems with the completeness of its reported liabilities was Enron, which filed for bankruptcy in December 2001.[21] Although the transactions and other arrangements were complex, it can be argued that Enron understated its liabilities through improper use of unconsolidated special purpose entities (SPEs).[22] Benston and Hartgraves note that Enron was not required by US GAAP in place at the time to consolidate the many SPEs it used if independent third parties had a controlling and substantial equity interest in the SPE.[23] Enron therefore treated the SPEs as separate entities and sold assets to them, creating profits without having to recognise the SPEs' liabilities. However, because the principal assets for the SPEs were shares in Enron, the fall in Enron's share price meant that it became liable for the SPEs' debt (which was guaranteed by Enron). When Enron's use of SPEs was reviewed by their auditors, Arthur Andersen, in 2001 it was decided to retroactively consolidate the entities which resulted in a massive reduction in Enron's reported net income and a massive increase in its reported debt. Within months of the announcement of a $1.2 billion reduction in shareholders' equity, Enron's shares were practically worthless.[24]

Although understatement of liabilities is a concern for auditors, especially if it creates doubt about the company's solvency, overstatement of provisions also raises issues for auditors. Commonly labelled 'cookie-jar' reserves, provisions for future expenditures, such as maintenance, allow the company to 'store' excess earnings for a 'rainy day'.[25] As discussed earlier, blatant use of this technique is now limited by IAS 37/AASB 137, but auditors are still required to test the appropriateness of any provision (including both those shown as liabilities and those recognised as contra assets, such as a provision for doubtful debts).

The introduction of IFRS 2/AASB 2 *Share-based Payment* has increased the authoritative guidance for auditors when assessing the reasonableness of the fair values assigned to equity-based transactions. The standard states that fair value may be determined by either the value of the shares or rights to shares given up, or by the value of the goods or services received, depending on the type of payment. A similar standard forms part of US GAAP. In the United States, the Public Company Accounting Oversight Board (PCAOB) inspected audit firms for the period 2004 to 2006 and reported that in some cases auditors were not properly evaluating whether their clients, particularly their newer or smaller company clients, had used appropriate values for share-based payment transactions. For example, some auditors were allowing equity instruments issued as consideration for the cancellation of outstanding debt to be valued at the carrying values of the debt even though there was evidence that the equity instruments' market values exceeded those carrying values.[26] In general, to properly audit these types of transactions auditors need to evaluate the substance of the arrangement and the accounting principles that could be applicable, rather than simply accept management's assertions of the nature, timing and valuation of the transaction.

Summary

The proprietary and entity perspectives of the firm

We began this chapter by exploring two theories: proprietary and entity theory, which help us understand our approach to accounting. Under proprietary theory, we see the owner or proprietor of the business as the party for whom the accounting information is prepared. The proprietor's interest or equity is represented by the net assets of the business. The assets generate income, which in turn increases equity or the wealth of the proprietor. The proprietorship perspective takes a 'financial' view of capital because capital is seen as the investment of the proprietor which increases or decreases, depending on the financial success of the business.

The diverse nature of the modern-day corporation has raised questions about the proprietorship perspective and led to the development of entity theory. Under this theory, the business for which accounts are prepared is legally and practically separated from its owners. Accounting provides information about the entity's use of its assets to generate income. This information is used by a range of stakeholders including current and potential shareholders, creditors, employees and tax authorities. Under this view, assets are resources controlled by the entity and liabilities are obligations of the entity, not the owners. Income generated from assets increases equity and the entity then makes decisions about the portion, if any, which will be distributed to shareholders. The entity is assumed to have a financial view of capital if users are primarily concerned with maintenance of nominal capital or purchasing power of capital. On the other hand, if the entity is focused on maintaining the operating capacity of assets (i.e. the physical productive capacity) then a concept of physical capital is useful leading to, in theory at least, the use of current value measurement to maintain capital.

Issues involved in defining liabilities and equity, applying those definitions, and why the definition and recognition criteria are important

The practice of accounting is based on a shared understanding of principles and concepts. Definitions help us interpret concepts such as assets, liabilities and equity. Since definitions must be stated in general terms, we also have recognition rules to assist accountants to apply definitions in practical situations. Recognition rules may be drawn from generally accepted accounting practices (e.g. recognise liabilities as soon as they are foreseen) and from specific accounting standards (e.g. a finance lease is to be recognised on the balance sheet when certain conditions are met).

The current definition of liabilities draws from the 1989 IASB/AASB *Framework*. It has two elements relating to the existence of a present obligation and a past transaction.

Determining whether a present obligation exists may be straightforward, for example, when contractual rights are specified. On the other hand, an obligation may be equitable or constructive, such as social obligations relating to product warranties, employee health benefits or environmental restoration. Practitioners must apply judgement in determining the amount and timing of liabilities. Guidance is provided in recognition criteria in the IASB/AASB *Framework*. The criteria focus on whether an outflow of economic benefits is probable and whether it can be measured reliably.

Definitions and recognition criteria are important for several reasons. Initially, they guide the practitioner in decisions about whether an item constitutes an asset, liability or equity. This in turn influences whether an item is shown on the balance sheet. Entities' choices about the amount at which items are to be recognised and the timing of their recognition are of fundamental importance because they affect the numbers in the accounts and can have economic consequences. We know that accounting information has a variety of uses and is important to a range of stakeholders. For example, investors are interested in the firm's future prospects; lenders are interested in the entity's ability to repay debt; and managers are interested in the amount of their compensation. Accounting information is relevant to decision making in each of these cases. Thus, the ability of accounting information to include timely and appropriate measures of liabilities and equity is a crucial concern in capital markets.

LO 3 Current measurement practices in relation to liabilities and equity

The majority of liabilities are measured on an historical cost basis (amortised historical cost). More recently, some 'fair value' measurements have been used to provide a current value of liabilities. Examples include some financial liabilities, lease liabilities and pension obligations.

Ideally, the liabilities recognised on the balance sheet should represent only those items for which an outflow of future benefits is expected to occur. Thus, provisions are created to show the outflows predicted in the future. However, standard setters argue that provisions may be used inappropriately to create 'reserves' during profitable years which can be called on in lean years, allowing companies to smooth reported earnings. They claim that this practice introduces a bias into the accounts which reduces the usefulness of information for decision making. Thus, current standards (e.g. IAS 37) require that a provision is raised only when there is a present obligation to an external party.

In some circumstances, it may be difficult to estimate outflows which relate to future events. If reliable measurement is not possible, but information about the future liability is relevant, managers may disclose a contingent liability. Many legal claims are disclosed in this way. Managers are uncertain about the amount involved (i.e. the outflow cannot be measured reliably) but they want to keep stakeholders informed about the possibility of a future outflow.

Liabilities must be distinguished from equity, which is the residual represented by the net assets of the entity. In practice, accountants must determine whether an item should be recognised as a liability or equity. Two points of guidance are the rights of the parties and the economic substance of the arrangement. Entities may differ in how they view 'capital'. It may be considered as financial capital (representing the money invested or its purchasing power) or as physical capital (the productive power of the entity).

LO 4 Challenging issues for standard setters and auditors

Standard setters are currently facing many challenges as they revise the *Framework* and standards relating to definition and recognition criteria for liabilities. The development of more sophisticated 'hybrid' securities, which have attributes of both debt and equity, have raised issues for practitioners. The standard setters are currently working on improved guidance to assist an informative and useful classification of these instruments. The determining factor should be the economic substance associated with the risk–return relationship established by the financial instrument. The debt/equity classification is important because it affects not only the balance sheet but also the level of profit reported by an entity since distributions associated with financial instruments (or parts of financial instruments) that are classified as liabilities are regarded as expenses or income. In contrast, distributions associated with equity instruments are treated as a distribution of profit after expenses and income have been taken into consideration. The debt/equity classification may have a significant impact on ratios used in debt covenants and in other contractual specifications.

The bankruptcy of the Enron Corporation in the United States and the global financial crisis of 2007–08 have focused attention on the extent to which assets and liabilities are appropriately recognised in the accounts. In the case of Enron, the existence of off-balance sheet Special Purpose Entities (SPEs) meant that investors were generally unaware of the extent of the firm's liabilities. The firm collapsed after the full amount of its debts were revealed. In relation to the financial crisis, questions were raised about the valuations applied to assets and liabilities and the use of measurement based on mark-to-market (fair value) accounting. Fair value accounting was accused of exacerbating the financial crisis by allowing firms to write up assets in boom conditions then requiring write-downs to (arguably) unrealistic levels when markets became illiquid. In addition, the crisis drew attention to whether items which had been removed from firms' balance sheets should in fact still be recognised due to ongoing commitments by the originating firm. The IASB has current projects in relation to measurement, disclosure and derecognition of financial instruments which will likely lead to changes in accounting practices for liabilities and equity.

Questions

1. With respect to the proprietary theory,
   (a) what is the objective of the firm?
   (b) how important is the concept of 'stewardship'?
   (c) what is the relationship between assets/liabilities and the owner?
   (d) how would you define income, expenses, profit?
   (e) what are three effects on current practice?
   (f) what are the theory's limitations?
2. With respect to the entity theory,
   (a) what are the reasons for concentrating on the entity as a unit of accountability rather than on the proprietor?
   (b) what is the objective of accounting?
   (c) how important is the concept of 'net worth'?
   (d) what is the reason for modifying the accounting equation to Assets = Equities?
   (e) on what side of the equation in (d) would retained earnings appear?
   (f) why is there a stress on profit determination?
   (g) how do the concepts of income, expenses and profits differ from the proprietary theory? What about interest charges, dividends and income tax?
   (h) what are three effects on current practice?
3. Liabilities are all 'obligations' under the IASB/AASB *Framework* definition of liabilities. What is an obligation, and why does the *Framework* rely heavily on it in the definition?

4. If a liability is a present obligation, does that mean that a legally enforceable claim must exist before a liability exists? Explain. Conversely, if a legally enforceable claim exists, does that mean that a liability must exist? Explain.

5. Under some countries' accounting regulations, unrealised foreign exchange gains and losses are not immediately recognised in a firm's income statement. Instead, unrealised gains are put into a deferred credit account. Is this a liability? Why or why not?

6. Hunter Ltd is attempting to bring its accounts in line with International Financial Reporting Standards (IFRS). Advise the accountant of Hunter Ltd whether a liability exists in each of the following cases and, if so, what the liability is.
   (a) The company is being sued for injuries sustained by an employee who claims that the workplace steps he fell down were unsafe. The outcome of the lawsuit is highly uncertain.
   (b) An order for raw materials has been placed with the firm's regular supplier.
   (c) There is a signed contract for the construction by Oh, Suzanna Ltd of a major item of plant for Hunter Ltd.
   (d) The firm has unsecured notes of $1 000 000 outstanding. Interest is payable six-monthly in June and December. It is now August.
   (e) At the end of the year, half of the firm's employees have non-vested sick leave owing.

7. Does the IASB/AASB *Framework* adopt the principle of conservatism? Why or why not? Do you think that conservatism is desirable in the definitions of assets, liabilities and equity, or in their recognition criteria? Why or why not?

8. How does owners' equity differ from liabilities? Give examples where they are closely aligned, and examples of where they are not.

9. In your opinion, when should the following be recognised as assets or liabilities? Explain whether, how and why your answer deviates from IFRS.
   (a) accounts payable
   (b) put options
   (c) call options
   (d) raw materials inventory
   (e) finance lease obligations
   (f) operating lease obligations
   (g) warranty commitments

10. When, if ever, should a firm recognise a pension (superannuation) liability, and why?

11. Explain the concept of capital maintenance and how it can apply to different concepts of capital.

12. A benefactor pays off a loan for a university. How should the university record the transaction, and why?

13. How should a mining company account for
   (a) a contract which stipulates that on maturity of a cash loan to the company, it must pay the principal in cash or provide a given quantity and grade of extracted minerals, whichever is the higher?
   (b) a contract which stipulates that $1 000 000 is to be spent on mine restoration at the end of the project in 10 years time?

14. How should Shannondoah Ltd account for a cash loan to the company when the contract requires that the principal will be redeemed in ordinary shares at maturity? Ten shares will be given for each $1000 bond. The current market value of the shares is $120.

15. Skipper Ltd financed the construction of its new office block by issuing securities for $50 000 000 on 30 April 2000. Buyers of the securities received a 30 per cent

ownership interest in the office block, and receive 30 per cent of the rent revenue related to letting the offices. The securities mature on 30 April 2015, when Skipper Ltd must redeem the securities at 30 per cent of the value of the office block or $50 000 000, whichever is higher. What should Skipper Ltd have recorded in its accounts on 30 April 2000, and what other journal entries should be recorded throughout the term of the securities?

Problems

PROBLEM 8.1

During 2009, the following events occurred in relation to Jessica's Revals Ltd, a property developer and real estate valuation firm.

(a) Jessica's Revals Ltd purchased land from Denis Gibson for $1 000 000. This land was adjacent to, and otherwise identical to, the block of land that Jessica's Revals Ltd had bought three years ago for $1 000 000 and had then spent an extra $50 000 improving to now have the same value as the land bought from Gibson. Record the two blocks of land in the accounts of Jessica's Revals Ltd.

(b) Jessica's Revals Ltd bought 500 ordinary shares in Charmers Construction Ltd for $18 000 cash on 7 September 2009. This was 5 per cent of the shares on issue by Charmers Construction Ltd. The shares are held for investment purposes. The parcel of shares had a market value of $16 000 at 31 July 2010. Record all the transactions that Jessica's Revals Ltd should record in relation to the shares.

(c) At 31 July 2009, Jessica's Revals Ltd valued its current assets at $20 000 above carrying amount and its fixed assets at $600 000 above carrying amount. In both cases, the valuations were based on market values. How should the firm account for the increase in values?

(d) Jessica's Revals Ltd purchased a development site for $81 000 and immediately sold that site to Kathy Pratt Real Estate for $130 000. The payment consisted of a 10-year non-interest-bearing note for $130 000. The first equal payment ($13 000) is due one year after the sale. The normal rate of interest for such a loan is 10 per cent per annum. Record the sale of the land.

(e) Jessica's Revals Ltd bought bricks with a recommended retail price of $18 000 and a cash price of $16 500. The firm paid for the bricks by paving part of the roadway leading into the brick manufacturing plant. The cost of the paving was $12 000 and the regular contract price to provide the paving was $17 000. Record the transactions.

(f) Jessica's Revals Ltd issued 1000 of its ordinary shares in payment for a tract of land. The market price of the shares was $83 per share at the time of acquisition but the seller had offered to sell the land for $82 000 cash. What journal entry should the firm make to record the land purchase?

PROBLEM 8.2

A block of units was constructed for you five years ago at a cost of $1 200 000. The land had been purchased for $100 000. You now wish to sell the property. You have consulted with your accountant and, to help you, she has provided you with the following calculation:

1. *Present value of $1 514 459*

   Based on your five-year experience, you believe that the average net cash inflow will be $240 000 per year for the next 20 years. This estimate is based on projections of future rentals, tax savings due to depreciation, expenditures for electricity, repairs, property taxes, and so on. A 20-year horizon was chosen because that is when you plan to retire. At the end of year 20, you believe the property can be sold for

$200 000. Your present rate of return is 15 per cent per year. On the basis of your estimates, your accountant calculated present value as follows:

Present value of ordinary annuity of $240 000, 20 periods, 15%	$ 1 502 239
Present value of $200 000, 20 periods, 15%	12 220
	$ 1 514 459

2. *Fair value $2 000 000*
   Two different real estate valuers were hired to give an estimate of the current value of the property. One said the property was worth $2 200 000 ($200 000 for the land, $2 000 000 for the building) and the other said it was worth $1 800 000 ($300 000 for the land, $1 500 000 for the building). The accountant took the average of the two estimates.

3. *Carrying amount $1 080 000*
   The accountant made the following calculations:

Original cost of building	$ 1 200 000
Accumulated depreciation (5 years × $44 000)	220 000
	980 000
	100 000
Land (historical cost)	$ 1 080 000

Depreciation was based on an expected useful life of 25 years and a residual value of $100 000.

4. *Current cost $1 750 000*
   The accountant used specific price indexes, published by the government, to determine the gross current cost of constructing the building today with reference to labour, materials and overhead. Her estimate was $1 800 000. Because the building is actually five years old, she ascertained the amount of accumulated depreciation to be $300 000, based on a 30-year economic life. The net amount of current cost was $1 500 000. The value of the land was considered to be worth $250 000, the average of the estimates by the two valuers.

Required
Comment on each of the four estimates with respect to its relevance and reliability to you as a potential seller of the property.

Additional readings

American Accounting Association Financial Accounting Standards Committee 2001, 'Evaluation of the FASB's proposed accounting for financial instruments with characteristics of liabilities, equity, or both', *Accounting Horizons*, December, pp. 387–400.

Laux, C, & Leuz, C 2009, 'The fair value crisis: Making sense of the recent debate', *Accounting, Organizations and Society*, vol. 34, April.

Ma, R, & Miller, M 1960, 'Conceptualising the liability', *Journal of Accountancy*, May, pp. 41–6.

Marquardt, C, & Wiedman, C 2005, 'Earnings management through transaction structuring: contingent convertible debt and diluted earnings per share', *Journal of Accounting Research*, pp. 205–43.

Moonitz, M 1960, 'Changing concepts of liabilities.' *Journal of Accountancy*, May.

St Kerr, G 1984, The definition and recognition of liabilities. Accounting Theory Monograph No. 4. Melbourne: Australian Accounting Research Foundation.

Page, M, & Whittington, G 2007, 'Financial reporting Fair Value: The price of everything and the value of nothing', *Accountancy*, September, pp. 92–93.

Schipper, K, & Yohn, T 2007, 'Standard setting issues and academic research related to accounting for financial asset transfers,' *Accounting Horizons*, March.

Scott, R 1979, 'Owners' equity, the anachronistic element', *Accounting Review*, October, pp. 750–63.

**8.1
CASE STUDY**

Disclosure of environmental liability

by Lindene Patton C.I.H., Senior vice-president and counsel, Zurich

Around the world, companies are being required to meet higher levels of disclosure of environmental liability ... In the United States, for example, the US Financial Accounting Standard Board (FASB) issued provisions in 2002 for accounting for environmental liabilities on assets being retired from service. The provision for accounting for asset retirement obligations required companies to reserve environmental liabilities related to the eventual retirement of an asset if its fair market value could be reasonably estimated.

The intent of the ruling was disclosure, but the conditional nature of estimating a fair market value caused corporations to take the position that they could defer their liability indefinitely by 'mothballing' a contaminated property. Companies effectively postponed the recognition of their environmental liabilities in the absence of pending or anticipated litigation.

Earlier this year, FASB clarified its intention by providing an interpretation that said companies have a legal obligation to reserve for environmental and other liabilities associated with the eventual retirement of manufacturing facilities or parts of facilities, even when the timing or method of settlement is uncertain. Among examples given by FASB:

- An asbestos-contaminated factory cannot simply be 'mothballed' without adequate reserves to cover the eventual cost of removing the asbestos
- Reserves must be established today for the eventual disposal of still-in-use, creosote-soaked utility poles

As a result of what may seem like a minor technical re-interpretation, companies may have to recognise immediately millions of dollars in liabilities in their income statements to comply with this change.

In Europe, regulators have also initiated efforts to promote disclosure. In 2001, the European Commission promulgated tougher, non-binding guidance for disclosing environmental costs and liabilities, and various countries in Europe have issued additional requirements related to environmental disclosure. In 2002, the Canadian Institute of Chartered Accountants published voluntary guidance that stressed the importance of disclosing all material risks, including environmental liabilities, in companies' annual reports.

Some financial institutions have also pledged to adhere to tenets of international initiatives such as the Equator Principles, which factor environmental and social considerations into assessing the risk of a project. Also, a group of pension funds, foundations, European investors and US state treasurers have endorsed UN efforts to promote a minimum level of disclosure on environmental, social and governance issues.

Recognition of environmental liabilities may also soon emerge as an issue for companies in Asia. While environmental issues may have taken a back seat to rapid economic development over the past 20 years, that situation may change as legislation and regulation catch up with development.

The responsibility for disclosing future environmental liability is clearly a growing issue for companies around the world. However, accurately estimating cleanup costs is not an easy task due to unknown contaminants, legacy liabilities related to formerly operated property, regulatory changes or unexpected claims related to natural resource damage.

Source: CEO (Chief Executive Officer), Thought Leadership, www.the-chiefexecutive.com.

Questions

1. The article states that the US standard setter FASB requires companies to record a provision in relation to environmental costs of retiring an asset ('to reserve environmental liabilities') if its fair value could be reasonably estimated. How do you think companies would go about estimating such a provision?
2. What aspects of the requirements were used by US companies to defer recognition of a liability?
3. In what ways does the recognition of the liability in relation to future restoration activity affect (a) net profit in the current year and future years; and (b) cash flow in the current and future years?
4. The article refers to changes in disclosure requirements relating to environmental liabilities in many countries around the world. How important is it that companies recognise the liability? To what extent is disclosure about the liability sufficient?

8.2
CASE STUDY

Post-retirement employee benefits

Part A — British Telecom (BT): The UK's largest pension scheme

At December 2007, BT had pension liabilities (under IAS 19) of £39 billion. The company's market capitalisation was £18 billion.

When different assumptions are used, the pension liability increases from £39 billion to £43 billion. The different assumptions are (a) discounting at the risk free swap rate and (b) excluding salary growth.

If actual pension asset returns are included in the company's finance income and changes in liabilities due to changes in discount rates are included in finance expenses, BT's 2007 profit before tax increases by £1.4 billion (from £2.5 billion to £3.9 billion).

BT held £8 billion of bonds in its pension asset portfolio but the portfolio comprised mainly equity securities. To meet its annual commitment for pension payments, the company needs £28 billion bonds at 5 per cent yield.

Reference
Ralfe, J 2008, 'Clearer view of pension costs in the offing', *Financial Times*, 18 February, p. 6.

Questions

1. Compare BT's pension liabilities and market capitalisation at December 2007. What are the implications of what you observe?
2. Should changes in pension assets and liabilities be included in net finance income? Give reasons for your answer.
3. The company has a pension asset/liability mismatch because it holds mainly equities, not long-dated bonds in its pension plans (pension asset portfolio). Explain the risk of this approach.
4. Companies must make assumptions when measuring the value of pension assets and liabilities. Assume you are an investor in BT. What information do you require about the assumptions made by the company?

Part B — Australian companies' superannuation shortfall

At 31 December 2008, the combined deficit in the defined benefit superannuation schemes operated by Australia's leading companies was $25 billion. Unfunded liabilities for the 54 biggest companies were less than $2 billion six months earlier.

Companies such as Qantas, Telstra, Rio Tinto, Westpac, BlueScope Steel, Amcor and ANZ all reported unfunded liabilities. Qantas contributed $66 million and Telstra $110 million into their defined benefit schemes.

The value of future superannuation liabilities reflects 10-year government bond yields, which fell from 6.5 per cent to 4 per cent over the period July to December 2008, raising the amount payable in 10 years time by 28 per cent to 0.68 cents for every dollar.

Defined benefit schemes guarantee employees fixed payouts regardless of movements in financial markets. They are only a small portion of total superannuation plans in Australia and are being phased out and replaced by defined contribution schemes (where the benefit depends on the amount contributed and the earnings on the contributions).

Reference

Patten, S 2009, Super shortfall balloons to $25bn, *The Australian Financial Review*, 14 April, p. 15.

Questions

1. What has caused the large increase in unfunded superannuation (pension) liabilities during the period July to December 2008?
2. Should the unfunded superannuation liability be shown on the balance sheets of companies such as Qantas, Telstra, Rio Tinto, Westpac, BlueScope Steel, Amcor and ANZ?
3. What are the implications for employees of belonging to defined benefit schemes? What are the implications for employers of providing defined benefit schemes?
4. Why are defined benefit funds being phased out and replaced by defined contribution schemes?

Endnotes

1. C Sprague, *The philosophy of accounts*, Kansas: Scholars Book Company, 1972, originally published in 1907, pp. 30, 67.
2. W Vatter, 'Corporate stock equities', in Morton Backer (ed.), *Modern accounting theory*, New York: Prentice-Hall, 1966, p. 251. Note that the argument supplied by Vatter applies only to revenue and expenses. For example, an increase in assets because of an owner's contribution of buildings gives rise to a debit to the asset account and a credit to a proprietorship account 'Capital'. In the income statement, debit accounts (expenses) reduce proprietorship, but in the balance sheet, debit accounts (assets) can increase proprietorship.
3. C Martin, *An introduction to accounting*, 2nd edn, New York: McGraw-Hill, 1978, p. 114.
4. W Paton, *Accounting theory*, New York: Scholars Book Company, 1962, originally published in 1922, p. 473.
5. ibid.
6. ibid.
7. W Paton and AC Littleton, *An introduction to corporate accounting standards*, Florida: AAA, 1940, p. 9.
8. ibid., p. 8.
9. G Husband, 'The equity concept in accounting', *Accounting Review*, October 1954.
10. D Cairns, 'The use of fair value in IFRS', *Accounting in Europe*, vol. 3, iss. 1, October 2006, pp. 5–22.
11. G Whittred, I Zimmer and S Taylor, *Financial accounting: incentive effects and economic consequences*, Sydney: Harcourt Brace, 1996.
12. International Accounting Standards Board (IASB) *Liabilities*, July 2009, www.iasb.org.
13. AAA, Supplementary Statement No. 1, 'Reserves and Retained Income', 1950.
14. International Accounting Standards Board (IASB) *Liabilities*, July 2009. www.iasb.org.
15. P Kimmel and TD Warfield, 'The usefulness of hybrid security classifications: evidence from redeemable preferred stock', *Accounting Review*, vol. 70, no. 1, January 1995, pp. 151–67.
16. International Accounting Standards Board (IASB) Financial Instruments with Characteristics of Equity, www.iasb.org, April 2009.
17. International Accounting Standards Board (IASB) IASB Amendments Permit Reclassification of Financial Instruments, www.iasb.org, October 2008.

18. International Accounting Standards Board (IASB) IASB Proposes Improvements to Derecognition Requirements as part of Review of Off Balance Sheet Risk, www.iasb.org, March 2009.

19. AAA Financial Accounting Standards Committee, 'Evaluation of the IASB's proposed accounting and disclosure requirements for share-based payment', *Accounting Horizons*, vol. 18, no. 1, 2004, pp. 65–76.

20. Auditing Standard ASA 570 Going Concern, June 2007.

21. J Madrick, 'Report of Investigation by the Special Investigative Committee of the Board of Directors of Enron Corp — Review — Statistical Data Included', *Challenge*, May 2002.

22. G Benston and A Hartgraves, 'Enron: What happened and what we can learn from it', *Journal of Accounting and Public Policy*, vol. 21, no. 2, 2002, pp. 105–27; WC Powers Jr, (Chair) RS Troubh, HS Winokur Jr, Powers Report: Report of Investigation by the Special Investigative Committee of the Board of Directors of Enron Corp, February 1, 2002.

23. An SPE may be treated as it if were an independent, outside entity for accounting purposes if two conditions are met: (1) an owner independent of the company must make a substantive equity investment of at least 3 per cent of the SPE's assets, and that 3 per cent must remain at risk throughout the transactions; and (2) the independent owner must exercise control of the SPE (Powers Report, 2002, paragraph 4, page 6). However, it is not clear that the 3 per cent limit is legally binding, (Madrick 2002, op. cit.).

24. Madrick 2002, op. cit.; Benston and Hartgraves, 2002, op. cit.; Powers Report, 2002, op. cit., paragraph 6, page 6.

25. A Levitt, 'The numbers game', speech to the NYU Centre for Law and Business, New York, September 28, 1998, www.sec.gov.

26. Public Company Accounting Oversight Board (PCAOB), 'Report on the PCAOB's 2004, 2005, and 2006 inspections of domestic triennially inspected firms', Release No. 2007-010 October 22, 2007, www.pcaobus.org.

9 Revenue

LEARNING OBJECTIVES

After reading this chapter, you should have an appreciation of the following:

1 the nature of revenue and various approaches taken to defining revenue, including the behavioural view of revenue

2 issues related to the recognition of revenue and the criteria used in the revenue recognition process

3 guidance provided by standard setters in relation to revenue recognition and measurement

4 standard setters' current activities in relation to revenue recognition and measurement

5 issues for auditors arising from revenue recognition and measurement.

Revenue is a key element in financial statements and of considerable importance to preparers and users of financial statements. Reported revenue reflects the firm's past operations and is used to predict future performance. Although determining revenue is a crucial part of performance measurement, its measurement is not always straightforward because of the many different business models which exist. In this chapter we consider the nature of revenue by exploring its definition, recognition and measurement. We discuss issues related to revenue recognition and measurement, giving some historical background and outlining three commonly accepted criteria for revenue recognition. An overview of the guidance provided in IAS 18/AASB 118 *Revenue* is also provided.

Firms' policies relating to the timing of revenue recognition can have significant impact on their reported results. Market regulators such as Australian Securities and Investments Commission (ASIC) in Australia and the SEC in the United States have taken action in many cases where they have considered that firms have used inappropriate recognition policies. Standard setters have also identified revenue recognition as an area where improved guidance is needed. This chapter outlines international initiatives being undertaken in relation to standards for revenue recognition and measurement and for reporting firms' financial performance. Finally, we discuss issues arising for auditors in relation to revenue recognition and measurement.

LO 1 ▸ REVENUE DEFINED

Revenue is a key accounting element and fundamental to reporting on a firm's activities, so its definition is important. We know that revenue has to do with the gross increase in the value of assets and capital, and that the increase eventually pertains to cash. For the main operations of the business, the cash inflow is created predominantly by the production and sale of the output of the entity. We can therefore identify two flows connected with the major operations of the business: the physical and the monetary flows.

The physical flow involves the event of producing and selling the firm's output or product. The monetary flow involves the event of increasing the value of the firm (due to production or sales to customers of the firm's output). Paton and Littleton refer to both the physical and monetary flows when discussing revenue. They call revenue the 'product of the enterprise' capturing the physical flow of producing the firm's output. They also add that revenue is 'represented finally by the flow of funds from the customers' thus capturing the monetary flow.[1] Thus, we conclude that revenue is directly related to the monetary event of value increasing in the firm, which arises out of production or sale of output.

Revenue is defined in IAS 18/AASB 118 *Revenue*, paragraph 7, as having a flow characteristic:

> Revenue is the gross inflow of economic benefits during the period arising in the course of the ordinary activities of an entity when those inflows result in increases in equity, other than increases relating to contributions from equity participants.

In the IASB *Framework* (the AASB *Framework* in Australia, from 1 January 2005), revenue forms part of income. This is made clear in paragraphs 70(a) and 74 of the *Framework*:

> Income is increases in economic benefits during the accounting period in the form of inflows or enhancements of assets or decreases of liabilities that result in increases in equity, other than those relating to contributions from equity participants.

The definition of income encompasses both revenue and gains. Revenue arises in the course of the ordinary activities of an entity and is referred to by a variety of different names including sales, fees, interest, dividends, royalties and rent.

In the United States, the FASB defines revenues as follows:

Revenues are inflows or other enhancements of assets of an entity or settlements of its liabilities (or a combination of both) during a period from delivering or producing goods, rendering services, or other activities that constitute the entity's ongoing major or central operations.[2]

The IASB definition is consistent with the FASB's definition of revenue and focuses on inflows or other asset enhancements arising from an entity's ongoing major or central operations. Assets received or enhanced by income may include cash, receivables and goods and services received in exchange for goods and services supplied (*Framework*, para. 77). The definitions note that income may also result from the settlement of liabilities.

Since income is defined to include both revenue and gains (*Framework*, para. 74), further clarification about gains is provided. For example, gains that meet the definition of income may or may not arise in the course of ordinary activities. Gains are included as part of income since they represent future economic benefits and are thus no different in nature from revenue. Therefore, they are not considered a separate element in the *Framework* (para. 75). The definition of income also includes unrealised gains, which has implications for revenue recognition rules. These implications are explored later in this chapter.

In contrast to the IASB approach, the FASB makes a distinction between revenues and gains, although both are included in profit. Gains are increases in net assets from 'peripheral or incidental transactions' and from other events that may be largely beyond the control of the firm. Revenues pertain to the ongoing major or central operations. However, Martin has suggested that there appears to be no reason that revenues and gains should not follow the same rules for their recognition and measurement. Fundamentally, both represent increases in net assets and they should therefore be treated identically.[3] An application of this principle in practice is explored in theory in action 9.1 in relation to the treatment of gains on remeasurement of property held by property trusts.

9.1
THEORY IN ACTION

No income gained from revaluations

by Robert Harley

On February 27, Westfield Group declared an annual profit of $5.58 billion. It was a great headline number, up more than 30 per cent on last year, but Frank Lowy's investors did not see a cent of additional payout.

Why? Because the result included $5.1 billion worth of asset revaluations which, under AIFRS — the Australian equivalent of International Financial Reporting Standards — were reported as profit, even though they add nothing to income.

Westfield is not alone. The latest property results reinforce the problems the sector is having, and will continue to have, with statutory accounting, which insists that cash and non-cash items (such as revaluations) be combined as profit.

"The market is still coming to grips with the appropriate way to disclosing the true underlying performance of property companies and listed property trusts," says joint chief executive of Mirvac Funds Management, Adrian Harrington.

"It is not going to be until property revaluations head down that people will truly understand the impact of putting revaluations through the P&L [profit and loss statement] and the confusion that will create [for] investors," he says.

GPT Group chief financial officer Kieran Pryke holds a similar view: "The financial statements are no longer useful. We had a reported profit of $1.3 billion, but the actual money was $560 million.

"AIFRS has made the production of financial statements a compliance exercise; the market does not use the financial statements to assess financial performance but is relying upon supplementary information that is not subject to any proscribed process or a director's sign-off," says Pryke.

"I am not sure these conditions are conducive to an orderly market."

For the International Accounting Standards Board in London, the logic seems simple. Property investors gain their return through both cash income and capital gain. Both should be included in profit. However, many of Pryke's investors regard real estate as a cash flow business.

"Profit should refer to how much money I have made, not necessarily how much value I have," he says.

In its Real Estate Investment Trust reporting wrap, Goldman Sachs JBWere notes that a few REITS, notably Westfield, Tishman Speyer Office Fund, Multiplex Group and Bunnings Warehouse Property Trust, did not present a distribution-reconciliation statement on the basis of the accounting system before AIFRS.

"We believe investors should insist on these statements so exact composition of distributions can be compared on a like for like basis, GSJBW notes.

Property Council of Australia chief executive Peter Verwer says AIFRS had aimed to give global investors comparable numbers wherever they were investing. "It hasn't worked because the framers of the standards did not understand property markets," he says.

He notes, however, that in recent weeks, "the Australian Accounting Standards Board has shown more willingness to revisit key issues".

Source: The Australian Financial Review, 14 March 2007.

Questions

1. Explain why Westfield's result for 2006 was 30 per cent better than the previous year. How do reporting requirements of AIFRS differ to Australian Generally Accepted Accounting Principles, (AGAAP) for companies in the property sector?
2. Why does the IASB consider that revaluation gains are part of income? (Refer to material in the chapter.)
3. What is meant by the statement 'IFRS has made the production of financial statement a compliance exercise; the market does not use the financial statements to assess financial performance'?

Behavioural view of revenue

As outlined, revenues represent increases in the total value of assets (or a decrease in the value of liabilities) and capital other than additional investments by owners. These increases usually occur because the firm undertakes certain activities; in other words, there is performance by the firm. Revenue generally comes about because the entity does something to make it happen.

Revenue is not simply a sum of money. As Paton and Littleton put it, revenue indicates the 'accomplishment' of the firm.[4] It is a measure of the entity's 'gross performance' as a profit-making business. When expenses are seen as representing the 'effort' of the firm, then the matching of revenues and expenses results in profit: the 'net accomplishment' of the firm. This is a behavioural view of revenues, expenses and profit.

In a similar vein, Bedford stresses an operational view of revenue and profit, where profit is defined in terms of certain operations performed by the entity rather than being merely the result of the application of accounting methods.[5] Profit arises only from those activities that are designated business operations. Thus, certain increases and decreases in value are excluded, such as those from government bond transactions, gifts and contributions, because they are not considered profit-generating business activities. The general business operations specified by Bedford are:

- acquisition of money resources
- acquisition of services
- use of services
- recombination of acquired services
- disposition of services
- distribution of money resources.

Myers relates the concepts of revenue and profit to certain critical events and decisions made by the managers of the firm. He suggests that profit is earned at the moment of making the most critical decision or of performing the most difficult task in the cycle of a complete transaction. However, he stresses that the critical event will be at a different point depending on the nature of the business. For example, the critical event for a manufacturer (i.e. sale of the product) may be different from the critical event for a financial institution (making a loan). Despite inconsistencies in practice, Myers's critical event theory remains useful in helping the accountant determine the point at which revenue should be recognised.[6]

These positions all emphasise that revenue and profit come about because of something the firm does. This is a behavioural view of revenue and profit. All the activities undertaken by the firm to make a profit, taken as a whole, are called the 'earning process'. Applying Bedford's business operations to a manufacturing firm, we find its earning process consists of the sequence illustrated in figure 9.1.

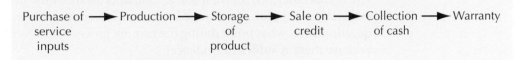

FIGURE 9.1 Earning process of a manufacturing firm

In contrast to Myers, Paton and Littleton argue that revenue and profit accrue throughout the earning process — that is, there is a continual change in value of the total assets and capital as the firm undertakes the activities specified in the process.[7] The FASB's definition of revenue calls attention to 'the inflows or other enhancements of assets of an entity or settlements of its liabilities' due to 'delivering or producing goods, rendering services'. Note that the definition does not specify that revenue is only the amount of sales made to customers. Defining revenue is only the first step in measuring it in actual situations. A set of rules based on the definition is necessary in order to objectively identify and measure the amount of revenue in practice. These rules are commonly referred to as realisation or recognition principles.

LO 2 ― REVENUE RECOGNITION

Historical perspective

During the nineteenth century, income (profit) for a business was determined on the basis of an increase in net worth. Chatfield states that this was done either 'through a policy of replacement accounting or by way of periodic asset appraisals'.[8] The now familiar recognition or realisation principle was not always a part of standard accounting practice. As May stated:

> A review of accounting, legal, and economic writing suggests that the realisation postulate was not accepted prior to the First World War. In 1913, leading authorities in all these fields in England and America seemed to agree on the 'increase in net worth' concept of income.[9]

The increase in net worth view of income was gradually supplanted by the notion that income had to be 'realised'. This change arose because the use of specialised non-current assets by firms became significant in the period between World War I and the 1930s. Determining the value of these specialised assets was difficult, making calculation of changes in asset values more difficult to ascertain.

In the United States, abuses arising from appraisal valuations in the 1920s contributed in part to the disastrous economic events leading to the Great Depression of the 1930s. Some people saw the accounting profession as being partly responsible for the calamity because it had permitted companies to value assets over-optimistically. In the face of these criticisms, accountants adopted a conservative attitude and the recognition or realisation principle was an outcome of this defensive posture. Chatfield points out that the first authoritative use of the word 'realisation' occurred in 1932 in correspondence between a special committee of the American Institute and the New York Stock Exchange.[10] The special committee supported the realisation criterion and rejected the asset appraisal method. Subsequently, upward revaluations of non-current assets were not permitted under US GAAP. However, they were commonly observed in the United Kingdom and Australia prior to the adoption of IASB standards in 2005.

Criteria for revenue recognition

The events described above made accountants aware of the need for sufficient objective evidence to support any change in value if it were to be recorded as revenue. The key question is: At what point during the earning process can revenue be recorded as earned because there is sufficient evidence?

Revenue recognition may take place at a number of stages in a firm's operating (or earnings) cycle, depicted in figure 9.2. This was outlined by Coombes and Martin as follows:

revenue has been recognised at several points in the earnings cycle, for example:

(i) at point 5 in the building industry for long-term construction contracts
(ii) at point 7 where it is the responsibility of the purchaser to collect the goods

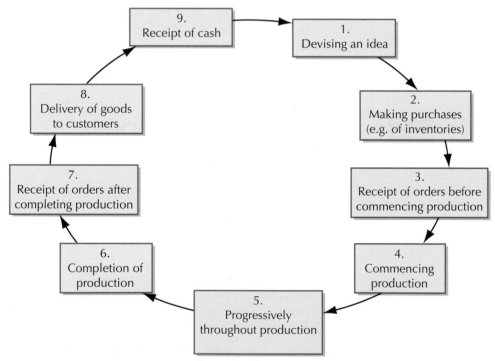

FIGURE 9.2 The operating cycle
Source: AARF, ED 51B.

(iii) at point 8 in most cases

(iv) at point 9 by some professional practices and for instalment credit sales.[11]

We need to formulate criteria to help us decide what is sufficient objective evidence — that is, we need to know the type of evidence we require before we have confidence in a given amount of revenue or gain. Over the years, based on the need for objective evidence, three criteria have evolved to ascertain whether revenue or gain should be recognised. Recognition criteria are based on the desire for both relevant and reliable accounting information but, traditionally, emphasis is placed on the latter. The three criteria are:

- measurability of asset value
- existence of a transaction
- substantial completion of the earning process.

These criteria are discussed below.

Analysis of criteria for revenue recognition

Measurability of asset value

Revenue can be viewed as an inflow that increases the value of the total assets of the firm, with a concurrent increase in equity. Thus measurability of asset value is a reasonable criteria for recognising revenue. If there is no inflow of asset value that can be objectively determined, revenue cannot be calculated objectively. The use of fair value measurement in standards such as IAS 39/AASB 139 *Financial Instruments: Recognition and Measurement*, IAS 40/AASB 140 *Investment Property* and IAS 41/AASB 141 *Agriculture* also focuses on the enhancement of assets, without any actual or physical inflow of assets. In such cases, the key issue is still objectivity. This requires that there is a valid basis by which to measure the enhancement (increased value) of the asset(s).

The need for reliable or verifiable measurement has led to conservative approaches to valuing assets. The most conservative position is that an increase in asset value should be recorded when actually realised. Under fair value accounting, changes in the value of assets are reported as expenses or revenues arising from holding the assets. This is entirely consistent with the accrual accounting approach, but inconsistent with historical cost conservatism and the realisation concept. The incremental recognition of changes in asset values is less of an issue where there are ready markets for assets, such as shares in publicly traded companies. However, it becomes problematic when market values or reliable inputs to valuation models are not readily available.

Must the asset be liquid?

The FASB states that revenues and gains are generally not recognised until realised or realisable.[12] This viewpoint was supported by the AARF in Theory Monograph No. 3. The term 'realised' means that the asset received is cash or claims to cash and 'realisable'[13] means the asset received is readily convertible to known amounts of cash or claims to cash. Readily convertible assets have interchangeable units and available quoted prices in an active market.

In most cases, the entity receives an asset from a sale transaction and the value of the asset received is the amount of revenue recorded. But must the asset received be liquid, such as cash or receivables, before revenue can be recorded? What if a firm sold its product and received raw materials or a non-current asset in exchange? At one time, the dominant view was that the asset received had to be liquid. Paton and Littleton outlined this viewpoint:

> Revenue is realised, according to the dominant view, when it is evidenced by cash receipts or receivables, or other new liquid assets.[14]

In Theory Monograph No. 3 (p. 12) it was reported that the literature has 'confused the term realisation with recognition'. The 'everyday' meanings of the two words are considered to be significantly different:

> 'Realise' has been defined as '... to convert (securities, paper money etc.) into cash, or (property of any kind) into money ... to obtain or amass (a sum of money, fortune etc.) by sale, trade or similar means ... On the other hand, 'recognise' means 'to treat as valid, as having existence ...'.[15]

This led the authors of the monograph to propose a definition of 'realisation' (p. 14) designed to overcome this confusion:

> 'realisation' should be defined strictly in terms of a cash receipt or a legal claim to cash and should not refer to the broader problem of revenue recognition.[16]

This is a reasonable stance to take, given that recognition can be made by the business at any point which is considered to satisfy the more complex recognition criteria, whereas realisation will take place only when the cash or equivalent in assets is actually received by the business.

According to a committee report of the American Accounting Association, the reason for the FASB's position in requiring revenues to be realised or realisable before they were recognised was to prevent management from depleting the working capital of the firm by paying out dividends when the firm was low on liquid assets, or by paying dividends out of invested capital.[17] Another reason for the insistence that the asset received be liquid before revenue could be recorded was the legal provision that dividends be distributed out of profits. Hatfield stated:

> Another use of the term profits limits it to so much of the increment in proprietorship as may, in accordance with legal provisions or the maxims of business expediency, be distributed as dividends of a corporation. In legal discussions the term profits of a corporation frequently means profits available for dividends.[18]

Some accountants questioned whether they should formulate rules which, in effect, interfered in the managerial decision-making process concerning the firm's working capital position and its ability to pay dividends. After all, if an entity wanted to sell most of its output for non-current assets, thereby limiting its cash position, it was the entity's problem, not the accountant's. Accounting is needed to help managers make decisions, not to make decisions for them. Also, the rule was already being violated by the equity method which permits the absorption of a proportion of the investee firm's profit into the valuation of the investor firm's long-term investment in the investee.

Recognition requires an inflow of assets or a measurable (quantifiable) change in the value of an asset, whereas realisation requires an inflow of liquid assets. For example, a bank that holds shares in public companies will mark the investment to market and recognise any gain or loss at balance date (i.e. use fair value). Let's say that a bank holds 1000 shares in B Ltd which were purchased at the beginning of the financial year for $1 per share. At reporting date, they have a market value of $1.20 per share. The asset (listed company shares) is valued at $1200 at reporting date and revenue is increased by the gain of $200. If the year-end value was 80 cents per share, then the incremental expense of holding the shares of $200 would be recognised in the income statement. The gain/loss has not been realised, but is recognised each accounting period. When a gain or loss is realised through the sale of the shares then the adjustment is directly against the asset, to remove it from the books, and to cash (or whatever asset is received for the shares). This approach leads to consistent values reported in the balance sheet, provided that all such assets can be 'measured reliably'.

Collectability

An aspect of the criterion of measurability is whether collectability of the cash is reasonably assured. Measurability of asset values relates to their collectability. Collectability is a matter of judgement, usually based on the previous experience of the firm. The longer the collection period, the more uncertain it is that all the cash will be collected. Determining collectability is a matter of resolving the uncertainty associated with the realisation of revenue.

In Theory Monograph No. 3, the authors discuss in detail the tests related to the resolution of uncertainty.[19] In 1977, Hendriksen outlined the underlying issue:

> It is the uncertainty of the expected receipt and the search for verifiable measures that have led accountants to the adoption of specific rules for the timing of revenue.[20]

Uncertainty resolution is therefore fundamental to the recognition of revenue. Coombes and Martin are of the following opinion:

> If uncertainty resolution is accepted as the underlying criterion for revenue recognition, it seems fruitful to adopt measurability and permanence as the conditions to be met before uncertainty is resolved.[21]

In this definition, 'measurability' relates to the objective ability to assign value to the sale. The term 'objective' can be broadly interpreted as 'unbiased', and subject to verification by another competent investigator.[22] The second factor of 'permanence' implies that, once recognised, there should be no reason for subsequently 'reversing' the revenue out of the accounts.

Existence of a transaction

When an external party in an arm's-length transaction expresses willingness to pay a given price for the firm's product, the transaction constitutes objective evidence of an increase in value in the firm. The outside party provides corroboration of the value of the output. Presently, except in specified cases, the firm must be a direct participant in the transaction. Note that if we insist on the firm being a party to the transaction before revenue can be recognised, then historical cost becomes the most feasible basis for asset valuation. It is not surprising, therefore, to find that critics of the 'transaction' criterion tend to be advocates of current cost and exit price accounting (types of fair value accounting). They argue that the firm does not need to be a party to the transaction, but that a market transaction in general is sufficient. Based on such an approach, assets can be revalued and a gain recorded before the sale.

We should not lose sight of the fact that the desire for a transaction is due to the need for objective evidence. Is it possible to have objective evidence concerning the price of a firm's output without insisting on an external transaction involving the firm? Many accountants believe that a market transaction, even without the direct participation of the firm, provides sufficient evidence of the value of the firm's inventories. The fact is that at present there are numerous instances where market values are used to value inventories or other assets and revenue or gain is recorded. For example, inventories of certain products, such as wheat and barley, can be valued at current market prices. In the United States, ARB 43 states:

> For certain articles, however, exceptions are permissible. Inventories of gold and silver, when there is an effective government-controlled market at a fixed monetary value,

are ordinarily reflected at selling prices. A similar treatment is not uncommon for inventories representing agricultural, mineral, and other products, units of which are interchangeable and have an immediate marketability at quoted prices and for which appropriate costs may be difficult to obtain.[23]

Why do we allow a business selling one of these products to record revenue, even though there is no transaction in which the business is a direct participant? The answer is that the profession recognises that sufficient objective evidence exists before the moment of sale. The output is practically guaranteed to be sold. The point is that it is objective evidence that is the critical factor, not the transaction itself.

Too many instances of the use of market prices as the basis of valuation currently exist for anyone to say that market prices do not constitute sufficient objective evidence. It may be true that in some cases they are not reliable, but we cannot demand that in all cases a firm must be a direct participant in the transaction before revenue or gain can be recognised.

The transaction test will be appropriate in the majority of cases to validate the recognition of revenue. However, the authors of Theory Monograph No. 3 consider that there is a problem associated with the 'vagueness inherent in the word transaction'.[24] As a consequence, the transaction test is often used in conjunction with associated tests, such as the realisation test. Martin and Coombes state:

> In recent years, the transaction test has become less persuasive. More recent accounting standards mean that valuation gains may appear as income, for example IAS 39 *Financial Instruments: Recognition and Measurement* and IAS 41 *Agriculture*. The requirement for a transaction to have taken place may be seen as a necessary but not a sufficient condition to establish revenue.[25]

Substantial completion of the earning process

This criterion, not explicitly stated in the *Framework*, focuses on the notion that revenue is not generated (earned) until the firm has performed most of the activities for which the firm earns revenue. For this criterion to be applicable, revenue is not regarded as having been earned until the firm has done something. For example, the signing of a contract in most cases does not create revenue because there is no performance by the seller at that point.

When most of the operations that constitute the earning process have been undertaken by the enterprise, then the costs associated with those operations can also be determined. The total cost can be ascertained with little uncertainty, because whatever future costs there may be can be easily estimated. The objective evidence we seek to support value increases is related to the objective determination of costs.

The completion-of-earning-process test suffers from the subjective difficulties associated with the tests outlined in this chapter:

> The difficulty is that revenue may result from a number of activities, from production to sale to collection and is in reality a continuous process: and
>   The problem faced by those who would adopt an earning point test is the selection of that point at which earning is considered to be accomplished.[26]

Myers considered the completion of earnings problem by advocating a 'critical event' criterion:

> profit is earned at the moment of making the most critical decision or of performing the most difficult task in the cycle of a complete transaction.[27]

LO 3 ⊣ REVENUE MEASUREMENT

The three general criteria for revenue recognition discussed above have been considered by standard setters in determining appropriate guidance. The *Framework*, paragraph 83, provides two criteria for revenue recognition:

(a) it is probable that any future economic benefit associated with the item will flow to or from the entity; and

(b) the item has a cost or value that can be measured with reliability.

While the *Framework* provides some guidance in relation to recognition it does not cover measurement. IAS 18/AASB 118 *Revenue* is more specific. It states that revenue is to be measured at the fair value of the consideration received or receivable (para. 9). Further, it provides specific rules for recognition and measurement of different types of revenue, namely (a) sale of goods, (b) rendering of services and (c) interest, royalties and dividends (figure 9.3). A discussion of this guidance follows.

FIGURE 9.3 Revenue recognition and measurement rules in IAS 18/AASB 118 *Revenue*, paragraphs 14, 20, 29 and 30

Sale of goods

14. Revenue from the sale of goods shall be recognised when all the following conditions have been satisfied:

    (a) the entity has transferred to the buyer the significant risks and rewards of the ownership of the goods;

    (b) the entity retains neither continuing managerial involvement to the degree usually associated with ownership nor effective control over the goods sold;

    (c) the amount of revenue can be measured reliably;

    (d) it is probable that the economic benefits associated with the transaction will flow to the entity; and

    (e) the costs incurred or to be incurred in respect of the transaction can be measured reliably.

Rendering of services

20. When the outcome of a transaction involving the rendering of services can be estimated reliably, revenue associated with the transaction shall be recognised by reference to the stage of completion of the transaction at the reporting date. The outcome of a transaction can be estimated reliably when all the following conditions have been satisfied:

    (a) the amount of revenue can be measured reliably;

    (b) it is probable that the economic benefits associated with the transaction will flow to the entity;

    (c) the stage of completion of the transaction at the reporting date can be measured reliably; and

    (d) the costs incurred for the transaction and the costs to complete the transaction can be measured reliably.

Interest, royalties and dividends

29. Revenue arising from the use by others of entity assets yielding interest, royalties and dividends shall be recognised on the bases set out in paragraph 30 when:

    (a) it is probable that the economic benefits associated with the transaction will flow to the entity; and

    (b) the amount of the revenue can be measured reliably.

FIGURE 9.3 *(continued)*

> 30. Revenue shall be recognised on the following bases:
>   (a) interest shall be recognised using the effective interest method as set out in AASB 139, paragraphs 9 and AG5–AG8;
>   (b) royalties shall be recognised on an accrual basis in accordance with the substance of the relevant agreement; and
>   (c) dividends shall be recognised when the shareholder's right to receive payment is established.

Sale of goods

From a theoretical perspective, the sales point best meets the three general recognition criteria (measurability of asset value, existence of a transaction, and substantial completion of the earning process) listed in the previous section. Therefore, the sales point in the earning process is selected as being generally the most appropriate time to measure and record revenue because it meets the criteria for recognition. At the time of sale, a transaction takes place, the seller receives a measurable asset, and the earning process is substantially complete.

Explanation of sale

What is a sale? How do we know that a sale has taken place? Using the law as a guideline, the usual event giving rise to a sale is that the product is delivered by the seller to the customer, or the services are rendered. As stated by Martin:

> The verifiable evidence of revenue often consists of an external sales transaction, so that revenue cannot usually be recognised before the point of sale.[28]

In a few instances, the seller may make delivery not by moving the goods but by delivery of a document of title. Must title to a product pass to the customer for the exchange to be considered a sale? In most cases, title to goods does pass to the customer because the legal notion of a sale includes the transfer of title. But emphasis should be placed on the economic substance of the transaction rather than on technical legal details. The passing of title is one aspect to consider in determining whether a sale has been made (IAS 18/AASB 118, para. 15), but it should not be stressed as the main consideration, at least from an accounting point of view. The sales-type lease is an example of how accounting methods may differ from the legal viewpoint. The standard setters have stated that a lease that transfers substantially all of the benefits and risks associated with ownership of property should be accounted for as an acquisition of an asset by the lessee and a sale by the lessor. Despite the contract, which calls the exchange a lease, from an accounting standpoint the transaction is a sale. If the lessor is transferring one of its products to the lessee, then sales revenue and cost of sales are to be recorded. Criteria for ascertaining whether a lease is a sales-type lease (finance lease) are listed in IAS 17/AASB 117 *Leases*. The main consideration for determining whether a sale has occurred is the economic substance of the transaction or event, not the legal form.

The rule that a sale takes place when a seller delivers goods to a customer is simple enough. However, business transactions can be varied and complex and generate such questions as: When should an entity record sales revenue if the goods are set aside for a customer to meet their convenience? In such a case, delivery is not insisted on yet the sale may be recorded. What if the product is delivered but the customer has the right to return it? Rights of ownership, discussed in IAS 18/AASB 118, provide guidance.

If significant risks of ownership are retained, then the transaction is not a sale and revenue is not recognised (para. 16).

Exceptions to sales basis

Situations exist where revenue is permitted or required to be recorded other than at the time of sale. There are three accepted exceptions to the sales recognition principle. They are:

- revenue recognised during production
- revenue recognised at the end of production
- revenue recognised when cash is received after the sale is made.

Since recognition principles are based on the demand for objective evidence, exceptions relate to insufficient evidence before sale or at the time of the sale. The exceptions to the general rule relating to the sales basis can or should be used only under specified conditions, as explained below.

During production

Revenue can be recognised in increments in some cases while the product is still in production. IAS 18/AASB 118 permits revenue recognition based on the percentage-of-completion method. IAS 11/AASB 111 *Construction Contracts* provides guidance for the use of this method for long-term construction contracts. These contracts include construction for specific projects usually carried on at the job site. In some cases, they may include the manufacturing or building of special items on a contractual basis in a manufacturer's own plant.

The contention that a better measure of periodic revenue results from using the percentage-of-completion method is not based on the criteria for recognition. Rather, its justification is founded on the argument that revenue accrues throughout the operating cycle. Revenue does not suddenly appear when a sale is made, but is generated in increments in a continuous process. Therefore, it is reasonable to view revenue as an orderly, gradual increase throughout the period of production — the most critical event of the earning process — but only if there is sufficient evidence of earning revenue. Revenue can be recognised only when it is probable that economic benefits will flow to the entity (IAS 18/AASB 118, para. 22). The use of the percentage-of-completion method for construction contracts is appropriate only when reasonably reliable estimates can be made of the extent of progress towards completion, costs and contract revenue.

The emphasis appears to be on the first general criterion for recognition, which has to do with the measurability and collectability of the asset. Because there is a contract between buyer and seller, the measurability of the total sales value of the item is established. Collectability is a matter of judgement. It depends on assurances that buyers can be expected to satisfy their obligations. The critical estimate is the percentage of completion. Three ways have been identified to help determine the stage of contract completion (IAS 11/AASB 111, para. 30):

(a) the proportion that contract costs incurred for work performed to date bear to the estimated total contract costs;
(b) surveys of work performed; or
(c) completion of a physical proportion of the contract work.

The second general criterion for recognition of revenue (existence of a transaction) is met by the signing of the contract which stipulates the total sales value. Although this is an executory contract, it does objectively establish the price of the item and reveals the willingness of an outside party to pay that amount. The contract normally will specify the enforceable rights of each party. The seller has the right to require progress payments as evidence of the buyer's ownership interest and intent to complete the contract. Assuming the percentage of completion is reasonably reliable, then the proportionate amount of the total expected revenue recorded each period can be considered to be rationally determined.

If the earning process is considered to be complete only when the project is finished, then the third generally applied criterion for revenue recognition (substantial completion of the earnings process) cannot be said to be met. However, the intent of the 'substantial completion' criterion is to have revenue recorded reflecting extent of performance by the firm; that is, to ensure that the firm has undertaken the necessary operations to earn the current revenue. The costs incurred are assumed to reflect the performance of the firm.

As discussed earlier under the sales recognition principle, it would be inappropriate to record the total revenue at time of sale if most of the necessary operations to earn that revenue have not yet been undertaken. But for the percentage-of-completion method, the proportionate amount of revenue recorded for the current period is related to the amount of costs incurred, which represents the performance by the firm for that period. Therefore, revenue for the period is based on the substantial completion of a portion of the total work being attempted.

Case study 9.1 explores revenue recognition in relation to real estate property companies. Some companies apply IAS 18 to recognise revenue on a completed contract basis. However, other firms have applied the completed contract method as per IAS 11. The importance of revenue recognition and the diversity of practice led IFRIC to issue an interpretation to provide practical guidance in relation to this issue.

End of production

The recognition of revenue based on end of production rather than sales is a sensible procedure if production is the critical event and the subsequent sale is simply a routine transaction to be taken for granted. Such a situation exists only where the demand for the output is assured. Obviously, there must be sufficient evidence that the demand for the goods exists before their actual sale.

Cash received after sale

The instalment method and the cost recovery method are the appropriate procedures in relation to the recognition of revenue based on cash received after a sale. The cash received is the amount of revenue. Under the instalment method, the cost of the product is allocated by the ratio:

$$\frac{\text{Cash collected during the period}}{\text{Total sales price (total cash expected)}}$$

Under the cost recovery method, an amount of expense equal to revenue is recognised until all the costs are recovered. Thereafter, any additional cash received is profit.

The instalment and cost recovery methods reveal a conservative position in relation to revenue recognition, because they assume the sale of the product does not constitute sufficient evidence that revenue has been earned. Only the actual receipt of cash from the customer will satisfy the evidence requirement. These methods are necessary because either the first criterion for revenue recognition, measurability (collectability), or the third, substantial completion, is not met. Under the third criterion, the firm does not record revenue because it has not yet earned it by undertaking the necessary activities. Under the first criterion, the seller has no assurance that all the cash will be collected from the sale.

Rendering of services

IAS 18/AASB 118 paragraph 20 requires that revenue associated with rendering of services is to be recognised by reference to the stage of completion of the transaction at reporting date. Thus, revenue is recognised in the period in which the service is rendered. The recognition of revenue on this basis provides useful information about the service activity and performance of the firm in the period, which would not be available if the service was required to be complete before revenue was recognised. Paragraph 23 states that an entity is generally able to make reliable estimates, enabling recognition of revenue, when it has agreed to the following with other parties:

(a) each party's enforceable rights regarding the service to be provided and received by the parties;
(b) the consideration to be exchanged; and
(c) the manner and terms of settlement.

Services may involve a single act and time, or multiple acts and times. Revenue recognition must consider the nature and timing of the acts. If there is a significant act which must be completed, recognition should not occur until this act has been performed. Where the services consist of an indeterminate number of acts over a specified period, revenue should be recognised on a straight-line basis (para. 25). The amount of revenue recognised should reflect the service provided. For example, ASIC found that companies acting in an agency relationship, such as travel agents, were reporting revenue on a gross basis. They showed the value of transactions undertaken by their clients, rather than the net amount of commission to which they were entitled. Although profit was not affected (because the companies also made a corresponding overstatement of expenses), ASIC considered the practice was contrary to revenue recognition requirements and potentially misleading for financial statement users.[29]

Interest, royalties and dividends

Interest, royalties and dividends can be recognised when received, satisfying all three of the general recognition criteria (measurability, transaction and substantial completion). However, for some items, the passing of time signifies revenue has been earned. In this case, accrued revenue is recorded, even though there is no external transaction. An example is interest revenue accrued at the end of the accounting period. In effect, a service is being sold — the use of money — as each day passes. IAS 18/AASB 118 paragraph 30 provides that interest should be accrued using the effective interest method; royalties should be accrued in accordance with the substance of the relevant agreement; and dividends are to be recognised when the shareholder has the right to receive payment. In the first two cases, the practical treatment may be to accrue revenue on a straight-line basis over the life of the agreement.

LO 4 → CHALLENGES FOR STANDARD SETTERS

Developments in revenue recognition and measurement

The IASB and FASB have undertaken a joint project in relation to revenue recognition and measurement because revenue transactions are not well served by existing guidance literature. In addition, transactions have become more complex; for example, they may combine goods, services and financial transactions. The standard setters have noted that inconsistencies exist between the IASB *Framework* and some standards. For example, the application of recognition criteria in the *Framework* and IAS 18 may create deferred assets and liabilities which do not accord with the *Framework's* definition of assets and liabilities.

Further, the standard does not deal well with transactions involving components (multi-element revenue arrangements).[30] For example, the 'bundling' of principal products with ancillary products and ongoing services, as occurs in the technology sector, makes revenue recognition complicated. The FASB has indicated there is a void in revenue recognition guidance and a lack of a conceptual basis for resolving the relevant issues.[31] Revenue recognition policies of US companies have been the subject of the majority of the SEC's requests for restatement of financial statements. Theory in action 9.2 provides a UK example where auditors have required restatement of revenue recognised in the accounts.

9.2
THEORY IN ACTION

Revenue recognition is Isoft's curse

by Philip Stafford

Exactly how Isoft accounts for its sales has dogged the healthcare software company for most of its six-year life on the stock exchange.

It was the initial cause of the troubles the healthcare software company is now mired in — in January it told the market that full-year revenues would be far below market expectations. This was owing "to a significant degree of rescheduling on the National Programme for IT".

On Tuesday, Isoft had to admit that an investigation by Deloitte had found that some revenues had been recognised earlier than they should have been.

In June it had already said it had decided to change its accounting policies, which would cut revenues by about £70 m in 2005 and £55 m in 2004.

On Tuesday, it denied that the irregularities it had uncovered were connected with these changes in accounting policy. It said the irregularities would not have a material impact on the revenue figures for the year to April 30 which they expect to be £195 m to £200 m. The accounts have not been published.

The problems of revenue recognition at Isoft are surprising for a company set up and run by a team of highly qualified accountants from two of the Big Four firms.

There has long been some contention in the City about Isoft's method of accounting for revenues.

Traditionally it recognised the value of the product licences at the time of delivery, while the value of subsequent support and services was recognised in the accounts as they were performed rather than when they were paid for.

Analysts have questioned this but Isoft has rebutted them.

Eyebrows were also raised about the signing of a contract for €56 m (£38 m) in the Republic of Ireland. It was signed on April 30, the last day of Isoft's financial year and unusually, a Saturday, although the group has always said it didn't take the revenue from it in that year.

Isoft is not the first software company to have become entangled in questions over how to account for revenues. Others include companies such as Innovation Group, Cedar and AIT.

"The biggest problem is distinguishing between buying the software and buying the services to maintain it," says David Toms, an analyst at Numis Securities. "The issue is that the customer wants the end product — working — which may be two contracts, and the software company wants to separate it out."

But the question of historic revenue recognition has had a knock on effect that goes to the heart of Isoft's problems. Although it has drawn a line under previous accounting policies, Isoft still has to align the rest of its accounts with the restated, reduced revenue figures.

Source: Financial Times, 9 August 2006.

Questions

1. When did Isoft traditionally recognise revenue? Is the policy acceptable under GAAP?
2. What accounting issues were identified by analysts in relation to recognition of revenue for software companies?
3. Why did the company restate revenue and/or change its accounting policies?

The FASB/IASB project aims to develop a comprehensive set of principles for revenue recognition that will eliminate the inconsistencies in the existing authoritative literature and accepted practices.[32] The project tackles key conceptual issues that underlie financial reporting, including the distinction between liabilities and equity, liability recognition (including guidance relating to definition and recognition criteria), and general principles for recognising revenue.[33]

The FASB and IASB have proposed the following fundamental principles for revenue recognition and measurement:

- A reporting entity should recognise revenues in the accounting period in which they arise and measure them at their fair value on the date that they arise if it can determine both their occurrence and measurement with sufficient reliability.
- A reporting entity should measure revenues arising from an increase in its assets or a decrease in its liabilities (or a combination thereof) at the fair value of that increase or decrease.[34]

These principles are an extension of previous guidance. However, they encompass a change in emphasis in some areas, which may lead to changes in accounting practice. For example:

- Revenue is recognised in the period in which it arises. There is an emphasis on timely recognition of revenue, rather than the realisation of revenue.
- Revenue arises from an increase in assets or a decrease in liabilities. Revenue can result from changes in asset values that occur in the production cycle and from holding assets (i.e. from remeasurements). Both elements of revenue are included in the measurement of comprehensive income.
- Revenue recognition and measurement reflect fair value. The fair value approach has been adopted as a working principle, but this will be affected in the future by decisions in the Board's project on measurement. The fair value approach is controversial and does not have unanimous support of standard setters. For example, the Accounting Standard Setting Board of Japan has expressed concern about the use of fair value.[35]
- Measurement should be reliable. This is consistent with the qualitative characteristics of financial information included in the *Framework*.

Further, the IASB has tentatively agreed that two criteria must be met to recognise revenue. These are:

- *the elements criterion*, which requires a change in assets or liabilities to have occurred, that is, (1) an increase in assets has occurred that increases equity, without a commensurate investment by owners, and (2) a decrease in liabilities has occurred that increases equity, without a commensurate investment by owners (such as the forgiveness by owners of a debt owed to them by the entity)
- *the measurement criterion*, which requires that the change in assets or liabilities can be appropriately measured, that is, (1) assets or liabilities are measured by means of a relevant attribute, and (2) the increase in assets or decrease in liabilities is measurable with sufficient reliability.[36]

The measurement criterion does not contain a probability criterion, such as that in the IASB and AASB *Frameworks*. The decision not to use a probability criterion reflects the IASB's view that probability should be part of the measurement of elements of financial statements and should not be a criterion for recognition. Measurability is still an important element of the new criteria, but there is less emphasis on substantial completion of the earnings process. The approach taken in the project is to focus on the change in value of assets and liabilities rather than the completion of an earnings process.[37]

A situation where companies have sought to measure revenue in a manner not supported by IASB standards is explored in theory in action 9.3. Companies with insurance contracts, which are accounted for under IAS 39, have provided additional information consistent with the 'embedded value' framework. Under this framework, companies recognise the expected value of future insurance contacts when they are written. Thus revenue is recognised earlier than permitted under IASB standards. Theory in action 9.3 explores the incentives for companies to provide measures of earnings based on embedded value.

**9.3
THEORY
IN ACTION**

Banking group attacks IFRS with double set of accounts

by David Jetuah

HBOS, the banking group, intends to publish two sets of accounts for the foreseeable future in order to make the value of its new investment business comprehensible to investors, it said in a blast at international financial reporting standards.

In announcing its annual results the banking giant presented its investment business figures under embedded value criteria in addition to IFRS requirements.

The embedded value (EV) rules mean that HBOS can provide more detail on the value of contracts with future expected revenues.

IFRS only allows for the recording of the revenues once they have been accrued.

Ian Gordon of Dresdner Kleinwort said: 'The reported numbers under IFRS are misleading. The move to IFRS has been unhelpful. The issue is more damaging for HBOS than for other banks because this part of its operation is growing very fast. IFRS overstates the profitability of businesses which have a more mature profit. It is inappropriate to punish businesses which are growing fast. They've now had to go the extra mile in providing the disclosure and it's significant change of perception.'

HBOS has said that underlying profit before tax for the UK investment business under EV parameters was £262 m higher than reported under IFRS and the contribution from new business in the UK investment arm was £474 m higher than reported under IFRS — the full EV contribution being £245 m compared to a loss of £229 m under the IFRS basis.

The full EV basis, unlike the IFRS basis, recognises profits on new business at the point of sale with the contribution from existing business only including changes in the value of future cashflows compared to predictions.

Under IFRS, insurance contracts are accounted for under IAS 39. In relation to UK GAAP, this delays the recognition of profit in respect of some investment contracts leading to significant 'losses' for HBOS.

Deloitte technical partner Ken Wild emphasised the need for a happy medium to be established.

'I think it's great that companies are deciding to disclose both, but it questions the way in which standards such as IAS are devised where you have fairly robust principles such as these. I think the most useful thing is an understanding of both elements.'

Source: Accountancy Age, 8 March 2007, www.accountancyage.com.

Questions

1. Why does HBOS provide a second set of financial results?
2. What is the revenue recognition rule of IFRS, according to this article? What are the differences in profit for HBOS under IFRS and embedded value?
3. What do you consider are the incentives to report embedded value results? To what extent are managers likely to manipulate embedded value results?

Fair value measurement

The emergence of assets with different characteristics (such as financial instruments) and greater use of fair value measurement in specific standards such as IAS 39/AASB 139 *Financial Instruments: Recognition and Measurement*, IAS 40/AASB 140 *Investment Property* and IAS 41/AASB 141 *Agriculture* has generated considerable interest in revenue recognition and related issues about when and how changes in the value of assets and liabilities should be recognised and measured. Under a mixed measurement attribute model, all items are measured at fair value at acquisition (i.e. an acquisition cost or entry price) and thereafter carried at historical cost or written down historical cost. Some items are remeasured to fair value subsequent to acquisition.

As discussed earlier, the definition of revenue adopted by the IASB means that revenue can result from changes in the value of net assets. Several IASB standards require that gains and losses arising from remeasurement of assets are included in either in operating income or in 'comprehensive income' (i.e. income which includes all gains and losses from the period, whether realised or unrealised). Standards allowing or requiring remeasurement of assets include IAS 16/AASB 116 *Property, Plant and Equipment*, IAS 39/AASB 139 *Financial Instruments: Recognition and Measurement*, IAS 40/AASB 140 *Investment Property*, IAS 41/AASB 141 *Agriculture* and IAS 19/AASB 119 *Employee Benefits*. Greater use of fair value measurement in standards means that gains and losses are recognised in the period in which they occur, irrespective of whether they are realised or not. Consequently, the FASB and IASB have turned their attention to how best to display information about income items in an entity's financial statements. Their project on financial statement presentation is discussed below.

Financial statement presentation

The IASB has a joint project with the FASB in relation to financial statement presentation (a continuation of their work on reporting financial performance). The project is relevant to a discussion of revenue recognition as it is concerned with how items of revenue will be reported in the financial statements.

The project was undertaken to establish standards for the presentation of information in the financial statements to enhance the usefulness of that information in assessing the financial performance and position of an entity. The IASB noted that there were differences between countries in relation to presentation, classification and definitions of items and key performance indicators. In addition, the use of a mixed-attribute measurement model (i.e. a model that uses both historical cost and fair value measurement) raised concerns about its effect on the presentation of financial performance and position.

The project covers issues relating to the display and presentation in the financial statements of all recognised changes in assets and liabilities from transactions or other events, except those related to transactions with the owners. It will consider items that are presently reported in the income statement, cash flow statement, and statement of changes in equity. IAS 1 permits but does not require a single comprehensive income statement.

In the course of its deliberations about financial statement presentation the Board has reached the following tentative conclusions:

- *An all-inclusive, single income statement.* This is a change from past practice where multiple income statements have been presented. All changes to assets and liabilities will be shown in the income statement, whereas in the past only some items were included in the income statement. A guide to possible presentation formats is shown in table 9.1 overleaf.

- *Realisation is not the basis for inclusion of items.* The aim of the income statement is to provide useful information for decision making. The fact that an item is not realised will not preclude it from being included in the income statement. This is a change in practice that may be favoured by some constituents such as analysts who want more fair value measurements and inclusion of all items that affect equityholders' wealth. However, it may be opposed by others, for example preparers who do not favour a fair value approach. The use of fair value measurement is controversial in many countries, as some financial statement preparers and users consider that it may lack reliability.

- *Separate disclosure of performance and remeasurement.* The income statement will distinguish between income flows and valuation adjustments. Changes in fair value will disclose the cause of the change: performance during the period, changes in economic conditions, or changes in market expectations. However, classification of items may not be straightforward and judgement will be required. Some financial statement users object to requirements which increase subjectivity in the financial statements and reduce the reliability and comparability of material presented.[38]

TABLE 9.1 Financial statement presentation

Statement of Financial Position	Statement of Cash Flows	Statement of Comprehensive Income
BUSINESS	**BUSINESS**	**BUSINESS**
Operating assets Operating liabilities	Cash flows from operating activities	Operating income and expenses
Subtotal (A1)	Subtotal (A1)	Subtotal (A1)
Investing assets Investing liabilities	Cash flows from investing activities	Investing income and expenses
Subtotal (A2)	Subtotal (A2)	Subtotal (A2)
TOTAL (A) = Subtotals (A1) + (A2)	TOTAL (A) = Subtotals (A1) + (A2)	TOTAL (A) = Subtotals (A1) + (A2)
DISCONTINUED OPERATIONS	**DISCONTINUED OPERATIONS**	**DISCONTINUED OPERATIONS**
TOTAL (B) Sum of Net assets of Discontinued operations	TOTAL (B) Sum of Cash flows from Discontinued operations	TOTAL (B) Sum of Income/expense from Discontinued operations
FINANCING	**FINANCING**	**FINANCING**
Financing assets	Cash flows from financing assets	Financing income
Subtotal (C1)	Subtotal (C1)	Subtotal (C1)
Financing liabilities	Cash flows from financing liabilities	Financing expenses
Subtotal (C2)	Subtotal (C2)	Subtotal (C2)
TOTAL (C) = Subtotals (C1) + (C2)	TOTAL (C) = Subtotals (C1) + (C2)	TOTAL (C) = Subtotals (C1) + (C2)
INCOME TAXES	**INCOME TAXES**	**INCOME TAXES**
Income tax assets		
Income tax liabilities		
TOTAL (D) Sum of Net income tax asset/liability	TOTAL (D) Sum of Cash flows from income taxes	TOTAL (D) Sum of Income tax expense/benefit
EQUITY	**EQUITY**	—
TOTAL (E) Sum of Equity	TOTAL (E) Sum of Equity	—

Source: IASB November 2007, www.iasplus.com.

LO 5 → ISSUES FOR AUDITORS

The primary issue for auditors surrounding revenue is the risk that recorded revenue is overstated by managers. Overstatement of revenue can arise if transactions or events underlying recorded revenue have not occurred or do not pertain to the entity, the amount of revenue has not been recorded appropriately, or revenue for the period relates to transactions for a future accounting period. In addition, there is the risk that disclosures about revenue are not accurate, for example, sales to related parties are not disclosed correctly. Overstatement of revenue is regarded as a greater problem than understatement of revenue because it is more likely to be driven by managers' attempts to deceive financial statement users and the associated efforts to conceal the true events make the overstatement difficult to detect. Case study 9.2 explores ways in which managers may overstate revenue. In addition, the natural bias in accounting against overstatement of profits suggests that auditors are more likely to be questioned by regulators and investors over a failure to detect errors that lead to overstated revenue than to understated revenue.

Evidence of the importance of the issue of revenue overstatement can be found in the United States Public Company Accounting Oversight Board (PCAOB) report of its inspections of auditors for the period 2004–06.[39] The report contains a set of common issues identified during inspections of audit firms and is aimed at assisting audit firms in improving or maintaining the quality of their work. The PCAOB noted that material misstatements due to fraudulent financial reporting often result from a misreporting of revenue.[40] Auditors need be sensitive to the heightened risks surrounding clients who are likely to be evaluated more on revenue growth than on profit, and auditors should seek evidence to support their opinion beyond relying on results of analytical procedures or of testing of other areas (e.g. accounts receivable and inventory).

Hurtt, Kreuze and Langsam review several large frauds and the SEC's views in applying accounting principles and standards to revenue recognition.[41] They suggest that more than half of all financial reporting fraud involves overstating revenue. Typically, the frauds have their origins in the highest levels of management and are more likely when managers' compensation is based on a bonus tied to targeted revenues, managers show an interest in using aggressive accounting policies to boost the share price, and managers have a history of committing to analysts and other outsiders that they will achieve aggressive or unrealistic forecasts. Both the PCAOB and Hurtt et al. suggest that revenue recognition could be a difficult issue for complex transactions and/or when significant uncertainty surrounds determining the substantial completion of the transaction. Auditors are responsible for assessing the basis for managers' decisions about the existence and value of revenue recognised in the current accounting period.

Overestimating revenue can occur within accounting standards by making estimates that later prove to be too optimistic. For example, revenue (and expenses) for construction contracts that take several years to complete can be recognised prior to the completion of the contract if the outcome of the contract can be estimated reliably (IAS 11/AASB 111). If costs on the project later exceed the estimated costs at the time of the revenue recognition, an adjustment is made in that later period to reverse profit that is no longer expected to be earned. In the interim period, auditors have to determine how much leeway they will allow managers in their estimates of costs to completion and thus how much revenue can be recognised.

Other cases of revenue overstatement can be attributed simply to fraud. In 2004 Bristol-Myers Squibb Co agreed to pay US$150 million to settle a case with the SEC related to accounting fraud involving US$1.5 billion of inflated revenue from 2000 to 2001.[42] The company had engaged in 'channel-stuffing' — improperly inducing wholesalers to purchase more drugs than demand warranted. This practice involves sending goods prematurely to buyers, often with deferred payment terms, and recognising the revenue when the goods are shipped (i.e. point 8 in figure 9.2). Even though this is the common point for revenue recognition, there is a weakness in the validity of the buyers' orders (point 7) that suggests there is doubt about the eventual completion of the earning process. A related practice involves backdating sales made during the early part of the new accounting period to the last part of the old accounting period — known as improper sales cut-off. More blatant fraud examples are found where managers simply invent sales transactions. Research by Dechow et al. suggests that the financial statements can show the likelihood that firms have overstated revenue (see case study 9.3).

The PCAOB has found frequent deficiencies in audit firms' performance of audit procedures related to revenue accounts.[43] In particular, auditors were not sufficiently investigating significant unexpected results of their testing. Too often, when auditors sought explanations from managers about any issues arising from their work, the auditors were not obtaining corroboration of managers' explanations. In other words, the auditors were accepting managers' statements about the accounts without verifying the reliability of managers' explanations by obtaining other evidence that the revenue should be recognised. Theory in action 9.4 explores a case where questions were raised about the auditors' approval of managers' revenue recognition policies.

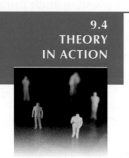

9.4
THEORY
IN ACTION

EPG's auditor queried on sales

by Ashley Midalia

Auditors for the failed Estate Property Group, Moore Stephens, allowed the group to backdate profits and incorporate questionable sources of revenue into its accounts, a liquidator's lawyer was told yesterday.

EPG's financing arm, Australian Capital Reserve, collapsed last year owing $300 million to retail investors and, since early last month, ACR's liquidator, PricewaterhouseCoopers, has been conducting a preliminary examination of the key players associated with EPG in the NSW Supreme Court.

Counsel for the liquidator, Ian Pike, yesterday questioned Moore Stephens audit partner Chris Chandran about two property sales made in 2005 by EPG subsidiary companies to an apparently unrelated company, AIPT Management.

The sales of the properties in Sydney's outer west accounted for $47.5 million of the group's total revenue of $56 million for the 2004–05 financial year and had the effect of making the group's accounts appear significantly healthier than would otherwise have been the case.

One EPG subsidiary, Estate Project Development, sold a property in Villawood for $30.5 million and a second subsidiary, Estate on Miller, sold a property in Werrington for $17 million. The Werrington sale accounted for the entire $13.2 million profit reported by Estate on Miller for 2004–05, the hearing was told.

While contracts for both sales were initially exchanged on June 30, 2005, the transactions were not settled until months later. Moreover in the case of the Werrington property, the contract of sale was rescinded and a new contract signed on October 28, yet the revenue from both sales was booked to the 2004–05 accounts.

Asked about the effect on the EPG's bottom line of excluding the property sales, Mr Chandran said: "It would reduce revenue, it would reduce cost of goods sold and it would reduce profit."

Mr Pike suggested to Mr Chandran that, under applicable accounting standards, the revenue should not have been recognised until control in the properties — "a matter of substance, not form" — had passed to AIPT.

But Mr Chandran said Moore Stephens had sought to "take a conservative approach" and defended the auditors' decision to approve the EPG's companies' 2004–05 accounts. "That was the judgement we made," he said.

Mr Pike questioned Mr Chandran over whether control of the properties could be said to have genuinely passed to AIPT at all since, under the vendor financing arrangements entered into by the parties, the EPG companies retained effective control of the development of the properties and stood to receive a 50 per cent share of profits derived from the subsequent sale of the developed lots.

Source: The Australian Financial Review, 9 May 2009, www.afr.com.

Questions
1. Contracts for the sale of the two properties were initially exchanged during the year ended 30 June 2005, and eventually were finalised before the end of 2005, so why were the auditors criticised for allowing the revenue to appear in the 2004–05 accounts?
2. Why is there doubt over whether the revenue should have been recognised at all?

Summary

LO 1 The nature of revenue and various approaches taken to defining revenue, including the behavioural view of revenue

Revenue represents a physical and a monetary flow. Revenue has been defined by standard setters as an inflow of economic benefits. Examples of revenue are sales, fees, interest, dividends, royalties and rent. Revenue forms part of income (which also includes gains) and arises in the course of ordinary activities. The behavioural view of revenue suggests that revenue (and profit) come about because of something done by the firm. All the firm's activities form part of its earning process. Within this process, a point for recognising revenue must be determined.

LO 2 Issues related to the recognition of revenue and the criteria used in the revenue recognition process

Originally, net income was determined on the basis of the increase in net worth of a firm. The concept of income and definitions were developed through court cases and a distinction between capital and income emerged. Over time, the emphasis on changes in net worth was overtaken by the notion that revenue must be realised. Generally accepted revenue recognition criteria endeavour to guide accountants as to when revenue is realised. The three criteria are measurability of asset value, existence of a transaction, and substantial completion of the earnings process.

LO 3 Guidance provided by standard setters in relation to revenue recognition and measurement

Accounting standards such as IAS 18/AASB 118 *Revenue* have provided specific guidance about revenue recognition to supplement the general criteria. IAS 18/AASB 118 clarifies when revenue is recognised in relation to sale of goods, rendering of services and interest, royalties and dividends. Revenue recognition is not a straightforward process because of the wide range of different business revenue-generating activities and circumstances. Many questions have been raised in practice in relation to revenue recognition and many related examples are provided in the chapter.

LO 4 Standard setters' current activities in relation to revenue recognition and measurement

Standard setters such as the IASB and FASB have expressed the view that revenue transactions are not well served by current guidance literature. They have indentified inconsistencies in existing guidance and diversity in observed practice. In addition, transactions have become more complex requiring a review of present guidance. Thus, the IASB and FASB have undertaken a project which aims to provide a comprehensive set of principles for revenue recognition and measurement.

Standard setters are making greater use of fair value measurement in recent standards such as IAS 39/AASB 139. Fair value measurement gives rise to unrealised gains and losses which are considered to form part of income. Consequently, the presentation of income from operations separately from that relating to remeasurement has been considered. The IASB and FASB are working on a financial statement presentation project that is investigating how best to present in the financial statements the change in assets and liabilities arising from transactions and other events. The asset–liability approach, that income is measured as a change in net assets, places less emphasis on the notions of 'realisation' and 'earned'.

LO 5

Issues for auditors arising from revenue recognition and measurement

Revenue overstatement is likely to be driven by managers' attempts to deceive financial statement users. It may occur when managers' compensation is based on bonuses tied to targeted revenues. Managers with a history of achieving aggressive or unrealistic profit forecasts may be managing earnings. The Public Company Accounting Oversight Board or PCAOB (in the USA) has documented failures by auditors to detect misreported revenue. Auditors need to be sensitive to the risks surrounding clients that are likely to be evaluated on revenue growth and should gather direct evidence to support their opinion that revenue is not misstated. Some revenue misstatement could be attributed to over-optimism, for example with estimates of the progress of construction contracts. However, other revenue misstatements are due to fraud (e.g. shipping goods prematurely to buyers without a firm order, or backdating sales made in the early part of the new accounting period).

Questions

1. What is revenue? Is revenue essentially an event or an object?
2. What is the difference between revenue and gains? How does the *Framework* definition of 'income' treat revenues and gains?
3. Explain the 'earning process'. How does the earning process concept relate to the operational view of revenue?
4. What are the differences between general criteria for revenue recognition and revenue recognition principles contained in IAS 18/AASB 118 *Revenue*?
5. Why are revenue recognition principles needed? Does it matter which principles are adopted, as long as they are applied consistently across time? Discuss.
6. What is the significance of the criterion of measurability of the consideration received?
7. Explain the concepts of realisation and recognition as they relate to the measurement and disclosure of revenues under the historical cost system and under a system of mark-to-market or fair value for financial instruments.
8. What do we mean when we suggest that applying the principles adopted in accounting standards which make use of fair value measurement, such as IAS/AASB 39/139, 40/140 and 41/141, leads to an even greater mix of values presented in an entity's balance sheet?
9. Suppose you are a manufacturer of plastic products. A new customer, X Ltd, has purchased a large quantity and gives you a note as payment. The note requires X Ltd to make four equal instalments over a period of 2 years. How do you determine the collectability of the note? When should revenue be recognised?

10. Should accountants insist that revenue be recognised by a firm only on receipt of a liquid asset in a sale transaction? Why or why not?

11. Is it important to have an external transaction to support the amount of revenue recorded? Name a case in present accounting practice where revenue or gain is not directly based on an external transaction and state the reasons for this exception.

12. If the criterion of 'existence of a transaction' is relaxed so that the firms involved need not be direct participants in the transaction, what are the implications?

13. What is meant by 'substantial completion of the earning process'? What is the significance of this criterion? How is the criterion incorporated into IAS 18/AASB 118?

14. Does the percentage-of-completion method meet the criterion of substantial completion of the earning process? Explain.

15. What are the reasons for selecting the point of sale as the general revenue recognition principle?

16. What is the significance of 'title passing' in determining whether a sale has taken place?

17. What are the reasons proposed for recognising revenue at the end of production?

18. 'Revenue should be recognised only where it is supported by the existence of an external transaction.' Discuss.

19. Explain how Myers' concept of 'critical event' can influence the point at which revenue is recognised.

20. What are the conditions for use of the 'cash received' basis for revenue recognition?

21. When should revenue be recognised for the following businesses?
    (a) a soft-drink manufacturer
    (b) a legal firm
    (c) a theatre that sells season tickets to musical productions
    (d) a magazine publisher producing monthly titles
    (e) a gold-mining company
    (f) a farmer who grows wheat
    (g) a company which sells houses on an instalment plan; terms of payment extending to 20 years; buyers assume all risks of ownership; buyers pay a deposit of 25 per cent of the sale price
    (h) a contractor building a bridge for the government

22. On 20 December, E Ltd sold a portion of its inventory to W Ltd for $200 000 cash. The cost of the inventory was $80 000. In a related transaction, E Ltd agreed to repurchase the inventory from W Ltd 2 months later for $200 000, to be paid in four equal monthly instalments at 10 per cent interest. What transactions should be recorded by E Ltd?

23. Lee Ltd agreed to manufacture Product A according to Smith Ltd's specifications over a 2-year period. Because special machinery is needed to produce Product A, Smith Ltd is to pay for it. Lee Ltd purchased the machinery for $1 000 000. It debited Machinery and credited Cash. A month later, Lee Ltd received $1 000 000 from Smith Ltd as reimbursement of the cost. What entry should Lee Ltd make for the cash received? When Lee Ltd uses the machinery each year, what entry should be made?

24. If revenue is recognised, does that mean that the revenue has been realised? Explain your answer and give an example to support your view.

25. Kalbarri Ltd began operations on 1 January 2008 by purchasing 3000 orange tree saplings at a cost of $4 per sapling. Delivery charges were $500 and it cost $1200 to plant the trees on Kalbarri Ltd's land, which 2 years earlier cost $60 000. During 2008, the saplings produced fruit that was used to generate 1000 seedlings. The only

other expense during the year was herbicidal spraying, which cost $400. At the end of the year the saplings had a market value of $4 per sapling and the seedlings $1 per seedling. Show all journal entries for the calendar year 2008 and the calculation of profit for the year.

26. Why have the IASB and FASB begun a project to reconsider revenue recognition and measurement? What apects of their approach in this project may cause changes to the way companies recognise and measure revenue?

27. What is meant by 'revenue cut-off'? Why do auditors verify the date of sales transactions around the end of a financial period?

28. Explain why an auditor would be interested in the terms of the senior executives' remuneration contracts, in particular, how bonuses for outstanding performance are calculated.

Problems

PROBLEM 9.1 — In the following examples, indicate whether it was proper for X to record the particular amount of revenue according to accepted recognition principles (accrual system). Your answer should be 'yes' or 'no'. Give reasons for your answers.

1. X received a cheque for $500 from a customer in full payment for an item to be shipped DDP (delivered duty paid) destination. The common carrier now has possession of the item. X recorded $500 as revenue.

2. A customer purchased a television set from X for $600 and paid cash. However, since he was going to Europe, he asked X to deliver the television set next month. X immediately recorded the $600 cash as revenue.

3. X sold a motor vehicle to Y for $10 000 in December. Y paid a deposit of $1000 and agreed to pay the balance by monthly instalments beginning in January of the next accounting year. Y's credit rating is good. X recorded $1000 as revenue for the year ended 31 December.

4. X purchased a $10 000, 10 per cent corporate debenture at par on 1 March of this year. Interest is paid every 1 March and 1 September. X received $500 cash interest on 1 September and recorded the $500 as total interest revenue for the year ended 31 December.

5. X operates a garage. He repaired Y's car for $600 last year. There is no reason to doubt Y's ability to pay. X received payment this year and recorded the payment of $600 as revenue this year.

6. X delivered $2000 worth of merchandise on consignment to Y, the consignee. X recorded $2000 as sales revenue.

7. X is a management consultant and was asked by Y to conduct a study on the feasibility of selling a new product, D. The study was not completed until 20 January Year 10 but, at the end of Year 9, X estimated that she had rendered $2000 worth of services and recorded that amount as Service Revenue.

PROBLEM 9.2 — State whether revenue (or gain) is to be recorded in the following cases:

1. The market value of an orchard is increased because of the physical growth of the trees.

2. A tax refund is received because of an adjustment of the tax amount paid 3 years ago.

3. Cash is received from a lawsuit won for patent infringement. The lawsuit was initiated a year ago.

4. The production of paper for inventory is completed. The market price is stable. The sales price of the inventory is $80 000.

5. A building with a carrying amount of $50 000 is destroyed by fire. The building was insured on the basis of its current market price. A cheque for $60 000 is received from the insurance company.
6. Mr Evans owned a block of land which cost him $60 000. He exchanged it recently for a business building and the land on which the building stands. The land and building he received have a current market value of $70 000.
7. X Ltd received 200 additional shares as its portion of a share dividend from Y Ltd. Each share sells for $50 on the stock exchange.
8. Seldom Ltd received a block of land from the city of Fairdeal on condition that the company build a factory there. The condition was fulfilled recently. Title to the land was conveyed to the company. The fair market value of the land is $200 000.

PROBLEM 9.3

In early 2008, Apex Construction Ltd contracted to build an office building. The project took 3 years. The project was accepted by the buyer in late 2009. The company bid $600 000 and its estimated total cost at the time of the bid was $400 000. The actual costs incurred and cash collections were as follows:

	2009	2010	2011	2012	Total
Costs	$100 000	$250 000	$ 50 000		$400 000
Collections	0	100 000	200 000	$300 000	600 000

Required
Calculate the amount of revenue for each year under each of the following recognition principles:
(a) sales recognition principle (completed contract method)
(b) production recognition principle (percentage-of-completion method)
(c) instalment recognition principle (cash received method).

PROBLEM 9.4

Revenue was recognised when the events below occurred (accrual system). State whether it was proper or improper according to accepted recognition principles.
1. A customer's order is received for 100 boxes of nails. It is approved by the credit department.
2. A repairer did some work a year ago, but waited until now to record the revenue because it took that long to collect the bill.
3. A retail merchant sold some silverware to a customer who took the merchandise with her. The merchant charged the customer's account.
4. An order is received by a merchant. It is approved by the credit department and a shipping order is sent to the shipping department of the firm. The order specifies EXW (ex works) shipping point.
5. Goods have just been shipped DDP destination to a customer.
6. A customer signs a sales order for a certain 1912 motor vehicle for his antique collection, but asks that it be delivered to him 3 months later since he will be in Europe until then.
7. Cash was collected from a tenant on 31 December 2010 for January and February 2011 rents.
8. A vacuum cleaner was delivered to a customer 'on approval'. The trial period expires after 20 days.
9. Goods were shipped on consignment to a consignee.
10. A contract is signed by a customer who agrees to have the firm build a yacht for her according to her specifications. It is estimated that construction will take 6 months. The customer will pay in full when the yacht is completed.

11. A truck is delivered to a customer and a conditional sales contract is signed by him. Title is to remain with the firm (seller) until the customer makes full payment in 6 months.
12. A refrigerator is delivered to a customer. The customer made a nominal down payment and is expected to make monthly payments for the next 36 months. The credit rating of the customer is good. The full sales value was recorded as revenue.

PROBLEM 9.5

Steele Ltd is a manufacturer of paper products, such as paper towels and facial tissues. Consider the following events:

1. One of Steele Ltd's largest customers, Rudd Ltd, sent in an order in December 2011 for 200 000 boxes of paper towels. Each box sells for $9. The price is stable over the next 3 months and it is relatively certain that the order will be filled, probably in January 2012.
2. Goods with a sales price of $300 000 are shipped EXW shipping point to Arnold Stores. As of 31 December, Arnold Stores has not received the goods.
3. Goods were sent throughout 2011 to various customers. The selling price of these goods was $12 000 000. The customers were billed for the sale. Of the total, $2 000 000 has not been paid by 31 December.
4. Steele Ltd developed a new product and sent some samples to customers on consignment. The cost to Steele Ltd of these items was $300 000 and the sales price $420 000.
5. Favour Ltd, a new customer, purchased in November $150 000 of products but wished to pay for the goods by equal monthly instalments over 16 months at 2 per cent interest per month. Each payment is to be $11 047. Steele Ltd believes Favour Ltd will be able to make the payments. By 31 December, $11 047 cash was collected from Favour Ltd, of which $3000 was interest.
6. Total inventory on 31 December of all the different products amounts to $1 700 000. Steele Ltd is quite sure it can sell the products in 2012 for $2 800 000. Estimated costs of disposition are $400 000.

Required

According to generally accepted accounting principles, determine the total amount of sales revenue Steele Ltd should report on its income statement for 2011.

PROBLEM 9.6

D Ltd holds the franchise to Dizzy Hamburgers. In 2011, it sold to T the right to operate Dizzy Hamburgers as a franchise. An initial franchise fee of $300 000 was received from T. Of this amount, $150 000 was payable when the agreement was signed and the balance was payable in three annual payments of $50 000 each. The credit rating of the franchisee is such that interest at 8 per cent would have to be paid to borrow money.

Required

Prepare entries to record the sale of the franchise to T under each of the following assumptions:

(a) The deposit is not refundable, no future services are required by the franchisor and collection of the note is reasonably assured.
(b) The franchisor has substantial services to perform and the collection of the note is very uncertain. D Ltd will charge an annual fee of $4000 for services rendered.
(c) The deposit is not refundable, collection of the note is reasonably certain, the franchisor has yet to perform substantial services and the deposit represents services already performed.

Cascade Ltd has two divisions. Each division is a wholly owned subsidiary and is in a different line of business. The following activities occurred in Year 1.

Division A is in construction. Presently, it has only one project, a dam, which it started in May. The contract price is $2 000 000. Expected date of completion is May Year 3. Division A has decided to use the percentage-of-completion method. During Year 1, it purchased $250 000 of materials of which $190 000 were used. Labour costs were $350 000. Overhead costs were determined to be $100 000. Administration costs were $80 000. Estimated additional costs in order to complete the project are $720 000. This amount is for items yet to be used and includes administration expenses of $100 000. Billings were $700 000 and cash collected $65 000.

Division B operates a farm. During Year 1, it produced 10 000 m³ of barley and 20 000 m³ of rye. Of these, 8000 m³ of barley were sold at $5.00 per cubic metre and 12 000 m³ of rye were sold at $3.00 per cubic metre. On 31 December, the market price per cubic metre of each was as follows: $5.50 for barley; $3.20 for rye.

Total operating expenses during the year were $50 000. Division B estimates that its cost of selling these crops is $0.50 per cubic metre. The selling expenses of the crops sold are included in the operating expenses, but do not include expenses for selling the beginning inventories.

Division B had 1000 m³ of barley and 2000 m³ of rye in beginning inventory. All were sold during the year. The barley was sold at $5.00 per cubic metre and the rye for $3.00 per cubic metre. On 31 December Year 0, Division B had estimated the sales price of barley to be $5.40 per cubic metre and rye to be $2.90 per cubic metre. Costs of selling were estimated to be $0.50 per cubic metre.

Required

Prepare separate income statements for Divisions A and B for Year 1. For Division B, use the end of production revenue recognition principle.

Camdend Ltd, which began operations on 1 January Year 1, appropriately uses the instalment method for its instalment sales. The following data were obtained from its records for Year 1:

Instalment sales	$700 000
Cost of instalment sales	420 000
General expenses	70 000
Cash collections on instalment sales	300 000

Required

A. Record the journal entries relating to the instalment sales, using a deferred gross profit account.
B. Calculate the realised gross profit, showing it as the difference between revenue and cost of goods sold.

Brockelsby Station Ltd commences operations on 1 January 2011 by purchasing 100 000 hectares of grazing land and purchasing 800 head of cattle at auction for $1 060 000. The auctioneer's fee payable by the seller was 1 per cent of that price. It cost Brockelsby Station Ltd $55 000 to transport the cattle to the farm. If Brockelsby Station Ltd were to sell the cattle it would incur a 1 per cent auctioneer's fee and point of sale costs of $55 000.

The first reporting date for Brockelsby Station Ltd is 30 June 2011. At this date the net market value of cattle is $1 220 000. This was after the sale of 20 calves for $8000 during the 6 months to 30 June 2011.

Required

A. Prepare all journal entries to record the establishment of Brockelsby Station Ltd.
B. Prepare journal entries to reflect the change in net market value of cattle at 30 June 2008 and the sale of calves during the period.
C. Assume the only transaction was veterinary fees of $20 000. Show the calculation of reported profit/loss for Brockelsby Station Ltd at 30 June 2008.

(Note: All transactions are cash transactions. Brockelsby Station Ltd has been established to buy, breed, sell or slaughter and process cattle for sale at retail outlets.)

PROBLEM 9.10

See Pty Ltd began operations on 1 January 2011 by purchasing 5000 apple tree saplings at a cost of $2 per sapling. It cost $3600 to transport and plant the trees on land purchased 3 years earlier for $100 000. During 2011, the only expenses were insecticide spraying and pruning costs totalling $8000. On 15 August an additional 1000 saplings were purchased for $3 each (with transport and planting costs of $1800). In November a bushfire destroyed 25 per cent of the planted trees. The year-end market valuation of the remaining trees was $11 000.

Show all journal entries for the calendar year 2011 and the calculation of profit/loss for the year. Assume all transactions are cash-based.

Additional readings

CFA Institute Centre for Financial Market Integrity 2007, *A comprehensive business reporting model: financial reporting for investors*, July, CFA Institute Centre Publications.

Dechow, P, Ge, W, Larson, C, & Sloan, R 2009, 'Predicting material accounting misstatements', Working paper. SSRN: http://ssrn.com.

Deloitte 2009, *IASPlus Revenue recognition*, www.iasplus.com.

European Financial Reporting Action Group (EFRAG) 2006, 'The performance reporting debate', PAAinEurope Discussion Paper No. 2, November — comment letters, www.efrag.org.

International Accounting Standards Board (IASB) 2001, *Framework for the preparation and presentation of financial statements*, IASB, London.

International Accounting Standards Board (IASB) 2009, *Revenue recognition*, www.iasb.org.

International Accounting Standards Board (IASB) 2009, *Financial statement presentation*, www.iasb.org.

Tarca, A, Brown, PR, Hancock, P, Woodliff, D, Bradbury, M, & van Zijl, T 2008, 'Identifying decision useful information with the matrix format income statement', *Journal of International Financial Management and Accounting*, vol. 19, no. 2, pp. 185–218.

**9.1
CASE STUDY**

Property development companies: When to recognise revenue?

Many listed property development companies use the completed contract method when recognising revenue. Under this method, revenue is recognised upon handover of the property to the buyer and not on a progressive basis during the construction phase. For example, Jose (2008) states that the United Arab Emirates (UAE) has many listed property companies which follow IFRS. Companies such as Union Properties and Rak Properties take a conservative approach and recognise revenue only when the sale is complete (the completed contract method).

Listed property development companies that apply IAS 18 have specific guidance in the Appendix (pp. 19–20). It states that real estate sales are sale of goods and that:

Revenue is normally recognised when legal title passes to the buyer. However, in some jurisdictions the equitable interest in a property may vest in the buyer before legal title passes and therefore the risks and rewards of ownership have been transferred at that stage. In such cases, provided that the seller has no further substantial acts to complete under the contract, it may be appropriate to recognise revenue. In either case, if the seller is obliged to perform any significant acts after the transfer of the equitable and/or legal title, revenue is recognised as the acts are performed. An example is a building or other facility on which construction has not been completed.

In some cases, real estate may be sold with a degree of continuing involvement by the seller such that the risks and rewards of ownership have not been transferred. Examples are sale and repurchase agreements which include put and call options, and agreements whereby the seller guarantees occupancy of the property for a specified period, or guarantees a return on the buyer's investment for a specified period. In such cases, the nature and extent of the seller's continuing involvement determines how the transaction is accounted for. It may be accounted for as a sale, or as a financing, leasing or some other profit sharing arrangement. If it is accounted for as a sale, the continuing involvement of the seller may delay the recognition of revenue. A seller also considers the means of payment and evidence of the buyer's commitment to complete payment. For example, when the aggregate of the payments received, including the buyer's initial down payment, or continuing payments by the buyer, provide insufficient evidence of the buyer's commitment to complete payment, revenue is recognised only to the extent cash is received.

Some listed property companies, for example Emaar Properties in the UAE, have applied the 'percentage of completion' method by relying on IAS 11. Under the percentage of completion method a company recognises revenue in stages according the extent to which the construction has been completed. A spokesperson from Emaar Properties stated that 'Companies would always want to be liquid right from the beginning and the cash flow to start early' (Jose, 2008).

In July 2008 the IASB issued IFRIC 15 *Agreements for the Construction of Real Estate*. It was issued to standardise accounting practice across jurisdictions for the recognition of revenue by real estate developers for sale of units, apartments or houses before construction is complete, i.e. off the plan sales. IFRIC 15 provides guidance on how to determine whether an agreement for the construction of real estate is within the scope of IAS 11 *Construction Contracts* or IAS 18 *Revenue* and, accordingly, when revenue from the construction should be recognised.

An agreement for the construction of real estate is a construction contract within the scope of IAS 11 only when the buyer is able to specify the major structural elements of the design of the real estate before construction begins and/or specify major structural changes once construction is in progress (whether they exercise that ability or not). If the buyer has that ability, IAS 11 applies. If the buyer does not have that ability, IAS 18 applies.

References

IASB 2008, *IFRIC issues clarification on agreements for the construction of real estate*. Press release, 3 July. www.iasb.org.

Jose, CL 2008, 'Booking profit now or later?' *The Business Weekly*. www.zawya.com.

Questions

1. For companies which construct and sell residential property units, what would be the conservative accounting treatment for revenue under IFRS? Identify the sections of IAS 18 which support this treatment.

2. Emaar Properties uses the percentage of completion method under IAS 11. Explain when revenue is recognised under this method. Why would a company want to use the percentage of completion method?
3. How does the IFRIC 15 affect revenue recognition for property development companies?
4. Why do you think the IFRIC issued IFRIC 15?

9.2
CASE STUDY

The following article describes several revenue recognition violations identified by the US securities market regulator, the SEC.

Improper revenue recognition

by H. Lynn Stallworth and Dean Digregorio

US Securities and Exchange Commission (SEC) enforcement activity aimed at curbing earnings management and fraudulent financial reporting has increased markedly in recent years. In 2003, the SEC filed a record number of accounting and auditing enforcement actions against both companies and individuals. The individuals charged included senior managers and lower-level staff, accountants and sales managers, external auditors, and even customers. Most of these enforcement actions focused on earnings management, with violations of Generally Accepted Accounting Principles (GAAP) for revenue recognition constituting the most common offense. The SEC has also frequently cited violations of its Staff Accounting Bulletin (SAB) No. 101 revenue recognition guidelines . . .

In recent years, revenue recognition has become increasingly complex due to factors such as international competition and rapidly evolving business models. Constant process and technology innovation also create challenges, as both Internet-based and traditional brick-and-mortar businesses continue to develop innovative distribution channels and sales agreements that complicate revenue recognition. For example, Web-based companies must determine how revenue should be recognized for online sales, licensing, subscription, service, and maintenance agreements. Unless effective controls are in place, the real-time nature of online transactions can easily lead to accounting violations such as recording revenues before goods are actually shipped or services are provided. Progressive fulfillment practices such as outsourcing and drop-shipping can also cause revenue-recognition problems due to delays in recording liabilities and related expenses . . .

Revenue-recognition violations

Companies manage earnings for a variety of reasons, but the pressure to achieve targeted earnings is usually the primary motivation. To boost revenues, companies might recognize sales prematurely, or during a period prior to the one dictated by GAAP. Methods include using improper sales cut-offs for legitimate transactions, treating consignment sales as if they are final, and entering into parking, bill-and-hold, or channel-stuffing agreements. More flagrant violations include recording fabricated transactions, or fictitious sales. The SEC has taken action against companies for each of these types of violations.

Improper sales cut-off To ensure consistency with GAAP requirements, companies must record sales during the period in which goods are shipped or services are performed. Although the complexity of some business models may make this determination difficult, the accounting literature clearly indicates that intentionally holding the books open past the end of a period — until the company reaches a pre-determined revenue target — represents a violation of GAAP.

According to SEC investigations, Minuteman International Inc., a manufacturer of commercial floor care products, engaged in improper sales cut-offs as a routine practice between 1989 and 2001. During the first three quarters of each year, the company left its sales register open past quarter-end, until its target revenue — as determined by the company's chief executive officer — had been reached. Sales invoices were backdated to the last day of the quarter, even though shipping transactions were actually processed after the quarter had ended. This activity resulted in the overstatement of quarterly revenues, as well as incentive bonuses for the company's sales staff. The SEC settled charges with Minuteman in May 2003.

Consignment sales recorded as revenue   Consignment sales typically are characterized by a mutual agreement in which the buyer, or consignee, has an unconditional right to return purchased merchandise to the seller, or consignor. Usually, title does not formally pass to the consignee, nor is the consignee required to pay the seller, until the goods are sold to a third party. As discussed in SAB No. 101, the risks of ownership have not passed to the buyer before this stage of the transaction, nor is the collectibility of the receivable ensured. Consequently, revenues from the delivery of goods on consignment should not be recognized until the goods are sold by the consignee.

Consignment sales serve a legitimate business purpose. They allow sellers to gain access to distribution channels that might otherwise not be available. However, abuses arise when the shipment of consigned goods is booked as a revenue transaction or when the true arrangement is disguised or hidden. For example, firms may have a valid sales agreement in place, then negotiate the consignment feature as a side agreement and backdate it to precede the original sales agreement.

In April 2003, the SEC settled charges with electrical component manufacturer Thomas & Betts Corp., which was accused of committing consignment sales violations between 1998 and 2000. The company created a new type of sales arrangement known as a 'power buy'. The terms of individual agreements varied, though generally they included unusually large sales volumes and price discounts, extended payment terms, shipment to third-party warehouses where goods were stored and insured at the seller's expense, unqualified rights to return products, and assistance from the seller in procuring an end user for the products. In some cases, these conditions were negotiated in side agreements.

Thomas & Betts booked revenues from the power buys when goods were shipped. In substance, however, the power-buy arrangements constituted consignment sales and should not have been reported as revenues by the seller until the goods were subsequently sold by the buyers. GAAP requires the buyer to make payment, or to be obligated to make payment without the contingency of product resale, before revenue can be recorded.

The SEC's complaint against the firm alleged that three of the firm's executives approved or were aware of many of the side agreements. All three executives consented to the entry of final judgments against them and were eventually required to pay disgorgement, prejudgment interest, and other penalties.

Parking, bill and hold, and channel stuffing   Parking, bill-and-hold, and channel-stuffing sales arrangements each essentially represent the same type of premature revenue recognition scheme. As the end of an accounting period approaches, the firm negotiates sales with customers who either may not need the offered goods or may not have the ability to take delivery of the goods within that period. The goods may be temporarily held by an intermediary (parking), left in the seller's inventory (bill and hold), or shipped to the buyer (channel stuffing). Typically, deferred payment terms are included within the agreements.

In April 2003, the SEC settled charges of premature revenue recognition through improper bill-and-hold sales with Candle's Inc., a designer and distributor of women's footwear, apparel, and fashion products. Although the company's stated practice was to recognize revenue when products are shipped, Candle's recorded purchase orders received for future shoe deliveries as revenue in the current period, even though shoes had not yet been shipped. SAB No. 101 includes specific criteria that preclude this type of transaction from being recognized as current period revenue. According to the bulletin, transactions must be initiated at the request of the customer, the customer must have a legitimate business reason for requesting delayed delivery, and goods must be segregated from the seller's stock and may not be available to fill other orders. Candle's failed to meet these criteria, eventually prompting the SEC to issue a cease-and-desist order.

Back-to-back swaps Even less defensible than the revenue manipulation methods discussed thus far are the fabrication of transactions through back-to-back swaps, also referred to as round-trips. This earnings-management technique requires the cooperation of a customer, related affiliate, or other organization. One firm 'sells' an asset at a gain to another organization and agrees, in turn, to purchase assets from the 'buyer' during either the current accounting period or a subsequent period. Both firms inflate earnings by recording gains on the assets transferred to the other party.

Enron engaged in this type of transaction, with the cooperation of Merrill Lynch, by trading Nigerian barges. Homestore.com Inc., an Internet provider of residential real estate listings and related services now known as Homestore, also used this technique. In 2001, Homestore participated in a fourparty round-trip transaction designed to allow the company to recognize its own cash payments as advertising revenue. Homestore purchased unneeded products and services at inflated prices from two vendors. The vendors then used the cash to purchase online advertising from the fourth firm, a media buyer, which in turn purchased online advertising from Homestore, thus returning the cash as advertising revenue. Although Homestore argued that the transactions were merely barter, the complaint filed by the SEC in September 2003 charged that the purpose of the transactions was to artificially and fraudulently inflate Homestore's advertising revenues to exceed analysts' expectations.

Fictitious sales Perhaps the most egregious form of revenue manipulation is the creation of fictitious sales. Under this type of scheme, company goods may be ordered but never shipped, shipped but not ordered, or never ordered or shipped. Furthermore, the company may fabricate purchase orders and shipping records, or even neglect to produce such documents altogether.

Anicom Inc., a now-bankrupt distributor of wire and cable products, reported revenues from sales to fictitious customers — and engaged in other fraudulent practices — to boost revenues. Most of Anicom's sales consisted of drop shipments, or shipments in which the company arranged for a vendor or manufacturer to ship the product directly to the customer. According to the company's stated policies, Anicom recognized revenue and the associated cost of sales when products were shipped to the customer. At the end of financial quarters between 1998 and 2000, however, Anicom manipulated revenue by recording sales for orders that customers had not yet placed, creating charges that sometimes exceeded the customer's existing credit line. Because customers had not actually placed these orders, Anicom did not order products from vendors or manufacturers for shipment. Customer credits were entered into Anicom's billing system during subsequent quarters to eliminate the receivables previously generated by improper sales. In 1999, the company also recorded sales to an entirely fictitious company that was created solely for the purpose of obscuring uncollectible accounts receivable write-offs on Anicom's books. In March 2003, the SEC indicted six former Anicom executives and employees for 30 counts of fraud-related violations.

Source: Internal Auditor, vol. 61, no. 3, June 2004, p. 53.

Question
The violations outlined involve techniques to boost revenue, including
- improper sales cut-off
- consignment sales recorded as revenue

- parking, bill and hold and channel stuffing
- back-to-back swaps
- fictitious sales.

Describe each of these techniques and explain whether they would be in breach of Australian accounting standards. In your answer, refer to the recognition criteria of IAS 18/AASB 118 *Revenue* presented in figure 9.3.

9.3
CASE STUDY

New research finds red flags to uncover accounting fraud

Newswise — Growth companies suffering deteriorating operating performance are most likely to cook their books, according to a comprehensive analysis of Securities and Exchange Commission enforcement releases by Patricia Dechow, an accounting professor at the University of California, Berkeley's Haas School of Business.

Other common characteristics of firms who manipulate financial results include unusually high growth in cash sales but declines in cash profit margins and earnings growth; declines in order backlog and employee headcount; and abnormally high increases in financing and related off-balance sheet activities such as operating leases.

Those were the findings from the most comprehensive analysis ever of Securities and Exchange Commission Accounting and Auditing Enforcement Releases, which the agency issues to document enforcement actions against companies, auditors, and officers for alleged accounting misconduct.

Dechow and her coauthors develop(ed) a model to help identify firms that manipulate earnings or commit fraud. They examined more than 2,000 SEC releases from 1982 to 2005, which resulted in a final sample of 680 firms alleged to have manipulated financial statements.

"A consistent theme among manipulating firms is that they have shown strong performance prior to the manipulations," the researchers noted in their paper. "Manipulations appear to be motivated by managements' desire to disguise a moderating financial performance."

Managers may want to disguise such performance to ensure their stock-based compensation remains valuable or to raise capital at better prices, Dechow notes.

Based on the research, Dechow and her co-authors devised a so-called Fraud-Score, or F-Score, to be used by investors, auditors, and regulators as a preliminary assessment of "earnings quality" to determine whether further investigation into possible fraud is warranted.

Enron, for instance, received an F-score almost twice a high as the average firm. "Enron comes up as a very high risk firm," Dechow says.

Overall, alleged manipulations are more common in large firms. About 15 percent of the manipulations occur in the largest 10 percent of firms, most likely because of the SEC's incentive to identify only the most material and visible manipulations involving large losses to numerous investors.

In addition, more than 20 percent of manipulating firms were in the computer industry, but the computer industry only comprised 11.9 percent of public companies. Retail firms made up 13 percent of manipulating firms, compared with 9.7 percent of public companies. And service firms such as telecommunications and health care made up 12.4 percent of manipulating firms, compared with 10.4 percent of public companies.

The most manipulations occurred in 1999 and 2000, perhaps because slowing growth during this time gave managers incentive to manipulate earnings.

Other findings of the research include:

- Investors have abnormally high expectations about the future growth opportunities of manipulating firms, as evidenced by unusually high price-earnings and market-to-book ratios prior to manipulations.

- Manipulating firms tended to have abnormally low free cash flows. Many firms were actively seeking new financing to cover negative operating and investing cash flows.
- Cash sales, surprisingly, increased during manipulations. That's because many firms (Coca Cola, Sunbeam, Computer Associates) allegedly front-loaded their sales and engaged in unusual transactions at the end of the quarter.
- More firms issued either debt or equity in years in which they manipulated financials compared with other years. And cash from financing more than doubled during manipulating years compared with other years.
- Companies engaged in abnormally high leasing activities during manipulation periods, consistent with managements' increased use of the flexibility granted by lease accounting rules to manipulate their firms' financial statements.
- Accruals increase in manipulating years. Accruals are the difference between reported earnings and actual cash flows, so high accruals indicate more accounting adjustments being made to boost earnings.
- Revenue is by far the most commonly manipulated line item on income statements, with 55 percent of sample firms allegedly manipulating revenue. Types of revenue manipulations include front-loading sales from future quarters (Coca Cola and Computer Associates), creating fictitious sales (ZZZZ Best), incorrect recognition of barter arrangements (Qwest), and shipping goods without customer authorization (Florafax International).
- Manipulations of inventory and cost of goods sold occurred in 25 percent of sample firms. Manipulations of allowances, including the allowance for doubtful debts (an estimate of how many customers who purchased goods on credit will not pay), occurred in 10 percent of sample firms.

Source: University of California, Berkeley Haas School of Business, 5 July 2007, Newswise Inc., www.newswise.com. Based on Working Paper, 'Predicting material accounting misstatements', by Patricia Dechow, Chad Larson, Weili Ge, and Richard Sloan.

Questions

1. What is meant by the term 'earning management'? What are the incentives for managers to manage earnings?
2. What types of firm score poorly on the F score?
3. Explain the relationship of cash flow and earnings management. Is it possible for managers to 'manage' cash flows?
4. What are the practical applications of the F score? In what ways can the F score assist auditors?

Endnotes

1. W Paton and AC Littleton, *An introduction to corporate accounting standards*, Florida: AAA, 1940, pp. 46–7.
2. FASB, Concepts Statement No. 6 *Elements of financial statements of business enterprises*, 1985.
3. C Martin, *An introduction to accounting*, New York: McGraw-Hill, 1987, p. 389.
4. Paton and Littleton op. cit.
5. N Bedford, *Income determination theory: an accounting framework*, Kansas: Addison-Wesley, 1965.
6. J Myers, 'The critical event and recognition of net profit', *Accounting Review*, October 1959.
7. Paton and Littleton op. cit., p. 48.
8. M Chatfield, *A history of accounting thought*, Illinois: Krieger, 1977, p. 257.
9. G May, 'Business income', *Accountant*, 30 September 1950, p. 316.
10. Chatfield op. cit., p. 260.
11. R Coombes and C Martin, *The definition and recognition of revenue under historical cost accounting*, Theory Monograph No. 3, Melbourne: AARF, 1982, pp. 6–7.
12. FASB, Concepts Statement No. 5 *Recognition and measurement in financial statements of business enterprises* December 1984, para. 83.

13. Coombes and Martin, op. cit.
14. Paton and Littleton op. cit., p. 49.
15. Coombes and Martin, op cit.
16. ibid.
17. 'Report of the committee on concepts and standards, external reporting', *Accounting Review*, Supplement, 1974.
18. HR Hatfield, *Accounting, its principles and problems*, reprinted by Scholars Book Company, Houston, Texas, 1971, originally printed 1927, p. 250.
19. Coombes and Martin op. cit., pp. 18–27.
20. E Hendriksen, *Accounting theory*, Homewood, Ill.: Irwin, 1977, p. 189.
21. Coombes and Martin op. cit., p. 19.
22. M Moonitz, *The basic postulates of accounting*, Accounting Research Study No. 1, New York: AICPA, 1961.
23. Accounting Research Bulletin No. 43, chapter 4, 'Inventory pricing', para. 16.
24. Coombes and Martin op. cit., p. 15.
25. ibid., pp. 15, 16.
26. ibid., p. 17.
27. Myers op. cit., p. 55.
28. Coombes and Martin, op. cit.
29. G Pound, 'Room for improvement', *CA Charter*, August 2003, p. 58.
30. IASB, 'Revenue recognition', 1 March 2003, www.iasb.org.
31. FASB, 'Project updates: Revenue recognition', 2004, www.fasb.org.
32. IASB op. cit.
33. Deloitte Touche Tohmatsu, 'IASB agenda project: Revenue recognition, liabilities and equity: Concepts', 2004, IASPlus website, www.iasplus.com.
34. ibid.
35. ibid.
36. IASB, op. cit.
37. Deloitte Touche Tohmatsu, 'Project update: Concepts of revenue and liabilities', *IASPlus Newsletter* (Asia–Pacific edition), April 2004, p. 11, IASPlus website www.iasplus.com.
38. IAS Plus: IASB Agenda — Financial Statement Presentation, Financial Statement Presentation (previously called Performance Reporting and Reporting Comprehensive Income), www.iasplus.com/agenda/perform2.htm
39. Public Company Accounting Oversight Board (PCAOB), 'Report on the PCAOB's 2004, 2005, and 2006 inspections of domestic triennially inspected firms', Release No. 2007-010 October 22, 2007, www.pcaobus.org.
40. ibid, p. 5.
41. DN Hurtt, JG Kreuze, and SA Langsam, 'Auditing to combat revenue recognition fraud', *The Journal of Corporate Accounting & Finance*, vol. 11, no. 4, May/June 2000, pp. 51–59.
42. B Martinez, 'Bristol-Myers settles SEC fraud case', *The Wall Street Journal*, (Eastern Edition), New York, NY, August 5, 2004, p. A.3.
43. PCAOB op. cit., p. 6.

10

Expenses

LEARNING OBJECTIVES

After reading this chapter, you should have an appreciation of the following:

1 the nature of expenses and the way they are defined in the accounting literature

2 recognition criteria and the matching concept as they are applied to expenses in the accrual accounting system

3 criticisms of the matching process and accountants' use of allocations

4 challenges for standard setters and issues for auditors relating to expense recognition and measurement.

Business entities engage in a range of revenue-generating activities which may give rise to expenses. Determining the correct amount of expense to be recorded in an accounting period is very important, as it affects a firm's reported financial position and performance. However, calculating the amount of expense and when it should be recognised is not a straightforward process. In the first section of this chapter, we explore the nature of expenses and the definitions presented in the literature. We discuss standard setters' definitions of expenses and explain the relationship of expenses and losses. Expenses represent either an increase in liabilities or a decrease in assets, with a subsequent effect on equity. We explain how this definition is applied in practice and discuss the behavioural view of expense.

Recognition criteria for expenses are fundamental to accounting practice. In the second section of the chapter, we discuss guidance provided in the IASB/AASB *Framework* and accounting standards for recognition and measurement of expenses. We explore how expenses are determined using the matching approach. Methods of allocating expenses (associating cause and effect, systematic and rational allocation, and immediate recognition) are outlined. Existing practices, such as matching and conservatism, give rise to issues for accounting standard setters and auditors. We discuss current issues for standard setters and auditors in the final two sections of the chapter.

LO 1 → EXPENSES DEFINED

The discussion of assets, liabilities and equity, and revenue (chapters 7, 8 and 9) provides some background for us to understand the nature of expenses. We know that an expense has to do with a decrease in value of the firm. Expenses arising in the course of the ordinary activities include, for example, cost of sales, wages and depreciation. They usually take the form of an outflow or depletion of assets such as cash and cash equivalents, inventory, and property, plant and equipment (*Framework*, para. 78).

In the *Framework* paragraph 70, expenses are defined as follows:

> Expenses are decreases in economic benefits during the accounting period in the form of outflows or depletions of assets or incurrences of liabilities that result in decreases in equity, other than those relating to distributions to equity participants.

Expenses encompass losses as well as expenses which arise in the course of ordinary activities of the entity. Losses may or may not arise in the course of ordinary activities of the entity. However, the *Framework* states that losses represent decreases in economic benefits and are therefore not different in nature from other expenses. Therefore, they are not regarded as a separate element (para. 79). Firms have sought to distinguish between expenses and losses occurring within and outside ordinary activities by categorising items as abnormal or extraordinary in the income statement. This practice is not permitted under IAS 1/AASB 101 *Presentation of Financial Statements*. Paragraph 85 states that an entity must not present any items of income or expense as extraordinary items, emphasising the *Framework*'s all-encompassing definition of expense.

The view represented in the IASB/AASB *Framework* differs from that promulgated by the Financial Accounting Standards Board (FASB), the US standard setter. Concepts Statement No. 6 (paragraphs 68–9) distinguishes between expenses and losses. The latter are decreases in net assets from 'peripheral or incidental transactions' and from other events that may be largely beyond the control of the firm. Expenses pertain to the ongoing major or central operations. It is interesting to note the point made by Henderson, Peirson and Brown concerning this dichotomy:

> The FASB distinction between expenses and losses does not seem to be very useful. It requires a judgment about whether a transaction is part of the entity's 'ongoing major or central operations'. Not having to distinguish between expenses and losses has distinct advantages . . . management will no longer be able to decide that an outflow of assets is a loss and omit it from the determination of operating profit.[1]

The differences between the FASB and IASB frameworks will be the subject of discussion as the boards seek to converge their frameworks and standards. Substantial revisions and extensions to the IASB *Framework* are underway.

Changes in assets and liabilities

As discussed in chapters 7 and 8, revenues and expenses are directly related to the value aspects of assets and liabilities. By their nature, revenues and expenses come about because of events (namely, increases in the value of liabilities or decreases in the value of assets) in the operation of the business. In reality, the events increasing assets and decreasing liabilities may be difficult to observe. What makes a definition of expenses operational is the concept of physical flows involving the entity, thus the *Framework* definition refers to outflows or depletions of assets or incurrences of liabilities.

The *Framework*'s definition makes no reference to the relationship of expenses to revenue, although both are defined in terms of future economic benefits. Although revenues and expenses occur as the firm undertakes the activities that will generate profit, it is preferable to correlate revenues with the actual events of production and sale and to correlate expenses with the using up of goods or services in support of those events, rather than with those events themselves. The definitions in the *Framework* all revolve around future economic benefits, thus ensuring their consistency, using the definition of assets as the point of reference. Case study 10.1 explores issues relating to carbon emissions and considers whether inflows or outflows of economic benefits are expected under trading schemes.

Expenses and 'costs'

The *Framework* implies that the using up of assets entails a cost to the entity. This is in accord with the previous argument that expenses represent a value change. The value change refers to the sacrifice which the firm must make in acquiring the services. If there is no cost to the firm, then there is no expense. For example, if an employee renders services without pay, perhaps in order to gain experience, certainly the company should not record a wages expense. If a machine is donated to a firm and even though the asset would be stated at fair value, it would be theoretically incorrect, under historical cost accounting, for the firm to record depreciation. Sometimes an expense is referred to as an 'expired cost'. For example, a special committee of the American Accounting Association (AAA) in 1957 presented the following definition:

> Expense is the expired cost, directly or indirectly to a given fiscal period, of the flow of goods or services into the market and of related operations.[2]

LO 2 → EXPENSE RECOGNITION

Once we have determined if an outflow is an expense to the firm, the next step is to decide when it should be recognised. The *Framework* specifies two criteria for the recognition of expenses in paragraph 83:

> An item that meets the definition of an element should be recognised if:
> (a) it is probable that any future economic benefit associated with the item will flow to or from the entity; and
> (b) the item has a cost or value that can be measured with reliability.

For an expense to be recognised in the financial statements, it must meet both of the recognition criteria. Firstly, it must be 'probable' that the outflow of future economic benefits has occurred. The *Framework* states that the concept of probability is in keeping with the uncertainty that characterises the environment in which an entity operates. Assessments of the degree of uncertainty attached to the flow of future economic benefits are to be made on the basis of evidence available when the financial statements are prepared (para. 85).

If the probability criterion was interpreted as being more or less than 50 per cent, its application could be at odds with the qualitative characteristic of prudence (*Framework*, para. 37). Prudence is 'the inclusion of a degree of caution in the exercise of the judgements needed in making the estimates required under conditions of uncertainty, such that assets or income are not overstated and liabilities or expenses are not understated'. Bear in mind that another qualitative characteristic, neutrality, requires the information in financial reports to be free from bias (para. 36). Thus, preparers ideally must exercise caution in their judgements and estimations, but not create a bias in the information reported. For example, the overstatement of expenses reflecting excessive prudence and lack of neutrality would not be acceptable as the information would not be reliable.

The second criterion requires that the expense can be 'measured with reliability'. This provides for the case where estimates are required (e.g. depreciation expense, provision for doubtful debts) but appropriate evidence to support the validity of the estimates will be necessary. The *Framework*, paragraph 31, indicates that information is reliable:

> when it is free from material error and bias and can be depended upon by users to represent faithfully that which it either purports to represent or could reasonably be expected to represent.

The *Framework* indicates that an expense is to be recognised in the income statement when a decrease in future economic benefits related to a decrease in an asset or an increase of a liability has arisen and can be measured reliably (para. 94). This means, in effect, that recognition of expenses occurs simultaneously with the recognition of an increase in liabilities or a decrease in assets. For example, the change in value of assets gives rise to depreciation, amortisation or impairment expense. The change in value of liabilities for employee benefits gives rise to gains or losses to be included in income. From the standard setters' point of view, an expense or loss arises following a change in value of an asset or liability. In practice, determining when to recognise expenses or losses can be a subject of debate. Case study 10.2 presents material about recognition of revenue, expenses and liabilities related to an airline's frequent flyer program. This case shows that accepted practice for accounting for frequent flyer points has changed over time, most recently in response to guidance from IFRIC (the IASB's standards interpretations committee).

EXPENSE MEASUREMENT

The measurement of additions to liabilities and depletion of assets in the current period may seem a simple task. However, liabilities may increase because of the acquisition in the current period of key operating equipment with an estimated operating life of many years. Investments may be made in the current period in livestock which will not reach maturity and subsequently generate revenue for a number of years. This means that in measuring expenses in the current period, a number of decisions need to be made as to how expenses should be allocated across future periods of resultant revenue. There are a number of accounting standards that provide guidance on such matters, but offer a choice in the method of expense and revenue apportionment. For example, IAS 16/AASB 116 *Property, Plant and Equipment* allows for the value of a depreciable asset to be measured in a number of ways after recognition (e.g. the cost model or the valuation model) and for several alternative depreciation options (e.g. the straight-line, diminishing value and units of production methods). The decision criteria are meant to be supported by the accrual accounting concept of matching expenses against revenues in the period to which they relate. The complexity of this process and the underlying discretion in adoption of allocation and measurement techniques are key issues for students of accounting and are the focus of this section.

Allocation of expenses

One approach to measuring expenses is to allocate them to periods to which they relate. The matching concept forms the basis of accrual accounting. The IASB/AASB *Framework* recognises the matching concept in paragraph 95 which states 'Expenses are recognised in the income statement on the basis of a direct association between the costs incurred and the earning of specific items of income'. The matching process involves the simultaneous or combined recognition of revenues and expenses that result directly and jointly from the same transactions or other events. For example, the various components of expense making up the cost of sales are recognised at the same time as the income derived from the sale of the goods (para. 95).

For many accountants, relating effort (expenses) and accomplishments (revenue) for a given period is the main function of accounting. However, in practice, proper matching is a difficult task, and involves a great deal of judgement on the part of the accountant. The accountant must identify which assets have been used up (expired) and the amount that should be written off against revenue for the period. Paton and Littleton state:

> The problem of proper matching of revenue and costs is primarily one of finding satisfactory bases of association — clues to relationships which unite revenue deductions and revenue ... Observable physical connections often afford a means of tracing and assigning. It should be emphasised, however, that the essential test is reasonableness, in the light of all of the pertinent conditions, rather than physical measurement.[3]

Indeed, the matching concept is of critical importance in historical cost accounting. It guides the accountant in deciding which costs should be expensed and matched against revenue for the period, and which costs remain unexpired, to be recorded as assets in the balance sheet. To overcome problems associated with determining and measuring costs to be expensed and to be carried forward, three basic methods of matching are commonly relied on. These are:
- associating cause and effect
- systematic and rational allocation
- immediate recognition.[4]

The first is the ideal way of determining an amount of expense, whereas the second and third are alternatives if the first cannot be used. The methods are discussed below.

Associating cause and effect

The ideal way of matching expenses with revenue is by associating cause with effect. Cause-and-effect relationships are difficult to prove. However, based on what appears to be a reasonable observation, accountants decide that certain goods and services used up must have helped in the creation of the revenue for that period. Examples are sales commissions, cost of sales, and salaries and wages. It seems reasonable to assume that the efforts of the sales personnel helped to generate the sales revenue for the current period. Therefore, their efforts, as represented by the commissions paid or payable to them, should be associated with the current revenue. Similarly, the revenue from selling products is usually related to the cost of those products sold; and the services rendered by employees are assumed to have helped to create the current revenue.

Under revenue recognition principles (see chapter 9), there is no cost of sales if there is no revenue. For example, in long-term construction contracts, when the completed contract method (similar to the sales basis) is used, there are no costs of construction (expense) recorded, as long as there is no construction revenue recognised. The costs incurred in the project are placed in an asset account. When the project is completed and 'sold', only then are the total accumulated costs in the asset account transferred to the expense account to be matched against the revenue. The assumption is that at that point the effort represented by the expense helped produce the revenue. If the percentage-of-completion method is used, the actual construction costs incurred for the given period are assumed to have helped in the creation of the current revenue; therefore, an expense is recorded for the amount of the construction costs. In fact, a common technique for ascertaining the ratio of completion is to use the actual construction costs over the total expected construction costs of the project.

However, associating cause and effect may be difficult to apply in practice. One reason is that, in practice, the 'costs attach' concept is the basis on which the cause-and-effect rule rests. According to Paton and Littleton:

> Ideally, all costs should be viewed as ultimately clinging to definite items of goods sold or services rendered. If this conception could be effectively realised in practice, the net accomplishment of the enterprise could be measured in terms of units of output rather than of intervals of time ... In the more typical situation the degree of continuity of activity tends to prevent the finding of a basis of affinity which will permit convincing assignments, of all classes of costs incurred, to particular operations, departments, and — finally — items of product. Not all costs attach in a discernible manner, and this fact forces the accountant to fall back upon a time-period as the unit for associating certain expenses with certain revenues.[5]

However, Paton and Littleton themselves admit that in the typical situation one cannot find a basis for 'costs attach'. In effect, accountants do not directly associate costs with revenue, but match costs to intervals of time. An assumption is made that costs assigned to a given period as expenses must therefore have helped to generate the revenue for that period.

Critics also point out that the rule of cause and effect implies that a certain amount of revenue can be attributable to a certain amount of expenses. For example, suppose the total revenue is $100 000 and the total expenses are $60 000. Let's say that of the total expenses, one-quarter, or $15 000, is for salaries and wages. If we argue cause and effect, we are claiming that salaries and wages, that is, services rendered by employees, generated one-quarter of the revenue, or $25 000. But no accountant would make such an assertion, and certainly it cannot be proven.

Systematic and rational allocation

Associating cause and effect cannot be used for all expenses. When it cannot be done, an alternative is to use a systematic and rational allocation procedure. The aim is to recognise expenses in the accounting periods in which the economic benefits associated with these items are consumed or expire (*Framework*, para. 96). The principle of allocating the cost of an asset to current and future periods is well known in accounting. The matching process begins by associating expenses to segments of time. When this is accomplished, the amount of expense is assumed to correlate with the revenue for that period.

IAS 16/AASB 116 *Property, Plant and Equipment* defines depreciation as 'the systematic allocation of the depreciable amount of an asset over its useful life' (para. 6). Thus, depreciation expense is a well-known example of the allocation process. But what is depreciation? A typical answer is that it is a procedure whereby cost is allocated in a systematic and rational manner to periods in which the benefits are expected to be received. Indeed, IAS 16/AASB 116 paragraph 60 states that the depreciation method used must reflect the pattern in which an asset's future economic benefits are expected to be consumed.

Considering depreciation as an allocation of costs is unsatisfactory for a number of reasons. It confuses an event with a valuation method. Is depreciation a procedure or is it a real-world event? We said earlier that an expense represents a monetary event caused by a physical event. Depreciation therefore is a phenomenon that occurs, and the expense recorded is the monetary effect. The intermingling of event and measurement method is due to the costs attach theory.

In the United States, the Committee on Terminology saw depreciation as 'exhaustion of usefulness'.[6] Similarly, the term 'decline in service potential' of an asset aptly describes depreciation. However, there are others, including economists, who see depreciation as a decline in the value of an asset, which is not necessarily the same as the position taken by accountants. A decline in value usually means a decrease in the market price. Accountants see long-term non-current assets as 'bundles of future services' that become smaller and smaller because of (1) physical factors such as wear and tear through use, and (2) economic factors such as obsolescence.

Depreciation is the decrease or decline of that bundle of services. How is that decline to be measured? Accountants have chosen to use cost allocation. A number of different procedures can be derived from the principle but as long as they are rational and systematic they are considered acceptable.

Cost allocation is a matching concept which leads to a variety of procedures. For instance, for depreciation we have the straight-line, units-of-production, sum-of-the-years-digits, diminishing-balance and other methods. The idea is to find a particular method that more or less coincides with the pattern of services or benefits provided by the asset to future periods of time. This is no simple task. Because of the inherent difficulties in applying the principle, many firms select allocation methods based on reasons that have little to do with the pattern of benefits. In addition, accounting practice may ignore matching all together, when it suits the preparers of financial statements. For example, prior to 2005 many entities opposed the expensing of stock options, even though such a procedure aimed to match revenue with expenditure incurred in its production.

One of the weaknesses of cost allocation is that it relies on estimates and assumptions, which may be arbitrary. How do we know ahead of time what the benefits or services rendered by the asset will be for each future period? How do we objectively select a time horizon or determine the residual value?

An example of the arbitrary allocation of a cost based on time was the amortisation of goodwill. Before widespread adoption of IASB standards in 2005, many entities amortised goodwill over 20 years or less, often on the straight-line basis. Some companies argued that goodwill did not decrease in value, and therefore should not be subject to amortisation. From 1 January 2005, IFRS do not require goodwill to be amortised, thereby avoiding the arbitrary assumptions which were used in the amortisation process. IFRS 3/AASB 3 *Business Combinations* paragraph 54 states that, after acquisition, goodwill acquired in a business combination will be measured at cost less any impairment losses. Thus, an estimation process to determine goodwill amortisation is no longer necessary. However, it will be necessary for an entity to assess annually the extent, if any, to which goodwill has been impaired (or reduced in value), which is another type of estimation.

An area where allocations are currently used is in relation to share-based payments. IFRS 2/AASB 2 *Share-based Payment* requires that companies record an expense in relation to all remuneration given to employees, whether in the form of cash, other assets or equity instruments of the entity. Three forms of share-based payment are identified. These are:

1. equity-settled share-based payments (the entity receives good and services as consideration for its own equity instruments)
2. cash-settled share-based payments (the entity acquires good and services by incurring liabilities for amounts based on the value of its own equity instruments)
3. other transactions (the entity receives or acquires good and services and the entity, or the supplier, has the choice of whether the transaction is settled in cash or equity instruments).

The goods and services received in a share-based payment transaction must be recognised when they are received (IFRS 2, para. 7). A corresponding increase in equity is recorded for equity-settled plans and an increase in liabilities is recognised for cash settled share-based payments.

Equity-settled plans are most commonly observed (e.g. in the United Kingdom and Australia most plans are equity-settled, not cash-settled). The goods and services received in an equity-settled share-based payment transaction and the corresponding increase in equity must be measured at the fair value of the goods or services received, unless that value cannot be reliably estimated (IFRS 2, para. 10). The fair value of the goods and services received is usually measured by reference to the fair value of the equity instruments granted, at grant date. Fair value should be based on a market price (IFRS 2, para. 11) but if such a price is not available then an option pricing model (such as Black-Scholes-Merton or a binomial model) must be used.

Thus, the equity-based plan gives rise to an asset or an expense and a corresponding increase in equity (in relation to shares issued). If the equity instrument vests immediately, the expense in relation to goods and services provided is recognised immediately and there is a corresponding increase in equity. However, if the equity instrument does not vest until certain conditions are met (such as completion of a period of service, or an increase in the price of the entity's shares) then the fair value of the goods and services received is recorded across the vesting period. That is, an allocation process is used to apportion the remuneration expense (the fair value of goods and services to be received) over the vesting period. For example, if the fair value at grant date of options issued to employees is $12 000 and the vesting period is four years, then an expense of $3000 will be recognised in each of the four years. Theory in action 10.1 explores issues relating to accounting for share-based payment plans and theory in action 10.2 explores their effectiveness as motivational tools.

Options deal dwarfs salary of ANZ chief

by Stuart Washington

ANZ chief executive John McFarlane's total pay as shown in yesterday's annual report was $7.2 million. But this figure is dwarfed by the $19.7 million gain he received from cashing in options throughout the year.

The sheer size of the options payout enjoyed by Mr McFarlane highlights the large gap between the accounting treatment and the reality — with $2.1 million shown as "share-based payments" in Mr McFarlane's total pay, in contrast with the $19.7 million benefit he actually enjoyed.

It also flies in the face of suggestions Mr McFarlane did not receive a pay rise, despite his reported total pay increasing by less than 1 per cent on last year's figure.

To ANZ's credit — unlike many of its peers in the ASX 50 — the gain on the options transactions is reasonably clearly outlined in the annual report.

Yet ANZ still falls short of US disclosure practices by failing to show a year-end price for another 1 million vested options (which means Mr McFarlane can cash them in whenever he chooses). These were worth another $10.1 million to Mr McFarlane as of September 30. On the same date, the bank boss held just over 2 million ANZ shares worth $55.7 million.

The Sydney Morning Herald has previously highlighted the lack of meaningful disclosure in many annual reports of large options transactions by chief executives in Australia's largest companies.

In some cases, including McFarlane's, the deals more than double executives' reported pay totals.

In particular, established chief executives in reasonably successful companies appear to enjoy a late-career benefit of a series of successive share-ownership plans that result in large payouts. Mr McFarlane has been CEO since October 1997, with his extended contract coming to an end in September next year.

On Monday the *Herald* revealed Westpac chief executive David Morgan received a $3.8 million cash payment when he exercised 250,000 "stock appreciation rights" from a 1997 share plan. The gain on this transaction was not disclosed in the annual report, nor was it disclosed to the stock exchange.

This was on top of a $6.3 million gain Mr Morgan received from exercising options. Again, the share-based payments dwarf his reported $8.4 million pay figure.

In Mr McFarlane's case he exercised 2 million options which met the performance hurdles of ANZ beating the ASX 200 banks index and beating the ASX 100 index, since their issue.

He is also eligible for 175 000 performance shares.

Source: Sydney Morning Herald, 15 November 2006, www.smh.com.au.

Questions

1. Since 2005, IFRS 2/AASB 2 requires companies to record an expense in relation to stock options plans. Explain the requirements of IFRS 2/AASB 2 and how they differ to previous requirements. (Students will need to consult additional resources. See the list at the end of this chapter.)
2. Provide an overview of the advantages and disadvantages of the requirements of IFRS 2/AASB 2.
3. The article states that certain executives gain much more on options plans than is shown in their company's accounts. For example, the ANZ CEO gained $19.7 m cashing in options, but his pay was shown as $7.2 m in the 2006 annual report. Given that IFRS 2 requires the recording of an expense for share-based payments, explain how this could occur.
4. In light of your answer to question 3, do you consider that the requirements of IFRS 2 should be changed? Why or why not?

Share option plans worthless

by Patrick Durkin

Almost three quarters of employee share options plans issued by the top 50 ASX-listed companies since 2003 are now worthless, research by the law firm Deacons has found.

For the companies listed in the bottom two-thirds of the S&P/ASX 300 Index, almost 90 per cent of the plans are worthless.

Executives at major listed companies including Macquarie Group, Toll Holdings, Tabcorp and Babcock & Brown are just some of those who have watched millions of dollars in share options disappear after the All Ordinaries had its worst calendar year on record in 2008, plummeting 43 per cent.

Yesterday, the share market fell to its lowest point this year, with the S&P/ASX 200 Index losing another 5.2% for the year.

Employee share option schemes have been embraced over recent years, especially by smaller listed companies trying to compete with their higher-paying rivals in the battle for executive talent.

The plans set the share price at which executives can take up the options and usually vest three years after being issued.

The schemes delivered big windfalls at the height of the boom, with options often being exercised at a fraction of the company's rising share price. But most of the windfalls executives thought they had pocketed have evaporated.

Executives at Macquarie Group and Toll Holdings have been hit particularly hard because they are the only two companies in the top 50 which exclusively use option plans, rather than performance rights plans.

"Performance rights plans provide at lease some protection from sharp market falls because they have a nil exercise price and the performance hurdle usually involves comparing the company's total shareholder return against a group of similar companies," said Andrew Spalding and Shane Bilardi, authors of the research undertaken last month.

"Provided that the company matches or outperforms its peers, the rights can still vest even in a falling market."

The average exercise price for Macquarie options is $61.23, the company's most recent annual report shows. At current levels, its share price would need to more than double before the option plans regain any value for executives.

Tabcorp options would also need to more than double, being on average 54 per cent out of the money.

Timbercorp's share price would need to increase 13 times, with options on average 92.5 per cent out of the money.

Fortunately for executives at the blue chips, many ASX top 50 companies have moved exclusively to performance rights plans or use them in a combination with option plans.

"It seems most of the top 50 companies have learnt a lesson from the Dotcom crash and moved to performance rights schemes rather than employee option schemes to ensure that their incentive schemes continue to motivate their employees during downturns in the market," the authors said. "The same cannot be said for many companies outside the top 100, and this could have an adverse impact on their ability to retain and motivate their key employees."

The exercise prices of options issued under the plans of the top 50 listed companies are on average 4 per cent above their current share price. But even that result is flattering because of the strong performances of QBE, Woolworths, Fortescue Metals and Origin Energy and the fact that the worst performers — Asciano, Centro and Babcock — have dropped out of the top 50.

The exercise prices of options issued under the plans of the companies in the bottom two thirds of the top 300 are on average 49 per cent above their share prices.

Remuneration Strategies Group director Gary Fitton said that any gearing plans put in place before the crash were simply outdated.

"Companies tend to adopt a fairly copycat approach and some investors are now asking whether different performance hurdles should be used, given the historically low watermark for the market.

"You may see more internal performance measures being adopted and a return to more earnings orientated measures."

Source: The Australian Financial Review, 16 January 2009, p. 4, www.afr.com.

Questions
1. Outline the difference between an option plan and a performance rights plan.
2. The article states that almost three-quarters of employee share option plans issued by the top 50 ASX firms are now worthless. Explain how options can be worthless when companies have billions of dollars of assets.
3. What does an environment of falling share prices reveal about the effectiveness of incentive plans as motivational tools?

Immediate recognition

This last principle for recognising and measuring expenses can be viewed as one that accounts for all other possibilities not covered by the first two principles. An example of the use of immediate recognition is the recording of advertising expenses. The effect of advertising may have long-lasting benefits, but they are often difficult to determine. For example, customers may purchase a product because they were influenced by an advertisement they saw two years previously. Since the benefits cannot be determined in a credible manner, the cost of advertising is usually recognised immediately as an expense. Similarly, research expenditure is recognised immediately as an expense under IAS 38/AASB 138 *Intangible Assets.* Standard setters (the IASB in this case) hold the view that research expenditure does not meet the recognition criteria for an asset, that is, future economic benefits are not probable, or cannot be measured reliably.

Impairment expenses are another item given immediate recognition. Although both tangible and intangible assets may be subject to depreciation or amortisation requirements, the allocation process may involve errors in judgement or asset value may be affected by other unexpected events. When an asset's recoverable amount is considered to be less than its carrying value, an immediate expense is recognised in the income statement in accordance with IAS 36/AASB 136 *Impairment of Assets.* Thus, impairment expenses arise because of a decline in the value of assets, consistent with the *Framework*'s definition of expenses.

Criticisms of allocations

Paton and Littleton furnished a logical framework for conventional accounting.[7] The matching concept is one of the key features in this framework. Paton and Littleton related the matching of expenses against revenues with the notion of matching effort with accomplishment. They saw the business process as a flow of costs, a flow that inevitably ends up on the income statement as costs expire. Determining the amount of costs that have expired is one of the main tasks of the accountant. However, as indicated by Sprouse,[8] the matching process has made the balance sheet secondary to the income statement; it serves simply as a repository of unexpired costs as they await their time to expire on a future income statement. This approach reduces the usefulness of the balance sheet for users' decision making. In more recent years standard setters have focused on definition and recognition criteria for assets and liabilities which ensure the balance sheet is not 'secondary' to the income statement.

Current practice is also criticised by Thomas, who contends that much of what accountants report is 'rubbish', because accounting information is based mostly on allocations.[9] Thomas argues that allocations are theoretically unjustified. To be justified, three criteria are suggested:

- *Additivity.* The whole must equal the parts. If an allocation is made of a total, the partitioning of it must exhaust the total, no more and no less. That is to say, when the allocated amounts are added together, the total is the same as before the allocation.
- *Unambiguity.* An allocation method should yield a unique allocation — a clear-cut choice of the method should be made. The way the allocation is to be conducted should be clear.
- *Defensibility.* Once an allocation method is selected, the person making the selection must be able to provide conclusive argument for his or her choice, and defend it against other possible alternative methods.

Thomas argues that allocations in accounting do not meet these criteria, especially the third criterion. It is possible to defend particular allocation methods; in fact, a variety of methods exist, each of which can be defended. However, there is no conclusive way to choose one in preference to the others, except arbitrarily.

Accountants defend allocations on two grounds. One argument is that a given input provides services in the current and future periods and the cost allocation pattern reflects the cost of the services received in the given periods. The other argument is that allocated data serve a useful purpose because readers of accounting reports, which include allocated data, find them useful.

If the first argument is made, Thomas insists that accountants must show that the services provided by the given input contributed towards a certain amount of cash inflow or revenue or cost savings. But accountants cannot, Thomas maintains, because allocation assertions in the first place are 'incorrigible'; that is, they are not capable of verification or refutation by objective, empirical means. Thomas states that 'there is nothing in the external world for allocations to approximate'.[10] He contends:

> Conventional allocation assertions do not refer to real-world partitionings; when an incorrigible allocation divides an accounting total, there is no reason to believe that this reflects the division of an external total into independent parts ... Conventional allocation assertions do not refer to real-world economic phenomena, but only to things in asserters' and their readers' minds.[11]

If Thomas means that a pattern of services or contributions related to an input does exist in the real world but accountants' assertions about this pattern are so far removed from the actual pattern as to render their assertions unrealistic, many accountants can accept such a criticism. But Thomas goes further than that. He contends that the pattern of services or contributions does not exist in the external world, only in the minds of accountants. Accountants have convinced themselves and others that such divisions exist when in fact they do not. Thomas remarks, 'our assertions refer to the contents of our minds, not to the external world'.[12]

Another reason the contributions argument in support of allocations is invalid is due to the 'interaction' of the inputs. An input's individual contributions to the output, or revenue, or cash inflow during a particular period cannot be known because all the inputs interact with each other to generate an output total that is different from what they would yield separately. For example, labourers working with machines produce more output than would be the case if the labourers worked with their bare hands and the machines were left untended. Whenever inputs interact, calculations of how much revenue or cash inflow has been contributed by each input are meaningless.

We can see why Thomas insists on the points he makes, because by correlating a division of services provided by an asset with the actual usage of the asset, such as by hours used or kilometres driven, it can be argued that division does have real-world referents and, therefore, allocations are sensible. Allocations may not be accurate, but they would be rational. The task then would be to devise better ways to approximate the divisions, not necessarily to abandon allocations. But Thomas argues that the divisions do not exist in reality. If this is true, any argument given to defend allocations is useless. At any rate, he contends, determining individual patterns of contributions is meaningless because of interaction.

The second argument, that allocated data serve a useful purpose and therefore such data must be useful, is rejected by Thomas. He contends that empirical studies claiming existing accounting information is useful do not really demonstrate that it is so. He maintains that people have been conditioned to believe that allocated information is valid. 'Conventional allocation assertions are on a group pragmatic level.'[13] Such assertions describe phenomena with words that are used by others but are internal to the asserter. Accountants are making claims they cannot validate. The solution is to prepare allocation-free reports. Thomas suggests current exit price reports or net quick assets funds statements. Despite such arguments, standard setters continue to make allocation proposals. Abandoning allocations would be a drastic departure from what accountants understand, believe in, and are accustomed to at present. Allocation is a substantial portion of accounting. Even the definition of an asset implies allocation. An asset is seen essentially as a bundle of future services, and these services are rendered over current and future periods.

Defence of allocations

Eckel supports Thomas in saying that allocations are arbitrary, but only because the objective of allocations is not defensible.[14] The objective of allocations in conventional accounting is to determine profit by a process of matching, in particular by cause and effect. The effectiveness of matching depends on the existence of a unique and identifiable cause-and-effect relationship between costs and revenues. But this cannot be demonstrated as Thomas argues. The objective of allocations, however, could be changed. For example, it could be changed to: Profit for the period will be the result of the difference between recognised revenue and the cost allocated to the period on the basis of a straight-line amortisation over n years. This redefines the process of profit from cause and effect to a particular relationship only: straight-line.

Zimmerman has demonstrated that allocations of costs for internal purposes are useful as devices for controlling and motivating managers, and therefore are justified.[15] In his analysis, Zimmerman showed that cost allocations appear to represent certain hard-to-observe costs that arise when decision-making responsibilities are assigned to managers within the firm. That is, cost allocations, when coupled with incentive schemes that encourage managers to pay attention to reported costs, help to lessen some of the control and coordination problems that arise when managers within the firm are given the right to make certain decisions. He concluded that as long as the benefits of cost allocations (e.g. fewer delay costs) exceed the costs of cost allocations (e.g. more record-keeping costs), using allocation techniques is rational. Zimmerman suggested that allocated fixed costs can serve as a measure for difficult-to-calculate opportunity costs. Using a queuing system to model a service department of a company, Miller and Buckman concluded that Zimmerman's explanation is valid for cases where economies of scale are small.[16] Their study sets out certain instances for the allocation of fixed costs by a service department in setting a charge to a user department.

LO 4 → CHALLENGES FOR ACCOUNTING STANDARD SETTERS

Matching

A sound theoretical framework for the financial statements would mean that both the balance sheet (statement of financial position) and income statement present information with the characteristics of relevance and representational faithfulness (IASB, 2008).

IASB standards have been written and revised over a period of more than 30 years. The *Framework* aims to provide common definitions and recognition criteria, to improve consistency between standards.

In addition, the *Framework* specifically states that the matching concept should not be applied in such a way as to allow the recognition of items in the balance sheet which do not meet the definition of assets or liabilities (para. 95). As noted in chapter 9, guidance for revenue recognition included in IAS 18/AASB 118 gives rise to items in the balance sheet that do not meet the *Framework*'s definition of assets or liabilities. The IASB is tackling this inconsistency in projects it is currently undertaking. An example of debatable recognition of expenses or losses within an accounting period is presented in theory in action 10.3. In 2008 the French bank Société Générale incurred large losses as a result of the unauthorised activities of an individual trader. Although they were incurred in 2008, the losses were included in the 2007 accounts, allowing the bank to offset the loss against profits earned in 2007.

10.3 THEORY IN ACTION

Loophole lets bank rewrite the calendar

by Floyd Norris

It is not often that a major international bank admits it is violating well-established accounting rules, but that is what Société Générale has done in accounting for the fraud that caused the bank to lose 6.4 billion euros — now worth about $9.7 billion — in January.

In its financial statements for 2007, the French bank takes the loss in that year, offsetting it against 1.5 billion euros in profit that it says was earned by a trader, Jérôme Kerviel, who concealed from management the fact he was making huge bets in financial futures markets.

In moving the loss from 2008 — when it actually occurred — to 2007, Société Générale has created a furor in accounting circles and raised questions about whether international accounting standards can be consistently applied in the many countries around the world that are converting to the standards.

While the London-based International Accounting Standards Board writes the rules, there is no international organization with the power to enforce them and assure that companies are in compliance.

In its annual report released this week, Société Générale invoked what is known as the "true and fair" provision of international accounting standards, which provides that "in the extremely rare circumstances in which management concludes that compliance" with the rules "would be so misleading that it would conflict with the objective of financial statements," a company can depart from the rules.

In the past, that provision has been rarely used in Europe, and a similar provision in the United States is almost never invoked. One European auditor said he had never seen the exemption used in four decades, and another said the only use he could recall dealt with an extremely complicated pension arrangement that had not been contemplated when the rules were written.

Some of the people who wrote the rule took exception to its use by Société Générale.

"It is inappropriate," said Anthony T. Cope, a retired member of both the I.A.S.B. and its American counterpart, the Financial Accounting Standards Board. "They are manipulating earnings."

John Smith, a member of the I.A.S.B., said: "There is nothing true about reporting a loss in 2007 when it clearly occurred in 2008. This raises a question as to just how creative they are in interpreting accounting rules in other areas." He said the board should consider repealing the "true and fair" exemption "if it can be interpreted in the way they have interpreted it."

Société Générale said that its two audit firms, Ernst & Young and Deloitte & Touche, approved of the accounting, as did French regulators. Calls to the international headquarters of both firms were not returned, and Société Générale said no financial executives were available to be interviewed.

In the United States, the Securities and Exchange Commission has the final say on whether companies are following the nation's accounting rules. But there is no similar body for the international rules, although there are consultative groups organized by a group of European regulators and by the International Organization of Securities Commissions. It seems likely that both groups will discuss the Société Générale case, but they will not be able to act unless French regulators change their minds.

"Investors should be troubled by this in an I.A.S.B. world," said Jack Ciesielski, the editor of The Analyst's Accounting Observer, an American publication. "While it makes sense to have a 'fair and true override' to allow for the fact that broad principles might not always make for the best reporting, you need to have good judgment exercised to make it fair for investors. SocGen and its auditors look like they were trying more to appease the class of investors or regulators who want to believe it's all over when they say it's over, whether it is or not."

Not only had the losses not occurred at the end of 2007, they would never have occurred had the activities of Mr. Kerviel been discovered then. According to a report by a special committee of Société Générale's board, Mr. Kerviel had earned profits through the end of 2007, and entered 2008 with few if any outstanding positions.

But early in January he bet heavily that both the DAX index of German stocks and the Dow Jones Euro Stoxx index would go up. Instead they fell sharply. After the bank learned of the positions in mid-January, it sold them quickly on the days when the stock market was hitting its lowest levels so far this year.

In its annual report, Société Générale says that applying two accounting rules — IAS 10, "Events After the Balance Sheet Date," and IAS 39, "Financial Instruments: Recognition and Measurement" — would have been inconsistent with a fair presentation of its results. But it does not go into detail as to why it believes that to be the case.

One rule mentioned, IAS 39, has been highly controversial in France because banks feel it unreasonably restricts their accounting. The European Commission adopted a "carve out" that allows European companies to ignore part of the rule, and Société Générale uses that carve out. The commission ordered the accounting standards board to meet with banks to find a rule they could accept, but numerous meetings over the past several years have not produced an agreement.

Investors who read the 2007 annual report can learn the impact of the decision to invoke the "true and fair" exemption, but cannot determine how the bank's profits would have been affected if it had applied the full IAS 39.

It appears that by pushing the entire affair into 2007, Société Générale hoped both to put the incident behind it and to perhaps de-emphasize how much was lost in 2008. The net loss of 4.9 billion euros it has emphasized was computed by offsetting the 2007 profit against the 2008 loss.

It may have accomplished those objectives, at the cost of igniting a debate over how well international accounting standards can be policed in a world with no international regulatory body.

Source: The New York Times, 7 March 2008, www.nytimes.com.

Questions

1. Outline the events which led to Société Générale recording a 2008 loss in the company's 2007 accounts. How did the bank justify its action?
2. On what grounds has the bank's approach been criticised?
3. Evaluate the role of the auditors in this situation.
4. Comment on the implications of this case for the consistent application of IFRS in the European Union and elsewhere.

Conservatism

The matching concept requires a great deal of judgement in determining whether a given amount of cost is applicable to the future or to the current period. It is noteworthy that accountants demand objective evidence for the recognition of revenue, but there has been limited discussion of objective evidence in relation to recognising expenses. Instead the plea is for reasonableness or appropriateness, not for objective evidence. To be reasonable is a virtue, but what is the standard of reasonableness in applying the matching concept? It is general acceptance of a procedure. Whatever is deemed acceptable practice is considered reasonable and appropriate. For instance, the way to deal with inventories is to expense them by using one of the accepted methods (such as FIFO or average cost) and the way to handle plant and equipment is to depreciate them by using one of the accepted depreciation methods.

One reason for the lesser requirement for objective evidence in recognising expenses as compared with revenues is the convention of conservatism. This convention calls for the recording of expenses, losses and liabilities as soon as possible, even though the evidence may be weak; however, it requires that revenues, gains and assets be supported by more substantial evidence before they are recorded. According to IAS 11/AASB 111 *Construction Contracts* (para. 22) 'contract revenue and contract costs associated with the construction contract shall be recognised as revenue and expenses respectively by reference to the stage of completion of the contract activity at the reporting date. An expected loss on the construction contract shall be recognised as an expense immediately . . .' So provision is made for the loss immediately, but not for overall gains of the contract. Although the loss on the entire contract has not been fully realised because the project is not completed, the total expected loss is to be recognised immediately. This is true even when the completed contract method is used.

Some argue that conservatism underlies the probability and reliability criteria espoused in the *Framework*. The term 'probable' means that a future event is likely to occur to confirm the loss or expense. Thus, a bad debts expense is recorded because it is probable on the date of the financial statements that the entity will be unable to collect a certain amount to which it is entitled. This probability is based mainly on past experience. A loss due to the threat of expropriation is to be recorded if expropriation is imminent and the amount of the loss is estimable. Imminence may be indicated by public or private declarations of intent by a government. Accrual of a loss related to litigation, claim or assessment would be required if the probability of the loss is such that the two conditions mentioned above are met.

It is argued that, because of conservatism, if it is probable that the value of net assets has decreased, an expense must be recognised. The kind of evidence required to determine this probability is vague. Conventional treatment is followed, and convention dictates that one be conservative. The admonition 'anticipate no profits but anticipate all losses' is commonly followed. The interpretation of the matching concept in practice, therefore, is biased by the effect of the convention of conservatism. Conservatism does not focus on evidence, but on the fear of overstatement of net assets and profits. Misleading information can be the result.

Under previous Australian guidelines (SAC 4), conservatism was considered a bias to be avoided. The current *Framework* is not so explicit, although it does nominate neutrality as a qualitative characteristic of financial information. Information with a conservative bias is not neutral information. The extent to which conservatism is practised through the recognition of provisions has been restricted by the introduction of IAS 37/AASB 137 *Provisions, Contingent Liabilities and Contingent Assets*. In addition to the recognition criteria of the *Framework* relating to 'probability' and 'reliability', the standard requires an entity to have a present obligation (legal or constructive) before recognising a provision (para. 95).

Thus, a provision cannot be recognised unless the entity cannot avoid meeting the obligation; that is, it 'has no realistic alternative to settling the obligation' (para. 17). Consequently, management's ability to create provisions which reduce income in the current period and allow for income to be increased in future periods, has been curtailed. Provisions such as those for maintenance and restructuring cannot be included in the financial statements unless the recognition criteria are met. Therefore, a provision for maintenance must reflect an obligation to an external party. A provision for restructuring arises only when a detailed formal plan, meeting certain criteria (para. 72), has been formulated. In addition, the standard states that contingent liabilities cannot be recognised, that is, included in the expense of the period (para. 27).[17] Since the contingent liability does not meet recognition criteria, it cannot be recognised and does not provide a means to overstate expenses and thereby present a conservative view of financial position and performance.

Issues for auditors

Auditors face issues surrounding the distinction between expenses and assets, the period in which expenses are recognised, and appropriate measurement of expenses. The definition of expenses in the *Framework*, paragraph 70, as 'decreases in economic benefits ... in the form of outflows or depletions of assets' focuses attention on the choice between debiting expenses or assets when recording outflows of assets (or incurrence of liabilities). The collapse of the US telecommunications company WorldCom in July 2002 revealed its accountants had been having problems in applying principles surrounding the definition of expenses.[18] WorldCom was a major provider of long-distance telephone and Internet services, growing rapidly during the 1990s through acquisitions of other companies.[19]

One accounting irregularity that was revealed after the collapse of WorldCom was inappropriate capitalisation of operating expenses as assets. During 2001 and 2002 the company treated as capital investments US$3.8 billion paid as fees to other telecom companies for the right to access their networks.[20] The payment of fees for the use of a network represents outflows of assets which should have been matched with the revenue generated from the provision of telephone and Internet services to customers in the same period.

Treating expenses as assets is a relatively uncomplicated way to overstate profit for the period, and auditors usually require strong evidence to support capitalisation of expenditure. However, attempts by managers to overstate expenses (and understate assets) can also lead to problems for auditors. When accounting for its acquisitions during the 1990s, WorldCom would write down the value of certain assets it acquired.[21] When assets are recognised at a lower cost, future depreciation charges are also lower, helping managers to report greater profits. The practice of overstating one-time charges associated with acquisitions and restructures is known as 'big bath' accounting. WorldCom also appeared to practise 'cookie-jar' accounting by including a charge for future expected company expenses at the time of the acquisition.[22] Cookie-jar accounting allows for profit to be increased in the future when the charges are reversed on the basis of new evidence that original expectations of future costs were too pessimistic.

The practices of big bath and cookie-jar accounting violate the principles of systematic and rational allocation of expenses to the appropriate accounting periods. Auditors could be tempted to give less attention to the possibility that expenses are overstated than understated because of the belief that a conservative approach to profit measurement is desirable. However, the *Framework*'s nomination of neutrality as a desirable qualitative characteristic and the introduction of IAS 37/AASB 137 would appear to require auditors to gather sufficient evidence to ensure that they do not sign off on accounts with overstated expenses.

Another difficult area for auditors related to expenses is accounting estimates, such as provisions for inventory obsolescence, warranties, losses on lawsuits, and construction contracts in progress. An accounting estimate means an approximation of the amount of an item in the absence of a precise means of measurement.[23] Expenses arise from estimates when there is no underlying transaction for a certain amount which produces a debit that must be classified, such as whether a cash payment results in a debit to expenses or assets. Auditors have to test the assumptions and processes used by management when arriving at an estimate and consider whether there is any other evidence to support the reasonableness of the amount claimed.

An accounting estimate that created difficulties for WorldCom was the provision for doubtful debts. WorldCom's many acquisitions created operational difficulties in merging different billing and customer collection practices and systems. These difficulties resulted in a jump in the length of time receivables had been on the company's books without collection from an average of 63 days in 1999 to 77 days in June 2000. Evidence subsequently emerged that during this period customer accounts that were known to be uncollectable were not written off. Finally, in September 2000, WorldCom recognised a bad debt expense of US$685 million which clearly included expenses that should have been recognised in previous periods.[24]

Summary

LO 1 The nature of expenses and the way they are defined in the accounting literature

The ideal case tells us that expenses are a monetary event which relates to a decrease in the net assets of the firm. The decrease in value pertains eventually to the outflow of cash. Although the decrease may be simple to observe and calculate in the ideal situation, in a world of uncertainty it is not. To render a definition of expenses operational, it must be associated with a physical activity of the entity, something the entity does. Thus we say, in the earning process, that production and sales generate revenue and the using up of goods and services in support of those functions causes expenses to occur. To provide practical guidance, standard setters have defined expenses in terms of decreases in economic benefits arising from the outflow or depletion of assets or the incurrence of liabilities. Based on this definition, expenses encompass both expenses and losses incurred in the normal operations of the entity.

LO 2 Recognition criteria and the matching concept as they are applied to expenses in the accrual accounting system

The recognition criteria for expenses are consistent with those of the other accounting elements discussed in the *Framework*. An expense is to be recognised in the financial statements when it is probable that future economic benefits associated with the item will flow from the entity, and the item has a cost that can be measured reliably. The decrease in future economic benefits relates to a decrease in an asset or an increase in a liability. This means, in effect, that recognition of expenses occurs simultaneously with the recognition of an increase in liabilities or a decrease in assets.

Conventional theory sees revenue as the accomplishment resulting from the efforts expended by the firm; thus, for any given period, matching effort (expenses) with accomplishment (revenue) yields the net accomplishment, or periodic profit. This is an imaginative way of visualising the earning process. Even with an operational definition and an imaginative view of the earning process, recognising expenses in practice is difficult without more specific criteria. Accountants use three matching methods: (1) associating cause and effect; (2) systematic and rational allocations; and (3) immediate recognition.

Applying the three matching methods is not a straightforward process and involves a great deal of judgement. In fact, most of the problems of profit determination have to do with matching. Accruals and deferrals are connected to the matching process. The accountant must decide whether a cost pertains to future revenues and therefore should be deferred; or whether a cost is related to past revenues and therefore should be written off against previous profit; or whether a cost, although not yet paid, is related to current revenues and therefore should be accrued. In making these decisions, official pronouncements by authoritative bodies, conventions, conservatism and expediency play an important role. Some rules are very specific, such as expensing research costs; others are vague, such as recording a loss if it is 'probable' that a liability has been incurred.

Criticisms of the matching process and accountants' use of allocations

The matching process has become an essential part of accounting practice. However, there are many criticisms of this approach. An emphasis on matching gives priority to the income statement and reduces the usefulness of the balance sheet which becomes a repository for unexpired costs. Standard setters have sought to rectify this situation by defining elements of financial statements in relation to each other and presenting definition and recognition criteria which are consistent with each other. The matching process requires considerable judgement on the part of financial statement preparers. The doctrine of conservatism means that expenses, losses and liabilities are recognised as soon as possible, even if evidence for them is weak. In addition, personal incentives may influence managers' judgement in the allocation process. The asymmetrical treatment of revenue and expenses may create a conservative bias and misleading financial statements.

Matching methods may be difficult to apply in practice. For example, accountants do not actually associate cause and effect but rather match costs to intervals of time. The allocation method of assigning costs is criticised as being theoretically unjustified. Thomas argues that allocations breach criteria such as additivity, unambiguity and defensibility and that the arbitrary nature of the allocation process reduces the usefulness of financial statements. He suggests alternative approaches, such as current exit price reports and net quick assets funds statements. However, standard setters continue to recommend allocation methods, and abandoning this approach would be a fundamental change from current accounting practice which may not be acceptable in the financial community.

Challenges for standard setters and issues for auditors relating to expense recognition and measurement

The *Framework* provides a basis for determining whether amounts meet the definition and recognition criteria of expenses. However, judgement is required when deciding whether items represent assets or expenses, the amount of items and the period in which they should be recognised. In applying the *Framework*, standard setters argue that concepts such as 'matching' and 'conservatism' are not helpful if they distort the information presented and thus reduce its usefulness for decision making. In reality, matching and conservatism are accounting practices, not accounting principles. Standard setters argue that financial statement users (current and future investors, lenders and other creditors) are better served by neutrality (not conservatism), which together with completeness and accuracy (freedom from error) and relevance form the basis of the fundamental qualitative characteristics of financial information.

A feature of developed capital markets is the range of contracts which exist between managers and capital providers. Contractual arrangements can provide incentives which may influence managers' decisions about the recognition of expenses, as shown in the WorldCom case discussed in the chapter. Auditors have a key role in ensuring that financial statements comply with the requirements of accounting standards and are not distorted by inaccurate recognition of expenses.

Questions

1. How is the cash outflow of an entity related to expenses?
2. What is the 'monetary event' associated with the notion of expense? How is the 'using up of goods or services' related to expense?

3. What is the difference between expense and loss? How does the *Framework* apply to expenses and losses?
4. Explain the connection between accruals and deferrals on the one hand and the process of matching on the other. Give two examples.
5. Name the three basic methods of matching. Give an example of each. How do they align with the expense recognition criteria outlined in the *Framework*?
6. What are some of the problems connected with the cause-and-effect method?
7. What are some of the problems related to the immediate recognition method?
8. What is the 'allocation problem' as argued by Thomas? What is your opinion of this problem? How is it dealt with under the *Framework*?
9. How has allocation been defended by some researchers?
10. Determine whether an asset or expense should be charged for the following costs, and state your reasons.
    (a) cost of removing two small machines to make way for a larger new machine
    (b) cost of repairing a floor damaged when a new machine was dropped while being unloaded
    (c) cost of a new calculator, $48
    (d) cost of major repairs to equipment (the need for repair was discovered immediately after acquisition, and there is no warranty on the equipment)
11. What guidance is provided by the *Framework* in relation to the convention of conservatism?
12. Standard setters have been criticised for being 'balance sheet biased'. What does this mean? What evidence is available to support this criticism?
13. Explain the arguments for and against expensing share (stock) options.
14. Leonard Ltd is a small firm. For the six-month period ending 30 June of the current year, it made sales totalling $40 000. These sales were on credit and were all made in the last four months. To determine its bad debts expense, it uses an ageing schedule of accounts receivable that has proven to be relatively accurate. For the six-month period, the following calculation was made of accounts receivable multiplied by the uncollectable percentage:

60 days and under	$ 30 000 × 1%	= $	300
61 90 days	10 000 × 3%	=	300
91–120 days	8 000 × 6%	=	480
Over 120 days	4 000 × 12%	=	480
Total	$ 52 000		$ 1560

There was no remaining balance in Provision for Doubtful Debts at the end of the six-month period. Leonard Ltd recorded $1560 as a bad debts expense, which was one of the expenses deducted from sales revenue of $40 000 on the income statement. Is the $1560 the proper amount of expense to match against the $40 000 sales revenue? Explain. Where the Provision for Doubtful Debts is inadequate, leading to a significant expense affecting current year profits but relating to revenue from a previous period, is it consistent with the matching concept to write off the debt in the current period?
15. Decide whether the following expenditures should be put into an asset or expense account.
    (a) The cost of an insurance policy, which had been purchased by Y Ltd to cover goods in transit to the company from suppliers for the current year.

(b) The salary for the general manager in charge of plant operations for Z Manufacturing Ltd. The cash component of the salary is $100 000; employer-contributed superannuation is $20 000, and the general manager is offered 40 000 share options in the company to be exercised after two years at 50 per cent of the market value of the shares at the date the options are exercised. Cover each component of the general manager's remuneration in your answer.

(c) The legal fees incurred in the unsuccessful prosecution of a patent infringement suit.

(d) The fees paid to a consultant who designed a more efficient layout for plant operations.

(e) The fees paid to an underwriter for handling the share issue when T Ltd was first established.

16. The following items are typical expenses. Identify the asset or service that is used up.
(a) income tax expense
(b) interest expense
(c) cost of goods sold
(d) warranty expense
(e) goodwill amortisation expense
(f) research and development expense
(g) life insurance expense (on life of chief executive)
(h) superannuation expense
(i) rates expense

17. An entity receives 100 emission trading allowances from the government. It purchases an additional 50 allowances for $3000 each.
(a) What is the average cost of the allowances? What journal entries are required to record these transactions?
(b) How should the entity record sale of one allowance for $4000? What entry is required if the entity uses all 150 allowances?

Problems

PROBLEM 10.1 For Ryder Ltd for the financial year 1 January to 31 December 2009, record all necessary journal entries relating to the selected events described. Use generally accepted accounting principles. The records are still open on 31 December 2009.

1. On 2 January, Ryder Ltd granted certain executives options to purchase 10 000 shares of its ordinary share capital at $180 per share in exchange for services to be performed over the next 3 years. The quoted market price of the shares on 2 January was $175 per share. The executives believe that the market price is likely to rise to $250 per share over the next 3 years.

2. On 1 July, Ryder Ltd acquired a patent on a product with a remaining legal life of 15 years. The estimated economic life of the patent on the acquisition date was eight years. The cost of the patent was $64 000.

3. Ryder Ltd developed a process in 2009 on which it received a patent on 1 October. In 2011, developmental costs of the process amounted to $140 000. Legal fees to obtain the patent were $13 600. Ryder Ltd decided that the legal life of 20 years approximated its economic life.

4. In December 2009, Ryder Ltd acquired all the shares of Victorian Communications Ltd, publisher of the *Victorian News*. The excess of cost over the fair value of the net assets of the company was $80 000. This amount of goodwill was attributable to the newspaper's established circulation list, the editorial reference library, established news development resources, community loyalty and established advertising clients. The consolidated financial statements do not include any impairment of the goodwill.

5. Ryder Ltd acquired five heavy trucks in 2007 for $35 000 each. Based on a 5-year study, it was decided that the total kilometres driven for each truck over its useful life of 5 years would be 200 000 km. The residual value of each was estimated to be $5000. The company decided to use the units-of-service (output) method for the trucks in determining depreciation. The actual total kilometres driven for the five trucks in 2009 were 120 000 km. Other equipment which was purchased in 2007 with an original cost of $5 000 000 is being depreciated by the straight-line method over a useful life of 10 years. No residual value is expected. Because of a labour dispute, the plant was shut down between 1 August and 30 October. The equipment and trucks were not used during that time.

6. Ryder Ltd had the exterior of its office building painted in November. The cost was $20 000.

7. An unusual storm, which Ryder Ltd believes is not likely to recur in the foreseeable future, occurred in February. The storm caused extensive damage to the office building. The loss was $50 000. This amount is over and above the amount received from the insurance company.

8. On 1 January 2007, Ryder Ltd acquired a warehouse at a cost of $150 000. The company adopted the straight-line method of depreciation and has been recording depreciation over an estimated economic life of 10 years with no residual value. At the beginning of 2009, a decision was made to adopt the diminishing-balance method of depreciation for the warehouse. Due to an oversight, however, the straight-line method was used for 2009.

9. A lawsuit against the company which was initiated in 2008 was settled out of court. Ryder Ltd paid the plaintiff $125 000.

10. Ryder Ltd acquired its factory building on 2 January 1999 for $300 000. At that time the useful life was estimated to be 20 years. At the beginning of 2009, it was decided that the useful life on the acquisition date should have been 30 years.

11. From September 2009 to December 2009, one of the company's major products was advertised on television. The cost of these one-minute commercials was $200 000. The company experienced a dramatic increase in the sale of this product. It is believed that the larger amount of sales will continue indefinitely because the commercials have made the product better known to the public.

12. Ryder Ltd sells a product with a one-year warranty. On 31 December 2009, the company estimated that the cost of repairs for the items sold in 2009 but to be returned for repairs in 2012 would be $68 000.

13. In October, Ryder Ltd agreed to purchase 7500 tonnes of material in 2010 at the fixed price of $100 per tonne. The contract is not subject to cancellation. On 31 December 2009, the replacement cost of the materials was $88 per tonne.

14. One of Ryder Ltd's divisions is in the construction business. The following information relates to one of its projects, started in 2009:

Total contract price	$520 000
Billings	350 000
Costs incurred	424 000
Estimated additional costs to complete the project	106 000

The division uses the completed contract method.

15. Ryder Ltd acquired a new machine by trading in a similar machine. The old machine originally cost $90 000 and had accumulated depreciation of $20 000 at the date of exchange. The new machine could have been purchased for $50 000 cash. Ryder Ltd received $5000 also on the exchange.

16. Ryder Ltd has just learned that one of its customers, Dayton Ltd, has declared bankruptcy. Dayton Ltd owes $60 000 to Ryder Ltd. It does not appear that Ryder Ltd will receive anything. This amount constitutes 40% of the ending balance of Accounts Receivable.

17. One of Ryder Ltd's divisions received a donation consisting of 3 hectares of land with an old building on it. The intention is for the company to build a manufacturing plant on the land. On 2 January 2009, when the company took title to the property, the appraised value of the land was $3 00 000 and of the building was $100 000. The building's useful life at that time was 10 years. The company is using the building for the storage of a variety of items.

PROBLEM 10.2 ⊢ Mangold Ltd received several donations. Record the journal entries for the following events:
1. Cash of $10 000 is received from a shareholder as a donation.
2. The cash donation is used to pay salaries and wages expenses.
3. Equipment is received at the beginning of the year from Lin Pty Ltd as a donation. The fair value is $20 000. The carrying amount for Lin Pty Ltd is $15 000. Estimated useful life at the time of receipt of the equipment is 10 years.
4. The equipment received from Lin Pty Ltd is used in operations for the year.
5. Land is received from a shareholder as a donation. The fair value is $50 000.
6. The land is sold for $55 000.

PROBLEM 10.3 ⊢ The Flying Fox Group of companies owns the tollway from the centre of a major city to the airport. Under the agreement with the state government, Flying Fox must upgrade the road every 10 years. Flying Fox has established a provision account to allocate the future cost of upgrading the road over the next 10 years. Outline the accounting entries to provide for such a provision. Is this approach consistent with the matching principle? How does this approach relate to IAS 16/AASB 116 *Property, Plant and Equipment* and IAS 37/AASB 137 *Provisions, Contingent Liabilities and Contingent Assets*?

Additional readings

Aboody, D, Barth, ME, & Kasznik, R 2004, Firms' voluntary recognition of stock-based compensation expense, *Journal of Accounting Research*, vol. 42, no. 2, pp. 123–150.

Alfredson, K, Leo, K, Picker, R, Loftus, J, Clark, K, & Wise, V 2009, *Applying international accounting standards*, chapter 6, Share-based payment, Brisbane: John Wiley and Sons Australia, Ltd, pp. 195–226.

American Accounting Association Committee. 'The matching concept.' *Accounting Review*, April 1965.

de la Torre, I 2008, Creative accounting exposed, Palgrave Macmillan.

FASB 2004 'FASB issues final statement on accounting for share based payment' FASB News Release, 19 October, www.fasb.org.

IFRIC 13 Customer Loyalty Programs, IASCF, 2008.

Nelson, MW, Elliott, JA, & Tarpley, RL 2003, How are earnings managed? Examples from auditors, *Accounting Horizons*, vol. 17.

Robinson, D, & Burton, D 2004, 'Discretion in financial reporting: The voluntary adoption of fair value accounting for employee stock options.' *Accounting Horizons*, vol. 18, no. 2, pp. 97–108.

Zeff, S 2006, 'Political lobbying on accounting standards — national and international experience', in Nobes, C & Parker, R, *Comparative international accounting*, chapter 9, 9th edn, London: Prentice Hall.

10.1
CASE STUDY

Emissions trading: recognising the cost of pollutants

Current developments in environmental issues

by Charlotte Wright

Accounting for emission allowances

Emissions allowances are credits or allowances that a company receives from a regulatory agency that represent the "right" to emit a specified amount of pollution. Emission allowances arise as a consequence of emission trading programs. Emission trading programs are widely used by governments in an effort to regulate the emissions of a variety of pollutants, including greenhouse gases. For example, in the U.S. sulfur dioxide emission credits are issued by the Environmental Protection Agency (EPA) in compliance with the Clean Air Act. Similar emission trading programs targeted at reducing greenhouse gasses exist globally and are becoming increasingly popular.

In an emission trading program the government sets a limit on the amount of pollution that a company (or company group) can emit. Companies are given credits or allowances that permit them to emit a specified amount of pollution in any given year. Once issued, these allowances can be sold or traded if, for example, in any given year a company's emissions are low and they do not need all of their credits. A company with excess emissions has the choice of paying a fine or purchasing unused credits from another company. In this example, the company with unused credits may sell its credits to the company with excess emissions. These programs have become a popular means of controlling emission of pollutants since, in effect, they reward low polluters and fine excess polluters. Based on supply and demand, if a large number of firms need to buy allowances, the demand for allowances will increase and the price will go up. Theoretically, at some point it becomes cheaper for a company to reduce emission of greenhouse gasses than to continue to purchase allowances.

One popular trading program is referred to as a "cap-and-trade" program where the regulatory agency establishes the amount of permissible emissions per plant. The plant owners are given a number of allowances, typically denominated in tons of emissions per year. The allowances become immediately tradeable, and companies must decide whether to buy, sell, or hold their allowances. At the end of the year (or the allowance period) companies must report their actual emissions and deliver a sufficient number of allowances to cover the emissions or pay a fine. Typically allowances are only good for a specific year and cannot be banked by a company to be used in future years when their pollution levels are higher.

Emission credits are traded in established markets. One of the most active markets in the U.S. is the over-the-counter market for sulfur dioxide credits established under the Clean Air Act. Emission trading markets are also prominent outside the U.S. For example, in the European Union (EU) each country in the EU is allocated allowances for greenhouse gas emissions within its borders, and there is an active market for carbon dioxide allowances.

Currently in the U.S., financial accounting for emission allowances is on an accrual basis. When the allowances are issued by the regulatory agency they have zero cost basis to the reporting entity. If the entity purchases allowances in the market, the allowances are recorded as "allowances inventory" using the lower of cost or market valuation approach. Sales of allowances result in recognition of gains or losses. For example, if an entity receives 100 allowances from the government and purchases an additional 50 allowances for $3000 each, the total cost of the 150 allowances is $150 000. Each allowance has an average cost of $ 150 000/150 = $ 1000. If the entity sells an allowance for $4000, $1000 is charged to expense and a profit of $3000 is recognized. If the entity uses all of the allowances, the full $150 000 is charged to expense.

Upon issuance of Statement No. 153, "Exchanges of Nonmonetary Assets" the FASB received numerous questions regarding whether emission allowances should be accounted for at fair value and whether allowances are properly accounted for as inventory. The Emerging Issues Taskforce put the topic on its agenda but later removed it citing the need for a comprehensive examination of all of the accounting issues related to the allowances and to the cost of pollution. The IASB faces similar issues. The International Financial Reporting Interpretations Committee (IFRIC) originally issued an interpretation entitled "Emission Rights" wherein allowances are accounted for at fair value and systematically recognized in income over the period in which the rights accrue. Recently this interpretation was withdrawn. Both the IASB and the FASB have concluded that there is a need for a comprehensive model of accounting for emission trading programs, and both boards have added the topic to their respective agendas. The projects include questions regarding liability accrual at the time pollution emissions occur.

Source: Petroleum Accounting and Financial Management Journal, Spring 2007, vol. 26, no. 1, p. 64. Reproduced by permission of the Institute of Petroleum Accounting, University of North Texas, © 2007.

Questions

1. What are emission allowances? Do they meet the IASB *Framework* definition of assets or expenses?
2. How do businesses obtain emission allowances?
3. How are emission allowances accounted for in the USA?
4. Why are the IASB and FASB involved in setting guidelines for accounting for emission trading?

10.2
CASE STUDY

Accounting for frequent flyer points: fact or fiction?

Accounting requirements under IFRS have changed the way airlines account for frequent flyer points. In the past, deferred cost accounting practices were used. Under this method, the upfront sale of points to banks, credit card companies, mortgage brokers and general retailers was recorded as revenue in the income statement at the time of sale. The expense related to the sale, that is the cost of travel, was recorded at a later period, when the airline provided the travel service, or gave up the 'free' seat.

The Australian Financial Review (AFR) reported in December 2004 that the sale of points to third parties, rather than giving them away to loyal customers, made the schemes profitable for Qantas and major network carriers in the United States and Europe. The newspaper claimed that when Qantas sought additional debt or equity capital, it would have to treat its frequent flyer point liability on the same basis as other global firms, in the name of equality and transparency.

Qantas responded immediately to the *AFR* article. The company stated that it establishes a liability and takes a charge to the profit and loss account for the cost of providing a 'free' seat at the time the frequent flyer revenue is received, not when Qantas gives up the 'free' seat (the cost/provision approach). The company said it complies with Australian accounting standards and would comply with international accounting standards when they were introduced. It would not have to change its accounting practices when it next sought to raise capital.

From 1 July 2008 Qantas must apply IFRIC 13 *Customer Loyalty Programmes*. The interpretation applies to the recognition and measurement of obligations to supply goods and services to customers if they redeem 'award' points. IFRIC 13 requires the deferred revenue approach. Building on IAS 18 paragraph 3, the interpretation views awards granted as separately identifiable components of an initial transaction (in Qantas's case, the sale of an airline ticket). The ticket sale is split into two components, the provision of service and the associated award. The revenue allocated to the award is deferred and recognised when the award is redeemed. The award is to be measured at fair value and measurement guidance is included in the interpretation.

References

Sandilands, B 2004, 'Popular cards fail to fuel flyers' fantasies,' *The Australian Financial Review*, 9 December, p. 4.

'Qantas: no change' 2004, *The Australian Financial Review*, 13 December, p. 51.

Questions

1. Describe the accounting process used to account for frequent flyer points prior to the adoption of IFRS. How was the matching principle breached by this practice?
2. How could companies benefit from this accounting practice? Consider both the short and long term.
3. Why was Qantas keen to correct the errors reported in *The Australian Financial Review* article?
4. Explain the difference between the cost/provision and the deferred revenue approaches.
5. What impact do you expect adopting the deferred revenue approach to have on Qantas's financial statements?

Endnotes

1. S Henderson, G Peirson, and R Brown, *Financial accounting theory — its nature and development*, 2nd edn, Melbourne: Longman Cheshire, 1992, p. 247.
2. American Accounting Association (AAA), Accounting and Reporting Standards for Corporate Financial Statements, Florida, 1957.
3. W Paton and AC Littleton, *An introduction to corporate accounting standards*, Florida: AAA, 1940, p. 15.
4. FASB, Statement No. 4 Basic Concepts and Accounting Principles Underlying Financial Statements of Business Enterprises, October 1979, paras 157–60.
5. Paton and Littleton, op. cit.
6. Accounting Terminology Bulletin No. 1, 'Review and resume', August 1953, para. 50.
7. Paton and Littleton, op. cit.
8. R Sprouse, 'The balance sheet — embodiment of the most fundamental elements of accounting theory', in S Zeff and T Keller (eds), *Financial accounting theory I*, 2nd edn, New York: McGraw-Hill, 1973, p. 166.
9. AL Thomas, 'The FASB and the allocation problem', *Journal of Accountancy*, November 1975; A Thomas, 'The allocation problem', *Studies in Accounting Research No. 9*, Florida: AAA, 1974.
10. ibid., p. 3.
11. ibid., p. 53.
12. ibid., p. 56.
13. ibid , p. 59.
14. L Eckel, 'Arbitrary and incorrigible allocations', *Accounting Review*, October 1976.
15. J Zimmerman, 'The costs and benefits of cost allocations', *Accounting Review*, July 1979.
16. B Miller and AG Buckman, 'Cost allocation and opportunity costs', *Management Science*, May 1987.

17. IAS 37/AASB 137 paragraph 10 defines a contingent liability as a possible obligation that arises from past events and whose existence will be confirmed only by the occurrence or non-occurrence of one or more uncertain future events not wholly within the control of the entity; or a present obligation that arises from past events but is not recognised because (a) it is not probable that an outflow of resources embodying economic benefits will be required to settle the obligation, or (b) the amount of the obligation cannot be measured with sufficient reliability.

18. K Eichenwald, 'For WorldCom, acquisitions were behind its rise and fall', *The New York Times*, 8 August 2002; P Elstrom, 'How to hide $3.8 billion in expenses', *Business Week*, 8 July 2002, p. 41.

19. ES Browning, 'Is the praise for WorldCom too much?' *Wall Street Journal*, 8 October 1997, C-24.

20. Elstrom, op. cit.

21. Eichenwald, op. cit.

22. ibid.

23. Auditing Standard ASA 540 *Audit of Accounting Estimates*, April 2006, paragraph 6.

24. Eichenwald, op. cit.

Part 3

Accounting and research

11 Positive theory of accounting policy and disclosure   359

12 Capital market research   403

13 Behavioural research in accounting   445

14 Emerging issues in accounting and auditing   477

11

Positive theory of accounting policy and disclosure

LEARNING OBJECTIVES

After reading this chapter, you should have an appreciation of the following:

1 contracting theory — why the firm can be described as a 'nexus of contracts'

2 agency theory — how accounting is used in contractual specifications to reduce the agency costs of equity and debt

3 price protection and shareholder/manager agency problems — constraining opportunistic accounting reporting by managers

4 shareholder–debtholder agency problems — how managers' *ex post* accounting decisions can transfer wealth from lenders to equityholders

5 the difference between *ex post* opportunism and *ex ante* efficient contracting — contracting and the information perspective

6 signalling theory — how accounting can be used to signal information about the firm

7 political processes — how accounting can be used to reduce the political costs faced by the firm

8 conservatism, accounting standards and agency costs — accounting standards as an agency constraint

9 additional empirical tests of the theory

10 evaluating the theory — key criticisms of contracting theories of accounting choice

11 issues for auditors.

Earlier chapters distinguished between two main classifications of accounting theories: normative and positive. Normative theories are prescriptive in nature and are based on value judgements about what is an appropriate course of action (e.g. the IASB supports decision usefulness as the primary objective of accounting information). Capital market research became more dominant after the 1970s largely because it became clear that until researchers knew whether, and how, investors use financial statements, it was unreasonable to expect them to develop theories prescribing how accountants should prepare financial statements. However, capital market research has not provided all the insights accounting researchers, practitioners and regulators need. For example, it was difficult to predict how the market would react to accounting information when the reasons managers adopted particular accounting practices were not known. Also, capital market research did not specifically deal with other important stakeholder issues such as the impact of accounting regulation on lenders or other non-shareholder users of accounting reports. As such, whereas capital market research constituted the first wave of positive accounting theory, the second wave tackled the following issues:

- Why do managers prepare accounting reports if there is no regulation requiring them?
- Why do managers make systematic accounting decisions and lobby standard setters to try to influence which accounting practices are permitted under standards?
- What motivates managers' accounting decisions?
- If firms are required to change their accounting practices, what actions might managers take that will affect the reactions of capital market investors and other parties?

This chapter examines the second wave of positive theory. In doing so, it focuses on contracting theory, political cost theory, signalling, and information perspective explanations of accounting determinants and consequences. It examines both the determinants and the consequences of managers' accounting decisions. In particular, it focuses on accounting policy choice and the management of accruals.

BACKGROUND

Early demand for theory

Capital markets research during the 1970s provided a major step forward in explaining the effects of accounting on investment in share capital, in particular the effects of accounting on share prices and share sale/purchase volumes. However, it was inconclusive regarding the mechanistic and no-effects hypotheses and gave inconsistent support for predictions that investors used accounting information systematically in making decisions about whether to buy or sell shares. This caused researchers to appreciate the difficulties of predicting market reactions to accounting releases when they did not have a strong theory to explain why managers prepared accounting reports in the first place, nor why they chose to apply particular accounting principles.

In order to understand the significance of accounting choice, it is necessary to understand the fundamental economic principles and premises on which it is based. The literature investigating the capital market information content of profits accepted the efficient markets hypothesis (EMH) as a descriptive reality, or at least accepted that the world functioned 'as if' it described reality.[1] Like classical price theory, EMH relies on perfect market assumptions such as freely available information, zero transaction costs, no taxes and no monopolistic control (all participants are price takers). Under these assumptions, prices are immediately and costlessly adjusted to reflect accounting information. However, although these conditions might 'on average' be descriptive of the stock market,[2] there are other circumstances where these conditions do not approximate reality.[3] That is, there are aberrations.

The strict EMH assumptions of early positive accounting research meant that capital market researchers could not always explain why share prices did not respond immediately to accounting information in the manner predicted. Similarly, when share prices continued to reflect accounting information days after its release, the assumption of zero transactions costs and free information clearly did not hold. One question asked was whether accounting reports were primarily aimed at supporting decision making in capital markets or do they have some other purpose? After all, if accounting reports were not prepared with the major intention of informing capital markets of the value of the shares, why *should* the capital market react to the release of accounting reports? Thus, as they investigated market reactions to firms' accounting practices and earnings releases, researchers made several significant observations that prompted interest in developing a positive theory of accounting policy choice. These observations are described below:

- Prior to any regulation requiring them to do so, many firms provided accounting reports. Further, these reports were audited and both the preparation of accounts and their auditing consumed real resources. Therefore, rational managers would not allow firms to incur these costs if they did not perceive that there were net benefits from the provision of the accounting information. That observation led researchers to question what would be the benefits to firms if they voluntarily incurred the costs to prepare financial statements.
- Companies lobby in relation to proposed accounting standards. Again, lobbying is a costly activity[4] and rational managers would engage in it only if the benefits outweighed the costs. Researchers began asking what would be the benefits of lobbying.
- Firms made consistent patterns of accounting policy choice among competing alternatives and these accounting policy choices appeared to be related to characteristics (attributes) of the firms. Researchers were curious to explain the reasons for these associations.
- On the whole, firms tended to choose accounting methods that applied conservative measures of profit, assets and equity. Again, researchers were prompted to ask 'Why?'

The information hypothesis, that accounting is produced to enable investors in capital markets to make good investment decisions, could not satisfactorily explain these observations. Consequently, researchers developed a theory built on premises of costly contracting and monitoring. So that you can understand the literature of accounting policy choice (the 'economic consequences' literature), we explain the fundamental aspects of contracting and agency theories in the following sections of this chapter. These theories provide another rationale for the production of accounting reports. We also discuss the role played by accounting in the political and contracting processes. Positive theorists argue that political markets are less efficient than capital markets and therefore give rise to greater opportunities for wealth transfers via political lobbying for government intervention. Underlying the policy choice literature are the assumptions that people act in their own self-interest, that they are economically rational, and that accounting numbers play a central role in the distribution of wealth. Positive accounting theory ignores non-financial aspects of individuals' utility functions by generally assuming that all individuals attempt to maximise their financial wealth.

LO 1 → CONTRACTING THEORY

Contracting theory characterises the firm as a legal nexus (connection) of contractual relationships among <u>suppliers and consumers</u> of factors of production. The firm exists because it costs less for individuals to transact (or contract) through a central organisation than to do so individually. For example, if you want to buy an ice-cream, you have at least two options. One option is to contract separately with the dairy farmer for the milk and cream to make the ice-cream and any chocolate coating, a cane-grower to buy sugarcane, a crusher to extract the juice from the cane, a refiner to produce the sugar, a logger to provide the timber to produce the stick for the ice-cream, a metal worker to produce various items to create a refrigerator to set the ice-cream, an electrician to wire the refrigerator, and so on. By the time you have produced your ice-cream, it is likely to be winter 2020 and you will prefer a bowl of soup! Option 2 is to buy the ice-cream from a firm such as the local corner store or supermarket. This firm will already have direct or indirect contracts with all of those providers of resources used to produce the ice-cream. It is, as such, a nexus of contracts because it centralises, or links, the contracts between you as a consumer and the various suppliers.

In a more general sense, rather than all individual suppliers of the factors of production (land, labour and capital) individually contracting with consumers for their output, contracts are struck by the 'the firm' between classes of suppliers and consumers of factors. There are, for example, contracts:

- documenting the terms and conditions of employment of managers by shareholders
- documenting the terms and conditions under which lenders provide financial resources
- of employment for factory and other workers
- for the supply of goods
- for the sale and delivery of goods and services.

Thus, once we allow for the reality of contract transactions costs, including financial and non-financial costs of negotiating the terms of the sale of milk from a dairy farmer, Coase argues that firms will exist. The reason is that firms are the most efficient form of contract nexus in organising and coordinating economic activity and reducing contracting costs.[5] Although it is important to recognise that firms involve a multiplicity of contracts, positive accounting theory usually focuses on two types of contract: management contracts and debt contracts. Both of these contracts are agency contracts, and agency theory provides a rich source of explanation for existing accounting practice.

LO 2 ⊢ AGENCY THEORY

Firms are the most efficient form of contracting and were originally both owned and managed by individuals or families. However, over the past 100 years there has been an agency divergence between owners (shareholders and debt providers) and managers as firms developed into the large corporations we know today requiring professional management. Jensen and Meckling are generally credited with having developed agency theory in a 1976 publication.[6] However, there are antecedents in the work of Alchian and Demsetz,[7] among others. Jensen and Meckling describe an agency relationship as arising where there is a contract under which one party (the principal) engages another party (the agent) to perform some service on the principal's behalf. Under the contract, the principal delegates some decision-making authority to the agent.

In such a situation, both the principal and the agent are utility maximisers and there is no reason to believe that the agent will always act in the principal's best interests. The agency problem that arises is the problem of inducing an agent to behave as if he or she were maximising the principal's welfare. For example, where the agent is the firm manager, the manager has incentives to increase consumption of perquisites such as the use of a company car, expense account, or the size of bonus payments at the expense of the principal (in this instance, the shareholders). Alternatively, the manager (agent) may seek to avoid personal stress from overwork, and not be as conscientious as possible in endeavours to maximise the firm's value. Because the agent has decision-making authority, he or she can transfer wealth in this manner from the principal to the agent if the principal does not intervene.

This agency problem, in turn, gives rise to agency costs. At the most general level, agency costs are the dollar equivalent of the reduction in welfare experienced by the principal owing to the divergence of the principal's and the agent's interests. Jensen and Meckling divide agency costs into:

- monitoring costs
- bonding costs
- residual loss.[8]

Monitoring costs are the costs of monitoring the agent's behaviour. They are expenditures by the principal to measure, observe and control the agent's behaviour. Examples of monitoring costs are mandatory audit costs, costs to establish management compensation plans, budget restrictions and operating rules. These monitoring costs are incurred in the first instance by the principal. However, the principal protects against ultimately bearing the costs by adjusting the remuneration paid to the agent so that the agent bears the costs. For example, a manager (agent) with a good reputation would be expected to behave in the interests of shareholders (principals). As such, shareholders would probably monitor the manager's performance very little and remunerate the manager well. If the manager had a poor or uncertain reputation, shareholders would probably monitor that manager's performance much more. Also, shareholders would not be prepared to pay the manager as much as a manager who had a good reputation and acted in shareholders' interests. That is, shareholders (principals) pay managers (agents) less as the cost of monitoring increases. The way the principal protects against bearing agency costs is by paying according to the level of expected monitoring costs. This is known as price protection.

Similarly, under debt contracts, managers (this time acting on behalf of shareholders) are the agents for lenders (i.e. the principals). The greater the risk of lending, the more lenders will want to monitor the performance of the firm they invest in by providing debt. As compensation for the monitoring costs, the rate of interest the lenders demand will be higher, or the period over which they will be prepared to lend to the firm will be shorter. Thus, the rate of interest or the term of the loan are the ways that lenders 'price-protect'.

If there is efficient price protection, agents may ultimately bear the monitoring costs associated with contracts. Therefore, agents are likely to establish mechanisms to guarantee they will behave in the interests of the principal, or to guarantee they will compensate the principal if they act in a manner contrary to the principal's interests. The costs of establishing and complying with these mechanisms are known as *bonding costs* since they are the costs of bonding the agent's interests to those of the principal. Bonding costs are also borne by the agent. For example, managers (agents) may voluntarily provide shareholders (principals) with quarterly financial statements that the managers have a comparative advantage in preparing, or managers might contract not to disclose certain information to competitors. The costs incurred by managers in relation to these bonding activities include:

- the time and effort involved in producing more regular (quarterly) accounting reports
- the constraints on the manager's activities because the quarterly reports will reveal opportunistic behaviour
- the income forgone by being prohibited from selling firm secrets to an opposing firm.

Agents will be prepared to incur bonding costs only to the extent that these costs reduce the monitoring costs they bear. That is, they will stop incurring bonding costs when the marginal cost of bonding equals the marginal reduction in the monitoring costs they bear.

Despite monitoring and bonding, it is likely that the agent's interests still will not correspond exactly with those of the principal. Furthermore, the agent is likely to make some decisions that are not entirely in the principal's interests. For example, the manager might change the accounts to maximise his/her bonus or put in less work effort than shareholders would prefer. As such, the net value of the agent's output is less than if the agent's interests were completely aligned to the principal's. This deadweight loss is known as the *residual loss*. The residual loss, then, is the wealth effect of the fact that, even with monitoring and bonding expenditures, actions taken by an agent (or, indeed, an agent's inaction) will sometimes differ from the behaviour that would maximise the principal's interests or wealth.

Given that bonding and monitoring mechanisms will be observed in contracts defining agency relationships, two questions arise: (1) who has the incentive to incorporate such mechanisms into contracts? and (2) who bears the costs of these mechanisms? Agency theory, in answering these questions, borrows from the EMH. If managerial and shareholder information markets are strong-form efficient, then the market will have information regarding the incentives and opportunities for an agent to act in a manner contrary to the interests of a principal. It will therefore incorporate all this information in the agent's price of remuneration. That is, the principal will remunerate the agent according to the principal's expectations of how much the agent's behaviour is likely to be contrary to the principal's interests. In these circumstances the principal will be price-protected. Because price protection is a cost borne by the agent (agents receive less remuneration than they otherwise would), the agent has incentives to bond to the principal's interests and bear the costs of behaviour monitoring. This incentive is increased by the fact that, in addition to price protection, principals can 'settle up' with agents for dysfunctional behaviour. *Ex post* settling up occurs when, having observed an agent's performance, the principal revises the returns paid to the agent (e.g. managerial salary) to ensure that the level of the agent's remuneration and the level of the agent's effort are aligned. For example, shareholders may decide that managers are acting less (more) in shareholders' interests than was first expected. In such situations, the shareholders may decide to pay managers less (more) salary for the term of the managers' contracts. The *ex post* settling up at the end of one period is effectively price protection for the start of the next period.

Fama points out that the market for managerial labour may also discipline managers who act opportunistically.[9] The market incorporates into a manager's salary the expectation that the agent will act opportunistically, which is based on his or her propensity to do so in the past. As such, managers who are looking for new jobs will be paid according to the market's expectation of their behaviour in serving shareholders' interests. This expectation is based on the manager's past performance. Moreover, managers whose actions depress the value of their firms can be exposed to removal in the event of a takeover. However, as Amershi and Sunder point out, the takeover market for company control is an expensive form of disciplining managers because of the high premiums paid to take over a firm.[10]

Despite these various forms of governance, all of the agent's dysfunctional conduct will not be eliminated, since bonding mechanisms operate at a cost and the agent will bear these only up to the point where the marginal cost of doing so equals the marginal benefit. Thus, there is residual opportunism, the costs of which will be borne by the agent in a strong-form efficient market because the loss of reputation and potential loss of long-term returns to the agent act as a deterrent (the 'residual loss').

When we relax the assumption of perfectly efficient markets, agents perceive that they will not be fully penalised (via price protection and settling up) for behaviour that is contrary to the interests of the principals. They therefore have incentives to engage in opportunistic behaviour which, in turn, increases the residual loss. With incomplete price protection and settling up, the residual loss is borne partially by the principal as well as (or instead of) the agent.

The appeal of agency theory lies in the fact that it attributes a role for accounting — as part of the bonding and monitoring mechanisms — which is closely related to the traditional stewardship role of accounting. Our attention is now directed to specific agency relationships, particularly those which have been considered routinely by positive accounting theory. Reference is also made to the use of accounting numbers in the contracts between the contracting parties.

LO 3 ⊢ PRICE PROTECTION AND SHAREHOLDER/ MANAGER AGENCY PROBLEMS

The separation of ownership and control means that managers, as the agents of shareholders, can act in their own interests. But agents' interests may be contrary to the interests of the shareholders. This problem was recognised as long ago as 1776, when Adam Smith referred to it in *The Wealth of Nations*.[11] Partial ownership or non-ownership of a firm by management provides incentives for managers to behave in a manner contrary to the interests of shareholders because management does not bear the full cost of any dysfunctional behaviour. For example, imagine a scenario where there are no taxes, there is one owner of a firm, and that owner is also the manager. The owner–manager is likely to be indifferent as to whether he or she purchases non-pecuniary benefits directly, or whether the business purchases those benefits on his or her behalf. Either way, the financial impact is the same. Assume that the firm has a net present value of $1 000 000 and the owner–manager's other assets are worth $1 000 000. If the firm spends $100 000 on benefits for the owner, such as a higher bonus, the owner is no better or worse off because the firm is a direct extension of the owner. Either way, the owner–manager has assets worth $2 000 000.

Now assume that the owner–manager sells 30 per cent of the firm. As a 70 per cent owner, the manager is no longer indifferent as to whether benefits to him or her are purchased by the firm or by the manager. Again assume that the manager purchases benefits for himself or herself at a cost of $100 000, and immediately consumes the benefits. The manager's assets are now worth $1 600 000 — that is, a 70 per cent interest in the firm is worth $700 000 and the other assets of the manager are worth $900 000. But if the firm purchases the benefits for the owner, the manager's assets are worth $1 630 000 — that is, a 70 per cent interest in the firm is worth $630 000 (70% × 1 000 000 − 70% × 100 000) and the manager's other assets are worth $1 000 000. In this case, the manager would prefer that the firm purchases any benefits for him or her because a fraction of the cost of those benefits is paid for by the other owner(s).

The proportion of the cost that the manager bears decreases as the manager's ownership in the firm decreases. Hence, the smaller the ownership interest of the manager in the firm, the more likely the manager is to overconsume perquisites and other benefits on the job, or to shirk in other ways. Again the incentive exists for as long as the marginal benefit to the shareholder exceeds the marginal cost — that is the likelihood of job loss or the increase in monitoring costs that the manager bears when the other owners price-protect against dysfunctional behaviour.

Price protection in this case takes two forms. When the owner–manager sells a portion of his or her interest in the firm, investors pay for the shares what they think the shares are worth. The price incorporates a discount for the extent to which the manager is expected to consume more benefits on the job than is in investors' interests. As such, the price the owner–manager is paid for the shares reduces as the market's expectation of behaviour contrary to its interests increases, even if the new owners do not closely monitor the manager's performance. If the new owners do monitor the manager's performance closely, they will remunerate the manager on the basis of an assessment of the likelihood of behaviour contrary to their interests. Either way, if markets are efficient, the new shareholders receive a normal rate of return on average. The managers ultimately bear the cost of shareholders monitoring their performance and of their expected behaviour that reduces owners' wealth. Hence, they are the parties who have the incentives to contract to have their actions monitored, and to limit their actions that reduce firm value. If they provide sufficient credible up-front assurances that they will act in shareholders' interests, the market pays a higher price for its ownership interest, and there is likely to be less monitoring.

Reasons for differences in shareholders' and managers' incentives regarding firm policies represent a number of specific problems. These problems include the *risk-aversion* problem, the *dividend-retention* problem and the *horizon* problem.[12] The risk-aversion problem means that managers prefer less risk than do shareholders. Shareholders have the capacity to diversify their investment portfolios so that they are not risk-averse with respect to their investment in any particular firm. By investing in a variety of firms (e.g. blue chip, mining, industrial) or types of investments (e.g. shares, property, commodities), shareholders can minimise their exposure to investment risk from any one source. Diversifying their investments in this manner tends to hedge their exposure to risk of loss from their investments. Shareholders' risk aversion is further reduced by the fact that limited liability means that they have no obligation to cover future decreases in firm value except to the extent that their shares are not fully paid. Since their claim against the firm is essentially an option against the future value of the firm, their interests are best served if management invests in certain risky projects in order to maximise the value of the business.

However, managers generally prefer to invest in less risky, lower net present value (NPV) projects because they have significant undiversified human capital invested in the business they are managing. That is, the manager's most valuable asset is their own human capital — management expertise — and all of this is invested in the one firm. Losing the job or being paid less has a significant effect on the manager's wealth. Further, this risk cannot be fully hedged or diversified because the manager usually is employed in one management position only. Diversification through investment in other firms can only partially reduce the manager's risk since the manager's human capital is such a major asset that the risk associated with it far exceeds the risk associated with other investments. As such, managers are risk-averse with respect to their management of the firm just in case high-return but high-risk investments by the firm reduce the value of their human capital. Managers therefore rationally prefer to minimise their own risk rather than maximise the value of the firm.

An example of risk aversion arises if the management of an established coal-producing company has the opportunity of buying a highly speculative gold mine and operating it. The returns to shareholders could exceed 100 per cent per annum after tax for the foreseeable future. On the other hand, the mine could fail dismally, producing negative returns to the firm and causing losses, so that shareholders' funds were negative. Providing there is a sufficient probability of very high returns to shareholders, shareholders would want management to invest in the gold mine. After all, shareholders would reap the high returns and, because of limited liability, lose only an amount up to the value of the unpaid amounts owing on their shares if the operation were unsuccessful.

On the other hand, managers would be averse to the investment in the mine because if it failed, the value of their most valuable asset — human capital — would fall and they may lose their job. Although they may obtain other employment, it would not necessarily be at the same level of status and/or remuneration because of their reputation for managing a failed operation. Further, the time and effort spent seeking employment could be 'costly' to the manager.[13] Clearly, then, shareholders and managers have different incentive and risk preferences.

This in turn leads to several other agency contracting problems. The first is the dividend-retention problem which occurs when managers prefer to pay out less of the company's profits in dividends than shareholders prefer. This problem can arise because managers retain money in the business to pay for their own salaries and benefits and to increase the size of the 'empire' they control (empire building). Consider a situation where the firm's best investment opportunity will earn an 8% rate of return for shareholders, but shareholders could invest personally to earn returns of 15%. Under these circumstances, shareholders want to be paid dividends to invest them in the higher earning investment rather than leave the money in the firm to be invested at a lower return. However, managers may prefer to retain the funds in order to increase the size of the firm under its management and increase the scope of their power. If management does retain funds that otherwise could be paid as dividends, then shareholders lose 7% (15% − 8%).

The horizon problem stems from a difference in the time horizon interests of shareholders and managers with respect to the firm. Shareholders are theoretically interested in the cash flows of the firm for an infinite number of periods into the future, since the theoretical value of their shares is the discounted present value of the future cash flows attributable to the share. Even if shareholders own shares in order to speculate, the value of their shares is the present value of all future cash flows to whoever holds the shares for as long as the shares exist. As such, even the speculative shareholder has a long-horizon interest in the firm because the firm's future cash flows affect how much other investors will pay for the shares. On the other hand, managers are interested in the cash flows of the firm only for as long as they intend to stay with the firm. Obviously this is situation-specific and we would expect it to become more pronounced as the age of the manager increases or a manager anticipates moving to another firm in the near future. The incentive is to take actions to promote an appearance of firm profitability in the short term, at the expense of long-term profitability. Such actions would be taken to create an impression of good immediate management by reporting higher profits as an indicator of good management.

Contracting can be used to reduce the severity of these problems. One way to do that is to tie the manager's remuneration to the share price. After all under EMH, the share price reflects the owner's (principal's) interests and expectations about the riskiness of investments and all future cash flows attributable to the shareholder for the life of the firm. As such, it reflects the market's assessments of the extent of the wealth effect for shareholders of management's risk-aversion and dividend-retention preferences. It also provides a longer term incentive to maximise share prices than the short-term incentive of profit maximisation. However, this can introduce inequities. Since part of the share value is determined by general market or industry effects that the manager cannot control, it is unlikely that managers would accept remuneration based solely on share price movements. Nonetheless, providing some remuneration tied to share prices (payments based on share price movements or by paying in shares or options) can help to reduce the horizon and risk-aversion problems.

Profit is often regarded as being more directly related to managerial performance than share prices. As such, accounting profit is often used either instead of, or in conjunction with, share values in remunerating managers. For example, a manager's remuneration package may include a fixed salary plus a bonus where the manager is paid a percentage of profits in excess of some base profit combined with some bonus tied to the value of the firm's shares. In this way, accounting numbers are also used in determining the contractual payoffs to managers. Hence, as a consequence, managers have a strong interest in the way profits are calculated, and in the selection of accounting policies.

Specific contractual means of motivating managers to act in shareholders' interests include:

- providing a bonus plan where the upper limit of the bonus partially depends on the firm's dividend payout ratio (to reduce the dividend-retention problem)
- paying managers more on the basis of share price movements as the manager approaches retirement (to reduce the horizon problem)
- paying bonuses at a progressive rate as reported profits increase (to minimise the risk-aversion problem)
- remunerating managers less with share-based compensation as the manager's ownership in the firm increases (to reduce the risk-aversion problem).

At this point it is important to emphasise that accounting numbers are more frequently used in determining management compensation contracts. The major reason is the broad applicability of accounting numbers to a greater variety of contexts:

- simply because the vast majority of firms do not have a listed share price
- firm market value is non-observable by virtue of thin trading or untraded ownership interests (e.g. proprietary companies or unincorporated entities)
- the level of management being remunerated is lower than the chief executive officer, and the division/area/section under the manager's control reports its own earnings
- managers' efforts are more directly linked to earnings performance than to share price performance (e.g. the firm has a high beta, and share price fluctuations are at least as much a function of the market as of managerial performance).

Hence, earnings-based bonus plans are the more important part of executive compensation schemes and typically provide for managers to share in some portion of reported profits. Since compensation is tied to the level of reported profits, it has been hypothesised that, in the presence of these plans, managers will select accounting procedures that shift reported profits from future periods to present periods. Transfers of profits between periods affect the present value of the manager's bonus and increase its certainty. This has been called the 'bonus plan hypothesis'.[14] The bonus plan hypothesis is often phrased as: 'Firms with management compensation plans use profit-increasing accounting policies.'

That said the use of earnings as a basis for executives' compensation is now well-entrenched worldwide, with the use of shares and share options also well-entrenched in listed firms on liquid stock markets. Interestingly, it introduces some accounting issues that have the potential to affect reported earnings, and thus the components of management compensation that are tied to reported earnings. Theory in action 11.1 demonstrates the significance of regulation to management compensation and how firms are likely to take real economic decisions to counteract new rules that would change arrangements for contractual payments to top managers.

Objections to crackdown

by Steven Scott (with Marsha Jacobs)

The Rudd government's proposed crackdown on employee share schemes could drive up executive cash bonuses and lead to further tax volatility, human resources professionals have warned.

And caps on executive payouts proposed by Prime Minister Kevin Rudd would only force companies to beef up other parts of remuneration packages.

The warnings from the Australian Human Resources Institute are contained in a submission in the Productivity Commission's inquiry into executive remuneration.

The submission — based on a survey of members and focus group interviews of HR directors from 20 leading ASX companies — argued any regulation of executives' golden handshake payments would merely drive up senior salaries.

Mr Rudd has criticised executive termination payments and ordered the commission to inquire into possible regulation to limit excessive risk-taking.

Companies surveyed by the Institute said that, if there was a termination pay cap, they would be forced "to find some other way of spreading the present value of the forgone benefits into other remuneration elements, either pre or post termination".

The Institute also called on the government to scrap its proposal to tax employee share schemes up front, taxing instead at the point at which shares or rights could be sold, or risk a "policy push back to a 'cash and cash bonus' only structure [which] would lead to potentially higher GDP and tax volatility in the long term".

In a separate submission, the Australasian Compliance Institute called for tighter controls of executive bonus payments via the introduction of key performance indicators directly linked to industry-benchmarked frameworks.

Source: The Australian Financial Review, 29 May 2009, p. 13, www.afr.com.

Questions

1. What are the likely components of a chief executive officer's (CEO) management compensation package that might be affected by the proposed changes?
2. How is the introduction of a 'cap' (upper limit) on termination payments likely to affect CEOs' remuneration if firms make no adjustments to the compensation packages?
3. How could researchers evaluate the general impact of a 'termination pay cap' on the structure of management compensation packages?
4. What sort of key performance indicators are likely to be included in CEOs' compensation packages? What role might accounting numbers play in these indicators?

LO 4 — SHAREHOLDER–DEBTHOLDER AGENCY PROBLEMS

When we discuss the role of debt contracts in an agency context, we assume that the manager is either the sole owner of the firm, or has interests that are totally aligned with the interests of the owners. That is, the principal in this instance is the debtholder, or lender; the agent is the manager acting on behalf of the shareholders or other owners. Given that firm value comprises the value of debt plus the value of equity, one way to increase the value of equity is to increase the value of the firm; another is to transfer wealth away from debtholders. The former involves efficient contracting, and the latter involves opportunistic behaviour.

Smith and Warner recognised that the agency problem of debt can give rise to four main methods of transferring wealth from debtholders to shareholders:

- excessive dividend payments
- asset substitution
- underinvestment
- claim dilution.[15]

The excessive *dividend payment* problem arises when debt is lent to a firm on the assumption of a certain level of dividend payout. Debt is priced accordingly, but the firm then issues a higher level of dividends. Issuing higher dividends reduces the asset base securing the debt and reduces the value of the debt. At the extreme, there is an incentive for management to borrow and then pay out all of the borrowed funds as dividends (a liquidating dividend), leaving debtholders with nothing, and shareholders with the funds. Shareholders benefit under such a scheme because they have received the cash, but limited liability means that they are not personally liable for the debts of the firm in the event of bankruptcy.

Asset substitution is based on the premise that lenders are risk-averse. They lend to a firm with the expectation that it will not invest in assets or projects of a higher risk than that which is acceptable to them. They price debt accordingly, via the rate of interest charged or the term of the loan. After all, they do not share in the increased returns that high-risk projects can provide. However, they do share in the possible losses to the extent that the losses reduce the security available to meet their claims. On the other hand, shareholders generally have diversified portfolios and, with limited liability, are risk preferrers in relation to their investment in any particular firm. This is because they participate in the 'upside risk' where high-risk assets provide high returns, but limited liability means that they do not participate in the downside risk. Should investment in further high-risk assets cause financial distress, shareholders are liable only for the amounts unpaid on their shares. Thus, managers have incentives to accept debt finance and invest in higher risk assets to increase the potential returns to shareholders.

Underinvestment occurs when owners have incentives not to undertake positive NPV projects because to do so would increase the funds available to the debtholders, but not to the owners. For example, imagine a firm that is facing bankruptcy. It has shareholders' funds of negative $90 000. The firm could invest in a project that would provide a positive NPV of $50 000. However, the entire $50 000 accrues to the debtholders of the firm, not to the shareholders: it will reduce the net debt to $40 000. Only if the project earned a positive NPV in excess of $90 000 would wealth-maximising owners have an incentive to invest in the project. On the other hand, the lenders' interests are best served if the firm invests in all positive NPV projects because any positive NPV increases the funds available to repay at least some of the debt.

Claim dilution occurs when the firm issues debt of a higher priority than the debt already on issue. This increases the funds available to increase the value of the firm and the value of the ownership interest, but it decreases the relative security and value of the existing debt. That is, it dilutes the value of the existing debt because that debt has now become riskier in the presence of higher priority debt. Again, lenders can anticipate claim dilution and price-protect; however, an alternative is for the owners to include in the debt contract a covenant which stipulates that they will not borrow debt of a higher priority or earlier maturity. (Note that lower priority debt also increases agency costs if the proceeds are used to pay dividends.)

As in the case of management contracts, if capital markets have rational expectations, then shareholders bear the agency costs of attempts to transfer wealth away from debtholders. Lenders will price-protect via interest rates or the withholding of funds, and this provides managers acting on behalf of shareholders with the incentives to voluntarily contract to curtail their actions. These debt contracts often contain restrictions (or covenants) that are designed to protect lenders' financial interests. Covenants are often written in terms of accounting numbers.

Debt covenants are terms and conditions written into debt contracts that restrict the activities of management or require management to take certain actions. The covenants are designed to protect the interests of debtholders by requiring, for example, that the firm maintains a certain level of assets as security for the debt. Breach of a debt covenant constitutes technical default on the contract and provides lenders with rights to institute agreed-upon actions such as the seizure of collateral. Therefore managers have incentives to ensure that the terms of covenants are not violated. Managers of the borrowing corporation are required to certify that it has no knowledge of any breach of the debt contract, and the firm's auditor is normally also required to certify that it has no knowledge of any breach. The covenants contained in debt contracts generally fall into one or more of four categories:

- Covenants that restrict the production–investment opportunities of the firm. These covenants are designed to reduce asset substitution and underinvestment.
- Covenants restraining dividend payouts and typically tying dividend payments to a function of profit. These covenants deter excessive dividend payments.
- Covenants restraining the financing policy of the firm. These are aimed at the claim dilution problem and usually take the form of restricting the use of higher debt (or leverage).
- Bonding covenants that require the firm to provide certain information to lenders, such as financial statement reports and disclosures to regulatory authorities. These help bondholders determine whether covenants have been violated or are close to violation.

Note that accounting numbers and financial reports are used extensively in forming these contracts.

Whittred and Zimmer provided evidence about the terms of debt covenants found in trust deeds supporting listed public debt in Australia — debentures, unsecured notes and convertible notes.[16] They found that as the priority of debt in the event of winding-up increases, the covenants become more restrictive. For instance, debentures (the most senior debt) were the only form of debt to use interest coverage constraints.[17] Additionally, for all classes of covenants, such as a restriction on the firm's ratio of total liabilities to total assets, those applied to debentures were more restrictive. On the other hand, Whittred and Zimmer found few covenants that directly restricted dividend policy or that directly constrained production–investment decisions. It is not surprising that there are few covenants directly restricting dividend policy, since legislative requirements disallowing dividend payments from capital (Corporations Act, s. 254T) and debt covenant restrictions on leverage serve essentially the same purpose in Australia. These constraints ensure that dividend payments do not increase the firm's leverage to an unacceptable level. It is also not surprising that there are few covenants that interfere with production–investment opportunities, since many of the investment decisions are unobservable. After all, it is difficult to monitor compliance with a covenant requiring managers to invest in all positive NPV projects without actually performing the management function? Whittred and Zimmer's findings were endorsed by Stokes and Tay in a later study relating to convertible notes (convertible notes are debt instruments that can be converted into shares under specified circumstances).[18]

In a more recent study of Australian debt contracts, Cotter found that bank loan agreements often contain leverage covenants where leverage is measured as the ratio of total liabilities to total tangible assets.[19] Intangible assets are often excluded from measures of leverage because they have traditionally been deemed to be likely to lose their value quickly and have subjective values that cannot be easily verified. However, in the case of some firms, brand names or mastheads such as Coca-Cola, Nike, *The Australian Financial Review* or other well-known corporate brands, the intangible assets may be the most valuable assets of the firm, and have a tradeable and hence collateral value. Cotter also found that debt contracts often used interest coverage and current ratio clauses. She found that interest coverage constraints ranged from requiring firms' ratios of earnings before interest and tax (EBIT) divided by interest expense to be at least 1.5:4. Current ratios were required to be between 1 and 2.

Stokes and Whincop examined the restrictive covenants underlying preference share contracts as well as the hypothesis that debt incorporates more specific restrictions on management discretion than equity.[20] Preference shares represent an interesting form of finance since they are a hybrid, having elements of both debt and equity. Some preference shares have more debt-like characteristics than others. For instance, some permit the repayment of capital to shareholders, and others allow unpaid dividends to accrue to future years. Others are more like equity, as they allow conversion into ordinary shares. The authors found that preference shares that are more like debt rely on more restrictive terms than those that are more closely aligned to equity. Such restrictive terms included restraints on the issue of preference shares ranking in priority, as well as restrictions on the level of preference shares as a percentage of ordinary shares. A number of these constraints were expressed in the form of accounting numbers.[21] The Stokes and Whincop findings are consistent with the agency assumption that managers align their interests to those of owners in relation to debt contracts.

The following is a list describing the nature of common Australian debt covenants involving accounting numbers:

- Maintenance of working capital above a certain dollar value or ratio. The requirement to maintain liquidity combats excessive dividend payments and also, to some extent, underinvestment. It combats underinvestment by requiring managers to retain funds within the firm. Since those funds must be invested somehow, managers are likely to invest them in positive NPV current assets.
- Restrictions on merger activity, either requiring debt repayment in the event of merger or repayment if, after merger, the group net tangible assets exceed a given percentage of total long-term debt. Such constraints combat asset substitution by ensuring that an acceptable indicator of risk level (e.g. tangible assets to long-term debt) is not exceeded. Also, asset substitution is combated by deterring mergers with firms having higher risk profiles than the borrowing firm.
- Restrictions on investments in other firms such as limitations on the level or proportion of assets permitted to be invested in financial assets or requirements that net tangible assets exceed a certain percentage of long-term debt or long-term debt and owners' equity. These constraints combat asset substitution in the same manner as restrictions on merger. They attempt to limit investments in firms with higher risk profiles than the borrowing corporation.
- Restrictions on additional borrowings such as requirements for the maintenance of ratios of total tangible assets to total liabilities, requirements that the firm be able to maintain an interest coverage of three times if it is to issue new debt, or prohibitions on borrowing where the new debt has higher priority than existing debt. These covenants combat claim dilution.

The existence of debt suggests that managers, acting for shareholders, have incentives to transfer wealth away from debtholders to shareholders. Since they are restricted by debt covenants, managers also have incentives to adopt accounting procedures that enable them to 'get around' these covenants. Researchers have hypothesised that as the firm's leverage (debt ÷ assets) increases, the manager selects accounting procedures that shift reported profits from future periods to present periods (the 'debt to equity hypothesis' or 'debt hypothesis').[22] The premise is that, as leverage increases, the firm gets closer to covenant restraints, and thus managers' incentives to transfer wealth away from debtholders increase proportionately. On the basis of Australian evidence, an increase in profit will not evade many covenants, since only interest coverage constraints actually use profit in the algorithm. However, increases in profit are generally accompanied by increases in net assets and reductions in leverage. We can rephrase the hypothesis to say that, as the firm's leverage increases, the manager selects accounting procedures which increase assets or decrease liabilities, since many Australian debt agreements constrain liabilities as a proportion of assets. Reducing reported leverage in this manner decreases the likelihood of breaching the firm's leverage-based debt covenants. Interestingly, different economic circumstances and reputations mean that the roles of debt covenants and accounting numbers in debt contracts are not constant, either between firms, or even for the same firm over time.

**11.2
THEORY
IN ACTION**

Debt contracting

CVC deal with UBS helps Stella performance

CVC Asia Pacific has renegotiated the terms of tourism and hospitality operator Stella Group's debt, initially estimated at about $900 million, with lender UBS, in a deal that is said to have removed immediate concerns about the group's financial structure.

The deal is significant in that it removes concerns about one of CVC's portfolio assets and that it places UBS in a position to syndicate the Stella debt after years of it dragging down the local group's balance sheet.

It is thought the restructure involves a demerger of the Stella operations into three key business units: travel, hospitality and the UK-based Stella Travel Services.

The travel and hospitality divisions account for the bulk of the business and are said to be roughly the same size.

Stella operates the BreakFree, Peppers and Mantra Hotels holiday accommodation brands across Australia. The company also operates about 1200 travel agencies through Harvey World Travel, Travelscene and Gullivers Travels.

Early last month, CVC bought out the 35 per cent minority stake held by Octaviar, the former MFS, in Stella for $3.2 million. CVC acquired the 65 per cent stake in Stella for $409 million early last year.

This latest restructure is said to have involved CVC contributing further equity and an overhaul of the lending terms, including covenants and rates.

Source: Excerpts from *The Australian Financial Review*, 3 August 2009, p.18, www.afr.com.

Questions

1. Explain why the Stella Group's debt position would have 'dragged down' the CVC Asia Pacific organisation's balance sheet?
2. From a lender's perspective, what are the costs associated with high leverage? How can these costs be mitigated?
3. From a shareholder's perspective, what are the costs of high leverage? How can these costs be mitigated?
4. What are some incentives that might explain why CVC chose to restructure the Stella Group by contributing further equity (by buying Octaviar's 35 per cent stake).
5. What are the potential 'covenants' and 'lending terms' that are likely to have been overhauled in the Stella Group's financial restructure?

LO 5 → *EX POST* OPPORTUNISM VERSUS *EX ANTE* EFFICIENT CONTRACTING

Agency contracts provide incentives for agents to act in a manner that is contrary to the interests of the principals. However, the fact that there is price protection means that it is in the interests of the agents to contract to reduce agency costs. How strong these incentives are is unclear. One approach is to argue that agents are opportunistic and seek to transfer wealth from principals because the agents consider that price protection is incomplete and that any *ex post* settling up for dysfunctional behaviour is also incomplete. This line of argument is termed the 'opportunistic'[23] perspective. It is also termed an *ex post*[24] approach because it takes the contracts of the firm as given and argues that, *ex post* (i.e. after the contracts are in place), agents have incentives to transfer wealth from the principals because the contractual terms and renegotiations of existing contracts are unlikely to completely 'settle up' or eliminate the benefits they can derive (i.e. agency contracts are incomplete). The early research in agency theory examined *ex post* opportunistic behaviour. The bonus plan hypothesis and the debt to equity hypothesis are both examples of predictions based on theory developed from the opportunistic perspective.

Applying the opportunistic perspective of contracting theory to debt contracts implies that managers will act in a manner that attempts to transfer wealth from lenders to shareholders. So, for example, if managers perceive that the firm is financially distressed, they will take actions to ensure that the firm does not breach debt covenants and that lenders are unaware of the extremity of the problem for as long as possible. Such action would enable the firm to continue operating and to pay dividends to shareholders, while simultaneously reducing the amount likely to be available to settle debts when the firm ultimately fails. An example of the actions managers could take is to use accounting techniques that are profit-increasing in the current period(s) even though the underlying economic attributes are unaffected (e.g. by accelerating the recognition of income and/or delaying the recognition of expenses).

An alternative to the opportunistic approach is the efficient contracting approach. If contracts are efficient, they align the interests of agents and principals so that actions that benefit the agent also benefit the principal, and increase the value of the firm. Although recognising that agents have incentives to transfer wealth from principals, the 'efficient contracting', or *ex ante*, approach to agency theory argues that agents recognise that if they attempt to transfer wealth from principals, they will be penalised for that activity in the future. That is, there will be settling up that eventually removes the benefits of the opportunistic behaviour. This line of argument recognises that reputation effects will reduce the remuneration paid to agents in the future if they undertake dysfunctional behaviour. Therefore, agents will negotiate contracts that align their interests with those of the principals in the first instance. Even if the contracts do not completely constrain their activity, agents will behave as if the contracts already incorporated the constraints. This perspective is termed 'efficient' because agency costs are minimised in the long term. That is, the value of the firm, the value of the principals' claims, and the value of the agents' remuneration are all greater and more equitably allocated than under the opportunistic perspective. The approach is also termed *ex ante* because agents behave as if the contracts had been negotiated up front to limit their behaviour.

Under the efficient contracting approach, managers are likely to provide information that reflects as accurately as possible the firm's underlying economic circumstances. This reduces monitoring costs and enhances the manager's reputation, thereby increasing the value of the firm and the value of the manager's human capital. If the efficient contracting perspective were applied to a situation where a firm's debt covenants were likely to be breached because of a temporary situation that caused leverage to exceed the stipulated maximum, managers might switch to straight-line depreciation to prevent the technical default. Although this is also the action that management would take under the opportunistic approach, in this case it is efficient because it prevents a default that imposes unnecessary costs on both lenders and the firm. In the event of a technical default, both lenders and managers, acting on behalf of shareholders, would be required to devote resources to deciding whether to renegotiate the terms of the debt agreement, forgive the debt, refinance, or ignore the breach. Since lenders and shareholders alike would prefer to avoid these costs, the action is efficient in the context of a firm whose likely debt covenant violation is only temporary. It is, of course, opportunistic if the action is taken to 'cover up' a continuing problem.

Another example of efficient contracting applies when the firm uses accounting methods (such as diminishing-balance depreciation) because the pattern of expense recognition matches the use of the asset's service potential. The opportunistic approach might dictate the use of straight-line depreciation because it is profit increasing and therefore likely to increase management's bonus payments or avoid debt covenant violation. The essential difference is the long-term signalling quality of the accounting contract.

Although *ex ante* efficient contracting and *ex post* opportunism are theoretically distinguishable, they can be difficult to distinguish in practice.

LO 6 ┤ SIGNALLING THEORY

In addition to the contracting perspectives, Holthausen describes a further perspective on accounting policy choice — the information perspective.[25] Under this perspective, managers voluntarily provide information to investors to help their decision making. Managers undertake this role because they have a comparative advantage in the production and dissemination of information. Similar to the efficient contracting perspective, managers provide information for decision making because they have the comparative advantage and it reduces monitoring costs and the costs of *ex post* settling up. Holthausen then goes on to distinguish the contracting and information perspectives according to the timing of cash flows and accounting information. Under the information perspective, accounting information precedes (predicts) the cash flows affecting the value of the firm. The accounting information is used to indicate how the value of the firm and claims against it *will* change. Under the efficient contracting perspective, accounting reflects the changed cash flows that affect the firm: the accounting reports are used to monitor (confirm) economic events and transactions that *have occurred*.

The information hypothesis underlies most of the early capital market research. In capital market studies, managers were assumed to provide information for decision making by investors. As such, any change in accounting method should mean that the information has changed and investment decisions should change. In turn, changes in investment decisions should be reflected in share prices or in trade volumes and volatilities.

The information hypothesis is aligned with signalling theory, whereby managers use the accounts to signal expectations and intentions regarding the future. According to signalling theory, if managers expected a high level of future growth by the firm, they would try to signal that to investors via the accounts. Managers of other companies that are performing well would have the same incentive, and managers of firms with neutral news would have incentives to report positive news so that they were not suspected of having poor results. Managers of firms with bad news would have incentives not to report. However, they would also have the incentive to report their bad news, to maintain credibility in effective markets where their shares are traded. Assuming these incentives to signal information to capital markets, signalling theory predicts that firms will disclose more information than is demanded.

The logical consequence of signalling theory is that there are incentives for all managers to signal expectations of future profits because, if investors believe the signals, share prices will increase and the shareholders (and managers acting in their interests) will benefit. However, one problem therefore arises: how does a firm ensure that its signal is seen as credible by investors, given that other firms will also try to signal 'good news'? For a signal via the accounts to be credible to users, that signal must not be easily and costlessly replicated by another firm. Costs can include the long-term loss of credibility if actual performance does not match the level that has been signalled via the way in which profitability has been represented in the accounts.

One way is to provide additional credibility to earnings signals by providing dividend signals. These are costly as they involve cash payouts to shareholders. Furthermore, firms generally smooth their dividends and managers are very reluctant to reduce dividends. Thus, if dividends increase, managers are reasonably sure that they will not subsequently decrease. So the increase can create an expectation of future increased profits sufficient to support the higher level of dividends into the future.

Research into signalling incentives includes studies that investigate why firms voluntarily disclose bad news, reduce and increase dividends, smooth earnings and revalue and impair assets, and recognise internally generated assets. Theory in action 11.3 provides an example of how one firm has signalled its expectations regarding future profitability.

11.3 THEORY IN ACTION

What do profits signal?

Navitas earnings soar in slump

by Sara Rich

Education provider Navitas has achieved a 32 per cent rise in full-year profit and says the global financial crisis may be working in its favour, with another year of double-digit earnings growth expected.

Net profit for the year ended June 30 climbed to $49.2 million compared with $37.4 m a year ago, while revenue rose 36 per cent to $470.7 m.

The Perth-based company provides university pathway programs for domestic and international students, as well as language training, work-force education and student recruitment services.

Navitas chief executive Rod Jones said the company, which had low debt levels and good cashflow, had not been affected by the downturn and that student numbers were at record highs. Last financial year, the number of students in Navitas's university programs surged 26 per cent to about 20 000. In total, there are about 45 000 domestic and overseas students using the education provider's services.

"When employment opportunities reduce, many students turn back to education," Mr Jones said.

He said this had helped drive a 22 per cent increase in earnings before interest, tax, depreciation and amortisation to $77.1 m for the company.

Earnings per share climbed 32 per cent to 14.3c, while operating cashflow was up 33 per cent at $104.3 m.

Navitas declared a final dividend of 8.8c, up from 6.2c last year, taking the full-year payment to 14.3c, compared with the previous year's 10.9c.

Last financial year was the fifth year in a row that Navitas achieved more than 10 per cent growth in earnings, revenue and operating cashflow.

The company's share price climbed 5.45 per cent, or 15c yesterday to $2.90.

Source: Excerpts from *The Australian*, 5 August 2009, p. 24, www.theaustralian.com.au.

Questions

1. Navitas's announcement of soaring profit is a strong signal of the firm's earnings prospects. Other comments in the article reinforce that signal. What could Navitas do in relation to its profits to strengthen the signal even further? Explain your answer.
2. What factors might increase or decrease the credibility of the signal provided by Navitas's announcement and press attention?
3. What do you expect will be the impact of the 'soaring' profits on management compensation contracts of Navitas?

LO 7 → POLITICAL PROCESSES

Positive accounting theory also models the political process involving the relationship between the firm and other parties interested in the firm, such as government, trade unions and community groups. As in the context of debt and management compensation contracting, accounting is important in the political process as one of the sources of information about firms.

The major difference between the political market and the capital market is that there is generally less demand, and therefore less incentive, for the production of information in political markets. Economic analysis suggests that this results from the lower marginal benefit to individuals in the political process, because it is harder for individuals or groups to capture benefits from that information.[26] There are high information costs to individuals, heterogeneity (diversity) of interests, and organisational costs.

High information costs arise because in the political environment, the probability that one individual's actions will affect that person's wealth is small. Each individual is only one of many 'voters' in the political arena, there are many political decisions being made at any time, and many of them are likely to affect that individual's wealth. To be informed on all the issues is unlikely to be cost-beneficial given the low probability that the individual will affect the political outcome. Political costs can be diffused among individuals. Take for example, the political decision to increase the price of milk by 10 cents per litre. The costs are diffused across consumers but the total amount received by the milk corporation is substantial. The lobbying cost/benefit for individuals is high.

If consumers form interest groups and group lobby then this increases the likelihood of a particular political outcome. However, heterogeneity of interests within the group means that group actions will not necessarily be in a particular individual's interests. Further, the formation of interest groups is costly. Not only must group members incur the search costs of identifying each other to form the group, but the group incurs additional costs to lobby for its cause, inform its members, and so on. These transaction costs mean that individuals either will choose to stay rationally uninformed or if the individual gains are high enough they will form interest groups to capture economies of scale in the information-generation process, despite the organisational costs of doing so.

The amount of information generated for political and social purposes will therefore depend on the diffusive effects of government policy and the transaction costs of effective lobbying.[27] Hence, because of the greater information costs, diffused rewards, and high monitoring costs, there is greater scope for residual opportunism to occur. Positive accounting theorists often cite the 1931 and 1933 Securities Acts in the United States which followed the 1929 stock market crash as an example of political cost theory in practice.[28] The US government reacted to the public sentiment to avoid future crashes by passing the Securities Acts which increased government control over public companies. Empirical evidence suggests these Acts have done little to prevent future crashes. Basically, it is too costly for the public to become fully informed about the reasons for stock market crashes and to lobby in an informed manner for the appropriate corrective action. Further, the individual gains the public can expect to capture from doing so are low. Therefore, they stay rationally uninformed.

Accounting plays a role in political cost allocation because accounting numbers are often seen as evidence of a 'crisis' that politicians and other parties 'solve', thereby promoting their own interests. For example, if a particular firm or industry reports unusually high profits, employees may see these profits as resulting from the exploitation of their labour and lobby for higher salaries. Alternatively, firms have incentives to reduce reported profits if the profits are likely to be considered indicative of a mature industry and there is potential for politicians to remove subsidies or tariffs that protect the industry. In both of these examples, the employees and politicians have vested interests in selectively using accounting numbers to increase their remuneration (it is unlikely that employees would offer to accept lower wages in the event that their company or industry is incurring losses) or increase their profile and record of 'public interest' intervention by transferring funds from a 'mature' industry to another industry. Because of the transaction costs already mentioned, other 'players' in the political arena are unlikely to attempt to unravel the firms' accounting numbers (e.g. to argue that the profits reported to support political arguments are due to transitory gains and are unsustainable).

Since the political process is a competition for wealth transfers, politically sensitive firms are likely to understate profits. It is more difficult to criticise a firm with a lower profit for having an unfair level of government support. Hence, reducing reported earnings can sometimes reduce censure by politicians, public demands for price or rate decreases, and union pressure for wage rises. Accounting researchers use size as a 'proxy' for political sensitivity. Other things being equal, larger firms are expected to be more politically sensitive. The size hypothesis predicts that the larger the firm, the more likely the manager is to choose accounting procedures that reduce reported profits by deferring them from current to future periods.[29] We might also expect that managers will prefer accounting methods that reduce the variance of reported profits. Volatile profits may also attract political attention, because participants in the political process would not take into account the higher variance when profits are high.[30]

In Australia, the banking sector has often been subject to critical scrutiny by both the public and politicians for earning high profits and not passing them on to customers via reduced interest rates. Other industries where firms are often subject to political costs are the airline industry and telecommunications industry. Theory in action 11.4 presents an example of political processes that may have an effect on pharmaceutical companies' accounting reports.

11.4 THEORY IN ACTION

The politics of promoting products

Drugs code set to get tougher

by Emma Connors

The pharmaceutical industry faces a nervous wait as the competition regulator deliberates over proposed changes to the rules that govern the promotion of prescription drugs.

The last review of the industry code of conduct resulted in major changes when the Australian Competition and Consumer Commission ruled innovative drug companies would have to publicly disclose the details of hospitality given to health professionals at educational events.

Companies found to have broken the rules at these events or in other promotions can be fined up to $200 000. Those fines are set to increase when the latest edition of the code takes effect next year.

The draft code increases the maximum penalty for a breach of the code from $200 000 to $250 000 — a long way short of the maximum $1.1 million fine called for by the consumer organisation Choice.

Choice argues the fines are not large enough to deter companies from irresponsible promotion because of the substantial revenue increases that can be gained if such promotion delivers the company even a small increase in market share.

Medicines Australia, however, believes the other sanctions — including corrective letters to doctors and corrective advertising — that are imposed on companies that break the rules are often a better deterrent than fines.

Source: Excerpts from *The Australian Financial Review*, 4 August 2009, p. 5, www.afr.com.

Questions

1. What is the potential impact of the increased fines on the content of the accounting reports of firms in the pharmaceutical industry, particularly in relation to accounting information?
2. How does the article demonstrate political processes? In your answer, explain what, if anything, firms in the pharmaceutical industry can do to manage political costs.
3. What do you expect will be the impact of the increased fines on the (1) earnings and (2) management compensation contracts, of firms in the pharmaceuticals industry?

LO 8 — CONSERVATISM, ACCOUNTING STANDARDS AND AGENCY COSTS

In the above discussion on agency theory we implicitly assume that agency contracts are made simply between principals and agents within the firm. We are essentially talking about internal corporate governance with efficient contracting. That is, in a well functioning capital market with shareholder and corporate democracy there is an appropriate level of contracting that minimises agency costs. This assumes dominance (or control) by the principals (shareholders and debtholders) with little residual loss.

Another approach tilts towards an agent control model with restrictive power for debtholders and shareholders. This arises because managers have limited tenure and limited liability and this provides them with a bias to introduce noise into value estimates. In the extreme, if managers as agents have dictatorship power and seek to act in their own interests, then there may also be contagion effects that may affect the economy as a whole (e.g. by manipulating accounts so as to make excessive compensation payments such as the Enron case or the recent financial crisis).

Returning to the 1931 and 1933 Securities Acts in the United States mentioned earlier, one of the outcomes was to influence the development of conservative accounting statements. Traditional (prudent) conservatism in accounting means accelerating expenses and delaying revenue recognition: '… anticipate no profit but anticipate all losses.'[31] Conservatism arises because there is an asymmetric verification requirement that imposes a higher degree of verification for revenues when compared to expenses and this generally serves to reduce reported earnings.[32] Further, the valuation system was based on historical costs, and revaluations (especially taken to income) were not allowed in the United States. Moreover, the use of conservative historical costs effectively means that any increased asset values will leak into earnings as they are realised through transactions, rather than through the immediate jump in value. This was a reaction against some aggressive accounting methods used in the 1920s.

Recently, the International Accounting Board (IASB) argued that the conservative bias in accounting does not reveal the 'real' financial picture of the firm and reduces information available to investors. They propose that timely recognition of gains, as well as losses, are equally important. In response, conditional conservatism theorists argue that the demand for timely gain recognition is lower.[33] This means the market places a higher value on more timely loss recognition. A reason for this is the role that external reporting practices play in providing a corporate governance externality by: (a) *ex ante* — discouraging trophy investments, and (b) *ex post* — discontinuing negative cash flow investments. Trophy investments are when management invest in projects that extend management control or add to prestige. They are not necessarily positive net present value projects. If management know they are required by accounting standards to impair these investments in the near future then they will be careful in their investment behaviour.

On the other hand, information about fair value gains is not as highly demanded because negative price shocks are the driver for contract renegotiation, litigation is always against the non-recognition of losses, by banks and providers of debt capital, and by restricting gain recognition it places a constraint on the ability of management to pay out compensation to themselves or to shareholders. Basu argues the demand for conditional conservatism has increased over the years as a result of higher litigation and the demand for compensation based contracts. Auditors provide a demand for accounting numbers that are based on conservative financial numbers that can be independently verified more easily. In this context, regulators who advocate the inclusion of capitalised unverified future cash flows should be aware of the impact on managerial behaviour. In short, the principle of conservatism constrains managerial opportunistic behaviour with asymmetric requirement for recognising losses.

Finally, accounting principles that reduce the reported income reduce the manager's ability to report opportunistic accounting figures.[34] Therefore, the probability of managers and auditors being sanctioned increases (decreases) the less (more) the reported income accelerates and/or increases.

11.1 INTERNATIONAL VIEW

Do agency costs differ between countries?

In general, firm managers tend to choose income-increasing accounting methods to increase their own compensation, to avoid debt-covenant violation and to influence predictions of future cash flows. However, in bank-oriented countries this behaviour tends to be severely constrained. Banks have direct access to relevant information; they may control financial reporting policies and suggest the adoption of conservative income-decreasing accounting methods in order to protect their financial position.

The differences between financial systems may also have implications for the accounting information demanded. For example, in markets that rely on equity capital the main purpose of the accounting system is to reduce agency costs and provide strong investor protection. Thereby, the demand for financial information in these countries is mainly influenced by shareholders' needs. Conversely, credit protection is traditionally considered the main purpose of the accounting system in bank oriented countries. Given the interests and needs of debt holders, accounting tends to lead to a high degree of undervaluation of assets and/ or overvaluation of liabilities through managers' adoption of income decreasing accounting policies. In Europe, tax and financial systems tend to influence managers in the same direction because of a high degree of correlation between these systems. In a broad assessment, one may say that non-tax-aligned countries tend to be capital market oriented and tax-aligned tend to be bank oriented.[35]

Further, in countries with a strong enforcement system, there is higher litigation risk and a greater probability of managers and auditors being sanctioned. Therefore, in order to reduce this risk, managers in these countries would be more willing to adopt income decreasing accounting methods than those operating within a weak enforcement system where there is little risk of litigation. In Japan, where firms are more highly levered and rely to a greater extent on bank debt, Stulz shows that capital structure covenant contracts are more effective at monitoring managerial accounting discretion. In Asia, Ball et al. report that strong legal enforcement is associated with income-decreasing accounting methods. They further argue the existence of quality legal enforcement systems is a crucial factor for the success of accounting harmonisation

In Europe, de las Heras reports that accounting policy choice after the introduction of IFRS/IAS in 2005 is strongly influenced by differences in institutional factors such as the legal, tax, financial (debt v equity) and enforcement systems across Europe. That is, application of accounting standards is not homogeneous. The results also demonstrate that these different institutional factors better explain the differences in accounting policy choices under IFRS/IAS than individual European firm characteristics. With regard to firm characteristics, only the differences in the investment opportunity set and the level of ownership dispersion between companies have any impact on accounting policy choice. The greater the investment opportunity set available or the availability of growth options and the higher the ownership dispersion, the more willing managers will be to adopt income-increasing accounting methods. However, in countries with a strong enforcement system, the tendency to adopt income-decreasing accounting choices in order to increase the reported income is constrained.

References

Ball, R, Robin, A, & Wu, JS 2009 'Incentives versus standards: properties of accounting income in four East Asian countries,' *Journal of Accounting and Economics*, vol. 36, no. 1–3, pp. 235–270.

de las Heras, E 2009, 'Institutional determinants of accounting policy choices under IFRS', Unpublished PhD, Thesis (ch. 4), Universidad Autónoma de Madrid, Spain.

Stulz, R 1996, 'Does the cost of capital differ across countries? An agency perspective', *European Financial Management*, vol. 2, no. 1, pp. 11–22.

LO 9 — ADDITIONAL EMPIRICAL TESTS OF THE THEORY

As we have already mentioned, one of the advantages of models developed using positive theory is that the models can be tested empirically, thereby helping to corroborate or reject the 'real world understanding' developed by the theory. We start by discussing the tests of opportunistic behaviour and political cost motivations, that is wealth-transfer theories, then we discuss the tests of efficient contracting theories.

Testing the opportunistic and political cost hypotheses

Having established models for contracting in firms and in the political process, general hypotheses were developed to explain accounting choices which involved wealth transfers away from the principal.

One of the first studies was carried out by Watts and Zimmerman, who examined the positions that company managers took in their submissions to the US FASB's 1974 Discussion Memorandum on GPLA (general price level adjustment accounting).[36] The effect of GPLA is to restate firms' accounts according to a general inflation index, thereby increasing the value of assets but (in general) decreasing reported profit because of higher depreciation charges. GPLA could affect management compensation and debt contracts; however, since disclosures would be supplementary, there would be little direct effect under US proposals for new reporting requirements. Hence, the political process was deemed to provide the major incentives for the adoption of a particular lobbying position. Watts and Zimmerman argued that, because of political factors, the managers of large firms have greater incentives to reduce reported profit. Effects that were expected to vary with size were potential tax relief, rate regulation (for regulated firms) and bookkeeping costs.

Results were consistent with the proposition that the predicted lobbying position taken with regard to GPLA was driven mainly by very large firms. This suggested that political costs affect only the largest of firms. However, the results may also be influenced by the sample's inclusion of some very large oil firms which, at that time, were politically sensitive. Ball and Foster have since criticised the use of firm size as a measure for political costs and suggested more direct measures such as industry membership.[37]

Research has found strong support for the debt hypothesis. Numerous studies have found that managers make individual accounting policy choices that increase reported profits as they come closer to breaching their debt covenants, and also that they manipulate accounting profits in general in the years preceding and following violation of debt covenants. As discussed elsewhere in this chapter, it is possible to manipulate accounting profits using not only accounting policy choices but also discretion regarding matters such as estimates of the useful lives of assets (to influence depreciation amounts), estimates of doubtful debts, and estimates used in other provisions and write-offs. Sweeney found that managers of firms approaching the restrictions of their debt covenants are more likely to adopt key profit-increasing accounting strategies than firms that are not approaching technical default of those covenants. The strategies she investigated included the calculation of pension liabilities and determining which inventory cost flow assumption to adopt. She also found that firms approaching their debt covenant constraints were typically the first to adopt accounting standards that allowed companies to use profit-increasing methods or were slow to adopt an accounting standard that required companies to use profit-decreasing methods.[38]

Similarly, DeFond and Jiambalvo investigated the reporting behaviour of managers of firms that defaulted on their accounting-based debt covenants. Their results support the *ex post* opportunistic perspective of accounting policy choice. Similar to Sweeney they found managers of firms that breached debt covenants manipulated accounting profits in the years immediately preceding, and in the year following, the violation.[39]

Other researchers have conducted empirical tests of the size, bonus plan and debt to equity hypotheses on the basis of single accounting techniques. However, the profit figure, the focus of all three hypotheses, is the result of applying *many* accounting procedures to various transactions. For example, although the straight-line depreciation method might increase current profit, another procedure (say, last in, first out) might offset that increase. A stronger test, therefore, is to study the results of a portfolio of accounting procedures rather than focus on individual procedures. The first study to attempt this was carried out by Zmijewski and Hagerman.[40] The results of the study generally support their hypotheses that managers use multiple techniques.

One of the most popular topics in early positive accounting research was the choice of procedures for accounting for preproduction costs in the oil and gas industry. The choices available are full costing (FC) and successful efforts (SE). Relative to SE, FC has the effect of shifting profits to the current period and produces lower variance in profits. This suggests that FC would be favoured under the bonus plan and debt to equity hypotheses and that SE would be preferred under the size hypothesis because it shifts profits to future periods, but increases variance. Lilien and Pastena studied the extent to which firms shifted profits by using SE and FC.[41] All variables had the hypothesised sign and, apart from leverage, were statistically significant.

Further early accounting policy choice studies by Dhaliwal (accounting for pre-production costs),[42] Daley and Vigeland (accounting for research and development expenditures),[43] Dhaliwal, Salamon and Smith (depreciation),[44] and Bowen, Noreen and Lacey (accounting for interest)[45] strongly supported the debt to equity and size hypotheses, and provided mixed support for the bonus plan hypothesis. However, Watts and Zimmerman[46] suggested three further refinements:

- Details of the relevant contracts could be used.
- The size hypothesis could be refined since firm size could measure a variety of factors.
- Hypotheses could be derived from the other contracts already in place within a firm.

Tests using contract details

Healy's[47] paper represented a more powerful test of the bonus plan hypothesis than previous studies because it adopted a more comprehensive characterisation of bonus plans because they sometimes offer incentives to managers to select profit-decreasing accounting policies. Healy described the nature of accounting bonus schemes as involving the transfer to a bonus pool of an amount of money according to the following formulas:

$$P_t \{\max [(E_t - L_t),\, 0]\}$$

or

$$P_t (\min \{U_t,\, \max [(E_t - L_t),\, 0]\})$$

where

P_t = a maximum percentage
E_t = a variant on the profit figure
L_t = a stated lower limit expressed as a percentage of investment
U_t = an upper limit also expressed as a percentage of investment, sometimes tied to a variable of interest such as cash dividend payments.

In other words, the company transfers amounts which are equal to the maximum of profits less a lower limit, or zero. Where there is an upper limit, the amount transferred will be bound by this limit. Below a threshold level of profit, management earns no bonus. Between the threshold (lower limit) and a ceiling level of profit, management earns a bonus that increases as firm profits increase. Above the ceiling (upper limit), management earns a constant maximum level of bonus that does not increase as profits increase above the limit. This is represented diagrammatically in figure 11.1.

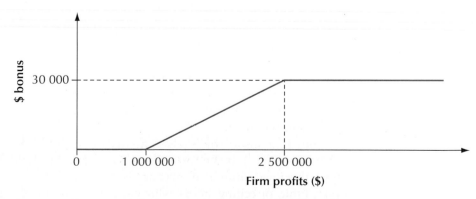

FIGURE 11.1 Allocation of funds to the bonus pool, based on accounting profits

If, in Healy's formula, the lower limit was $1 000 000, the upper limit was $2 500 000 and P_t was 2%, the manager would earn no bonus until the firm earned $1 000 000 in profits. Then the manager would earn 2% of the firm's profit less $1 000 000 to a maximum of $30 000 (2% × [$2 500 000 − $1 000 000]). If the firm earned $2 000 000 in profits, the manager would receive $20 000 as a bonus (2% × [$2 000 000 − $1 000 000]). If the firm earned profits of $5 000 000, the bonus would be the maximum: 2% × ($2 500 000 − $1 000 000), or $30 000.

Lower limits are set to lessen risk aversion by motivating managers to obtain profits that involve some risk taking. Assuming that a given level of profit is to be expected with relatively risk-free investments, the lower limit provides incentives for managers to take risks because the managers earn a bonus only for firm profits above a certain level, and the higher profits can be earned only if risky strategies 'pay off'. Upper limits are likely to reflect shareholders' expectations of a sustainable level of profits. For example, profits can be earned through 'real' or 'cosmetic' means: real profits reflect genuine economic activity, whereas cosmetic profits reflect the use of accounting or other techniques to 'window-dress', giving a more profitable appearance than is actually the case. Beyond a certain level of profit, current-period profits are unlikely to increase through 'real' economic activity because, according to the law of diminishing marginal returns, the firm runs out of positive net present value projects. To prevent managers from increasing profits and their bonuses by artificially inflating profits (e.g. by deferring research and development or repairs and maintenance expenditures, or by changing accounting methods from diminishing-balance depreciation to straight-line depreciation), the bonus plan formula is struck so that the bonus cuts out at a level of profit that is regarded as high but sustainable. The contractual specifications and their use of accounting numbers are therefore designed to reduce agency costs. The lower limit combats the problem of risk aversion; the upper limit combats the horizon problem.

Given these parameters, Healy discussed managers' incentives with respect to discretionary accruals. Discretionary accruals are the adjustments made by managers to cash flows when they calculate reported earnings. The manager selects these accruals from generally accepted accounting principles (which include the method of depreciating long-lived assets) and from activities such as the acceleration or delay of the delivery of inventory at the end of a financial year.

Healy formulated a decision rule, based on the defined parameters of the plan. When profit before discretionary accruals is significantly below the lower limit, the manager would have an incentive to 'take a bath' — that is, to make 'negative' discretionary accruals in order to write off as much profit as possible in the expectation that the next period's reported earnings would be above the lower limit. The next period's reported earnings could then be bolstered with discretionary accruals not used in the current period and carried forward to the next period. In the case where profits are above the lower limit, the manager would be expected to make 'positive' discretionary accruals to maximise his or her present bonus award. However, if the bonus plan uses an upper limit, and profit before discretionary accruals is substantially above that limit, any 'positive' discretionary accruals would be lost because profits above the upper limit are not compensated for. Therefore, the manager would have incentives to make 'negative accruals' down to the plan's upper limit. These accruals could be reversed to increase bonuses in the future.

Figure 11.2 shows the levels of accruals that would be predicted for given stages of the bonus plan. L is the lower limit, or profits threshold. The firm must earn profits above this lower limit, L, if there are to be any distributions to the bonus pool. U is the upper limit, or ceiling, above which additional profits do not attract a bonus. K is the maximum possible accruals and −K is the minimum possible accruals.

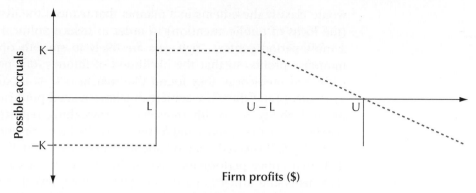

FIGURE 11.2 Accounting accruals as a function of bonus plan specifications

Healy studied 94 companies (1527 company years) each of which was assigned to one of three portfolios based on whether profits invoked the upper limit (UPP), the lower limit (LOW) or neither (MID). The portfolios LOW and UPP would be expected to have predominantly negative accruals, and the MID would be expected to have predominantly positive accruals. Healy's results were consistent with his hypotheses.

In a later study, Holthausen, Larcker and Sloan examined managerial behaviour using private data regarding firms' management compensation plans.[48] They found results that confirm Healy's findings, except that they did not find evidence that managers 'take a bath' when profits are below the threshold.

Healy, Kang and Palepu extended the bonus plan hypothesis research by examining the effect of changes in accounting procedures on the cash salaries and bonus compensation of chief executive officers.[49] They tested whether there was any statistical relationship between these factors and the firm's profits following a change in FIFO to LIFO inventory cost flow assumptions and from accelerated to straight-line depreciation. The change from FIFO to LIFO decreases reported profits and the change from accelerated to straight-line depreciation increases reported profits.

Healy, Kang and Palepu found that, after a change in accounting procedures, the salary and bonus award is based on actual reported profits. In other words, there is no adjustment for the change in accounting procedures. This suggests that management compensation schemes do not eliminate managerial manipulations of accounting choices. Moreover, if there are changes in the elements of the compensation model after a change in accounting policy (e.g. by a compensation committee), these element changes do not fully take into account the effects of the accounting changes. Examples of element changes include changes to weightings of management remuneration from salary, earnings-based bonuses and the like. The Healy, Kang and Palepu study demonstrated that although managers have an opportunity to change accounting procedures after the event, and thus their compensation awards, the benefits are likely to be small. This may explain the attitude which is taken by compensation committees when they appear not to fully adjust for accounting procedure changes.

Refining the specification of political costs

The second suggestion Watts and Zimmerman made to increase the power of positive theory tests was to improve the specification of the political cost variable.[50] Several papers have concentrated on the role of accounting in the political process and attempted to refine the size measure.

Using a sample of Australian firms, Godfrey and Jones investigated incentives for firms to smooth reported operating profits.[51] They predicted that during the period when it was possible to classify unusual recurring items as extraordinary, managers would classify these items in a manner that reduced the instability of operating profits (the focus of public attention) in order to reduce political costs. They argued that in a multi-period context, managers are likely to smooth operating profits rather than minimise profits, so that the likelihood of future profit peaks is reduced. Consistent with their prediction, they found that managers of companies with highly unionised workforces (and therefore subject to labour-related political costs) attempted to affect the probability of wealth transfers by smoothing reported net operating profit by classifying recurring gains and losses as extraordinary or operating.

DeAngelo observed that dissident shareholders usually cite poor earnings rather than share price performance as political evidence for company control.[52] The proxy statements and articles in *The Wall Street Journal* revealed that in 61 out of 86 proxy contests (71%), dissidents cited poor earnings. In only 11 cases (13%) were share prices cited and, in every case, earnings were also cited. DeAngelo found that the pre-contest accounting returns on equity of the sample firms were substantially below that of the market. On the other hand, for the 6 months up to the start of dissident activity, the market model prediction errors suggested that these firms had positive abnormal returns, in contrast to their accounting returns.

DeAngelo then predicted that during the election campaign, unexpected profits will be positive because managers, by using their discretion to manipulate accounting reports, will report favourable profits and try to increase their chances of winning the election. It was found that, during elections, managers reported profits materially exceeding those they had reported a year earlier. At the same time, the increase in profits was not associated with an increase in cash flows. These results contrast with the evidence of Liberty and Zimmerman, and DeAngelo suggests that they may be consistent with differing incentives to monitor management's accounting manipulations.

DeAngelo also found that where dissidents succeed in the proxy contest they appear to 'take a bath' in their first year of gaining office, but in the year that follows there is a highly significant turnaround in profits. This is then cited by the new managers as evidence that when they took control the company was in dire straits, but their management skills have helped get the company 'back on the rails'. However, the empirical evidence in this specific area is not consistent and, in another study by DeAngelo of management buyouts, there was no evidence of profit manipulation.[53]

Wong studied the effect of political and debt contracting costs on the choice of accounting for export tax credits available in New Zealand.[54] Until 1985, the New Zealand tax regime provided tax incentives for companies generating export profits. Between 1980 and 1985, there was significant pressure for the repeal of these laws, based on the premise that 'big business' did not pay its share of tax. Wong argued that the way in which tax credits were accounted for during this period was influenced by political costs. The two methods available to account for credits were:

- the tax reduction method (TRM), where credits are deducted from the taxation expense
- the credit-to-sales method (CSM), where the income tax is shown as a gross figure because the tax credit is apportioned directly to sales.

Although the profit after tax for any period is identical under both methods (thus the choice is intraperiod), TRM has the effect of lowering the overall tax rate (income tax expense divided by pre-tax profit) and the interest coverage ratio relative to CSM.

Wong tested three hypotheses:

- Companies with low reported tax rates are more likely to use CSM.
- Companies with large amounts of export tax credits are more likely to use CSM.
- Large companies are more likely to use CSM.

The third hypothesis reflects the presumed link between size and political profile. The first two hypotheses are based on the proposition that companies with high amounts of tax credits, or low reported tax rates, have the highest political costs in the context of the export tax credit debate. This is because it is easy to argue that their tax rates/credits reflect wealth transfers from society to the firms. Wong also tested the debt to equity hypothesis. Since CSM lowers interest-coverage constraints, companies closer to their interest-coverage constraints are more likely to use CSM. Tests supported all the hypotheses. The advantage of Wong's model is that he developed an explicit link between the politicisation of a particular issue, export tax credits, and its effect on accounting policy choice, thus enabling more powerful tests of the political cost hypothesis than do studies predicting a general association between firm size and accounting policy choice. Additionally, the study suggested that intraperiod accounting choices are relevant to the political process, although they have no effect on bottom-line results.

In another type of study using measures that explicitly link specific political costs to their effect on accounting policy choice, Wong examined the extent to which political costs influenced New Zealand firms to voluntarily disclose current cost data supplementary to historical cost financial statements.[55] Current cost accounting (CCA) generally reports lower profits than does historical cost accounting. Wong's results were consistent with the view that companies subject to wealth transfers by way of taxes and government regulation attempt to affect the probability of such transfers via an accounting choice: the voluntary disclosure of supplementary current cost financial statements. Similarly, Lemke and Page found support for the political cost hypothesis when they examined UK firms' responses to mandatory requirements to produce CCA accounts.[56] Like Wong, they used measures of the likely tax benefits from introducing CCA in an environment where there was potential for CCA to be required for purposes of calculating taxable income. They found that the tax-driven political cost incentives of firms had considerable explanatory power.

One of the best-known studies of the association between political costs and accounting discretion is Jones's 1991 paper that investigated whether the managers of firms subject to International Trade Commission import tax relief investigations in the United States between 1980 and 1985 manipulated their accounting accruals in order to demonstrate their need for government support.[57] Jones argued that a combination of accounting policy choices and estimates (e.g. the amount of doubtful debts to provide for, or the useful life of depreciable assets) might be used to manage profits downwards to present the firms and their industry in a manner that demonstrated that need. Jones found that the sample firms had negative discretionary accruals, thus decreasing profits, in the year of the investigations. They did not have negative discretionary accruals in the years before or following the investigations, however. The Jones study not only demonstrated the role of discretionary accruals to reduce firms' exposures to political costs, but also provided a model for calculating discretionary accruals that encompasses a wide range of accounting discretion.

Using data concerning 72 companies listed on the Australian Stock Exchange (now the Australian Securities Exchange), Panchapakesan and McKinnon further tested the validity of using firm size as a measure of political cost exposure.[58] The variables they examined were market share, industry membership, capital intensity, number of employees, number of shareholders, social responsibility disclosure, level of press coverage and firm size. Their results suggest that all the variables examined are implicated in political visibility with the exception of industry membership and capital intensity. Thus, their tests supported the continued use of firm size as a measure of political cost exposure. However, their results also suggest that the political visibility construct is a complex one, and that researchers should give serious consideration to measures of social responsibility disclosure such as the number of words or the area of words and photographs devoted to social responsibility issues in the financial press.

Testing the efficient contracting hypothesis

Throughout the research literature investigating accounting choices, there have been several significant studies that investigate the efficient contracting perspective. This literature concentrates mainly on the 'efficient' selection of accounting procedures, that is, accounting decisions that are made up front (*ex ante*) by management and claimholders on the firm to reduce the agency costs of contracting.

Interest capitalisation

One of the earliest empirical *ex ante* efficient contracting studies of accounting policy choice was Zimmer's study of accounting for interest by Australian real estate developers.[59] Zimmer provided an explanatory theory as to why firms would capitalise interest rather than expense it in order to reduce the costs of contracting. His theory stands in contrast to previous research on capitalisation or expensing of interest for *ex post* (after the fact) opportunistic reasons.[60]

Zimmer's theory establishes a link between real estate firms' financing methods and accounting choices. He hypothesises that real estate firms that finance projects by project-specific loans are more likely to capitalise interest. Real estate firms that undertake development projects on behalf of customers have an incentive to ensure that the customer bears the risks of the project. As a result, they will seek to make the price of the project depend on the developer's costs, including the interest. In the absence of *ex ante* contracting, the *ex post* opportunistic hypotheses predict that customers will then be exposed to managerial manipulations of the amount of funds used, and consequently to manipulation of the interest charged, through arbitrary accounting allocations. A means of controlling this is to 'tie' the funds to the project, that is, project-specific financing. The lender's funds are then secured by the assets of the project, and are protected from asset substitution and claim dilution since the lenders have the first (secured) claim over specific assets. Also, the only interest attributed to the project is the interest on the project finance, so the purchase guards against arbitrary interest allocations to the project increasing the project cost and the price the purchaser pays.

Zimmer expected that *ex ante* contracts between the firm and the customer which are 'cost plus' in nature led to capitalisation of interest for two reasons. First, although capitalisation typically increases managers' bonus awards, management compensation committees would allow interest capitalisation and recoup revenue through a cost-plus contract. Second, a consistent application of capitalising interest on specifically financed projects would save time in negotiations with auditors and the customer's cost investigators.

An *ex post* opportunism hypothesis — that capitalisation is more likely where firms are more highly leveraged, since capitalisation leads to an increase in reported profit and a reduction in leverage — was also tested by Zimmer. The evidence is strongly consistent with his first *ex ante* hypothesis (firms are more likely to capitalise interest if they use project-specific finance) and weakly supportive of his second *ex ante* hypothesis. However, as he observes, this result is also consistent with the *ex post* argument, since there may be a relationship between project-specific finance and the amount of debt in the capital structure. A further finding is that larger firms are more likely to capitalise interest, which is inconsistent with the conventional size hypothesis and suggests that larger firms are more likely to attract project-specific financing.

Changes in chief executive officer

Dechow and Sloan tested whether the horizon problem (mentioned earlier in relation to management contracts) would motivate chief executive officers (CEOs) in their final years of office to improve reported short-term profit performances, and thus their bonuses, by cutting back on research and development expenditures.[61] Their results suggest that CEOs did spend less on research and development in their final years in office. However, the effects on management compensation were minimised through CEO share ownership. Further, there was no evidence that the reduced expenditures were associated with either poor firm performance or reductions in investment spending over time. In fact, in the first year of the new CEO's term in office, research and development expenditures increased. This result is interesting because it indicates that although actions such as the reduction of research and development expenditure appear opportunistic and may even be opportunistically motivated, it might be more efficient for shareholders to allow indirect settling-up mechanisms (via share-based compensation) and compensatory action (new-CEO-increased research and development expenditures) to ensure equitable wealth distributions between shareholders and managers rather than take direct control over the actions of their managers. The Dechow and Sloan study seems to indicate that management contracts can balance share-based and profit-based incentives to ensure that attempts to transfer wealth from shareholders to managers are largely ineffectual. Thus, accounting and other contracting terms can reduce agency costs when the incentives for opportunism are strong.

Other studies

Responding to Watts and Zimmerman's calls for additional research to investigate the motivation for accounting choices, Skinner investigated whether traditional explanations of accounting choice (based on existing contracts and opportunistic decision making) have ignored another possible explanation: that accounting reflects the underlying investment, production and financing opportunities of the firm.[62] Using data from the United States, Skinner tested whether accounting decisions were correlated more with contracting variables or with variables that represented the firm's underlying economic attributes (e.g. opportunities for growth). He found evidence that the firm's economic attributes affected the nature of the firm's debt and management compensation contracts, and that the traditional opportunistic contracting variables were associated with accounting policy choices. He found only limited evidence of a direct association between the underlying economic attributes and the accounting decisions.

In contrast, Bradbury, Godfrey and Koh found that the goodwill accounting decisions of New Zealand firms were more related to the economic attributes of the firms than to traditional contracting variables.[63] They attribute some of the difference between their results and Skinner's to the fact that accounting in New Zealand is less constrained than in the United States, so there are more opportunities for managers to adopt policies that reflect the firm's economic position. Bradbury, Godfrey and Koh also use more refined measures of both their dependent and independent variables, which enables them to 'tease out' some of the implications.

LO 10 ⟶ EVALUATING THE THEORY

Although the development of positive accounting theory has been welcomed by many academics, it is fair to say that it has not been well received by all. In the past, accounting researchers provided comment and suggestions for reform based on research findings to help in developing accounting standards to prescribe how practitioners should account. By concentrating on positive questions rather than normative questions, Howieson argues that academics now risk neglecting a very important role in the community.[64] In contrast, Schipper has argued that academics provide extremely valuable input to the regulatory process by ensuring that regulators (1) can understand and predict the economic and social impact of alternative accounting standards, and (2) are informed of why managers make particular accounting choices and whether it is really 'after the fact' opportunism that is driving those choices or 'before the fact' efficient contracting. Schipper suggests that academics should focus on positive accounting research as an input to the standard-setting process.[65]

Other major criticisms of positive accounting theory fall into two main categories: methodological and statistical criticisms, and philosophical criticisms. These criticisms are now discussed.

Methodological and statistical criticisms

A major criticism of positive accounting theory is that the empirical evidence relating to the explanation of accounting policy choice, and the effect on share prices and firm contracts, is weak and inconclusive. Specifically, the methodological and statistical criticisms are that:

- the explanatory variables in some studies are insignificant and not of the predicted sign
- the predictive power (R^2) of the hypothesised models is low
- there is collinearity among the contracting (explanatory) variables
- the cross-sectional models are poorly specified
- crude measures, such as firm size, to operationalise political costs are not well defined in a theoretical sense, nor in a measurement sense (errors in variables).

McKee, Bell and Boatsman, for example, replicated Watts and Zimmerman's 1978 study by expanding the original sample size.[66] They found a deterioration in the predictive power of the model, and changes in the size, direction and significance of the coefficients. They concluded that the theory failed to correctly classify a disturbingly large number of observations and that economic factors were not adequate predictors of lobbying behaviour. However, other researchers have evaluated the aggregated evidence from positive accounting studies and concluded that there is significant evidence of empirical regularities which are consistent with the leverage and size variables.[67] Further, Christie statistically tested the hypothesis that positive accounting theory can explain the choice of accounting procedures by summing the results of tests across published studies.[68] He concluded that there are six variables common to one or more of the early positive accounting research studies that consistently demonstrate statistically significant, high explanatory power. They are:

- managerial compensation
- interest coverage
- leverage
- size
- dividend constraints
- risk.

Christie also observed that positive accounting theory is still developing as a paradigm. Like other social sciences, there is a tendency to publish results supporting a theory in its earlier stages. Once the 'core' of the theory is generally accepted, the theory and its methods are developed and refined by exploring abnormal results. This happens in Lakatosian research programs, for example. Christie pointed out that although there are insignificant results in some published studies, there is a significant set of empirical regularities.

In reviewing Christie's paper, Leftwich pointed out that Christie's tests make us more confident that there are significant relationships between certain variables and accounting choices. However, Leftwich[69] also commented that, although the theory is driven by contracting and monitoring costs, there was little attempt to operationalise or measure those costs. For example, there is a significant body of literature describing the nature of covenants found in lending agreements, but at that stage there was no attempt to determine the costs of monitoring the covenants or of renegotiating them in the event of default. Research published since Leftwich's discussion has now removed those concerns, however. In particular, research by Beneish and Press used US data to show that the cost of technical violation of debt covenants significantly reduced the value of equity.[70]

Watts and Zimmerman further point out that, at present, the mainstream literature explains accounting policy choice on the basis of two arguments: managerial opportunism and efficiency.[71] Neither explanation precludes the other, and accounting choices can be made that are motivated by both arguments. The relative strength of each explanation is uncertain and this will be reflected in tests.

Philosophical criticisms

Since its emergence as an alternative model to normative theory, positive accounting theory has been subjected to philosophical criticisms. These criticisms are presented below, along with a brief summary of the responses of positive accounting theorists.

Tinker, Merino and Neimark suggested that positive accounting theory is, contrary to its claims, value-laden, since researchers choose the topics to be investigated and the methods and assumptions to be applied.[72] They therefore impose a value judgement about what is worthy of investigation. Indeed, this is true of all research. Watts and Zimmerman suggest that, since positive accounting theory serves an information demand, people who require accounting theories for such reasons will choose from among those that are available.[73] Therefore, although value judgements are exercised, they will be constrained by the competition among theories.

Christenson characterises positive accounting theory not as an accounting theory, but as a sociology of accounting because it concentrates on human behaviour rather than on the behaviour or measurement of accounting entities.[74] In response, Watts and Zimmerman comment that accounting entities can be recognised only in terms of the behaviour of the individuals related to the firm — shareholders, managers, accountants, auditors.[75] This follows from recognising firms as a nexus of contracts and accounting as a political, economic and social product.

A number of papers have taken the view that the methodology of positive accounting theory is inappropriate for the purpose it purports to serve.[76] For example, Christenson links the positive approach in accounting to the nineteenth century school of thought known as logical positivism. The logical positivists held the view that only the methods of the natural sciences provided 'positive knowledge' of 'what is'. Christenson suggests that, as a philosophy of science, positivism is no longer taken seriously. He further argues that positive accounting research ignores the fundamental methodological approach of 'falsification' proposed by Popper.[77] Watts and Zimmerman dismiss these criticisms as being misplaced.[78] The methodology of positive accounting theory draws from that used in positive economics (including the finance discipline) which, they argue, provides useful descriptions and predictions about the way the world operates. They further argue that the word 'positive' is used in a sense to distinguish between positive (empirical) propositions and the normative propositions that were prevalent when positive theory was emerging. Even detractors of positive accounting theory recognise that to criticise accounting theory for failing to conform to such 'metatheories' of science, such as falsificationism, is inappropriate.[79]

In concentrating on criticising Watts and Zimmerman's original papers, critics have largely ignored the increasing body of evidence which supports the fundamental hypotheses of positive accounting theory. Finally, the demand for conservative accounting practices provides a stewardship source for accounting that potentially reduces the possibility of accounting manipulation by managers and counters the current claims by regulators for the introduction of 'unbiased' fair value accounting. This may be the most important role that it plays in the future.

LO 11 → ISSUES FOR AUDITORS

As discussed earlier in the chapter, the demand for auditing can be explained by agency theory as part of the monitoring and bonding activities and costs. Accounting numbers are used in contracting to determine management compensation and as the basis of debt covenants. These accounting numbers are required by law to be audited, but there is some evidence that auditing would be demanded in the absence of the law.

Watts and Zimmerman examine the history of auditing in the United Kingdom and the United States to test whether auditing was demanded to reduce agency costs and increase firm value, or simply to satisfy legal requirements.[80] Watts and Zimmerman find evidence that audits existed in the early history of corporations (as early as 1200). These audits evolved gradually into the type of audit required by the first English companies act in 1844. They also find that the differences in the development of professional auditing between the two countries reflect differences in the timing of capital market development in the two countries. Their evidence supports the conclusion that legislation requiring audits codified the best practice, rather than driving the demand for auditing.

It is difficult, if not impossible, to test theories about the demand for auditing using contemporary data because countries with developed capital markets require companies listed on public exchanges to disclose audited financial data at least annually. However, there are some specific situations that researchers have exploited to test the explanations from agency and signalling theories. Rather than examine the choice to purchase an audit or not, the tests examine the determinants of the choice of a higher quality auditor.

DeAngelo[81] argues that larger auditors, such as those commonly referred to as the 'Big 4',[82] are higher quality than other auditors because larger auditors have 'more to lose' by failing to report a discovered breach in a particular client's records. If a large audit firm compromises its independence on one audit to please that client, its reputation will suffer and the firm could lose all its other clients. The incentive for an auditor to compromise independence for one client depends on that client's importance. This importance is measured as a proportion of total audit firm value, which is dependent on that client relative to all the other clients.[83] DeAngelo explains that the audit firm's value is equal to the present value of future quasi-rents. Quasi-rents are *ex post* rents after costs have been sunk, that is, revenues minus marginal costs excluding the sunk costs.[84] Quasi-rents arise because it is costly for clients to switch auditors, so auditors can increase their prices above marginal costs in subsequent periods.

Datar, Feltham and Hughes suggest that users of financial statements believe that large auditors are higher quality because they understand the 'more to lose' argument.[85] They argue that companies issuing shares in an initial public offering (IPO) use audit quality to signal the quality of the company and its shares. One method of signalling the new firm's quality is for the promoter to retain a large proportion of the shares.

This is a valuable signal because it is costly. An alternative signal of share quality is employing a costly, high quality auditor. Therefore, Datar, Feltham and Hughes predict that promoters of IPOs in companies using a high quality auditor (Big 4 auditor) will have lower holdings of shares at the time of the IPO than promoters of IPOs in companies using a lower quality auditor.

Research conducted using US data did not support Datar, Feltham and Hughes's predictions.[86] This is possibly because, although promoters could prefer higher quality auditors, those auditors are likely to increase their audit fees to protect them against the litigation risk associated with IPOs. Using data from Canada where the litigation risk for auditors is relatively lower, Clarkson and Simunic found evidence to support Datar, Feltham and Hughes's predictions that audit quality is used to signal investment quality.[87]

Another method of testing the demand for auditing is to examine the question of audit quality across countries that vary in the strength of their corporate control mechanisms. Fan and Wong argue that in emerging markets, such as those in East Asia, agency conflicts between controlling owners and minority shareholders are difficult to control through conventional control mechanisms, such as boards of directors and takeovers.[88] They find that firms with agency problems in their ownership structures are more likely to employ Big 5 auditors where the firms raise capital frequently. These firms receive smaller share price discounts due to their agency conflicts than other firms, which Fan and Wong attribute to the monitoring role of the high-quality auditor. They also find that the Big 5 auditors seem to charge higher fees in these situations.

Finally, researchers have refined the concept of high-quality auditors to include those auditors that specialise in certain industries or contracts. Craswell, Francis and Taylor find that even after controlling for the effect of a Big 4 auditor brand name, industry specialist auditors charge higher audit fees.[89] Godfrey and Hamilton show that firms with high discretionary research and development (R&D) expenditures choose auditors that specialise in auditing R&D contracts, particularly for small clients who are not constrained to use large auditors for size reasons.[90] The auditors provide assurance that the expenditure on the R&D growth options is reported correctly, and therefore the risk of underinvestment is lower.

Summary

Positive accounting theory has been a major force in academic accounting research. Its departure from the approach of previous normative accounting theory lies in its development of a theoretical model of contractual exchange between persons who use accounting numbers to effect payoffs between them, and in the empirical testing of this model. Researchers perceived a need for a model of accounting policy choice as an explanation as to why accountants account as they do. Early positive accounting theory research proposed that accounting numbers would play a role in contracts used to minimise the costs of agency relationships. Once the contractual terms were specified, it was proposed that managers would choose accounting policies to transfer wealth to managers or shareholders, away from the principals with whom contracts were written. Subsequent research used more specific models and shifted its emphasis to efficient *ex ante* selection of accounting policies designed to reduce contracting and monitoring costs.

LO 1 — Contracting theory — why the firm can be described as a 'nexus of contracts'

Firms exist to specialise in connecting consumers of goods and services with the suppliers of the factors of production that produce those goods and services. It is more economic for firms to undertake contracting between agents rather than individuals.

LO 2 — Agency theory — how accounting is used in contractual specifications to reduce the agency costs of equity and debt

Among the factors of production that unite to create the firm are capital and labour. Capital may be provided by lenders or investors (principals), and labour is provided by managers who have decision-making authority (agents). Because agents' incentives differ from those of their principals, contractual specifications can be used to try to align the interests of both parties. Accounting numbers can be used in those contracts because they are measurable and observable. For example, managers might receive bonus payments if they achieve profits in excess of some target; or lenders might take action to renegotiate the terms of their loans if the firm's gearing ratio rises above 60%.

LO 3 — Price protection and shareholder/manager agency problems — constraining opportunistic accounting reporting by managers

Agency problems include the risk-aversion problem, the dividend retention problem, and the horizon problem. Shareholders can price protect by tying managers' remuneration to share prices or accounting numbers or some combination thereof. For example a manager close to contract closure or retirement would be tied to the share price as a reflection of long-term value, rather than having a bonus plan linked to the amount of dividends paid out or progressively linked to earnings based upon pre-agreed accounting formulas.

LO 4 **Shareholder–debtholder agency problems — how managers' *ex post* accounting decisions can transfer wealth from lenders to equityholders**
If firms have debt contracts in place with covenants that limit the amount that firms can borrow to, say, a certain proportion of total tangible assets, managers acting on behalf of shareholders have incentives to use income- and asset-increasing accounting measures to ensure that they do not technically violate the debt covenant, even though the firm's financial situation is poor. In this way, the interest rate and other factors are not renegotiated, the lenders end up taking on more risk than expected, and the effect is to transfer wealth from the lenders to shareholders.

LO 5 **The difference between *ex post* opportunism and *ex ante* efficient contracting — contracting and the information perspective**
Ex post opportunism occurs when, once a contract is in place, agents take actions that transfer wealth from principals to themselves. In contrast, efficient contracting occurs when agents take actions that maximise the amount of wealth available to distribute between principals and agents, and the information perspective simply argues that managers provide information to existing and potential investors with the intention of providing the best information possible to help decision making. Signalling theory relates to each perspective by predicting that managers will provide information that forms the basis for expectations reflected in contractual terms or investment decisions.

LO 6 **Signalling theory — how accounting can be used to signal information about the firm**
Accounting reports are often used to signal information about a firm, particularly where earnings trends are highlighted to indicate likely future earnings. This is achieved by voluntarily disclosing bad news, reducing and increasing dividends, smoothing earnings, impairing assets, and recognising internally generated assets

LO 7 **Political processes — how accounting can be used to reduce the political costs faced by the firm**
Often, firms try to avoid public attention that is 'costly' to them, either financially or in terms of public perception and reputation. One way to do that is to reduce their reported earnings or reduce the volatility of their reported earnings so that they are not a target of public attention.

LO 8 **Conservatism, accounting standards and agency costs — accounting standards as an agency constraint**
Prudent traditional practice shows a bias by accountants in recognising expenses over revenue. Emphasis is placed on verifiability and using historical cost in measurement. Conditional conservatism is argued to arise from a demand in the market for accounting techniques that place more emphasis on timely recognition of losses compared to gains. This is brought about by a demand for management and debt contracting, shareholder litigation and taxation. Accounting regulators' arguments for neutrality and rejection of conservatism fails to recognise the role conservatism plays in reducing earnings management and curtailing compensation and dividend payouts.

LO 9 **Additional empirical tests of the theory**
Empirical tests provide evidence that managers use accounting numbers to counter political pressure, to gain political advantages such as export credits, to set targets for managers that have upper and lower compensation limits, to reduce debt covenants, to provide dividend constraints, and to generally play a significant role in constraining management manipulation.

LO 10 → **Evaluating the theory — key criticisms of contracting theories of accounting choice**
Positive accounting theories have been criticised on the grounds of their usefulness, their methodological and statistical rigour, and their philosophy. In response, positive accounting researchers argue they develop a theory that has an information role; that is, managers, auditors, lenders and others demand theories that help them to predict the effects of accounting choices on their welfare and in setting up efficient contracts. Moreover, through its contribution to explanation and prediction, positive theory helps parties such as standard setters to understand the consequences of their actions in removing the conservative bias of accounting practices.

LO 11 → **Issues for auditors**
Auditors have a bonding and monitoring role in agency theory. Auditing is now a legal requirement but there is evidence that auditing was voluntarily undertaken in the past. Research has also shown that higher quality auditors are demanded in situations where clients wish to signal that their accounts are of higher quality or where there are severe agency conflicts or weak control mechanisms. Industry specialist auditors are able to demand higher audit fees, and clients demand research and development contract specialist auditors when firms have highly discretionary expenditures on research and development growth options.

Questions

1. What is the difference between normative and positive accounting theory? Give examples of each.
2. What were some of the factors that led to the development of positive accounting theories of accounting policy choice?
3. Why might managers choose accounting methods that increase current period reported earnings?
4. Why might managers choose accounting methods that reduce current period reported earnings?
5. What does it mean when researchers claim that for a signal to be credible, it must be 'costly' to replicate? Consider an example where accounting information is used for signalling purposes. Is the signal credible? What are the potential costs of replicating that accounting signal?
6. What is the debt hypothesis? Explain the logic (theory) behind it.
7. Why might managers' interests differ from those of shareholders? What can shareholders do to ensure that they do not suffer financially because managers' interests differ from their own?
8. Why might politicians choose, rationally, not to be fully informed about issues they are charged to resolve?
9. What are debt covenants, and why are they used?
10. What are the costs of breaching a debt covenant? How significant do you think these costs might be?
11. Agency relationships give rise to agency costs that are borne, at least initially, by different parties. Briefly explain how agency relationships arise and give rise to agency costs.
12. Explain the three types of agency costs and their relationships to each other in the context of
    (a) debt contracts
    (b) equity contracts.

13. Although managers have incentives to transfer wealth from shareholders to themselves or from lenders to shareholders, there are various factors that can limit the wealth transfers. What are those factors, and how do they work to constrain the wealth transfers?

14. Because of *ex post* settling up and price protection, much opportunistic behaviour is prevented or compensated for. What is price protection, and how does it reduce the cost of opportunistic behaviour?

15. Who bears agency costs?

16. Bonus plans are used to reduce the agency costs of equity. Describe the agency relationship giving rise to the agency cost of equity and explain how bonus plans can reduce particular types of agency problems.

17. Explain the role, if any, played by accounting numbers in specifying the contractual terms of bonus plans designed to reduce agency problems.

18. Explain the main agency costs of debt, and how debt contracts can be designed to reduce those costs. In particular, explain how accounting specifications within the contracts can be used to reduce the agency problems.

19. When Kezza Ltd approached Steffs Banking Corporation Ltd for an unsecured loan of $100 million, Kezza Ltd had a good credit rating. However, the economy was depressed and Steffs Banking Corporation Ltd was concerned about lending such a large sum. You have been asked by Steffs Banking Corporation Ltd to provide a short report to the finance manager, Mike Hanshee, explaining how debt agreements and restrictive covenants can be used to safeguard debt in general. Mike wants the report to explain which agency costs of debt are controlled by specific covenants. Furthermore, he is interested to know how accounting numbers can be used in the debt covenants to help control any opportunistic behaviour on the part of Kezza Ltd.

20. In the context of positive accounting theory, political costs can reduce the value of firms significantly.
    (a) Give examples of how firms can be exposed to political costs.
    (b) Give examples of how a firm's exposure to political costs can influence the nature and/or content of the firm's annual report, particularly in relation to its accounting information.

21. Positive accounting theory has been criticised by many. Outline the criticisms and comment on their validity.

22. Positive accounting theory does not prescribe how accounting reports should be prepared. How, then, can it make any contribution to the advancement of accounting as an information system? Do you think that positive accounting theory has played any role in the development of accounting practices or regulation?

23. Are the contracting and information perspectives of positive accounting theory different in any significant ways? If so, how and why? Which of the two perspectives is more consistent with the efficient market hypothesis, and why?

24. What is unconditional and conditional accounting conservatism? How would an unbiased (neutral) approach to recognition of all gains and losses reduce the stewardship (monitoring) role of accounting?

25. The role of financial accounting is to provide information for making economic decisions to buy and sell shares? Evaluate this argument from a contracting perspective.

26. Explain the role of auditing in agency theory and the information perspective.

Additional readings

Ahmed, AS, Billings, BK, Morton, RM, & Stanford-Harris, M 2002, 'The role of accounting conservatism in mitigating bondholder–shareholder conflicts over dividend policy and in reducing debt costs', *Accounting Review*, vol. 77, no. 4, pp. 867–90.

Ball, R, Robin, A, & Wu, JS 2003, 'Incentives versus standards: Properties of accounting income in four East Asian countries', *Journal of Accounting and Economics*, vol. 36, no. 1–3, pp. 235–70.

Beatty, A, & Weber, J 2003, 'The effects of debt contracting on voluntary accounting method changes', *Accounting Review*, vol. 78, no. 1, pp. 119–42.

Cahan, SF, & Wei, Z 2006, 'After Enron: Auditor conservatism and ex-Andersen clients,' *Accounting Review*, vol. 8, no. 1, pp. 49–82.

Cheng, Q, & Warfield, TD 2005, 'Equity incentives and earnings management', *Accounting Review*, vol. 80, no. 2, pp. 441–76.

Christenson, PO, Feltham, GA, & Sabac, F 2005, 'A contracting perspective on earnings quality', *Journal of Accounting and Economics*, vol. 39, pp. 265–94.

Guay, WR, Kothari, SP, & Watts, RL 1996, 'A market-based evaluation of discretionary accrual models', *Journal of Accounting Research*, vol. 34, Supplement, pp. 83–104.

Skinner, D 1994, 'Why firms voluntarily disclose bad news', *Journal of Accounting Research*, vol. 32, no. 1, Spring, pp. 38–60.

Watts, R 1977, 'Corporate financial statements: A product of the market and political processes', *Australian Journal of Management*, pp. 53–75.

Watts, R 2003, 'Conservatism in accounting Part I: Explanations and implications', *Accounting Horizons*, vol. 17, no. 3, September, pp. 207–221.

Watts, R, & Zimmerman, J 1979, 'The demand for and supply of accounting theories: The market for excuses', *Accounting Review*, vol. 54, April, pp. 273–305.

11.1 CASE STUDY

An area of positive theory considers the political incentives underpinning certain accounting choices. This case study illustrates the significant pressure that business can apply on government in the process of setting business regulation.

Further concessions sought on share plans

by John Kehoe

Business is putting pressure on the federal government to make further concessions on the taxation of employee share schemes, warning the current position does not fully align the interests of directors and executives with shareholders.

Mining giant Rio Tinto and the Australian Institute of Company Directors told a Senate committee inquiry into employee share schemes that the tax rules on options were too "harsh" and that forcing departing employees to pay tax on shares was contrary to sound remuneration practices.

The government backed down earlier this month on its controversial budget decision to tax employee shares upfront, a proposal that stemmed from concerns that executives were rorting shares and options plans by deferring their tax liability and then never paying the tax due. Most of the pre-budget rules were restored, after a backlash from business and unions.

Assistant Treasurer Nick Sherry tripled the income threshold – from $60,000 to $180,000 – below which $1000 of shares could be received tax-free, deferred the taxing point on shares where there are restrictions preventing the taxpayer from disposing of the securities and allowed employees to defer tax on up to $5000 of shares through salary sacrifice arrangements.

Despite welcoming the government's revised position, AICD chief executive John Colvin said ... "The revised proposal still does not adequately recognise the fundamental imperative to promote ongoing share ownership by employees and directors."

Source: Excerpts from *The Australian Financial Review*, 20 July 2009, p. 5, www.afr.com.

Questions

1. This article describes certain components of executive remuneration. What are those components?
2. Why would an employee's remuneration package contain non-cash components?
3. What sort of benchmarks and hurdles are likely to be included in a 'sound remuneration' package?
4. Why do you think unions reacted negatively to the government's proposal to tax employee share schemes up-front?

11.2 CASE STUDY

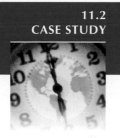

It is often difficult, if not impossible, to distinguish operating efficiencies from changes in reported results brought about by accounting rule changes, as the following article demonstrates.

Results blamed on accounting

by Duncan Hughes

Argo Investments managing director Rob Patterson claims "nonsensical" new accounting changes have distorted the $3.1 billion fund's annual performance and he is backing industry moves for changes.

Mr Patterson, who joined the fund 39 years ago, was speaking after the fund announced a full-year loss of $64.4 million for the 12 months to June 30 compared with a profit of $294 million in the corresponding period.

He said: "The results were thrown around by the new international accounting standards. We believe they do not account for long-term investments in equity securities where our profits come from collecting income."

The Australian Listed Investment Companies Association and individual companies are lobbying local accounting governing bodies to have the Accounting Standard 139 amended to better reflect their underlying performance.

ARGO INVESTMENTS LIMITED

Full year	2009	2008
Pretax ($m)	174.8	196.1
Net ($m)	–64.4	294.1
EPS	–11.1c	52.0c
Final div	27c ff	30c ff
Shares (last)	$6.63 (+30c)	

The fund outperformed the benchmark 10-year result of the All Ordinaries Accumulation index with 8.8 per cent annualised capital growth to 7.3 per cent. Over 12 months, the fund was down 16.8 per cent compared with the benchmark's 22.1 per cent.

Mr Patterson dismissed suggestions that underlying performance would be affected by the 10.4 per cent fall in operating profit to $163.4 million, the second-highest in the company's history, and claimed the fund's investment approach was more popular than ever.

Source: Excerpts from *The Australian Financial Review*, 4 August 2009, p. 47, www.afr.com.

Questions

1. How does this article and the underlying profit decrease demonstrate signalling theory? In your answer, explain what, if anything, is costly to replicate and therefore gives the signal credibility.
2. Apply the theories described in this chapter to explain the decrease in reported earnings from the information perspective.
3. How is the application of Accounting Standard 139 likely to have affected Argo Investment's approach to the structuring of CEOs' remuneration packages?

Endnotes

1. As described in the previous chapter, the EMH predicts that investors immediately incorporate information into share prices. The semi-strong version of the EMH predicts that investors immediately incorporate publicly available information into share prices.
2. R Ball, 'What do we know about market efficiency?', Working paper 31, Sydney: University of NSW, School of Banking and Finance, 1990.
3. E Chamberlin, *The Theory of Monopolistic Competition*, Harvard: Harvard University Press, 1933.
4. Lobbying includes making submissions on exposure drafts to accounting standard-setting bodies, convening meetings to raise public awareness and concerns about proposed accounting standards, and writing to authorities and individuals who have the power to influence the outcome of the accounting standard-setting process. Each is expensive, in terms of both time and the cost of specialist labour involved in preparing the submissions.
5. R Coase, 'The nature of the firm', *Economica*, vol. 4, November 1937, pp. 386–405.
6. M Jensen and W Meckling, 'Theory of the firm: Managerial behaviour, agency costs and ownership structure', *Journal of Financial Economics*, vol. 3, October 1976, pp. 305–60.
7. A Alchian and H Demsetz, 'Production, information costs and economic organization', *American Economic Review*, vol. 62, December 1972, pp. 777–95.
8. Jensen and Meckling, op. cit.
9. E Fama, 'Agency problems and the theory of the firm', *Journal of Political Economy*, vol. 88, April 1980, pp. 288–307.
10. A Amershi and S Sunder, 'Failure of stock prices to discipline managers in a rational expectations economy', *Journal of Accounting Research*, vol. 25, Autumn 1987, pp. 177–93.
11. A Smith, *The wealth of nations*, New York: Cannan, originally published 1776, p. 700.
12. C Smith and R Watts, 'Incentive and tax effects on executive compensation plans', *Australian Journal of Management*, vol. 7, December 1982, pp. 139–57; W Llewellen, C Loderer and K Martin, 'Executive compensation and executive incentive problems: An empirical analysis', *Journal of Accounting and Economics*, vol. 9, November 1987, pp. 287–310.
13. In the contracting framework, costs are both financial and non-financial. Non-financial costs include such things as time, effort, stress and reduction in self-esteem.
14. R Watts and J Zimmerman, 'Positive accounting theory: A ten year perspective', *Accounting Review*, January 1990, p. 208.
15. C Smith and J Warner, 'On financial contracting: An analysis of bond covenants', *Journal of Financial Economics*, vol. 7, June 1979, pp. 117–61.
16. G Whittred and I Zimmer, 'Accounting information in the market for debt', *Accounting and Finance*, November 1986, pp. 19–33.
17. An interest coverage constraint requires the firm, in the year that it issues the debt, to maintain a profit that is a specified number of times greater than the company's interest expense.
18. D Stokes and KL Tay, 'Restrictive covenants and accounting information in the market for convertible notes: Further evidence', *Accounting and Finance*, November 1988, pp. 57–73.
19. J Cotter, 'Utilisation and restrictiveness of covenants in Australian private debt contracts', *Accounting and Finance*, vol. 38, no. 2, 1998, pp. 181–96.
20. D Stokes and M Whincop, 'Covenants and accounting information in the market for classes of preferred stock', *Contemporary Accounting Review*, vol. 9, Spring 1993, pp. 463–78. See O Williamson, 'Corporate finance and corporate governance', *Journal of Finance*, vol. 43, July 1988, pp. 567–91.
21. Stokes and Whincop, op. cit.
22. Watts and Zimmerman, op. cit., p. 216.

23. RW Holthausen, 'Accounting method choice: Opportunistic behavior, efficient contracting and information perspectives', *Journal of Accounting and Economics*, January 1990, pp. 207–18.

24. Watts and Zimmerman, op. cit., pp. 131–56.

25. Holthausen, op. cit.

26. See, for instance, A Downs, *An economic theory of democracy*, New York: Harper & Row, 1957.

27. Watts and Zimmerman, op. cit., p. 225.

28. See, for example, Watts and Zimmerman, op. cit., p. 225. In the early years of the twenty-first century, Enron and WorldCom crashes, particularly, have given rise to political lobbying for changes to accounting regulations and regulatory processes in a manner similar to the reactions of the 1930s.

29. Watts and Zimmerman, op. cit., p. 235.

30. ibid., p. 234.

31. RL Watts, 'Conservatism in accounting Part I: Explanations and implications', *Accounting Horizons*, vol. 17, no. 3, September 2003, pp. 207–221.

32. However, this is not always the case if depreciation charges based on historic costs are held artificially low.

33. S Basu, The conservatism principle and the asymmetric timeliness of earnings, *Journal of Accounting and Economics*, vol. 24, 1997, pp. 3–37. Basu reports coefficients of 0.209 and 0.664 for gains and losses.

34. R Ball, A Robin and JS Wu, 'Incentives versus standards: Properties of accounting income in four East Asian countries', *Journal of Accounting and Economics*, 2003, vol. 36, pp. 235–70.

35. C Leuz, D Nanda and PD Wysocki, 'Earnings management and investor protection: An international comparison, *Journal of Financial Economics*, 2003, vol 69, no. 3, pp. 505–27.

36. R Watts and J Zimmerman, 'Towards a positive theory of the determination of accounting standards', *Accounting Review*, vol. 53, January 1978, pp. 112–34.

37. R Ball and G Foster, 'Corporate financial reporting: A methodological review of empirical research', *Studies on current research methodologies in accounting: A critical evaluation*, supplement to *Journal of Accounting Research*, vol. 20, 1982, pp. 161–234.

38. AP Sweeney, 'Debt-covenant violations and managers' accounting responses', *Journal of Accounting and Economics*, vol. 17, 1994, pp. 281–308.

39. M DeFond and J Jiambalvo, 'Debt covenant violation and manipulation of accruals', *Journal of Accounting and Economics*, vol. 17, 1994, pp. 145–76.

40. M Zmijewski and R Hagerman, 'An income strategy approach to the positive theory of accounting standard setting/choice', *Journal of Accounting and Economics*, vol. 3, August 1981, pp. 129–49.

41. S Lilien and V Pastena, 'Determinants of intramethod choice in the oil and gas industry', *Journal of Accounting and Economics*, vol. 5, April 1983, pp. 145–70.

42. DS Dhaliwal, 'The effect of the firm's capital structure on the choice of accounting methods', *Accounting Review*, vol. 55, January 1980, pp. 78–84.

43. LA Daley and RL Vigeland, 'The effects of debt covenants and political costs on the choice of accounting methods: The case of accounting for R&D costs', *Journal of Accounting and Economics*, vol. 5, December 1983, pp. 195–211.

44. DS Dhaliwal, G Salamon and E Smith, 'The effect of owner versus management control on the choice of accounting methods', *Journal of Accounting and Economics*, vol. 4, July 1982, pp. 41–53.

45. R Bowen, E Noreen and J Lacey, 'Determinants of the corporate decision to capitalise interest', *Journal of Accounting and Economics*, vol. 3, August 1981, pp. 151–79.

46. Watts and Zimmerman, op. cit., p. 245.

47. P Healy, 'The effect of bonus schemes on accounting decisions', *Journal of Accounting and Economics*, vol. 7, April 1985, pp. 85–107.

48. R Holthausen, D Larcker and R Sloan, 'Annual bonus schemes and the manipulation of earnings', *Journal of Accounting and Economics*, vol. 19, 1995, pp. 29–74.

49. P Healy, S Kang and K Palepu, 'The effect of accounting procedure changes on CEO's cash salary and bonus compensation', *Journal of Accounting and Economics*, vol. 9, January 1987, pp. 7–34.

50. Watts and Zimmerman, op. cit.

51. JM Godfrey and KL Jones, 'Political cost influences on income smoothing via extraordinary item classification', *Accounting and Finance*, November 1999.

52. L DeAngelo, 'Managerial competition, information costs and corporate governance: The use of accounting performance measures in proxy contests', *Journal of Accounting and Economics*, vol. 10, January 1988, pp. 3–36.

53. L DeAngelo, 'Accounting numbers as market valuation substitutes: A study of management buyouts of public stockholders', *Accounting Review*, vol. 61, October 1986, pp. 400–20.

54. J Wong, 'Political costs and an intraperiod accounting choice for export tax credits', *Journal of Accounting and Economics*, vol. 10, January 1988, pp. 37–51.

55. J Wong, 'Economic incentives for the voluntary disclosure of current cost financial statements', *Journal of Accounting and Economics*, vol. 10, April 1988, pp. 151–67.

56. KW Lemke and MJ Page, 'Economic determinants of accounting policy choice: The case of current cost accounting in the UK', *Journal of Accounting and Economics*, vol. 15, March 1992, pp. 87–114.

57. J Jones, 'Earnings management during import relief investigations', *Journal of Accounting Research*, vol. 29, 1991, pp. 193–228.

58. S Panchapakesan and J McKinnon, 'Proxies for political visibility: A preliminary examination of the relation among some potential proxies', *Accounting Research Journal*, Spring 1992.

59. I Zimmer, 'Accounting for interest by real estate developers', *Journal of Accounting and Economics*, vol. 8, January 1986, pp. 37–51.

60. R Bowen, E Noreen and J Lacey, 'Determinants of the corporate decision to capitalise interest', *Journal of Accounting and Economics*, vol. 3, August 1981, pp. 151–79.

61. P Dechow and R Sloan, 'Executive incentives and the horizon problem: An empirical investigation', *Journal of Accounting and Economics*, vol. 14, March 1991, pp. 51–89.

62. DJ Skinner, 'The investment opportunity set and accounting procedure choice: Preliminary evidence', *Journal of Accounting and Economics*, vol. 16, 1993, pp. 407–45.

63. ME Bradbury, JM Godfrey and PS Koh, 'Investment opportunity set influence on goodwill accounting: New Zealand evidence', Unpublished manuscript, presented at Asia–Pacific Journal of Accounting and Economics Symposium 2002.

64. B Howieson, 'Whither financial accounting research: A modern-day Bo-Peep?', *Australian Accounting Review*, vol. 6, no. 1, 1996, pp. 29–36.

65. K Schipper, 'Academic research and the standard setting process', *Accounting Horizons*, vol. 8, no. 4, 1994, pp. 61–73.

66. AJ McKee, TB Bell and JR Boatsman, 'Management preferences over accounting standards: A replication and additional tests', *Accounting Review*, vol. 59, October 1984, pp. 647–59.

67. R Holthausen and R Leftwich, 'The economic consequences of accounting choice: Implications of costly contracting and monitoring', *Journal of Accounting and Economics*, vol. 5, August 1988, pp. 77–117; Watts and Zimmerman, op. cit.

68. A Christie, 'Aggregation of test statistics: An evaluation of the evidence on contracting and size hypotheses', *Journal of Accounting and Economics*, vol. 12, January 1990, pp. 15–36.

69. R Leftwich, 'Aggregation of test statistics: Statistics versus economics', *Journal of Accounting and Economics*, vol. 12, January 1990, pp. 37–44.

70. MD Beneish and E Press, 'Costs of technical violation of accounting-based debt covenants', *Accounting Review*, April 1993, pp. 233–57.

71. Watts and Zimmerman, op. cit.

72. T Tinker, B Merino and M Neimark, 'The normative origins of positive theories: Ideology and accounting thought', *Accounting, Organizations and Society*, vol. 7, 1982, pp. 167–200.

73. Watts and Zimmerman, op. cit.

74. C Christenson, 'The methodology of positive accounting', *Accounting Review*, vol. 58, January 1983, pp. 1–22.

75. R Watts and J Zimmerman, *Positive accounting theory*, Englewood Cliffs, NJ: Prentice Hall, 1986.

76. Tinker, Merino and Neimark, op. cit.; Christenson, op. cit.

77. For an explanation of 'falsification', see KR Popper, *The logic of scientific discovery*, London: Hutchinson, 1959.

78. Watts and Zimmerman, op. cit.

79. R Hines, 'Popper's methodology of falsification and accounting research'. *Accounting Review*, vol. 63, October 1988, pp. 657–62.

80. RL Watts, and J Zimmerman, 'Agency problems, auditing, and the theory of the firm: some evidence', *Journal of Law and Economics*, vol. 26, no. 3, October 1983, pp. 613–33.

81. LE DeAngelo, 'Auditor size and audit quality', *Journal of Accounting and Economics*, vol. 3, no. 3, December 1981, pp. 183–99.

82. Big 4 auditors: KPMG, PricewaterhouseCoopers, Deloittes, and Ernst and Young. The number of 'Big' auditors has shrunk over time due to mergers (e.g. between Price Waterhouse and Coopers & Lybrand) and the collapse of Arthur Andersen in 2002.

83. LE DeAngelo, 'Auditor independence, "lowballing", and disclosure regulation. *Journal of Accounting and Economics*, vol. 3, no. 2, 1981, pp. 113–27.

84. H Chung and S Kallapur, 'Client importance, nonaudit services, and abnormal accruals', *The Accounting Review*, vol. 78, no. 4, 2003, pp. 931–55.

85. S Datar, GA Feltham and JS Hughes, 'The role of audits and audit quality in valuing new issues', *Journal of Accounting and Economics*, vol. 14, 1991, pp. 3–49.

86. D Simunic and M Stein, 'Product differentiation in auditing: Auditor choice in the market for unseasoned new issues, Certified General Accountants' Research Foundation, Vancouver, 1987; RP Beatty, 'The initial public offerings market for auditing services, in Proceedings of the 1986 auditing research symposium, University of Illinois, Urbana-Champaign, IL, 1989, pp. 1–40; GA Feltham, JS Hughes and D Simunic, 'Empirical assessment of the impact of auditor quality on the valuation of new issues', *Journal of Accounting and Economics*, vol. 14, 1991, pp. 1–25; cited in PM Clarkson and DA Simunic, 'Auditor choice, risk and ownership', *Journal of Accounting and Economics*, vol. 17, no. 1–2, 1994, pp. 207–28.

87. Clarkson and Simunic, op. cit.

88. JPH Fan and TJ Wong, 'Do external auditors perform a corporate governance role in emerging markets: Evidence from East Asia', *Journal of Accounting Research*, vol. 43, no. 1, 2005, pp. 35–72.

89. AT Craswell, JR Francis and S Taylor, 'Auditor brand name reputations and industry specializations', *Journal of Accounting and Economics*, vol. 20, no. 3, December 1995, pp. 297–322.

90. JM Godfrey and J Hamilton, 'The impact of R&D intensity on demand for specialist auditor services', *Contemporary Accounting Research*, vol. 22, no. 1, Spring 2005, pp. 55–93.

12 Capital market research

LEARNING OBJECTIVES

After reading this chapter, you should have an appreciation of the following:

1 the philosophy of positive accounting theory

2 the strengths of positive theory

3 the scope of positive accounting theory

4 capital market research and the efficient markets hypothesis

5 the influence of accounting information on investor behaviour and share prices

6 trading strategies and mechanistic behavioural effects

7 issues for auditors.

The distinction between the 'moral' order (that which ought to be) and the 'physical' order (that which is), together with the extent to which one can be derived from the other, is a dilemma that has challenged philosophers for centuries. The accounting community, similarly, is divided in the priority it gives to 'normative' as opposed to 'positive' theories. Prescriptive theories are referred to as 'normative', since they are derived from the notion of a norm, a standard, or a model which is seen as an ideal. Normative accounting theory, for example, prescribes the 'correct' or 'best' way to account. Theories that explain or predict real world phenomena and are tested empirically (according to their correspondence with observations from the real world) are referred to as 'positive' theories.

An appreciation of the difference between positive and normative accounting theories is necessary for any understanding of accounting theory and accounting regulation. This is especially so because positive accounting theorists have strongly supported the historical cost system, which has been the norm for several centuries. More recently, supporters of fair value measurement have been influential through the adoption of International Financial Reporting Standards in Europe and Australia in 2005. That is, the relative importance of positivism and normativism in accounting has been keenly debated over the last 40 years. This chapter examines how capital markets react to accounting information.

LO 1 ▸ PHILOSOPHY OF POSITIVE ACCOUNTING THEORY

Positive theory seeks to understand accounting phenomena by observing empirical events and to use these results to make predictions about a wider set of observations and/or to predict future events. This differs from descriptive theory, which focuses only on describing events, and from normative theory, which prescribes what should occur. Milton Friedman championed positive theories in economics. He stated:

> The ultimate goal of a positive science is the development of a 'theory' or 'hypothesis' that yields valid and meaningful (i.e. not truistic) predictions about phenomena not yet observed.[1]

Consistent with Friedman's view, Watts and Zimmerman asserted:

> The objective of [positive] accounting theory is to *explain* and *predict* accounting practice ... *Explanation* means providing reasons for observed practice. For example, positive accounting theory seeks to explain *why* firms continue to use historical cost accounting and why certain firms switch between a number of accounting techniques. *Prediction* of accounting practice means that the theory predicts unobserved phenomena.[2]

Unobserved phenomena are not necessarily future phenomena; they include phenomena that have occurred, but on which systematic evidence has not yet been collected. For example, positive theory research seeks to obtain empirical evidence about the attributes of firms that continue to use the same accounting techniques from year to year versus the attributes of firms that continually switch accounting techniques. We might also be interested in predicting the reaction of firms to a proposed accounting standard, together with an explanation of why firms would lobby for and against such a standard, even though the standard has already been released. Testing these theories provides evidence that can be used to predict the impact of accounting regulations before they are implemented.

Positive accounting theory also has an economic focus and seeks to answer such questions as those below:
- What are the costs and benefits of using alternative accounting methods?
- What are the costs and benefits of regulation and the accounting standard-setting process?

- What is the effect of reported financial statements on share prices?
- Which accounting valuation models are superior in predicting future prices, returns, earnings or cash flows?

In order to answer these questions, positive accounting theories are based on some assumptions about the behaviour of individuals:

- Managers, investors, lenders and other individuals are assumed to be rational, evaluative financial utility maximisers (REMs).
- Managers have discretion to choose accounting policies that directly maximise their utility (self-interest) or to alter the firm's financing, investment and production policies to indirectly maximise their self-interest.
- Managers will take actions that maximise the value of the firm.

Positive accounting theorists argue that any proposed normative accounting model be tested and verified to assess its impact before being made an accounting standard. They argue against the use of anecdotal evidence and naive acceptance of political or academic prescriptions. Positive theorists argue their theory is more scientific in its methodology. Watts and Zimmerman comment:

> the theory and methodology underlying the economics-based empirical literature in accounting ... is based on the scientific concept of theory.[3]

LO 2 — STRENGTHS OF POSITIVE THEORY

Jensen argues that normative accounting theory precedes positive accounting theory.[4] In order to prescribe an appropriate accounting policy, he believes it is necessary to know how the world actually operates. To support his argument, he provides the following example using one form of a market value adjustment to the accounts to improve decision making:

> [A]ccountants have been justifiably concerned with the effects of general price level adjusted accounting (GPLA) on accounting numbers. But a manager interested in maximising the value of his firm also must estimate either explicitly or implicitly how such accounting procedures will affect firm value. And how GPLA affects firm value is a purely positive issue in the sense that the term is used in the social sciences.[5]

Jensen goes on to say:

> In the end, of course, we are all interested in normative questions; a desire how to accomplish goals motivates our interest in these methodological topics and in positive theories.[6]

Thus, we need to know how the financial world currently makes (or will make) adjustments to historical cost (i.e. do they actually make use of GPLA in their decisions) before normatively prescribing a change in accounting standards.

Dissatisfaction with prescriptive standards

One criticism of changing accounting standards is that they make certain prescriptions for accounting and auditing practice which are not entirely based on identified, empirical observations or methods. Watts and Zimmerman assert that valid prescription requires specification of both an objective and an objective function.[7] An objective might be monitoring and controlling management perquisites, or economic decision making and predicting future cash flows or alternatively, it might be a more equitable distribution of wealth.[8] Neither is an *a priori* superior objective, and positive theorists question whether accountants have any advantage over other individuals or societal groups in formulating accounting objectives. A positive example of an objective function is the specification of how the measurement of assets at their fair values affects the distribution of wealth between shareholders, lenders and managers. Note that this goes further than just specifying a normative objective to change accounting to measure fair values.

A normative theory based on value judgements, however, produces irrefutable prescriptions, even if it is developed logically. Normative accounting theory, in making prescriptions, specifies neither an objective nor an objective function that is independent of subjective preferences. The problem with this approach is that the validity of its prescriptions is irrefutable. According to Popper, *no* amount of empirical testing — that is, tests of a theory against 'real-world' data — can *prove* a theory to be correct, but a theory should be refutable, or capable of falsification.[9] Should the main objective of accounting be to provide information to investors so that they can predict future value, to provide a yardstick to assess the valuation of stock markets by reporting current values, to control management compensation payouts by requiring conservative accounting practices, or to disseminate wealth evenly throughout society? Because these objectives are subjective there is no means of assessing the appropriateness of their objectives. For example, assume that one normative objective prescribes that accountants should measure assets at current selling prices to provide lenders with information about the solvency of the firm. Assume that another normative theory prescribes that accountants should measure assets at their current cost to show investors how well their funds have been managed to maintain the operating capacity of the firm. Several factors prevent either theory being falsifiable:

- It is not possible to prove or refute the claim that financial accounts should provide lenders with a measure of the firm's solvency because this is a value-laden judgement.
- It is not possible to prove or refute the claim that an objective of financial accounts should be to report to investors about maintenance of the operating capacity — again, because this is a value-laden judgement.

The theories, therefore, cannot be ranked objectively because it is impossible to prove or refute claims that either objective is more important than the other. Thus, by Popper's standards, normative and prescriptive theory is methodologically weak.

There is a further methodological problem with normative and prescriptive theories: even if they were falsifiable, the choice of the objective function would still have to be justified. If we were to attribute to normative accounting theories an objective such as the improvement of the quality of information in accounting reports, it would be necessary to show that their prescriptions did actually serve that purpose. For instance, would users (including regulators, unions, debtholders, shareholders and management) find the accounting information produced by fair value actually improved decision making by shareholders? To answer this question, it would be necessary to ascertain the usefulness of balance sheets and income statements prepared on the basis of historical cost, and to show that the alternatives to historical cost were more useful.

This raises further questions. Does the profit number, prepared according to historical cost accounting principles, convey adequate information to market participants, and are they deceived by 'manipulations'? Are markets inefficient because of inadequate information disclosure or is accounting information becoming less relevant? Furthermore, why is it that after almost 40 years of proclamations of the merits of alternative fair value measurement techniques only a handful of companies voluntarily adopted them as supplementary disclosures? And, finally, have International Financial Reporting Standards (IFRSs) using fair value measurement had undesirable economic and social impacts on businesses and society, and have these accounting standards been decided without political interference? These questions illustrate the view of positive theorists that writers of prescriptive accounting standards may have failed to fully understand the effect of the adoption of fair value measurement methods.

From the above discussion, it should be clear why proponents of positive accounting theory may be viewed as taking the role of 'devil's advocate'.

First, they argue that theory should be able to generate hypotheses capable of falsification through empirical testing. Second, they deem it desirable to understand the historical application of accounting practice arising from the commercial market place, rather than make wholesale normative changes. Such an approach overcomes the need to supply an objective for accounting, given that no objective is *a priori* superior to any other. Third, if it is necessary to re-assess historical cost rules-based accounting principles, then fair value accounting lacks a theory and has not as yet supplied a systematic and empirical conceptual framework that underpins its use. Finally, it is one of the imperatives of positive accounting theory that there be at least some attempt to model the connection between accounting numbers, firms and markets and to analyse problems within an economic framework.

LO 3 — SCOPE OF POSITIVE ACCOUNTING THEORY

It is instructive to view the development of positive accounting theory in two stages. The first and chronologically earlier stage involved research into accounting and the behaviour of capital markets. The literature from this stage *did not* explain accounting practice. Rather, it investigated the connection between the announcement of accounting data and the reaction of share prices. The studies suggest that financial statements prepared according to historical cost methods did provide information which is used by the capital market in the valuation of the shares but, at the same time, accounting does not monopolise the information set used to value firms. That is, the assumption that accounting numbers are the primary driver of share prices was not observed and this supports the argument that perhaps accounting reports may best serve a stewardship function. Finally, the theories of financial economics, particularly the efficient markets hypothesis and the capital asset pricing model, were incorporated into this literature.

The second-stage literature sought to explain and predict accounting practices across firms. There were two central focuses. First, there was an attempt to explain whether firms make particular accounting choices for opportunistic reasons, such as to transfer wealth away from other claimholders to managers. This opportunistic perspective is often labelled *ex post*, since it assumes that managers choose accounting policies *after the fact* to maximise their own self-interest. The second perspective assumes that firms select accounting practices for efficiency reasons; that is, accounting policies are put in place *ex ante* to reduce the costs of contracting between the firm and its claimholders. It is important to remember that these two views are not mutually exclusive. The selection of an accounting method *ex ante* for reasons of efficiency does not preclude managers from the opportunistic selection, *ex post*, of accounting methods. The reason for this is that it is either impossible or inefficient to attempt to eliminate all residual opportunistic behaviour by managers. The efficiency perspective, similarly, does not require that accounting policy is actually selected *ex ante* — only that the choice is made as if it were chosen *ex ante* to maximise firm value rather than made opportunistically. Both focuses of this second stage of positive accounting literature draw extensively from the property rights contracting literature. First, however, we outline capital market research, which constituted the initial and ongoing research work in the positive accounting paradigm.

LO 4 → CAPITAL MARKET RESEARCH AND THE EFFICIENT MARKETS HYPOTHESIS

Two types of capital market research are particularly important to positive accounting theory: (1) those studies that attempt to determine the impact of the release of accounting information on share returns, and (2) those studies that consider the effects of changes in accounting policy on share prices. Most research in these areas has been conducted within a prevailing paradigm in financial economics — the efficient markets hypothesis (EMH). The EMH draws on microeconomic price theory, which is characterised by its emphasis on the demand and supply of information in markets.[10] In a competitive capital market the marginal cost of information equals the marginal revenue.

It was Fama and his associates who first coined the phrase 'efficient market' as being a 'market that adjusts rapidly to new information'.[11] Fama later formalised the definition of an efficient market as one 'in which prices "fully reflect" available information' based on assumptions that:[12]

- there are no transaction costs in trading securities
- information is available cost-free to all market participants
- there is agreement on the implications of current information for the current price and distributions of future prices.[13]

The implication of these assumptions is that in a capital market that is efficient, information is fully incorporated into share prices when it is released. As such, it is impossible, on average, to earn economic profits by trading on information. However, we are aware that these assumptions are not satisfied in any market. Hence, to accommodate different types of information sets and to enable empirical testing, Fama distinguished between three information sets:

- The 'weak form' of market efficiency where a security's price at any particular time fully reflects the information contained in its sequence of past prices — that is, investors cannot profit from extracting information based on cycles in prices (Dow theory), price patterns (head and shoulders), or other rules such as odd-lot behaviour, moving averages and relative strength.
- The 'semistrong form' form asserts that a security's price fully reflects all publicly available information, in addition to past prices. This means that there are no profitable trading strategies available to make excess profits from analysing publicly available economic, political, legal or financial data. Or more importantly by adjusting accounting reports for fair values that are not reported.
- The 'strong form' suggests that a security's price fully reflects all information, including information that is not publicly available; for example, private information only available to managers, directors or financial analysts who have access to insider information.

Of the three forms, the semistrong form is the one most directly related to accounting research, because accounting information is part of the subset of publicly available information. Normative accounting theorists and accounting standard-setting bodies give considerable effort to arguing the merits of the form in which accounting statements are disclosed to investors for decision making. However, if prices reflect all publicly available information (including current values of assets and liabilities), then normative arguments for 'proper' measurement and reporting are considerably weakened.

Note that, when we speak of the market as being efficient we do not suggest that every, or any, investor has knowledge of all information. Market efficiency does not mean that all financial information has been 'correctly' presented by a firm or 'properly' interpreted by individual decision makers. Nor does it imply that managers make the best management decisions or that investors can predict future events with absolute precision. Market efficiency in the context of the EMH simply means that security prices reflect the aggregate impact of all relevant information, and do so in an unbiased and rapid manner; that is, market prices are a 'fair game' and are close to 'fundamental value'. Markets are not perfect but they do anticipate and incorporate relevant data.

12.1 THEORY IN ACTION

Is relevant information incorporated into the price of shares?

Deregulation aids earnings at GrainCorp

by Carrie LaFrenz

Higher than expected grain receivals and export tonnages have propelled GrainCorp to a second full-year earnings upgrade, and the company is tipping a net profit of up to $63 million.

Australia's largest grain handler on the east coast expects net profit to be between $53 million and $63 million in 12 months to September 30, compared with a net loss of nearly $20 million last year.

GrainCorp managing director Mark Irwin told *The Australian Financial Review* the key drivers of better earnings were a result of the deregulated bulk wheat export market.

"The deregulated market has meant that our system has attracted more post-harvest grain than we anticipated. It pulled on-farm grain into our system because the exporters are happier to buy in the system rather than on-farm," he said.

The improved performance was underpinned by higher grain receivals, on target to exceed 9.5 million tonnes, compared with previous guidance of 9.2 million tones and 9.4 million tonnes.

Greater than expected high margin export volumes of 4.5 million tonnes to 5 million tonnes versus 4 million tonnes forecast previously, and higher than budgeted export sales, also helped earnings.

GrainCorp shares jumped 50 c, or 6.7 per cent, to finish at $8 yesterday after the upbeat news.

In mid-May the company upgraded full-year net earnings expectations to between $37 million and $42 million from its February forecast of between $23 million and $28 million.

This is a significant turnaround in performance after posting back-to-back losses of nearly $20 million in financial years 2007 and 2008.

ABN Amro Morgans analyst Belinda Moore said the amount of the upgrade was larger than expected; her previous net profit forecast was $44.5 million.

"It is also clear that a deregulated wheat market has provided GrainCorp with new and improved earnings streams," she said.

There was a lower net interest expense after a three-month contribution from the recent equity raising, she said.

A key risk to GrainCorp's forecast is the onset of an El Nino event, which is associated with lower than normal rainfall in spring. The Bureau of Metrology noted there was a high probability of El Nino developing.

Mr Irwin said there was still the prospect of another good winter grain harvest, but that finishing rain across the grain belt was an absolute necessity.

"We still have a long way until we see next harvest," he said. "The profile looks good, but it's all about spring rains in late August and September."

Source: The Australian Financial Review, 4 August 2009, p. 19, www.afr.com.

Questions

1. What impact has the unexpected increase in earnings had on GrainCorp's share price?
2. Apart from higher than expected grain receivals, what other factors have had a positive impact on earnings?
3. Does the article suggest market efficiency? Why or why not?

Whereas the EMH is a theory about the pricing mechanism of security markets, capital market research (CMR) is empirical research which uses statistical methods to test hypotheses concerning capital market behaviour. Most CMR uses the *market model*,[14] which derives from the capital asset pricing model (CAPM),[15] to estimate the unexpected (or abnormal) returns on the ordinary shares of a company at the time of an event occurring (e.g. profit announcements).

Market model

Share prices and returns are affected by both market-wide and firm-specific events. Therefore, if we are attempting to research and identify the impact of firm-unique information such as the release of earned profits, the returns arising from general market-related information (e.g. state of the economy, inflation etc.) must be first controlled. For example, if a security's return on the profit announcement day was +2.0%, this could be due to favourable market information affecting all shares, favourable firm-specific information, or a combination of both. To isolate that part of a security's return that is unique to the firm, we use the market model:

Raw return on day t	=	Constant average daily return	+	Return due to market moves	+	Return due to firm news
$\hat{R}_{i,t}$	=	α_i	+	$\beta_i(\hat{R}_{m,t})$	+	$\hat{\mu}_{i,t}$

$$(12.1)$$

where

$\hat{R}_{i,t}$ = the return on the firm i in period t

α_i = the constant average return (regardless of the return on the market)

β_i = the beta estimate of firm i (which is a measure of sensitivity to the return on the market)

$\hat{R}_{m,t}$ = the return on the aggregate market portfolio during period t

$\hat{\mu}_{i,t}$ = the residual error in period t, the portion of the raw return due to firm-unique events (individual earnings, dividend announcements or management policies).

Estimates of α_i and β_i are determined by using ordinary least-squares regression which relates historical firm rates of return with historical market returns. The regressions are normally run using 60 pre-event monthly returns ($t = 0$ to -59) over a five-year period.

The market model has a number of assumptions which should be made clear:

- investors are risk-averse
- returns are normally distributed (the mean and standard deviation are sufficiently descriptive of security returns) and investors select their portfolios on this basis
- investors have homogeneous expectations
- markets are complete (all participants are price takers, there are no transactions costs, no taxes, and there are rational expectations by investors).

According to Fama's conception of efficient markets, the abnormal rate of return on firm i for the period $t(\hat{\mu}_{i,t})$ is equal to the realised rate of return ($R_{i,t}$) less the expected rate of return for the period t, for asset i ($E(R_{i,t})$), *given* the information set available at time $t - (\theta_{t-1})$.[16] This is expressed mathematically as:

$$\hat{\mu}_{i,t} = R_{i,t} - E(R_{i,t} : \theta_{t-1})$$

$$(12.2)$$

Taking expectations:

$$E(R_{i,t}) = \alpha_i + \beta_i E(R_{m,t})$$

$$(12.3)$$

the estimated abnormal rate of return for the shares for period t is the difference between the actual return and the expected return:

$$\hat{\mu}_{i,t} = \hat{R}_{i,t} - \alpha_i - \beta_i E(R_{m,t}) \qquad (12.4)$$

In an efficient market, such abnormal rates of return will average to zero across many periods (T):

$$\frac{1}{T}\sum_{t=1}^{T} \hat{\mu}_{i,t} = 0 \qquad (12.5)$$

The abnormal return derived from the market model $\mu_{i,t}$ captures that part of the total return not attributable to factors affecting the market portfolio but, rather, to firm-specific factors. It is for this reason that abnormal returns, $\mu_{i,t}$, are studied in capital market research when researchers are interested in the short-term reactions of share prices to accounting factors hypothesised to affect specific companies.

These concepts can be illustrated by the following example. Assume you are given the following one-period market model data on BHP Billiton (BHP) for the calendar quarter ending June 2009:

$$\alpha_{BHP} = 2.0\% \qquad\qquad R_{BHP} = 12.0\%$$
$$\beta_{BHP} = 0.7 \qquad\qquad R_M = 10.0\%$$

These data are displayed in figure 12.1. If the market index (e.g. the Australian All Ordinaries) had a return of 0 per cent, the expected return on BHP Billiton would be 2 per cent (α). However, the market had a 10 per cent return. The β_{BHP} of 0.7 indicates that a 10 per cent index return is *expected* to result in a 7 per cent return on BHP Billiton above the constant 2 per cent. Adding the 2 per cent and 7 per cent results in an *expected return* of 9 per cent. However, BHP Billiton's actual return was 12 per cent. The difference between the actual 12 per cent and the expected 9 per cent is the error during this time period, 3 per cent, and is called the abnormal return.

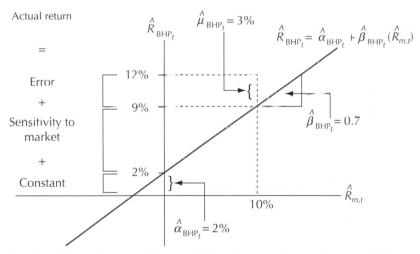

FIGURE 12.1 Sample market model for i = BHP and t = quarter ending June 2009

Two additional steps are usually taken before data from capital market research are analysed. First, an average *firm-unique return (AR)* is found for each month (or discrete period selected) for all firms in the study, by adding up and dividing as follows:

$$\text{Average market model residual in month } t: AR_t = \frac{\sum_{i=1}^{N} \hat{\mu}_{i,t}}{N}$$

where

> AR_t = average firm-unique return for month t
> $\hat{\mu}_{i,t}$ = firm-unique return on stock i during month t
> N = number of firms examined in a given month.

Second, a *cumulative average abnormal firm-unique return (CAR)* is found for each month by summing all average firm-unique returns for a particular month. Mathematically, using 18 monthly observations (6 after the specified event and 12 up to the event day) we have:

$$\text{Cumulative market model residual in month } t : CAR_t = \sum_{(t=-12)}^{6} AR_t$$

$$\text{where } -12 \leq t \leq 6$$

To empirically evaluate the price impact of accounting information, either the AR_t or the CAR_t values may be examined. If the released accounting numbers have incremental information (i.e. not previously known and acted on by the market) then there will be upward or downward residuals, if not then they will be zero (or close). If they are zero then either the accounting numbers do not have information content or the market has used other information and does not await the release of accounting reports before making pricing decisions.

Having the prerequisite understanding of the market model we now turn to a consideration of the empirical studies.

LO 5 — IMPACT OF ACCOUNTING PROFITS ANNOUNCEMENTS ON SHARE PRICES

Direction

A study by Ball and Brown is the foundation stone of positive accounting.[17] As already suggested, one motivation behind positive accounting theory was to determine the information content that accounting profit had for the stock market, in light of the criticisms by normative theorists of historical cost methods of calculating profit. The general view by normative theorists was that historical cost profit was meaningless, since it aggregated the results of applying diverse procedures to various types of economic data. On this point Ball and Brown noted:

> The value of analytical attempts to develop measurements capable of definitive interpretation is not at issue. What is at issue is the fact that an analytical model does not itself assess the significance of departures from its implied measurements. Hence it is dangerous to conclude, in the absence of further empirical testing, that a lack of substantive meaning implied a lack of utility.[18]

Ball and Brown tested the usefulness of the historical cost profit figure to investment decisions. They argued that if the information contained in the profit figure were useful and informative in making investment decisions, then share prices would adjust to reflect that information.

Ball and Brown argued that *unexpected* increases in profits represent new information for the market. In an efficient capital market, any change in expectations of a firm's cash flow (imbedded in current profits) will lead to changes in share prices and this will occur before, or very quickly after, the profit figure is released. Further, significant positive economic returns can be expected to cease after announcement date, since in a semistrong-form efficient market the market will move quickly to impound that information.

Ball and Brown used US data for 261 firms for the period 1946–66 to examine the price impact from unexpected profit announcements. They identified each announcement as either 'favourable' or 'unfavourable'. Favourable announcements were cases in which reported profits were greater than predicted by a naive mechanical forecasting model (i.e. greater than last year's profit). Unfavourable announcements were cases in which reported profits were less than last year. For each group, Ball and Brown calculated CARs for the 12 months before and the 6 months following the announcement. Results are shown in figure 12.2.

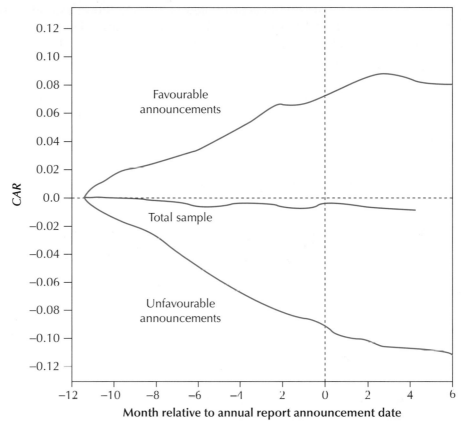

FIGURE 12.2 Share price movement around 'abnormal' profit announcements
Source: R. Ball and P. Brown, 'An empirical evaluation of accounting income numbers', *Journal of Accounting Research*, vol. 6, no. 2, Autumn 1968, p. 169. Reprinted with permission.

Note that the market anticipates favourable or unfavourable profit reports, and prices are adjusted accordingly. The CAR rises throughout the year for favourable profits and falls for unfavourable profits. This is evidence that the market is capable of forecasting firms' profits (more accurately than a naive profit model) and adjusting share prices accordingly. Further, some of the favourable, or unfavourable, announcements were not completely anticipated, and prices continued to adjust after the announcement. Although post-announcement price drifts were not instantaneous, they were fairly small and might not have been large enough to offset transaction costs (commissions and search costs). Overall, Ball and Brown concluded that much of the price adjustment to the change in profits (85–90%) occurs before the announcement month, and that this is attributable to the continuous release of information to the market in both accounting (e.g. quarterly profit) and non-accounting format (e.g. analysts, financial journalists).

Ball and Brown's results had several implications for financial accounting theory. First, there was significant information content in the historical profit figure despite the apparently haphazard way it was generated. Second, the evidence suggested there was a continuous release of information to the market and thus accounting was not the only source of information about firms — in fact it is fairly minor and may only serve as a feedback to the market. Third, the market seemed to be reasonably consistent in anticipating the information in accounting reports, and it was not possible to trade on accounting information, after its release, to earn economic profits after transaction costs were taken into account.

The studies which followed Ball and Brown's mostly supported their conclusions. In 1970, Brown replicated the study for Australian companies.[19] The results were similar, although he found that the adjustment during the year was slower and that there was more of a price adjustment in the 'announcement month'. Watts and Zimmerman suggest that this may be attributed to the fact that Australian companies issue half-yearly reports, not quarterly reports as in the United States.[20] This suggests that, in Australia, annual reports are a more important source of information about companies than they are in the United States. Watts and Zimmerman also suggest that this is because companies trading on Australian stock exchanges are smaller, on average, than companies trading on the New York Stock Exchange and that, apart from annual reports, there tends to be fewer sources of information about smaller firms.

Foster sought further evidence on Ball and Brown's finding that only 10–15 per cent of the information value of profits was conveyed by the annual announcements.[21] He asked whether this was attributable to the fact that quarterly profits had been announced in the interim. The other issue he investigated was whether the 10–15 per cent figure *understated* reality, since a part or all of the adjustment could have been made in the weeks or days during the month preceding the actual announcement. He analysed quarterly profit announcements and daily rather than monthly rates of return. An important finding was that approximately 32 per cent of the cumulative abnormal returns found over 60 trading days were experienced on the announcement date. This is a significant increase over the 10–15 per cent Ball and Brown reported and suggests that quarterly accounting profits are a timely source of information for the capital market. Foster's findings have been supported in subsequent studies using Australian data.[22]

Magnitude

The studies just discussed concentrated on the *direction* of unexpected profits and abnormal returns, that is, positive/negative abnormal returns are associated with unexpected increases/decreases in profits. However, it is also possible to investigate the relationship between the *magnitude* of the unexpected change in profits and abnormal returns. The theory underlying these tests is that if an accounting profit release has information content, the magnitude of abnormal returns will be related to the magnitude of unexpected profits. The first published work to investigate this question was by Beaver, Clarke and Wright.[23] Companies listed on the New York Stock Exchange were divided into 25 portfolios, based on the magnitude of each company's unexpected profits (as a percentage of expected profits). The mean annual abnormal rate of return for the 12 months ending 3 months after the firm's financial year was calculated for each portfolio. These measures, together with unexpected profits, were then ranked from highest positive to most negative and a strong relationship was found with magnitude.

In a further study of this relationship, Beaver, Lambert and Morse found that, on average, there was only a 0.1–0.15 per cent abnormal return associated with 1 per cent unexpected profits.[24] One reason for the small response measure is likely to be that the tests did not permit the possibility that firms might have different proportional relationships between unexpected profits and abnormal returns. That is, they did not allow for the fact that the sensitivity of the relationship between abnormal returns and unexpected profits (the earnings response coefficient, ERC)[25] can vary from firm to firm.

Information asymmetry and firm size

The information content of unexpected profits announcements may be inversely related to firm size; that is, the smaller the firm, the more information is contained in accounting reports. This differential information proposition relies on the fact that the amount of information available from sources other than accounting reports is an increasing function of firm size, and is developed from the theory of transaction costs and different incentives for information search. If the costs of information search are fixed and constant across firms, then the incentive to undertake research for mispricing is greater for large firms than for small firms. There are a larger number of shares in large firms and a more liquid market that makes it easier to sell and to hide your superior trading activities. Thus, armed with knowledge of mispricing, larger total profits can be made compared to knowledge of mispricing in a small firm.

But, Freeman[26] argues that the possibility of increased search costs associated with increased complexity of larger firms is offset by:

- larger firms providing a greater variety of information than smaller firms
- larger firms having a higher degree of exposure by constant reporting in the financial press and by the search activities of financial analysts.

Finally, institutional investors are more likely to trade in large firms owing to liquidity and contractual constraints. For example, institutions cannot hold a large percentage of the shares in small firms and expect to be able to sell the shares immediately without price discounts. Further, because institutions are a major source of demand for information, then financial analysts may concentrate their search activities on larger firms. In summary, the differential information hypothesis implies that the information contained in accounting releases should be more important for smaller firms than for larger firms.

Empirical research has shown that profit releases have greater information impact for small firms. Grant first compared the information content of annual profit announcements for smaller over-the-counter (OTC) firms against New York Stock Exchange firms.[27] He found that the reaction of the market to annual profit announcements was considerably greater for OTC firms. Atiase analysed the differential impact of quarterly profit announcements from American Stock Exchange and New York Stock Exchange firms. He concluded that the degree of a firm's security price change associated with a profit announcement was inversely related to firm size.[28]

Freeman focused on the timing differences in the adjustment process of small and large firms to profit announcements.[29] He showed that:

- security prices of large firms reflect profit information earlier than the security prices of small firms
- the magnitude of cumulative abnormal returns surrounding a profit announcement is larger for small firms than for large firms.

The above studies were confirmed by Shores who used a finer daily data set to examine market reactions.[30] Shores's results supported the hypothesis of a firm size differential.

Magnitude of profit releases from other firms

Other capital market research has investigated not only the responsiveness of firms' returns to their own profits announcements, but also the responsiveness of returns to other firms' profits announcements. This 'information transfer' research is based on the belief that unexpected profits for one firm in a particular industry would transfer across the industry. Thus, the first reporter contains the most information.

Foster examined information transfers using US data for 10 industries and found that the variance of abnormal returns for competing firms increased when another firm in the same industry made a profit announcement.[31] Clinch and Sinclair reported results similar to Foster's using Australian data concerning management forecasts instead of profits announcements.[32] Further, they showed that the last firm in the industry to announce its profits for a particular period had the smallest share price reaction. Following on from the Clinch and Sinclair approach, Freeman and Tse examined the potential for investors to revise their profit predictions in the light of other companies' profits announcements.[33] Consistent with previous results, they found significant price reactions by non-announcing firms to early announcers' sales and profit changes. They extended previous studies by examining the relation between actual information transfers (non-announcers' price reactions to the announcements of other firms in the industry) and potential information transfers (the strength of the co-movement of profits reported by firms in the industry). Consistent with their hypothesis, they found the association between late announcers' price reactions and early announcers' news was strongest for those industries with the highest profit correlations.

Volatility

Other researchers have used alternative 'indexes' of the information content of profits announcements. One alternative is the variance of the abnormal return, first used by Beaver.[34] The theory underlying this test is that if there is information content in profit announcements, we would expect to observe *larger* price changes on the announcement date. Beaver's results were consistent with this hypothesis, because in the announcement week the variance of firms' returns was 67 per cent larger than normal. The results of Beaver's study can be seen in figure 12.3.

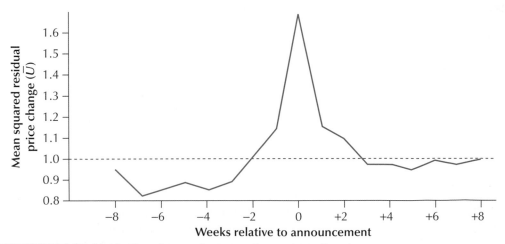

FIGURE 12.3 Residual price changes in squared unsystematic returns

Source: W Beaver, 'The information content of annual earnings announcements', *Empirical Research in Accounting: Selected Studies 1968*, supplement to *Journal of Accounting Research*, vol. 6, 1968, p. 91.

Grant noted that OTC firms experience a greater variance of abnormal returns than New York Stock Exchange firms at announcement date, which further supports the contention that the information content of profits will be greater where the firm is smaller and there are fewer alternative sources of information.

Other studies investigating the information content of profits announcements have used different research methods. These include the behaviour of implicit return variances derived from option pricing theory and movements in trading volume around the announcement date.[35] In general, they confirm that there is abnormal volatility in return or trading volume on or about the date of profits announcements.

Thus, while profit reports are relatively less important for large firms they play an increasing role as the size of the firm decreases and the access to other information is reduced. So in markets which have reduced information flows, accounting becomes more important.

Association studies and earnings response coefficients

Although profit release event studies clearly demonstrated that accounting profit at the same time captured a portion of the information set that is reflected in security returns, the evidence also suggested that competing sources of information pre-empted the information in annual profits by about 70–85 per cent. In this sense, the release of annual accounting figures is not a particularly timely source of information to the capital markets.

This observation led to another capital market approach labelled association studies. These studies measure the impact of accounting measures on share prices over a longer event window (usually one year or longer). Basically, the objective is to test the impact of accounting variables and a wider information set that is reflected in securities returns over a longer period. The ERC is obtained by running an ordinary least-squares regression with returns (or unexpected returns) as the dependent variable and profits (or unexpected profits) as the independent variable. The R^2 (the 'goodness-of-fit' of the regression model) and the slope (ERC) coefficient (the sensitivity of returns to profits) can then be used to assess the informativeness (value-relevance) of profits.

Determinants of firm value

Brown[36] applied a simplified version of Modigliani and Miller's[37] firm valuation model to depict the ERC as the reciprocal of the firm's cost of capital. The Modigliani–Miller (MM) model is given by equation 12.6:

$$V - \tau D = X(1 - \tau)/\rho + G \qquad (12.6)$$

where
$V - \tau D$ = capitalised value of the firm adjusted for the tax benefit of leverage
X = 'sustainable' earnings before interest and tax
$X(1 - \tau)$ = tax-adjusted earning
ρ = cost of capital
G = value of growth opportunities.

There are a number of linear regression models used to estimate the ERC. The more common models are:

$$\Delta P_t = \alpha_1 + \beta_1 E_t + \varepsilon_t \qquad (12.7)$$

$$\Delta P_t = \alpha_1 + \beta_1 E_t + \beta_2 \Delta E_t + \varepsilon_t \qquad (12.8)$$

$$P_t = \alpha_1 + \beta_1 NBV_t + \beta_2 E_t + \beta_3 \Delta E_t + \varepsilon_t \qquad (12.9)$$

where

P_t = the price of any share
E_t = a measure of earnings
NBV_t = net book value
Δ = the change variable.

The first two models are described as information models that relate earnings levels and changes to changes in price (ERC = β_1). The second model is derived from the research of Easton and Harris and simply adds changes in earnings as an additional explanatory variable (ERC = $\beta_1 + \beta_2$). The third model is a variant of the Ohlson model and is more commonly described as a valuation model because it combines the earnings coefficient (ERC = $\beta_2 + \beta_3$) with a net book or equity coefficient (β_1) to explain the stock price level. The book coefficient can then be further decomposed into its different components and tested for their incremental value relevance. For example, into total assets and liabilities, and then (say) assets decomposed into different asset classes (e.g. current, financial, tangible, intangible) in order to reveal the main drivers The valuation approach appears to be the approach adopted by the IASB because of its emphasis on 'fair value' measurement and the statement of financial position rather than taking an income approach.

Factors which can affect the ERC

There are a number of economic factors which can affect the association between profits and prices. These are examined below.

Risk and uncertainty

Researchers offer a definitive explanation as to why risk negatively affects the ERC.[38] Greater risk directly translates into a larger discount rate, which in turn reduces the discounted present value of the revisions in expected future profits, and the ERC. Hence, there is a significant negative association between beta and the ERC using reverse regressions of unexpected profits on raw returns.[39]

On the other hand, uncertainty has a rather more indirect effect on the ERC. Uncertainty about future operations can affect either the expected future economic benefits or the discount rate. In either case, the predicted impact on the ERC will be negative. Collins and DeAngelo found that uncertainty regarding a firm's future profits increased during a proxy contest for board seats and reduced the ERC.[40] Uncertainty can also be introduced by accounting manipulations that garble the 'true profits' signal about firm value.[41] In turn, these deficient accounting procedures produce low-quality profits that only have a weak association with prices. Lev states:

> While misspecification of the return/earnings relation or the existence of investor irrationality (noise trading) may contribute to the weak association between earnings and stock returns, the possibility that the fault lies with the low quality (information content) of reported earnings looms large.[42]

The concept of 'noise' in reported profits being responsible for lower ERCs was indirectly discussed via hypothesised agency/contracting arrangements.[43] An agency/contracting argument arises when managers of poorly performing firms manipulate reported accounting figures to avoid debt covenant violation or to enhance the likelihood of future bonuses. The predicted contracting-based relationship between low profitability and low ERCs was found by Jeter and Chaney to be significant, consistent with a market perception that poorly performing firms' profit reports contain more noise. Other studies suggested that 'noise' is induced by the use of liberal (as opposed to conservative) accounting policies.[44]

Audit quality

If the magnitude of the ERC is a function of the credibility of reported profits, and if the external auditing process is intended to enhance profit credibility,[45] then ERC magnitude should be a function of audit quality.[46] Analytical research suggests that audit firm size and audit quality are positively related,[47] and empirical evidence consistent with this argument is presented by others.[48] Additionally, Knapp presents evidence that audit committee members perceive that auditor size significantly influences the quality of the audit service provided.[49] Another facet of audit quality, audit industry specialisation,[50] was investigated and showed a significant positive association between audit industry specialisation among Big 6 auditors and client firm ERCs.[51]

The research findings of Choi and Jeter looked at audit quality in the context of uncertainty with regard to the future profit stream.[52] They compared pre- and post-qualification ERCs for 130 firms and found a qualified audit report signals to the market that the profit numbers generated by the firm are 'noisier', less reliable, and result in lower ERCs.

More direct evidence of a positive correlation between ERC magnitude and audit quality has been presented[53] by using Securities and Exchange Commission (SEC) sanctions against auditors as a measure of audit quality, where it was observed that there was a decline in the ERCs of companies whose (Big 6) auditors were subject to SEC sanctions.

Industry

An alternative approach to investigating the relationship between ERCs and uncertainty and/or the information environment was adopted by a few authors who argued that firms within a particular industry, because they face similar factor and product markets, should be more homogeneous in terms of outcome uncertainty than firms in other industries.[54]

They hypothesised that industries with the greatest perceived outcome uncertainty (due to either market uncertainties or lack of available information) would have the greatest ERCs. The finding of significant cross-industry variation in ERCs, although consistent with their argument, added little to our understanding of how industry-specific factors influence the sensitivity of the returns–profit relation. Like firm size, industry is unlikely to be important in its own right, but is capable of acting as a surrogate for other factors (such as risk) that determine the market's responsiveness to a profit innovation.

Interest rates

Collins and Kothari predict a negative temporal relation between ERCs and the risk-free rate of interest. The logic here is straightforward. The discount rate at any point in time is the sum of the risk-free rate of return and a risk premium. If the risk-free rate of interest rises, then, other things being equal, the present value of the revisions in expectations of future profit innovations falls; thus inducing a negative association between interest rate levels and ERCs. However, this argument ignores the possibility that changes in interest are simply changes in expected inflation and that the firm passes on the changes in inflation to its customers in the form of higher prices. In this case, ERCs would be unrelated to interest rate changes. Thus, the negative relation between interest rates and ERC implicitly assumes interest rate changes co-vary positively with changes in real interest rates.

There is another related concern regarding the temporal relation between interest rates and ERCs. The question is whether the interest rate is a causal determinant of ERCs given that a large component of nominal interest rates is inflation. The finance and macroeconomics literature documents that shocks to inflation are negatively related to both shocks to real economic activity and stock market returns.[55] Furthermore, real economic activity and business outlook is negatively related to expected rates of returns on shares and bonds.[56] This means that interest rates might be positively related to the risk premium. Thus, the interest rate effect on ERCs might be via a time-varying risk premium; that is, the expected return on the market minus the risk-free rate of interest.[57] Relatively little research has been done on this aspect of interest rates having a time-varying impact on the ERC, and it is an area for future research.

Financial leverage

The impact of leverage was analysed by Jeter and Chaney who found a negative association between leverage and the ERC.[58] They also found the strength of the association between beta and the ERC was insignificant after controlling for the effects of leverage, suggesting that a firm's debt to equity ratio better captures differences in risk more effectively than beta.

There are a number of other theories. The first is the 'default' theorem in which ERC is positively related to the profit persistence factor, and negatively related to the firm's default risk (i.e. the financial leverage level).[59] This suggests that as financial leverage steadily increases, the value of the firm falls in response and, hence, profits have less information for prices.

Second, the 'maximum debt' theorem argues that when financial leverage increases, share prices concurrently increase for two reasons. The first is that the tax deductibility of interest on borrowed funds creates a tax shield which increases with the level of corporate debt, thereby lowering the weighted average cost of capital.[60] The second relates to the positive signal that corporate leverage conveys. The willingness of managers to increase financial leverage is an expression of managers' confidence in the future and the belief that the firm will generate funds in excess of the adjusted weighted average cost of capital.[61]

Finally, the 'optimal leverage' approach assumes there is an ideal financial leverage position for each firm. That is the benefits of the tax shield will not be infinite. As a firm increases financial leverage, the level of risk and the possibility of bankruptcy increase, and to compensate for increased leverage, both debt and equity investors require higher rates of return. Further, agency costs also increase as debt and equityholders impose increasingly higher monitoring and bonding costs on the firm. Hence, the optimal leverage approach predicts that the direction of changes in share prices is conditional on the firm's financial leverage relative to its ideal. Hodgson and Stevenson-Clarke showed that if the firm is above the hypothesised ideal level of debt, then the ERC is lower.[62] Conversely, if the firm is below ideal leverage, the ERC is higher.

Firm growth

Growth opportunities will be reflected in higher ERCs. Growth opportunities include existing projects or opportunities to invest in projects that are expected to yield rates of return that exceed the risk-adjusted rate of return commensurate with the systematic risk of the project's cash flows. Collins and Kothari argued that the price reaction would be greater than that implied by the time series persistence of profits, because persistence estimates from historical data are likely to be 'deficient in accurately reflecting *current* growth opportunities'. They then demonstrated a significant positive correlation between the ERC and the market to book value of equity ratio which they used to measure expected growth.[63] Other research has been undertaken on the relation between a firm's life cycle and business strategy to explain the cross-sectional variation in ERCs.[64] It has been argued that, depending on a firm's stage in its life cycle, financial statement information is differentially informative about a firm's value, such that ERCs are predictably related to a firm's stage in its life cycle.[65]

This area of research has had limited work and offers the opportunity to undertake research into metrics that may predict future growth such as the level of intangibles, marketing, brand awareness, research and development, and so on.

Permanent and temporary profits

Other work in the area of ERCs has linked the finance theory emphasis on discounted cash flows and accounting measurements in the following manner:

- Profits announcements are analysed by investors who estimate how much of any unexpected profit will be permanent (i.e. they estimate profit persistence).
- With the belief that permanent (persistent) increases in profits will eventually appear as permanent increases in dividends, investors value shares at their revised expectation of the discounted cash flows attributable to the shares.

Thus, if a large (small) amount of unexpected profit was expected to persist, large (small) abnormal returns would be expected. There is therefore a positive relationship between the size of the revision to expected 'permanent' profit and ERCs. However, note that the sensitivity of the relationship is likely to vary between firms according to the risk factor used in discounting the revised expected cash flows attributable to the shares.

Ali and Zarowin examined the modelling of both profit persistence and ERCs, arguing that when the usual estimates of unexpected profits as the difference between current year profit and previous year profit are combined with the usual assumption that unexpected profits are purely permanent, the result is an overestimate of the permanent components of annual profit and the ERC.[66]

Non-linear modelling

One criticism of the ERC research is that the explanatory power of profits for prices is low (typically the R-squares are below 10%). The previously mentioned ERC studies applied linear statistical techniques to estimate the ERC, but some recent research has considered non linear techniques. A non-linear relationship rests on the premise that the absolute value of unexpected profits is negatively correlated with profit persistence. That is, as the surprise in profits increases, the likelihood that the profits surprise is permanent will decrease. Pragmatically, knowledge of these relationships is important, because valuation theory predicts that analysts and investors should place greater emphasis on forecasting high-persistence profits than low-persistence profits.

Freeman and Tse[67] argued unexpected profits–returns would be better explained by an S-shaped arctan relationship which is convex for bad-news firms and concave for good-news firms. Figure 12.4 provides an illustration of some hypothesised non-linear relationships. Measuring unexpected earnings (profits) as deviations from median quarterly analyst forecasts, Freeman and Tse found that the application of the non-linear arctan model resulted in increased ERCs and greater predictive power in the form of higher adjusted R-squares. They concluded that previous research which hypothesised and applied simple linear models may have misspecified the profits–returns relationship.

The arctan model of the relationship between profits and share returns postulates a symmetrical relationship between positive and negative unexpected profits. It is, however, possible that good news has a differential impact on share prices when compared with bad news. For example, increased unexpected profits may mean greater internal funds

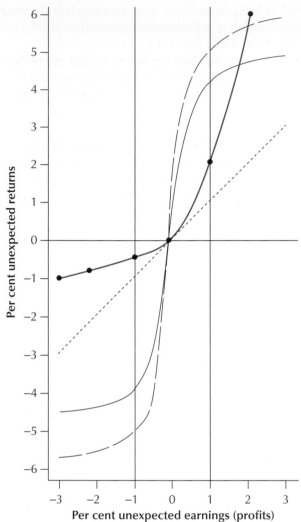

available to fund expansion, which leads to a lowering of leverage and financial risk and greater expectation of permanent increases in profits. On the other hand, lower unexpected profits may force firms to take on additional debt or resort to increased equity raising, with subsequent additional costs. The flatter relationship between negative unexpected profits and unexpected returns also represents the fact that, as the value of firms decreases, equity takes on more of the attributes of an option and also provides management with incentives to improve performance. This relationship is represented as an exponential function in figure 12.4.

Research in Australia shows that an arctan model is a descriptive representation of the relationship between profits and prices.[68] That is, large changes in profits are not incorporated in prices and the combination of profit levels and profit changes increases the explanatory power of the ERC by about 20 per cent. We can also observe that earnings between −1 per cent and +1 per cent in the arctan models represent expected permanent earnings or 'core' earnings.

FIGURE 12.4 Hypothetical non-linear functions relating unexpected returns (*UR*) to price-deflated unexpected earnings (*UE*). Unexpected returns are 0.04 arctan (300 *UE*) for the long-dashed line, 0.03 arctan (400 *UE*) for the solid line, 0.10 arctan (10 *UE*) for the short-dashed line, and the exponential function e^{UE}−1 for the dotted line.

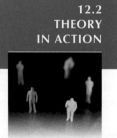

Managing costs doing business better

New Wattyl boss to target costs

by Jeffrey Hutton

Wattyl's incoming managing director will keep the country's second-biggest paint maker independent, aiming instead to cut costs as high levels of debt and sluggish housing demand hurt profits and narrow the company's options.

Tony Dragicevich will replace Wattyl's current managing director, John Nolan, on October 19, the company said yesterday. Mr Nolan has been in the role since May 2005.

"I didn't join the company to find a buyer," Mr Dragicevich said. "At the end of the day you have to do what's best for shareholders, but it's not on my agenda." "It's really about

The relative strengths of the associations between share returns and profits and share returns and cash flow for New York Stock Exchange firms was examined by Dechow.[80] Observing that the contemporaneous association between share returns and profits was stronger than that between share returns and net cash flows/cash from operations, Dechow argued that this was because the accrual process alleviates timing and matching problems which cause cash flow to be a noisy measure of firm performance. She further showed that cash flows play a more important role in the marketplace (a) the smaller the absolute magnitude of accruals, (b) the longer the measurement interval, and (c) the shorter the firm's operating cycle, and this demonstrates the ability of firm-specific factors to influence the magnitudes of both profit and cash flow response coefficients.

The previously mentioned research by Sloan who showed that investors do not understand the different persistent attributes of cash flows and accruals is probably the most important piece of research in this area. Sloan decomposed earnings into cash and accrual components and found significant economic profits can be made from investing in a hedged portfolio of high and low accrual firms. This is an area of continued research in financial accounting.

Balance sheet and balance sheet components

Ohlson argues that the balance sheet, together with profit, provides a higher proportion of the explanatory power for prices (see equation 12.9).[81] Subsequent research by Francis and Schipper indeed showed that profit and net book value account for approximately 60 per cent of price.[82] However, over the period 1952–94, profit declined in relevance from as high as 45 per cent down to 5–10 per cent, and asset and liability components in the balance sheet increased (see figure 12.6) from 20 per cent to 55 per cent.

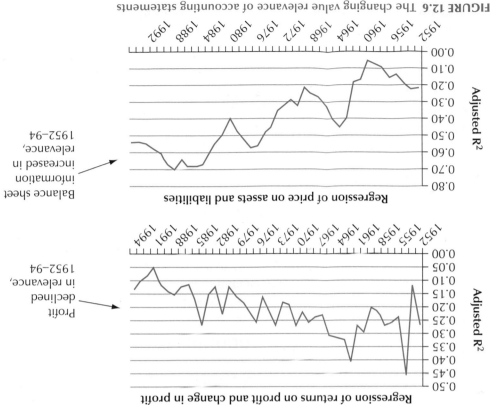

Regression of returns on profit and change in profit

Regression of price on assets and liabilities

FIGURE 12.6 The changing value relevance of accounting statements

Source: After J. Francis and K. Schipper, 'Have financial statements lost their relevance?' *Journal of Accounting Research,* vol. 37, no. 2, 1999, p. 340.

Decomposing profit and balance sheet items along lines suggested by investment analysts (see Lev and Thiagarajan) and adjusting for other macroeconomic conditions also increases the fundamental explanatory power of the accounting variables for price.[83] These modelling issues are fundamental to assessing the determinants of price and intrinsic value. Overall, with these adjustments and modelling refinements we might expect to get the explanatory power from fundamental accounting variables up to about 70–75 per cent.

Methodological issues

Many of the studies outlined in this chapter are developments of Ball and Brown's original paper.[84] As Williams and Findlay suggest, to argue that the results of the research are supportive of EMH and that that the form of accounting is not that important for valuation purposes derives, in part, from the fact that the EMH is assumed to be descriptively valid.[85] There was, as Watts and Zimmerman suggest,[86] no attempt to differentiate the EMH from two competing hypotheses — managers use accounting to systematically mislead the share market or that the market is efficient and ignores accounting changes that have no cash flow consequences. In other words, are markets aware of the implications of accounting manipulations and adjust for them or are they fooled by manipulations?

We now turn to a consideration of the literature that does attempt to discriminate between these hypotheses. The hypotheses at the centre of this literature are referred to as the mechanistic and the no-effects hypotheses, and the research seeks to determine whether accounting manipulations can 'fool' market participants and if there are trading strategies that arise from different forms of accounting.

LO 6 ◄— TRADING STRATEGIES

Post-announcement drift

In most studies of the information content of accounting numbers, capital market efficiency has been assumed or the test of efficiency has related to whether the accounting numbers have associated cash flow consequences. However, some researchers have questioned this assumption. The two findings which initially questioned the efficiency of capital markets are the presence of post-announcement drift that has been documented in a number of studies, including the original Ball and Brown paper,[87] and Ou and Penman's derivation of a trading rule whereby abnormal returns can be earned by trading on accounting information that is already public.[88] The post-announcement drift occurs where abnormal returns continue after a profit announcement, so that the information content of the profit announcement is not fully incorporated into the share price at the announcement date. A large fraction of the drift occurs on subsequent profit announcement dates and the drift consistently has the predicted sign for the extreme profits portfolios. These properties diminish the likelihood of an efficient markets explanation for the drift. Kothari comments:

The survival of the anomaly 30 years after it was first discovered leads me to believe that there is a rational explanation for it, but evidence consistent with rationality remains elusive.[89]

Further, the post-announcement drift has survived a battery of tests in Bernard and Thomas and many other attempts to explain it away.[90] It appears to be incremental to a long list of anomalies that are inconsistent with the joint hypothesis of market and accounting information efficiency.

Ou and Penman's studies examined whether the current year's financial statement accounting information could be used to forecast the sign of the following year's profit change sufficiently to enable positive abnormal returns. They found that using sixteen accounting variables to predict the possibility that a firm's profit will increase, and then buying shares if the probability exceeded 0.6 and selling shares if the probability was less than 0.4, they could earn market-adjusted returns of 12.6 per cent over a 2-year holding period.

The significance of the challenge to a major assumption underlying much of capital markets theory cannot be understated. As Ball has commented:

> The apparent predictability of abnormal returns after earnings announcements has become one of the most significant anomalies in financial markets research, for several reasons. First, the magnitude is daunting; for example, the estimated abnormal return from trading on 'old' earnings information exceeds the normal return on the market. Second, the anomaly is ubiquitous: earnings announcements occur every quarter for every stock. Third, the anomaly is scientifically indisputable; it appeared in Ball and Brown (1968) and has been replicated, consistently and with increasing precision, in one of the most carefully and thoroughly researched areas of the empirical financial economics literature. Fourth, taken at face value the anomaly implies that share markets, which are central to the economy and which one would think are paradigm examples of the competitive model, grossly fail the test of competitive economic theory. Fifth, the anomaly challenges the theory underlying most of the widely-used models in modern financial economics.[91]

Several studies, such as Sloan 1996, examine long-horizon stock market efficiency with respect to accrual management and analysts' optimistic profit growth forecasts. Their argument is that information from firms' owners and/or managers and financial analysts about firms' prospects, such as profit growth, reflects their optimism and that the market behaves naively in that it takes the optimistic forecasts at face value. Some studies show that discretionary accruals in periods immediately before initial public offerings and seasoned equity offerings are positive.

Evidence also suggests that the market fails to recognise the profit manipulation, which is inferred on the basis of predictable subsequent negative long-horizon price performance. Research also examines whether analysts affiliated with the investment-banking firm providing client services are more optimistic in their profits forecasts and share recommendations than unaffiliated analysts. A number of researchers report that affiliated analysts issue more optimistic growth forecasts than unaffiliated analysts,[92] and others find that affiliated analysts' share recommendations are more favourable than unaffiliated analysts' recommendations.[93] There are also many studies that show that financial analysts are fooled by profit figures and are optimistic in their forecasts.[94]

12.1 INTERNATIONAL VIEW

The controversy surrounding comprehensive income

Reported accounting income can be seen as an estimate of economic income that varies according to national boundaries possibly influenced by culture, tax, strength of the accounting profession, legislation and so on. Much of the international accounting research and standard setting efforts have revolved around moving noisy accounting representations towards ideal measures that provide more information on the underlying microeconomics of the firm. As a political process, there is the development, in the public interest, of 'a single set of high-quality, understandable and enforceable global accounting standards' (see www.iasb.org.uk).

The Discussion Paper[95] suggests that income should conceptually include all relevant events (including price restatements) and transactions during the period and display them ▼

as part of the total amount of comprehensive income. Separate statements of unrealised gains and losses that allow flexibility in reporting fair value changes as 'dirty surplus' reserve adjustments (as in the United Kingdom or SFAS 130 in the United States) will not be allowed. Standard setters ask: how should we allocate and report these events: (a) across operating, investing, and financing functions (similar to a cash flow disaggregation) or, (b) by nature or the economic characteristic of the activity by separating out transaction income from changes in prices that are unrealised (the disaggregation problem). The International Accounting Standards Board (IASB) initially expressed a preference for allocation by function, but now proposes allowing the functional allocation to be further dissagregated by nature.

This fair value approach and the point of revenue recognition (the IASB supports revenue being recognised when the customer is signed up and an exit price determined),[96] have been politically controversial and have not always had the unanimous support of national standard setters. For example, the Accounting Standard Setting Board of Japan initially expressed concern about the direction of the project and requested that it be stopped. Moreover, the European Financial Reporting Action Group (EFRAG) has been formed in order to make a contribution to the work of the IASB. EFRAG plans to be influential at an early stage by commenting on revenue recognition, which it believes has now become critical because of the approach taken by the IASB and FASB in linking revenue recognition to fair value remeasurement of financial assets. EFRAG has echoed the concerns of financial statement preparers about the lack of market prices, the obligation to provide reliable data and the duty of auditors to attest to the reported data.

Some empirical results show that traditional net operating income dominates comprehensive income as a valuation metric; however, there is a lack of research in Europe, Asia and Africa.[97] Thus, the IASB's decision to extend the recognition of income beyond traditional realisation concepts will not necessarily achieve the stated objectives of enhanced visibility and increased value relevance. Indeed, the proposed IASB comprehensive income performance report is a presentation format that could add further noise rather than information, to income reporting. The issue of how income is to be determined and reported is an international and a cultural issue.

References

Biddle, GC, & Choi, J-H 2006, 'Is comprehensive income useful?', *Journal of Contemporary Accounting and Economics*, vol. 2, no. 1, pp. 1–32.

Cahan, S, Courtenay, S, Gronewoller, P, & Upton, D 2000, 'Value relevance of mandated comprehensive income disclosures', *Journal of Business, Finance and Accounting*, vol. 27, nos. 9–10, pp. 1273–301.

Newberry, S 2003, 'Reporting performance: Comprehensive income and its components', *Abacus*, vol. 39, no. 3, pp. 325–39.

Schipper, KA, Schrand, CM, Shevlin, T, & Wilks, TJ 2009, 'Reconsidering Revenue Recognition', *Accounting Horizons*, vol. 23, no. 1.

Winners/losers and overconfidence

The winner/loser effect is an example of a long-term association anomaly. This effect produces a trading strategy. Shares that produce extreme positive returns (winners) or extreme negative returns (losers) are ranked on their last three-year performance and placed in portfolios. Past winners tend to be future losers, and vice versa. The studies of DeBondt and Thaler[98] suggested that a statistically significant abnormal return of up to 15 per cent can be made from this strategy. These results have been confirmed in subsequent studies that adjusted for size and differential performance.[99]

DeBondt and Thaler attribute these long-term return reversals to investor overconfidence and biased self-attribution. Overconfidence about private information also causes investors to downplay the importance of publicly disseminated information. Further, in forming expectations, investors are hypothesised to give too much weight to the past profit performance of firms and too little to the fact that performance tends to mean-revert. There is also a belief that the market is slow to react to events and in incorporating new information. There are also momentum effects observed, with shares that have high returns over the past year tending to have high returns over the following 3 to 6 months.[100] This is attributed to conservatism bias, whereby investors are slow to update their beliefs, which contributes to investor underreaction.

Other research examines whether indicators other than profit generate long-horizon abnormal stock performance. Examples include tests based on cash flow yield and sales growth;[101] tests of market overreaction stemming from analysts' optimism; and tests of the market's overreaction to extreme accrual portfolios.[102] The common finding is that the financial market overreacts to accounting indicators of firm value and corrects itself only over a long horizon.

The overreaction is explained by market participants' naive fixation on reported numbers and their tendency to extrapolate from past performance. However, because there is mean reversion in the extremes, the market's initial reaction to extreme indicators of value overshoots fundamental valuation and, in turn, provides an opportunity to earn abnormal returns. The overreaction hypothesis is extended by Bradshaw, Richardson and Sloan[103] who examined whether professional analysts understand the mean reversion property of extreme accruals. They found that 'investors do not fully anticipate the negative implications of unusually high accruals', and hence fail to incorporate them in their profits forecasts.

Ou and Penman analysis further extended this research by exploiting traditional rules of financial-ratio-based fundamental analysis to earn abnormal returns.[104] This research finds that the resulting fundamental strategies pay double-digit abnormal returns in a 12-month period following the portfolio formation date. The conclusion of the market's sluggish adjustment to the information in the ratios is strengthened by the fact that future abnormal returns appear to be concentrated around profit announcement dates when the profit predictions of the analysis come true. Finally, the multivariate fundamental analysis to estimating fundamental values of shares and investing in mispriced shares has been extended by the use of the Ohlson residual profit model combined with analysts' forecasts to estimate fundamental values and show that abnormal returns can be earned.

Mechanistic or behavioural effect

Cosmetic accounting

Two hypotheses have been developed:
1. The market reacts mechanistically to changes in accounting numbers, regardless of whether they are cosmetic or whether they have cash flow implications; as such, the market is systematically deceived by accounting changes which increased or decreased profits (the 'mechanistic' hypothesis).
2. The market ignores accounting changes which have no cash flow consequences — that is, the market does not react to accounting changes other than those switches that increase the present value of tax savings or otherwise affect the firm's cash flows (the 'no-effects' hypothesis deriving from the EMH).

The 'tests' of these two hypotheses consider the behaviour of abnormal rates of return at and around the time of a change in accounting policy. According to the no-effects hypothesis, there should be no abnormal returns when there is a 'cosmetic change' in accounting policy, since there will be no effect on cash flows. Under the no-effects hypothesis, creative accounting change is understood by capital market participants, and they are able to unravel and determine its effects. On the other hand, if an accounting policy has an effect on cash flows (e.g. as a result of tax regimes), we would expect to see abnormal returns at the date of announcement. Therefore, the no-effects hypothesis is a joint hypothesis of the EMH, the CAPM and zero monitoring costs.[105] In contrast, under the mechanistic hypothesis we would expect to see abnormal returns at the date of announcing accounting changes even though the change has no effect on cash flows — that is, cosmetic or creative accounting can fool market participants.

One of the first studies that attempted to discriminate between these competing hypotheses was undertaken by Kaplan and Roll.[106] They studied two accounting changes:

1. a change in accounting for investment tax credits from deferral to immediate recognition
2. a switch back from accelerated depreciation to straight-line depreciation.

Both changes were 'cosmetic', and both would be expected to increase the profits of the company in the year of implementation.

Kaplan and Roll's results showed that the market was 'fooled' for some time. For the firms that changed to the immediate recognition of the investment tax credit, the CARs behaved 'strangely', showing negative abnormal returns at announcement date, then rising to a peak about nine weeks after announcement before reverting to around zero. The behaviour of the control group of firms was also unusual, as the CARs suggest that abnormal cumulative excess returns of 9 per cent could be earned by purchasing these shares at announcement date.

Manipulating accounting numbers

Income calculated under GAAP is a noisy imperfect measure of 'economic income' or 'fundamental value'. This is because accounting standards are not precisely defined or consistent across countries; accountants are affected by subjectivity and cultural interpretations in their estimates, and manage or manipulate financial statements to varying degrees. How do we interpret and classify the wide scope of literature in this area? Regardless of the country, management has insider knowledge of the quality of the firm's performance. Management can choose to move accounting numbers towards fundamental value (implying an informational perspective) or away from fundamental value (i.e. taking an opportunistic perspective). (See figure 12.7.)

Under the opportunistic perspective, fraud is the most extreme variant of earnings management and it is used by managers to deceive financial statements users. Industry regulation is when firms are controlled and have incentives to increase or reduce earnings so that they can increase the prices they charge or obtain subsidies from the government or are not in breach of accounting-based risk ratios (e.g. banking regulation). Equity offerings occur when managers try to manipulate the accounts in order to raise share prices to increase the total of their wealth held in equity or options or to increase the price of initial or seasoned equity offerings. Debt covenants refer to managing the accounts so that debt or other covenants are not breached and firms are not in default and do not incur the increased costs associated with default. Finally, management compensation is when managers manipulate accounts so as to maximise utility from bonus schemes that are tied to accounting numbers.

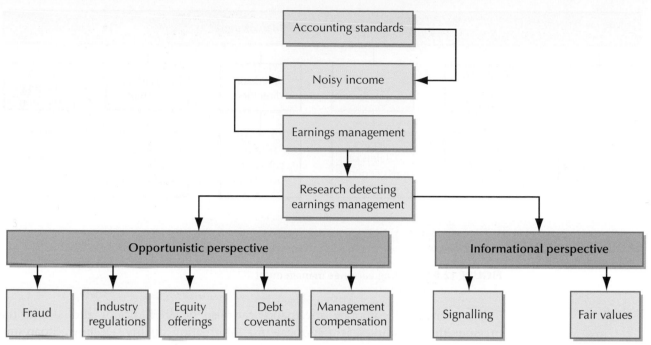

FIGURE 12.7 Two viewpoints of accounting manipulation

The informational perspective mainly revolves around signalling theory. Signalling refers to the practice whereby managers use insider knowledge of the financial statements to signal economic information about the firm to interested parties. For example, the income-smoothing literature signals that current income is permanent income. Fair value accounting refers to managers making accounting choices (not) complying with accounting standards but reflecting the underlying fundamentals of the business. The use of appropriate fair values, although theoretically defensible, raises issues about why managers might use different accounting techniques.

Detecting the quality and probability of accounting management

The capital market evidence suggests that managers' cosmetic changes to accruals affect share prices. The evidence also shows that prices will revert to fundamental value but that may take some time — even up to a year or more. What also is of interest to capital market researchers is the type of research that can help indicate the quality of the accrual management. Figure 12.8 provides an overview, with the arrow providing a blunt indicator of earnings-quality detection.

We can use share price reaction as an indication of quality. However, research by Sloan[107] and others has shown that the market as a whole does not have a sophisticated understanding of accruals, and hence overreacts to positive income-increasing accruals. The reaction of financial analysts can also be used to assess quality because of their expertise. However, research in this area has generally suggested that analysts may be biased and focused on industry-specific factors rather than firm-specific variables. Auditors' reports and opinions can also be used to proxy for quality but there is some debate over whether auditors are truly independent.

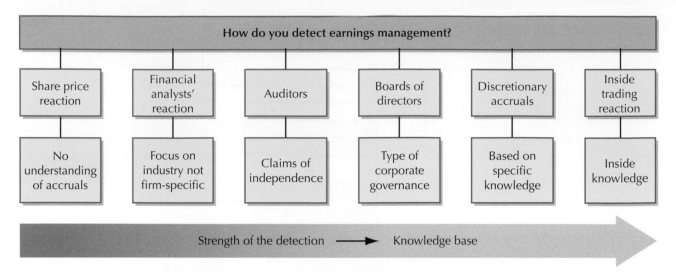

FIGURE 12.8 Detecting earnings management

The strength of corporate governance can also be an indicator and, unlike the previous three examples, is a surrogate for information quality. Dechow, Sloan and Sweeney[108] found that opportunistic accounting manipulations are more likely to occur when there is a desire to attract financial resources and the company has a board of directors dominated by a CEO who serves as the chairman of the board, does not have an audit committee and is less likely to have an outside block of directors. The type of accrual is also important. Marquardt and Wiedman[109] show that in new equity offering cases, firms particularly manage earnings through higher accounts receivables, whereas in management buyouts, accounts receivable are managed lower. For firms avoiding an earnings decrease, only the unexpected part of special-item accruals differs significantly. Finally, if we examine insider trading according to income increasing and decreasing accruals, we are able to predict future returns and earnings more accurately because of insiders' specialised knowledge of the firm and the implications of specific accruals.[110]

| 12.3 THEORY IN ACTION | **Financial analysts and their mixed reaction to switching to international accounting standards** |

AIFRS — a work in progress

In a Catch 22 scenario, increased understanding of Australia's equivalent of International Financial Reporting Standards (AIFRS) has caused mixed reactions among Australian financial analysts as to its potential to help investment decision-making, according to a KPMG report.

The report, *A Work In Progress* assesses Australian financial analysts' response to the first financial results published under AIFRS since its inception in January 2005. It replicated a similar report conducted in late 2004 on the same subject.

While it showed an encouraging uplift in analyst understanding, increased analyst knowledge around AIFRS has also led to debate on its value with 30 per cent saying it facilitated a strengthening of the capital markets, 30 per cent saying it didn't and 40 per cent still undecided.

Additionally, a 17 per cent increase in the number of analysts who are confident in distinguishing a change resulting from either business performance or accounting changes under AIFRS, coincided with an 11 per cent drop in those saying AIFRS provided more insight into a company's true financial performance.

"This highlights one of the most significant challenges for countries like Australia who are adopting IFRS: how to ensure the benefits are realised," said Geoff Wilson, KPMG's partner in charge of audit and risk advisory.

"While the analyst response is somewhat concerning, there were many positives to draw from the report, including the increased quality of company communication and reduced fears of market volatility because of AIFRS.

At the time of AIFRS' inception, analysts were calling for company briefings on its expected impact. Nearly half the analysts surveyed said all or most companies they follow provided briefings or additional information explaining how AIFRS is affecting the financial information they report. While this is a significant improvement since our first report, there is still work to be done as the remaining analysts (56 per cent), said they received briefings from just a few, one or none of the companies they track," Wilson said.

Andrea Waters, KPMG partner in charge of IFRS conversion services concluded: "In 2004, our report identified that analysts expected there to be market volatility when results under AIFRS were released. To date, this anxiety appears to have been quelled. In 2004 a majority of analysts said they would mark down a company's shares if they didn't understand why its results looked different under AIFRS. In 2006, analysts appear to be less likely to mark down shares of companies showing volatility after switching to AIFRS. However, business should see this time as an opportunity to ensure communications are hitting the mark with stakeholders and the AIFRS impacts are well understood by the market," she said.

Source: Australian Institute of Company Directors, 'A Work in Progress', *The Boardroom Report*, vol. 4, iss. 11, June 6, 2006, F.

Questions

1. On the evidence presented in this article, are financial analysts well equipped to efficiently factor into prices the impact of switching to international financial reporting standards?
2. What do you think will be the impact on share prices if analysts disagree on the information content?
3. What other methods could be used to assess the value relevance of AIFRS?

LO 7 ISSUES FOR AUDITORS

The empirical evidence reviewed in this chapter shows that accounting earnings have information content, and that market reactions to accruals tend to be biased because investors do not appear to fully appreciate the reversing nature of accruals. Research also shows that the nature of the long-term association between accounting earnings and share prices is influenced by a number of factors. The earnings response coefficient studies show that qualified audit reports and SEC sanctions against auditors signal lower quality earnings and result in lower ERCs.

There is some evidence of an association between auditing and the cost of capital. Blackwell, Noland and Winters investigated the effect of purchasing an audit on the cost of debt capital for a sample of companies that are not legally required to be audited.[111] They found that small private firms that purchase audits are charged lower interest rates. However, most economic activity occurs in firms that are required to purchase an audit, so researchers have investigated the cost of capital effects associated with different quality auditors. As discussed in chapter 11, it is generally believed that large or 'Big' auditors are higher quality than other auditors. Also, auditors that specialise in certain industries or contracts are higher quality after controlling for the Big auditor effect. Mansi, Maxwell and Miller provide evidence that higher quality auditing lowers the cost of debt capital.[112] They found that the effect on the cost of debt is most pronounced in firms that have lower quality debt, which suggests that auditors provide value to firms through both their information and insurance roles.

This means that lenders appear to believe that higher quality auditors are associated with higher quality financial information and that the larger auditor provides greater insurance against debt default. Securities laws provide recourse for investors against auditors, so the results suggest lenders value being able to sue a well-resourced large auditor instead of a smaller auditor.

The association of higher quality auditors with the cost of equity capital has also been investigated. Khurana and Raman studied the association of Big auditors with equity prices across several countries (including the United States, Australia, Canada and the United Kingdom).[113] They also found information and insurance effects, but only in the United States. They attributed this result to the higher litigation environment in the United States relative to the other countries. Li and Stokes investigated the Australian environment further and found that the choice of a Big auditor is associated with a lower cost of capital when a firm switches from a non-Big auditor to a Big auditor.[114] They interpreted their findings as supporting the information, or brand-name reputation, argument. In addition, they found evidence of a lower cost of equity capital for clients where there had been greater audit effort, and those clients were audited by an industry specialist.

Researchers investigated the effect on equity prices when there is an exogenous, or external, shock to the system. These shocks include the rare event of the failure of an audit firm. In 1990, the seventh largest accounting firm in the United States, Laventhol & Horwath, filed for bankruptcy. The main reason cited for its demise was the large amount of litigation against it.[115] These events meant that the insurance protection provided by the audit firm to its clients was suddenly withdrawn. If the protection was valuable to investors, we would expect to see a drop in Laventhol & Horwath's clients' share prices. Menon and Williams found evidence that the share prices did fall on average, and the effect was greater for initial public offerings than seasoned public offerings because securities laws provided more protection for the auditors in the latter case. The fall of Arthur Andersen LLP in 2002 following the Enron collapse appears to have had an adverse effect on its clients' share prices.[116] Because the 'Andersen effect' was more severe for clients audited from the same office as Enron (i.e. Houston), the results seem to indicate that investors had concerns about the quality of audits performed by certain partners and staff of the audit firm.

Many of the studies examining the association between auditor choice and cost of capital (reviewed in this chapter) and the demand for audit quality (reviewed in chapter 11) face a similar methodological problem. The researchers are unable to conduct controlled experiments to prove a causal link between auditor choice and cost of capital. Evidence from archival data[117] that a client using a larger auditor is likely to have a lower cost of capital could be explained in three different ways:

1. Investors value either the quality of the audit work and/or the insurance protection provided by the large auditor, and therefore pay more for shares or charge lower interest.
2. The company is perceived as being a good investment for other reasons, and the economic benefits from the lower cost of capital enable the managers to pay the higher fees charged by a large auditor. In this case the cost of capital causes auditor choice.
3. The auditor choice and cost of capital could both be caused by other factors, such as the quality of the company's management or investment opportunities.

The researchers are careful to attempt a control of these alternative explanations, and use techniques such as control variables, simultaneous equations and complex statistical analysis, as well as conducting numerous sensitivity tests. Finally, the process of research involves many separate attempts to investigate theory using different methods and samples, and in different contexts, to build confidence in the results.

Summary

LO 1 — **The philosophy of positive accounting theory**

The philosophical objective of positive accounting theory is to explain and predict the application of accounting practice. It also seeks to explain how and why capital markets react to accounting reports. In contrast, normative or inflation theorists often argue for a change in accounting method without putting forward any supporting empirical evidence and without trying to understand the rationale for current and past use of accounting principles and rules. Positive theory has an empirical economic focus. It assumes investors and financial accounting users and preparers are rational utility maximisers. Positive theorists reject arguments based on anecdotal evidence, and call for the testing of normative assumptions.

LO 2 — **The strengths of positive theory**

The strengths of positive theory lie in the fact that hypotheses are framed in such a way that they are capable of falsification by empirical research. Researchers aim to provide an understanding of how the world works rather than prescribing how the world should work. In capital market research that means understanding the association of accounting numbers and stock prices. Researchers attempt to understand the connection between accounting information, managers, firms and markets and to analyse those relationships.

LO 3 — **The scope of positive accounting theory**

Positive theory developed in two stages. The first stage involved research into the impact of accounting and the activity of capital markets. The second-stage literature sought to explain and predict the application of accounting practices across firms.

LO 4 — **Capital market research and the efficient markets hypothesis**

Two types of capital market research are particularly important to positive accounting theory: (1) those studies that attempt to determine the impact of accounting information on share returns, and (2) those studies that consider the effects of changes in accounting policy on share prices. Most research in these areas has been conducted by testing the semistrong form of the efficient markets hypothesis (EMH). Event studies, association studies and the mechanistic behavioural approaches are examples of research, which tests relationships in capital markets.

LO 5 — **The influence of accounting information on investor behaviour and share prices**

The major results suggest the following:

- Historical cost profit releases have information content for the marketplace in terms of *CARs* and the effect on volatility and trading volume.

- Information asymmetry (which is affected by firm size) affects the responsiveness of price changes, the nature of price changes, and the volume of trade following profit announcements.
- There is a continuous information set which is used by the market and, therefore, accounting reports are not the only sources of information.
- Longer term association studies show that a number of factors including risk and uncertainty, firm size, industry, interest rates, financial leverage, potential growth, and permanent and temporary profits have a role in determining firm value.
- Adding profit levels (as well as changes in profit), decomposing profits into separate components, adding cash flows, accruals and balance sheet components, as well as taking into account broader macroeconomic factors further increases the explanatory power of accounting variables.

LO 6 Trading strategies and mechanistic behavioural effects

There is increasing evidence that markets can be fooled by accounting numbers, evidenced by post-announcement drift, trading rules from financial statement information, changes in accounting techniques, accrual levels, winner–loser strategies and financial analyst optimism. The relationship between accounting methods and the impact of behaviour on share markets is an ongoing research area in accounting which will play a significant role in the research literature in the years to come.

LO 7 Issues for auditors

The empirical research provides evidence of benefits to companies through lower cost of equity and debt capital when they voluntarily purchase an audit or purchase a high-quality audit. Investors value the insurance protection provided by the possibility of taking legal action against a large auditor who has deep resources. In addition, investors value the assurance provided by the auditor about the quality of the company's financial information. Researchers are unable to run controlled experiments on auditor choice and face methodological challenges in designing studies using archival data that enable these conclusions to be drawn with confidence.

Questions

1. What is positive accounting theory? How does it differ from normative accounting theory? What was/were the major dissatisfaction(s) with normative accounting theory which led to the development of a positive theory of accounting?
2. Explain the meaning of an efficient market. What is meant by the following terms: weak-form efficiency, semistrong-form efficiency and strong-form efficiency? Which form is the most important to accounting research? Why?
3. Explain the importance of examining the impact of profits on share prices for financial analysis. Can this analysis be used to make abnormal returns from share markets?
4. Does a study of the information content of profits announcements explain why firms use particular accounting practices? Does it help to predict which firms will use particular accounting practices?
5. Give reasons that non-linear models relating unexpected returns to share prices would provide a more precise estimate of the earnings response coefficient (ERC).
6. Why would share prices have a greater reaction to the profit announcements released by small firms compared with those released by large firms? Do you think this research has any implications for 'measurement' issues in accounting or for the formulation of accounting standards?

7. Outline the research that has been undertaken on the impact of permanent and temporary increases in profits. Why is this research important?
8. How will risk and uncertainty affect the valuation of a firm and, through this valuation model, the ERC?
9. The impact of profits for valuation has diminished over the years. What is the impact? How has the research adjusted to reflect this fact?
10. Outline a research project which explains how share prices are determined. Would this project include factors other than accounting data?
11. Briefly explain and outline the research on the 'mechanistic' hypothesis. What are the implications of this research?
12. Why would financial analysts be fooled by accounting numbers and provide optimistic and biased estimates of profits? Can you offer a positive economic reason for their actions?
13. Outline the different procedures that can be used to determine whether accounts have quality accruals or whether they create more noise.
14. What are the two main explanations for the association between the choice of a high-quality auditor and a lower cost of debt or equity capital?
15. Why do we have to be careful drawing conclusions about causality based on studies using archival data?

Additional readings

Brown, P 1970, 'The impact of the annual net profit report on the stock market', *Australian Accountant*, July, pp. 273–83.

Deitrick, JW & Harrison, WT 1984, 'EMH, CMR and the accounting profession', *Journal of Accountancy*, February, pp. 82–94.

Wyatt, AR 1983, 'Efficient market theory: Its impact on accounting', *Journal of Accountancy*, February, pp. 56–65.

12.1
CASE STUDY

This case study discusses the impact of an increase in accounting metrics but a fall in share price.

DJ sales pick up but shares dive

by Rachel Hewitt

David Jones shares yesterday suffered their biggest one-day drop this year, despite the retailer unveiling a better fourth-quarter sales result. The shares were hammered more than 8 per cent to $4.81 — the biggest fall since November last year — as the department store chain booked a 6.9 per cent dive in full-year like-for-like sales.

However, after falling almost 11 per cent in the third quarter, comparable sales rebounded in the fourth, to be down just 1.2 per cent on the back of stronger trading.

David Jones chief Mark McInnes refused to say the worst was over for department stores, warning the economy was still open to "an external shock". "It's not about being less confident, it's more about recognising that the jury's out ... as to the recovery and the pace of recovery of the economy," he said.

Mr McInnes said the fourth quarter sales of $512.3 million were much better than expected "and after the previous three quarters, which were terrible, it was a great relief".

Credit Suisse retail analyst Grant Saligari said the result was "fairly well in line" with market expectations. He attributed the slide in the share price to a strong run over the past month. "I think you're just seeing a little bit of profit-taking off the back of that," Mr Saligari said. He said the strong cyclical rally in the market over several months was reflected in the share prices of retailers such as David Jones and JB Hi-Fi, while "some of the more staple stocks such as Woolworths, which have lower risk profiles, are coming back to the field a little bit."

Austock securities analyst Thomas Hodson compared David Jones' recent share performance to Harvey Norman's, "where there was a strong run up in the share price hoping that the good news and strong momentum would continue". The DJs sales result wasn't a disaster, but there probably wasn't enough in terms of upside surprise or news to really keep the momentum going," Mr Hodson said.

Other retail stocks also took a hit yesterday, with Harvey Norman down 4.28 per cent to $3.13 and JB Hi-Fi off 3.82 per cent to $16.11. DJ's shares have doubled since March, and surged 10.17 per cent on June 30 after Mr McInnes upgraded the store's full-year profit guidance to between 9 and 12 per cent growth.

Mr McInnes yesterday reaffirmed this year's profit guidance and said the company's next financial year, in which it expects to deliver flat to 5 per cent profit growth, would be one of "stability" before a return to retail growth. We're not predicting any sales growth in FY10 — we don't see that coming until FY11 and FY12," he said.

The retailer outlined a new focus on online marketing, with former marketing general manager Georgia Chewing appointed to the new role of head of digital marketing and e-tail business. Mr McInnes said that over the next year David Jones would focus on improving its communications networks online.

"Twitter is only like 12 months old and Facebook three years old, and those are completely changing the way people are communicating, and so we want to make sure our brand has a presence in those new technology distribution markets," he said. "And if there's an opportunity for e-tail expansion and we can get a return on investment then we'll take it."

DJ's latest full-year sales totaled $1.986 billion. Cosmetics continued to be the store's best performer, achieving double-digit growth during the fourth-quarter. Young men's and women's fashion, children's wear, manchester, kitchenware, home office electronics and small appliances were among other strong performers. However, trading in big items such as televisions remained tough.

Like Myer chief Bernie Brookes a day earlier, Mr McInnes was bemused at this week's retail trade figures which showed department stores' sales fell 8.8 per cent in June compared with May. "Our sales both at a total level and a like-for-like level in June were up on last year, so it has to be the discount department stores that have had a difficult month – but it certainly wasn't us," Mr McInnes said.

He did not believe the flagged relisting of Myer influenced yesterday's DJ share price plunge.

Source: Herald Sun, 6 August 2009, pp. 37–8, www.heraldsun.com.au.

Questions

1. Why do you think David Jones' shares have dropped in value when fourth-quarter profits have increased?
2. What other economic information is the market using besides accounting reports?
3. One analyst suggests that there wasn't enough in 'upside surprise or news to really keep the (share price) momentum going'. What does this comment suggest to you about market efficiency?
4. Given the analyst's comment in question 3 how would you classify the market efficiency: weak-form; semistrong-form; strong-form? Explain your answer.

The following article discusses the situation of a firm expanding its core operations offshore.

Nufarm buys US companies

by Geoff Easdown

Agricultural chemicals group Nufarm has bought two US-based sorghum companies to help grow its seeds division into a $50 million business. The company will add Texas-based Richardson Seeds and MMR Genetics to its sorghum platform, which was started with the acquisition last year of Queensland sorghum specialist Lefroy seeds.

Brent Zacharias, the head of Nufarm's seeds division, said the acquisitions would deliver significant growth and complement Nufarm's sorghum business.

Nufarm managing director Doug Rathbone said Richardson and MMR would strengthen Nufarm's seeds platform. "Sorghum has been a target crop for our seeds business," Mr Rathbone said, noting that Nufarm would gain a range of benefits from the purchases.

Richardson Seeds produces and markets sorghum seed hybrids. It is a market leader in the US and holds expanding market positions in Mexico, South America, Europe, Japan and the Middle East.

MMR Genetics, previously 47 per cent owned by Richardson Seeds, is a global leader in the development of elite sorghum germplasm.

Combined sales of Richardson Seeds and MMR in 2008 totalled about $US22 million.

Mr Zacharias said he considered it important that Nufarm was retaining the existing management and employees of Richardson Seeds, including company president Larry Richardson of MMR.

Nufarm fell 7 c to $10.90.

Source: Herald Sun, 6 August 2009, p. 60, www.heraldsun.com.au.

Questions

1. List the ways that you think Nufarm is changing its core operations.
2. If the acquisition is expected to deliver significant growth, why do you think the share price is falling? In your answer, consider the potential impact of both market-wide events and firm-specific information.
3. Does this article suggest market efficiency? Explain your answer.
4. Does the volatility hypothesis predict greater or less variance in the share price on the days following the announcement date? What other factors might affect the volatility of the share price following the announcement?

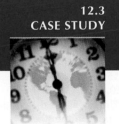

This case study considers the market reaction to information released by a firm that has diversified its operations.

Market cheers Axa's Asian plan

by John Durie

The fund manager got off lightly yesterday despite a sharp slump in sales, thanks to its diversification plans. Axa's Andy Penn yesterday showed that the stockmarket is in a forgiving mood. Just getting close to expectations with no negative surprises was enough to win market backing.

It doesn't work for everyone, as David Jones learned, with expectations running ahead of actual returns, sending its stock price down 8.4 per cent to $4.81. It was partly caught in a general sell-off of the so-called high beta stocks, which have run hard on hopes of an economic bounce because, as with Axa, the sales figures were in line. The mistake was not satisfying hopes of another profit upgrade.

Axa eased but still closed up 2.3 per cent at $4.42 a share after disclosing a sharp slump in sales and a profit that was no better than in line with estimates. Penn's advantage is that he was the first to report from the funds management sector.

But the good news for AMP's Craig Dunn et al is that Penn didn't set the bar very high. Those with a much better domestic franchise should jump over it easily.

As always, how analysts responded depended on their estimates. So news that surplus capital stood at $1.5 billion pleased those expecting less and disappointed those tipping more. The bottom line is that it shows Axa is well funded.

As for growth, well that's another question altogether, and hard to find in this environment. In Axa's case, it's all in Asia, which accounts for two-thirds of operating earnings and a platform for growth, once all the problems are ironed out.

Overall operating earnings were down 13 per cent, with funds under management down some 28 per cent. This shows Axa's Andy Penn is keeping a close eye on costs, and diversification is once again proving to be the best line of defence.

Source: The Australian, 6 August 2009, p. 26, www.theaustralian.com.au.

Questions

1. Axa's share price increased by 2.3 per cent when its annual results were announced. What does this reaction suggest about market efficiency?
2. The article indicates that Axa experienced a sharp slump in sales, yet its share price increased. Explain why sales is not the most relevant indicator of Axa's value?
3. List the factors that appear to have had an impact on Axa's share price and indicate the likely direction of that impact; that is, an increase or decrease.

Endnotes

1. M Friedman, 'The methodology of positive economics', in M. Friedman (ed.), *Essays in positive economics*, Chicago: University of Chicago Press, 1953, p. 7.
2. R Watts and J Zimmerman, *Positive accounting theory*, Englewood Cliffs, NJ: Prentice-Hall, 1986, p. 2.
3. ibid.
4. M Jensen, 'Organisation theory and methodology', *Accounting Review*, April 1983, pp. 319–39.
5. ibid., p. 320.
6. ibid.
7. Watts and Zimmerman, op. cit., p. 7.
8. ibid., p. 8; Watts and Zimmerman suggest that the adoption of any objective other than economic efficiency, such as a more equitable distribution of wealth, is a subjective value judgement,
as it involves choosing between individuals.
9. K Popper, *The logic of scientific discovery*, London: Hutchinson, 1968.
10. J Hirschliefer, *Price theory and applications*, 2nd edn, Englewood Cliffs, NJ: Prentice-Hall, 1980.
11. ibid., p. 1.
12. E Fama, 'Efficient capital markets: A review of theory and empirical work', *Journal of Finance*, May 1970, pp. 383–417, p. 383).
13. ibid., p. 389.
14. E Fama, *Foundations of finance*, New York: Basic Books, 1976, pp. 63–8.
15. We will not present an in-depth discussion of the CAPM. Interested readers are referred to the seminal articles: W Sharpe, 'Capital asset prices: A theory of market equilibrium under conditions of
risk', *Journal of Finance*, September 1964, pp. 425–42; J Lintner, 'The valuation of risk assets and the selection of risky investments in stock portfolios and capital budgets', *Review of Economics and Statistics*, February 1965, pp. 13–37; or to any text in introductory finance.
16. Fama, op. cit.
17. R Ball and P Brown, 'An empirical evaluation of accounting income numbers', *Journal of Accounting Research*, vol. 6, no. 2, Autumn 1968, pp. 159–78.
18. ibid., p. 160.
19. P Brown, 'The impact of the annual net profit report on the stock market', *Australian Accountant*, July 1970, pp. 273–83.
20. Watts and Zimmerman, op. cit., pp. 48–9.

21. G Foster, 'Quarterly accounting data: Time-series properties and predictive-ability results', *Accounting Review*, January 1977, pp. 686–98.
22. Examples include: P Brown and P Hancock, 'Profit reports and the sharemarket', in I Telley and P Jubb (eds), *Capital, income and decision-making: introductory readings in accounting*, Sydney: Holt, Rinehart and Winston, 1977, pp. 281–8; S Easton and NA Sinclair, 'The impact of unexpected earnings and dividends on abnormal returns to equity', *Accounting and Finance*, May 1989, pp. 1–19.
23. W Beaver, R Clarke and W Wright, 'The association between unsystematic security returns and the magnitude of earnings forecast errors', *Journal of Accounting Research*, Autumn 1979, pp. 316–40.
24. W Beaver, R Lambert and D Morse, 'The information content of security prices', *Journal of Accounting and Economics*, March 1980, pp. 3–38.
25. The term 'earnings response coefficient' and the acronym 'ERC' were first used in PD Easton and ME Zmijewski, 'Cross-sectional variation in the stock market response to accounting earnings announcements', *Journal of Accounting and Economics*, July 1989, pp. 117–42.
26. RN Freeman, 'The association between accounting earnings and security returns for large and small firms', *Journal of Accounting and Economics*, vol. 9, 1987, pp. 195–228.
27. EB Grant, 'Market implications of differential amounts of interim information', *Journal of Accounting Research*, vol. 18, no. 1, 1980.
28. R Atiase, 'Pre-disclosure information, firm capitalization and security price behaviour around earnings announcements', *Journal of Accounting Research*, vol. 23, 1985, pp. 21–36
29. Freeman, op. cit.
30. D Shores, 'The association between interim information and security returns surrounding earnings announcements', *Journal of Accounting Research*, vol. 28, no. 1, 1990.

31. G Foster, 'Intra-industry information transfers associated with earnings releases', *Journal of Accounting and Economics*, December 1981, pp. 201–32.
32. GJ Clinch and NA Sinclair, 'Intra-industry information releases: A recursive systems approach', *Journal of Accounting and Economics*, April 1987, pp. 89–106.
33. R Freeman and S Tse, 'Intercompany information transfers', *Journal of Accounting and Economics*, June/September 1992, pp. 509–23.
34. W Beaver, 'The information content of annual earnings announcements', *Empirical research in accounting: selected studies 1968*, supplement to *Journal of Accounting Research*, vol. 6, 1968, pp. 67–92. The apparent advantage of such a method is that it avoids the necessity of specifying a model for expected profits — this is necessary in the studies using mean abnormal returns — since there is no need to partition the sample into 'good news' and 'bad news' firms.
35. J Patell and M Wolfson, 'Anticipated information releases reflected in call option prices', *Journal of Accounting and Economics*, August 1979, pp. 117–40; J Patell and M Wolfson 'The ex ante and ex post price effects of quarterly earnings announcements reflected in option and stock prices', *Journal of Accounting Research*, Autumn 1981, pp. 434–58.
36. P Brown, *Capital markets-based research in accounting: an introduction*, Coopers & Lybrand and AAANZ, 1994.
37. F Modigliani and MH Miller, 'Corporate income taxes and the cost of capital: A correction', *American Economic Review*, vol. 53, no. 3, 1963, pp. 433–43.
38. Easton and Zmijewski, op. cit.
39. DW Collins and SP Kothari, 'An analysis of intertemporal and cross-sectional determinants of earnings response coefficients', *Journal of Accounting and Economics*, vol. 11, 1989, pp. 143–81; R Lipe, 'The relation between stock returns and accounting earnings given

alternative information', *Accounting Review*, vol. 65, 1990, pp. 49–71.
40. DW Collins and L DeAngelo, 'Accounting information and corporate governance: Market and analyst reactions to earnings of firms engaged in proxy contests', *Journal of Accounting and Economics*, vol. 13, 1990, pp. 213–47.
41. Beaver, Lambert and Morse, op. cit.; Normative theorists would argue this is done to observe deficient accounting standards, whereas agency theorists would argue that it is done in order to enhance contracting mechanisms.
42. B Lev, 'On the usefulness of earnings and earnings research: Lessons and directions from two decades of empirical research', *Journal of Accounting Research*, vol. 27, Suppl., 1989, p. 155.
43. DC Jeter and PK Chaney, 'An empirical investigation of factors affecting the earnings association coefficient', *Journal of Business Finance and Accounting*, vol. 19, no. 6, 1992, pp. 839–63.
44. M Pincus, 'Accounting methods and differential stock market response to the announcement of earnings', *Journal of Accounting, Auditing and Finance*, vol. 8, no. 3, 1993, pp. 221–46.
45. AUS 202 Objective and General Principles Governing an Audit of a Financial Report states, paragraph 02: '… the auditor's opinion enhances the credibility of the financial report …'
46. L DeAngelo, 'Auditor size and audit quality', *Journal of Accounting and Economics*, vol. 3, 1981, pp. 183–99.
47. N Dopuch and D Simunic, 'Competition in auditing: An assessment', Paper presented at the Symposium on Auditing Research IV, University of Illinois, at Urbana-Champaign, 1982.
48. RA Davidson and D Neu, 'A note on the association between audit firm size and audit quality', *Contemporary Accounting Research*, vol. 9, no. 2, 1993, pp. 479–88; H Jang and C Lin, 'Audit quality and trading volume reaction: A study of initial public offerings', *Journal of Accounting and Public Policy*, vol. 12, no. 3, 1993, p. 263;

C Lennox, 'Are large auditors more accurate than small auditors?', *Accounting and Business Research*, vol. 29, no. 3, 1999, pp. 217–77.

49. MC Knapp, 'Factors that audit committee members use as surrogates for audit quality', *Auditing: A Journal of Practice and Theory*, vol. 10, no. 1, 1991, pp. 35–52.

50. It is argued that industry specialisation contributes to auditors' credibility and audit quality by enhancing the level of assurance provided by the audit.

51. J Krishnan and JS Yang, 'Auditor industry specialisation and the earnings response coefficient', Temple University Working Paper, Philadelphia, 1999.

52. SK Choi and DC Jeter, 'The effects of qualified audit opinions on earnings response coefficients', *Journal of Accounting and Economics*, vol. 15, 1992, pp. 229–47.

53. K Moreland, 'Criticisms of auditors and the association between earnings and returns of client firms', *Auditing: A Journal of Practice and Theory*, vol. 14, no. 1, 1995, pp. 94–104.

54. Jeter and Chaney, op. cit.

55. E Fama and G Schwert, 'Asset returns and inflation', *Journal of Financial Economics*, vol. 2, 1977, 115–46; E. Fama, 'Stock returns, real activity, inflation, and money', *American Economic Review*, vol. 71, 1981, pp. 545–65.

56. E Fama and K French, 'Permanent and temporary components of stock prices', *Journal of Political Economy*, vol. 96, 1988, pp. 246–73; E Fama and K French, 'Business conditions and expected returns on stocks and bonds', *Journal of Financial Economics*, vol. 25, 1989, pp. 23–49; R Balvers, T Cosimano and B McDonald, 'Predicting stock returns in an efficient market', *Journal of Finance*, vol. 45, 1990, pp. 1109–28.

57. S Kothari, 'Capital markets research in accounting', *Journal of Accounting and Economics*, vol. 31, 2001.

58. Jeter and Chaney, op. cit.

59. D Dhaliwal and S Reynolds, 'The effect of the firm's capital structure on the relationship between earnings changes and stock returns', Working Paper, University of Arizona, 1989; DS Dhaliwal, KJ Lee and NL Fargher, 'The association between unexpected earnings and abnormal security returns in the presence of financial leverage', *Contemporary Accounting Research*, vol. 8, no. 1, 1991, pp. 20–41.

60. Modigliani and Miller, op. cit.

61. SA Ross, 'The determination of financial structure: The incentive-signalling approach', *Bell Journal of Economics*, vol. 8, 1977, pp. 23–40.

62. A Hodgson and P Stevenson-Clarke, 'Accounting variables and stock returns: The impact of leverage', *Pacific Accounting Review*, vol. 12, no. 2, 2000, pp. 37–64.

63. Collins and Kothari, op. cit.

64. J Anthony and K Ramesh, 'Association between accounting performance measures and stock prices: A test of the life cycle hypothesis', *Journal of Accounting and Economics*, vol. 15, 1992, pp. 203–27.

65. There is another stream of literature that derives predictions about the behaviour of ERCs as a function of a firm's life cycle that is rooted in the resolution of uncertainty about the parameter values of the time-series properties of earnings.

66. A Ali and P Zarowin, 'Annual earnings and estimation error in ERCs', *Journal of Accounting and Economics*, June/September 1992, pp. 249–64.

67. RN Freeman and SY Tse, 'A nonlinear model of security price responses to unexpected earnings', *Journal of Accounting Research*, vol. 30, no. 2, Autumn 1992, pp. 185–209.

68. A Hodgson and P Stevenson-Clarke, 'Earnings, cashflows and returns: Functional relations and the impact of firm size', *Accounting and Finance*, vol. 40, 2002, pp. 51–73.

69. Lipe, op. cit.

70. An implication is that a time series model which constrains profit components to have the same time series properties (e.g. the random walk model for profits) is not descriptively valid.

71. RG Sloan, 'Do stock prices fully reflect information in accruals and cash flows about future earnings?', *The Accounting Review*, vol. 71, no. 3, 1996, pp. 289–315.

72. YK Chia, R Czernkowski and J Loftus, 'The association of aggregate and disaggregated earnings with annual stock returns', *Accounting and Finance*, vol. 37, no. 1, 1997, pp. 111–28.

73. RM Bowen, D Burgstahler and LA Daley 1987, 'The incremental information content of accrual versus cashflows', *Accounting Review*, vol. 42, no. 4, 1987, pp. 723–47.

74. ibid.

75. JLG Board and JFS Day, 'The information content of cashflow figures', *Accounting and Business Research*, vol. 20, 1989, pp. 3–11.

76. A Ali, 'The incremental information content of earnings, working capital from operations, and cashflows', *Journal of Accounting Research*, vol. 32, no. 1, 1994, pp. 61–74.

77. Freeman and Tse, op cit.

78. A Ali and PF Pope, 'The incremental information content of earnings, funds flow and cashflow: The UK evidence', *Journal of Business Finance and Accounting*, vol. 22, no. 1, 1995, pp. 19–34; Hodgson and Stevenson-Clarke, op. cit.

79. CSA Cheng, C Liu and TF Schaefer, 'Earnings permanence and the incremental information content of cashflows from operations', *Journal of Accounting Research*, vol. 34, no. 1, 1996, pp. 173–81.

80. Dechow, op. cit.

81. Ohlson, op. cit.

82. J Francis and K Schipper, 'Have financial statements lost their relevance?', *Journal of Accounting Research*, vol. 37, no. 2, 1999, pp. 319–52.

83. B Lev and R Thiagarajan, 'Fundamental information analysis', *Journal of Accounting Research*, vol. 31, 1993, pp. 190–225.

84. Ball and Brown, op. cit.

85. E Williams and C Findlay, 'Beyond Neoclassical economic theory as a foundation for financial accounting', *Abacus*, December 1980, pp. 133–41.

86. Watts and Zimmerman, op. cit., p. 69.

87. Ball and Brown, op. cit.; CP Jones and RH Litzenberger, 'Quarterly earnings reports and intermediate stock price trends', *Journal of Finance*, March 1970, pp. 143–8; RJ Rendleman, CP Jones and HA Latane, 'Empirical anomalies based on unexpected earnings and the importance of risk adjustments', *Journal of Financial Economics*, November 1982, pp. 269–87; R Freeman and S Tse, 'The multi-period information content of accounting earnings: Confirmations and contradictions of previous earnings reports', *Journal of Accounting Research*, vol. 27, Supplement, 1989, pp. 49–79; VL Bernard and J Thomas, 'Evidence that stock prices do not fully reflect the implications of current earnings for future earnings', *Journal of Accounting and Economics*, vol. 13, 1990, pp. 305–40.

88. J Ou and SH Penman, 'Financial statement analysis and the prediction of stock returns', *Journal of Accounting and Economics*, November 1989, pp. 295–329; J Ou and SH Penman, 'Accounting measurement, price-earnings ratio, and the information content of security prices', *Journal of Accounting Research*, vol. 27, Supplement, 1989, pp. 111–44.

89. Kothari, op. cit., pp. 105–231.

90. V Bernard and J Thomas, 'Post-earnings announcement drift: delayed price response or risk premium?', *Journal of Accounting Research*, vol. 27, 1989, pp. 1–48; V Bernard and J Thomas, 'Evidence that stock prices do not fully reflect the implications of current earnings for future earnings', *Journal of Accounting and Economics*, vol. 13, 1990, pp. 305–40.

91. R Ball, 'The earnings–price anomaly', *Journal of Accounting and Economics*, June/September 1992, pp. 319–45.

92. R Rajan and H Servaes 1997, 'Analyst following of initial public offerings', *Journal of Finance*, vol. 52, 1997, pp. 507–29; H Lin and M McNichols, 'Understanding relationships and analysts' earnings forecasts and investment recommendations', *Journal of Accounting and Economics*, vol. 25,

1998, pp. 101–27; Dechow, Hutton and Sloan, op. cit.

93. R Michaely and K Womack, 'Conflict of interest and the credibility of underwriter analyst recommendations', *Review of Financial Studies*, vol. 12, 1999, pp. 653–68; Lin and McNichols, op. cit.; H Lin and M McNichols, 'Analyst coverage of initial public offering firms', unpublished working paper, Stanford University.

94. See P Dechow and R Sloan, 'Returns to contrarian investment strategies: Tests of naive expectation hypothesis', *Journal of Financial Economics*, vol. 43, 1997, pp. 3–27.

95. Deloitte Touche Tohmatsu *IASPlus* website, IASB Agenda Project: Reporting Comprehensive Income (Performance Reporting), www.iasplus.com.

96. KA Schipper, CM Schrand, T Shevlin, and TJ Wilks, 'Reconsidering Revenue Recognition', *Accounting Horizons*, vol. 23, no. 1, 2009.

97. GC Biddle and J-H Choi, 'Is comprehensive income useful? *Journal of Contemporary Accounting and Economics*, vol. 2, no. 1, 2006, pp. 1–32.

98. W DeBondt and R Thaler, 'Does the stock market overreact?' *Journal of Finance*, vol. 40, 1985, pp. 793–805; W DeBondt and R Thaler, 'Further evidence of investor overreaction and stock market seasonality', *Journal of Finance*, vol. 42, 1987, pp. 557–81.

99. T Brailsford, 'A test for the winner–loser anomaly in the Australian Equity Market 1958–87', *Journal of Business Finance and Accounting*, vol. 19, 1992, pp. 225–42; N Chopra, J Lakonishok and J Ritter, 'Measuring abnormal performance: Does the market overreact?' *Journal of Financial Economics*, vol. 32, 1992, pp. 235–68.

100. N Jagdeesh and S Titman, 'Returns to buying winners and selling losers: Implications for stock market efficiency', *Journal of Finance*, vol. 48, 1993, pp. 65–91.

101. J Lakonishok, A Shleifer and R Vishny, 'Contrarian investment, extrapolation, and risk', *Journal of Finance*, vol. 49, 1994, pp. 1541–78; R La Porta, 'Expectations and

the cross-section of stock returns', *Journal of Finance*, vol. 51, 1996, pp. 1715–42; Dechow and Sloan, op. cit.

102. R Sloan, 'Do stock prices fully reflect information in accruals and cash flows about future earnings', *Accounting Review*, vol. 71, 1996, pp. 289–316; D Collins and P Hribar, 'Earnings-based and accrual-based market anomalies: One effect or two?', *Journal of Accounting and Economics*, 2000; D Collins and P Hribar, 'Errors in estimating accruals: Implications for empirical research', Working paper, University of Iowa, 2000; H Xie, 'Are discretionary accruals mispriced? A re-examination', Working paper, University of Arizona, 1999.

103. M Bradshaw, S Richardson and R Sloan, 'Earnings quality and financial reporting credibility: An empirical investigation', Working paper, University of Michigan, 1999.

104. Lev and Thiagarajan, op. cit.; J Abarbanell and B Bushee, 'Fundamental analysis, future earnings, and stock prices', *Journal of Accounting Research*, vol. 35, 1997, pp. 1–24; J Piotroski, 'Value investing: The use of historical financial statement information to separate winners from losers', *Journal of Accounting Research*, 2000.

105. Watts and Zimmerman, op. cit., p. 74.

106. R Kaplan and R Roll, 'Investor evaluation of accounting information: Some empirical evidence', *Journal of Business*, April 1972, pp. 225–57.

107. RG Sloan, 'Do stock prices fully reflect information in accruals and cash flows about future earnings?' *Accounting Review*, vol. 71, no. 3, 1996, pp. 289–315.

108. PM Dechow, RG Sloan and AP Sweeney, 'Causes and consequences of earnings manipulation: An analysis of firms subject to enforcement actions by the SEC', *Contemporary Accounting Research*, vol. 13, no. 1, Spring 1996, pp. 1–36.

109. CA Marquardt and CI Wiedman, 'How are earnings managed? An examination of specific accruals',

Contemporary Accounting Research, vol. 21, no. 2, 2004, pp. 461–91.

110. MD Beneish and ME Vargus, 'Insider trading, earnings quality and accrual mispricing', *Accounting Review*, vol. 77, no. 4, 2002, pp. 755–91.

111. DW Blackwell, TR Noland and DB Winters, 'The value of auditor assurance: Evidence from loan pricing', *Journal of Accounting Research*, vol. 36, no. 1, 1998, pp. 57–70.

112. SA Mansi, WF Maxwell and DP Miller, 'Does auditor quality and tenure matter to investors? Evidence from the bond market', *Journal of Accounting Research*, vol. 42, no. 4, 2004, pp. 755–93.

113. IK Khurana, and KK Raman, 'Litigation risk and the financial reporting credibility of Big 4 versus non-Big 4 audits: Evidence from Anglo-American countries', *The Accounting Review*, vol. 79, no. 2, 2004, pp. 473–95.

114. Y Li and D Stokes, 'Audit quality and cost of equity capital', Working paper, Monash University, 2009.

115. K Menon and D Williams, 'The insurance hypothesis and market prices,' *The Accounting Review*, vol. 69, no. 2, 1994, pp. 327–42.

116. PK Chaney and KL Philipich, 'Shredded reputation: The cost of audit failure', *Journal of Accounting Research*, vol. 40, no. 4, September, 2002, pp. 1221–45.

117. Archival data are data collected from records of past events. For example, details about a company's auditor and financial characteristics are obtained from the company's annual report. Details about share prices are obtained from daily reports of share prices. This contrasts with experimental data that are obtained from observations made of an experiment controlled by a researcher. An example from natural science can be used to illustrate this point: archival data about food eaten by a wild animal would be obtained by a researcher from analysing droppings found in the natural habitat; experimental data is obtained by a researcher from observing which bowl of food is preferred by a captive animal that has the choice between a number of food bowls provided by the researcher.

13

Behavioural research in accounting

After reading this chapter, you should have an appreciation of the following:

1 the behavioural perspective and the nature of behavioural accounting research

2 the contribution to our understanding of the role of accounting information within and outside the accounting entity provided by studying behaviour

3 the influence of accounting information on behaviour and on decision processes

4 the fact that organisations are complex environments and accounting disclosures are trade-offs between competing perspectives and interests

5 the inherent constraints on behavioural research

6 issues for auditors.

Chapter 12 discussed research into how capital markets react to the release of accounting information. A difficulty of capital markets research is that it does not investigate how information is actually processed by market participants because it concentrates on only two items, the release of information and the capital market reaction (if any), not what goes on between these two events. One of the responses to this limitation was the development of agency theory as described in chapter 11. Agency theory examines why firms choose particular accounting methods from a set of acceptable alternatives. Although agency theory is concerned with the actions of individual managers and other parties, it makes the important assumption that all individuals are motivated to maximise their self-interest. This assumption makes it easier to develop testable predictions for research but it does not really *explain* why people act as they do, because the same reason is given for different behaviours. For instance, when a manager chooses the FIFO method of inventory measurement, agency theory says this is because it is in the self-interest of the manager to do so. Similarly, if another manager chooses the weighted average method instead, the same reason is given by the theory, that is, the choice was in the manager's self-interest. As we make different choices for different reasons, 'self-interest' is a very incomplete explanation for people's behaviour. Clearly, if we are to have a better understanding about how people use accounting information, then we need to study people's *actual* behaviours and decision processes. This is the role of a third area of accounting research, popularly known as 'behavioural accounting research' (BAR).

This chapter introduces you to the field of behavioural accounting research by describing some of the key questions it investigates and some of the main research tools used by researchers. Along the way we will indicate some of the important findings so far from this research, particularly in the area of financial accounting. Like the capital markets and agency theory schools of research, behavioural accounting also has its limitations and these will be mentioned throughout the chapter where relevant.

LO 1 → BEHAVIOURAL ACCOUNTING RESEARCH: DEFINITION AND SCOPE

Behavioural accounting research has been defined as:

> The study of the behaviour of accountants or the behaviour of non-accountants as they are influenced by accounting functions and reports.[1]

Behavioural accounting research (BAR), capital markets research and agency theory research can all be called 'positive' research in the sense that they all are concerned with discovering 'facts': capital markets research asks '*how* do securities markets react to accounting information?'; agency theory asks '*what* are the economic incentives that determine the choice of accounting methods?'; and behavioural research asks '*how* do people actually use and process accounting information?' However, they are also very different in many respects. For instance, capital markets research looks at the macro level of aggregate securities markets, whereas agency theory and behavioural accounting focus on the micro level of individual managers and firms. Capital markets research and agency theory are both derived from the discipline of economics and dispense with people's actual motivations by assuming that everyone is a rational wealth maximiser. Behavioural accounting, on the other hand, is derived from other disciplines such as psychology, sociology and organisational theory, and generally makes no assumptions about how people behave; rather, its objective is to discover *why* people behave as they do. Consequently, each of these three schools of accounting research is designed to answer very different types of questions about the practice of accounting.

Research in behavioural accounting is immense and has covered many different spheres of accounting activity.[2] Some BAR studies have, for instance, been applied in the area of auditing to improve auditors' decision making. For example, when auditors are planning the way they will conduct an audit of a particular client, they must assess how much risk is associated with the client. The higher the risk, the more audit work that will have to be done. Assessing risk is a highly complex task that could have serious consequences for the auditor (and investors) if an incorrect assessment is made and the auditor consequently performs a poor audit. BAR has been used to help analyse the risk assessments of auditors and improve them. Another major area of BAR has been in the field of management accounting. For example, BAR has been used to help explore and understand the various incentive and disincentive issues associated with different types of budgeting processes and how organisational form and accounting systems can affect the behaviour of individuals within firms. However, since this is a text on financial accounting, the main focus of this chapter is on the information contained in financial statements for users external to the firm. The major type of BAR in this area has become known as human judgement theory (HJT) or human information processing (HIP) and encompasses the judgement and decision making of accountants and auditors and the influence of the output of this function on users' judgements and decision making.[3] The aim of research within this model is often more than that of explaining and predicting behaviour at an individual or group level. It is also concerned with improving the quality of decision making. In the context of financial accounting, that aim translates into improving decision making by both producers (including auditors) and users of accounting reports.

LO 2 WHY IS BAR IMPORTANT?

There are a number of very good reasons that BAR is important to accounting practitioners and others:
- We noted at the start of this chapter how other accounting research schools such as capital markets and agency theory are not equipped to answer questions about *how* people use and process accounting information. To fill this void we need research that specifically examines the decision-making activities of the preparers, users, and auditors of accounting information.
- BAR can provide valuable insights into the ways different types of decision makers produce, process and react to particular items of accounting information and communication methods. We can use these insights to improve decision making in a variety of ways as described later in the chapter when we discuss the 'Brunswik lens model' of decision making. Improving decision making is important, of course, to both users of financial information (who want to avoid making bad decisions which lead to losses) and to preparers and auditors of financial information (who want to avoid being sued). An understanding of the information-processing aspects of accounting is also important to you in your own career. As information professionals, accountants need to develop high levels of expertise in information gathering, processing and communication. BAR can help lead to training and knowledge that improves these skills, thus allowing you to perform better in the workplace and improve your chances of obtaining work, gaining promotions and achieving better pay.[4]
- BAR can potentially provide useful information to accounting regulators such as the Australian Accounting Standards Board (AASB). As the main objective of accounting is to provide 'decision useful' information,[5] members of the AASB are

constantly grappling with the problem of which accounting methods and what types of disclosures will prove 'useful' to the users of financial statements. Behavioural accounting researchers can directly study specific accounting options and report to standard setters on which methods and disclosures improved users' decisions.

- The findings of BAR can also lead to efficiencies in the work practices of accountants and other professionals. For example, the expertise of senior and experienced members of an accounting firm can be recorded and harnessed by BAR methods to develop computerised expert systems for a variety of decision-making contexts. These expert systems can be used to train inexperienced practitioners and to undertake routine tasks that would otherwise tie up the valuable time of experienced staff. Some accounting firms, for instance, have used BAR methods to develop expert systems to conduct risk assessments of potential audit clients. In the past, this time-consuming task would have been done by senior members of the accounting firm, but a detailed screening of potential clients can now be done by less qualified staff using the computer expert system, subject to a final review by the firm's partners.

Development of behavioural accounting research

The term 'BAR' first appeared in the literature in 1967,[6] but HJT research had its foundations in the psychology literature with the seminal work of Ward Edwards in 1954.[7] The application of the research to accounting and auditing can be dated to 1974 when Ashton published an experimental study of the internal control judgements made by auditors.[8]

The last 30 years have seen an explosion of BAR in general and HJT research in particular, especially in auditing, where the importance of judgement to the audit process is paramount. To some extent, the development of behavioural research in the area of financial accounting has been eclipsed by the dominance of contracting theory since the 1980s. Nevertheless, important insights into the link between accounting information and human behaviour have been forthcoming.

Many disciplines (e.g. political science, organisation theory, sociology and statistics) have played a role in BAR's growth, but by far the most important behavioural science in terms of contribution has been psychology. The growth of HJT research in accounting owes much to the adaptation of a research method already well used in the psychology literature, the Brunswik lens model.[9] This technique represented a powerful new research approach which could be applied to the old question of which data users take notice of. Ashton is credited with being the first accounting researcher to use this technique, followed closely by Libby who was the first to use it in a user-oriented context. Both researchers have continued to play a dominant role in the development of BAR.

Behavioural effects of international accounting diversity

A behavioural accounting study was conducted by Choi and Levich (1990). They investigated the impact of international accounting differences on capital market participants. Growth in international financial markets and diversity in financial reporting had been noted in previous research. Therefore the authors asked the following questions: (1) Is accounting diversity perceived to be a problem, and if so, why? (2) Are attempts made to cope with national accounting differences and are these coping mechanisms successful? (3) Do problems associated with accounting diversity lead to capital market effects?

In posing these questions, the authors sought to obtain empirical evidence about the behaviour of participants in capital markets that would assist regulators and standard setters involved in the international harmonisation of financial reporting. They surveyed 52 market participants (institutional investors, corporate issuers, investment underwriters, market regulators, stock exchange officials and representatives of rating agencies and data services) from the United States, the United Kingdom, Germany, Switzerland and Japan.

The authors reported that approximately half of those surveyed felt that accounting diversity affected their capital market decisions. The other half responded that diversity had no effect because they used successful coping mechanisms, or because diversity was not considered an important issue to begin with. Some investors who restated accounting information reported that diversity affected their decisions, indicating that restatement was not always sufficient to remove the problem of diversity. The researchers concluded that accounting differences were important, and that they affected the capital market decisions of a significant number of market participants, regardless of their nationality, size, experience, scope of international activity and organisation structure. Thus, the study provided evidence that accounting diversity did affect decision making, suggesting that activities to reduce diversity could be beneficial.

Reference

Choi, F, & Levich, R 1990, *The capital market effects of international accounting diversity*, Homewood, Dow Jones.

An overview of approaches to understanding information processing

The basic objective of HJT research is to describe the way in which people use and process pieces of accounting (and other) information in a particular decision-making context. We call our description of a person's decision-making processes a 'model'. So, for example, we may use HJT research techniques to 'model' (or represent) the way in which a bank loan officer processes various information items (or 'cues' as they are called) such as the profit and cash flow figures to make a decision about whether to approve a loan application from a company. Although the Brunswik lens model has been the dominant method of developing models of decision making, there are also two other major research approaches. One of these is called 'process tracing', which is an attempt to build a decision tree representation of a person's judgements, and the other is known as the 'probabilistic judgement' paradigm, in which decision processes are represented as probability statements based on Bayes's theorem. Each of these three approaches to describing (modelling) decision making is outlined below.

The Brunswik lens model

Since the mid-1970s, the Brunswik lens model has been used as an analytical framework and the basis for most judgement studies involving prediction (e.g. of bankruptcy) and/or evaluation (e.g. of internal control).[10] Researchers use the lens model to investigate the relationship between multiple cues (or pieces of information) and decisions, judgements or predictions, by looking for regularities in the responses to those cues. The decision maker (e.g. bank loan officer) is viewed as looking through a lens of cues (e.g. financial ratios) which are probabilistically related to an event, in order to reach a conclusion about that event (e.g. likelihood of loan default/ non-default).[11] The diagrammatic representation in figure 13.1 will help make this process clearer.

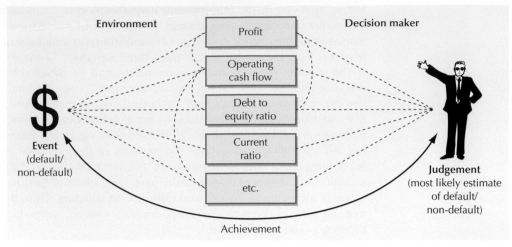

FIGURE 13.1 Diagrammatic representation of the lens model

Source: Adapted from R Libby, *Accounting and human information processing: theory and applications,* Englewood Cliffs, NJ: Prentice Hall, 1981, p. 6.

In developing a specific version of the Brunswik lens model, subjects are asked to make judgements for a large number of cases which are based on the same set of cues. For example, they may be asked to assess whether several firms are likely to fail, given the firms' working capital, price–earnings, earnings per share, quick, debt to equity and other ratios. A linear model, describing the functional relationship between the cues (ratios) and responses (likelihood of failure), is then constructed as a means of representing the way in which information is processed by individuals.[12] Using figure 13.1 as an example, our bank loan officer is given financial ratios and other accounting information for different companies. The bank loan officer is asked to make a judgement, on the basis of this information, about which of the companies will default on their loan payments and which companies will not default. A regression analysis is then conducted using the bank officer's responses (i.e. default/non-default) as the dependent variable and the financial ratios and other data as the independent variables that are attempting to explain the officer's judgements. As a result of the analysis we might, for instance, arrive at a model of the bank loan officer's judgements in the form of the following simplified equation:

Likelihood of default/non-default = a constant term − 0.15 profit + 0.25 cash flow + 0.50 debt to equity ratio + . . . other information cues . . . + error

Each of the beta weights in our regression model represents the relative importance of the information cues to the bank loan officer when making a judgement. So, in our equation above, the debt to equity ratio is viewed as being the most important cue to the bank officer because it has the highest beta weight, followed by cash flow and then profit.

The Brunswik lens model is a very powerful tool for helping us understand decision processes in very specific situations. Think about the ways the model in figure 13.1 can be used to improve decision making. First, look at the left-hand side of the diagram, that is, the relationship between the event of interest (default/non-default) and the variables being used to assess that event. One set of lens studies can examine the relationship between the event and the information cues being used by the decision maker to see whether the 'right' cues are being used; that is, whether the pieces of accounting information are useful predictors of the event. If the information cues are not relevant to the decision, then decision makers can be informed of this and taught which pieces of information are more helpful. Now consider the right-hand side of the diagram, that is, the relationship between the decision maker and the information cues. A Brunswik lens model study can be conducted to learn how decision makers actually use the accounting information cues and what weighting (importance) they assign to each cue. On the basis of our first set of studies we might find that the decision maker is not weighting the cues correctly. Perhaps, for instance, too much emphasis is placed on the profit figure when our analysis of the information cues suggests that more emphasis should be given to the debt to equity ratio and operating cash flow information instead. Armed with this information, we could then train decision makers to change the weightings they give to the different information cues to improve the accuracy of their judgements. In addition, we might discover that there are pieces of accounting information useful for making decisions that the decision maker is not presently using. Again, this information could be used in training sessions to improve the decision maker's performance. In general, the use of the Brunswik lens method has led to the discovery of valuable insights regarding:

- patterns of cue use evident in various tasks
- weights that decision makers implicitly place on a variety of information cues
- the relative accuracy of decision makers of different expertise levels in predicting and evaluating a variety of tasks
- the circumstances under which an expert system and/or 'model of human behaviour' outperforms humans
- the stability (consistency) of human judgement over time
- the degree of insight decision makers possess regarding their pattern of use of data
- the degree of consensus displayed in a variety of group decision tasks.

Because this information is useful in understanding decision-making processes, researchers have been (and still are) trying to determine the entire decision model or the decision processes used by various classes of users.

Process tracing methods

As described later in this chapter, models of decision making derived from using the Brunswik lens model usually have been found to have very good predictive powers. Indeed, a comparison of the predictions of a lens model equation and the decisions of a human decision maker usually shows that the lens model is a better predictor of the event of interest than the person from whom the model was derived. One of the reasons for this is that the statistical lens model removes much of the random error that creeps into human judgement owing to such things as tiredness, illness or lack of concentration. However, one important limitation of the Brunswik lens approach is that it is not a good descriptor of how people actually make decisions. The use of an equation format implicitly assumes that the decision maker is able to simultaneously process all the information items, but the majority of decision makers report that they analyse problems in a step-by-step process, looking at one piece of information first, assessing that, moving on to the next piece of information and so on until a decision is reached.

Although having a model that is a good predictor is very important, researchers and practitioners also want to have an explanation about how a decision is made. An explanation for the decision can help reveal weaknesses in the decision process that can then be removed with training and other means of improvement. These improvements will in turn lead to better predictions than before. In an attempt to capture the step-wise approach to decision making, some HJT researchers have used a different approach to modelling decision making called 'process tracing' or 'verbal protocol' methods.[13] In process tracing, the decision maker may again, for instance, be given a series of case studies to analyse but this time is asked to verbally describe each step gone through when making the decision. These verbal descriptions are recorded by the researcher and then analysed to produce a 'decision tree' diagram to represent the decision processes of the decision maker. Figure 13.2 presents a hypothetical decision tree model of a bank loan officer's default/non-default judgements. Each circle (or 'node') of the decision tree contains a question related to a step in the decision process. Depending on the answer to the question in a node of the tree, a decision might be reached (the square boxes in figure 13.2) or a further step is made towards reaching a decision. So, for example, in figure 13.2 the first step of the bank officer's decision process is to ask whether the debt to equity ratio is greater than 3. If the answer is 'yes', then the officer immediately concludes that the loan applicant will default. If the answer, however, is 'no', then the officer goes to the next stage of the decision process and asks whether the company's size is greater than $10 million. The answer to this question then leads to further questions and so on down the tree until a judgement is reached about the likelihood of the loan applicant defaulting.

In general terms, the decision trees derived from process tracing methods are intuitively good descriptors of people's decision processes. However, relative to Brunswik lens models, process tracing methods are not always good predictors of the event of interest. One reason for this is that decision makers often have difficulty explaining all the steps they go through. This is particularly true of tasks that decision makers do routinely and often because the task becomes so familiar that the decision processes are implicit and unconscious in the mind of the decision maker.[14]

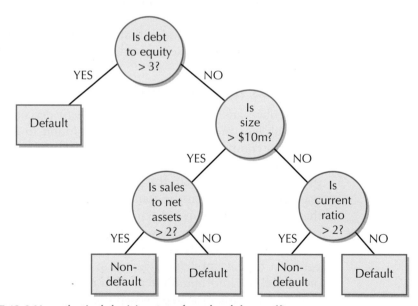

FIGURE 13.2 Hypothetical decision tree for a bank loan officer

Some researchers have tried to overcome the general limitations of both the lens and process tracing methods by combining the predictive and descriptive powers of the two approaches. One such alternative is a statistical technique known as 'classification and regression trees' (CART) that uses statistical methods to partition (or split) the output of a decision maker's judgements into decision 'nodes' that maximise the power of the model to correctly predict the classification of different cases into the right type of decision.

Howieson[15] used the CART method to model the share action recommendations ('buy', 'buy/hold', 'hold', 'hold/sell', 'sell') of three Australian investment analysts, using accounting and other information taken from the company reports written by the analysts. Figure 13.3 shows an extract of the CART decision tree derived for one of the analysts.

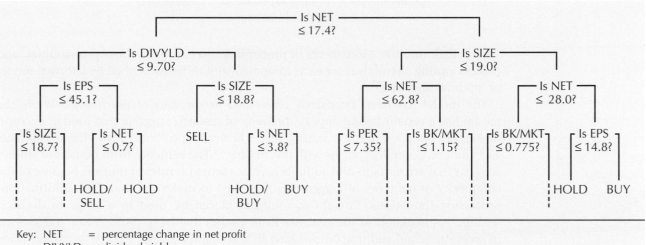

Key: NET   = percentage change in net profit
      DIVYLD = dividend yield
      SIZE   = firm size measured as market capitalisation
      PER   = current price to estimated earnings ratio
      EPS   = earnings per share
      BK/MKT = book to market ratio

FIGURE 13.3 Extract of CART decision tree for an Australian share analyst

Source: BA Howieson, 'A security analyst's action recommendations: an application of recursive partitioning to modelling judgement', *Australian Journal of Management*, vol. 16, no. 2, December 1991, p. 176.

The diagram shows how various accounting variables were used by the analyst to arrive at buy, hold or sell decisions. The CART models combined strong power to correctly classify analysts' recommendations with an intuitively appealing descriptor of their decision processes. However, it was found that the more data available for analysis, the more complex the resulting decision trees, making it more difficult to derive simple rules for training other analysts. The relative complexity of decision trees has been a common problem no matter whether process tracing or CART methods have been used to derive them.

Probabilistic judgement

The probabilistic judgement model is useful for looking at situations in accounting where initial beliefs about a prediction or evaluation need to be revised once further evidence becomes available. An investor's revision of an investment decision in the light of new evidence concerning the outcome of a lawsuit against a firm is an example of this type of situation.

This model argues that the 'normatively' correct way to revise initial beliefs, stated as subjective probabilities, is by applying Bayes's theorem, a basic tenet of conditional probability theory. Bayes's theorem states that the revised (posterior) probability in the light of additional evidence is equal to the original belief (base rate) multiplied by the amount by which prior expectations should be revised; that is, by the informativeness or diagnosticity of the new data.[16]

Thus:

Posterior odds	=	Likelihood ratio	×	Prior odds
(revised probability)		(amount by which prior expectations should be revised)		(initial probability or base rate)

Thus actual, intuitive assessments of probabilities, revisions of those probabilities, and choices among alternatives are each compared with those prescribed by a formal model or 'optimal answer'.[17]

The model has been extensively researched in the area of psychology. While the model has a certain logical appeal, the body of research suggests that human decision makers are not good intuitive statisticians.[18] Research specifically involving accountants and auditors generally concurs with this finding.[19] The evidence from numerous studies suggests that accountants and auditors invoke a series of 'rules of thumb', because of the complexity of the types of judgements they need to make and their own information-processing limitations. Probabilistic judgement can be used in a range of decision settings. A discussion of the evidence from studies involving probabilistic judgements in accounting and auditing follows later in this chapter.

A non-accounting example, drawn from Libby,[20] might help clarify the normative application of Bayes's theorem.

> Suppose that you are in charge of security for a large department store. A recent audit has indicated that losses owing to employee theft have risen to 10 per cent of sales. In response to your superior's concern, you institute a mandatory lie detector screening program for the employees. Previous research has shown that:
> - 2 per cent of employees steal
> - the probability that the employee will produce a 'deceptive' response on the lie detector if he or she did in fact lie (true positive) is 0.9
> - the probability of producing the 'deceptive' response if the employee did not lie (false positive) is 0.12.
>
> **Question**
> If the employee produced a deceptive response to the question, 'Did you steal from the store?' what is the probability that the employee did in fact steal?
>
> **Normative Bayes's solution**
> Posterior odds = Likelihood ratio × Prior odds
> $$= 0.90/0.12 \times 0.02/0.98$$
> $$= 0.153/1$$
> Probability $= 0.153/1.153$
> $$= 13\%$$

Libby argues that most people suggest that the probability is quite high, around 80 per cent.[21]

The finding that human decision makers do not apply Bayes's multiplicative rule when revising prior beliefs is pervasive in the HJT research literature. This led researchers in psychology to investigate what rules, if any, are used. They found that the explanation seems to lie in the use of rules of thumb or biases, which humans resort to in order to simplify complex judgement tasks.

Three categories of rules of thumb (known in the literature as 'heuristics') have been identified in the psychology literature: representativeness, availability and anchoring.[22] As previously mentioned, financial accounting researchers have accumulated much evidence that these rules of thumb or biases are also pervasive among accountants, auditors and users of financial statements. That is not to imply that these rules of thumb are necessarily dysfunctional or that they automatically lead to poor judgements. Rather, it may be that they represent an efficient and effective method of dealing with complexity and the limitations of human cognitive processes. A later section of this chapter explains how each of the three identified rules of thumb operates, and reviews evidence regarding the existence and effects of each in an accounting context.

Lens model studies — the evidence

Many studies have used the lens model framework to examine the accuracy of humans' predictions of business failure. This task is important and realistic for people such as investors, bank loan officers, other lenders and auditors. It has generally been researched by providing the subject with a number of numerical cues across repetitive cases of actual business success and failure, drawn from archival data. Thus, in this task (as opposed to others described later), a 'correct' solution exists as a benchmark against which to compare human performance.

Using the lens model as a research tool in this way allows analysis of the consistency of judgements, of whether a 'model of human behaviour' can predict more accurately than a human. It also enables analysis of the ability of the cues to predict the event in question (the 'environmental predictability' using an ideal cue weighting). In addition, it can give insights regarding the degree of consensus between decision makers.

The 'model of human behaviour' is developed using a mathematical representation of an individual's pattern of use of the cues. This model is then applied to the cases in question. The evidence consistently shows that humans are reasonably proficient at developing principles or models to solve the success/failure task using financial ratios, but are outperformed when their own models (inferred from the pattern of use of cues) are applied mathematically for two reasons: they misweigh cues, and they inconsistently apply their decision rules due to factors such as fatigue and boredom. Mathematical application of either the environmental model (using ideal cue weightings) or the 'model of human behaviour' is perfectly consistent over time, eliminating random error.

Libby was the first to research the task of assessing business failure, and several studies have followed.[23] What has emerged in the literature is the question of whether disclosing to the subjects the actual rate of failure is necessary to achieve realism in the task. The actual rate of business failure is very low, less than 5 per cent. Therefore subjects, unless they are told otherwise, bring to the judgement task the expectation that the number of failure cases will be marginal.

On the other hand, researchers cannot hope to gain evidence from this task setting unless a 'reasonable' number of actual failure cases are included in the materials provided. Researchers have generally used a failure rate of between 33 per cent and 50 per cent, and experiments manipulating the rate of failure and its prior disclosure/ non-disclosure have been carried out.[24] The results have been inconclusive[25] in terms of the extent to which prior disclosure of the sample failure rate matters, but it seems that task predictability[26] and information representativeness play a role.[27]

Other variations of this line of research include observing the effect of allowing subjects to choose their own ratios, examining the impact of information overload, and analysing the confidence level that decision makers place on their judgement and whether confidence influences accuracy. Abdel-Khalik and El-Sheshai concluded that it was the subject's choice of information, rather than his or her processing of the chosen cues, that limited accuracy.[28] Simnett and Trotman found that, although subjects were able to use all the information from ratios they themselves selected, they were unable to improve performance when asked to apply an ideal cue-weighting model. These authors concluded that when subjects are unable to choose their own ratios their information-processing performance declines.[29]

The information overload literature has implications for the presentation and disclosure issue in financial accounting. It provides evidence of lower consensus and lower decision-making consistency for individuals experiencing overload.[30] It is thought that, as the amount of information increases, initially the use and integration of the information increases. However, beyond some point, additional information results in a decrease in the amount of information integrated into the decision-making task.[31] Chewning and Harrell, in a financial distress prediction task, found evidence of the above theory once subjects were given more than 8 cues (financial ratios).[32] Libby noted that the addition of less valid cues to a set containing more valid cues decreased performance;[33] however, other studies have detected no such relationship.[34]

Overall, the literature on information overload has produced inconclusive results. One reason for the lack of clear outcomes across these different studies is that most researchers have not sought to determine whether the additional data provided were actually 'informative' (i.e. relevant to the decision at hand) in the first place. Further, there has been little attempt to see whether decision makers actually used the additional data provided by the researcher.[35]

The judgement confidence literature has consistently found that both expert and non-expert subjects are overconfident of their ability in specific judgement tasks.[36] This overconfidence seems to stem from three factors:

- the tendency for humans to seek out and overweight positive feedback
- the limited nature of feedback in many instances (e.g. in failure or distress prediction the correctness of a decision not to lend is rarely evaluated)
- the interdependency of actions and outcomes (e.g. the act of lending/not lending itself influences success or failure).[37]

Libby[38] and Zimmer[39] found that the accuracy of judgements increased with increasing confidence, but other studies have shown that confidence is not related to accuracy.[40]

After examining the lens model evidence collected from many decision tasks, including the prediction of failure, Libby sums up the findings of this category of research, as follows:

> In many important decision-making situations, the environmental predictability of available information is low. However, even in situations where environmental predictability is relatively high, poor judgemental achievement is the norm.
>
> Both human inconsistency and misweighting of cues contribute to the poor achievement. Combining quantitative information in repetitive tasks does not appear to be a function that people perform well. Thus, in these situations, replacing people with models (e.g. environmental regression models, models of man, and equal weighting models) shows promise for increasing predictive accuracy.[41]

Although this statement was made in 1981, the evidence gained since then has not violated the thrust of Libby's observation.

Theory in action 13.1 provides an example of how accounting influences behaviour by investors. This media release illustrates the growing influence of the Australian Shareholders' Association.

The power of interest group perceptions

ASA seeks to remove NAB director

The Australian Shareholders' Association (ASA) today called for shareholder support for a resolution to remove Mr Paul Rizzo, Chair of National Australia Bank (NAB) Risk Committee, from the board.

John Curry, Chairman of the ASA's Company Monitoring Committee in Victoria, said "The NAB Risk Committee has failed in its oversight of the bank's risk management, as evidenced by the significant provisions and hedging costs which the bank has incurred in relation to its portfolio of collateralized debt obligations".

"Mr Rizzo, as chairman of NAB's Risk Committee, should be held accountable for this failure."

The ASA has commenced a campaign to obtain the 100 signatures necessary to move a resolution at the NAB AGM on 18 December 2008 for the removal of Mr Rizzo. Mr Curry said, "We have emailed our members today and will be giving NAB shareholders the opportunity to sign the request at ASA meetings."

"Given the contact we have been receiving from disgruntled NAB shareholders, we do not expect to have any difficulty raising the required 100 signatures."

Upon obtaining the 100 signatures the ASA will request that NAB place a resolution before the AGM seeking the removal of Mr Rizzo, and circulate a statement in support of the resolution to all shareholders with the notice of meeting. The statement the ASA seeks to circulate in accordance with Section 249P of the Corporations Act 2001, is below.

A previous resolution moved by ASA members in 2005 to dismiss a NAB director, Geoffrey Tomlinson, received 39% of the vote.

National Australia Bank Limited (NAB)
Statement pursuant to Section 249P of the Corporations Act
National Australia Bank's Risk Committee has failed to adequately consider the underlying value of, or risks involved in, the significant portfolio of collateralised debt obligations (CDOs) held by the bank. These assets have resulted in large provisions that have significantly reduced shareholder value.

Whilst the entire board is responsible, Mr Paul Rizzo, as a director and chairman of NAB's Risk Committee, should be held accountable for the weak risk management culture which has led to the loss of shareholder value and bank credibility in relation to these assets.

When announcing the $181 million charge against the value of its portfolio of CDOs in March 2008, NAB claimed to be avoiding high risk business.

In May, the chairman of NAB, Mr Michael Chaney, wrote to shareholders stating "The volatility in world financial markets has highlighted the importance of robust risk management systems and prudent capital management in financial institutions. The efforts of our people to strengthen our risk framework and balance sheet in recent years has been validated by the company's resilience during the recent period of significant financial disruption".

In July the bank announced a further provision of $8309 million against the value of this portfolio.

In September, NAB announced additional costs of $100 million in 2008, $60 million per year for 5 years and a lesser yearly amount thereafter to hedge against default of the CDO portfolio.

In addition NAB still has a substantial portfolio of CDOs, corporate bonds and commercial mortgage backed securities that are neither provisioned nor hedged.

Shareholders will have an opportunity to hold Mr Rizzo accountable for this failure of risk management by supporting a resolution to remove him as a director of NAB at the forthcoming annual general meeting.

If you are unable to attend and wish to nominate the ASA as your representative at that meeting please insert the name "Australian Shareholders' Association" as your proxy on the proxy form and lodge it in accordance with the instructions shown on the form itself . . .

Source: Media Release posted by Australian Shareholders' Association, 8 October 2008, www.asa.asn.au.

1. On what type of information would the ASA decide that a company board or chairperson should be censured or removed for poor performance?
2. What is motivating shareholders to operate as a group to censure or remove company boards which do not appear to be managing the company in an appropriate fashion?
3. Is the ASA concerned about corporate governance or raising its own profile to increase membership and relative power? What type of value judgements did you make to answer this question?

Process tracing studies — the evidence

Brunswik lens models and process tracing style studies are different technologies with the same objective of modelling decision processes as completely as possible. Mention has already been made of the main differences between these two modelling methods. Brunswik lens models implicitly treat the decision process as a simple linear combination of the information cues whereas the decision trees derived from process tracing acknowledge the step-by-step nature of decision making, in which the information content of one piece of data interacts with that of other pieces of data. The majority of studies which have investigated the linearity of decision makers' judgements[42] conclude that the assumption of simple linear combinations of information cues is justified but some studies in business contexts[43] have found evidence of statistically significant interactions between information items suggesting that process tracing methods are advantageous modelling techniques for representing decision making in some contexts.

The relative predictive power of lens and process tracing models has been studied in business contexts by Larcker and Lessig[44] and Selling and Shank.[45] In a share selection scenario, Larcker and Lessig found that process tracing models outperformed the statistical linear models, but Selling and Shank found the opposite when the two approaches were compared in a task involving the prediction of bankruptcy. These differences in the studies may reflect our earlier comment that the type of decision task requires different styles of decision processing. As usual, the complexity of human decision making means that more in-depth research is needed to understand what types of decision task characteristics determine the most appropriate style of information processing.

Format and presentation of financial statements

In 1976 Libby observed that three basic options existed for improving decision making:

- changing the presentation and amount of information
- educating decision makers
- replacing decision makers either with a model of themselves or with an ideal cue-weighting model.[46]

Given the importance of the first suggestion to accountants, auditors, regulators and standard setters, surprisingly little research has been undertaken in ascertaining ideal accounting presentation formats. The studies that do exist have tended to examine radical changes to financial statement presentation in the form of multidimensional graphics (see figure 13.4). However, in response to calls in the literature, researchers have returned to the issue of ideal presentation of the more traditional table format.

The information load literature is also pertinent to the question of improving decision-making capabilities of users of financial statements.

The lens model is useful in examining financial statement presentation issues as well as in analysis of predictive judgements. It permits analysis of human judgement accuracy in terms of determining the extent to which the individual detects essential properties of the judgement task and consistently applies judgement policy. If changing the report format of information results in improving either of the above characteristics, human judgement accuracy should increase. The decision-usefulness objective, adopted in the conceptual framework, depends partly on the user's ability to interpret the data for a given investment or credit decision. The impact of a change in the report format on subjects' ability to detect a change in the financial status of the firm can similarly be examined within a lens model framework.

The multidimensional graphics most researched have been in the form of schematic or Chernoff faces as illustrated in figure 13.4.

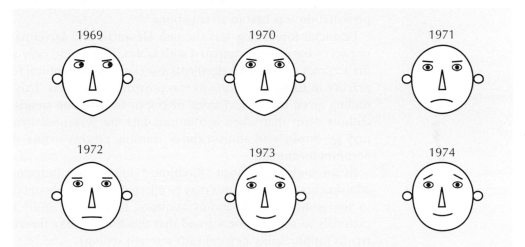

FIGURE 13.4 Chernoff faces representing changes in financial condition
Source: D Stock and CJ Watson, 'Human judgement accuracy: multidimensional graphics and humans versus models', *Journal of Accounting Research*, Spring 1984, p. 202.

The faces are constructed by mapping transformed financial variables onto facial features. Mathematical precision in terms of nose length, brow angle and mouth curvature is used to represent changes in financial position from one period to the next.

Interest in this mode of presentation arose in 1979 when Moriarity reported that subjects using financial information represented by such graphics outperformed a well-accepted financial distress model.[47] As previously noted, it has been a consistent research finding that models generally outperform humans and so this form of presentation offered promise. Stock and Watson found only weak confirmation of Moriarity's results in a prediction of bond ratings task.[48] However, they did find that accuracy performance using multidimensional graphics was superior to that attained with a conventional tabular presentation. This latter result held even when the subject had minimal accounting training. Stock and Watson concluded:

> ... a multidimensional graphics approach would be useful whenever cost or data availability makes good statistical models impossible to build, especially if the results using multidimensional graphics are at least as good as the results of a model.[49]

To date, financial statement preparers have not been prepared to publish graphics as radical as the Chernoff faces. However, the use of colour and more conventional graphs is common. Researchers in the fields of statistics, psychology, information systems, and education have investigated the relative advantages of various graphic and tabular forms of visual presentation for displaying both financial and non-financial information. To date, results are conflicting and questionable[50] but a common finding in accounting contexts is that presentation does influence decision making.

For example, Blocher, Moffie and Zmud[51] investigated the effects of different forms of presentation (tables and colour graphics) on accuracy and bias of internal auditors' decisions. They found that the relative effectiveness of different forms of presentation is a function of the amount of information that is presented to, and must be processed by, the decision maker. Graphic reports seem better for low levels of complexity and tabular reports for high levels of complexity.

Davis, using MBA students, investigated the impact of three graphical formats of financial statements (line graph, bar chart, pie chart) and the conventional table. That study found that the question the decision maker sought to answer from the statements and the forms of presentation interactively affected performance. No one form of presentation was best in all situations.[52]

Financial forecasting was the task Desanctis and Jarvenpaa chose for assessing the impact of bar graphs compared with tables. They found only a modest improvement in the accuracy of forecast judgements associated with graphical formats and then only after practice in using these formats was provided to subjects. This is a somewhat surprising finding given the alleged value of graphs in detecting trends and relationships.[53] The authors warn that when accounting data are presented in a graphical format, users may go through an adjustment or learning process before the graphical information becomes meaningful.

In an auditing context, Ricchiute[54] found that judgements regarding necessary adjustments to the accounts may be affected by the mode of presentation of information to the auditor: visual and/or auditory. Since most audit research presents written materials to subjects, he warned that this finding may threaten the generalisability of results (applicability beyond each research setting).

Recent research confirms that the impact of different presentation formats and styles remains a complex area that needs further context-specific investigation. In two studies based on a bankruptcy prediction scenario, So and Smith investigated the impact of colour graphics, gender, task complexity, and different presentation formats on the predictive accuracy of a sample composed mainly of undergraduate business students. In one of the studies[55] the decision makers used either colour or black-and-white bar charts of financial ratios as the basis for their judgements in different tasks that were either high or low in complexity (as measured by the level of inconsistency in the financial ratios). The results suggested that coloured graphics were not effective when the task was complex and that, interestingly, females made more effective use of colour than males. So and Smith concluded that more research needs to be conducted on the relationship between colour and information processing to aid in understanding the results they found.

In another study,[56] So and Smith obtained results confirming the call by Desanctis and Jarvenpaa mentioned earlier for more education on the use of graphics. So and Smith asked their decision makers to work with one of the following sets of data: a combination of tables and bar charts, or tables and Chernoff faces, or tables only. They found that in situations where the complexity of the information was high, the use of tables alone led to the highest accuracy, suggesting that the use of graphics and pictorial representations of data actually led to a decrease in the effectiveness of users' decision making. One of the reasons for this might be the desire of decision makers to choose the easier option when situations are complex, but graphical and pictorial representations of data are often more abstract and less detailed than the information found in tables. These findings are a concern in an age when many firms are turning to the Internet and multimedia-style presentations to communicate with stakeholders.

These examples demonstrate that Wainer and Thiessen's claim, that there is no well-developed and tested theory that can be used to specify the circumstances under which different forms of presentation are most appropriate, remains true.[57] That this situation still holds is probably, at least in part, attributable to the concentration of HJT research in an auditing context over the last decade. Much of that auditing research has taken place within the probabilistic judgement framework, the evidence from which is discussed in the next section.

Probabilistic judgement studies — the evidence

In many accounting contexts and especially in auditing, there is no 'correct' solution with which judgements can be compared in order to assess their accuracy. One way of coping with this lack of a benchmark criterion against which to judge performance is to examine the degree of consensus regarding a particular decision across a number of decision makers. Another way is to use a mathematical or statistical model. As discussed in an earlier section, probabilistic judgement research is based on analysis of whether humans revise their beliefs in line with Bayes's theorem once new evidence becomes available. HJT research within this model has consistently demonstrated that humans possessing a variety of skill levels and, observed over a variety of tasks, revise their prior probabilities to a lesser extent than Bayes's theorem prescribes. This conservatism has been attributed to the use of rules of thumb and biases which are adopted as a means of simplifying complex judgements in order for humans to cope.

Three rules of thumb are defined in the literature as follows:

* *Representativeness.* This rule of thumb states that when judging the probability that a particular item comes from a particular population of items, people's judgement will be determined by the extent to which the item is representative of the population. Items or events that are viewed by the decision maker as being more representative will be assessed as having a higher probability of occurrence than those that are less representative. For instance, a bank loan officer may judge the likelihood that a company will default on its loan by how similar it is to a stereotypical failed firm. As described later, research has shown that the use of this rule of thumb can lead to poor decisions because decision makers who use it often ignore other relevant data that are not part of the representative stereotype. One example of these errors relates to the rate at which the event of interest actually occurs in the total population (this is called the 'base rate'). The population rate of loan default might be, say, 5 per cent but the decision maker might ignore this important information and consequently overstate the rate of default when evaluating a sample of companies mainly because he or she is looking only for companies that have characteristics that correspond to the stereotype.

* *Availability.* The availability rule of thumb refers to the assessment of the probability of an event based on the ease with which instances of that event come to mind.[58] The consequence of use of this rule of thumb is that probabilities related to 'sensational' events are likely to be overestimated.

* *Anchoring and adjustment.* This rule of thumb refers to a general judgement process in which an initially generated or given response serves as an anchor, and other

information is used to adjust that response.[59] The consequence of this rule of thumb is the possibility of insufficient adjustment in the light of changing circumstances.

As previously stated, most of the research into probabilistic reasoning has used auditors as subjects. Auditors are ideal subjects for the study of human judgement, and probabilistic reasoning in particular, since many audit judgements entail the need to revise assessments in the light of additional evidence. In addition, in the United States the larger public accounting firms have been extremely cooperative in making available both funds and practising auditors for research.[60] A brief overview of research related to all three rules of thumb follows.

LO 3 → REPRESENTATIVENESS: THE EVIDENCE

Kahneman and Tversky[61] first reported the existence of representativeness and the tendency to ignore base rates. Since then, research in both the psychological and accounting fields has investigated the phenomenon. The evidence is inconclusive in that it shows base-rate information is sometimes neglected and sometimes used appropriately in assessing the probability of an event.[62] The use of base-rate information seems to be highly sensitive to a variety of tasks and contexts, and this has led to the hypothesis that probabilistic reasoning involves contingent processing.[63]

Joyce and Biddle[64] used an accounting adaptation of the employee theft/lie detector example previously given in this chapter to illustrate the application of Bayes's theorem. In this example related to management fraud, again a very low base rate was used. It was expected that, as in the previous example, subjects would pay insufficient attention to the low base rate and, therefore, have too high an expectation of fraudulent activity. Practising auditors were the subjects, and results indicated that, although the auditors did not ignore the base rate given, they also did not consider it sufficiently. Since audit judgements often involve low-base-rate, high-impact events (e.g. fraud), the authors were concerned about the implications of this result. However, Holt[65] cast doubt on the findings of Joyce and Biddle, arguing that it was the wording of the problems, leading to a framing effect, which had driven their results. Framing effects are defined as a cognitive perspective elicited by the task characteristics.[66] They are often illustrated by use of the half-empty/half-full glass analogy where a pessimist regards a glass as half empty and an optimist regards the same glass as half full.

Availability: the evidence

The basis of this rule of thumb is that likelihood judgements are based on retrieval from memory of relevant instances or construction of plausible scenarios. The more instances recalled, or the greater the ease with which one can recall instances or generate plausible explanations for an event, the higher will be the judged probability of occurrence of the event.[67] However, this requires a large sample of probabilities to improve prediction accuracy.

Moser[68] examined the availability rule of thumb in connection with investors' predictive judgements. He asked half of his 58 subjects to list reasons the target company's profits would increase and then reasons the company's profits might decrease. The remaining subjects listed reasons in the opposite order. Moser found that the first group of subjects made predictions of higher probability regarding an increase in profits for the company, despite there being no objective basis for their optimism. The outcome for which the subjects were able to generate the most supporting reasons was judged more probable. He concluded that some environmental event regarding a particular company that caused disproportionate news coverage might systematically influence predictive judgements. Individual investors might either overprice or underprice shares because of a tendency for all to think about the company from the same perspective — optimistically or pessimistically.

Anchoring and adjustment: the evidence

Joyce and Biddle[69] again used practising auditors as subjects in examining the effect of changes in internal control systems on the extensiveness of substantive tests (audit tests designed to search for the existence of dollar errors in the accounts). It was expected that the subjects would adjust for changes in internal controls by adjusting audit scope but that the adjustment would be insufficient as anchoring on the initial internal control would occur. No evidence of anchoring and adjustment was found. However, Kinney and Uecker[70] did find evidence of anchoring and adjustment in analytical review (ratio analysis) and compliance test (audit test of internal controls) tasks.

Expert judgement and rules of thumb

The research involving expert judgement is concerned with examining the thought processes of experts and the determinants of expertise. Newell and Simon[71] provided the analytical framework with their theory of bounded rationality. They suggested that humans possess a short-term memory with very limited capacity (4–7 chunks) and a virtually unlimited long-term memory. The structure of these memories and the characteristics of tasks combine to determine the way different types of problems are represented in memory (cognitive representation) which in turn determines the way problems are solved.

Much of the early work on expert memory involved medical practitioners[72] and chess masters.[73] The ability of experts to effectively expand their memory capacity in situations related to their expertise has been a consistent finding in the literature. It seems that a small set of cue values brings to mind a larger set of cues associated with a prototype. The explanation lies in the use of representativeness to recognise a familiar pattern and bring a prototype into short-term memory out of long-term memory.

Bouwman[74] found evidence of representativeness in an accounting task when he asked 15 students (novices) and 3 accountants (experts) to analyse four cases containing extensive financial information to determine any underlying problem areas. He found that the experts followed a directed strategy based on standard check lists, complex trends and stereotypes, and developed an overall picture of the company. The experts, when encountering a violation of the stereotype, attempted to uncover the cause, searching for both confirming and non-confirming evidence. The students, on the other hand, followed a simple undirected sequential strategy, evaluating information in the order presented, searching for a significant fact which could explain the situation. They searched only for confirming evidence and did not attempt to find causal explanations.

Numerous studies in auditing have confirmed that audit experts have better recall,[75] integrative abilities[76] and error frequency learning ability[77] than do novices. Audit experts exhibit evidence of all three rules of thumb and it is not clear that this necessarily results in inferior quality in decision making.[78] The double-entry nature of bookkeeping means that audit tests often overlap and mechanisms exist (e.g. partner review) which try to assure quality.[79] Process tracing methods may be a good way of learning more about the differences between the decision processes of experts and novices. This knowledge would be valuable for training purposes.

LO 4 → ACCOUNTING AND BEHAVIOUR

Accounting exists as a direct function of the activities of individuals or groups of individuals (defined as accounting entities). There are different viewpoints of accounting, indicating that there are a number of accounting perspectives possible. Even in a period of centralised government regulation of accounting disclosures by firms, there are thousands of choices and assumptions required between alternative accounting techniques in the preparation of financial statements for corporate entities. Even under the more stringent regulations of the Australian taxation legislation, there is considerable discretion in the techniques that can be applied to the calculation of taxable income. The main issue is that the techniques adopted, and the interpretation of reported information, are matters of perspective. There are many competing interests across the various people who interpret financial information reported by organisations. Basically, the users of accounting information represent a variety of perspectives and objectives, ranging from employee groups (unions), individual shareholders and investor groups to the management of an organisation. Accounting standard setters have often spent considerable time debating the technical validity of particular techniques proposed. However, even technical validity is a matter of perspective.

The aim of this section is to reinforce an underlying theme throughout this and a number of other chapters of this text: that accounting is a function of human behaviour and activity. As such, accounting information will influence behaviour, both in the methods adopted to measure and report information, and in response to the information disclosed. The responses to information are a function of human perspectives and are therefore not divorced from the personal aims and interests of users, whether acting as individuals or as a group of like interests. Consequently, accounting operates in a complex environment. Accountants should be conscious of this environment and appreciate the impact of accounting information on behaviour.

Burchell et al. summarised the significant role of accounting in a broad economic context:

> Accounting data are now used in the derivation and implementation of policies for economic stabilisation, price and wage control, for the regulation of particular industrial and commercial sectors and the planning of national economic resources in conditions of war and peace and prosperity and depression.
>
> No longer seen as a mere assembly of calculative routines, it now functions as a cohesive and influential mechanism for economic and social management.[80]

In addition, it is important to consider the factors which influence changes in accounting systems and the nature of reported information. Accounting is not a one-way process, with accounting information influencing behaviour or prompting a response on the part of some user group. Accounting information and systems are affected and changed by factors, most of which are beyond the direct control of accountants. According to Zimmerman, the accounting system is a fundamental component of an organisation's architecture, with senior managers constantly seeking to adapt the architecture to ensure the best structure of the firm. Zimmerman provides two important observations about the factors affecting the accounting system:[81]

1. Changes in the accounting system rarely occur in a vacuum. Accounting system changes generally occur at the same time as changes in the firm's business strategy and other organisational changes, particularly with regard to the partitioning of decision rights and the performance evaluation and reward systems.

2. Alterations in the firm's organisational architecture, including changes in the accounting system, are likely to occur in response to changes in the firm's business strategy caused by external shocks from technology and shifting market conditions.

Accounting information therefore significantly affects the behaviour of individuals both within an entity and external to it. However, the influence is two-way, with individuals (or groups of individuals) directly and indirectly affecting the structure of accounting systems and information disclosures. If behavioural research is to progress and provide valuable insights into these complex relationships, it will need to diverge from capital markets research which operates under assumptions that represent the individual or shareholder group as a set of interchangeable blanks (each sharing the same powers of interpretation, motives and beliefs) and which accepts that economies, societies and the entities within them are living complex organisms that do not act in isolation but affect each other in complex ways.[82]

LO 5 → LIMITATIONS OF BAR

This overview of BAR has shown that we have learnt a great deal about how different decision makers use accounting information. However, it has also revealed that there is significantly much more for us to learn in this area. The frequent (and frustrating) contradictions between the findings of similar studies simply mean that human information processing is far more complex than the development of current research theories and methods.

Maines has argued:

> Unfortunately, three criticisms levelled against this research have limited its impact. First, studies on the same topic have produced conflicting results, preventing conclusive guidance for policy decisions. In addition, the experimental subjects and settings used in these studies often differ from those found in real judgment settings. Finally, accounting researchers have questioned whether policy should be influenced by research on individual decision makers.[83]

These limitations of BAR have meant that it is yet to achieve the same level of dominance in the academic literature presently enjoyed by the capital markets and agency theory research schools. Overall, the major limitation of BAR is the lack of a single underlying theory which helps in the unification of the diverse research questions and findings of BAR. Unlike the capital markets and agency theory research schools which have grounded their research activities and theoretical development within a particular field of economics, BAR researchers have borrowed from a multitude of disciplines and contexts and have no common framework within which to develop useful generalisations for policy makers. There is also no signal that the development of such a theory is likely in the foreseeable future.

Nevertheless, it remains true that BAR is a valuable and practical research school. BAR methods have been used by many groups of decision makers to develop expert systems and other practical tools for information processing and training purposes in the workplace. BAR also offers the promise of revealing systematic errors (such as the different rules of thumb discussed previously) made by all decision makers within specific contexts that have implications for improvement at the macro level. For instance, research is starting to show how the types of incentives share analysts face in the workplace bias their decisions.[84] For example, they are less inclined to make sell recommendations than buy recommendations for companies with which they enjoy close business relationships.

Greater interest is now being shown in the development of non-financial measures of company performance such as the environmental and social performance indicators proposed in 'triple bottom-line reporting'. As there is little existing knowledge about what these non-financial measures should be or how they should be reported, BAR has a significant role to play in helping accounting practitioners and policy makers in developing emerging areas such as this. Further, continuing advances in research technologies and methods will enable future BAR researchers to develop richer hypotheses and tests of how decision makers process accounting information.

LO 6 ISSUES FOR AUDITORS

Just as behavioural accounting research can address questions about how people use and process accounting information, behavioural auditing research can investigate how auditors perform their audit tasks and make their judgements. Archival studies of auditor choice, examined in earlier chapters, often treat the process of auditing as a 'black box'. Results that Big or specialist auditors are associated with higher audit fees and a lower cost of capital are interpreted as evidence that these auditors are higher quality, but it is not direct evidence of better auditing performance. Behavioural research attempts to go inside this black box to examine the characteristics of better performing auditors and investigate factors that affect auditors' performance.

Early research started with fairly obvious questions. For example, does greater audit experience improve the quality of auditors' judgements?[85] Despite the apparent simplicity of this question, researchers soon found that the answers were not conclusive.[86] Auditors' performance varied between settings in ways which suggested that auditors had both general knowledge, which was common to all auditors, and specialised knowledge that is gained through practice and feedback in particular domains or contexts.[87]

One particular context that has been researched intensively is industry specific experience.[88] Auditors with experience in industry specific contexts appear to have higher quality auditor judgement when working within those contexts. This effect appears to occur because auditors acquire specialised knowledge when given the opportunity to receive industry-specific training either formally or informally through on-the-job experience within the industry audit team environment.[89] Owhoso, Messier and Lynch show that when auditors work within their industry specialisation teams they are more effective than other auditors at detecting both conceptual and mechanical errors.[90] If auditors are required to work outside their area of specialisation, they do not exhibit greater levels of performance. This research finding is supported by observations that large audit firms organise their practices along industry lines.

Owhoso, Messier and Lynch's results show that auditors' specialised knowledge is not transferable to other contexts. Hammersley suggests that this is because industry specialist auditors are able to use multiple cues more efficiently than other auditors within the industry specialist context.[91] Cues are pieces of information, and Hammersley was interested in the relative performance of specialist and non-specialist auditors in using apparently innocuous cues to make patterns that represent the existence of financial misstatements. Her results show differences in the ways that specialist and non-specialist auditors make sense of the cues when they are sprinkled throughout the information available to the auditors. She shows that specialist auditors tend to use more efficient and effective procedures to detect the presence of the misstatement, but only within their own field of specialisation.

The industry specialisation research focuses on auditor competence, which is one part of audit quality.[92] Behavioural researchers have also investigated the issues surrounding the other component of audit quality; auditor independence. Koch and Schmidt[93] examined the effects of disclosing conflicts of interest on auditors' reporting decisions. Initially, and consistent with Cain, Loewenstein and Moore,[94] they found that auditors are more likely to misreport when they disclose conflicts of interest because such disclosure mitigates their moral concerns. They feel they have a licence to misreport because investors should realise the existence of this possibility. However, Koch and Schmidt found that more experienced auditors are less likely to misreport in these circumstances. They also found that when auditors do not disclose their fees, they work to build a reputation for truthful reporting. Koch and Schmidt show that increasing the complexity of the experiment by incorporating more factors, such as experience and reputation, can produce richer results and a deeper understanding of auditors' behaviour.

Another way of investigating auditor independence is to examine investors' reactions to information about auditors. For example, Davis and Hollie[95] and Dopuch, King and Schwartz[96] investigated investor perceptions of auditor independence when auditors were receiving non-audit service fee revenue from their audit client. Both studies found that disclosure of non-audit fees reduces the accuracy of investor perceptions of auditor independence. These results are important because their evidence suggests that even when the auditor is independent in fact, the appearance of independence can be impaired and share prices adversely affected. Regulations such as the Sarbanes-Oxley Act (2002) were introduced to prevent auditor independence problems by restricting auditors' provision of non-audit services to their clients. Even if there is no actual independence impairment to prevent, these regulations could help auditors and their clients avoid problems caused by perceived independence impairments.

Experimental research has the potential to complement research using archival data by focusing on the behaviour of auditors and investors. However, the methodological challenges faced by behavioural researchers are also significant. There is often a tension between making the experiment sufficiently realistic by incorporating many contextual factors and making it simple enough so that the researcher can be sure that the observed outcome is caused by the manipulation of the specific factor under investigation. The researcher has to consider all the design issues before assembling the subjects because, unlike archival data research, there is no opportunity to collect additional data at a later date. Research continues to progress incrementally as researchers try different case instruments, contexts, and subjects.

Summary

LO 1 **The behavioural perspective and the nature of behavioural accounting research**
Behavioural research in accounting can be interpreted widely to include financial accounting, auditing and managerial accounting. The focus of this review has been human judgement theory (HJT) and the use of that theory in explaining, predicting and improving decision making. Research in this area has relied heavily, but not exclusively, on three models of human information processing: the Brunswik lens model, the process tracing model, and the probabilistic judgement model. A review of the research evidence demonstrates that prediction of company failure or distress has been heavily researched using the lens model. The consistent finding has been that failure is easier to predict than success and that the issue of disclosure of the prior probability of failure is important to realism in the task. To a lesser extent, the presentation and format of accounting information has also been researched using the lens model framework. It is, as yet, not possible to formulate an underlying theory as to which formats or modes of presentation are best in particular circumstances. This question awaits further research.

LO 2 **The contribution to our understanding of the role of accounting information within and outside the accounting entity provided by studying behaviour**
Process tracing methods have revealed that there may be contexts in which decision tree representations of human information processing may be more appropriate than the simple linear combinations of data implied by Brunswik lens models. Process tracing methods are particularly helpful when there are significant interactions between information cues.

LO 3 **The influence of accounting information on behaviour and on decision processes**
Within the probabilistic judgement model, auditor judgement has been extensively researched. Findings reveal that auditors and others use the same rules of thumb as have been prevalent in research in psychology, although often to a lesser extent. The rules of thumb of representativeness, availability, and anchoring and adjustment seem to be adopted in auditing and other business contexts in order to simplify complex judgement tasks and alleviate limitations in the cognitive processes of humans. Whether the presence of these rules of thumb reduces the quality of decision making in auditing or accounting remains in dispute. Auditing, in particular, is an activity where compensating mechanisms, such as partner review, exist as a means of assuring quality. More research is needed in a holistic sense in order to assess whether deleterious effects occur from the use of rules of thumb.

LO 4 ⊣ The fact that organisations are complex environments and accounting disclosures are trade-offs between competing perspectives and interests

Accounting exists as a direct function of the activities of individuals or groups of individuals (defined as accounting entities). Consideration needs to be given to the complex environment in which accountants operate and the competing demands for and of accounting information.

For example, disclosing environmental information and the likely cost of an environmental clean-up by an organisation may lead to support from environmental lobby groups; however, it may also attract a very different response from shareholder groups, who may take the view that the company is expending excessive resources to appease marginal interest groups.

LO 5 ⊣ The inherent constraints on behavioural research

Behavioural researchers and accounting practitioners need to recognise the complex nature of the users and uses of accounting information, and the influence of these users on accounting practice and disclosure.

LO 6 ⊣ Issues for auditors

Behavioural auditing research investigates characteristics of high-performing auditors and the factors that affect auditor judgement. Results have shown that industry specialist auditors outperform other auditors when they are in their specialist industry environment. They appear to process multiple pieces of information more efficiently and effectively to determine the existence of financial misstatements. Experimental research also shows that there are complex interactions between experience and context in auditors' reporting decisions. Additionally, this research shows that investors react as though they perceive auditor independence is impaired when auditors receive non-audit service revenue from their audit clients even if actual auditor independence is not affected. However, experimental researchers face challenges when they attempt to balance realism and simplicity in research design.

Questions

1. Consider a decision task, other than a bankruptcy prediction task, that uses accounting information (e.g. making recommendations for share investors). Assume that you are intending to conduct a Brunswik lens model experiment on your selected decision task. List seven information cues you think would be important variables to use in making your decision. Why did you choose these cues? Compare and contrast your list of information cues with a colleague. Discuss with each other the similarities and differences in your choices.

2. Most human judgement research is undertaken in an experimental setting. How would you respond to the assertion that experiments cannot be generalised to the real world? What are the weaknesses and strengths of this research method? (*Hint:* See RJ Swieringa and KE Weick, 'An assessment of laboratory experiments in accounting', *Journal of Accounting Research*, vol. 20, Supplement, 1982, pp. 56–93.)

3. Use the probabilistic judgement framework to describe an accounting or auditing related decision task.

4. Explain the implications for accounting if decision makers in an accounting context display any or all of the representativeness, availability, or anchoring and adjustment rules of thumb.

5. Describe how (and why) the information processing systems of expert accountants might be different from those of accounting students. How might the expertise of experienced accounting practitioners be effectively passed on to accounting students?

6. 'Most people are not good intuitive statisticians.' Discuss this statement in an accounting context, drawing on research using the probabilistic model.

7. Compare and contrast the efficient markets hypothesis and human judgement theory. Are they inconsistent with each other? Explain.

8. Does consensus always imply accuracy in studies of accounting decision making? Justify your answer.

9. Why is a 'model of human behaviour' generally superior to human judgements?

10. What alternatives exist for improving the format and presentation of accounting information? What is the research evidence regarding the merit of the various alternatives?

11. Human judgement theory does not purport to penetrate the 'black box' of cognitive processing. Verbal protocol research, however, has that ability. What are the strengths and weaknesses of this research methodology? (*Hint:* See GF Klersey and TJ Mock, 'Verbal protocol research in auditing', *Accounting, Organizations and Society*, vol. 14, no. 1/2, 1989, pp. 133–51.)

12. Reconcile normative accounting studies and human judgement theory.

13. Why do individuals form lobby groups to influence companies' behaviour and information disclosures? What types of information would shareholder groups require to determine whether company directors should be censured for poor performance?

14. What is more important for an organisation — the 'right' physical assets or the 'right' people? Explain.

15. Accounting is a function of human behaviour and activity. As such, is not all accounting research behavioural? Justify your answer.

16. List nine or more factors that will influence the accounting system adopted by a firm and the information disclosed. Which of these factors is a direct function of human behaviour?

17. What is an industry specialist auditor? Will an industry specialist auditor always perform better than a non-specialist auditor? Explain.

18. What is the difference between independence in fact and independence in appearance? Which is more important?

Additional readings

Burgstahler, D & Sundem, GL 1989, 'The evolution of behavioral accounting research in the United States, 1968–1987', *Behavioral Research in Accounting*, vol. 1, pp. 75–108.

Caplan, EH 1989, 'Behavioral accounting — a personal view.' *Behavioral Research in Accounting*, vol. 1, pp. 109–23.

Gibbins, M 1977, 'Human inference, heuristics and auditor's judgment process', CICA Audit Research Symposium, CICA.

Hogarth, RM & Einhorn, HJ 1992, 'Order effects in belief updating: the belief-adjustment model,' *Cognitive Psychology*, vol. 24, pp. 1–55.

Hopwood, AG 1989, 'Behavioral accounting retrospect and prospect', *Behavioral Research in Accounting*, vol. 1, 1989, pp. 1–22.

Johnson, PE, Jamal, K, & Berryman, RG 1989, 'Audit judgement research.' *Accounting, Organizations and Society*, vol. 14, no. 1/2, pp. 83–99.

Murray, D & Regel, RW 1992, 'Accuracy and consensus in accounting studies of decision making', *Behavioral Research in Accounting*, vol. 4, pp. 127–30.

Swieringa, RJ & Weick, KE 1982, 'An assessment of laboratory experiments in accounting', *Journal of Accounting Research*, vol. 20, Supplement, pp. 56–93.

13.1
CASE STUDY

One area of research in BAR is to discover the differences in the judgements of various 'experts' and to discover what characteristics and skills lead to expertise in a particular context.

Telstra opts for David Thodey as replacement for Sol Trujillo

by John Durie and Jennifer Hewett

An embattled Telstra board will try to improve relations with the Rudd Government and the market by today announcing its business head, David Thodey, as the replacement for chief executive Sol Trujillo.

Mr Thodey was one of three internal candidates for the position, with one British executive also making the shortlist . . . other internal candidates . . . were finance chief John Stanhope and Sensis boss Bruce Akhurst. Neither is expected to quit but just what management changes Mr Thodey has in mind are not known.

Mr Thodey, 54, is expected to move quickly to mend fences with the Government and end the acrimonious relationship that had developed between Canberra and Telstra.

The Telstra chairman, Donald McGauchie, has sounded much more conciliatory in recent months, and the Government has publicly and privately welcomed what it sees as a far more constructive tone.

But Canberra will be trying to drive a hard bargain in its negotiations over the building of its proposed $43 billion national broadband network, and this will severely test the new chief executive and the board.

Mr Thodey, an Australian, does not have a close relationship with key government ministers, but is regarded as relatively calm. And he has the political advantage of not being closely identified with Mr Trujillo's aggressive strategy against government regulation over the past few years.

But the new chief executive will need to persuade investors he will not make too many concessions to Canberra that would end up harming the Telstra shareholders. The cost of building the network and the charges to consumers will be dramatically affected by the returns Telstra wants, and intense and lengthy negotiations can be expected.

Source: Excerpts from *The Australian*, 3 August 2009, www.theaustralian.news.com.au.

Questions

1. Why would the Telstra board appoint an internal candidate to the position of chief executive, rather than an external candidate?
2. Why might David Thodey have been preferred to the other internal candidates one of whom had finance experience and the second of whom had other telco industry experience?
3. The article reports that David Thodey had internal experience. How might his skill set have changed during his time with Telstra and what might have been his main means of learning new skills?
4. Describe the complex environment in which Telstra is operating and identify the particular skills that the new chief executive might be able to use to influence that environment.

Will a focus on cash rather than debt change decision processes? The following extract considers the shifting focus towards the importance of cash flow in considering business success.

Reporting season's moment of truth

by Barbara Drury

This month's reporting season is the moment of truth for corporate Australia when it reveals the extent of any damage sustained during the global financial storm.

"This is probably the toughest reporting season in decades," says Fat Prophets founder Angus Geddes.

"It's time to pick the wheat from the chaff . . . the ones to focus on are coping well and will be in a strong position in future."

John Price, of Conscious Investor, encourages people to ask if all the indicators point to a business being successful in five years' time . . . key indicators to identify the top share investments in these turbulent times include . . .

Low debt

Too much debt was a feature behind last year's corporate casualties such as ABC Learning Centres, Allco Finance and Babcock & Brown.

"Companies with little or no debt will come out (of the current crisis) stronger," Price says. He looks for a debt-to-equity ratio of under 50 per cent.

Geddes says cash-flow problems are an important sign that a company's financial position is deteriorating. He cites Qantas, which sprung a nasty surprise on investors earlier this month, announcing a $500 million capital raising to pay down debt. "Qantas is one of the best-run airlines in the world but given the state of the global economy the airline market will be among the last to recover," he says.

Source: Excerpts from *The Age*, 25 February 2009, http://thebigchair.com.au.

Questions

1. If cash is the best measure of success, why have the accounting profession and regulators persevered with analysing debt-to-equity ratios?
2. What do analysts means by the term 'nasty surprise'?
3. Why does the market so readily interpret a cash-flow problem as a sign that a company's financial position might be deteriorating but was apparently prepared to focus on debt-to-equity ratios for a number of years?
4. The article refers to the need to 'sort the wheat from the chaff' by focusing on companies that are coping well. How are such judgements made?

Endnotes

1. T Hofstedt and J Kinard, 'A strategy for behavioral accounting research', *Accounting Review*, January 1970, p. 43.
2. G Siegel and H Ramanauskas-Marconi, *Behavioral Accounting*, Ohio: South-Western Publishing Co., 1989, p. 4 describes how widely BAR can be interpreted.
3. EM Bamber, 'Opportunities in behavioral accounting research', *Behavioral Research in Accounting*, vol. 5, 1993, pp. 1–29.
4. See pp. 386–7 of SE Bonner, 'Judgment and decision-making research in accounting', *Accounting Horizons*, vol. 13, no. 4, December 1999, pp. 385–98.
5. See paragraph 43 of SAC 2 Objective of General Purpose Financial Reporting, Melbourne: Public Sector Accounting Standards Board and Accounting Standards Review Board, August, 1990.
6. SW Becker, 'Discussion of the effect of frequency of feedback on attitudes and performance', *Journal of Accounting Research*, vol. 5, 1967, pp. 225–8.
7. W Edwards, 'The theory of decision making', *Psychological Bulletin*, July 1954, pp. 380–417.
8. RH Ashton, 'An experimental study of internal control judgments', *Journal of Accounting Research*, Spring 1974, pp. 143–57.
9. E Brunswik, *The Conceptual Framework of Psychology*, Chicago: University of Chicago, 1952.

10. AT Lord, 'Development of behavioral thought', *Behavioral Research in Accounting*, vol. 1, 1989, pp. 124–49.

11. R Libby and B Lewis, 'Human information processing research in accounting: The state of the art', *Accounting, Organizations and Society*, vol. 2, no. 3, 1977, pp. 245–68.

12. RH Ashton, *Human information processing in accounting, studies in accounting research* no. 17, American Accounting Association, 1982.

13. See GF Klersey and TJ Mock, 'Verbal protocol research in auditing', *Accounting, Organizations and Society*, vol. 14, nos. 1/2, 1989, pp. 133–51.

14. Bonner op. cit., p. 394.

15. See BA Howieson, 'A security analyst's action recommendations: An application of recursive partitioning to modelling judgement', *Australian Journal of Management*, vol. 16, no. 2, December 1991, pp. 165–85.

16. R Libby, *Human information processing: Theory and applications*, Englewood Cliffs, NJ: Prentice Hall, 1981, p. 55.

17. R Ashton, 'Human information processing research in auditing: A review and synthesis', in DR Nichols and HF Stettler (eds), *Auditing Symposium VI*, Kansas, 1982, p. 80.

18. JG Birnberg and JF Shields, 'Three decades of behavioral accounting research: A search for order', *Behavioral Research in Accounting*, vol. 1, 1989, p. 25.

19. See, for example, Libby, op. cit., p. 70.

20. ibid., p. 54.

21. ibid., p. 81.

22. A Tversky and D Kahneman, 'Judgment under certainty: Heuristics and biases', *Science*, September 1974, pp. 1124–31.

23. For example, C Casey, Jr, 'The usefulness of accounting ratios for a subject's predictions of corporate failure: Replication and extensions', *Journal of Accounting Research*, Autumn 1980, pp. 603–13; and I Zimmer, 'A lens study of the prediction of corporate failure by bank loan officers', *Journal of Accounting Research*, Autumn 1980, pp. 629–36.

24. For example, C Casey, Jr, 'Prior probability disclosure and loan officers' judgements: Some evidence of the impact', *Journal of Accounting Research*, Spring 1983, pp. 300–6; and KA Houghton and R Sengupta, 'The effect of prior probability disclosure and information set construction on bankers' ability to predict failure', *Journal of Accounting Research*, Autumn 1984, pp. 768–75.

25. See, for example, KA Houghton and D Woodliff, 'Financial ratios: The prediction of corporate success and failure', *Journal of Business Finance and Accounting*, Winter 1987, pp. 537–54.

26. C Casey, Jr and T Selling, 'The effect of task predictability and prior probability disclosure on judgement quality and confidence', *Accounting Review*, April 1986, pp. 302–17.

27. M van Breda and K Ferris, 'A note on the effect of prior probability disclosure and information representativeness on subject predictive accuracy', *Behavioral Research in Accounting*, vol. 4, 1992, pp. 140–51.

28. AR Abdel-Khalik and KM El-Sheshai, 'Information choice and utilization in an experiment on default prediction', *Journal of Accounting Research*, Autumn 1980, pp. 325–42.

29. R Simnett and K Trotman, 'Auditor versus model: Information choice and information processing', *Accounting Review*, July 1989, pp. 514–28.

30. See, for example, D Snowball, 'Some effects of accounting expertise and information load: An empirical study', *Accounting, Organizations and Society*, 1980, pp. 323–8.

31. HM Schroder, MJ Driver and S Streufert, *Human information processing*, New York: Holt, Rinehart and Winston, 1967.

32. Abdel-Khalik and El-Sheshai op. cit.

33. Libby op. cit., p. 37.

34. For example, CJ Casey, Jr, 'Variation in accounting information load: The effect on loan officers' predictions of bankruptcy', *Accounting Review*, January 1980, pp. 36–49.

35. See LA Maines, 'Judgement and decision-making research in financial accounting: A review and analysis', in RH Ashton and AH Ashton (eds), *Judgement and decision-making research in accounting and auditing*, New York: Cambridge University Press, 1995, p. 92.

36. See, for example I Solomon, A Ariyo and LA Tomassini, 'Contextual effects on the calibration of probabilistic judgments', *Journal of Applied Psychology*, August 1985, pp. 528–32 for a review of this literature.

37. HJ Einhorn and RM Hogarth, 'Confidence in judgement: Persistence of the illusion of validity', *Psychological Review*, vol. 85, no. 5, 1978, pp. 395–416.

38. R Libby, 'Man versus model of man: Some conflicting evidence', *Organisational Behaviour and Human Performance*, June 1976, pp. 1–12.

39. I Zimmer, 'A lens study of the prediction of corporate failure by bank-loans officers', *Journal of Accounting Research*, vol. 18, no. 2, 1980.

40. For example, see T Kida, 'An investigation into auditors' continuity and related qualification judgements', *Journal of Accounting Research*, Autumn 1980, pp. 506–23.

41. Libby op. cit., p. 27.

42. See Maines op. cit., pp. 79–80 for a review of these findings.

43. See, for example, P Slovic, 'Analyzing the expert judge: A descriptive study of a stockbroker's investment decision processes', *Journal of Applied Psychology*, vol. 53, pp. 255–63; and A Schepanski, 'Tests of theories of information processing behavior in credit judgment', *Accounting Review*, vol. 58, 1983, pp. 581–99.

44. D Larcker and VP Lessig, 'An examination of the linear and retrospective process tracing approaches to judgment modelling', *Accounting Review*, vol. 58, 1983, pp. 58–77.

45. T Selling and J Shank, 'Linear versus process tracing approaches to judgment modelling: A new perspective on cue importance', *Accounting, Organizations and Society*, vol. 14, 1989, pp. 65–77.

46. R Libby, 'Prediction achievement as an extension of the predictive ability criterion: A reply', *Accounting Review*, July 1976, pp. 672–6.

47. S Moriarity, 'Communicating financial information through multidimensional graphics', *Journal of Accounting Research*, Spring 1979, pp. 205–25.

48. D Stock and CJ Watson, 'Human judgement accuracy,

multidimensional graphics and humans versus models', *Journal of Accounting Research*, Spring 1984, pp. 192–205.

49. ibid., p. 201.

50. For example, I Benbasat and R Schroeder, 'An experimental investigation of some MIS design variables', *MIS Quarterly*, March 1977, pp. 37–50; H Wainer, M Lono and C Groves, *On the display of data: some empirical findings*, Washington DC: The Bureau of Social Science Research, 1982; and EJ Lusk and M Kersnick, 'The effect of cognitive style and report format on task performance: The MIS design consequences', *Management Science*, August 1979, pp. 787–98.

51. E Blocher, RP Moffie and RW Zmud, 'Report format and task complexity: Interaction in risk judgements', *Accounting, Organizations and Society*, 1986, pp. 457–69.

52. LR Davis, 'Report format and the decision maker's task: An experimental investigation', *Accounting, Organizations and Society*, vol. 14, no. 5/6, 1989, pp. 495–508.

53. G Desanctis and S Jarvenpaa, 'Graphical presentation of accounting data for financial forecasting: An experimental investigation', *Accounting, Organizations and Society*, vol. 14, no. 5/6, 1989, pp. 509–25; WF Wright, 'Graphical displays and improved decision making', in GD Garson and S Nagel (eds), *Computers and the social sciences*, Greenwich, CT: JAI Press, 1989.

54. DN Ricchiute, 'An empirical assessment of the impact of alternative task presentation modes on decision-making research in auditing', *Journal of Accounting Research*, Spring 1984, pp. 341–50.

55. S So and M Smith 'Colour graphics and task complexity in multivariate decision making', *Accounting, Auditing and Accountability Journal*, vol. 15, no. 4, 2003, 565–93.

56. S So and M Smith, 'Presentation format and information complexity in multivariate decision making', Unpublished working paper, University of South Australia, 2002.

57. H Wainer and D Thiessen, 'Graphical Data Analysis', *Annual Review of Psychology*, 1981, pp. 191–241.

58. JW Payne, J Bettman and EJ Johnson, 'Behavioral decision research: A constructive processing perspective', *Annual Review of Psychology*, vol. 43, 1992, p. 103.

59. ibid.

60. For instance, the Peat Marwick 'Research Opportunities in Auditing' program.

61. D Kahneman and A Tversky, 'On the psychology of prediction', *Psychological Review*, vol. 80, 1973, pp. 237–51.

62. RM Hogarth (ed.), *Insights in decision making: A tribute to Hillel J. Einhorn*, Chicago: University of Chicago Press, 1990).

63. Payne, Bettman and Johnson, op. cit., p. 104.

64. EJ Joyce and GC Biddle, 'Are auditors' judgements sufficiently regressive?', *Journal of Accounting Research*, Autumn 1981, pp. 323–49.

65. DL Holt, 'Auditors and base rates revisited', *Accounting, Organizations and Society*, 1987, pp. 571–8.

66. D Kahneman and A Tversky, 'Choices, values and frames', *American Psychologist*, 1984, pp. 341–50.

67. A Tversky and D Kahneman, 'Availability: A heuristic for judging frequency and probability', *Cognitive Psychology*, September 1973, pp. 207–32.

68. DV Moser, 'The effects of output interference, availability and accounting information on investors' predictive judgements', *Accounting Review*, July 1989, pp. 433–48.

69. EJ Joyce and GC Biddle, 'Anchoring and adjustment in probabilistic inference in auditing', *Journal of Accounting Research*, Spring 1981, pp. 120–45.

70. WR Kinney, Jr and WC Uecker, 'Mitigating the consequences of anchoring in auditor judgment', *Accounting Review*, January 1982, pp. 55–69.

71. A Newell and HA Simon, *Human Problem Solving*, Englewood Cliffs, NJ: Prentice-Hall, 1972.

72. See, for example, AS Elstein, LE Shulman and SA Sprafka, *Medical problem solving: An analysis of clinical reasoning*, Cambridge, Mass: Harvard University Press, 1978).

73. WG Chase and HA Simon, 'The mind's eye in chess', in WG Chase (ed.), *Visual information processing*, New York: Academic Press, 1973, pp. 215–81.

74. MJ Bouwman, 'The use of accounting information: Expert versus novice behaviour' in G Ungson and D Braunstein (eds), *Decision making: An interdisciplinary inquiry*, Boston: Kent, 1982, pp. 234–67.

75. For example, SF Biggs and TJ Mock, 'An investigation of auditor decision processes in evaluation of internal controls and audit scope decisions', *Journal of Accounting Research*, Spring 1983, pp. 234–55; SF Biggs, TJ Mock and PR Watkins, 'Auditor's use of analytical review in audit program design', *Accounting Review*, January 1988, pp. 148–67; F Choo and KT Trotman, 'The relationship between knowledge structure and judgements for experienced and inexperienced auditors', *Accounting Review*, July 1991, pp. 464–85; and DM Frederick, 'Auditors' representation and retrieval of internal control knowledge', *Accounting Review*, April 1991, pp. 240–58.

76. CL Moeckel, 'The effect of experience on auditors' memory errors', *Journal of Accounting Research*, Autumn 1990, pp. 368–87.

77. JL Butt, 'Frequency judgements in an auditing-related task', *Journal of Accounting Research*, Autumn 1988, pp. 315–30; and R Libby and DM Frederick, 'Experience and the ability to explain audit findings', *Journal of Accounting Research*, Autumn 1990, pp. 348–67.

78. See, for example, J Shanteau, 'Cognitive heuristics and biases in behavioral auditing: Review, comments and observations', *Accounting, Organizations and Society*, vol. 14, no. 1/2, 1989, pp. 165–77.

79. See, for example, R Hogarth, 'A perspective on cognitive research in accounting', *Accounting Review*, April 1991, pp. 277–90.

80. S Burchell, C Clubb, A Hopwood, J Hughes and J Nahapiet, 'The roles of accounting in organizations and society', *Accounting, Organizations and Society*, vol. 5, no. 1, 1980, pp. 5–27.

81. J Zimmerman, *Accounting for decision making and control*, Chicago: Irwin Publishing, 1997, pp. 633–89.

82. For a full discussion of these issues, see P Ormerod, *Butterfly economics*, London: Faber and Faber, 1998.

83. Maines, op. cit., p. 95.

84. See, for instance, V Bernard and J Thomas, 'Evidence that stock prices do not fully reflect the implications of current earnings for future earnings', *Journal of Accounting and Economics*, vol. 13, 1991, pp. 305–40; and JRM Hand, 'A test of the extended functional fixation hypothesis', *Accounting Review*, vol. 65, 1990, pp. 739–63.

85. RH Ashton and PR Brown, 'Descriptive modelling of auditors' internal control judgments: Replication and extension', *Journal of Accounting Research*, vol. 18, 1980, pp. 269–77.

86. R Libby and J Luft, 'Determinants of judgment performance in accounting settings: Ability, knowledge, motivation and environment', *Accounting, Organizations and Society*, vol. 18, pp. 425–50.

87. Libby and Luft, 1993; R Libby, 'The role of knowledge and memory in audit judgment', in RJ Ashton and AH Ashton, (eds), *Judgment and decision making research in accounting and auditing*, Cambridge University Press, 1995, pp. 176–206; J Bedard, 'Expertise in auditing: Myth or reality?', *Accounting, Organizations and Society*, vol. 14, 1989, pp. 113–31;

JS Davis and I Solomon, 'Experience, expertise an expert-performance research in public accounting', *Journal of Accounting Literature*, vol. 8, 1989, pp. 150–164; AH Ashton, 'Experience and error frequency knowledge as potential determinants of audit expertise', *The Accounting Review*, vol. 66, 1991, pp. 218–239; all cited in RA Moroney, and PJ Carey, 'Industry versus task-based experience and auditor performance', http://ssrn.com.

88. JC Bedard, 1989; JC Bedard and SF Biggs, 'The effect of domain-specific expertise on evaluation of management representation in analytical procedures', *Auditing: A Journal of Practice and Theory*, vol. 10, Supplement, 1991, pp. 77–95; S Wright and AM Wright, 'The effect of industry experience on hypothesis generation and audit planning decisions', *Behavioral Research in Accounting*, vol. 9, 1997, pp. 273–294; all cited in Moroney and Carey 2008.

89. S Bonner, 'Experience effects in auditing: The role of task-specific knowledge', *The Accounting Review*, vol. 65, 1990, pp. 72–92; J Bedard and MT H Chi, 'Expertise in auditing', *Auditing: A Journal of Practice and Theory*, vol. 12, supplement, 1993, pp. 21–45; all cited in Moroney and Carey 2008.

90. VE Owhoso, WF Messier, and J Lynch, 'Error detection by industry-specialized teams during the sequential audit review', *Journal of Accounting Research*, vol. 40, no. 3, 2002, pp. 883–900.

91. JS Hammersley, 'Pattern identification and industry-specialist auditors', *The Accounting Review*, vol. 81, no. 2, 2006, pp. 309–336.

92. LE DeAngelo, 'Auditor size and audit quality', *Journal of Accounting and Economics*, vol. 3, no. 3, December 1981, pp. 183–199.

93. CW Koch and C Schmidt, 'Disclosing conflict of interest — does experience and reputation matter?', August 2008, http://ssrn.com.

94. DM Cain, G Loewenstein, and DA Moore, 'The dirt on coming clean: Perverse effects of disclosing conflicts of interest', Journal of Legal Studies, vol. 34, 2005, pp. 1–25; cited in Koch and Schmidt, 2008.

95. SM Davis and DY Hollie, 'The impact of nonaudit service fee levels on investors' perceptions of auditor independence', *Behavioral Research in Accounting*, vol. 20, 2008, pp. 31–44.

96. N Dopuch, R King, and R Schwartz, 'Independence in appearance and in fact: An experimental investigation', *Contemporary Accounting Research*, vol. 20, no. 1, 2003, pp. 79–114.

14

Emerging issues in accounting and auditing

LEARNING OBJECTIVES

After reading this chapter, you should have an appreciation of the following:

1 current factors influencing accounting and auditing research, regulation and practice

2 issues surrounding the application of fair value accounting during the global financial crisis

3 possible directions in future international accounting standard setting arrangements

4 sustainability accounting, reporting and assurance

5 other non-financial accounting and reporting issues.

LO 1 CURRENT FACTORS INFLUENCING ACCOUNTING AND AUDITING RESEARCH, REGULATION AND PRACTICE

One of the major influences on accounting and auditing practice and research explored throughout this text is the growing internationalisation of accounting and auditing standards. This issue, together with recent developments in sustainability reporting and assurance, will be discussed later in this chapter. First, a number of other potentially controversial factors are examined.

XBRL

There is a technological revolution in progress that will affect the way that financial statements are prepared.[1] In late 2008 the US Securities and Exchange Commission (SEC) voted to require 500 of the largest public companies in the United States to file their 2009 financial reports using Extensible Business Reporting Language (XBRL), with other companies to follow. XBRL allows financial information to be presented in a more interactive and user friendly manner by 'tagging' individual data items so that they can be extracted by software to produce reports custom-designed by users.[2] The SEC hopes that XBRL will allow much faster analysis of company financial data by a wider group of users with less error. The current techniques used to extract details from financial statements contain errors because they either are manually performed or use a software program that produces output that only approximates the underlying data.

The financial statements are lodged with the SEC's public database (known as EDGAR), which is accessible via the web, making the data available to any interested user. Haka suggests that this development will mean greater availability of more accessible data and will possibly place company managers under greater scrutiny to explain their financial statements.[3] In addition to more usable data, Haka suggests XBRL could change the way financial analysts follow small companies. Currently, financial analysts tend to focus on large companies because of the greater availability of their data and the wider interest in these companies from investors. Financial analysts produce reports about the companies they follow, making even more information available to investors. Increasing the availability of financial data for small companies could make them more attractive to analysts. In turn, greater analyst following is likely to increase the liquidity of small companies' stocks. In addition, amateur investors may develop more confidence from the greater level of detail and comparability of data between companies.

However, chief financial officers seem to be about to lose their ability to choose the level of disaggregation of data in financial statements. They would claim that a fundamental part of accounting is the process of aggregation of similar items in order to give meaning to the information. At the extreme, if it were possible to provide investors with complete access to transaction level data, this would not be useful because the data would have little meaning. Meaning is added by accountants through the process of classification and aggregation to allow, for example, calculation of ratios of certain types of expenses to sales.

One XBRL-related issue is whether the current auditing approach of reconciling a paper version of the XBRL-related documents to the information in the official SEC filing is sufficient. Plumlee and Plumlee suggest that the provision of XBRL information is an extension of the traditional reporting paradigm that will alter the way financial and non-financial data can be used.[4] This paradigm shift requires auditors to consider much deeper questions than mere reconciliation of output. These questions include; what constitutes an error in XBRL, and what does materiality mean when individual pieces of financial data will be used outside the context of the financial statements? Materiality is traditionally assessed as the impact on users' decisions, and quantitative guidelines suggest that the item is to be considered in isolation and in aggregate, and in proportion to a relative base, such as profit (see AASB 1031 *Materiality*). If the data are accessible in isolation or in new combinations, these materiality guidelines cannot be interpreted in the same way. Plumlee and Plumlee join Haka in calling for more research to understand the advantages and disadvantages of XBRL and its impact on the future of financial reporting and auditing.

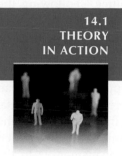

14.1 THEORY IN ACTION

Watch the SEC chairman explain why XBRL is important on YouTube.

SEC chair on XBRL

http://www.youtube.com/watch?v=oYaLeXowl5A

Questions

1. Why would XBRL help the SEC detect fraud instantly?
2. What do these statements mean?
   (a) 'The best investor protection is a growing economy and a rising market.'
   (b) 'Markets function best when all the information that market participants need is available to them when they want it and in a form they can use.'
3. Why doesn't the SEC simply prescribe a chart of accounts for all companies to use instead of devoting resources to developing XBRL?

The effects of corporate collapses and the Sarbanes-Oxley Act (2002)

As discussed in detail in earlier chapters, a number of high-profile corporate collapses and legal changes in the early 2000s changed both the image of accounting and auditing and its regulatory environment. Criticisms of auditor independence and corporate governance became 'front-burner' topics that have attracted much public comment and research attention.[5]

For example, in the United States prior to the Sarbanes-Oxley Act (2002) (SOX) audit firms reviewed each other under a system of peer reviews administered by the American Institute of Certified Public Accountants (AICPA). This process involved gathering information on audit firms' quality control procedures by interviewing staff and inspecting documentation. Fogarty criticised this process on the basis that the review process was not sufficiently rigorous and reviewers would be unlikely to detect important deficiencies.[6] It was suggested that staff could be trained to answer a reviewer's question and documents could be produced which showed a more thorough audit than actually took place.

Since 2004, the Public Company Accounting and Oversight Board (PCAOB), which was established under the SOX legislation, has conducted independent inspections of audit firms. However, despite the criticisms of the AICPA peer reviews which led to the change in regulation, Hilary and Lennox provide evidence that the peer reviews provided credible information about the quality differences between audit firms.[7] Although this appears to suggest that the regulatory change was not justified, Hilary and Lennox also note that differences between the review methods, and in particular how their findings are publicised, makes it difficult to draw this conclusion. In the AICPA system it seems that the reviewing firms were less likely to disclose auditing problems if they did not compete against the reviewed firms.[8] The reviewed firms appeared to be of higher quality if they were reviewed by another auditor who did not compete for the same clients. The evidence suggests it is difficult to completely eliminate the parties' self-interest incentives under a self-regulated quality control system. Perhaps a system with fewer personal incentives is preferred in times of trouble, even if it is not necessarily a better system.

Another key provision in SOX is a restriction on the provision of certain consulting (non-audit) services by audit firms to their clients. The financial statement auditor is banned from providing consulting services to their clients, except for some specific exceptions with the prior approval of the client's audit committee.[9] Following the corporate collapses in the early 2000s audit firms were criticised for compromising their audit independence by relying heavily on revenue from consulting services. Because US companies were not required to disclose fees paid to their auditors for audit and consulting services prior to 2000, there was little research evidence to support this view. However, early evidence using newly disclosed fees from 2001 supported the SOX ban on consulting.[10] Later evidence suggested there were other interpretations of the data, but the legislation had been passed and was unlikely to be changed.[11] Overall, the role of auditors, their techniques,[12] and their independence continue to be debated because of their role in creating trust in companies and their management.[13] In the near future, this debate is likely to intensify as the shake-up of the global financial system continues.[14]

14.2 THEORY IN ACTION

Ashton Kutcher is fair value's newest foe

Submitted by Melissa Lajara on Fri, 03/20/2009–0937

You know when an accounting standard has really arrived? When it's a topic of heated debate on a celebrity's Twitter page.

Actor Ashton Kutcher has a Twitter account, and late last night he and a few others began debating mark-to-market accounting. His verdict is that FASB 157 should be repealed, but isn't solely to blame for the financial crisis.

For the uninitiated, Twitter is a Web-based vehicle to "get the word out" — musings, events, links can all be uploaded as long as the message you create is 140 characters or less. You can follow other people's feeds, and they can follow yours. Many companies and media outlets embraced Twitter immediately, and some high-profile individuals — including Barack Obama, Karl Rove and Michael Phelps — are also known to "tweet."

Kutcher, who is married to Demi Moore and starred on "That 70's Show" and in movies including *The Butterfly Effect*, has a handful of posts about mark-to-market accounting and the financial crisis. He notes: "Greed caused the crash." Someone should tell him that the mark-to-market debate has its own Twitter. Ashton's tweet on FASB 157:

> **aplusk:** fasb 157 alone dnt cause the crash however it drove the banks down at a pace that was so fast we couldn't recover. Greed caused the crash

Source: CPA Blog, www.nysscpa.org

Questions
1. What is FASB 157?
2. How could an accounting standard cause a share market crash?

ISSUES SURROUNDING THE APPLICATION OF FAIR VALUE ACCOUNTING DURING THE GLOBAL FINANCIAL CRISIS

The causes of the global financial crisis (GFC) that swept around the world in 2008 and 2009 are complex and open to debate.[15] However, some regard the practice of fair valuing assets as a contributing factor to the rapid spread of the problem from its origins in the US subprime mortgage market to the rest of the world, and for exacerbating the depth of the crisis.[16] This is because the accounting standards (especially Financial Accounting Standard (FAS) No. 157 *Fair Value Measurements*) required write-downs in the value of investments held by banks during the turbulent market conditions.[17] These write-downs limited the ability of the entities to make loans. Marking financial assets to market (to reflect fair value) also affected the asset side of borrowing companies' balance sheets, restricting their ability to borrow.

The United States Securities and Exchange Commission (SEC) investigated the role of fair value in the crisis and issued a 211-page report in the last days of 2008.[18] The SEC was required to investigate the role of accounting standards, such as FAS 157 in the bank failures that occurred in 2008. The report concluded that 'bank failures in the US appeared to be the result of growing probable credit losses, concerns about asset quality, and in certain cases, eroding lender and investor confidence', and not merely marking financial assets to market value.[19] This view about the role of fair value accounting is supported by others, including former SEC chief accountants Conrad Hewitt and Lynn Turner, who praised mark-to-market accounting for increasing transparency, allowing users of financial statements to see an institution's true economic condition.[20]

The SEC offered eight recommendations for improving fair value accounting, and also recommended that accounting standard setters provide additional guidance for application of the standards in illiquid markets (where there are not enough willing buyers and sellers). The SEC noted that although the definition of fair value in SFAS 157 and IFRS are generally consistent, there are some differences.[21] In particular, SFAS 157 explicitly uses an exit price but IFRS fair value is neither explicitly an exit price nor explicitly an entry price. Also, the SEC suggests that IFRS and US GAAP differ in their accounting for financial instruments. One difference is the pre-October 2008 treatment of classifying certain financial assets. Since October 2008, both sets of standards allow non-derivative financial assets held for trading and certain financial assets to be reclassified in particular situations.[22]

Reactions by standard setters

In October 2008 the IASB changed the rules for reclassifying financial assets so that losses from changes in market values on those assets could be treated differently. Prior to the rule change, the international standards required such losses to be taken through the income statement. After the rule change, the assets could be reclassified under certain circumstances avoiding charging mark-to-market losses to the income statement. However, there were also rule changes requiring enhanced disclosures of financial instruments and the effects of the reclassification on the income statement. These changes were made through amendments to IAS 39 and IFRS 7.

The chairman of the IASB, Sir David Tweedie, has spoken publicly about the demands made on the IASB by European politicians who were requesting changes to standards that were consistent with the interests of the European banks.[23] Following the rule change, which was backdated to July 2008, one of those European banks, Deutsche Bank, reduced its write-downs and generated a surprise pre-tax profit.[24] Deutsche Bank's interim financial report for the third quarter of 2008 explains that the impact of the reclassifications increased income before income taxes by €825 million.[25] There is some suggestion that the securities markets were fooled by this accounting reclassification. Kessler claims that Deutsche Bank's shares rose nearly 19 per cent on October 30, the day it made the profit announcement. Whether or not this share price increase was due to fooling the market, or the market recognising that Deutsche Bank was now in a position to make more profitable loans, the effect of the pressured rule change on the IASB's credibility was profound. The ramifications of this pressure for future convergence between US GAAP and IFRS are discussed further in the next section.

The Group of 20 (G20) nations met in November 2008 and again in March 2009 in response to the developing financial crisis and made a number of recommendations for changes in financial market regulation, including accounting standards.[26] These recommendations included issues surrounding financial instruments, asset impairments and accounting for off-balance sheet items.[27] The IASB and FASB are working on responses to these recommendations. One response to the second G20 meeting was the ruling by the FASB to allow banks to use their own judgement in determining the fair value of assets, rather than using markets as the objective criteria.[28]

Overall, the focus on fair value accounting has the potential to divert attention from the underlying causes of the global financial crisis. Fair value accounting makes the problems with asset values transparent, but did not cause banks to change their business models in the early 2000s. Blundell-Wignall, Atkinson and Lee in a paper published by the OECD lay the blame for the financial turmoil on (1) global macro liquidity policies, and (2) a very poor regulatory framework that, far from acting as a second line of defence, actually contributed to the crisis.[29] These factors contributed to asset bubbles and excess leverage which were directed to mortgage securitisation and off-balance sheet activity, and began well before 2007. This analysis is similar to that made by the SEC in its 2008 study of mark-to-market accounting referred to above, and together they suggest that the solution to the crisis will involve more than changing the accounting rules.

Auditors and the global financial crisis

An alternative, or perhaps complementary, action to changing the accounting rules is to blame the auditor. Just as corporate collapses in the early 2000s triggered the audit independence restrictions in the Sarbanes-Oxley Act (2002) in the United States and CLERP 9 reforms in Australia, the GFC could lead to regulatory action against auditors. Sikka provides evidence that 28 distressed banks from the United States, United Kingdom, and other European countries received unqualified audit reports from major audit firms in the 2007 financial year (although three of these audit reports drew attention to matters disclosed in the notes to the accounts). As Sikka notes, very little attention has been paid so far in the press to the auditor's role in the crisis, although some commentators have questioned the value of audits when the auditors did not foresee the effect of the riskiness of the assets on some banks' balance sheets.[30]

The accounting profession and the regulators overseeing financial reporting and auditing around the world have proactively issued guidance to accountants and directors to assist them during the crisis. For example, the Auditing Practices Board in the United Kingdom published a bulletin in December 2008 on assessing going concern issues and determining the adequacy of disclosures in financial reports and the effect on the auditor's report.[31] Similar publications have come from the Canadian Institute of Chartered Accountants and The Institute of Chartered Accountants in England and Wales.[32] These publications emphasise the risk facing auditors when assessing asset values and considering the merit of management plans to mitigate going concern risks and liquidity issues during the anticipated recession. The publications also emphasise the importance of ethical standards when dealing with pressure from management to avoid unwelcome disclosures or write-downs. Analysis of the auditors' role in the global financial crisis is likely to continue in the immediate future.

LO 3 → POSSIBLE DIRECTIONS IN FUTURE INTERNATIONAL ACCOUNTING STANDARD SETTING ARRANGEMENTS

IASB and FASB convergence project

In November 2008, the Securities and Exchange Commission (SEC) in the United States released a 'Roadmap' for the potential use of IFRS by US companies by 2014.[33] The convergence with IFRS is contingent upon a number of milestones being achieved which would convince the SEC that using IFRS would be in the public interest and provide protection for investors. The convergence is being considered by the SEC because the investment markets are becoming increasingly global and new investment opportunities are available to US investors. In these circumstances, US investors could benefit from assistance in comparing financial statements for companies from different countries. The SEC will assess the progress towards the milestones in 2011 and then make a decision about whether the 2014 implementation date should proceed.

The milestones relate to:[34]

1. Improvements in accounting standards[35]
2. The accountability and funding of the IASC Foundation
3. The improvement in the ability to use interactive data for IFRS reporting
4. Education and training relating to IFRS
5. Limited early use of IFRS where this would enhance comparability for US investors
6. The anticipated timing of future rulemaking by the Commission; and
7. The implementation of the mandatory use of IFRS by US issuers.

The SEC Roadmap builds on the 2002 and 2006 agreements between the IASB and the FASB to commit to developing as soon as practicable high-quality, compatible accounting standards that could be used for both domestic and cross-border financial reporting, and to work towards a common set of high-quality global standards. Since those dates, the IASB and the FASB have been working on several projects under a joint work plan which covers the period to 2011. The SEC intends to review the standards that come out of those projects for their quality and comprehensiveness.

Another area of concern for the SEC is the robustness, inclusiveness, and promptness of the due process used to develop the standards. Overall, the SEC is concerned about the quality of the financial reporting and the investor protection that is provided by IFRS.

The second milestone relates to the governance of the IASB. The IASB reports to the International Accounting Standards Committee Foundation (IASCF). The IASCF is a non-profit, non-government organisation. It does not report to any sovereign government, so it does not receive the legal backing of a government. This makes the IASB vulnerable to interference and pressure from interested parties, including governments. This is in contrast to the FASB, which reports to the US Congress, or the Australian Accounting Standards Board, which is ultimately responsible to the Australian government. The IASCF is governed by 22 trustees whose backgrounds are geographically diverse. Funding for the IASCF comes largely through voluntary donations from a wide range of market participants. The SEC is concerned about the security and stability of the funding, and whether these arrangements have the potential to compromise the independence of the IASB.

The IASB is currently engaged in a constitutional review. One of the first outcomes of the review is the creation of a body which will give the IASB greater ability to withstand pressure from external parties. The membership of this new body, known as the Monitoring Group, is drawn from capital markets authorities from various jurisdictions who have an interest in supporting the development of high-quality international accounting standards.[36] The SEC supports the creation of the Monitoring Group and will assess its performance as an oversight mechanism.

The third milestone is related to the use of XBRL, discussed earlier in the chapter. The remaining milestones relate to changes in the United States regarding the capacity of accountants, companies and regulatory authorities to cope with changes in the accounting standards.

Issues in IFRS – US GAAP convergence

Despite the existence of the roadmap, it is not certain that the United States will adopt IFRS. The SEC chair, Mary Schapiro, recently said that she would not 'feel bound' by the roadmap. She added that she had some concerns about 'IFRS standards generally', and was not prepared to delegate standard-setting or oversight responsibility to the IASB.[37] A member of the Public Company Accounting Oversight Board (PCAOB) in the United States, Charles Niemeier, is also critical of the proposed convergence.[38] His main concern is that the move to IFRS would leave the United States with rules that are more difficult to enforce. He also claims that the IFRS are not more principles-based than US GAAP, merely younger and therefore there has been less time to make detailed corrections and additions.

Other parties have also expressed concerns in relation to the political pressure placed on the IASB in late 2008 which forced a rule change on banks' use of fair values.[39] However, some commentators have acknowledged that the SEC and FASB are not entirely immune from such political pressure. Former SEC chief accountants Conrad Hewitt and Lynn Turner have both spoken of pressure from US politicians, particularly in relation to issues of accounting for stock options and derivatives.[40] The FASB is also accused of buckling under pressure from Congress when it made the April 2009 changes to fair value reporting by banks.[41]

A further consideration in the move towards one global set of standards is the issue of competition between standards setters. Jamal et al. argue that there is research evidence that both IFRS and US GAAP produce valuable information for users of financial statements, and that there is no conclusive evidence that US GAAP is better than IFRS.[42] In this context, they argue, it is prudent to promote competition between the two sets of standards. All companies should be allowed to choose between the standards, and researchers can analyse these choices and their consequences to assist future regulatory changes to the set of standards. At this stage only foreign companies have the choice to use US GAAP or IFRS for reporting within the United States, but this still provides the opportunity for a limited amount of research on the competition between the standards.

The SEC has highlighted several of the key issues that need to be addressed before US companies begin to use IFRS domestically. The long lead time is necessary to address these issues and it is also required for affected parties to adjust. As discussed in chapter 11, management compensation and debt contracts typically contain numerous references to accounting numbers such as profit, debt and shareholders' equity. These numbers are calculated by applying the rules of accounting, including those specified in accounting standards. Any accounting standard change has the potential to redistribute wealth between the contracting parties. Allowing time for the change from US GAAP to IFRS, and smoothing the change by modifying both sets of standards to reduce the differences between them, gives the contracting parties time to renegotiate the contracts.

International auditing standards

Haka reports that some accountants suggest that the move to IFRS will require auditing standards and practices in the United States to change away from a model of assessing conformity with the rules in the accounting standards to an overall assessment of 'true and fair'.[43] The audit approach has important implications for the adoption of principles-based IFRS accounting standards because the existing approach focuses on enforcing rules rather than principles.

Auditing standards are also being internationalised for the same reasons as the accounting standards; that is, the globalisation of business and share markets creates demand for global standards. Many multinational firms voluntarily choose to have their financial statements audited according to International Standards on Auditing (ISAs)[44], and some countries either incorporate ISAs into their national auditing standards, or base their national standards on the ISAs.[45] ISAs are issued by the International Auditing and Assurance Standards Board (IAASB), which operates under the auspices of the International Federation of Accountants (IFAC). The IAASB has recently completed a Clarity project involving the redrafting of its standards in a form designed to enhance understanding and implementation of them, as well as aid their translation.[46] The IAASB's work program for 2009–11 aims to provide new standards and processes to improve and assess the effectiveness of the ISAs.

In the past the IAASB has been criticised for a lack of independence from the auditing profession.[47] This is because IFAC's members are accounting organisations and most members of the IAASB have been practising auditors.[48] Simnett regards the introduction of the Public Interest Oversight Board (PIOB) in 2005 to oversee the operations of the IAASB as a positive step because it separates the IAASB from the direct influence of IFAC, thereby increasing confidence that the auditing standards are properly responsive to the public interest. In addition, the cooperation over recent years between the IAASB and the US PCAOB has increased alignment between the two sets of standards.[49]

The PIOB and the Monitoring Group essentially perform the same function for the IAASB and the IASB respectively. Both oversight bodies have been established to counter suggestions of a lack of independence arising from the perception that the parties funding the organisations are in a position to influence the content and rigour of the standards. The IAASB and the IASB also share another problem. That is, they are both international standard setting bodies with no government directly responsible for enforcing the standards. The IAASB relies on national regulators to police its standards, and national professional accounting associations that are members of IFAC encourage their members to follow the standards.[50] The international acceptance of both sets of standards will depend, at least partly, on the success of the standards' enforcement and on retaining the trust of the various stakeholders using and relying on the standards. There is much at stake; successful harmonisation of accounting and auditing standards has the potential to benefit economic activity around the globe by reducing costs of financial reporting.[51]

LO 4 → SUSTAINABILITY ACCOUNTING, REPORTING AND ASSURANCE

What is sustainability accounting and reporting?

Sustainability accounting and reporting is a subset of social accounting. Gray, Owen and Adams regard social accounting as a combination of accounting for different things, in different media, to different users, for different purposes.[52] In other words, it goes beyond financial measurement of economic events and reporting to a defined set of users, often in accordance with accounting standards and regulations. Social accounting and reporting aims at observing and assimilating issues not necessarily covered by the traditional accounting function into a form that can be used for decision making by individuals not necessarily directly or only concerned with the financial success of the entity. Social accounting could be seen as fitting within categories four and five of the ontological assumption sets shown in table 2.1 (p. 31). Social accounting researchers often adopt naturalistic research approaches, using case studies and interviews to understand how accounting has been socially constructed and how it is experienced by participants.

The term 'sustainability' is used and interpreted in different ways. It can be regarded as meeting the needs of the present without compromising the ability of future generations to meet their own needs.[53] Under this definition, sustainability is concerned with both environmental protection (eco-efficiency) as well as justice between peoples and generations (eco-justice). This broad definition means that environmental reporting is a subset of sustainability, and companies that publish sustainability reports include information relating to their relations with their employees, communities and the environment. For example, J Sainsbury plc's corporate responsibility report[54] grew out of earlier environment reports. The 2008 report contains information about Sainsbury's policies and actions in providing healthy food choices for their consumers, using fair trade suppliers and local suppliers, supporting charitable events and organisations in local communities, promoting the health and wellbeing of their employees, and reducing their impact on the environment through waste and carbon emissions.

Recent developments in sustainability reporting

The landscape for sustainability reporting has changed in recent years due to a number of developments. One of the most widely used set of guidelines for sustainability reporting, published by the Global Reporting Initiative (GRI), was revised and released in October 2006.[55] The GRI guidelines form the basis of a sustainability disclosure framework and contain principles and guidance plus standard disclosures for all types of organisations. The principles define the content of sustainability reports, the quality of the information, and the report boundary. The standard disclosures include the organisation's sustainability strategy and profile, management approach, and performance indicators. The GRI guidelines are similar in purpose to the conceptual framework used to guide financial reporting.

Companies adopting the GRI guidelines can register their sustainability reports with the GRI, and by March 2009 nearly 1000 reports for 2008 were registered. The growth in sustainability reporting is confirmed by a recent survey by KPMG on corporate economic, environmental, and social performance disclosure.[56] The survey finds that over 90 per cent of Global Fortune 250 companies publish 'sustainability' or 'corporate responsibility' reports. KPMG also reported that 70 per cent of the reporting companies worldwide use the GRI guidelines, possibly due to the perceived credibility of the standards and the advantage gained from using a consistent set of standards which make the reports more comparable across companies. In addition to the impact of their own operations, companies are also reporting data on sustainability impacts arising in the company's supply chain.

The growth in reporting on environmental issues is also driven by the emergence of markets in permits to emit greenhouse gases or in credits earned by not emitting them. Companies affected by these markets are required to account for their greenhouse gas emissions and report under the prescribed rules to the relevant regulatory authority.[57] The development of mandatory emissions permit trading, in particular the establishment of the European Union Emissions Trading Scheme (EU ETS) in January 2005, has also contributed to a closer association between financial reporting and environmental, or sustainability, reporting. This is due to the need to consider how to account for emission rights, or permits, and the liabilities that accrue as the emissions are made.

The EU ETS was not the first carbon market established, but it is the largest, with an annual trade in permits of US$24 billion in 2006 and US$50 billion in 2007.[58] In the period prior to the introduction of the EU ETS the International Financial Reporting Interpretations Committee (IFRIC), a subsidiary body of the IASB, released a document prescribing the acceptable accounting treatment for emission rights.[59] IFRIC 3 *Emission Rights* required companies to treat all allowances as intangible assets. This meant that they had to recognise the fair value of any free allowances immediately as income, while the costs of the corresponding emissions would be recognised only gradually as they accumulated.[60] Cook describes the response to the document as a 'public outcry' and it was withdrawn in June 2005.[61] MacKenzie attributes the controversy to the fear that IFRIC 3's recommendations would produce increased earnings volatility as the income and expenditures were mismatched in time.[62] MacKenzie argues that companies prefer to treat emission rights as financial instruments and adopt hedge accounting under IAS 39. This would allow the company to then offset allowances and corresponding emissions, keeping 'carbon' off the balance sheet.[63]

A report by PricewaterhouseCoopers (PwC) and the International Emissions Trading Association (IETA) shows little support for the IFRIC 3 method of accounting, as well as substantial variation in accounting for emissions rights.[64] Their survey shows that six main methods of accounting for emissions rights are currently in use in European companies, with fifteen different approaches to classifying the EU ETS on the companies' balance sheets.[65] The most common approach is to recognise the granted allowances at nil value, with the obligation recognised at the carrying value of allowances already granted/purchased, with the balance at the prevailing market price.

PwC and IETA conclude that in addition to the lack of clarity and comparability of financial statements produced by companies with emissions rights, the absence of authority on this issue has caused both frustration and a waste of resources for these companies.[66] In addition, because their survey did not address the needs and views of external stakeholders it is not known what impact the variability in accounting for emission rights has on their ability to rely on this information for decision making. In response to the problems in accounting for emission that have arisen in Europe and the growing likelihood of other emissions trading schemes being established, the IASB has recently announced it will re-activate its project on Emissions Trading Schemes and a standard is expected in 2010.[67]

Climate change and sustainability issues are also affecting traditional financial reporting through decisions about asset impairments and risk disclosures. Climate change can pose a physical threat to asset values; for example, low-lying coastal land could be at increased risk of flooding. Also, the value of operational assets is adversely affected by falling demand for the products they produce. For example, a shift in demand from high-energy appliances towards low-energy appliances because of changing attitudes or increasing electricity costs would affect the value of the assets used to make high-energy appliances.

Further, insurance companies in the United States must now disclose to the insurance regulator how climate change is likely to affect their businesses, and by implication, their assets.[68] The regulations require insurance companies to make 'climate risk reports' that address the risks of higher claims from their clients due to extreme weather events. Insurers should also disclose their vulnerability to falling profits from their investments in companies that would be adversely affected by caps on carbon emissions (e.g. utility companies). Although the climate risk reports now required of insurance companies are not part of accounting regulations, they are evidence of a trend towards investors and other stakeholders demanding better information on how climate change is likely to affect companies' profits.[69] There are also potential obligations for disclosure of operational, market and credit risks of the carbon market under IFRS 7 *Financial instruments: disclosures*.[70]

The following extract is from PricewaterhouseCoopers and International Emissions Trading Association (IETA), Trouble-entry accounting — Revisited*.

Accounting approaches for the EU ETS — PwC view

The withdrawal of IFRIC 3 means that under the hierarchy for selecting accounting policies in IAS 8 'Accounting policies, changes in accounting estimates and errors' other accounting models are acceptable (as long as they are consistent with underlying IFRS).

The main accounting approaches which PricewaterhouseCoopers consider to be acceptable are summarised in the following table.

	Full market value approach (IFRIC 3)	Cost of settlement approach	
		Alternative Approach 1	Alternative Approach 2
Initial recognition — Granted allowances	Recognise when able to exercise control; corresponding entry to government grant at market value at date of grant.	Recognise when able to exercise control; corresponding entry to government grant, at market value at date of grant.	Recognise when able to exercise control; recognise at cost, which for granted allowances is a nominal amount (e.g. nil).
Initial recognition — Purchased allowances	Recognise when able to exercise control, at cost.	Recognise when able to exercise control, at cost.	Recognise when able to exercise control, at cost.
Subsequent treatment of allowances	Allowances are subsequently held at cost or re-valued amount, subject to review for impairment.	Allowances are subsequently held at cost or re-valued amount, subject to review for impairment.	Allowances are subsequently held at cost or re-valued amount, subject to review for impairment.
Treatment of deferred income	Government grant amortised on a systematic and rational basis over compliance period.	Government grant amortised on a systematic and rational basis over compliance period.	Not applicable.
Recognition of liability	Recognise liability when incurred.	Recognise liability when incurred.	Recognise liability when incurred.
Measurement of liability	Liability is re-measured fully based on the market value of allowances at each period end, whether the allowances are on hand or would be purchased from the market.	Re-measure liability at each period end. For allowances held, re-measure to carrying amount of those allowances (i.e. market value at date of recognition if cost model is used; market value at date of revaluation if revaluation model is used) on either a FIFO or weighted average basis. A liability relating to any excess emission would be re-measured at the market value at the period end.	Re-measure liability at each period end. For allowances on hand, at the carrying amount of those allowances (nil or cost) on a FIFO or weighted average basis. A liability relating to any excess emission would be re-measured at the market value at the period end.

Note: this summary does not deal with the accounting for emissions allowance by broker/traders.

Illustrative example

To illustrate the impact on the financial statements of these accounting approaches consider the following scenario:

- Companies A, B and C all have financial year ends of 31 December 2006
- Each receives 150 granted allowances at the start of the year
- The market price at grant date was £20 per allowance
- Each company requires 200 allowances to cover its obligation for the 2006 compliance year to be settled in February 2007
- The market price at 31 December 2006 was £25 per allowance

Accounting policies adopted

- Company A has adopted the Alternative Approach 1
- Company B has adopted the Alternative Approach 2
- Company C has adopted the 'full market value' approach (IFRIC 3)

TABLE 1: The companies' financial results and balance sheet for the 2006 year-end

Figures in £	Alternative approach 1 Company A	Alternative approach 2 Company B	IFRIC 3 Company C
Income statement			
Release of deferred income	3000 (i)		3000 (i)
Emissions cost	–4250 (ii)	–1250 (iii)	–5000 (i) (iv)
Net result	–1250	–1250	–2000
Balance sheet			
Intangible assets	3000 (i)		3000 (i)
Liability	–4250 (ii)	–1250 (iii)	–5000 (iv)
Net assets	–1250	–1250	–2000
Current year result	–1250	–1250	–2000
Revaluation reserve	—	—	—
Shareholders funds	–1250	–1250	–1250

Notes:

(i) 150 allowances received measured at market value at grant date £20 per allowance (150 * £20 = £3,000)

(ii) liability based on allowances held measured at carrying amount, and liability related to excess emission market value at period end [(150 * £20) + (50 * £25) = £4,250]

(iii) 50 shortfall in obligation measured at market value at period end £25 per allowance

(iv) 200 obligation measured at market value at period end £25 per allowance

- The financial results show that companies A and B have identical net results. However, company A effectively has a grossed up balance sheet in comparison with Company B.
- Company C has applied the IFRIC 3 approach and has a very different net result and balance sheet.
- It is important to note that each entity, making the same level of emissions and holding the same number of allowances will ultimately be required to make up the same shortfall in allowances. In the example each company will have to finance the shortfall of allowances, which if the price of allowances remained constant would cost each company £1,250. For company C, the decision to value the entire obligation at the prevailing market price of allowances means that there is a mismatch in the timing of recognition, with the following year recognising a credit to the income statement of £750 as the liability is settled. This highlights the volatility in earnings that can arise with the use of this method.
- Further differences in results could arise when considering when the shortfall is recognised. One approach could be to recognise the expected shortfall, and associated cost and liability, over the financial year. Others, meanwhile, recognise the cost and liability only when the emissions obligation exceeds the assets held. Hence, for two identical companies

receiving the same number of allowances and making the same level of emissions, whilst the liability at the year-end would be identical, the position at the half year or at each quarter would of course be very different between the two approaches.

- There is an additional consideration for entities using Alternatives 1 and 2, as the measurement of the obligation for which allowances are held will depend on whether the carrying amount of allowances is allocated to the obligation on a FIFO or on a weighted average basis. This is a particular issue where the balance sheet date is not at the end of the compliance period (for example, an interim balance sheet date, or a financial year-end which is not the same as the compliance period end).

- Entities using the FIFO method should measure the obligation at the carrying amount per unit of emissions, up to the number of allowances (if any) held at the balance sheet date, and at the expected cost (the market price at the balance sheet date) per unit for the shortfall (if any) at the balance sheet date.

- Entities using the weighted average method should measure the obligation using the weighted average cost per unit of emission expected to be incurred for the compliance period as a whole. To do this, the entity determines the expected total emissions for the compliance period and compares this with the number of allowance units granted by the government and/or purchased and still held by the entity for that compliance period, to determine the expected shortfall (if any) in allowances held for the compliance period. The weighted average cost per unit of emission for the compliance period is the carrying amount of the allowances held (which may be nil for those granted for nil consideration) plus the cost of meeting the expected shortfall (using the market price at the balance sheet date), divided by the expected total number of units of emission for the compliance period. In other words:

$$\frac{\text{Carrying amount of allowances held} + \text{Cost of meeting expected shortfall}}{\text{Expected total units of emission for the compliance period}} = \frac{\text{Weighted average cost per unit of}}{\text{emission for the compliance period}}$$

- Organisations that choose to actively manage their emissions asset and liability face further accounting decisions. For example, consider an organisation that reports quarterly and sells all of its 2007 allowances in March 2007. Some would claim that the income from the sale should be recognised immediately as a credit to the income statement. This would of course be partially offset by a debit to the income statement to reflect emissions in the year to date not covered by any allowances held. However there is a mismatch between recognising the value of 12 months allowances against the cost of three months of emissions. Alternatively, some would claim that the credit to the income statement be deferred and released over the remainder of the compliance year.

- Differences in accounting treatment concerning recognition of emissions obligations and allowances could therefore have a significant impact on financial reporting, particularly where the organisation reports quarterly or half-yearly results or has a financial year which is not co-terminus with the compliance year.[71]

Source: PricewaterhouseCoopers and the International Emissions Trading Association (IETA), 2007, pp. 27–8, www.ieta.org.

Questions

1. Recalculate each company's financial statements using the following assumptions:
   (a) Each company requires 250 allowances to cover its obligation for the compliance year
   (b) The market price at 31 December 2006 was £40 per allowance.
2. Recalculate each company's financial statements using the following assumptions:
   (a) Each company requires 100 allowances to cover its obligation for the compliance year
   (b) The market price at 31 December 2006 was £40 per allowance.
3. Comment on the differences between your solutions and the above example.

Trends in sustainability reporting assurance

An important ingredient in the usefulness of company financial reports is independent assurance of the reports. Independent assurance provides confidence to stakeholders about the credibility, relevance and reliability of the reports. In most countries annual financial reports must be audited, although interim financial reports could be reviewed only. The difference between an audit and a review is the level of assurance provided by the auditor regarding the reliability of the information provided by the company. This in turn is determined by the nature and extent of procedures performed by the auditor, the results of the procedures and the objectivity of the evidence obtained.[72] An audit provides a reasonable level of assurance and a review provides only a limited level of assurance. The audit provides a greater reduction in assurance engagement risk because the auditor performs greater and more effective evidence-gathering procedures to support the opinion on the financial statements.

Some companies are now seeking assurance for their sustainability reports. KPMG's survey of corporate responsibility reporting shows that 56 per cent of G250 (the largest 250 companies in the Fortune Global 500) that issued a corporate responsibility report included some form of third-party commentary.[73] Formal assurance increased from approximately 30 per cent in 2002 to 40 per cent in 2008. KPMG note that this is still a minority of the reports, despite evidence that consumers are concerned about 'greenwashing' claims. Greenwashing is the practice of disseminating disinformation so as to present an environmentally responsible public image.

The KPMG survey also shows that the numbers of large companies seeking formal assurance varies significantly by country. Over 50 per cent of large companies from France, Spain, South Korea, Italy and the United Kingdom include formal assurance statements in their corporate responsibility reports, compared to less than 20 per cent of large companies from Canada, United States and Romania.[74] The low level of assurance in the North American countries compared to the European countries could be reflective of the different regulatory environments, particularly with respect to emissions trading schemes. Demand for verified environmental information for regulatory purposes can drive the provision of assured information to a wider group of stakeholders. Scandinavian countries were among to first to mandate environmental reporting and companies made the information available to their external stakeholders. However, companies in these countries were slower to provide reports on wider social issues.[75] KPMG note there was a jump in the provision of assured corporate responsibility reports by companies in Denmark, Finland, and Sweden from 2005 to 2008, possibly driven by maturing reporting practices and new Swedish legislation requiring assurance reports.[76]

There appears to be a change in attitude towards sustainability reporting and assurance in the United States, with the provision of formal assurance statements in corporate responsibility reports increasing rapidly from 2 per cent in 2002 to 14 per cent in 2008.[77] This change in attitude could be due to the end of the Bush administration[78], and the activities of lobby groups such as Boston-based CERES (a co-founder of the Global Reporting Initiative).[79] A stimulus to providing high-quality environmental information is also coming from the growth of the Carbon Disclosure Project (CDP).[80] The CDP obtains data from corporations on their climate change risks, strategies, and greenhouse gas emissions and makes it freely available on their website. The primary aim of gathering the information is to inform investing and purchasing decisions by institutional investors, purchasing organisations and government bodies. Over 1500 companies from around the world voluntarily provided information to the CDP in 2008.[81]

Why seek assurance for sustainability reports?

As discussed in earlier chapters, the positive theory of auditing suggests that the demand for auditing arises from the separation of ownership and management. The process of price protection provides incentives for management to incur the cost of auditing where that cost is less than the benefits from increases in the share price. Auditing is argued to provide benefits by increasing the credibility of management-prepared financial statements and improving the quality of an entity's accounting system based on feedback from the auditing process.

Applying this theory to sustainability assurance suggests that companies with the most to gain from increasing the credibility of their reports are more likely to seek assurance. KPMG report that companies claim they seek assurance on their corporate responsibility reports to increase the credibility of their reports and processes and because they wish to improve the quality of reported information.[82] The companies with most to gain from more credible reports are likely to be those in highly visible, potentially high polluting industries. KPMG report that all mining companies in their sample that publish a corporate responsibility report have that statement independently assured. In addition, more than 50 per cent of the sample companies in the utility, oil and gas, chemicals and synthetics, and pharmaceuticals industries, provide assurance reports.[83]

Sustainability assurance standards

The standards for financial statement audits are extensive. For example, following the completion of the Clarity project to redraft International Auditing Standards (ISAs) in a form designed to enhance the understanding and implementation of them, the International Auditing and Assurance Standards Board (IAASB) provides 36 ISAs to govern auditing.[84]

However, there is limited authoritative guidance for assurance engagements on sustainability reports and carbon emissions information. ISAE 3000, *Assurance Engagements Other than Audits or Reviews of Historical Financial Information*, published by the IAASB, provides some general guidance but does not address specific issues in sustainability and carbon emissions reports. As such, it is likely to be applied inconsistently by assurance providers. Another commonly used guidance statement is AA1000AS[85] issued by AccountAbility. AA1000AS provides guidance on sustainability assurance reports that evaluate an entity's adherence to the AA1000 AccountAbility Principles and the quality of publicly disclosed information on sustainability performance.[86]

Research suggests that there are problems with assurance statements in sustainability reporting. O'Dwyer and Owen critically analyse assurance statements from reports shortlisted for the 2002 Association of Chartered Certified Accountants (ACCA) United Kingdom and European Sustainability Reporting Awards Scheme.[87] They report that there are doubts about the independence of the assurance exercise and there also appears to be a large degree of management control over the assurance process. Given these sustainability reports are drawn from a pool of high-quality reports, this is a disturbing finding. Their results are supported by the conclusions of Deegan, Cooper and Shelly[88] who examine a set of Australian reports and conclude the 'assurance statements do not, on average, appear to embrace the recommendations of the GRI (Global Reporting Initiative) or the Federation of European Accountants'.[89] This finding is also reinforced by KPMG's report of a wide variety of approaches to sustainability report assurance, including the type of assurance opinion, and whether all parts of the reports are subject to assurance.[90]

In response to the difficulties in the quality of assurance for sustainability reporting, the IAASB has begun a project to develop a new international standard for *Assurance Engagements on Carbon Emissions Information*.[91] The IAASB intends to issue guidance, probably in the form of a new ISAE, to increase the consistency of approach to assurance of sustainability reports and to provide assistance to financial statement auditors when considering the carrying value of emission trading rights.[92]

LO 5 — OTHER NON-FINANCIAL ACCOUNTING AND REPORTING ISSUES

The best clues to the directions for accounting standard setting in the immediate future are contained in the IASB's current list of projects.[93] The issues arising in most of these projects and their current progress are discussed elsewhere in this text. The IAASB also has a list of current projects in the development of international auditing standards.[94] Some of the auditing projects are affected by the progress on accounting standard setting. For example, the IAASB plans to examine the issues arising in auditing fair values used in accounting reports throughout 2009 and 2010.

However, for guidance on the future of accounting and auditing it is possible to look further afield than the agendas of the accounting and auditing standard setters. For example, there are areas outside traditional financial accounting where the concepts and skills used in accounting and auditing could provide a contribution. One of the areas where financial accountants and auditors are beginning to make a contribution is water accounting. Water accounting applies the accrual accounting concepts of identifying, measuring, recording and reporting information relating to water resources.

Water accounting

Water accounting is currently under development by the Water Accounting Standards Board (WASB)[95] in Australia, with similar projects at various stages of development elsewhere.[96] The WASB released the first edition of a *Water Accounting Conceptual Framework* (*WACF*) and Preliminary Australian Water Accounting Standards (PAWAS) in 2009. The *WACF* and PAWAS govern the preparation and presentation of general purpose water accounting reports (GPWARs) by particular entities. The GPWARs are designed to be useful for decision making by users who cannot command their own water information from those entities.[97] The ultimate aims of the water accounting project are to have an accounting and reporting system that will inform decisions about the allocation of water resources and to enhance public and investor confidence about the management of water in Australia. The first National Water Account (NWA) is due in 2010 and, following more testing and feedback, the PAWAS are expected to be further developed and released as the Australian Water Accounting Standards (AWAS).[98]

The impetus for the water accounting project is provided by the National Water Initiative (NWI) of the Australian government.[99] Although water has always been a scarce natural resource in Australia, the prolonged drought in southern Australia has created political pressures to share water among competing users in the country and city regions, particularly in Victoria.[100] The competing users include industry, farmers, households, community and sporting organisations, and the environment (e.g. for keeping lakes and rivers fresh and providing sufficient water for wildlife). Decision makers will rely on water accounting data about how much water there is, where it is, who is using it, and how it is being used. In addition to informing allocation decisions, the water accounting data will underpin water trading and investment in water infrastructure.[101]

The WASB's aim of developing water accounting standards and procedures to facilitate decision making by various users who are concerned about the sourcing, management, distribution and use of water is similar to the aims of financial accounting standard setters. The WASB has used the financial accounting conceptual framework and standard setting processes to underpin the development of water accounting. The *WACF* is based on the financial accounting standard model and relates to the objective and content of general purpose water accounting reports. The *WACF* prescribes[102] the purpose of general purpose water accounting reports; the reporting entity; the qualitative characteristics of information reported; the elements of those reports when those elements are recognised in general purpose water accounting reports and how they are measured; and compliance disclosures and assurance

The system of water accounting adopted by the WASB is an accrual system in which reports for most water reporting entities will include (a) a Statement of Physical Water Flows; (b) a Statement of Water Assets and Water Liabilities; (c) a Statement of Changes in Water Assets and Water Liabilities; (d) Disclosure Notes; (e) a Compliance Statement; and (f) an Assurance Statement. The adoption of the objective that the reports are to provide information for decision making has required the development of statements on the definition of the elements of those reports, such as water assets, liabilities and changes in water assets and liabilities. For example, the conceptual framework defines water assets as follows:

> Water assets are water, or the rights or other claims to water, which the water reporting entity either holds, or for which the water reporting entity has management responsibilities, and from which an individual or organisation that is a water reporting entity, or a group of stakeholders of a physical water entity, derives future benefits.[103]

The definition includes not only water in storage, but also rights and other claims to water. In addition, following the financial asset definition, the water asset definition considers the concept of future benefits flowing from these assets, and to whom they flow. Similarly, the definition of water liabilities considers the nature of a present obligation to deliver water, or otherwise decrease water assets (or increase other water liabilities). Rather than using financial currency as a unit of measurement, water accounting incorporates information about physical volumes and water quality, as well as asset location (e.g. underground or surface water storages).

Water accounting reports will provide information on stocks and flows of water resources, not just data and claims made by managers that rely on data sourced outside a formal accounting system, such as in sustainability reporting. In the same way that financial statement auditors add value to financial statements by increasing their credibility, it is expected that water reports would be audited. Auditors could provide assurance on water reports using the same skills and techniques used for auditing financial statements, although they would likely need to seek opinions on technical issues from engineers and experts in water quality.

Water accounting standard setting is an example of the ontological assumption that accounting is a concrete structure and process (see table 2.1, p. 31). The underlying premise is that stocks and flows of water are objective and concrete realities and are able to be accounted for using structured frameworks. Water accounting is also an unusual and innovative example of the extension of the financial accounting framework to a non-financial context. If it is ultimately successful, it could encourage the formalisation of standards in other non-financial reporting applications.

Water accounting vs greenhouse gas emission accounting

Another non-financial reporting project developed over recent years is greenhouse gas (GHG) emission accounting. One of the current major international sources of guidance for measuring and reporting GHG emissions is the Greenhouse Gas Protocol (GGP) standards.[104] Although the GGP accounting and reporting standards are based on, in part, generally accepted financial accounting and reporting principles, they also reflect the outcome of a collaborative process by various stakeholders from a variety of backgrounds.[105] The GGP standards allow for direct measurement of GHG emissions, but the main focus is on the process of converting activity data into GHG emissions via use of agreed emissions factors.[106] The activity data are captured by proprietary software or are entered into spreadsheets concurrently with specified activities or financial transactions such as invoice payment, issuance of inventory or entering of journal transactions.

One key difference between the water accounting standards and the GGP standards is the emphasis in the former on accounting for stocks and flows of water using an accrual process. The measurement approach for water accounting derives from the explicit adoption of the purpose to produce information to assist decision making, which is the same purpose adopted by the financial accounting conceptual framework. The GGP provides a standard to guide companies in preparing a GHG inventory that represents a true and fair account of their emissions, and emphasises the qualitative characteristics of relevance, completeness, consistency, transparency, and accuracy.[107] However, the GGP standards are designed to aid companies in their measuring and reporting decisions, rather than to ensure that all information required by the external stakeholders in their decision making is provided in the form they need. Although the information currently being provided under the GGP standards is likely to be of some use to external decision makers, it is incomplete and approximate. It does not attempt to provide a full accrual accounting of the company's activities on the stocks of greenhouse gases in the environment, with limited reporting of indirect emissions,[108] and measurement problems are created by the emissions factor approach.

Some of the issues arising from the emissions factor approach in the GGP standards are associated with the selection and application of the emission factors and the quality of the activity data. The acceptance of emissions factors as valid measurement tools mean that the GGP standards do not allow decision makers to have the level of confidence in the GHG reported information that the water accounting standards aim to provide. They also raise different issues for auditors. For example, the current approach to accounting for GHG emissions focuses on assessing levels of activity and selecting appropriate factors. Auditors can provide assurance over the processes and controls over this data, but are not able to provide an opinion as to whether the resulting reports are a fair presentation of the impact of the entity on the environment. Movement towards a fully integrated accrual accounting system for GHG emissions would provide opportunities for auditors to make such opinions.

However, despite the limitations of the GGP standards and other attempts to quantify GHG emissions, these systems mean that companies are reporting GHG emissions data for the first time in history. The GGP and the water accounting standards are both evidence of the pressure on governments to obtain data on scarce resources other than those traditionally captured by financial accounting systems. As such, they point to a broader, and perhaps ultimately more important, future for accounting in the twenty-first century and beyond.

Summary

LO 1 **Current factors influencing accounting and auditing research, regulation and practice**
Large companies in the United States are now required to file their financial reports with the SEC using XBRL. XBRL allows financial data to be tagged so that they can be extracted by software to produce custom-designed reports, allowing a wider group of users to quickly access and analyse company financial data. XBRL will loosen the control company managers currently have on data aggregation decisions and place the managers' performance under greater scrutiny. Some issues arise for auditing from XBRL reporting and from the changes to auditor independence laws following the corporate collapses of the early 2000s. The research evidence that auditor independence is compromised when auditors provide non-audit consulting services is mixed, but the Sarbanes-Oxley Act in the United States restricts auditors' provision of these services to their audit clients.

LO 2 **Issues surrounding the application of fair value accounting during the global financial crisis**
The role of fair value accounting in the global financial crisis has been investigated by the SEC. Although the SEC concludes that the global financial crisis has several causes, both the SEC and the Group of 20 (G20) nations have recommended changes to financial market regulation and accounting standards. Pressure by European banks and politicians on the IASB led to changes in the relevant standards in 2008, allowing some companies to reclassify financial assets and avoid large write-downs. Auditors are also coming under scrutiny for their role, in particular, in auditing financial statements of banks later suffering financial difficulties.

LO 3 **Possible directions in future international accounting standard setting arrangements**
The IASB and FASB are working on convergence of accounting standards and the SEC has a roadmap for the potential use of IFRS by US companies by 2014. According to the SEC, a number of milestones must be achieved before convergence is finalised, and there are indications that there are substantial difficulties to be overcome during the convergence process. Progress is being made on international auditing standards; they have been redrafted and there is growing international acceptance. Both the auditing and accounting standards boards must deal with issues relating to their independence and governance before both sets of standards are truly global.

LO 4 **Sustainability accounting, reporting and assurance**
Evidence suggests that a growing number of companies are issuing sustainability reports and having them either audited or reviewed by independent auditors. The popularity

of sustainability reporting and assurance varies by country, possibly reflecting differing regulatory environments, such as emissions trading schemes. The financial accounting standards for emissions rights and liabilities are not specific, although a new standard is under development by the IASB. In addition, sustainability assurance standards are being developed by the IAASB.

LO 5   Other non-financial accounting and reporting issues

Water accounting standards are being developed to govern water reporting in Australia and elsewhere. The standards are based on a conceptual framework that is similar to the financial accounting conceptual framework, containing statements about the reporting entity, qualitative characteristics of information, elements of reports, recognition, measurement of elements, and compliance disclosures and assurance. As such, it uses an accrual accounting approach that is not evident in other non-financial reporting standards, such as the Greenhouse Gas Protocol (GGP) standards. Both the GGP and the water accounting standards reflect attempts to provide data on scarce resources other than those traditionally captured by financial accounting systems, and are indicators of an important future for accounting.

Questions

1. What is XBRL? What are the arguments for and against disaggregation of data in financial statements?

2. 'I do not know of any auditing regulation that originated in a research study.' What does this statement mean for the relationship between auditing research and public policy?

3. What is the global financial crisis? Why has it created intense discussion about accounting for fair values?

4. What specific issues does the global financial crisis create for auditors?

5. What are the latest pronouncements from the IASB and FASB on fair values?

6. Leon Gettler wrote in a recent article:

   As former analyst Henry Blodget points out, the US is adopting the model used by Japan in the 1990s when it refused to acknowledge its banks were insolvent and pretended they were healthy. History, as Mark Twain said, does not repeat itself, but it rhymes.
   The G20, banks and standard setters should remember this: to borrow from Winston Churchill's line on democracy, fair value is the worst [form of accounting except for all the other forms that have been tried].'[109]

   (a) Does fair value convey 'reality' better than any other form of valuation?
   (b) Is it better for banks to report stable asset values or to provide information about those assets? What are the arguments for each view?

7. What are the arguments for and against convergence between the FASB and the IASB?

8. Is it important to harmonise both accounting and auditing standards around the world? Why?

9. What is sustainability reporting? How does sustainability reporting relate to social accounting?

10. Why do companies issue sustainability reports?

11. What advantages do companies perceive in obtaining assurance for sustainability reports?

12. Why has the practice of sustainability reporting (and assurance) varied around the world?

13. Who do you think should be involved in sustainability assurance? Accountants or physical scientists and engineers? Why?

14. What is the Carbon Disclosure Project? Who would use the information provided by the Carbon Disclosure Project? Why?

15. What is the Global Reporting Initiative? Is this the same as the Greenhouse Gas Protocol Initiative?

16. What is water accounting? Why would we want to account for water?

17. What is a water asset? What is a water liability? How would water assets and liabilities increase or decrease?

18. What attributes of water could be measured? Who would use information about these water attributes? What decisions would they be making?

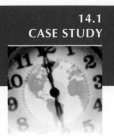

14.1
CASE STUDY

The following article outlines the objectives of The Group of Twenty (G20) at the conclusion of the London summit held in April 2009. (The G20 is an 'informal forum that brings together finance ministers and central bank governors to discuss key issues in the global economy'.)

Accounting related outcomes of the G20 meeting

In the Leaders Communiqué issued at the conclusion of its recent summit in London, the G20 has called upon international standard-setters to make significant progress towards a single set of high quality global accounting standards with particular emphasis on valuation and provisioning requirements. It considers this as an integral part of effective global reform of the financial system.

The Communiqué and supporting Declaration on Strengthening the Financial System emphasise that their objectives are strengthening transparency and accountability, enhancing sound regulation, promoting integrity in financial markets and reinforcing international cooperation.

The leaders have agreed that the accounting standard setters should improve standards for the valuation of financial instruments based on their liquidity and investors' holding horizons, while reaffirming the framework of fair value accounting.

They welcomed the FSF* recommendations on procyclicality that address accounting issues. They also agreed that accounting standard setters should take action by the end of 2009 to:

- Reduce the complexity of accounting standards for financial instruments;
- Strengthen accounting recognition of loan-loss provisions by incorporating a broader range of credit information;
- Improve accounting standards for provisioning, off-balance sheet exposures and valuation uncertainty;
- Achieve clarity and consistency in the application of valuation standards internationally, working with supervisors;
- Within the framework of the independent accounting standard setting process, improve involvement of stakeholders, including prudential regulators and emerging markets, through the IASB's constitutional review.

More details on the outcomes of the meeting, including the texts of the Leaders Communiqué and the Declaration on Strengthening the Financial System can be found at www.g20.org.

Note: *FSF = Financial Stability Forum, to be replaced by the Financial Stability Board (see Leaders Communiqué, and Declaration on Strengthening the Financial System, www.g20.org).

Source: The Institute of Chartered Accountants in Australia, 14 April 2009, www.charteredaccountants.com.au.

Questions

1. How would you 'improve standards for the valuation of financial instruments based on their liquidity and investors' holding horizons, while reaffirming the framework of fair value accounting'?
2. What is the IASB's constitutional review? What implications does this review have for the acceptability of IFRS?

14.2
CASE STUDY

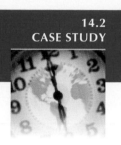

Authority 'fabricated' water data

by Carmel Egan

State Government water authorities have for eight years fabricated data they claimed was being collected at a river monitoring station that does not exist.

The revelation indicates the Government might be failing to deliver on commitments to release enough water to keep drought-stricken rivers flowing.

Water authorities are bound under the Water Act of 1989 to maintain river flow gauging stations at designated points.

But Government assurances have been undermined with an admission by Southern Rural Water it has been "calculating" river flow readings from a phantom gauging station near Sale.

West Gippsland Catchment Management Authority and Southern Rural Water have invented the readings taken at the last gauging station on the Thomson and Latrobe river system before it flows into the Gippsland lakes.

Gauging station number 226027 at Swing Bridge, five kilometres south of Sale, does not exist, despite $70,000 being set aside for its installation in 2000. Until last week, the authority was insisting the station was working to record the level of freshwater flowing to Lake Wellington in the internationally recognised Gippsland lakes and wetlands.

"There is monitoring there, it has been there a long time," said Southern Rural Water spokesman Craig Parker.

"It is a site that has historically been used as a compliance point but you might take up with the Department of Sustainability and Environment whether it will continue into the future. It is a partnership site where a number of agencies ... co-ordinate the management. West Gippsland Catchment Management Authority employ a person (to take readings).

"I am as certain as I can be," Mr Parker said before later confirming the gauging station had never been installed.

The Sale Swing Bridge, built in 1883, spans the Latrobe River at its junction with the Thomson River. The Victorian Water Act 1989 requires authorities to collect data to ensure the passing flows meet bulk-water entitlements allocated for the environment.

Freshwater levels at Swing Bridge have been calculated based on readings taken kilometres upstream at the Kilmany South and Bundalaguah, minus entitlements for irrigation and industry.

Southern Rural Water later told *The Sunday Age* one of the reasons the Swing Bridge monitoring station had never been installed was that it was impossible to split fresh water from the salt water wedge of tidal flows that run beneath.

But former general manager of Lake Wellington Rivers Authority, Ross Scott, said the technology had been available for a decade.

"They just don't want that site," said Mr Scott. "Forty per cent of the time they are not meeting the flows guaranteed under the bulk entitlements at the gauging stations further upstream at Kilmany on the Latrobe and Bundalaguah on the Thomson and there are absolutely no controls on extractions, legal or illegal, between those stations and Swing Bridge."

Conservationists and environmental groups have long accused the Government and water authorities of failing to properly monitor and control the quantity and quality of water reaching the Gippsland lakes and wetlands.

Last year chairman of the Gippsland Lakes Taskforce Professor Barry Hart admitted at a public meeting that the authority had failed to adequately monitor the vulnerable wetlands' health.

Southern Rural Water insists it is properly monitoring levels by calculation, observation, metering and a system of local landowners dobbing in suspected water thieves.

Source: The Sunday Age, 29 March 2009, p. 9, www.theage.com.au.

Questions

1. Explain the accusation that the water authority fabricated data. How was it done?
2. What are the difficulties faced by the water authority in providing accurate data? What water attributes are they supposed to measure?
3. Who are the stakeholders in this case? What are their interests?

Endnotes

1. M Lajara, 'SEC Mandates use of XBRL', NYSSCPA.Org, www.nysscpa.org; see also TJ Strader, 'XBRL capabilities and limitations', *The CPA Journal* (online), 2007, www.nysscpa.org.
2. Securities and Exchange Commission (SEC), 'Spotlight on tagged data and XBRL initiatives for EDGAR filings', 2009, www.sec.gov/spotlight/xbrl.shtml.
3. S Haka, 'Accounting tipping points and thought leadership', *Accounting Education News: The Newsletter of the American Accounting Association*, Winter 2009, vol. 37, iss. 1, pp. 3–4.
4. RD Plumlee and MA Plumlee, 'Assurance on XBRL for financial reporting', *Accounting Horizons*, vol. 22, no. 3, 2008, pp. 353–68.
5. J Francis, Editorial, 'Roundtable on auditing research', *European Accounting Association Newsletter*, issue 1, 2009, pp. 12–6.
6. TJ Fogarty, 'The imagery and reality of peer review in the US: insights from institutional theory' *Accounting Organizations and Society*, vol. 21, 1996, pp. 243–67, discussed in G Hilary and C Lennox, 'The credibility of self-regulation: Evidence from the accounting profession's peer review program', *Journal of Accounting and Economics*, vol. 40, 2005, pp. 211–29.
7. Hilary and Lennox, 2005, op. cit.
8. ibid., p. 228.
9. Section 201, Sarbanes-Oxley Act (2002) (US), www.soxlaw.com.
10. R Frankel, M Johnson and K Nelson, 'The relation between auditors' fees for nonaudit services and earnings management', *The Accounting Review*, vol. 77, supplement, 2002, pp. 71–105.
11. H Ashbaugh, R LaFond, and B Mayhew 'Do nonaudit services compromise auditor independence? Further evidence', *The Accounting Review*, vol. 78, no. 3, 2003, pp. 611–39.
12. M Power, 'Business risk auditing — Debating the history of its present', *Accounting, Organizations and Society*, vol. 32, 4/5, 2007, pp. 379–82.
13. M Power, *The audit society rituals of verification*, Oxford: OUP, 1999.
14. P Sikka, 'Financial crisis and the silence of the auditors', *Accounting, Organizations and Society*, 2009, doi:10.1016/j.aos.2009.01.004.
15. A Blundell-Wignall, P Atkinson, and SH Lee, 'The current financial crisis: causes and policy issues', 2008, *Financial Market Trends*, OECD.
16. Federation of European Accountants (FEE), 'Matters of specific relevance for statutory auditors during the financial crisis', Policy Statement, December 2008, Bruxelles.
17. M Lajara, 'SEC upholds fair value accounting', 2009, NYSSCPA.Org, www.nysscpa.org.
18. United States Securities and Exchange Commission (SEC) Report and Recommendations Pursuant to Section 133 of the Emergency Economic Stabilization Act of 2008: Study on mark-to-market accounting, December 2008, Washington.
19. SEC Press Release 2008-307, www.sec.gov.
20. C Patterson, 'SEC officials pressured over accounting rules', 2009, NYSSCPA.Org, www.nysscpa.org.
21. United States Securities and Exchange Commission (SEC), op. cit., p. 24.
22. ibid., p. 32.
23. G Kessler, 'Accounting standards wilt under pressure', *The Washington Post*, December 27, 2008, A01 www.washingtonpost.com; C Patterson, 'Tweedie: IASB yielded to political pressures', 2009, NYSSCPA.Org, www.nysscpa.org.
24. L Gettler, 'Can accounting watchdog resist the banks' pressure?', *The Age BusinessDay*, March 18, 2009, p.14; Deutsche Bank Interim Report, September 2008, www.db.com.
25. Deutsche Bank Interim Report 2008, September, www.db.com, p. 53, 63.

26. Leaders Communiqué 2009, www.g20.org.
27. The IASB responses to the G20 recommendations are available at www.iasb.org.
28. L Getter, 'Standard setters rendered toothless by G20', *The Age BusinessDay*, April 15, 2009, p. 14.
29. Blundell-Wignall, Atkinson and Lee, op. cit.
30. Sikka, op. cit.
31. The Auditing Practices Board, 'Going concern issues during the current economic conditions', Bulletin 2008/10, Kingston upon Thames.
32. Canadian Institute of Chartered Accountants 2009, 'Risk alert — auditing considerations in the current economic environment', Toronto; The Institute of Chartered Accountants in England and Wales 2009, 'Surviving the downturn: 8 strategies to help directors and their advisers manage through the recession', London.
33. Securities and Exchange Commission (SEC), 'Road map for the potential use of financial statements prepared in accordance with International Financial Reporting Standards by U.S. Issuers: Proposed Rule', Federal Register, vol. 73, no. 226, 2008.
34. ibid., 2008, p. 70817.
35. The discussion of this milestone in the SEC document suggests that both IFRS and US SFAS need to be improved.
36. Details of the IASB Foundation monitoring board's first meeting, www.iasb.org.
37. 'IASB's Tweedie meets new SEC chairman', *Accountancy Age*, www.accountancyage.com.
38. P Sukhraj, 'PCAOB member slams stateside IFRS plans', *Accountancy Age*, September 11, 2008, www.accountancyage.com.
39. G Kessler, 'Accounting standards wilt under pressure', *The Washington Post*, December 27, 2008, A01, www.washingtonpost.com.
40. C Patterson, 'SEC officials pressured over accounting rules', *CPABlog*, 2009, NYSSCPA.Org, www.nysscpa.org.
41. L Gettler, 'Standard-setters rendered toothless by G20', *The Age BusinessDay*, April 15, 2009, p. 14.
42. K Jamal, GJ Benston, DR Carmichael, TE Christensen, RH Colson, SR Moehrle, et al., 'A perspective on the SEC's proposal to accept financial statements prepared in accordance with International Financial Reporting Standards (IFRS) without reconciliation to U.S. GAAP', *Accounting Horizons*, vol. 22, no. 2, June 2008, pp. 241–48.
43. S Haka, 'Accounting tipping points and thought leadership', *Accounting Education News*, 2009, p. 4.
44. LM Smith, T Sagafi-Nejad and K Wang, 'Going international: Accounting and auditing standards', *Internal Auditing*, vol. 23, no. 3, July 2008, pp. 3–14.
45. IAASB Factsheet, www.ifac.org/IAASB.
46. IAASB, 'IAASB's Annual report focuses on the clarity standards as a foundation for global audit quality', Press Release, March 16, 2009, New York.
47. R Simnett, 'A critique of the International Auditing and Assurance Standards Board', *Australian Accounting Review*, vol. 17, no. 2, July 2007, pp. 28–36.
48. ibid., p. 29.
49. ibid., pp. 33–34.
50. ibid., p. 34.
51. Smith, Sagafi-Nejad and Wang, op. cit., p. 12.
52. R Gray, D Owen and C Adams, *Accounting and accountability*, Hertfordshire, UK: Prentice-Hall, 1996, pp. 3–11.
53. United Nations World Commission on Environment and Development (UNSCED), Our Common Future, the Brundtland Report, Oxford: OUP, 1987.
54. Sainsbury's corporate responsibility report: Our values make us different, 2008, www.j-sainsbury.co.uk.
55. Global Reporting Initiative, GRI Sustainability Reporting Framework, G3 Guidelines, www.globalreporting.org.
56. KPMG, International Survey of Corporate Responsibility Reporting 2008, www.kpmg.com.
57. For example, in preparation for an emissions trading scheme, the Australian Federal Government requires certain companies to report data on a greenhouse gases from 1 July 2008, National Greenhouse and Energy Reporting Act 2007 (NGER).
58. K Capoor and P Ambrosi, State and trends of the carbon market 2008, World Bank, Washington, May 2008, http://siteresources.worldbank.org.
59. IFRIC Interpretation 3: *Emission Rights*, December 2004.
60. D MacKenzie, 'Making things the same: gases, emission rights and the politics of carbon markets', *Accounting, Organizations, and Society*, 2008, doi:10.1016/j.aos.2008.02.004.
61. A Cook, 'Emission rights: from costless activity to market operations', *Accounting Organizations and Society*, doi:10.1016/j.aos.2007.12.001.
62. C MacKenzie, 'Making things the same: Gases, emission rights and the politics of carbon markets', *Accounting, Organizations, and Society*, doi:10.1016/j.aos.2008.02.004.
63. ibid., p. 10.
64. PricewaterhouseCoopers and International Emissions Trading Association, op. cit.
65. ibid., p. 4.
66. ibid., p. 44.
67. IASB, Information for observers: Accounting for Emissions Trading Schemes, SAC meeting, Agenda paper 4b, www.iasb.org.
68. J Ball, 'Insurers must disclose climate-change exposure', *The Wall Street Journal* (online), 2009, http://online.wsj.com.
69. For example, the 2006 revised version of the Australian Securities Exchange (ASX) 'Principles of Good Corporate Governance' requires appropriate disclosure of risks in the governance section of the annual report. These risks can include environmental risks; 'Principles of Good Corporate Governance and Good Practice Recommendations: Exposure Draft of Changes', ASX Corporate Governance Council, November 2, 2006, www.asx.com.au.
70. CPA Australia, 'Carbon Pollution Reduction Scheme: what may be the business impacts' (Discussion Paper), 2008, Melbourne.

71. PricewaterhouseCoopers and International Emissions Trading Association, op. cit.; analysis of the results of the Joint Survey undertaken by PricewaterhouseCoopers and IETA on the accounting approaches applied in practice and assessment of the key accounting approaches considered suitable under IFRS.

72. P Leung, P Coram, BJ Cooper, and P Richardson, *Modern auditing and assurance services*, 4th edition, 2009, Brisbane: John Wiley & Sons Australia, Ltd.

73. KPMG 2008, *International survey of corporate responsibility reporting*, www.kpmg.com.

74. KPMG 2008, op. cit., p. 58. Large companies are defined as the 100 largest companies by revenue, except for Sweden, where only 70 companies are included.

75. ibid.

76. ibid.

77. ibid.

78. A Davies, 'The rush to paint the White House green', *The Age Insight*, April 4, 2009, p. 3.

79. Ceres (pronounced "series") is a national network of investors, environmental organisations and other public interest groups working with companies and investors to address sustainability challenges such as global climate change, www.ceres.org.

80. Carbon Disclosure Project, www.cdproject.net.

81. Carbon Disclosure Project, op. cit.; in 2008 the CDP dealt with 385 institutional investors who collectively managed investor assets of US$57 trillion, www.cdproject.net.

82. KPMG, International Survey of Corporate Responsibility Reporting 2008, p. 62, www.kpmg.com.

83. ibid., p. 59.

84. IAASB Completes Clarity Project [Media release], www.ifac.org.

85. AA1000 Assurance Standard 2008, AccountAbility, London, www.accountability21.net.

86. The International Organization for Standardization has issued ISO 14064, which deals with quantification, reporting, validation and verification of greenhouse gas (GHG) assertions. It also specifies requirements for selecting GHG verifiers, establishing the level of assurance, objectives, criteria and scope, determining the validation/verification approach, assessing GHG data, information, information systems and controls, evaluating GHG assertions and preparing validation/verification statements.

87. B O'Dwyer and DL Owen, 'Assurance statement practice in environmental, social and sustainability reporting: a critical evaluation' *The British Accounting Review*, vol. 37, iss. 2, 2005, pp. 205–29.

88. C Deegan, BJ Cooper, and M Shelly, 'An investigation of TBL report assurance statements: Australian evidence', *Australian Accounting Review*, vol. 16, iss. 39, 2008, pp. 2–18.

89. Fédération des Experts Comptables Européens, www.fee.be.

90. KPMG 2008, op. cit., p. 55.

91. IAASB, Approved Project Proposal 'Assurance engagements on carbon emissions information', December, 2007, www.ifac.org/IAASB.

92. IAASB, December 2007, op. cit., p. 5.

93. IASB, work plan awww.iasb.org.

94. IAASB Project Timetable as of March 2009, http://web.ifac.org.

95. The Water Accounting Standards Board (WASB) was previously known as the Water Accounting Development Committee (WADC), and is an independent advisory Board to the Bureau of Meteorology, www.bom.gov.au/water/wasb/, and the WADC was established in February 2007. The WASB succeeded the WADC in April 2009, with the same membership as existed for the WADC at the time, and a similar aim. Both the WASB and the WADC envision the development of water accounting taking place over the next 20 years. The Water Accounting Standards Board reports to the Bureau of Meteorology, which is charged under the *Water Act 2007* with responsibility for water accounting in Australia.

96. The information presented in this section on the Water Accounting Standards is based on the Australian project. Other organisations are also tackling these issues. For example, see www.wateraccounting.com.

97. WASB, op. cit.

98. ibid.

99. For further details see www.bom. gov.au/water/wasb/.

100. Australian Government National Water Commission, www.nwc.gov.au.

101. ibid.

102. Statement of Water Accounting Concepts 2 Objective of General Purpose Water Accounting Reports (SWAC 2).

103. Water Accounting Standards Board, Water Accounting Conceptual Framework for the Preparation and Presentation of General Purpose Water Accounting Reports, Commonwealth of Australia, Canberra, 2009.

104. World Business Council for Sustainable Development and World Resources Institute, The greenhouse gas protocol, a corporate accounting and reporting standard (revised edition), www.ghgprotocol.org.

105. ibid., p. 9.

106. ibid., p. 44.

107. ibid.

108. ibid., p. 25.

109. L Gettler, 'Standard-setters rendered toothless by G20', *The Age BusinessDay*, April, 15, 2009, p. 14.

LIST OF KEY TERMS

A

a posteriori: once a statement has been developed, its validity is assessed based on objective empirical evidence.

a priori: the application of syntactic rules to test the validity of a statement 'from first principles', as opposed to testing the validity of a statement from observation of real-world events.

abnormal item: a large or unusual item of revenue or expense incurred during normal operations that is required to be disclosed separately because of its size and impact on the operating profit.

abnormal return: the difference between the expected and the actual return. For example, if the market average return on a particular investment is 10% and a return of 17% is achieved, then 7% represents an abnormal return.

accounting conceptual framework: a structured theory of accounting that is a coherent, interrelated theoretical description of the purpose, structure and components of accounting. It is intended to guide accounting practice.

accounting theory: logical reasoning in the form of a set of broad principles that (1) provide a general framework of reference by which accounting practice can be evaluated and (2) guide the development of new practices and procedures. Accounting theory is a logically derived description, explanation, prediction or prescription of accounting practice.

accumulated benefits fund: a superannuation fund that provides a pension directly from the total contributions of the pension recipient; also known as a defined contribution fund.

additivity: the ability to add together values that are expressed in like values. For example, past costs cannot be added to future expectations or current market prices.

agency costs: costs that arise from agency relationships, for example because of the separation of ownership from control of an entity. Three types of agency costs have been identified: (1) monitoring costs, (2) bonding costs and (3) residual loss. Agency costs can be initially incurred by both principals and agents. However, principals are able to adjust how much they pay agents, so agents will ultimately bear at least some, and possibly all, of the incurred agency costs.

agency relationship: arises where one party (the principal) engages another party (the agent) to perform some service on the principal's behalf. Decision-making authority is delegated to the agent. In accounting theory, the principals most usually considered are investors and lenders. The agents most usually considered are managers.

agency theory: a theory developed to explain and predict the actions of agents (e.g. managers) and principals (e.g. shareholders or lenders). The theory assumes that both the agent and the principal are utility maximisers (i.e. they seek to maximise their returns) whose interests are not necessarily aligned. As a result, an agency relationship has agency costs.

agent: a person appointed by a principal to manage the principal's affairs. *See* agency relationship.

agreements equally proportionately unperformed (AEPUs): a type of contract where both parties have yet to perform the same percentage of their individual obligations under the contract; also referred to as a wholly executory contract.

amortisation: systematic allocation of a prepaid expense to the periods in which the benefit from the expense is received. For example, the payment of building insurance 3 years in advance would be amortised (allocated) across each of the 3 financial years covered by the insurance, rather than fully expensed in the year the insurance is paid.

anomalies: problems that cannot be solved and which contradict the dominant pattern.

arctan model: a non-linear, S-shaped relationship between accounting numbers and share prices. Extreme gains or losses have a declining impact on prices because they are only temporary gains and losses.

asset: a resource controlled by an entity as a result of past events and from which future economic benefits are expected to flow to the entity.

asset substitution: occurs when managers invest in riskier investments than debtholders expected at the time they entered into the debt agreement. This reduces the value of the debt. Debtholders do not benefit from the increased returns that high-risk projects can provide; however, they can share in the possible losses. Debt lenders are therefore assumed to be risk averse and prefer firms to engage in less risky projects that increase the recoverability of their debt.

B

behavioural accounting research (BAR): the study of the behaviour of accountants or the behaviour of non-accountants as they are influenced by accounting functions and reports. BAR research is concerned with improving the quality of decision making.

beta (β): a measure of systematic risk; the non-diversifiable (market) risk in an investment.

biological assets: a living animal or plant.

bonding costs: costs incurred by agents when they establish mechanisms to signal to principals that they will behave (or have been behaving) in the interests of the principals, or that they will compensate the principals if they fail to act in the principals' interests.

bonus plan hypothesis: the prediction that managers of firms with bonus plans are more likely to choose accounting procedures that shift reported earnings from future periods to the current period. This happens because a risk-averse manager is assumed to prefer a guaranteed bonus in one year, as opposed to a possible bonus the next year. It assumes that managers are paid bonuses based on firm profits.

Brunswik lens model: a model that provides an analytical framework for investigating the decisions, judgements or predictions made by information users. The model has been used to consider the decision-usefulness of accounting information.

C

capital: the money invested in, or the productive capacity of, the entity, provided by the residual equityholders. It is the difference between the sums of the total assets and total liabilities.

capital asset pricing model (CAPM): a model that predicts the returns on a firm's securities as a function of marketwide risk and the risk-free asset.

capital maintenance: maintenance of the value of the original and any subsequent capital base (the base is equivalent to the input by the firms' owners). The value maintained depends on the concept of capital and how it is measured.

capital maintenance adjustment: the amount a firm would need to retain, in addition to the amount of capital originally invested, to maintain the value of the capital.

capital market research (CMR): empirical research using statistical methods to test hypotheses concerning capital market behaviour.

cash flow: the inflow and outflow of cash or cash equivalent assets/liabilities.

claim dilution: where a firm enters into a debt agreement that has a higher priority than debt that has already been issued.

commander theory: the focus of accounting activity is drawn from the perspective of those who control (or command) the economic resources of an entity. The unit of experience and the point of view taken should be of the people who have the power to deploy assets. In most modern corporations, this is the management team, which is often a group separate from the owners (shareholders).

comparability: comparable financial statements are produced in a consistent manner allowing users to compare the reports of entities at one time and over time.

conceptual framework: a coherent system of interrelated objectives and fundamentals that is expected to lead to consistent standards and that prescribes the nature, function and limits of financial accounting and reporting. A conceptual framework attempts to provide a definitive statement of the nature and purpose of financial accounting and reporting. It can consist of various levels, from stating the objective of financial reporting, to identifying and defining the basic elements of an accounting report.

constructive obligation: an obligation that is inferred from the circumstances of a particular situation, rather than a legal obligation.

contingent asset or liability: an asset or liability whose 'existence' for a particular entity depends on the outcome of future events or the non-occurrence of possible future events. For example, a liability arising from a legal decision that is yet to be handed down is a contingent liability.

continuously contemporary accounting (CoCoA): an accounting system based on exit values, which are deemed to occur in the normal course of business; that is, the values are not determined by the prices they would realise in immediate liquidation.

contributed capital: capital that is contributed to the entity from members, such as those acquiring ordinary shares.

control: the power to govern the financial and operating policies of an entity or business so as to obtain benefits from its activities.

convertible note: a document that is evidence of a company's indebtedness for a specific amount, paying a fixed interest rate until maturity. On maturity, convertible notes may be converted to ordinary shares or redeemed in full.

cost: the amount of cash or cash equivalents paid or the fair value of the other consideration given to acquire an asset at the time of its acquisition or construction or, where applicable, the amount attributed to that asset when initially recognised in accordance with the specific requirements of other standards.

costs attach theory: a theory based on the assumption that the value of any commodity, service or condition used in production passes to the object or product for which the original item was expended and attaches to the result, giving it value. There are two components of the theory: (1) displacement cost, which denotes what has been given up and is synonymous with opportunity cost, and (2) embodied cost, which relates to the factors of production and what has been outlaid rather than forgone.

critical event: the point at which revenues should be recognised by an entity. The event relates to the stage of the *operating cycle* which is most appropriate to the revenue earning activity in which the entity is engaged.

current cost: cost to acquire an asset at current prices. This cost normally reflects the change in expected returns from holding the asset. Current and replacement cost are likely to differ the older the asset is, because of factors that normally relate to technological advances or changes in market demand.

current cost accounting: accounting based on the current buying price of assets; that is, expensing and matching resource usage using current replacement values.

D

debenture: a fixed-term loan to a company, secured by either a fixed or floating charge over a company's assets, that pays a fixed rate of interest. A trustee is appointed to protect the interests of debtholders.

debt contract: a contract between a lender and a borrower of funds. The contract sets the terms and conditions of the loan and usually contains debt covenants devised to restrict the borrower's behaviour and protect the lender.

debt covenant: a term or condition written into a debt contract that restricts or prescribes the behaviour of management to ensure that debtholders' interests are protected. For example, a covenant may require that the firm may not allow its ratio of debt to total tangible assets to exceed 60%.

debt hypothesis: the prediction that the larger a firm's debt to equity ratio, the more likely it is that the firm's manager will select accounting procedures that shift reported profits from future periods to the current period. Such action reduces the chances of a firm technically breaching a debt covenant.

deduction: reasoning from general to specific statements; opposite of induction. A logical argument that proceeds from a general statement to a specific conclusion; the opposite of induction.

deductive reasoning: the act of logically reaching a specific conclusion from known or supposed general facts.

defeasance: the release of a debtor from the primary obligation for a debt.

defined benefits fund: a superannuation fund under which the amounts paid to an employee through the fund are (at least partially) a defined proportion of the employee's salary.

deprival value: the loss that would be expected to be incurred by the firm if it were deprived of the service potential or future economic benefits of assets at the reporting date.

derived measurement: a measurement that depends on the measurement of two or more other properties. Examples in accounting are profit, which is derived from the deduction of expenses from revenue, and asset values, which are derived from the historic purchase cost less accumulated depreciation.

descriptive pragmatics: a method of accounting theory construction which relies on repeatedly observing the methods and techniques of practising accountants.

differential information hypothesis: implies that the information in accounting reports should be more important for smaller firms than for larger firms, because of the alternative information sources available regarding large firms. For example, financial analyst reports and media coverage are more likely to be available on large firms than on smaller firms.

discretionary accruals: accruals that are recorded based on management's choice rather than necessity; that is, accruals recorded at the manager's discretion. *See* 'taking a bath'.

dividend retention: a result of managers retaining the company's profits in the company in an attempt to 'empire build' the company and hence maximise their own personal benefits, rather than pay out the higher level of dividends that the shareholders prefer.

dogmatism: accepting the truth of a statement because it has been made by someone from the establishment, an expert or someone in authority, rather than examining the statement for logical or empirical content.

E

earning process: the full range of activities undertaken by a firm to generate revenues.

earnings response coefficient (ERC): the security price reaction evident from investors' reactions based on their assessment of the earnings persistence of the release of unexpected profits information.

economic resource: a resource that can be used to generate an economic benefit. For example, a company's property, plant and equipment are regarded as an economic resource.

economic value: subjective value which relates to the preference or desire people have for one item as opposed to others.

efficient contracting: minimises agency costs and ultimately increases the wealth available to agents and principals. Agents (in recognition of price protection and *ex post* settling up) enter into contracts aligning their interests with those of the principal, or behave as if their individual interests are aligned.

efficient market hypothesis (EMH): prediction that the capital market adjusts rapidly to new information. Three forms of capital market efficiency have been proposed: (1) Weak-form efficiency assumes that a security's price at a particular time reflects the information contained in its sequence of past prices. (2) Semi-strong efficiency assumes that a security's price fully reflects all publicly available information, including and in addition to past prices. (3) Strong-form efficiency suggests that a security's price fully reflects all information, including information that is not publicly available.

empirical research: analysis of practices, activities or behaviour based on direct observation and/or experience.

enterprise theory: adopts the viewpoint that organisations have a key role in society and have responsibilities to report on activities to a range of stakeholders, including shareholders, employees, creditors, government agencies and the public.

entity theory: adopts the viewpoint that the firm is a separate entity with its own identity and is not merely an extension of the activities and objectives of its owners. Accounting procedures are adopted from the viewpoint of the separate entity.

entry price value: a 'buying' price value.

environmental report: stand-alone document reporting on the environmental performance of an organisation.

environmental reporting: the disclosure of information on environment-related issues and performance by an entity, for example, disclosure of emissions targets.

epistemology: the study of the acquisition of knowledge. Concerned with the origin, nature, methods and limits of human knowledge.

equitable obligation: an obligation that arises out of a moral or social obligation, rather than as a legal requirement.

equity: the residual interest in the assets of the entity after deducting all its liabilities.

equity method: the method of accounting whereby the investment is initially recognised at cost and subsequently adjusted for the post-acquisition change in the investor's share of net assets of the associate. The profit or loss of the investor includes the investor's share of the profit or loss of the investee.

ethical/environmental investment funds: investment funds which screen potential investments for not only economic performance, but also social and environmental attributes, for example, whether the company conducts experiments on animals or is involved in armaments.

ex ante (efficiency) perspective: assumes that accounting policies are selected 'before the event' to maximise the value of the firm and to reduce agency costs.

ex post opportunism: managers are assumed to act opportunistically. Accounting policies are therefore chosen 'after the event' in order for managers to maximise their own wealth by transferring wealth from other parties.

ex post settling up: an agent's past behaviour is taken into account in either renegotiation or entering into new principal/agent contracts, so that agents are penalised for not acting in principals' interests.

excessive dividend payments: a method of transferring wealth from debtholders to shareholders. Dividends are paid at a rate that is higher than was expected when the debt was priced and borrowed by the firm.

exchangeability: refers to the ability of an asset to be sold separately from other assets

exit price accounting: accounting for assets, liabilities and expenses by valuing them at current selling prices

exit price value: an asset's expected selling price; used to estimate its value.

expense: decreases in economic benefits during the accounting period in the form of outflows or depletions of assets or incurrences of liabilities that result in decreases in equity, other than those relating to distributions to equity participants.

externality: cost that results from the organisation but is borne by other parties, for example, greenhouse gas emissions from an industrial site.

extraordinary item: items of revenue and expense attributable to events of a type that are outside the ordinary operations of the company or the economic entity and are not of a recurring nature.

F

fair value: the amount for which an asset would be exchanged in an arm's-length transaction between knowledgeable, willing parties.

falsification: all hypotheses must be framed so that they are capable of being falsified if they are not true. Under this epistemological approach, science advances by falsifying weak hypotheses and replacing them with stronger hypotheses which are not as easily falsified.

fiat measurement: arbitrarily established and indirect measurement, for example, when expenses are determined as a function of revenue according to accounting standards.

finance lease: a lease where the rights and obligations associated with ownership reside with the lessee. It is a noncancellable lease where the lease generally is for 75% or more of the useful life of the leased property, or the present value of the minimum lease payments equals or exceeds 90% of the fair value of the lease property at the inception of the lease.

financial capital: the amount of capital required to maintain the initial financial investment in the firm; the monetary value invested in residual equity. Financial capital can be adjusted by an inflation index to reflect real financial capital.

firm: in contracting theory, the firm is classified as a legal nexus (connection) of contractual relationships among suppliers and consumers. It is assumed that firms exist because they are an economically rational alternative to individuals transacting in the market.

forward exchange contract: a type of hedging agreement where two parties enter into a contract to exchange currencies at an agreed exchange rate in the future.

framing effects: in behavioural accounting research, judgement or decision problems are often developed to support the research. Devising problems creates framing effects, in that the wording of the problem can drive or influence results in a manner that cannot be measured or adjusted.

free-rider: a user of accounting information who bears little of the cost of producing the information and therefore has incentive to demand increased levels of disclosure.

fund theory: adopts the view that the firm is a set of funds, where a 'fund' is a unit of operations, a centre of interest, with a specified purpose or set of activities, consisting of assets and equities. The focus is on an impersonal fund, rather than adopting a personality perspective, such as the proprietor of an entity.

fundamental measurement: where numbers can be assigned to the property by reference to natural laws (such as length).

future economic benefits: access to assets or resources to support the activities of an entity resulting from a prior expense.

G

gain: increases in net assets from peripheral or incidental transactions (from events that are not part of an organisation's mainstream trading activities). Gains arise from subsidiary rather than main activities and are often largely beyond the control of the firm.

going concern: the ability of the business to continue operations in the foreseeable future.

H

heuristics: a type of probabilistic reasoning used by individuals using rules of thumb in order to simplify complex judgement tasks. Three heuristics have been identified: (1) representativeness — the degree to which a particular event corresponds to an appropriate mental model; (2) availability — the assessment of a probability of an event based on the ease with which instances of that event come to mind; and (3) anchoring — a general judgement process in which responses by an individual serve as an anchor (or base) in an individual's decision process when additional information is introduced.

historical cost accounting: the traditional system of accounting, based on double-entry bookkeeping and reporting of transactions at the amount paid or liable. Gains and losses are only recognised when actually realised. The matching principle underlies the historical cost method, where expenses are offset against the revenues they support.

holding gains and losses: separately measuring gains and losses on assets and liabilities determined by the increase or decrease over the reporting period of their current costs. An opportunity gain or loss is made by management because they make the decision to buy early.

horizon differences: shareholders (principals) and managers (agents) have different time horizons with respect to the firm. The classical valuation of security prices (the value of a share is the present value of all future cash flows attributable to it) means that shareholders have an infinite horizon. Managers are assumed to be interested only in the cash flows attributable to their intended employment in the company.

human information processing (HIP): a subset of behavioural accounting research that examines how and why decisions are made by accountants or users of accounting information.

human judgement theory (HJT): a subset of behavioural accounting research that concentrates on examining the judgements made by users of accounting information, such as auditors.

hypothesis: a predictive statement derived from a theory. Hypotheses can be stated in the null (no association between variables of interest) or positive/negative forms.

I

income: an increase in an asset or a decrease in a liability will result in income, unless the increase or decrease results from an equity contribution (such as cash raised through share capital). Because of this broad definition, income is further dissected into revenue and gains.

induction: reasoning from the particular (specific) to the general; the opposite of deduction.

inductive tests: testing the truth of a proposition by observing a subset of real-world observations or events. The epistemological development of a theory under this method requires widespread and repeated tests under varying conditions.

information asymmetry: the difference in the quantity and quality of information available to a firm's managers compared with the information that is available to others about a firm. The existence of information asymmetry results in people outside the firm being unsure of the true meaning and nature of the information that managers disclose.

information content of accounting information: impact of accounting information on decision making. Capital market research assesses the information content of profits by empirically testing the direction and/or magnitude of the abnormal return of a security's return.

information hypothesis: prediction that accounting information is produced to enable investors to make good investment decisions.

information transfer: the information released by one firm in a particular industry may also provide information applicable to the pricing of securities for other firms in the same industry. Information transfer assumes that the release of unexpected profits information for one firm in a particular industry will have a flow-on effect to the pricing of securities of other firms in the same industry.

intangible asset: a non-physical asset, such as goodwill, patents or trademarks.

interest rate swap: occurs when two entities enter into a contract to swap interest payments but remain obligated to their original creditors.

interval scale: a scale that uses numbers which have rank order and equal intervals, such as a temperature scale, but uses an arbitrary point of reference. An example in accounting is standard costing and variance analysis.

investor theory: adopts the view that the objective of accounting is to serve the information needs of those who provide capital to an entity. This relates to both debt and equity funds.

L

lease: an agreement conveying the right from a lessor (owner of the asset) to a lessee (another party) to use property for a stated period of time in return for a series of payments by the lessee to the lessor.

leverage: the use of debt to finance an entity, often measured as the amount of debt to equity or as the amount of liabilities to assets.

liability: present obligations of an entity arising from past events, the settlement of which is expected to result in an outflow from the entity of resources embodying economic benefits.

life-cycle analysis: an analysis of the environmental impact of a product or process from raw materials until disposal, that is, tracking the environmental impact from the mining or collection of the raw materials, through production, to sale to the consumer and ultimately the disposal at the end of its useful life.

liquidation value: the value of an item derived from immediate 'fire sale' (forced sale) liquidation.

lobbying: actions taken by interested parties to influence the actions or outcomes of decisions made by another.

logical positivism: a school of thought where the view is held that only the methods of the natural sciences provide 'positive knowledge' of 'what is'. It is a theoretical approach where all meaningful statements must be capable of verification. Hence, all logical positive theories must be capable of being empirically tested.

loss(es): decreases in the value of net assets as a result of peripheral or incidental transactions. For example, if a retail firm's retail outlet building is uninsured and destroyed by a fire, this is a loss.

M

management contracts: contracts between managers (agents) and owners (principals). *See* agency theory.

market efficiency: the degree to which the market efficiently reflects information subsets. For example, a market that reflects all information contained in past prices is deemed to be a weak-form efficient market. *See* efficient market hypothesis.

market model: a model of how returns on a security have been determined. The model controls marketwide and firm-specific risk, thus allowing the specific security price effect of an action to be assessed. For example, the market model can be used to assess the security price impact of the release of accounting information.

market value: the value of an asset placed on it by the market for that asset. The market is normally represented by many buyers and sellers operating at arm's length.

matching concept: the accepted accounting process of recognising revenues, then deducting the expenses incurred to support these revenues. This requires that expenses are allocated to a specific accounting period.

materiality: the quality applicable to information which, if it was omitted, misstated, or not disclosed in the financial statements, could adversely affect users' decisions about the allocation of scarce resources.

measurement: the process of determining the monetary amount at which an asset, liability, income or expense is reported in the financial statements.

mechanistic hypothesis: assumes that the capital market is deceived by accounting changes, regardless of the cash flow implications of the change

monetary items: assets and liabilities which are accounted for at the dollar amounts for which they will be redeemed or repaid; claims to fixed amounts in dollar terms.

monitoring costs: costs associated with observing (monitoring) the agent's behaviour, for example, mandatory audit costs.

multivariate models: models of behaviour or events that include two or more factors that explain the variable of interest.

N

naturalistic method: an unstructured research design, which has no preconception of the research problem or the form of the ultimate discovery. Under this epistemological approach, information is discovered by unobtrusive researchers without a predetermined research methodology.

negative heuristic: the central core or basic assumptions or propositions that have been accepted by scientists as the central core of a research program.

net realisable value: the selling price of an asset less expected selling costs.

no-effects hypothesis: the capital market only reacts to accounting changes that have a cash-flow consequence.

nominal: scale using numbers as labels, for example, numbers on the shirts of football players.

non-monetary items: claims to assets or liabilities which may appreciate or depreciate in value.

normative theory: a prescriptive theory that is stated in terms of what should occur in order to achieve the theory's objective. Normative accounting theories prescribe the 'correct' way to account.

null hypothesis: a prediction or proposition extracted from a theory that states a positive association between the variables of interest.

O

ontology: study of the nature of 'being' or the conception of what exists.

operating (earnings) cycle: the different points at which revenue might be recognised by a firm.

operating lease: a lease under which the lessor (owner of the property that is leased) effectively retains substantially all the risks and benefits associated with ownership of the property.

opportunity cost: the value of the next best alternative forgone.

ordinal scale: using numbers to rank or order between alternatives, for example, ranking firms according to the amount of their profitability.

owners' equity: the residual interest in the assets of the entity after deducting its liabilities. A firm's equity cannot be defined independently of its assets and liabilities. Rather, it is the balance remaining when the two are netted.

P

paradigm: a particular school of thought. A paradigm incorporates the background knowledge and research procedures that provide the guidance and rules for scientists working within the paradigm.

percentage-of-completion method: relates to the periodic estimation of profit from an ongoing contract or activity. This method is applied to construction contracts under IAS 11/AASB 111.

physical capital: the firm's ability to produce a given level of output or services; operating capability.

political cost hypothesis: prediction that managers of larger firms have greater incentives to reduce reported profits and hence reduce their perceived ability to bear political costs.

political costs: wealth transfers away from a firm due to its political exposure. The amount of the transfer is often related to the size and/or visibility of the firm. For example, extractive industry firms may incur political costs due to the actions of protesters; tariffs may be reduced, based on an industry's ability to compete internationally.

political economy theory: used to describe a process by which an organisation will try to pre-empt a threat to organisational legitimacy, that is, the organisation is a powerful participant in society able to lobby and change expectations of performance.

political perspective of standard setting: acknowledges the role of accounting in economic markets and recognises that accounting information is an artificial construction of specific types of information. This construction is guided by the interests and priorities of various parties, who lobby to achieve the types of accounting standards they prefer.

positive accounting theory: an empirically tested theory that describes, explains or predicts accounting practice.

post-announcement drift: occurs when the abnormal returns due to a particular profit announcement are not immediately reflected in a security's price at the announcement date, but are reflected progressively after the announcement date. The existence of post-announcement drift raises questions about whether the capital market is efficient.

pragmatic: the effect of words or symbols on people; their real-world effect.

predictive value: the relevance of the accounting information to facilitation of decisions about the future actions and value of an entity.

preference shares: a form of equity in a company that receives preference over ordinary shares in either or both dividend payments and the distribution of assets on the winding-up of a company.

present value: a value based on the calculation of future net cash receipts associated with the future services or benefits of an asset. Three variables are required to measure present value: future cash amounts, discount rate and time horizon (length of time).

price protection: the ability of principals to transfer the bearing of agency costs to the agent. For example, when an agent's contract is negotiated, principals are in a position to be able to adjust the contract to compensate for the costs that they expect to incur due to the agent's self-interested actions.

principal: the individual or group who appoints an agent to act on their behalf.

private-interest theory: assumes that regulation, and hence standard setting, is regulated by the relative political power of various interest groups.

probabilistic judgement paradigm: a model used to assist in situations where initial predictions need to be adjusted in light of additional information. The initial likelihood estimation is adjusted by a likelihood ratio, which is the amount by which prior expectations should be revised.

probable: the conceptual framework uses the expression 'probable' to mean more rather than less likely, that is, there is more than a 50% likelihood that something will occur.

profit: the excess of revenues over expenses. Profit is generated only when a firm's beginning amount of capital is maintained.

profit persistence: the expectation of investors that unexpected profit changes (increases or decreases) will continue and eventually be reflected in permanent changes in dividends.

proprietary theory: adopts the perspective of the owner (proprietor) in determining accounting methods and reporting. The purpose of the firm, the nature of capital and the meaning of accounts are defined in terms of the owner's perspective.

public-interest theory: justifies the mandatory requirement of accounting standards as a means of reducing the likelihood of market failures in response to public demands for the control of accounting information.

R

ratio scale: type of scale where the rank order is known, intervals are equal and the scale has a unique origin or natural zero point. Under a ratio scale we can compare the relative performance of firms and legitimately use accounting numbers as ratios.

realisation: the point at which the sale of an asset, product or service results in a transfer of assets (normally cash) or reduction in liabilities for an entity. The revenue may have been previously recognised, but now that assets have flowed to the entity (or liabilities reduced), the transaction is referred to as 'realised'.

recognition criteria: guidelines used or adopted to determine whether an asset or liability should be formally included (recognised) in an entity's financial statements and records.

recognition of financial statement elements: the item 'recognised' appears on the face of financial statements. Australian standards require that financial statement elements, such as assets and liabilities, are recognised when there is a probability that the elements exist and they can be measured reliably.

recognition principle: revenues are recognised in the period during which the major economic activities necessary to the creation and disposition of goods and services have been accomplished (provided objective measurements of the results of those activities are available).

regulatory capture theory: assumes that individuals are economically rational and hence will act in their own self-interest. Therefore, although the purpose of standard setting is to protect the public interest, this is not achieved because the regulatee comes to control or dominate the regulator.

relevance: relevant financial information helps users make predictions about future situations or confirms the past predictions of users.

reliability: a qualitative characteristic that ensures information corresponds with the events it reports. Reliable financial information faithfully represents transactions and events without bias or undue error.

REM: (rational, evaluative utility maximiser) the term is often applied to predict how managers will act and is derived from the assumption that individuals will act in a manner to maximise their self-interest.

replacement cost: the amount that would be paid to acquire the best asset available to undertake the function of the asset that is to be replaced.

reproduction cost: the amount that would be paid now to reproduce an asset identical to the one currently being used.

residual loss: monitoring and bonding activities cannot completely align principals' and agents' interests because it is not cost-effective to do so. Therefore, the costs associated with the continuing difference are known as a residual loss. For example, residual losses result when agents use company resources such as stationery or printing facilities for their own use.

restoration: the process of restoring, for example, an abandoned mine site.

revenue: the gross inflow of economic benefits during the period arising in the course of the ordinary activities of an entity when those inflows result in increases in equity, other than increases relating to contributions from equity participants.

risk aversion: unwilling to accept a fair gamble. Agency theory assumes that managers prefer a low rather than a high level of risk because, compared with investors, they are unable to diversify their risk level associated with working for one firm. Hence, managers are assumed to prefer to invest the firm's money in lowrisk investments. It is predicted that they prefer to minimise their own risk rather than maximise the value of the firm.

S

scientific method: an epistemological approach whereby systemic, structured or controlled research design leads to the acquisition of knowledge or conclusions.

semantics: the correlation of a word, sign or symbol with a real-world object or event.

share dividend: a return of profit to shareholders that is issued by way of new shares rather than a cash dividend; also referred to as a bonus share issue.

signalling theory: assumption that managers of all firms have incentives (albeit different) to maintain their credibility with the market through reporting the firm's performance. Therefore, signalling theory predicts that firms will disclose more information than is demanded. Signalling theory goes on to predict what information firms will signal, how and when.

social contract: a theory describing the interaction between individuals or organisations within society through implicit or explicit boundaries of behaviour (implicit boundaries are moral obligations, explicit boundaries are regulatory requirements).

social reporting: sometimes referred to as social accounting or social responsibility disclosure. It is the disclosure of information on social-related issues and performance; for example, the reporting of policies on equal opportunity and minorities.

statement of cash flow: provides information about the cash payments and cash receipts of an entity during a period.

statement of changes in equity: a financial statement prepared in accordance with IAS 1/AASB 101 for inclusion in general purpose financial reports. The statement reports on the changes in the entity's equity for the reporting period. Changes in equity disclosed may include movements in retained earnings for the period, items of income and expense recognised directly in equity, and movements in each class of share and each reserve.

statement of comprehensive income: a financial statement that reports on the entity's revenues and expenses for the reporting period.

statement of financial position: a financial statement that presents assets, liabilities and equity of an entity at a given point in time.

subjective value: an estimate of the current value of an asset or liability based on the estimated benefit or cost over the term of a liability or life of an asset, as determined by management.

sustainability: the equitable consumption of resources that does not compromise the needs of future generations.

syllogism: a set of propositions from which a logical conclusion is drawn.

syntactic relationship: an analytical or logical methodology for formulating propositions.

T

'taking a bath': involves decreasing profits, through the use of discretionary accruals, in one year to enable profits to be increased in future years. This increases a manager's future earning potential.

technical perspective of standard setting: based on the belief that accounting involves the measurement of facts and that standard setting should be concerned with measurement issues and ensuring that accountants provide factual information.

thin trading: occurs when a company's shares are not traded frequently (or only at relatively low volumes). Its existence reduces the efficiency of the market.

transaction costs: costs associated with negotiating the terms of a contract. Transaction costs can include the costs of legal advice and the time spent by managers in developing a contract or the costs of brokerage when selling shares.

triple bottom-line reporting: the reporting of economic, social and environmental performance of an entity. It is also a possible means of quantifying a trade-off between these three aspects of performance.

trust deed: written contract between the lender and the borrower detailing the terms and conditions of a debenture.

U

underinvestment: occurs if entering into a project has a net present value level that will repay at least some of the firm's debt, but not provide any benefits to the owners of the firm. In such cases, owners have no incentive to enter into the project.

unrealised gain: a change in the value of an asset (or reduction in the value of a liability) which has not actually been taken by an entity, but reflects the change in the current or market value of an asset or liability. Unrealised gains are recognised at a point in time, normally balance date.

unsecured note: written evidence of a company's indebtedness which is issued when the lender does not have security over the company's assets.

utility: in economic theory, the utility of a commodity is its ability to satisfy human wants. At its broadest level, a commodity is regarded as useful because of what it can be used to produce.

V

value: within accounting the term 'value' commonly refers to economic value, which is a function of expectations about the future benefits that will be derived from an asset or cash generating unit.

value of a good: the market price of a good is believed to reflect its value.

W

wholly executory contract: a contract where each party to the contract has yet to perform exactly the same percentage of its obligations under the contract; also referred to as agreements equally proportionately unperformed (AEPUs).

INDEX

A

AAA, *see* American Accounting Association (AAA)

AARF, *see* Australian Accounting Research Foundation (AARF)

AASB   231,

AASB standards, *see also* International Accounting Standards (IAS)
  AASB 108 *Accounting Policies, Changes in Accounting Estimates and Errors*   100, 141
    alternate measurement concepts   199–200, 205
    financial analysts' reaction to switch   432–3
    historical background   74–5
    impact on risk management strategies case study   155–6
    Improvements Project   75
    principles-based standards   76
    true and fair provision   342–3
  AASB 111 *Construction Contracts*   303, 322, 344
  AASB 116 *Property, Plant and Equipment*   193, 197–8, 236, 272
    depreciation valuation   333, 335
    revaluation of assets   309
  AASB 117 *Leases*   231, 233, 302
  AASB 118 *Revenue*   292, 303
    revenue recognition guidance   301–2, 305, 314
  AASB 119 *Employee Benefits*   198, 268
    amendments   275
    revaluation of assets   309
  AASB 102 *Inventories*   193
  AASB 132 *Financial Instruments: Disclosure and Presentation*   275–6
  AASB 136 *Impairment of Assets*   196–7, 198
  AASB 137 *Provisions, Contingent Liabilities and Contingent Assets*   100, 268, 269, 270, 344
    amendments   275
  AASB 138 *Intangible Assets*   100, 195, 238
  AASB 139 *Financial Instruments: Recognition and Measurement*   147, 148, 193, 198, 309
    fair value concept case study   210–12
    impact on risk management strategies case study   155–6
    revenue recognition   297
    trading securities   199
  AASB 140 *Investment Property*   193, 236, 297
    revaluation of assets   309
  AASB 141 *Agriculture*   148, 297
ABC Learning Centres   246
abnormal items   330 *see also* extraordinary items

abnormal rate of return   414–15
  behaviour hypothesis   429–30
  BHP Billiton's one period market model data   411
  calculations   410–12
  predictability of   426–7
  variance in   416
accelerated method of depreciation   96
Account Ability   492
accounting
  accountability   166
  accruals, *see* accruals in accounting
  cosmetic   429
  deferrals   347, 354–5
  economic realism   113–14
  fraud enforcement case study   326–7
  fraudulent   311–12, 315, 430–1, 431
  fraudulent financial reporting case study   323–5
  freedom from bias   113
  general scientific period   6–7
  goodwill   189, 219, 232, 235, 336, 389
  historical phases   185–6, 203
  inconsistencies in practice   96–7
  intraperiod choices   386–7
  non-financial   493–5, 497
  normative period   7–9, 146
  pre-theory period   5–6
  public   185
  social   485–6
  sociological construct   391
  socio-systemic structure   34
  specific scientific period   8
  tax credit   386–7
  transaction approach   165
accounting information   104–7
  competing sources   417
  continuous release to market   413–14, 436
  current cost accounting approach   177
  decision making purposes   105
  decision rules for long-term/short term approaches   191
  determining relevant models for reporting   186–7
  disclosures   469
  impact on behaviours   464
  overload   456
  overproduction   57
  prediction models for users   105
  relevance in business evaluation   172
  rule change impact on reporting case study   399–400
  stewardship purposes   104, 162–3, 166, 203, 407
  supply and demand   55–6
accounting models
  bank oriented countries   380–1
  emissions trading schemes   487–90

factors affecting   464–5
  interpreting validity   26
accounting practice, permissive mode of operation   96
Accounting Principles Board (APB)   7, 96
Accounting Procedures Committee   6–7
accounting publications and bulletins, notable   6–7
Accounting Regulatory Committee (ARC)   67
accounting reporting, systems transition   26–7
accounting research   381–9, 486
  business failure rate predictions   455–6
  mainstream   114
  positive   446
Accounting Series Release (ASR)   190, 191
Accounting Standard Setting Board of Japan   307, 428
Accounting Standards Committee (ASC)   192
Accounting Standards Review Board (ASRB)   60
  due process mechanism failure   61
  susceptibility to influence from interest groups   62
Accounting Standards Steering Committee   192
accounting theory
  development progress   32–6
  direct approach testing   25
  historical timeline   14
  implementing approaches according to crisis   8–9
  inconsistencies within   5
  practical 'real world' applications   4–5
accruals in accounting   333, 347, 354
  discretionary   384–5, 387
  prediction levels for bonus plan   385
accumulated benefit funds   268
accurate measurement   142, 152
acquisition costs   193, 197
  inconsistencies within   195
adaptive behaviour in accounting   184–5, 204
additivity factors in accounting   187, 189, 204
agency contracting problems   366–8, 418
agency costs   380, 384, 420
  reducing   389
  types of   363–4
agency problems   363
agency relationships   362, 364
agency theory   56–7, 80, 116, 362–5, 373, 394
  objectives of   446
agents
  control models   379
  decision-making authority   362–3

agents *(continued)*
  incentives for disciplined behaviour   365
AIFRS   432–3
allocation-free reports   340
allocations, *see under* expenses
Alumina's share price and earnings case
    study   50–1
American Accounting Association
    (AAA)   35
  audit investigation committee   40, 120
  expenses committee   331
  An Inquiry into the Nature of Accounting   8
  A Statement of Basic Accounting Theory   8
  *A Tentative Statement of Accounting
    Principles Affecting Corporate
    Reports*   6
American Institute of Certified Practising
    Accountants (AICPA)   35, 78, 479
  A Statement of Accounting Principles   6
amortised costs   165, 199, 255, 336
Anicom Inc   325
anthropological approaches   20
appropriation, types of   274–5
appropriation statements   224
ARC   67
archival data research   467
arctan models   421, 424
Argo Investments reaction to rule change
    case study   399–400
arm's length transactions   193, 197,
    299–300
Arrow-Debreu economy   4
Arthur Andersen   60, 85, 434
ASA   457
ASC   192
ASIC, *see* Australian Securities and
    Investments Commission (ASIC)
ASOBAC   40, 120
ASRB, *see* Accounting Standards Review
    Board (ASRB)
asset provisioning on earnings   163
asset substitution   370, 371, 372
asset-liability view   164
assets
  adaptability in resale conditions   189
  agricultural assets fair value
    measurement   242–3
  classification   228
  collectability   299
  conservative measurement
    approach   236
  contra   280
  debenture   220
  future economic benefits   228–30
  held-to-maturity   199
  IASB *Framework* definition   228
  measurability criteria   297–9
  measurement   235–8
  non-current   169
  non-marketable fixed   190
  property   229
  recognition criteria   233–4, 235, 247
  recognition rules   232–5

revaluation standards   309
tangible   236–8
associating cause and effect method   347
association studies   417, 435, 436
ASX   62
audit fees   41, 124, 393
auditing
  accounting estimates   346
  American history   392
  Andersen effect   434
  audit firm inspection reports   245–6, 280
  British history   392
  credibility and quality factors   419,
    433–4
  effect of fair value in assessing
    profits   150–1
  equity-based transaction guidelines   280
  expert valuation opinions   201
  forms of statutory regulation   71–2
  information presentation formats   460
  insurance protection   434, 436
  misstatement risks in measurement
    models   201, 202, 205
  overstatement of revenue   311
  non-auditing services to clients   121,
    124, 467, 469, 480
  peer review systems   78
  peer review systems criticisms   479–80
  probabilistic judgement model   461
  quality assessment methods   468
  small private firms   433
  specialised   393, 396, 434
  timing irregularities   279
  training programs   144
  signalling quality of company
    shares   392–3
  XBRL-related issues   478–9
Auditing and Assurance Standards Board
    (AUASB)   78
Auditing Practices Board (UK)   482
auditing research   43
  competence research   466–7
  empirical research and theories   40–1
  testing/judgement process   40, 462–3
auditing standards
  conceptual framework   119–21
  criticisms post global financial
    crisis   482–3
  historical background   77
  impairment losses guidelines   151
  oversight bodies   82
  redrafting international   485, 496
  rewriting   78
auditors
  association with cost of capital   434
  cut-off test   279
  determining quality of evidence
    201, 205
  distinguishing between research and
    development costs   202
  expense issues   345–6
  failure to detect misreported revenue
    311–12, 312–13, 315

fair value approaches to client's
    processes   243
  independence   120, 467, 469, 496
  litigation risks   393, 434, 482
  market impact   78–9
  oversight   71–2
  restrictions under *Sarbanes-Oxley
    Act*   467
  risk assessments   447
  rules of thumb decision making
    process   463
  shift in profit measurement
    methods   150–1, 153
  specialised   396, 434
  targets of class actions   245–6
  value to big and small firms   433
Australian Accounting Research
    Foundation (AARF)   61
  Accounting Theory Monograph 3   297,
    298, 299, 300
  Accounting Theory Monograph
    10, *Measurement in Financial
    Accounting*   168
  ED 42A-B 'Proposed Statements of
    Accounting Concepts'   13
  ED 42A-D 'Proposed Statements of
    Accounting Concepts'   13
Australian Accounting Standards Board
    (AASB)   231
  AASB 120 *Accounting for Government
    Grants*   100
Australian International Financial
    Reporting Standards (AIFRS)   432–3
Australian Securities and Investments
    Commission (ASIC)   62–3
  independent enforcement role   72
Australian Securities Exchange (ASX)   62
Australian Shareholders' Association
    (ASA)   457
Axa's diversification operations case
    study   439–40

B
backdating share options   72–3
backlog depreciation   182, 223
back-to-back swaps   325
balance sheets
  current cost accounting   219
  exit price accounting   184, 222, 225
  government   267
  reduced usefulness   348
  role in historical cost accounting   170
bank covenants, impact on small
    businesses   79
banking industry's crisis case study   85–7
banking industry's fraudulent financial
    reporting   342–3
banking industry's option payouts   337
banking industry's write-down of
    investment securities   244–5
banking regulation issues   68–9
BAR, *see* behavioural accounting
    research (BAR)

Barclays Bank's ownership structure 262–3
Barclays Bank's investment securities write-down 244–5
base-rate information 462
Bayes's theorem 449, 462
   normative applications 453–4
behavioural accounting research (BAR)
   applications in accounting 447–8
   computerised expert systems 448, 465
   definitions 446
   limitations of 465–6, 469
   Telstra's chief executive officer (CEO) appointment case study 471
   types of 447
behavioural accounting theory 12
behavioural research 12
Bell and Edwards system 162, 171, 172, 173, 203–4
BHP Billiton's one period market model data 411
big bath accounting 345
bill and hold arrangements 323
bonding covenants 371
bonding costs 363–4
bonds as capital 189–90
bonus plan hypothesis 9–10, 368, 373
   allocation of funds to bonus pool 383
   empirical research 383–5
   levels of accounting accruals 385
Bradken costs attaching to business division case study 214–15
bright line accounting standards 102, 103
British stream of research 35
British Telecom (BT) pension case study 288
Brunswik lens model of decision making 447, 448, 449–51, 455–6
   diagrammatic representations 450
   financial statement presentations 459, 468
   weaknesses 451
business pressure on government regulation setting case study 398–9
business profit concept 172–4
business risk auditing 120–1, 124

C
CAAA 35
Canada
   conceptual framework 13
   environmental liability guidelines 287
Canadian Academic Accounting Association (CAAA) 35
cap-and-trade emission rights scheme 100–1, 353
capital
   contributed 274–5
   earned 274–5
   interpreting definitions 169
   real financial proprietorship concept 172–3
capital asset pricing model (CAPM) 154, 196, 410

capital leases 65
capital maintenance 146
   adjustments 149
   inconsistent measurement standards 149
   measurement methods 153
   objectives of 273–4
capital markets 35, 377
capital markets research 375–6
   historical background 360–1
   objectives of 446
   statistical models 410–12
   types of 408, 417, 435
capital valuation, measuring 145
CAPM 154, 196, 410
capture theory 57–8, 61–2, 80
Carbon Disclosure Project (CDP) 491
cash flow
   aggregated 424
   alternative outcome of information content 424
   data as information content 424–6
   discounting future 196, 205, 421
   distributable 174, 182
   importance in perception of success case study 472
cash-settled share-based payments 279, 336
CCA, see current cost accounting (CCA)
channel stuffing agreements 323
Chartered Accountants of Canada (CICA) 35
Chernoff faces framework 459, 460
chief executive officers (CEOs) share ownership impact on management compensation 389
CICA 35
circularity of reasoning 115, 123
claim dilution 370, 371, 372
classification and regression trees (CART) method 452–3
   decision tree 453
Clean Air Act 353, 354
CLERP 1 62, 63
CLERP 9 78, 121, 482
climate change impact on financial reporting 487–8
CoCoA 184
Coles off-balance sheet leases 65
collaterized debt obligations (CDO) 86
Committee of Sponsoring Organizations (COSO) 120–1
Committee on Accounting Procedure 193
Committee on Basic Auditing Concepts 40
companies, accountability to owners 260
companies, political sensitivity 378
company law 70, 273
   corporate governance 71
completed contract method 334
completion-of-earnings-process 300
comprehensive income 16, 427–8
computerised expert systems 448, 465

conceptual framework 7–8
   building blocks for regulated financial reporting 95
   criticisms 122–3
   cross-cutting issues 127–30
   government intervention 94
   IASB/FASB convergence program projects 108
   internal circularity 115
   issues within national level 107
   measurement statements 13
   objectives of 97–8, 122
   policy models 116–18, 124
   public sector 109
   reasons for implementing 97
   role of 94–7, 122
   standards setting 64
   water accounting 494
conservative approaches 165
   negative consequences of 344
conservative bias 344, 348, 429
   impact on opportunistic behaviours 379–80, 395
construction contracts 311
   diversity in revenue recognition criteria case study 321–2
   percentage-of-completion method 303–4
   techniques for calculating expenses 334
contingent liabilities 270–2, 282
   note disclosures 271
continuously contemporary accounting (CoCoA) 184
contra assets 280
contracting theory 361–2
   alternatives to 374
   reducing severity of agency problems 367–8
contributed capital 274–5
control by entity 230
conventional recognition rules 233, 340
convertible debt 276
convertible notes 371
cookie-jar accounting 280, 345–6
corporate collapses 60–1, 64, 345
   effects of 479–80
corporate governance in financial reporting 70–1, 81, 380
corporate responsibility reports 491, 492
corporate scandals 85, see also Enron Corporation
corporate sector
   lobbying power 58, 62
   standards setting influence 63
Corporations Act 2001 78, 121
Corporations Act 2001 s 249P 457
COSO 120–1
cost recovery method 304
cost savings 175–6
costs attach concept
   business divisions case study 214–15
   expenses 334

credit crisis, impact on small
    businesses 79
credit market support in United States 8–9
Credit Suisse investment securities
    misevaluation 240–1
creditors' rights 272–3
    protection buffers 274
credit-to sales method (CSM) 386–7
critical event theory 295, 300
CSM 386–7
current cash equivalents (CCE) 184
current cost accounting (CCA) 171–83
    comparison of earnings with historical
        cost accounting 181
    criticisms 180–3
    evaluation tools 172
    history of 162
    level of objectivity 180, 181
    objectives of 171–2
    physical capital 217–21
    profit reporting 387
    resource management relevance 177
    technological change concerns 180–1
    valuation methods 176–7
CVC Asia Pacific's debt contract 372
cyclical industries' investments
    case study 47

D

David Jones share profit announcement
    case study 437–8
debenture assets 220, 371
debt
    convertible 276
    market reaction to
        announcement 422–3
    offsetting 277–9
    public 371
    subordinated 276, 277
debt contracts 362, 363, 369–73
    export tax accounting 386
    restrictions, *see also* debt
        covenants 371–3
    tourism and hospitality financial
        restructure 372
debt covenants 371–3, 382, 430
debt to equity hypothesis 373, 382
decision making processes
    current value 105
    models 447–62, 468
    training to use information cues 450–1
decision tree model 452
decision-theory approach 105–6
    processes 105
decision-usefulness approach 24–6, 35,
    42, 168
    financial assets 239
    financial reporting 109–10, 186
    financial statements 459
    standards setting 64
default theorem 420
depreciating assets, valuation
    principles 178

depreciation 335
    accounting 157
    backlog 182, 223
    criticisms of definition 23–2
    diminishing-balance 24
    diminishing value 333, 335, 375
    exit price accounting approach 187
    history 146
    straight-line 217
    valuation methods 196–7, 333,
        335, 375
deregulation of export markets 409
derivatives, measurement models 238–9
derived measurements 138–9, 145,
    152, 153
derived profit, measuring 145
descriptive pragmatic approach 20–1
Deutsche Bank's accounting
    reclassification 481–2
differential information hypothesis 415
distributable cash flow 174, 182
dividend payments, excessive 370, 371
dividend policies 298
    impact of current cost accounting 177
    proprietary theory 259
    revenue recognition 305
    untenable payment 214
dividend signals 376
dividend-retention problems 366,
    367, 394
Domino's Pizza exchange rates on
    earnings case study 213
double-entry accounting 5, 21, 33–4,
    146, 259
doublethink accounting 23
DPS 1.1 Statement of Provisional
    Accounting Standards (PAS) *Current
    Cost Accounting* 193

E

earned capital 274–5
earning process 347
earnings 369
    credibility signals 376
    impact of exchange rates case study 213
    measurement based on embedded
        value 308
    retained 274
earnings management 323, 430, 431–2
    methods to detect 432
    techniques 325
earnings response coefficients (ERC)
    factors affecting 418–21
    financial leverage impact 420
    permanent and temporary profits 421
earnings-based bonus plans 368
economic realism 113–14
economic rights, relationship with
    economic substance 273
economic substance
    classification 276
    criteria 234, 265
    relationship with economic rights 273

ED 42A-B 'Proposed Statements of
    Accounting Concepts' 13
ED 42A-D 'Proposed Statements of
    Accounting Concepts' 13
educational accounting resources and
    programs 145
Edwards and Bell system 162, 171, 172,
    173, 203–4
effective interest method 305
efficient contracting theory 374–5,
    388, 395
efficient markets hypothesis (EMH)
    360–1, 408, 410, 435
    methodological criticisms 426
EFRAG 428
embedded value recognition method 308
emissions allowances, accrual accounting
    model 354
emissions trading schemes
    accounting methods for financial
        reporting 489
    case study 353–4
    development in European Union 486–7
    Framework application 100–1
emphasis of matter accounts 79
empirical analysis in accounting 6–7,
    28–9
empirical auditing research 40–1
employee leave benefits, liability
    valuation 265
employee share schemes taxation case
    study 398–9
Enron Corporation 85, 104, 280, 283, 325
    consequence of collapse 60, 64
    F-Score 326
entity perspective in financial
    reporting 109, 179, 204
entity theory 260–3, 281
    accountability reporting 261
environmental liability case study 287–8
environmental reporting 486, 491
Equator Principles 287
equity method for long-term
    investments 259
equity-settled share-based payments 336
European Financial Reporting Action
    Group (EFRAG) 428
European stream of research 35
European Union
    agricultural assets fair value
        measurement 242–3
    auditing regulatory bodies 71
    corporate governance 71
    dissent over IFRS 8 62
    Emissions Trading Scheme
        (ETS) 486–7
    Emissions Trading Scheme (ETS)
        accounting methods 488–90
    Emissions Trading Scheme (ETS)
        financial accounting methods 489
    environmental liability guidelines 287
    financial instruments measurement
        methods 240–1

financial reporting jurisdictions 70
independent enforcement bodies 74
International Accounting Standards
(IAS) adoption 75
International Accounting Standards
(IAS) adoption case study 87–8
lobby against International Accounting
Standards (IAS) 39 67–8
single entity reporting 70
evidence, determining quality 201
ex ante settling up 374, 380, 395, 407
empirical research 388
ex ante uncertainty 56
ex post settling up 364, 373, 380, 382,
395, 407
empirical research 388
see also opportunistic behaviours
ex post uncertainty 56
exchange rates impact on earnings case
study 213
exchangeability of assets 187, 190, 231–2
exclusion of anticipatory calculations 189
executive compensation schemes 368, 369
exit price accounting 183–90
additivity factors criticism 189
additivity factors for financial
statements 187, 204
criticisms about profit
measurement 188–9
criticisms on valuation of
liabilities 189–90
market prices objectivity 187–8
objectives of 184–5
risk assessments 188
short-term approach 190
expected profit 174
expenditures, capitalizing and
expensing 195
expenses
advertising 339
allocation methods 333–9, 341, 347
allocation methods, criticisms
339–41, 348
allocation methods for internal
purposes 341
associating cause and effect
method 334
conservative approach 332
cost allocation methods 335–6
definition 330–1
expired costs 165, 331
immediate recognition method 339
impairment 339
objective evidence 344
overstatement 332
recognition criteria 332, 340, 347
expert judgement 463
Telstra's chief executive officer (CEO)
appointment case study 471
Extensible Business Reporting Language
(XBRL) 16, 478–9, 496
external appraisers 201–2, 236
extraordinary items 330, 385–6

F
fair market value 184
fair value accounting
application during global financial
crisis 481, 496
banking communities' perceptions case
study 253–5
criticisms in context of global financial
crisis 68
determining criteria 239
financial assets measurement case
study 210–12
impact on reliable measurement 143
relevance versus reliability case
study 156–7
share-based payment 279
fair value cost approach 242, 253
fair value in active markets 193
fair value in non-active markets 193
fair value income approach 242, 253
fair value market approach 242–3, 253
fair value measurement 242–4
intangibles valuation case study 154–5
liabilities 282
revaluation models 309
value hierarchy 242
false accounting case study 210–12
FAS, see Financial Accounting Standards
(FAS)
FASB, see Financial Accounting Standards
Board (FASB)
fiat measurements 15, 139–40, 152
FIFO 180, 197, 222, 385, 446, 490
finance leases 233
determining criteria 102, 231
liabilities 268
recognition criteria 234
social public-private partnerships 267
financial accounting
impact on accounting theory
development 34
influence of capital market 35
Financial Accounting Standards (FAS)
FAS 13 102–3
FAS 157 Fair Value Measurement
254, 480
FAS 157 Fair Value Measurement, effect
on banking case study 85–7
FAS 159 The Fair Value Option for Financial
Assets and Financial Liabilities 254
Financial Accounting Standards Board
(FASB)
amendments to ASR 190 191–2
collaboration with IASB on financial
reporting 54
concept statements for fair value
reporting 143
concept statements for financial
reporting 98, 129
conceptual framework definition 94
convergence program, see IASB/FASB
convergence program; IASB/FASB
joint projects

criticisms 112–13
distinguishing between expenses and
losses 330–1
environmental liability guidelines 287
joint conceptual framework project with
IASB 13
joint lease accounting project with
IASB 64–6
liquid assets guidelines 298
political influences 117–18
profit measurement theories 164
role as active share market
regulator 72–3
financial analysts' reaction to international
accounting standards 432–3
financial analysts' reaction to share
prices 431–2
financial capital
exit price accounting 222–6
proprietary theory 259
financial capital maintenance 162,
171, 204
difference from physical capital 174–5
proprietary theory 281
financial disclosure, hierarchical fair value
measurements 144
financial information
correcting market perceptions 61
determining objectives 5
public good service 60–1
financial instruments 66–7, 210
associated measurement rules 238
classification and measurement
methods 240t
decision-usefulness approach 239
hybrid 275–6
IASB derecognition project 278–9
improving valuation standards using fair
values framework case study 498
interim standards 67
financial leverage theories 420
financial mapmaking 113
financial reporting 109
active parties within 70
climate change impact on 487–8
conceptual framework building
blocks 95
decision-usefulness approach 109–10
entity perspective 109, 179, 204
hierarchy of important elements 98
internal control mechanisms 143
liability exclusions 271
not-for-profit sector guidelines case
study 127–8
objective of external 97–8
overlegislating 56–7
publishing two sets of accounts 308
qualitative characteristics 110–1
regulatory framework 69–74
regulatory framework case study 84–5
share options disclosure 337
shifting from future to present
periods 374, 382–3

financial reporting *(continued)*
  stewardship purposes 110
  underlying profit guidelines 106
financial statements
  exit price accounting 187, 204–5, 224,
  impact of fair value reporting 142–5
  information for capital markets 407
  misleading data 171
  normative approaches 25
  optimum resource allocation
    approach 177
  parent company method 259
  presentation 309–10, 315
  presentation and format types 458–61
  presentation examination using
    Brunswik lens model 459
  revaluation gains in property 293–4
  Securities Exchange Commission (SEC)
    public database 478
  value relevance 425–6, 425
firm size as measure of political cost
  exposure 387–8
firm size differential and information
  asymmetry 415
firm valuation model 417, *see also*
  Modigliani-Miller model
firms, impact from profit release
  information 415
firm-unique return (AR) 411–12
first-in, first-out (FIFO) method of
  inventory valuation 180
fixed-interest securities 189–90
forecasting 26
  forecasting growth amidst financial
    turmoil 39
  public disclosure on predicted
    earnings 38
Form 20-F 75
*Framework for the Preparation and Presentation
  of Financial Statements* 99,
    see also International Accounting
    Standards Board (IASB) *Framework*
France
  accounting tradition 70
  auditing regulatory bodies 71, 72
  historical cost accounting 236
  independent enforcement bodies 72
Fraud-Score model 326–7
fraudulent companies 325
free market approach to standards
  setting 55–6
free-rider problem 55, 56
frequent flyer programs case study 354–5
F-Score model 326–7, *see also* Fraud-
  Score model
fully funded pension plans 269
fundamental measurements 138, 152
fundamental qualitative characteristics in
  financial reporting 110
future economic benefits 247, 331,
  332, 347
future services in real world
  application 229–30, 335

G
G20 London summit meeting case
  study 497
G4+1 standard setting group 75, 231
GAAP 236, *see also* UK GAAP; US GAAP
gains, unrealised 293, 315
gambling industry shares case study
  49–50
general journal entries
  current cost accounting 220–1
  exit price accounting 222–3
general price level adjustment accounting
  (GPLA)
  impact on firms 381–2
general purpose water accounting reports
  (GPWARs) 493, 494
Generally Accepted Accounting Principles
  (GAAP) 236
Germany
  accounting tradition 70
  historical cost accounting 236
  two-tier enforcement system 74
global financial crisis, contributing
  factors 481–2
global financial interdependence case
  study 48–9
Global Reporting Initiative (GRI) 486
going concern assumption 169, 170,
  204, 280
  information for investors 177
goodwill accounting 189, 219, 336
  evaluation methods 232
  internally generated 235
  New Zealand 389
government intervention in free
  markets 55, 57, 59–60, 80
GPLA 381–2
GPWARs 493, 494
GrainCorp's share price earnings from
  deregulation 409
Great Wall Street Crash (US) 6, 296
  consequences on reporting
    legislation 12
greenhouse gas emissions accounting
  (GHG) 495
Greenhouse Gas Protocol (GGP)
  standards 495, 497
greenwashing practice 491

H
hedge accounting 487
hedged portfolios 425
hedged liabilies 148, 156
heritage assets valuation case study 252
HIP 447
historical cost accounting 21, 162–71
  asset values write-down 167
  benefits of 166–7
  challenges towards 146
  comparison of earnings with current
    cost accounting 181
  criticisms 23, 42, 163, 168–71, 198–9,
    204, 248

decision-usefulness approach 168
financial statements 196
history of 162
holding gains 173
information for investors 170–1
inventory valuation 193
matching costs theory 164–5, 333
objectives of 162–3
popularity within business
  communities 199
relevance in business evaluation 168–9
stewardship purposes 162–3, 166
tangible assets 236
useful applications 24
variations across industries' profit 182
HJT 447, 448, 449
holding gains 172, 173–4
  criticisms 176
  historical cost accounting 173
  inclusion as profit 175, 204
  reporting obligations 192
  unrealised 179–80, 182
  valuation methods 180
holding losses 172, 204
  inclusion as profit 173–4
horizon problems 366, 367, 389, 394
human information processing
  (HIP) 447, *see also* human
  judgement theory (HJT)
human judgement theory (HJT) 447,
  448, 449
hybrid securities 265, 276, 282–3, 372
  usefulness of classifications 277
hypothetico-deductive metholodogy
  25, 114

I
IAASB, *see* International Auditing and
  Assurance Standards Board (IAASB)
IAS, *see* International Accounting
  Standards (IAS)
IASB, *see* International Accounting
  Standards Board (IASB)
IASB/FASB convergence program 76–7, 94
  criticisms 111–13, 118
  descriptive approach 111
  exposure drafts on future
    projects 108–11, 130
  fair value measurement concerns 147–8
  governance issues 483–4
  non-operational approach 111
  phases in joint projects 108
  principles-based standards 104, 107,
    129, 147–8
  professional approach criticisms 111
  revenue recognition project 307,
    314–15
  revising framework 107–9
  revising framework case study 129–30
  scientific criticisms 111, 113
  standard setters 76
IASC 74, 99
IASC Foundation 75

IASG   192
ideal cue weightings   455, 456
IETA   488–9
IFAC, *see* International Federation of
    Accountants (IFAC)
IRFIC, *see* International Financial
    Reporting Interpretations Committee
    (IRIC)
IFRS, *see* International Financial Reporting
    Standards
impairment expenses   339
impairment loss   196
impairment of assets case study   213–14
improper sales cut-offs   323
income, definitions of   292–3
income statements   163
    current cost accounting   177, 219–20a
    entity approach   261
    exit price accounting   184, 187
    historical cost accounting   203
    impact from outsourcing jobs
        offshore   165
    measurement methods   150
    presentation   309–10
    prioritising   348
    single comprehensive   309
Income Tax Assessment Act 1936   195
income tax law   195
income-decreasing accounting
        methods   381, 383
income-increasing accounting
        methods   381, 382
independent enforcement bodies
        72–4, 81
    two-tier system   74
inductive approach   20
industry profit variations, historical
        cost and current cost valuation
        methods   182
inflation accounting   29
Inflation Accounting Steering Group
        (IASG)   192
information asymmetry and firm
        size   415, 436
information cues   449, 450–1, 466
information demand purposes   56
information hypothesis   375–6
information models   418
information transfer research   416
Infosys Technologies outsourcing offshore
        jobs   165
instalment method   304
in-substance defeasance   277, 278
intangible assets
    collateral value   371–2
    inconsistent asset recognition
        criteria   235
    revaluation models   238
    valuation methods   69, 248
    valuation methods case study
        252–3
    valuation methods using fair value case
        study   154–155

interest groups   377, 457
international accounting differences,
        impact on participants   448–9
International Accounting Standards Board
        (IASB)   7
    amendments to IAS 39   68
    assets definition   102
    collaboration with FASB on financial
        reporting   54
    compromised credibility   481–2, 484
    concept statements for financial
        reporting   99, 241
    conditions for revisions   99
    derecognition of financial instruments
        project   278–9
    European dissent   62
    European Union adoption of
        standards   75
    fair value valuation models   193–4
    FASB convergence, *see* IASB/FASB
        convergence program
    financial instruments standards   67
    financial statement presentation   310
    Framework. see International Accounting
        Standards Board (IASB) *Framework*
    independence from lobbying efforts   69
    influence of US GAAP on standards   62
    joint projects with FASB   13, 64–6,
        147, 149
    lease accounting reviews   66
    liabilities definition   103, 263
    liabilities guidance   266–7
    Liabilities project amendments   275
    oversight mechanism   75, 78
    principles based standards   101
    range of users   105
    revenue recognition guidance   307–8,
        314, 342
    threats to credibility   78
    valuation approach   418
International Accounting Standards Board
        (IASB) *Framework*   94, 99
    asset definition   228
    conservatism principle   234–5
    equity   272
    expenses definition   330
    expenses recognition criteria   332
    financial reporting guidelines   99
    financial statements using historical cost
        accounting   196
    inadequacies   100
    inconsistencies in revenue recognition
        standards   305–6
    matching costs theory support   170
    measurement standards   200–1
    mixed measurement methods   198
    qualitative characteristics exposure
        draft   110–11
International Accounting Standards
        Committee (IASC)   74, 99
International Accounting Standards (IAS)
    IAS 1 *Presentation of Financial
        Statements*   99, 149, 309, 330

IAS 11/AASB 111 *Construction
        Contracts*   303, 322, 344
IAS 16 *Property, Plant and
        Equipment*   149, 241
IAS 16/AASB 116 *Property, Plant and
        Equipment*   193, 197–8, 236, 272
    depreciation valuation   333, 335
    revaluation of assets   309
IAS 17 *Leases*   268
    fair value measurement   241
    inherent arbitrariness   102–3
IAS 17/AASB 117 *Leases*   231, 233, 302
IAS 18/AASB 118 *Revenue*   292, 303
    revenue recognition guidance
        301–2, 305, 314
IAS 19/AASB 119 *Employee Benefits*
        198, 268
    amendments   275
    revaluation of assets   309
IAS 29 *Financial Reporting in
        Hyperinflationary Economies*   149
IAS 2/AASB 102 *Inventories*   193
IAS 32/AASB 132 *Financial Instruments:
        Disclosure and Presentation*   275–6
IAS 36 *Impairment of Assets*   111, 150
IAS 36/AASB 136 *Impairment of
        Assets*   196–7, 198
IAS 37/AASB 137 *Provisions, Contingent
        Liabilities and Contingent Assets*   100,
        268, 269, 270, 344
    amendments   275
IAS 38 *Intangible Assets*   69, 149
IAS 38/AASB 138 *Intangible Assets*   100,
        195, 238
    development expenses recognition
        criteria   235
    expenses   339
    goodwill restrictions   235
    intangible assets   238
IAS 39 *Financial Instruments: Recognition
        and Measurement*   66, 67, 210, 238,
        254, 278, 481
    amendments   68, 88, 278, 481
    criticisms   101
    fair value measurement   241
    inconsistencies with *Framework*
        99–100
    liabilities   268
    revaluation of assets   309
IAS 39/AASB 139 *Financial Instruments:
        Recognition and Measurement*   147,
        148, 193, 198, 309
    fair value concept case study   210–12
    impact on risk management strategies
        case study   155–6
    revenue recognition   297
    trading securities   199
IAS 40/AASB 140 *Investment
        Property*   193, 236, 297
    revaluation of assets   309
IAS 41 *Agriculture*   241, 242–3
IAS 41/AASB 141 *Agriculture*   148, 297
    revaluation of assets   309

International Accounting Standards (IAS) (continued)

IAS 8 *Accounting Policies, Changes in Accounting Estimates and Errors* 99

IAS 8/AASB 108 *Accounting Policies, Changes in Accounting Estimates and Errors* 100, 141

alternate measurement concepts 199–200, 205

financial analysts' reaction to switch 432–3

historical background 74–5

impact on risk management strategies case study 155–6

Improvements Project 75

principles-based standards 76

true and fair provision 342–3

International Auditing and Assurance Standards Board (IAASB) 78

international sustainability assurance standard development 493

sustainability assurance standards publications 492–3

International Emissions Trading Associations (IETA) 488–9

International Federation of Accountants (IFAC) 77, 78, 485

corporate governance guidelines 71

International Financial Reporting Interpretations Committee (IFRIC)

IFRIC 13 *Customer Loyalty Programmes* 355

IFRIC 15 *Agreements for the Construction of Real Estate* 322

IFRIC 3 *Emission Rights* 100–1, 487, 489

accounting mismatches 101

International Financial Reporting Standards (IFRS)

alternate measurement concepts 199–200f

cross border acquisitions application 126

IFRS 2 Share-based Payment 268, 279, 280, 336

IFRS 3/AASB 3 Business Combinations 268, 336

IFRS 3/AASB Business Combinations (Appendix A) 193

IFRS 7 Financial Instruments: Disclosures 488

amendments 68, 278, 481

impact on financial statements case study 48–9

impact on share option schemes case study 158

shareholder perspective 15

small and medium enterprises (SMEs) 104

small and medium enterprises (SMEs) case study 125–7

subsequent measurement of liabilities 269

transition concerns in United Kingdom case study 45–6

transition towards 13

US GAAP convergence issues 484

International Organization of Securities Commissions (IOSCO) 67, 74, 239

cross-border listings standards 75

International Public Sector Accounting Standards Board (IPSASB) 77

conceptual framework for public sector 109

International Standards of Auditing (ISA) 71, 78, 151, 485

ISA 540 *Audit of Accounting Estimates* 151

redrafting standards 492

interval scale 135–6, 152

arithmetical calculations 137

weakness 136

invariance in scales 136–8, 152

inventory ledgers, exit price accounting 225

inventory valuation methods 96, 151, 193, 195, 197

market value 299–300

investor overconfidence 429, 456

investor psychology 171

investors' needs via historical cost accounting information 170–1

IOSCO, *see* International Organization of Securities Commissions (IOSCO)

ISA, *see* International Standard of Auditing (ISA)

ISAE 3000, *Assurance Engagements Other than Audits or Reviews of Historical Financial Information* 492

ISoft restatement of revenue 306

Italy

auditing regulatory bodies 71, 72

independent enforcement bodies 72

J

Joint Stock Companies Regulation and Registration Act 1844 146

Joint Working Group of Standard Setters (JWC)

'Financial Instruments and Similar Items' risk assessment draft 188

judgement in accounting 118

judgement/decision making research (JDM) 40

K

KPMG audit methodology

internal control mechanisms 121

program guides 144

KPMG fair value impact financial statement interview 142–5

L

Lakatosian research program 21, 34, 390–1

last-in-first-out (LIFO) method of inventory valuation 96, 180, 197, 385

Latin American financial reporting systems 35

lease accounting 64–6

classification 65

principles-based versus rule-based standards 102–3

ledger accounts

current cost accounting 221

exit price accounting 223–4

Lend Lease's profit announcement and investor reaction case study 47

lessees' rights 231

liabilities 15

common measurement methods 268, 282

conservative approach 265

contingent 270–2

definition 103, 263

hedging activities 148, 156

impact of companies on environment 265

offsetting 277–9

owners' claim 258

past transaction 264

pension schemes 156

planned maintenance 263

present obligation 263

public-private partnerships 266–7

recognition criteria 264–6, 282

subsequent measurement 269

understatement 280

valuation methods 198

LIFO 96, 180, 197,385

linear regression models 417

liquid assets 297–8

liquidating dividends 370

liquidation-oriented profit 174

Littleton and Paton system, *see* Paton and Little system

loan capital, gains and losses 179

loans, fair value measurement 255

lobby groups 58, 361, 399, 491

European 67

influence power 63

special-interest 66

lobbying for political outcome 377

lodgement supervision 72

long term approach to valuation 190–1

long-term association anomaly 428–9

long-term debt, valuation methods 226

long-term investments, equity method 259

losses, unrealised 315

M

mainstream accounting research 35, *see also* North American stream of accounting research

management accounting 34

management contracts 362, 370

managers

chief executive officers' share ownership impact on compensation 389

concealment concerns 280

current cost accounting information 177

forms of discipline for
    misconduct   364
incentives for disciplined
    behaviour   365
information needs   172
motivational contractual incentive
    strategies   367–8
motivational tools   341
motive for valuation models   237, 244
policies regarding incentives   366–7, 394
risk-aversion strategies   366–7
shifting future to present reporting
    periods   374, 382–3
wealth transfers from debtholders   372
managers as wealth maximisers   9–10, 29
mark to market case study   85–7
market failure   57, 60
    correcting perceptions towards   61
market forces price factors   178
market model   410–12
market opportunity costs   176
market priced capital   146
market prices objectivity   187–8, 299–300
market reaction to diversification
    operations case study   439–40
market-based comparisons measurement
    model   155, 248
matching costs theory   164–5, 333–9
    associating cause and effect
        method   334, 347
    criticisms   170
    historical cost accounting   333
    immediate recognition method   347
    rational allocation method   347
    systematic allocation method   347
materiality criteria   234, 479
maximum debt theorem   420
measurement
    accurate   142
    comparability   188
    conventional models   147
    current value model   237–8
    exit price accounting approach   184
    fair value valuation models   242–4
    historical background   145–7
    international standards   199–200f
    liabilities   268–70
    methods of defining   134
    mixed attribute   199–200, 247, 248
    mixed attribute case study   253–5
    potential measurement bases   241
    reliability   141, 266
    reliability and accuracy in valuation
        methods case study   154–5
    reliability hierarchy   142–5
    reliability of valuation models   237
    sources of error   140–1
    types of   138–40
    types of scales   134–8, 152
mechanistic hypothesis   430, 435
Metcash's bonus retention pay
    approach   22
microeconomic price theory   408

Ministerial Council   62
mixed attribute measurement models   15,
    199–200, 205
    impact on financial statements   309
Modigliani-Miller (MM) model   417
monetary assets, valuation principles   179
monitoring costs   363, 364
Monitoring Group   484, 485
multi-decade leases   65
multidimensional graphics
    presentation   459–60

N

National Companies and Securities
    Commission (NCSC)   62, *see also*
    Australian Securities and Investments
    Commission (ASIC)
National Water Account (NWA)   493
natural zero point   135
naturalistic research approaches   20, 30,
    31–2, 43, 486
    comparison with scientific
        approaches   32
Navitas' future profitability signal   376–7
net present value measurement
    method   154
Netherlands's independent enforcement
    bodies   72
neutrality concept   234, 346
    liabilities   265–6
New Zealand
    conceptual framework   13
    export profit incentives   386
    goodwill accounting   389
News Corp assets write-down   167
nexus of contracts   362, 391, 394
no-effects hypothesis   429–30
nominal scale   135
non-current assets   169, 176
    exit price accounting   184–5
    long-term   335
    specialised   295
    upward revaluations   296
    valuation methods   180, 196
non-derivative assets   481
non-financial liabilities   270
non-industry groups   58, 59
non-linear statistical techniques
    421–2, 424
    unexpected profit   422
non-marketable fixed assets   190
non-monetary assets, valuation
    principles   178–9, 261
Nordic countries' market regulation   73
normalised earnings case study   49–50
normative accounting   7–9, 20, 33, 42
    criticisms   8
normative theory   24–8, 116, 360, 404
    auditing application   40
    difference from positive accounting   29
    historical cost profit tests   412
    methodological criticisms   406–7
    share investments   28

North American stream of accounting
    research   35
Norwalk Agreement   76–7, *see also* IASB/
    FASB convergence program
note disclosures   236, 239
not-for-profit sector
    financial reporting guidelines case
        study   127–8
    future economic benefits   228
    standards setting   108–9
Nufarm offshore expansion case
    study   439

O

objectives-oriented approach to standards
    setting   122
off-balance sheet lease liabilities   64–6,
    267, 283
Ohlson model of residual profit   418, 429
ontology framework   30–2, 43, 113–14
    basic classification sets   31
operating leases   65, 103, 233
    public-private partnerships   267
    recognition criteria   234
opportunistic behaviours   373, 374–5,
    381–2, 395, 407
    conservative bias   379–80
    research into   385
opportunity cost concept   185
optimal leverage approach   420
optimum resource allocation   176–7
option pricing models   336, 417
ordinal scale   135, 152
    arithmetical calculations   138
outsourcing offshore jobs, impact on
    income statements   165
outsourcing offshore jobs, impact on share
    prices case study   439
oversight monitoring groups   484, 485
owners' equity   272–5
    classifications   274–5
    distinguishing from liability   276
ownership control   230, 233

P

Pacioli, Luca   34, 146
Pacioli's treatise   5
parent company method   259
parking techniques   323
partial standards approach to standards
    setting   119
past transaction liabilities   264, 281
Paton and Littleton system   146, 162
    matching costs theory   339
    revenue   292, 298
PCAOB   78, 245, 280, 479
peer review systems   78, 479
pension plans   268–70, 289
pension liabilities
    recognition criteria   269–70
    valuation methods   241
percentage-of-completion
    method   303–4, 322, 334

performance rights plans   338–9
performance share plans   158
perpetual capital notes   276
pharmaceutical industry, impact from political processes   378–9
physical capital   281
   current cost accounting approach   217–21
physical capital maintenance   149, 162, 175–82, 204
   adjustment   175
   capital maintenance features   178
   criticisms   183
   difference from financial capital   174–5
   United Kingdom   192
   valuation principles   178–9
PIOB   78, 485
policy models   116–18
   constitutional approach   117
political cost theory   377–9, 382, 387
political markets   59–60, 377
political power   117
   non-neutral   59–60
political process
   impact on accounting methods   386–7
   impact on companies' accounting information   378–9
   influence in standards setting   63–4, 117–18
politically sensitive industries   382
positive accounting   9–12, 16, 20, 33, 43
   types of contracts   362
positive accounting research   116
positive accounting theory   28–9, 377–9
   Ball and Brown study   412–14
   criticisms   396
   difference from normative accounting   29
   early research   360–1
   empirical research   381–3, 395
   methodological criticisms   390–1
   objectives of   404–6, 435
   philosophical criticisms   391–2
positive era in accounting   8, see also specific scientific period
post-announcement drift   426–8, 436
post-employment obligations   268–70
   employee benefits case study   288
pragmatic approaches   6–7, 42
   criticisms   20–1
preference shares   275–6
   covenants   372
Preliminary Australian Water Accounting Standards (PAAWAS)   493
prescriptive theories   404, 406–7
present obligation liabilities   263, 264, 281, 282
present value discounting techniques   196–7, 198
price protection   363–4, 365–6, 370–1
PricewaterhouseCoopers' accounting approaches towards emissions trading   488–9

primary user group reports   109
principles-based standards, challenges in IFRS settings   147–8
private interest theory   59–60, 62–3, 80
probabilistic judgement model   449, 453–5
   auditing application   461
process tracing model   449, 451–3, 458, 463, 468
   applications in share investments   458
'producer' private interest groups   59–60
professional accounting associations   35
   auditing standards   77–8, 82
   lobbying power   58
   professional conduct   118
   standards setting influence   61–2
professional monopoly   119, 124
professional values   118, 119
profit
   alternate approaches to predicting   38
   cosmetic   384
   disaggregated   423–4
   failure to detect manipulation   427
   frequency of announcements   414
   historical background   295
   historical cost accounting   169
   managerial remuneration   368
   market reaction to accounting information   415
   noise concept   418
   non-linear statistical model   422
   overstatement   345
   persistence models   421
   price impact from unexpected   413
   responsiveness from competing firms   416
   share prices around abnormal profit announcements   413
   shifting from future to present reporting periods   372–3, 382–3
   smooth operating   385–6
   understating reports for political reasons   378
profit measurement, exit price accounting approach criticism   188–9
profit reporting
   credibility of audit process   419
   historical cost and current cost valuation methods   182
   market's slow reaction case study   437–8
proforma earnings guidelines   106
project-specific financing   388
project-specific loans   388
property development revenue recognition case study   321–2
property valuation
   external appraisers   201–2
   mixed model approach   197–8
   revaluation models   237
proprietary theory   179, 258–60, 273, 281
provisions
   guidelines   282, 345
   limiting use   270–1
   overstatement   280

proxy contests   386, 418
psychological pragmatic approach   21, 42
Public Company Accounting and Oversight Board (PCAOB)   78, 245, 280, 479
public database for financial statements   478
public interest groups   59, 80
Public Interest Oversight Board (PIOB)   78, 485
public interest theory   57, 80
   applications   60–1
   government intervention   63
public sector
   accounting standards   77
   conceptual framework   109
   legal action claim   271
Public Transport Authority of Western Australia   271
public-private partnerships   266–7

Q
Qantas's frequent flyer program case study   354–5
Qantas's superannuation shortfall   289
quantitative data   105, 134
quasi-rents   392

R
ratio scale   136, 138, 152
   arithmetical calculations   137
rational allocation method   335–6, 347
real estate companies' diversity in revenue recognition case study   321–2
realisation principle   295–6, 298
realism in accounting   26
recruitment industry's impairment of assets case study   213–14
regulation theories   54, 57–63
regulatory bodies   35
regulatory capture theory   57–8, 61–2, see also capture theory
relative value measurement model   155
reliability in measurement   141, 152
   trade-offs   148
   trade-offs guidelines   157
research expenditures   235, 339, 389
residual claim   258, 261, 272
residual interest   258, 272, 273
residual loss   364, 365
residual opportunism   364
retail industry's share profit announcement case study   437–8
retained earnings appropriating   274–5
returns on invested (ROI) capital   65–6
revaluation gains in property   293–4
revenue
   behavioural approach   294–5, 314
   consistency in value reporting   298–9
   deferred approach   354–5
   definitions   292–3
   earning process   295
   fraud enforcement case study   326–7

measurability analysis 297–9
operational approach 294
overstatement 311, 315
overstatement case study 323–5
premature recognition
schemes 324–5
recognition criteria 295–300,
307–8, 314
recognition criteria, conservative 304
recognition criteria guidance 301–2
recognition criteria in operating
cycle 296
recognition inconsistencies 342
recognition tests 300
rendering of services criteria 305
restatement 306
timing relevance 302
revenue-expense viewpoint 164–5
risk assessments 188, 447
risk management strategies
impact of international accounting
standards case study 155–6
pension liabilities 148
risk-aversion problems 366, 394
rogue traders 10–11
royalty relief measurement method 155,
253, 305
rule of thumb biases 454–5, 462
rule of thumb decision making
process 468
rule-based standards, benefits 101

S
SAC, *see* Statement of Accounting
Concepts (SAC)
sale of goods 302–4
backdating 312, 315
consignment sales 324
exceptions 303–4
fictitious 325
fraudulent practices 323–5
sales type leases 302, *see also* finance
leases
SAP, *see* Statement of Accounting Practice
(SAP)
Sarbanes-Oxley Act 2002 (US) 12, 479
auditors' provision restrictions 467
balancing regulatory requirements case
study 84–5
financial reporting overhaul 103–4
introduction 60
Sarbanes-Oxley Act 2002 (US) s 404, 85
scales in measurement 134–8
invariance 137
types of 135–6
schematic faces framework 459
scientific accounting approaches 29–30,
114, 115
common misconceptions 37, 43
comparison with naturalistic
research 32
criticisms 30
external influences 35

scientific accounting journals 35
sector neutral standards 77, 108
Securities Acts 377–8
conservative influence 379
Securities Exchange Commission (SEC)
Accounting Series Release (ASR)
190, 191
auditor sanctions 419, 433
EDGAR public database 478
financial reporting concept release 76
fraudulent enforcement case
study 323–5
Roadmap 483
role as active share market
regulator 72–3
securities market law 70
securities market regulators 72
selected zero point 135–6
self- regulation 71
self- regulation for auditing 77, 479
self-preservation 118
semantics approaches 21–4
market reaction to accounting
information 22
measurement 134, 152
semi-strong form market 408, 412, 435
SFAC, *see* Statements of Financial
Accounting Concepts (SFAC)
SFAS, *see* Standards of Financial
Accounting Statements (SFAS)
share analysts' behavioural
research 465–6
share investment
normative theory 28
quality assessment methods 431–2
trading strategies 426–8, 436
use of auditing as signal of share
quality 392–3
share option scheme case study 158
share price movement and earnings case
study 50–1
share price movement around abnormal
profit announcements 413
share prices
adjustment levels 414
impact from market deregulation 409
market overreaction 429
volatitility following announcement
case study 439
share-based payment 144, 279
effectiveness as motivational
tool 338–9
forms of measurements 336
issues in accounting 337
measurement methods 241
shareholders
dissident 386
evaluating managers' performance 172
minimising investment risks 366–7
policies regarding incentives 366–7
shareholders' equity, restating 223–4
shareholders' group class action against
auditors 246

shareholders' reactions to normalised
earnings case study 49–50
shareholders' reactions to reported
earnings case study 47
short-term approach to valuation
190–1, 205
decision rules 191
signalling theory 375–7, 395, 431
future profitability signals 376–7
single comprehensive income
statement 309
single-entry accounting 145–6
small and medium enterprises
(SMEs) 104
differential reporting 127
International Financial Reporting
Standards (IFRS) case study 125–7
smaller-over-the-counter (OTC) firms 415
abnormal rate of return variance 417
social accounting 485–6
social public-private partnerships 267
Societe Generale rogue trader
scandal 10–11, 342–3
sociological accounting system 34
Southern Rural Water 499
space services 229
SPEs 280, 283
specific scientific period in accounting 8
SSAP, *see* Statutory Statement of
Accounting Principle
stakeholder demands for financial
information 4, 12
stakeholders' effect on financial
reporting 34
standard cost accounting 136
Statement of Financial Accounting
Concepts (SFAC)
SFAC 1 97
SFAC 2 98, 115, 157
Standards of Financial Accounting
Statements (SFAS) SFAS 123 (R)
144
SFAS 157 *Fair Value Measurement*
144, 242
standards setting
capture theory 61–2
corporate sector influence power 63
government intervention 81
impact of special-interest lobby
groups 66
independent national 64
interpreting 104
lobby groups 58
offshore 69
overload 57
partial standards approach 119
role of 56
staff training 75
state government fabricated water data
case study 499–500
Statement of Accounting Concepts (SAC)
SAC 1 *Objectives of Financial Reporting by
Business Enterprises* 13, 200

Statement of Accounting Concepts (SAC)
(*continued*)
SAC 2 *Qualitative Characteristics of Accounting Information* 13, 200, 98, 157
SAC 3 *Qualitative Characteristics of Financial Information* 13, 200
SAC 4 *Definition and Recognition of the Elements of Financial Statements* 170
replacement 13, 200
withdrawal 63
SAC 5 *Measurement of the Elements of Financial Statements* 13, 112, 200
Statement of Accounting Practice (SAP)
SAP 1 Current Cost Accounting 193
financial statements 218–19
Statement of Basic Auditing Concepts (ASOBAC) 40, 120
statistical models for decision making 56, 452–3
statutory requirements for financial reporting 70, 81
Statutory Statement of Accounting Principle (SSAP) 16 192
Step-Up Preference (SPS) Securities 277
stock exchange as market regulator 73
Stora Enso's agricultural assets fair value measurement 242–3
straight-line depreciation 217, 333, 335, 375, 382
straight-line revenue accrual 305
Strategic Systems Audit 121
strong-form efficient markets 364–5, 408
structured accounting theories 7–8
subordinated debt 276, 277
sum-of-the-years digits depreciation 335
superannuation liabilities shortfall case study 289
superannuation plans 268–70
supplementary data 167, 191, 192
sustainability accounting 485–6
sustainability reporting 486–92
formal assurance 491, 492, 496–7
guidelines 486
standards guidance 492–3
syntactic approaches 20, 21–4
criticisms 21–2
market reaction to accounting information 22
systematic allocation method 335–6, 347

T
Tabcorp normalised earnings case study 49–50
Talent2Go impairment of assets case study 213–14
tangible assets 236–8
tax credit accounting methods 386–7
tax reduction method (TRM) 386–7

taxation legislation 6, 70
Taxation Ruling IT 1350 'Value of Trading Stock on Hand at End of Year: Cost Price: Absorption Cost' 195
Telstra Corp
expert judgement case study 471
forecasting approaches 39
superannuation shortfall 289
termination pay cap schemes 369
theory of efficient markets 55–6, 80
theory-testing approach 35–6
trading securities, measurement standards 199
transaction test 300
triple bottom-line reporting 466
trophy investments 380
true income 24, 42
true profit 23, 24

U
UK GAAP 26, 127
uncertainty resolution in revenue recognition 299
unconsolidated special purposed entities (SPEs) 280, 283
underinvestment approach 370, 371
underlying profits, reporting guidelines 106
underperforming loans, impact on banks 163
unexpected profit 174
unfunded pension plans 269
Australian case study 289
United Kingdom
accounting systems growth 6
asset revaluation 237
British Telecom (BT) pension case study 288
conceptual framework 13
current cost accounting 192–3
differential reporting 127
heritage assets case study 252
IFRS reporting for local authorities 26–7
IFRS transition case study 45–6
independent enforcement bodies 74
restatement of revenue 306
self-regulation for auditing 72
United States
accounting systems growth 6
credit market support 8–9
current cost accounting reporting requirements 191–2
effect of special-interest lobby groups 66
financial reporting jurisdictions 70
financial reporting systems 35
government auditing regulator 78
increase in sustainability reporting 491

independent enforcement bodies 72
insurance companies' climate risk disclosures 487–8
lease accounting criteria 65
legislative reporting requirements 12
litigation against auditors 434
profit measurement theories 164
revenue definition 293
sub-prime crisis 278
theoretical approaches to financial crisis 8–9
units of production depreciation 333, 335
US GAAP
Form 20-F 75
historical cost accounting 236
convergence issues 484
rule-based standards 76

V
valuation
exit price accounting 184
frequency of 198
valuation models 418, *see also* Ohlson model of residual profit
value in exchange principle 185, 190–1, 205
value in use principle 185, 190–1, 205
verbal protocol methods 452, *see also* process tracing model
volatile markets 28
voluntary information to investors 375–6, 387, 395

W
warranty claims 266
Water Act 1989 (VIC) 499
water accounting 493–4
accrual system 494, 497
state government fabricated data case study 499–500
Water Accounting Conceptual Framework (WACF) 493
Water Accounting Standards Board (WASB) 493, 494
Wattyl's financial restructure 422–3
weak form of market efficiency 408
wealth transfer methods 370–1, 372, 395
weighted average method 490
wholly executory contracts 231, 234, 264
winner/loser effect 428–9
Woolworths off-balance sheet leases 65
WorldCom 85, 104, 345
write-off/write-down transactions 163, 167, 240, 248
Barclays Bank 244–5

X
XBRL 16, 478–9, 496